D1454731

The Communication Capstone

The Communication Capstone

The Communication Inquiry and Theory Experience

Editors:

Brian H. Spitzberg, Daniel J. Canary, and Heather E. Canary
San Diego State University

cognella®
SAN DIEGO

Bassim Hamadeh, CEO and Publisher
Todd R. Armstrong, Publisher
Tony Paese, Project Editor
Alia Bales, Production Editor
Jess Estrella, Senior Graphic Designer
Trey Soto, Licensing Coordinator
Natalie Piccotti, Director of Marketing
Kassie Graves, Vice President of Editorial
Jamie Giganti, Director of Academic Publishing

cognella® | ACADEMIC PUBLISHING
3970 Sorrento Valley Blvd., Ste. 500, San Diego, CA 92121

Brief Contents

Detailed Contents

Preface

Communication and the Capstone Course

CAPSTONE COURSES ARE COMMON IN COMMUNICATION-related degree programs and represent a variety of pedagogical models. This textbook, *The Communication Capstone: The Communication Inquiry and Theory Experience,* abbreviates to *CITE,* a homonym for "sight," as in "insight," as well as an abbreviation for "citation," involved in research and credibility. *CITE* seeks to address these kinds of questions in four important ways.

First, *CITE* provides broad, senior-level review of the discipline authored by experts in their respective fields. There are many textbooks for the student entering the university or the major of communication. However, there are few written for the student about to graduate and seeking a synopsis of his or her discipline. As such, the chapters have been authored by scholars, all of whom have been published in peer-reviewed journals, and many of whom are award-winning researchers and instructors. The textbook is written with minimal compromise to reading level or lowest common denominators. The text seeks to specify the most essential knowledge and learning outcomes that we expect a graduate with a degree in communication to know, both in terms of what we know and how we know it. The purpose of this text is to ensure a senior level of knowledge of a set of core concepts, principles, and empirical facts about communication as a field of study, a profession, and a fundamental process in people's lives and in society as a whole. Think of it as a text that covers the 200 or so things anyone with a degree in communication ought to know.

Second, *CITE* facilitates assessment of the value and effectiveness of a major or minor. The text and its ancillary materials facilitate completion of the communication major or minor, and assessing if the curricula have done a good job of educating students regarding the field of communication. In particular, because this capstone textbook partially parallels information introduced in the major's gateway courses, it gauges the extent to which the same corpus of key concepts and principles has been reinforced and integrated throughout the communication curriculum. Because this course covers content from courses across most majors, but not all students will have taken all courses in their major, some of the materials will be new and some will be review.

Third, the design of *CITE* involves the linking of learning objectives directly to assessments. Each chapter specifies a set of learning objectives—the things students are supposed to know—and the exam items are written directly from these learning objectives. In this design, it is crystal clear what communication majors are expected to know, and performance in the course is directly tied to this knowledge. In viewing the capstone experience as an "exit" experience in the degree, the text's learning objectives and the examination items developed from those learning objectives represent a fairly direct index of the sum total of the content knowledge students have learned about communication.

Fourth, *CITE* is flexibly designed to be selectively taught by your instructor. That is, there are more chapters and topics than will likely be assigned over the course of a given class. Thus, most instructors will select those chapters that best reflect the particular majors or minors involved in their program. Further, many instructors may find that there is a need to supplement the *CITE* textbook with readings or assignments that cover topics not currently included in this text. The field of communication is very diverse, and different programs and institutions represent their degrees with very diverse curricula and subjects. No text can comprehensively cover the entire discipline. As a consequence, while *CITE* attempts to provide a broad representation of the discipline, in your particular class your instructor is likely to select some subset of chapters to cover, and may also supplement the chapters in the text. This is inevitable, by design, and reflects an appropriate adaptation of the materials to the audience.

CITE is focused intentionally more on cognitive learning objectives of communication curricula than on applied forms of knowledge. Because different colleges and universities have different learning objectives for the communication skills and abilities to be assessed in the capstone, this text is intended to provide the intellectual content for the major or minor as a whole. Such knowledge then can provide a scholarly context within which skills such as presentations, group interaction, leadership, interviewing, service learning, community engagement, or other project-based activities can be guided by the instructor.

Each chapter follows a similar format. It begins with a list of approximately a dozen student learning objectives from which test items are derived. Most chapters then provide a summary exposition of the (a) history; (b) key assumptions or guiding principles; (c) key terms; (d) ethical issues; and (e) core concepts, methods, models, and/or theories relevant to their topic areas. For the contextual chapters, each chapter examines a few select but exemplary theories or significant studies that provide important insights into the subject. Clearly, there are far more theories and principles than can possibly be covered in one textbook, so the theories selected are intended to reflect exemplary theories in each area, but this selection is far from exhaustive, and may well be supplemented by your instructor.

CITE's organization is guided by the idea that a discipline is primarily defined by its approaches to and contexts or functions of knowledge. A discipline helps to organize, and is organized by, the knowledge it has accumulated in the past, how it claims to know things, what it claims to know, and how it claims things should or should not be known. These approaches to knowing (methodology), understanding (theory), evaluating (ethics), and practice (skills) represent the core contents of a discipline.

The sequence of units in the course follows a particular logic. The first part examines who we are as a discipline and where we have come from. Thus, a chapter examines the history of the discipline (Chapter 1), and another chapter introduces the basic axioms of verbal and nonverbal communication (Chapter 2). The second part examines how we know what we claim to know (Chapter 3). It is difficult to understand and evaluate a claim about a theory or skill if the methods by which that claim was reached are not understood first. Thus, the chapters in this unit examine the major conceptual and methodological paradigms in the field; that is, the tools we use to construct what we know. The second chapter in this unit reviews how we know what we already know by examining the process of background research and formatting styles for writing about such research (Chapter 4). The third chapter in this section explains how we think we know by examining theories and models as conceptual tools to guide any other research method (Chapter 5). Then, the major methodological toolboxes of the field are examined, ranging from the more historical and critical (critical and rhetorical, Chapter 6) to more qualitative (interpretive and ethnographic, Chapter 7; performative, Chapter 8), naturalistic (conversation analysis, Chapter 9), and quantitative and experimental (Chapters 10 and 11) methodologies.

The third part examines what we know primarily in regard to core contexts and functions of communication. The chapters examine the role of gender in communication (Chapter 12); interpersonal and relational communication (Chapter 13); argument, persuasion, and influence (Chapter 14); conflict management (Chapter 15); group and team communication (Chapter 16); organizational and leadership communication (Chapter 17); intercultural communication (Chapter 18); health communication (Chapter 19); political communication (Chapter 20); public speaking (Chapter 21); and mass and mediated communication (Chapters 22 and 23).

The final unit of the text asks how *knowing why* matters to your life by examining careers and communication (Chapter 24). The communication degree and the knowledge and skills it offers are examined in light of the evolving job market and its potential professional trajectories.

Thus, *CITE* is based on these principles:

1. We cannot know what needs to be known until we know *what is already known*. Thus,

2. Knowing what is already known allows us to know *how we claim to know* what we claim to know. Thus,

3. Knowing what we know and how we know it allows us to know *what we are talking about*. Thus,

4. Knowing what we are talking about allows us to *competently evaluate* what we, and others, claim to know. Thus,

5. Knowing what we know, how we know it, and how to evaluate it, allows us to know *where we can go* with what we know.

That is, a student first needs orientation to the core subject matter, its history, and its key terms and principles. But, when presented with specific knowledge claims about content (e.g., females are more nonverbally expressive than males), it is natural for a student to ask "How do we know that?" Thus, after the initial orientation to history and key concepts, the text moves to establish that communication is a scholarly domain with serious methodologies that systematize the ways we know what we claim to know. With this foundation, students then are better equipped to process the kinds of content claims made in particular functional and contextual areas of communication covered in the remainder of the course. Put simply, a person first needs to have a working vocabulary of concepts to discuss a subject matter at all. Second, that person then needs to know why claims made about those concepts are credible before being presented with such claims. Third, only when the topography of the discipline is explained, and the ways in which that discipline knows what it knows is explained, is a person equipped to fully understand what the discipline claims to know, the ethical implications of such knowledge, and what can and should (and should not) be done with such knowledge. The bookends of this organization also have the chronological advantage of "looking back" (history), "looking at the present" (orienting), and "looking ahead" (careers).

As a final note about the *CITE* text, instructors and students alike may find it of interest to know that all royalties from this textbook are contractually committed to assisting students. No royalties or fees are provided to or for any of the authors or editors. This textbook was written as a labor of love by scholars who have a deep sense of identification with their discipline, in the hope of improving the Capstone experience, and providing students a more comprehensive appreciation of the discipline their degree represents.

Acknowledgments

No project such as this arises *ex nihilo*, and thanks are due to those who contributed their talents and efforts. Among these are those who facilitated this project administratively (Dr. William Snavely and Dr. Heather Canary), those who assisted with editing (Daniel J. Canary and Dr. Heather Canary), exam item pool development (John Paul Whaley, Laura Horton, and Colter Ray) and the Cognella team (Todd Armstrong, Tony Paese, and Alia Bales) who managed strategic editing and marketing of this text. Of particular note is a former undergraduate and graduate student, Alanna McLeod, who devoted substantial time and effort, as well as her extraordinary intellect and keen eye for detail, to the editing of a late draft version of this book. Alanna volunteered to do this out of sheer desire to assist the project and to occupy the amazing clockwork of a mind that she possessed. Her one-time presence in the School of Communication's hallways and faculty offices is missed by all those who knew her. Thanks are also due to the extended family of current and former Aztecs at San Diego State University who contributed chapters, friendship, and continuing collegial support. Finally, having

designed and taught our Capstone course for well over a decade, thanks to all the students who, upon the precipice of graduation, engaged the materials of this ever-evolving text and contemplated the meaning of their degree.

We are especially grateful to the many reviewers who gave helpful feedback for this version of the book:

Betsy Wackernagel Bach
(University of Montana)

Steven A. Beebe
(Texas State University)

Bradley J. Bond
(University of San Diego)

Leila Brammer
(University of Chicago)

Janie Harden Fritz
(Duquesne University)

Elizabeth M. Goering
(Indiana University–Purdue University Indianapolis)

LaKresha Graham
(Rockhurst University)

Annette M. Holba
(Plymouth State University)

Jimmie Manning
(University of Nevada, Reno)

Joseph P. Mazer
(Clemson University)

Nina-Jo Moore
(Appalachian State University)

Alfred G. Mueller II
(Neumann University)

Rick Olsen
(University of North Carolina Wilmington)

Armeda C. Reitzel
(Humboldt State University)

Sarah E. Riforgiate
(University of Wisconsin-Milwaukee)

Tara J. Schuwerk
(Stetson University)

Anne M. Stone
(Rollins College)

Michelle T. Violanti
(University of Tennessee, Knoxville)

Introduction

Knowing What a Communication Degree Means

Y OU EXIT THE AUDITORIUM AFTER RECEIVING YOUR bachelor's degree, and a local news reporter sticks a microphone in front of you and asks, "And what was your major?" You say, "Communication." She then asks, "So, what is that major? Tell us something about communication that we don't already know."

You enter the personnel office of an organization in which your job interview will take place, and after the initial introductions, the interviewer inquires: "So, you're a communication major. Tell me something useful that this degree prepared you to do for our organization."

After failing to get that previous position, you interview again at another organization. The first prompt from the interviewer is, "How about you tell me an interesting story and offer a moral to it?"

You go to dinner for Thanksgiving and your uncle asks what you are studying in college. You (proudly) answer, "Communication," and he follows with, "I didn't know you could major in that. So, what can you do with that major?"

A degree in any major in higher education is supposed to mean that the degree recipient knows things that a person without such a degree does not know, either intuitively or with a modicum of experience or research (i.e., something beyond an incidental Google search). So, what *do* you know that your interviewer, your family, your employer, your noncollegiate peers, or others in general society do not know? This text seeks to address many of these kinds of questions and more.

***

You are a graduating senior in the discipline of communication. Presumably you selected the communication major because it called to you and because you feel an affinity to its contents, its values, and its potential for your future. Perhaps you stumbled into the major for lack of a clarion call from some other major. At either end of this spectrum of motives, this text seeks to ensure that you know the history, the scope, and the nature of the discipline that will be inscribed on your degree, which will travel with you for the remainder of your life as a significant reflection of your bona fides and of your own curriculum vitae. We hope that upon completion of this course you will not only have a deep sense of pride in your selection of major or minor, but also that your instructors will have pride in you representing the education they strove to provide you.

You should not be surprised that although the book is written in the American Psychological Association (APA) style, the format and authorial "voice" varies across chapters. For example, ethnographers and scientific scholars not only use different methods to study communication, but they also represent their approaches to communication in different writing and authorial styles. Recognizing the voice of authorship is an important step toward both developing your own voice and toward developing multiple voices for writing to put in your own communication toolbox.

The National Communication Association (NCA; www.natcom.org), the largest professional association of communication scholars and students in the world, has an extensive website with resources on the nature of the field. Its learning objectives for the discipline are perhaps more general, but they are not that different from the ones developed throughout this text. The NCA learning outcomes are reproduced on the next two pages.

The National Communication Association's
Learning Objectives for the Communication Discipline

The National Communication Association engaged in an intensive and iterative process to develop and fine-tune learning objectives for the discipline. We present their central assumption and results of that work below:

Central Assumption

A central assumption at the foundation of these Learning Outcomes in Communication (LOC) is that communication constructs the social world and is relational, collaborative, strategic, symbolic, and adaptive.

LOC #1: Describe the Communication discipline and its central questions.

- Explain the origins of the Communication discipline.
- Summarize the broad nature of the Communication discipline.
- Categorize the various career pathways for students of communication.
- Articulate the importance of communication expertise in career development and civic engagement.
- Examine contemporary debates within the field.
- Distinguish the Communication discipline from related areas of study.
- Identify with intellectual specialization(s) in the Communication discipline.

LOC #2: Employ communication theories, perspectives, principles, and concepts.

- Explain communication theories, perspectives, principles, and concepts.
- Synthesize communication theories, perspectives, principles, and concepts.
- Apply communication theories, perspectives, principles, and concepts.
- Critique communication theories, perspectives, principles, and concepts.

LOC #3: Engage in communication inquiry.

- Interpret communication scholarship.
- Evaluate communication scholarship.
- Apply communication scholarship.
- Formulate questions appropriate for communication scholarship.
- Engage in communication scholarship using the research traditions of the discipline.
- Differentiate between various approaches to the study of communication.
- Contribute to scholarly conversations appropriate to the purpose of inquiry.

LOC #4: Create messages appropriate to the audience, purpose, and context.

- Locate and use information relevant to the goals, audiences, purposes, and contexts.
- Select creative and appropriate modalities and technologies to accomplish communicative goals.
- Adapt messages to the diverse needs of individuals, groups, and contexts.
- Present messages in multiple communication modalities and contexts.

National Communication Association, Selection from "What Should a Graduate with a Communication Degree Know, Understand, and Be Able to Do?" What is Communication? Copyright © by National Communication Association. Reprinted with permission.

- Adjust messages while in the process of communicating.
- Critically reflect on one's own messages after the communication event.

LOC #5: Critically analyze messages.

- Identify meanings embedded in messages.
- Articulate characteristics of mediated and non-mediated messages.
- Recognize the influence of messages.
- Engage in active listening.
- Enact mindful responding to messages.

LOC #6: Demonstrate the ability to accomplish communicative goals (self-efficacy).

- Identify contexts, situations, and barriers that impede communication self-efficacy.
- Perform verbal and nonverbal communication behaviors that illustrate self-efficacy.
- Articulate personal beliefs about abilities to accomplish communication goals.
- Evaluate personal communication strengths and weaknesses.

LOC #7: Apply ethical communication principles and practices.

- Identify ethical perspectives.
- Explain the relevance of various ethical perspectives.
- Articulate the ethical dimensions of a communication situation.
- Choose to communicate with ethical intention.
- Propose solutions for (un)ethical communication.
- Evaluate the ethical elements of a communication situation.

LOC #8: Utilize communication to embrace difference.

- Articulate the connection between communication and culture.
- Recognize individual and cultural similarities and differences.
- Appreciate individual and cultural similarities and differences.
- Respect diverse perspectives and the ways they influence communication.
- Articulate one's own cultural standpoint and how it affects communication and worldview.
- Demonstrate the ability to be culturally self-aware.
- Adapt one's communication in diverse cultural contexts.

LOC #9: Influence public discourse.

- Explain the importance of communication in civic life.
- Identify the challenges facing communities and the role of communication in resolving those challenges.
- Frame local, national, and/or global issues from a Communication perspective.
- Evaluate local, national, and/or global issues from a Communication perspective.
- Utilize communication to respond to issues at the local, national, and/or global level.
- Advocate a course of action to address local, national, and/or global issues from a Communication perspective.
- Empower individuals to promote human rights, human dignity, and human freedom.

Source: https://www.natcom.org/learning-outcomes-communication

PART I

Knowing Who We Are and Where We've Been
The Discipline and Its History

CHAPTER 1

Communication as a Discipline
History and Intellectual Content

William F. Eadie

LEARNING OBJECTIVES

After reading this chapter, you should be able to do the following:

- Identify the century in which the earliest universities emerged that resembled modern universities.
- Identify and differentiate the five canons of rhetoric.
- Identify and differentiate the distinctive historical roots of journalism and speech schools.
- Identify the role that historical events (e.g., World War II) had on the evolution of the communication field.
- Identify the cognate disciplines most aligned with the emerging discipline of communication.
- Identify and differentiate the unique characteristics of the "three histories" of the communication discipline.
- Identify the role of the New Orleans Conference on the contemporary discipline of communication.

As with any human phenomenon, communication seems simple on the surface. It becomes complex only when it fails to go smoothly. Taking note of those times, which are part of everyone's experience, provides a window into the reasons for studying communication systematically. Another rationale for studying communication results from taking notice of technological developments that have changed the nature of communication within society. We have sometimes feared the potential power of new media technologies; because of this, we have been motivated to understand explicitly how media affect their users. Finally, because societal and cultural conflicts often seem to stem from "problems with communication," we have been motivated to explain how communication functions to shape our understanding of cultures and societies.

In this chapter, I trace how communication became an academic discipline in U.S. universities. The various strands of scholarship that formed this discipline are examined, and the five general, historical types of communication scholarship are reviewed that various groups of scholars pursued as the academic discipline of communication was forming. These five types of scholarship persist and form the basis for what communication students currently study.

Before focusing specifically on communication, I include some comments on the development of higher education in the United States. These developments facilitated the emergence of communication as an academic discipline.

Shifts in U.S. Higher Education

Although higher education in the United States can be traced to the 17th century (Harvard records its founding as occurring in 1636), it was not until the late 19th century that anything resembling a contemporary university emerged. Early higher education in the United States was limited to men. Further, it was generally the case that sons of businessmen and land owners were sent to college so that they might develop appropriate intellectual, cultural, and spiritual maturity to allow them to join their fathers' enterprises following graduation. Curricula for these institutions focused on the liberal arts: history, philosophy, literature, and religion (many colleges were sponsored by religious institutions), with some grounding in the sciences provided. Education in communication was provided through the study of rhetoric—the art of persuasion—which was considered a branch of philosophy. Education in communication was also provided through debates on societal issues. Often, these debates were held in forums open to the entire campus, and they attracted avid participation from students.

In 1862, Congress passed the **Morrill Act,** which extended and changed the nature of higher education in the United States. The law's land grants to each state allowed for the expansion of higher education, and these new public institutions were designed to advance agriculture and industry. In the process, these *land-grant institutions* offered professional education to well-qualified students, even if those students did not come from business or land-owning families. The missions of these institutions often stressed advancing democratic principles by helping anyone with talent and drive succeed.

Over time, professional education shifted from on-the-job training to college classrooms. This shift had the effect of limiting the amount of liberal arts taught in the curricula, although a solid grounding in the liberal arts continued to be valued. For the most part, however, colleges that offered an exclusively liberal arts education were private, whereas public institutions shifted their curricula to include both the liberal arts and the professions. As the need for specialization beyond the bachelor's degree grew, so did the demand for degrees at the master's and doctoral levels.

Journalism and Speech as Academic Disciplines

Journalism was one of the professional areas of study that shifted from an **apprenticeship model** to programs at land-grant universities. Journalism was the province of printers, so aspiring journalists learned their craft as part of learning the printing trade. Early university models replicated the apprentice model and focused on printing, but eventually stand-alone journalism departments (or "schools," as they were often called to indicate their professional focus) emerged.

Speech had its intellectual roots in rhetoric, an area of study that was commonly taught in English departments. Speech teachers often focused on the Roman orator Cicero's (1948) five canons of rhetoric, which directly applied to practical speaking situations: **invention** (constructing the content to be presented), **disposition** (organizing the content into a coherent presentation), **style** (using language appropriate to the audience and to make the message clear), **memory** (the ability to keep all of the pieces of presentation in one's head), and **delivery** (the presentation of the content in a lively fashion and, with adjustments for actual conditions, in a manner similar to how one planned the presentation).

Through much of the 1800s, instruction in the United States was heavily influenced by the *elocutionist movement*, which pursued an agenda of identifying very specific actions of body, face, voice, and delivery to express particular emotions, intentions, and sentiments. Textbooks on elocution contained illustrations of orators posed with precise gestures or postures for specific emotions, and speakers were assessed based on their degree of replication of those depictions. Speech teachers often worked with students outside of formal class settings, coaching them for speeches and debates for the edification of the campus and local communities. When universities began to be organized into departments, it seemed natural for the speech teachers to be placed in the English department.

As English departments were being formed, the **Modern Language Association (MLA)** was founded. The MLA represented not only those who taught English, but also those who taught languages other than English. Because the MLA was, from its beginning, a large and complex scholarly society, it was easy for a group of people, such as the speech teachers, to feel excluded. At a MLA conference in 1912, a second scholarly group was formed as a faction of scholars who sought to distinguish itself from the MLA, very likely in response to this sense of exclusion of its members' interests and pedagogical objectives. The group that split from the MLA referred to its nascent association as the **National Council of Teachers of English (NCTE),** and it consisted of high school and college English teachers.

At the same conference, individuals from a group favoring the formation of a separate scholarly organization decided to act. This group contained a number of professors from large land-grant universities, several of which aspired to offer doctoral degrees in speech. None of the group members were high school teachers, although high school teachers represented a significant proportion of the membership of NCTE. Although they wanted to break away from English for several reasons, some of the group members wanted to establish separate speech departments so that they could design their own curricula, including for advanced degrees, and could have a disciplinary identity separate from English.

Thus, the scholarly society that eventually became known as the **National Communication Association (NCA;** https://www.natcom.org) was established. The organizers initially tried several names before settling on the National Association of Teachers of Speech, a name that stuck until the end of World War II.

Although journalism was organized into professional schools, speech struggled to form college and university departments. Often, there were too few faculty to warrant a separate department, so speech professors sometimes found common cause with faculty who worked to correct what were called "speech disorders," and sometimes with theatre faculty, on the grounds that both groups dealt with teaching students how to perform. This "big tent" approach worked, even though members of both groups eventually formed their own scholarly societies and split their departmental identities from speech. It took a while, though; the last president of the association from speech disorders was Elise Hahn, in 1958, and the last president from theatre was Patti P. Gillespie, in 1987.

Tracing the Roots of Communication

Interest in communication emerged from a number of scholarly roots, and communication became a topic of study in a number of disciplines. The emergence of social science scholarship at colleges and universities probably did more to spur the study of communication than any other single development, however.

Everett Rogers's (1997) history of communication study credited three European thinkers with influencing how scholars began to think about the concept of communication. None of these thinkers were social scientists as we understand the concept today, but all of them influenced the development of social science study in the United States. The three thinkers were Sigmund Freud, the founder of psychoanalysis; Charles Darwin, who formulated the theory of evolution; and Karl Marx, whose analysis of the relationship between economics and society spawned both a social and political revolution.

These three thinkers, as well as others, helped to set the stage for U.S. universities to be organized not just around fine and performing arts, humanities, and sciences, but also around the social sciences as well. Social science disciplines dealt with how individuals think and behave as well as how they organize themselves into groups, organizations, societies, and cultures. It was natural for communication, as an important part of every broad social science area of research, to become a topic of specialized study.

As communication grew as a topic, it attracted scholars from a variety of other disciplines, including political science, psychology, and linguistics. Sociologists, however, continued to constitute the primary discipline for communication scholarship.

The Three Histories of the Communication Discipline

The formal beginnings of journalism and speech as separate fields of study from English and the development of interest in the effects of mass communication on society all occurred shortly after the turn of the 20th century. Although all three groups of scholars were interested in some aspect of communication study, members of each group went their own way, albeit with some influence from members of the other two groups.

Thus, three *histories* of communication developed: a speech history, a journalism history, and a communication history. Each history could point to a different set of intellectual ideas that were put forward by individuals who, at least for a while, did not interface with each other.

Speech History

In its **speech history,** public speaking remained a substantial focus of speech scholarship, but communication processes affecting group discussion and the effectiveness of persuasive messages were also a concern. **Journalism** scholars studied primarily the content of newspapers and magazines, but they, too, developed interest in how news is perceived by the public; that is, whether print or radio as a news medium makes a difference in how news is understood and how the public distinguishes news from propaganda.

In the process, members of each group became somewhat familiar with at least some work being done by other groups. The members of the communication group led the way in terms of renown because their scholarship was on a topic of public interest, and also because the work they did relative to that scholarship was innovative. Their scholarship led to theory development that produced unexpected findings (e.g., one group theorized that individuals, in most cases, are not directly influenced by messages they read or hear over the airwaves; rather, they are influenced by discussing those messages with others they trust).

The beginning of World War II in Europe changed the focus of scholarship. The U.S. government organized a panel of experts to move to Washington D.C., and interact with each other to help resolve key problems the country was expected to face. A propaganda group was part of that movement, and it consisted of some of the individuals who had been doing communication research on the topic, including a seemingly odd man out named Wilbur Schramm.

Schramm was right about interest in communication burgeoning following World War II. Developments occurred both from the places where communication scholarship had gone on before the war, as well as from new, unexpected quarters. Sociologists such as Paul Lazarsfeld and Bernard Berleson continued their work, but now they had the comfort of university professorships within which to operate. Social psychologist Carl Hovland assembled a very bright and motivated set of professors into the Yale Communication and Attitude Change program, and this group quickly became highly influential. Kurt Lewin, another social psychologist, studied group phenomena and contemporary social problems, generating interest in how "group dynamics" could affect both attitudes and performance.

Then, there were the **technologists**. Technological advances during the war had come in support of the war effort. Now an upgrade was needed of the technology that ordinary citizens used every day, starting with the telephone. The problem was that telephone service was sometimes unreliable and unavailable. Researchers at Bell Labs created a mathematical theory that measured the quantity of information that flowed through the system, as well as how that information flow can be distorted.

Speech scholars, whose interests had for some time included communication research, found themselves in the midst of a revolution where their ideas were not in the mainstream. To remedy this situation, a group of these scholars began the National Society for the Study of Communication. This organization was supposed to be deliberately interdisciplinary and was organized around study groups that reflected scholarly or practical problems the group's members wanted to research. The group soon began the *Journal of Communication* as its marquee publication, but the structure of the society seemed to hold it back. For one, it remained doggedly a speech organization, attracting very few members from other disciplines. Second, its study groups had to operate mostly through correspondence, and speech scholars had not organized institutes where members could interact on a daily basis (mostly because they worked at universities that had no funding to support this level of scholarship). Finally, the early scholarship published by this group did not attract much attention.

Journalism History

In part, some reluctance existed among both journalism and speech scholars to embrace communication research. Most journalism faculty thought of themselves primarily as professionals who had taken on the difficult role of training and mentoring the next generation of journalists. They knew from experience that journalism could be a tough but often satisfying life, and they wanted to prepare their students adequately for what was to come. They were interested in trends in their profession, so scholarship focused on the content of journalism, as well as how that content was assembled. They were somewhat interested in the development of new technologies. But, piece-by-piece, bit-by-bit data collection and theory building did not interest them. In fact, scholars who did this kind of work had no place in the Association for Education in Journalism (AEJ) to present their scholarship. They resorted instead to meeting either before or after the annual AEJ convention in what were called "rump" sessions.

Speech professors had their share of individuals who were focused on teaching, particularly on developing public speaking, debate, group communication, and oral interpretation of literature skills. The dominant mode of scholarship in speech focused on the history and criticism of public address, however, so the quick growth of interest in communication, plus the volume of scholarship being produced by leading researchers of communication frightened the historians and critics, who typically worked much more slowly and deliberately. There was talk of "war" between the rhetoricians and the "behaviorists," and skirmishes (intellectual and political, not generally physical) did, indeed, break out in some speech departments. At the national level, the Speech Association of America was dominated by traditionalists who primarily valued the study and performance of great speeches and oratory but not to the extent that communication scholarship was excluded. Many of the association's leaders saw communication as a valuable, if sometimes difficult to understand, addition to the study of speech.

Communication History

Meanwhile, some actions taken by the scholarly societies in speech and journalism helped to pave the way for growth of communication study. Most notably, in 1964, members of AEJ met and approved a substantial overhaul to that association's constitution. Although the membership turned down a proposal to rename the entire organization to the Association for Education in Communications, it still approved a proposal to add a division of theory and methodology so the mass communication scholars had a place within AEJ to hold their sessions.

On the speech side, the Speech Association of America hired professional staff and set up a national office in New York City in 1963. The staff quickly began to pursue a number of projects on behalf of its membership, and one of those projects focused on how to bring communication study into a more central location within speech. Money to plan and execute a major conference on this topic was secured from the U.S. Office of Education. In 1968, that conference was held in New Orleans, Louisiana, and is commonly referred to as the **New Orleans Conference**.

The conference planners did an excellent job of selecting participants. Rather than set up a confrontation with the scholars of rhetoric over the inclusion of communication, the planners invited a sufficient number of articulate, open-minded individuals and gave them key roles in the conference sessions. Tension had also been brewing between the so-called "old guard" and what had been dubbed the "young Turks." Conference planners diffused potential hurt feelings by inviting a selection from each group.

The conferees made significant recommendations for making communication a central part of speech scholarship. The recommendations were published as a book (*Conceptual Frontiers in Speech-Communication: Report of the New Orleans Conference on Research and Instructional Development*; Kibler & Barker, 1969). In particular, the group recommended that the focus of speech scholarship should be "spoken symbolic interaction," a far cry from the traditional understanding of speech scholarship as focused on public speaking, group discussion, the history and criticism of speeches, and oral interpretation of literature. The group made a number of other recommendations regarding an agenda for studying communication from a speech perspective, and the group set an agenda to have communication scholarship become known and used in society.

Most important, the group recommended that the term "communication" be combined with "speech" whenever appropriate. In fact, it recommended that the Speech Association of America revise its name to include communication and that the names of the speech journals be revised to incorporate communication as well.

The recommendations, taken collectively, caused sweeping changes in how speech scholars understood what they did. The conference proceedings were widely read and discussed, and there was a groundswell of sentiment that the recommendations should be adopted. Most notably, by 1970, the Speech Association of America had become the Speech Communication Association.

The leadership of the National Society for the Study of Communication had decided by the mid-1960s that the model of scholarship they had established was not working, so they set out to remake their organization to focus on major aspects of communication scholarship. They also added an international focus and renamed themselves the **International Communication Association (ICA)**.

The initial set of four interest groups represented a broad-brush view of communication. Division 1 was named "Information Systems," encompassing both human and technological means of transmitting and receiving information. Division 2 was named "Interpersonal Communication," representing the primary area of communication scholarship favored by speech faculty. Division 3 was named "Mass Communication," representing the primary area of communication scholarship favored by journalism faculty. Division 4 was named "Organizational Communication," which represented a fast-growing area of communication scholarship that had been established as part of the previous structure. Not long thereafter, Division 5, "Intercultural Communication," was added as a means of providing a scholarly basis for the international focus ICA was trying to promote. By the mid-1970s, ICA had hired an executive director, set up an office, and started a second journal, *Human Communication Research*. It had also held its first annual meeting at an international site, Montreal, Quebec, Canada.

The Association for Education in Journalism was the slowest of the three major scholarly societies to embrace the idea of communication. AEJ remained dominated by practitioners-turned-teachers, even though more and more doctoral programs were producing mass communication scholars who were finding jobs in journalism schools. In the early 1980s, AEJ acquired office space off campus in Columbia, South Carolina, and hired its own paid staff. It also approved a name change to the **Association for Education in Journalism and Mass Communication**. Thus, AEJ became **AEJMC**, finally embracing communication as part of its identity.

During the time between 1964, when AEJ first allowed the *mass communication* scholars to be included in its annual meeting, and 1982, when AEJ became AEJMC, speech and journalism scholars embraced the idea of communication being integral to what they do as scholars. They revised their curricula to focus on communication as a central concept of what students learn, and they included the word "communication" in their department and school titles. By 1982, students at many U.S. universities could choose to major in something with "communication" in its title, and many of them did. Communication swelled in popularity as a university major in the United States.

By 1982, the histories of journalism, speech, and communication had converged sufficiently enough that an academic discipline of communication was born.

What Communication Scholars Study

Communication has been criticized as a discipline for being so broad in scope that it includes just about anything that someone wishes to study, and to a degree that criticism is warranted. "Communication research regularly invokes a broad range of ontological, epistemological, and methodological viewpoints, a blend of empirical and critical work, and a mix of qualitative and quantitative methods" (Zelizer, 2016, p. 227). Part of the problem comes from having inadequate means of defining subareas of scholarly interest. These areas have most often been defined by what has been called context (i.e., how many people are involved in the communication process). Typically, *communication contexts* have been labeled "interpersonal," "group," "organizational," "public," and "mass communication." In addition, major areas of study have been defined by the topic of communication, such as political communication, health communication, family communication, and relational communication. This approach is illustrated in **Figure 1.1**, which distinguishes contexts by the number of participants, the agency of the communicator(s), the formality of the situation, and the degree to which communication is adapted to the specific individuals and relationships involved (Powers, 1995).

From a historical point of view, I propose dividing communication scholarship into five broad areas based on how

FIGURE 1.1: Some Typical Contextual Domains of the Discipline

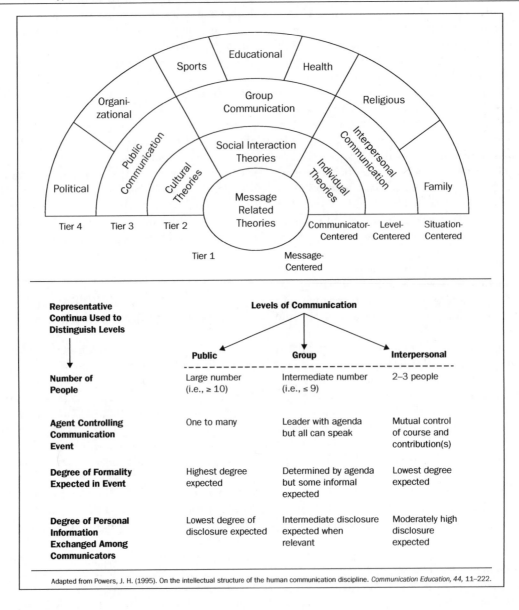

Adapted from Powers, J. H. (1995). On the intellectual structure of the human communication discipline. *Communication Education, 44,* 11–222.

communication *functions* (see **Table 1.1**). These areas of scholarship had each received a good deal of attention prior to 1982, the establishment of communication as an academic discipline, and scholarship in each area has persisted. These areas are as follows: (a) communication as shaper of individual and public opinion; (b) communication as language use; (c) communication as information transmission; (d) communication as developer of relationships; and (e) communication as definer, interpreter, and critic of culture. I treat each area of scholarship in the sections that follow.

TABLE 1.1: Content Analogues for the Communication Discipline

	Communication as Shaper of Public Opinion	Communication as Language Use	Communication as Information Transmission	Communication as Developer of Relationships	Communication as Definer, Interpreter, and Critic of Culture
Exemplar theory	Agenda setting	Rhetorical apologia	Uncertainty reduction	Relational dialectics	Speech codes
Methods used	Primarily quantitative: survey, content analysis, experiment	Primarily nonquantitative: critical, analytical, discourse/conversation analysis	Primarily quantitative: survey, experiment	Both quantitative and nonquantitative: survey, interview, ethnography, and other observational methods	Both quantitative and nonquantitative: survey, experiment, field observations, ethnography, critical/cultural analysis
Sample historical scholars	Paul Lazarsfeld, Harold Lasswell, Bernard Berleson, and George Gerbner	Alfred Korzybski, S. I. Hayakawa, Kenneth Burke, Marshall McLuhan, Stephen Toulmin, George Grice, Roland Barthes, and John Waite Bowers	Claude Shannon, Warren Weaver, Carl Hovland, Leon Festinger, David Berlo, Wilbur Schramm, and Steven Chaffee	George Herbert Mead, Gregory Bateson, Paul Watzlawick, Carl Rogers, Martin Buber, Mikhail Bakhtin, Erving Goffman, Clifford Nast, and Edna Rogers	Stuart Hall, Edward T. Hall, Geert Hofstede, William Gudykunst, Everett Rogers, and Theodor Adorno
Sample contemporary scholars	Maxwell McCombs, Ellen Wartella, Robert Entman, Larry Gross, and Nancy Signorelli	Sonja Foss, Karen Foss, Karlyn Kohrs Campbell, Kathleen Hall Jamieson, Celeste Condit, and Wayne Beach	Charles Berger, Marshall Scott Poole, Linda Putnam, Howard Giles, Joseph Walther, and Joseph Cappella	Leslie Baxter, Dawn Braithwaite, Brian Spitzberg, Judee Burgoon, Michael Roloff, Daniel Canary, William Rawlins, and Kurt Lindemann	Stephen Hartnett, Dana Cloud, Raymie McKerrow, Barbara Biesecker, and Thomas Nakayama
Sample insights on communication phenomena	Media don't tell people what to think; they tell them what to think about. Time-consuming media matters; heavy consumers of media have a more greatly distorted view of their environments than do light consumers.	A good deal of the ability to understand messages can be attributed to recognition of the genre of the communication situation. Close examination of how language is used on conversation can provide insights into how messages are interpreted, both in the short and long term.	A primary goal of interaction among new acquaintances is reduction of uncertainty through exchange of information. Organizations may have formal goals, but the actual goals are formulated through finding predictable patterns that help organizations function well and then institutionalizing those patterns.	Messages may not matter as much as expectations and whether they are violated in maintaining effective relationships. Relationships are continually influenced by evolving needs and patterns of interaction among members.	Cultural practices are often so firmly ingrained that they resist being replaced. Media can prove to be a powerful cultural tool by bringing audiences ideas about potential new cultural developments. These ideas and their impacts must be subject to critique in order to be effective, however.

Communication as Shaper of Individual and Public Opinion

Public opinion and propaganda were key areas of study that drove early communication scholarship. With the development of technological means of communication, particularly radio and television, came the fear that the ability to communicate directly to large numbers of people at once would create a great deal of power for those who owned television and radio stations. Some were worried that such power could be used to control the public and allow for the rise of charismatic figures who might undermine the democratic principles of governance outlined in founding documents.

As U.S. President Franklin Roosevelt embarked in 1940 on a run for an unprecedented third term in office, these fears became palpable. Paul Lazarsfeld and colleagues were able to obtain funding to study how radio affected voting patterns in that election. They focused on voters in Erie, Pennsylvania, and Decatur, Illinois, and conducted extensive interviews with a panel of those voters. Their 1944 book, *The People's Choice*, based on the Erie study, put some of the fears about media influence to rest because the researchers concluded that radio by itself had very little effect on voting behavior (Lazarsfeld, Berelson, & Gaudet, 1944). Rather, as the Decatur study confirmed, voters relied heavily on their conversations with people they considered to be influential (called "opinion leaders") to interpret what they were hearing and to help them make up their minds (Katz & Lazarsfeld, 1955). Thus, influence occurred in a ***two-step flow***, from a source to one receiver, who influenced a subsequent receiver.

Communication as Language Use

Language has been a central focus of study from the time of recorded history, and spoken language in particular has been characterized as uniquely human. Scholars have studied language from a variety of disciplinary perspectives, but to study how language is used necessarily comes close to understanding the communication process.

The relationship between symbols and reality that characterizes much of this work on language use is placed center stage in Robert L. Scott's (1967) landmark essay, "On Viewing Rhetoric as Epistemic." Scott drew on both classical and contemporary sources to argue that rhetoric—the use of language and other symbols for persuasive purposes—functions more to create what we

know than to reflect it. Thus, rhetoric was **epistemic**—a study of ways in which rhetoric influences what and how we know what we know. In Scott's view, language use defines our understanding of reality, not the other way around. Consequently, the nature of reality is tentative and subject to continual reinterpretation.

This idea has profound consequences. It means that communication—using language and other symbols—not only reflects our understanding of the world around us, but also serves to shape that world as well. Studying our use of symbols as texts, then, helps us to get at what we know. Organizational theorist Karl Weick (1995) has a helpful aphorism for understanding this idea: "How can I know what I think until I see what I say?"

Scholars have many ways of understanding texts. These include conversational analysis, which examines a carefully made transcript for subtleties of meaning; discourse analysis, which also focuses on transcripts, although at less of a *micro level*; and ethnography, which examines texts at relatively more *macro levels* in order to link them to the situations in which the actors find themselves. A variety of methods of analyzing texts as rhetoric have also yielded significant insights.

The study of communication as language use has also been approached from a quantitative perspective. Often, the focus of quantitative studies is on the factors that influence how messages are interpreted, as well as on those that influence success in achieving the goal of the message. For a more detailed explanation of this sort of scholarship, see Roloff and Wright (2009).

Communication as Information Transmission

The information transmission definition of communication is the one many people would think of if they were asked to define the concept of communication. They would see communication as moving a message from a source to a receiver and having it arrive in the same form as it was transmitted.

Although this definition has the advantage of being simple and easily grasped, it has problems that arise almost immediately on further examination. For one thing, even in the electronic environment for which the definition was originally created, signals are always subject to some sort of distortion during the transmission process. Although engineers are, in most cases, capable of reducing this distortion to a manageable level, transmission never works perfectly. Furthermore, human transmission does not have the same capabilities to be engineered; humans possess interpretive skills that may help to make up for what is lost in transmission.

The primary function of information is to reduce uncertainty, and uncertainty reduction has provided one means for productive theorizing about communication. The most well-known example of this sort of theory was put forward originally by Charles Berger and Richard Calabrese (1975).

Starting from the assumption that the primary goal of developing relationships with others is the reduction of uncertainty, Berger and Calabrese offered a series of concepts that could contribute to that goal: (1) the amount of verbal communication; (b) nonverbal affiliative expressiveness, or the degree to which an individual's non-verbal behaviors encourage interaction; (c) information seeking; (d) self-disclosure; (e) reciprocity, or the degree to which information sharing is mutual; (f) similarity; and (g) liking. The theory was built by examining the relationships among these key concepts. Some of these relationships are fairly obvious (e.g., similarity and liking are positively related), whereas others might be less so (e.g., information seeking and liking are negatively related).

Given that uncertainty affects both cognition and behavior, the information transmission approach to communication has been used to theorize about a wide variety of communication situations, including media effects. Mostly, this work has been quantitative in nature, using one or more messages as independent variables, and using changes to one or more cognitions that can be measured as dependent variables. An excellent review of how theories of media effects have changed and developed over time is available (see Neuman & Guggenheim, 2011).

Box 1.1 Ethical Issues

Communication ethics refers broadly to the morality, the values involved in or applied to, and the rightness or wrongness of communication events. One approach to such ethics is to articulate a set of grounding or self-evident ethical values or goals. The National Communication Association, the largest professional association of the communication discipline, developed a public policy concerning ethical communication.

Credo for Ethical Communication

Approved by the NCA Legislative Council, 1999; Reaffirmed by the Legislative Assembly passing the report and recommendations of the Taskforce on the Public Policy Platform, 2011. Reaffirmed by the Legislative Assembly with edits, 2017.

Questions of right and wrong arise whenever people communicate. Ethical communication is fundamental to responsible thinking, decision making, and the development of relationships and communities within and across contexts, cultures, channels, and media. Moreover, ethical communication enhances human worth and dignity by fostering truthfulness, fairness, responsibility, personal integrity, and respect for self and others. We believe that unethical communication threatens the quality of all communication and consequently the well-being of individuals and the society in which we live. Therefore we, the members of the National Communication Association, endorse and are committed to practicing the following principles of ethical communication:

- We advocate truthfulness, accuracy, honesty, and reason as essential to the integrity of communication.
- We endorse freedom of expression, diversity of perspective, and tolerance of dissent to achieve the informed and responsible decision making fundamental to a civil society.
- We strive to understand and respect other communicators before evaluating and responding to their messages.
- We promote access to communication resources and opportunities as necessary to fulfill human potential and contribute to the well-being of individuals, families, communities, and society.
- We promote communication climates of caring and mutual understanding that respect the unique needs and characteristics of individual communicators.
- We condemn communication that degrades individuals and humanity through distortion, intimidation, coercion, and violence, and through the expression of intolerance and hatred.

- We are committed to the courageous expression of personal convictions in pursuit of fairness and justice.
- We advocate sharing information, opinions, and feelings when facing significant choices while also respecting privacy and confidentiality.
- We accept responsibility for the short- and long-term consequences for our own communication and expect the same of others.

Source: National Communication Association. (1999, 2017). Credo for Ethical Communication. Retrieved from: https://www.natcom.org/sites/default/files/Public_Statement_Credo_for_Ethical_Communication_2017.pdf

Communication as Developer of Relationships

Interest in communication between individuals has been approached from a number of perspectives, and both social psychologists and speech professors have had a history of studying interpersonal and group interaction. The common denominator of these studies has been a focus on interaction—the process of interchange between and among individuals—as well as how those interactions serve to change the dynamics of a relationship. Two programs of research illustrate alternative approaches to the study of relational communication.

The stage model was developed by Mark Knapp (1978; Knapp, Vangelisti, & Caughlin, 2014). Knapp's model uses stages to characterize the kind of communication that goes on at various points in the development or dissolution of a relationship. According to Knapp's model, a brief *initiation* stage starts the relationship. In this stage, the relationship participants exchange pleasantries and "small talk" designed to indicate a degree of attraction and interest. From there, interaction will quickly shift to an exchange of information about each other. In this *experimentation* stage, individuals will "try out" information about themselves. For example, they give information about topics that are important to them (e.g., interests or opinions) to see how the other person reacts to this information.

Assuming that the experimentation is successful, participants will *intensify* the interaction. They may start to disclose things about themselves that they generally do not tell others as well as opinions about important information that their partner may have disclosed or on topics that they know their partner finds important. This partnership builds during the *integration* phase, where the relationship participants find ways of expressing solidarity with each other. Often, these symbols of solidarity and partnership are more nonverbal than verbal. These expressions of relational commitment culminate in *bonding*, which Knapp described as public commitments designed to indicate the expectation that the relationship will be a long-lasting one.

The stages of relationship termination follow a somewhat reverse order. Instead of expressing relationship solidarity, individuals begin to *differentiate* themselves from the other, to find some topics that are to be avoided or to set up boundaries where conversations do not go, eventually to find that the relationship has stagnated and the two are merely tolerating each other, leading to *avoiding* each other emotionally and physically, and finally relationship termination. Knapp has posited that relationships find their levels, and realization that communication patterns have shifted toward the separation side can prompt decisions about leveling off a relationship. Many of these "leveled-off" relationships eventually drift apart rather than race toward formal termination.

A very different approach is represented by Leslie Baxter and her associates' work on "relational dialectics" (Baxter, 2004). Baxter's work assumes that people "rub up against each other," verbally and otherwise, as they develop relationships, and that daily interaction brings tensions that may either be ignored or addressed. It is how relationship partners deal with these tensions that determines the quality of a relationship as it progresses. Sometimes the tensions result in an agreement (tacit or explicit) on relationship rules, and sometimes the tensions will result in conflict. These tensions, however, are part of everyday interaction, and relationship partners must continually manage them in some way.

Some of the common patterns of relationship tension revolve around openness and closedness (i.e., how much relational partners know about each other on an ongoing basis and how much privacy is allowed each partner), certainty and uncertainty (i.e., how much behaviors within the relationship are predictable and how much uncertainty or experimentation with new behavior is allowed to exist in the relationship), and connectedness and separateness (i.e., how much relational togetherness and unity of identity is present and desired, as well as how much individual identity is tolerated or encouraged within the relationship).

Communication as Definer, Interpreter, and Critic of Culture

If collective human activity can be said to define culture, then communication as the primary symbolic human activity must have a role in how we both define and understand culture. The role of communication in culture is most easily seen in how we use media. As Marshall McLuhan (1964) noted, media can be viewed as extensions of ourselves. Media use symbolic activity both to influence and reflect culture as we understand it.

How to study the relationship between collections of symbolic activity (typically called a "text") and culture has promoted discussion. To a great extent, such study relies on critical interpretation of the text by a scholar who uses a framework for analysis. That framework often involves researchers looking for the expression of hierarchy (i.e., who has power and who does not, who gets to make the rules, and who must follow them). By analyzing cultural texts, scholars argue, we get a window into the culture itself, what its strengths and weaknesses might be, and how the critic can offer an analysis of changes in culture that will produce more appropriate, productive texts.

From a strictly cultural perspective, texts may be examined in an attempt to determine the characteristics of culture as displayed by the interaction. Gerry Philipsen (1975) did the pioneering work on what has become known as speech codes theory, a means based in ethnography to discern cultural practices from observing members of the culture interacting. Philipsen's work has spawned an entire body of ethnographic research examining either cultural or performance practices.

Although critical/cultural work is inherently interdisciplinary, it is often rooted in the work of writers (e.g., Habermas, Foucault, and Butler) whose work contains a healthy communication component but whose theories are not communication theories per se. So, while there have been a number of insightful analyses produced by communication scholars (see, e.g., Biesecker, 2011; Hartnett, 2013; Morris & Sloop, 2006), these analyses tend to be based in established social theories rather than contributing specifically to the development of communication theories. Condit (2013) has offered a standard other than theory building for such scholarship: that the analysis must contribute to some "scholarly conversation" in communication. Whether such a standard will ultimately be adopted for this scholarship is still an open question.

Conclusion

Scholars have debated whether communication is a "discipline" or a "field," and my position is that communication is a discipline because its scholarly practitioners have made it so. Speech and journalism professors did the difficult work of assembling communication curricula and convincing colleagues at their universities that these curricula were not only worth studying, but also warranted departmental name changes to include the word "communication" in the department title. These curricula were based initially on a variety of scholarship that had been conducted by researchers representing a number of different disciplines, including journalism and speech, but as the discipline has grown and developed curricula are increasingly based in scholarship conducted by scholars who call "communication" home.

The five threads of communication scholarship outlined in this chapter (see **Table 1.1**) remain actively researched, and others, such as communication as performance and communication as the development of identity, may well have been added since 1982. Furthermore, communication has grown not only in popularity but also in stature within the academy, and not only in the United States, but globally. Understanding the historical and intellectual roots of communication can help people who study it to appreciate what they have learned all the more. As a field of study, and as a discipline for organizing knowledge, communication has much to offer.

CHAPTER 2

Orienting to Communication
The Nature of Communication

Brian H. Spitzberg & Peter A. Andersen

LEARNING OBJECTIVES

After reading this chapter, you should be able to do the following:

- Distinguish and differentiate symbolic and nonsymbolic, verbal and nonverbal, and intentional and unintentional processes.

- Distinguish and differentiate thought (reference), symbol (sign), and referent (signified) components of communication.

- Identify the applied implications of the axiom that, in social contexts, communication is inevitable.

- Distinguish and differentiate both analogic (nonverbal) and digital (linguistic) and content (report) and relationship (command) levels of communication.

- Distinguish and differentiate both nature (genetic) and nurture (environment) processes of communication.

- Identify the applied implications of the axiom that communication generally reduces entropy.

- Identify the applied implications of the axiom that communication generally involves distortion and inaccuracy.

- Identify the applied implications of the axiom that communication is contextually contingent.

- Identify the applied implications of the axiom that communication is a systemic (holistic, nonsummative, complex, irreversible) process.

- Identify the applied implications of the axiom that communication is socially constructed and constructive.

- Identify and differentiate features and defining characteristics of nonverbal communication, and specify exemplars of nonverbal and verbal channels or codes of communication.

- Identify parallel ways in which verbal and nonverbal behaviors can complement, replace, or contradict one another.

- Identify key learning implications of the Wobegon and transparency illusion biases.

The History of Human Communication, Writ Large

As a communication major with higher education preparation, what do you know that the average person on the street does not know? Answers to this question lie in the specific content knowledge that you have mastered through the courses you have taken. Another significant component of your knowledge, however, arises from a perspective or viewpoint toward communication. This chapter intends to provide an orientation to the most fundamental characteristics of symbolic, verbal, and nonverbal communication. It is important to have an understanding of the basic phenomenon under study before examining the ways in which it is studied. The following axioms represent a bird's-eye view of communication that should be understood by communication majors and scholars but are not intuitively apparent to a typical inexpert person.

Whereas all ancient forms of life have biochemical and physical means of transferring information from one cell to another, and from one organism to another, the advent of human language probably dates from 1 million (Dediu & Levinson, 2013, 2014) to 100,000 years ago (Miyagawa, Berwick, & Okanoya, 2013). **Figure 2.1** displays the currently hypothesized deep history of human language development (see also Bolhuis, Tattersal, Chomsky, & Berwick, 2014).

Examples of symbolic forms of expression include linear etchings of shells dating to around 500,000 years ago (Joordens, et al., 2015) and hashed drawings on cave walls created approximately 70,000 years ago (Henshilwood et al., 2018). Most languages are thought to have evolved from protolanguages. Languages culturally evolved from various original families (Pagel, 2009). Prior to the spread of agriculture, as many as 12,000 to 20,000 distinct languages may have existed, but today there are approximately 6,000 to 7,000 "mutually

FIGURE 2.1: The Timeline of Language Origins Among *Homo* Hominidea

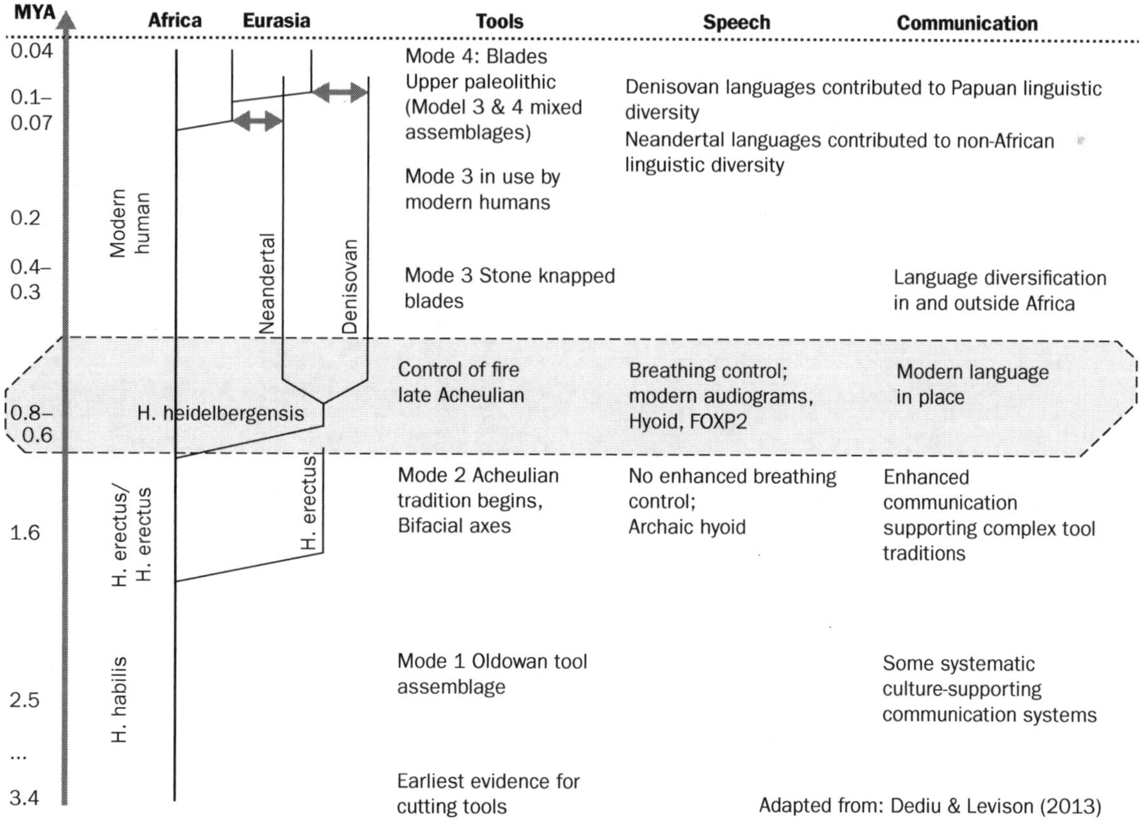

MYA	Africa	Eurasia	Tools	Speech	Communication
0.04			Mode 4: Blades Upper paleolithic (Model 3 & 4 mixed assemblages)	Denisovan languages contributed to Papuan linguistic diversity	
0.1–0.07				Neandertal languages contributed to non-African linguistic diversity	
	Modern human		Mode 3 in use by modern humans		
0.2		Neandertal / Denisovan			
0.4–0.3			Mode 3 Stone knapped blades		Language diversification in and outside Africa
0.8–0.6	H. heidelbergensis		Control of fire late Acheulian	Breathing control; modern audiograms, Hyoid, FOXP2	Modern language in place
	H. erectus/ H. erectus	H. erectus	Mode 2 Acheulian tradition begins, Bifacial axes	No enhanced breathing control; Archaic hyoid	Enhanced communication supporting complex tool traditions
1.6					
	H. habilis		Mode 1 Oldowan tool assemblage		Some systematic culture-supporting communication systems
2.5					
...					
3.4			Earliest evidence for cutting tools	Adapted from: Dediu & Levison (2013)	

unintelligible languages" (Pagel, 2009, p. 405). Furthermore, "it has been estimated that of the 6,000 languages spoken in the world, as much as 50% will become extinct in the near future" (Fernando, Valijärvi, & Goldstein, 2010, p. 48).

Throughout human history, numerous important events have marked the discontinuous development of communication. For example, research indicates that the earliest figurative cave paintings and stencils arose around 40,000 years ago (Brahic, 2014; Zorich, 2016). A highly selective display of some of the more obvious communication-relevant events is presented in **Figure 2.2** (panels a and b). As far as extant historical documents indicate, writings on the importance and precepts of competent communication date at least back 4,500 years to the *Instructions to Kagemni* and *Instructions of Ptah-hotep* (Gray, 1946; Hutto, 2002), and millennia

later, Aristotle's *Rhetoric* was among the first efforts to study communication systematically, with an intent of drawing generalizable conclusions about principles of effective persuasion.

In the second millennium of the Common Era (CE), Guttenberg's invention of the printing press is widely considered one of the most significant historical events in regard to its impact on human development. Although much of society was illiterate and incapable of affording printed books, the ability to efficiently produce highly transportable knowledge in large quantities meant that time and space were suddenly collapsed by an order of magnitude. Knowledge became more rapidly cumulative than ever before in history. Many different people could learn from the same book, as they did with symposia in the past, but now this process was multiplied within time, across space, and across audiences.

FIGURE 2.2A: Significant Historical Events Relevant to Communication (Panel A)

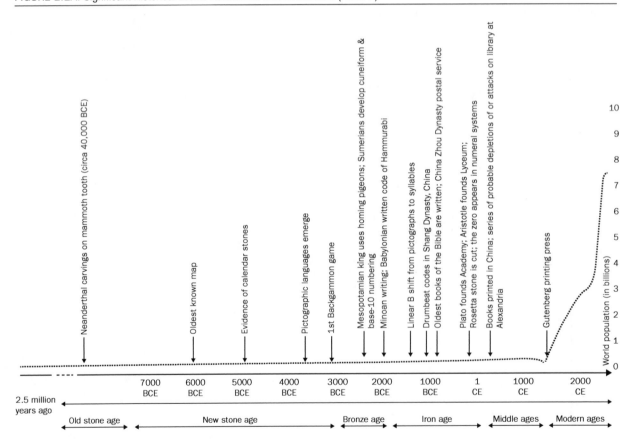

FIGURE 2.2B: Significant Historical Events Relevant to Communication (Panel B)

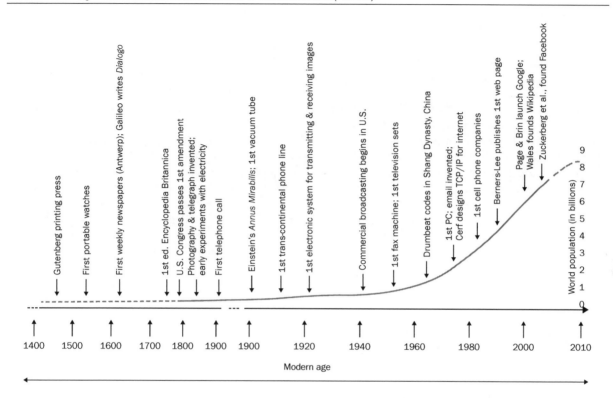

Axioms of Language and Communication

In the 1960s, the study of communication was rapidly expanding to include more than just rhetorical criticism of public address and toward a variety of alternative methodological approaches, including experimental, survey, conversation analytic, ethnographic, and performance-based methods. In this process, engineers (Shannon & Weaver, 1949), anthropologists, and psychologists (Watzlawick, Beavin, & Jackson, 1967) pioneered the articulation of basic precepts of the communication process (see also: Finkel, Simpson & Eastwick, 2017). Some of what follows represents some of these, along with other, fundamental axioms of communication that frame all other attempts to understand and use communication.

When two scientists working for what today is AT&T attempted to define communication, they realized what an expansive process it is. **Communication** is defined as "all of the procedures by which one mind may affect another" (Shannon & Weaver, 1949, p. 95). Thus, communication

becomes largely synonymous with interpersonal influence, or the processes by which one or more persons influence other(s). One interesting way of thinking about communication as influence is that for communication to have occurred a person must exit an encounter different from when they entered the encounter. If one is not changed by a communication event in some way, however slightly, how can we say that communication occurred?

Axiom 1: Communication Comprises (a) Symbolic and Nonsymbolic, (b) Verbal and Nonverbal, and (c) Linguistic and Nonlinguistic Forms

Humans obviously communicated in ways that facilitated their survival for millennia without language—they communicated nonverbally. Pointing a finger to refer to something in the direction of the finger is a universal cue that develops naturally and is understood cross-culturally (Liszkowski, Brown, Callaghan, Takada, & de Vos, 2012). A person yawning or crying is communicating information to others, but not symbolically or verbally. Smiles are universally understood to represent positive feelings but can be **intentional** or unintentional. The great cathedrals of Europe often are constructed with several rhetorical features (e.g., highest point of the city, vast interiors, focused stained-glass apertures, and steeples pointing to heaven) that represent several meanings (e.g., a person can always find God by locating the highest point of the city; a person feels small and humble before the vastness of God; a person can see the "light" of God's majesty; and a person is reminded of God's presence in heaven). Such meanings may or may not be intentional, but they are nevertheless interpretable, and therefore communicative. Thus, communication can be verbal or nonverbal, intentional or unintentional, and symbolic or nonsymbolic. A **sign** is any form of communication that is used to refer to something else for the purpose of communicating something. Signs are typically understood to be relatively universal (e.g., pointing to something; fire signifying a source of heat). When signs become conventionalized for a given group, culture, language, or relationship, they become a subset of signs known as **symbols**.

Language, in most ordinary uses (excluding specialized languages such as programming languages, mathematics, musical notation, etc.) consists of signs (anything used to represent something else that is understood as having meaning; e.g., "stop" signs, bathroom signs, finger pointing, the peace symbol, words, etc.), **meanings** (an interpretation or sense-making), and a **code** (a set of conventions for understanding and action), all of which comprise a conventional symbol system. This system itself possesses *morphology* (rules for word formation), **phonemics** (rules for sounding and pronunciation), **syntax** (rules for word arrangement in phrases and sentences), and **semantics** (rules for meaning attribution to words and sentences). Symbols, along with the codes that represent the conventions for using those symbols, are subsets of the concept of signs. Some signs are more analogic or iconic (i.e., structurally or functionally related to their underlying meanings), such as pictographic alphabets, whereas others are more contingent on context, social convention, and coconstruction (e.g., arbitrary symbol alphabets). Symbols and signs are elements of a code, but the code also includes programming instructions, or rules, for the use and interpretation of those signs and symbols.

Language has the properties of **productivity** (the capability of generating new words and language), **recursivity** (the capability for self-reference, or using itself to refer to itself, such as in dictionaries, or asking someone "What did you mean by that [gesture, statement, etc.]?"), and **displacement** (the capability of referring to things not present in time or space). Language, which occurs more frequently in the mind than between people, is only one form of communication (Chomsky, 2011). Furthermore, although any given language is finite at any given time in its basic elements, any language can produce an infinite number of possible sentences of distinct meaning (Chomsky, 2011); that is, language has the capacity for infinite uniqueness of messages. For example, consider the following sequence of sentences: This is a sentence. This is a sentence in this *CITE* textbook. This is a sentence in this *CITE* textbook in a class. This is a sentence in this *CITE* textbook in a class in which you are enrolled. This is a sentence in this *CITE* textbook in a class in which you are enrolled and currently (dis)interested. This is another sentence. ... Each sentence is grammatically and semantically expandable into new sentences that have never before been written or uttered. Thus, language is infinitely creative in its potential meanings.

Axiom 2: Communication Involves Thought (Reference), Symbol (Sign), and Referent (Signified)

Language operates in a triangle of meaning (Cassirer, 1953; de Saussure, 1959; Ogden & Richards, 1923). Symbols are anything conventionally used to stand for something else. Letters, words, language, numbers, and other code systems (e.g., sign language, music notes, mathematical operation symbols, etc.) are all symbols because they are arbitrarily formulated by people to have relatively standardized meanings within a given language or group of people who learn the conventions and rules (e.g., semantics, syntax) regulating those symbols. For example, consider the word "word" itself. Its translation across a variety of languages reveals how arbitrary (i.e., conventional) it is: *iječ* (Croatian), *le mot* or *le term* (French), ბოძგა (Georgian), *Wort* (German), λέξη (Greek), מִלָּה (Hebrew), शब्द (Hindi), 字 (Chinese), ワード (Japanese), *la palabra* (Spanish). Words were invented by humans, and the word for words has also been invented and reinvented by different cultures. The *idea* of words, of things that conventionally stand for something else, represent the cognitions that words represent. The word "word" reflects more than just the idea, but also *refers to* actual spoken or written words themselves. **References** are the ideas, thoughts, cognitions, feelings, and subjective concepts that a person is attempting to encode into a message (i.e., the idea of a word). The **referent** is a thing or set of things in the objective sensory world to which messages and references refer (i.e., the physically written or spoken words themselves). For example, a communicator may want to talk about the death penalty. The ideas that this communicator has about the death penalty are references, the messages communicated (e.g., in writing, conversation, public speech, etc.) about these references are symbols (and the nonsymbolic behaviors employed as media through which these symbols are transmitted), but the actual law that is passed, or the actual execution of a prisoner in the world, is the referent of this communication process. Words *refer to* the *references* we have in our minds about *referents* in the world.

Dozens of perspectives, and hundreds of theories, can frame this process of influence, but some tend to be more fundamental, or foundational, than others. The following foundational axioms are presented here in very brief form. Most students of communication will have encountered some version of each of these in their studies, and they are presented here as an introductory orientation to *CITE*. Some of these axioms may seem paradoxical, but that is part of the wondrous complexity of communication, which, in its self-reflexive, subjective, subjunctive, ironic, humorous, complex, subtle, and imaginative capacity, constitutes one of the defining features of humankind.

Axiom 3: In Social Contexts, Communication Is Inevitable

Any time a minimum of one person is within sensory exposure to another person or persons communication occurs. Watzlawick and colleagues (1967) characterized this axiom pithily as "one cannot *not* behave," and therefore, "one cannot *not* communicate" (p. 29). The way a person dresses, smells, sounds, and appears in general sends a "message" to those who can sense that person's behavior. A president *not* talking about an important public issue is a way of influencing the degree to which the public interprets the meaning of that issue as important, thereby affecting public policy—that is, silence communicates (Perez & Dionisopoulos, 1995). Giving someone the "silent treatment" or simply avoiding that person or certain topics, is also a way of saying something to that person (Wang, Fink, & Cai, 2012). *Not* calling or texting someone after a date is understood as communicating something about that person's interest in the relationship.

It is important to emphasize, however, that although communication is inevitable, it is also impossible for it to be entirely shared. We are prisoners of our own skin; we do not have telepathy or the ability to mind-meld with others. Because of personal idiosyncratic histories of experience, in a complex matrix of culture, environment, genetics, and unique relationships and encounters during a lifespan, there is always a unique **connotative** set of meanings for any word, symbol, or gesture, which is combined with the more conventional **denotative** ("dictionary") meanings of symbols.

Axiom 4: Communication Occurs on Both Content (Report) and Relationship (Command) Levels

Not only does communication necessarily occur in social contexts, it occurs on at least dual levels. All communication can be understood simultaneously at two interdependent levels: content and relationship (Watzlawick et al., 1967). The content of any message is typically its digital, verbal, or symbolic aspect; typically, the linguistic content is more intentional in its references. The **content** (or **report**) level resembles a dictionary definition of the communication. The relationship level typically resides more in the analogic, nonverbal aspects of the message that refer to or frame the content level. A simple example is a mother who says, "I love you," but does so with a cold, awkward, and stiff nonverbal demeanor, which communicates one message in content but quite another about the relationship. A subtler example is a husband who is sitting in a comfortable chair and says to his wife, "Hey honey, get me a beer while you're up." The content may be understood generally as a simple *request*, but the vocalics may make it sound more like a **command**. Either way, the content is always understood in part by the nature of the relationship, implied by the way in which the content is framed in its expression (e.g., Is the wife a prosocial provider or a servant to her husband?).

Axiom 5: Communication Comprises Both Nature (Genetic) and Nurture (Environmental) Influences

Human communication, both in its expression and its interpretation, is generated by both strong genetic influences and strong socialization, environmental, cultural, and creative processes (Iarocci, Yager, & Elfers, 2007; Ordoñana et al., 2013; Pourcain et al., 2014). Indeed, parents' behavior is molded by the genetic tendencies of their children (Avinun & Knafo, 2014). For example, twin studies indicate that genes can predict substantial variation in your communication dispositions, including up to 70% of the variation in your friendliness or affiliation, 65% of your social anxiety, 58% of your aggressiveness (Beatty, Heisel, Hall, Levine, & La France, 2002), and around 30% of your media use habits (Kirzinger, Weber, & Johnson, 2012). In any given situation, genetic and peripheral influences may be dominant in influencing communication, and in other situations, learned, analytic, rational, and cognitive influences may be more dominant.

Although communication behavior is always somewhat unique to a particular situation, its tendencies reflect significant similarity both within cultures and across cultures. Thus, although different cultures have relatively unique gestures (e.g., the "okay" gesture), rituals (e.g., a greeting ritual), and languages, given the evolutionary roots of behavior in general and communication in particular, humans are far more *similar* in their communication across cultures and sexes than they are different. Most communication processes are **universal**, meaning that they occur in relatively similar forms and functions across cultures. We all have language capacity and learn whatever language(s) we are exposed to during our early development (Chomsky, 2011). We all use eye contact to regulate speaking turns. We all use gestures to illustrate our talk. We all construct noun–verb phrases. We all have a sense of past, present, and future, which are incorporated to some degree or another into our languages (Núñez & Cooperrider, 2013; Pollio, Jensen, & O'Neil, 2014). We all need attachment, affection, and belonging (Floyd & Hesse, 2017). We all form groups, negotiate status, and desire mates (Bugental, 2000). We all evolved from a mitochondrial "Eve," and it shows in the degree to which we use communication to achieve everyday activities and relationships.

Axiom 6: Communication Generally Reduces Entropy

One of the primary functions of communication is to reduce uncertainty (Pierce, 1961; Wiener, 1948; Wilden, 1972). **Entropy** has many meanings, but in information sciences and communication it basically is "a measure of the degree of randomness … in the situation," such that a situation low in entropy "is highly organized, it

is not characterized by a large degree of randomness or of choice" (Shannon & Weaver, 1949, p. 103). Through communication, we are constantly engaged in a process of combatting entropy; we are constantly engaged in a process of creating order, regulating both nature and behavior, and managing to pursue pattern and structure rather than randomness. Communication, although often entertaining, fun, joyous, painful, awkward, and surprising, is also always something from which we take meaning. In these meanings, we find a modicum of control—a sense of why things are as they are. Communication is our attempt to control a universe that often seems indifferent to our actions.

Axiom 7: Communication Involves Distortion and Inaccuracy

In general, you are rarely as competent a communicator as you think you are. Competent communication can be highly accurate, and redundancy is one of the means through which such accuracy can be achieved. However, communication is also frequently capable of distortion and bias. Communication may be a particularly effective means for reducing uncertainty and error, but it is also fully capable of introducing error and uncertainty as well, both intentionally and unintentionally. Communication is often biased, distorted, manipulated, misused, and used incompetently. The persistence of crime, conflict, terrorism, neglect, deprivation, and extraordinary disparities in caring for our species, and the species with which we share the Earth, also indicates that *communication cannot fix everything*. One of the first and most insidious barriers to greater competence in communication is a human tendency to be unaware of the room for improvement that is intrinsic to the communication process.

Axiom 8: Communication Is Contextually Contingent

Closely related to the previous axiom is the presumption that communication is contextual (Spitzberg, 2013a; Spitzberg & Brunner, 1991). The effects of things on communication, and the effects of communication on other things, depends on the situation. The contextual nature of communication does not contradict the fact that many aspects of communication are universal. It is both. In some instances, a communication process or pattern will be more similar across situations and cultures than it will be different, and in other cases it will be more dissimilar. Students of communication will often hear a claim by an instructor and ask, "Doesn't that depend on … ?" The most appropriate response by the instructor should usually be, "Yes, it does, and what do you think it depends on; how does it depend on that, and why?" It is not enough to simply say that the effect of something on communication, or the effect of communication on something, *depends*. Communication scholarship seeks to understand the conditions under which it depends and in what ways it depends.

Axiom 9: Communication Is a Systemic Process

Communication is systemic, which broadly means it is holistic, complex, and irreversible (Berlo, 1960). Each of these concepts could be discussed at length, but only a couple of principles will be elaborated, here.

Communication is holistic (nonsummative). A system can only be fully understood as a whole (i.e., **holism**). All components of the system affect (i.e., are interdependent with) all other parts of the system (i.e., the butterfly effect). Interdependence means that each component of a system depends on all other components of that system to function properly (Watzlawick et al., 1967). As with organs in your body, or a family that loses one of its members, the actions of any one component of a system influence the functioning of the other components. This degree of subtlety can be illustrated by how a job interview can turn on one misplaced word choice (Scott, Sinclair, Short, & Bruce, 2014). As such, in any given communicative or rhetorical situation, simply analyzing the situation by breaking it down into its component parts and pieces will not provide a full understanding of what that system is capable of (i.e., the system differs from the sum of its components; that is, it is **nonsummative**). Collectively, to say that communication is systemic is also to say that it can only be understood as an entire, or **holistic**, process, taking into account all of the interrelationships that influence it. No message in a relationship can be understood apart from understanding the individuals involved, their relationship history, the situation in which it occurs, the culture in which it occurs, and so on. To extract a detail

of a message may facilitate focus, but a full understanding will require a more comprehensive account of the various factors that may affect the function of that behavior, both past and present.

Communication is complex. Systems are characterized by both multifinality (i.e., any given path, behavior, message, tactic, or strategy can lead to multiple possible outcomes) and equifinality (i.e., any given multiple possible paths, behaviors, messages, tactics, or strategies may yield the same outcome) (Adams, Hester, Bradley, Meyers, & Keating, 2014; von Bertalanffy, 1968, 1975; Wilden, 1972). As such, communication behavior is differentially adaptive (i.e., facilitative of system survival or functioning), such that as the system interacts with its social environment, different behaviors will have different effects at different times and in different contexts. An intrinsic degree of unpredictability exists in every system. All characterizations of tactical communication are at best probable rather than certain (Spitzberg, 2013a, 2014). That is, no single communication behavior guarantees that a particular outcome will occur—it only increases or decreases the probability of certain outcomes based on past experience and context.

Communication is irreversible. An old saying states that "you cannot step in the same river twice." The aphorism is based on the intuitive understanding that the complex system of the river is such that it is constantly changing. By the time a foot is lifted and placed back into the river, an indefinite number of features of the river will have already shifted and changed such that it is not the exact same river as it was with the first step. Further, the initial step itself altered the architecture of the river, changing, however infinitesimally, the river so it is no longer its former self. Communication systems are similar. No message can be fully erased because it has already become part of the history of the system, and there is no capacity for rebooting the system. Communication is **irreversible** (Watzlawick et al., 1967). If you have ever been in a heated argument with someone you care about and have spontaneously said something mean or hurtful, all the apologies and pleadings to "please forget that I said that" cannot actually erase it from having been spoken. It has become part of the communication system in which it was uttered, and it has changed that system now and in the future.

Axiom 10: Communication Is Socially Constructed and Constructive

Beyond the fundamental needs of safety and security (e.g., food, shelter), most of what is important to humans is determined by social processes of communication. We find our mates through communication. We keep our families together through communication. We form and maintain organizations, societies, political systems, and cultures through communication. We figure out who we are through a communication process that lets us know where we stand in society and whether we meet its expectations of achievement and status. Issues of what kind of relationship we have with another are almost entirely established and evolved through communication. And, the categories and concepts we come to accept as important (how we dress, how we behave, how we govern, how we form bonds, what we value) are constantly negotiated and renegotiated through social intercourse (Berger & Luckmann, 1966; Searle, 1995). As Giddens (see Turner, 1986) might argue, we are born into a system, but the system only exists in the future by our continuity of contributions to that system through our communication with others. Much of the meaning of our everyday lives is therefore **socially constructed**, maintained, and constantly altered through symbolic behavior.

The Nature of Nonverbal Communication

Now that the nature of communication, symbols, and language has been briefly introduced, it is important to examine the mode of communication that the human species began with—**nonverbal communication**. Although definitions vary, nonverbal messages include all messages that are *nonlinguistic, analogic,* and typically governed by the right **brain hemisphere** (Andersen, Garrison, & Andersen, 1979). A better label would be *nonlinguistic communication* because spoken versus unspoken is not a key distinction (Andersen, 2008; Dunbar, 2017).

Nonverbal Communication Is Nonlinguistic

Much of communication does not rely on language at all. Nonverbal communication does not use language. "The real distinction between verbal and nonverbal communicative behavior lies in the system by which action is organized. Verbal behavior is organized by language systems, whereas nonverbal behavior is not" (Eisenberg & Smith, 1971, p. 20). **Verbal behavior**, or language, is a unique human communication system that relies on arbitrary symbols to convey meaning. The term "arbitrary symbols" refers to the fact that people create and use messages that represent ideas (people, places, and things) but are not uniformly fixed to those ideas. So, different words can refer to the same idea, and the same word can represent different ideas. For instance, "affect" can reference emotions (a noun) as well as causing something (a verb). Written or spoken words, computer codes, numbers, and sign languages are arbitrarily symbolic, and thus linguistic. By contrast, nonverbal communication is a direct, biological system that does not use arbitrary symbols. Infants are excellent communicators, but they cannot talk; they use vocalizations, touch, facial expressions, and interpersonal distance very effectively without uttering a word.

Nonverbal Communication Is Analogic

Analogic messages tend to have a direct, intrinsic, nonarbitrary relationship to the things they represent (Andersen, 1986; Wilden, 1972). By contrast, **digital communication** uses arbitrary symbols, such as the word "dog" or "perro," rather than an image of a canine. Analogic messages often take abbreviated forms of other behaviors: a pat on the back is a miniature hug; a shaken fist is a pretend punch; and a furious person, like an angry dog, looks to be about to bite someone. Affection can be conveyed analogically, without words, via smiles, hugs, caresses, kisses, close distances, or prolonged eye contact (Andersen 2008; Guerrero & Floyd, 2006). Additionally, analogic messages can take on an infinite number of degrees or values. Affection can be communicated through a light touch or a passionate embrace; smiles can range from slight smirks to broad grins; distance can range from nearly touching to being miles away (Andersen, 2008). Digital codes, by contrast, have only two values: on or off, yes or no. Digital communication is like a light switch; analogic communication is like a light dimmer.

A defining characteristic of nonverbal communication concerns its nonarbitrary analogic code, not the channel (see **Table 2.1**). It is the nature of the **code**—analogic and nonlinguistic—and not the **channel**, that makes

TABLE 2.1: Exemplars of Parallel Nonverbal and Verbal Codes

	Nonverbal Exemplars	Verbal Exemplars
Haptics (contact codes)	Personal space	"Keep out" signs
	Conversational distance	"Welcome" signs
	Territory	Signs posting rules regarding access
	Hugs, pats, slaps	"No kissing" sign
Kinesic (and oculesic) codes	Posture	American Sign Language
	Facial expressions	Lip reading
	Expressive gestures (middle finger)	Verbal translation: "F—k you"
	Eye contact, gaze aversion	No photography signs
Physical appearance codes	Hair, eye, skin color	T-shirts with slogans
	Height and body shape	Writing on team jackets or uniforms, verbal tattoos
	Facial features (e.g., nose shape)	Name labels
	Adornments, makeup	ID bracelets, dog tags, etc.
Voice (vocalic) codes	Vocal qualities (pitch, volume, warmth, animation, etc.)	Spoken words
	Singing, shouting, whispering	Musical notation
	Pauses, silences, interruptions	"Shhhh," "Quiet!" "Don't interrupt!"
Environmental and artifact codes	Architectural features	Signs identifying rooms, buildings, streets
	Furniture arrangement	Plaques, diplomas
	Pictures, flowers, aesthetics	"Seat yourself" signs
	Temperature, noise, lighting	"You are here" sign
Time (chronemic) codes	Pacing, wait time, punctuality	Clocks, watches, timers, calendars
	Perceptions of time (e.g., island time)	Verbal phrases (e.g., "Time is money," "Time's a'wastin'")
Olfactory codes	Perfume, deodorant (smell-a-vision)	Verbal expressions ("You stink!"; "Stop and smell the roses"; "Ah, that 'new car' smell," etc.)
	Natural body odor	"Whoo! You've been working up a sweat"; "Oooh. Morning breath!"

Source: Adapted from Guerrero & Farinelli (2009).

a message nonverbal (Andersen, 2008; Watzlawick et al., 1967). Moreover, use of the vocal channel does not mean that a message is verbal. Gestures are usually analogic and nonverbal, but sign language and arbitrary emblems with dictionary definitions are verbal. A hug is a form of nonverbal, touch communication, but braille print, a verbal, linguistic form of communication, uses touch. Nonverbal messages can take many forms, but so can verbal messages. At the same time, substantive differences exist between verbal and nonverbal codes (see **Table 2.2**). Both the differences and the complementary features between verbal and nonverbal communication make their integration fundamental to everyday interaction.

TABLE 2.2: Distinguishing Nonverbal and Verbal Communication

	Nonverbal Communication Is	Verbal Communication Is
Fundamental differences	Analogic	Digital
	Nonlinguistic	Linguistic
	Right hemispheric	Left hemispheric
Origins	Primarily biologically based	Primarily learned
	Phylogenetically ancient	Phylogenetically recent
	Developmentally primary	Developmentally secondary
	Relatively pancultural	Culturally based
Codes	Iconic	Notational/symbolic
	Continuous	Discontinuous/intermittent
	Nonunitized	Unitized
Channel(s)	Multichanneled	Monochanneled
	Simultaneously redundant	Awkwardly redundant
Cognition	Encoded/decoded as a gestalt	Encoded/decoded discretely
	Syncretic/holistic	Analytic
	Spontaneous	Symbolic
	Relatively honest	Relatively manipulated
Functional distinctions	Used to convey global meanings	Used to convey precise information
	Affective and emotional	Logical and cognitive
	Relational	Content oriented

Source: Adapted from Andersen (2008).

Nonverbal Communication Is Hard-Wired in the Human Brain

The human brain is a remarkable organ in many ways. One of its many amazing features is that it is both one organ and a number of separate organs. Just as specific parts of the brain control the left hand or the right foot, each of the two brain hemispheres is primarily responsible for one of two broad types of communication: verbal or nonverbal (Andersen et al., 1979; MacNeilage, Rogers, & Vallortigara, 2009). Indeed, throughout the animal kingdom, the two sides of the brain evolved to perform different functions (MacNeilage et al., 2009). This functional separation enables people to send or receive both nonverbal and verbal messages simultaneously.

In almost all people, the right hemisphere is dominant in controlling nonverbal communication, whereas the left hemisphere is dominant in controlling language (Andersen et al., 1979; Herve, Zago, Petit, Mazoyer, & Tzourip-Mazoyer, 2013). A severe injury to a person's left brain hemisphere will impair that person's verbal communication abilities, whereas a similar injury to the right brain hemisphere will impair nonverbal communication abilities (Andersen et al., 1979). The right hemisphere of the brain functions to understand spatial relations, direction, facial recognition, facial expression, tone of voice, cries, music, environmental sounds, interpersonal touch, body motions, and other nonverbal behaviors (Andersen et al., 1979; MacNeilage et al., 2009).

Nonverbal Communication Is Continuous

Nonverbal communication is continuous (Andersen, 1986; Watzalwick et al., 1968). You cannot stand a nondistance from someone; you are near or far, not simply present or absent. There are no blank facial expressions—a motionless face can be perceived as sad, annoyed, or withdrawn

(Andersen, 2008). Even hand movements and gestures have no negative value. Still or folded hands are often perceived as relaxed or composed. Smiles run the gamut from smirks to grins to beaming smiles (Andersen, 2008). You cannot make yourself invisible, so your physical appearance always sends messages about yourself (recall from earlier in this chapter: "One cannot not communicate," Watlawick et al., 1967).

Words are digital and can be turned off, but nonverbal messages are continuously available to receivers. Nonverbal communication occurs whenever a receiver assigns meaning to a person's behavior. Analogic systems cannot be shut off; they continuously function as computers (Wilden, 1972, 1980). A rheostat, the hands on a clock, and a volume knob on a (nondigital) radio are examples of analogic codes with continuous functions. Nonverbal communication works the same way.

Nonverbal Communication Is Phylogenetically Primary

Phylogeny is the evolutionary history of a type or species of organism. In the world's long evolutionary history, the nonverbal behavior of animals has constituted its primary and more ancient communication system. Over many millions of years, animals developed greater complexity in various forms of nonverbal communication, including echolocation, whistles, heat sensors, olfactory communication, cries, and facial expression, to name but a few (Floyd, 2014). The ancient origins and sophistication of these systems suggest that these are a primary communication system that is, in many ways, more robust than verbal and linguistic systems. As with other animals, human beings communicated nonverbally a million years or more before they developed language (Andersen, 2008; Bateson, 1972; Guerrero & Floyd, 2006). Furthermore, nonverbal communication has continued to evolve to become even more complex and rich; nonverbal paralanguage became music, kinesic body movements became dance, and our vocal intonations and facial expressions are more complex than those of any other animal. The evolutionary primacy of nonverbal communication supports that the most basic and salient communication system is nonverbal, and because this system houses so much of emotional and relational communication, it is usually given great weight in everyday communication (Andersen, 2008; Guerrero & Floyd, 2006).

Nonverbal Communication Is Developmentally Primary

In the life of every human being, nonverbal communication develops long before verbal communication. Although humans acquire language quickly in the first years of life, newborn infants instantly can send and receive basic vocalic, kinesic, proxemic, olfactory, and tactile messages (Andersen, 2008; Camras, 1982; Stern, 1980). Human infants are adept at communicating their needs and emotions and at establishing relationships with their caregivers. The basic relational forms of nonverbal communication that are so crucial to infant development continue to persist throughout life (Guerrero & Floyd, 2006), particularly in the communication of turn-taking, immediacy, intimacy, affection, persuasion, and comfort. Spend time with any baby and you will observe the complexity and competence of their nonverbal displays. Language is learned by the time a human is one or two, but humans are born already possessing considerable nonverbal communication skills.

Nonverbal Communication Is More Universal and Cross-Cultural Than Verbal Communication

Nonverbal behaviors are more universal than verbal communication. To understand a language, a person must be taught that language, but nonverbal communication is a more biological system with considerable cross-cultural similarity (Andersen, 2008). Ekman and Friesen (1975) showed pictures of facial expressions for people around the world and found great similarities across cultures in facial displays of emotions. Similarly, blind children who have never seen a facial expression display the same expressions of joy, fear, anger, and other emotions as do sighted children (Eibl-Eibesfeldt, 1979). A meta-analysis provided evidence that facial expressions are recognized cross-culturally at better-than-chance levels (Elfenbein & Ambady, 2002). The same is true for gestures. Congenitally blind children use the same number and types of gestures as do sighted children (Iverson & Goldin-Meadow, 1997). At least some hand gestures have cross-cultural meanings, such as an open hand—a sign of peace and greeting in most cultures—and a fist—a sign of hostility and anger in most cultures; in general, gestural behavior is similar across cultures (Kinsbourne, 2006). The intonation and rhythmic patterns of voices show considerable similarity across cultures (Frick, 1985). Given these universal features, the difficulty of cross-cultural communication can be reduced through the use of nonverbal behavior. Smiling, opening one's hand, frowning, laughing, shrugging, and patting one's own stomach, along with other various affectionate behaviors, are messages that have substantial translation cross-culturally (Andersen, 2008; Guerrero & Floyd, 2006).

Nonverbal Communication Is Naturally Redundant

The multichanneled nature of nonverbal communication is the main reason that nonverbal communication is *naturally redundant*, and is thus more accurate and believable than verbal communication. A basic principle of communication theory is that redundancy increases accuracy (Andersen, 2008). Verbal communication is ill-suited to provide a lot of redundancy except through persistent repetition. Indeed, verbal redundancy is taxing, fatiguing, nagging, and condescending. Nonetheless, redundancy is needed to have clear and error-free communication. Redundancy increases accuracy (I said it again!) because noise, poor reception, and inattention can prevent accurate communication. As Bateson (1972) demonstrated, redundancy increases the signal/noise ratio and promotes communication fidelity.

Nonverbal communication, however, is multichanneled and simultaneously redundant. These properties make nonverbal communication straightforwardly redundant without the nagging, boring, condescending qualities of verbal communication. A friend who makes eye contact, sits close, smiles, touches, and spends time with you competently sends clear messages of intimacy. Even an imperceptive receiver is unlikely to miss such a display. Thus, consistent nonverbal communication is a clear and efficient system. In short, nonverbal communication enables messages to overcome noise and define relationships with others.

Nonverbal Messages Are the Primary Form of Emotional Communication

Certainly, words can convey powerful emotional messages, including fear, anger, and love, to mention but a few, yet emotional communication is mostly nonverbal. Emotions and emotional expressions were selected over the millennia because of the evolutionary advantage afforded by the ability to rapidly read others' emotions. In everyday communication, talking about our feelings is common, but spontaneously revealing feelings through nonverbal communication is much more common. Revealing our feelings verbally is too personal and "uncool." The natural system of communicating emotion is nonlinguistic, analogic, nonverbal communication (see **Table 2.3**). Research suggests that emotions constitute more than private experiences; they allow interpersonal information to be shared (Andersen & Guerrero, 1998; Parkinson, 2005).

Nonverbal Communication Is Multichanneled

When we communicate, we simultaneously send proxemic, physical appearance, kinesic, and oculesic messages (to mention but a few). Nonverbal communication is inherently **multichanneled** (Andersen, 1986; LaFrance & Mayo, 1978). When people communicate love, anger, excitement, affection, or any message, they accomplish this through multiple channels. In fact, it is hard to communicate nonverbal messages through only one channel. Imagine communicating intimacy or power with only your face or your hands; such an expression would seem awkward, wooden, and even deceitful. Excitement, for example, could be communicated verbally with a statement such as, "Wow, I'm excited!" Such excitement, however, will usually be accompanied by a set of multichanneled nonverbal messages that may include screams, wide eyes, smiles, clapping hands, running, jumping up and down, hands covering the mouth, an open mouth, and expressive gestures, to name only a few possibilities (Andersen, 2008).

Honest, believable nonverbal messages are generally consistent across channels, with each channel complementing and strengthening the meaning of the message. It is hard to be believable in 10 different channels if one is not being honest. It is the multichanneled nature of nonverbal communication that may cause nonverbal communication to be believed over verbal communication.

The power of nonverbal communication is partly due to the fact that it contains numerous codes or channels, often simultaneously. We communicate through our physical personae, our body movements, our facial expressions, our spatial and touch behaviors, our tones of voice, our uses of time, our eye behaviors, and even the ways we smell. These nonverbal cues are every bit as important as the words we speak or write. Let us explore some of the most potent channels of nonverbal communication in some more depth.

Physical Appearance: Usually, the first message we send to a person during our early interactions is via **physical appearance**. When someone first meets someone else,

TABLE 2.3: Nonverbal Profiles for Selected Emotions

Emotion	Kinesic Cues	Vocalic Cues	Haptic Cues
Happiness	Smile with skin crinkled around the eyes Cheeks raised Backward head tilt Open body position Raised arms	Moderately loud and varied volume Fast tempo Moderately high pitch Large pitch variation	Swinging, shaking, lifting
Sadness	Frown (sometimes with bottom lip trembling) Slumped posture	Low volume Slow tempo Low-pitched speaking High-pitched crying Monotone	Stroking, squeezing, lifting
Fear	Open mouth with tense lips Raised eyebrows Eyes wide open and dilated Backward head tilt Backward transfer of weight	Loud if in attack mode or quiet if in escape mode Fast tempo High pitch (if in attack mode) Small pitch variation	Trembling, shaking, squeezing
Anger	Square-shaped mouth or lips pressed together Furrowed eyebrows Backward head tilt Raised arms Clenched fist Erect posture	Loud Fast tempo High, rising pitch (if frustrated) Low pitch (if annoyed)	Squeezing, hitting, trembling
Surprise	Raised and arched eyebrows Eyes open wide with whites showing all around the iris Jaw dropped Hands over mouth	Fast tempo High pitch	Squeezing, lifting, shaking

Source: Adapted from Guerrero & Ramos-Salazar (2015).

that person's gender, race, clothing style, age, ethnicity, stature, body type, height, physical attractiveness, and mood all reveal that person's physical and psychological persona (Andersen, 2008).

Kinesics (Body Language): Another powerful nonverbal cue, based on body movements, is **kinesic** communication. Our bodies, legs, faces, and hands are capable of sending thousands of different messages (Andersen, 2008). The best cues to our moods and feelings are displayed on our faces, which are capable of communicating dozens of emotions. Although facial expressions have nuances, or "accents," in different cultures (Matsumoto, 2006), basic facial expressions have universal meanings

that are recognized across cultures throughout the world (Ekman & Friesen, 1975). Similarly, our hands are capable of numerous gestures that include illustrators—gestures that accompany speech—and emblems—gestures with dictionary meanings in a given culture, although emblems may actually be a gestural form of verbal communication (Andersen et al., 1979). Likewise, body postures, sitting positions, and walking styles can convey a variety of messages about power, pride, sexuality, extraversion, mood, and a host of other communication cues.

Oculesics (Eye Behavior): Our eyes are the most important windows to the outside world, and seeing, along with hearing, is one of our most important channels of communication. The eyes not only receive messages; they also send them through *oculesic* behaviors. These oculesic behaviors are vital forms of communication. Eye contact is the most important oculesic behavior. From early in life, babies are aware of eye contact as a form of communication (Lavelli & Fogel, 2005). Eye contact is an invitation to communicate and is vital in controlling and regulating verbal behavior. During face-to-face interaction, the absence of eye contact is perceived as distracted, rude, shy, disinterested, inattentive, and/or deceptive. Eye contact is used to send messages of affection, intimacy, flirtation, warmth, love, and concern (Andersen, 2008). Prolonged stares, however, particularly with blank or negative facial expressions, can be intimidating or even hostile, and continuous eye contact while speaking communicates power and confidence. Furthermore, oculesic cues can be subtle and even subconscious. Pupil dilation occurs in dim light, but also in response to images or events we find attractive, arousing, or inviting. Dilated pupils also send subtle messages to other people such that people with dilated eyes are perceived as more attractive, warmer, more loving, or friendlier (Andersen, 2008).

Proxemics (Spatial Behavior): How we use interpersonal space and distance—that is, **proxemic behavior**—is another potent form of communication. Most important is **personal space**—an invisible bubble about an arm's length in radius that surrounds us wherever we go (Andersen, 2008). Except for friends, lovers, and family members, most people are not allowed in our personal space bubble. Invasions of our space are perceived as rude, threatening, harassing, and inappropriate, with the exception being someone we find very attractive or high in status. If our space is invaded, we erect body barriers or buffers, back away, turn away, give people hostile stares, or leave the scene. The use of personal space signals our relationships with other people (Hall, 1968), though it varies from culture to culture. People who are within about a foot and a half of each other are using intimate space, an area reserved for our closest friends and family members, along with toddlers, because they do not recognize personal space boundaries. Most interactions occur in a moderate one-half- to four-foot space, and people are perceived as odd and inappropriate if they stand closer or farther than that distance. Hollywood stars, sport celebrities, and political figures are afforded much more personal space, partly as protection from the fans and public, but also as a sign of their status.

Proxemic behavior also includes territoriality; that is, the use of home space that is "owned" by the occupant. Some territory is fixed space, such as your home, locker, or yard, that is legally protected against outside intrusion by others, particularly strangers. A person's territory is even protected by the Fourth Amendment to the U.S. Constitution, which affirms "the right of the people to be secure in their persons, houses, papers, and effects" as a fundamental foundation of the Bill of Rights. Some territory is temporary, such as your desk in a college class, your table at a cafeteria, or your parking space. Even when seats are not assigned in a college class, when someone sits in "your" seat you may be upset or wonder why the person failed to recognize it as yours (Andersen, 2008).

Haptics (Touch Behavior): One of the most potent forms of communication is touch, or **haptic** behavior. Touch contains the greatest power to communicate love, intimacy, comfort, and warmth, but it also has the ability to dominate, harass, control, and injure. Touch is one of the most affectionate and loving forms of nonverbal communication, and research has shown that touch is intrinsically rewarding or reinforcing even in the youngest infants (Field, 2002). Indeed, babies who are touched frequently are much more likely to thrive physically, emotionally, and cognitively than babies deprived of touch. No form of communication is more powerful than touch when sending messages of love or affection, and it is the central form of communication in sexual interaction. Touch has also been shown to have powerful persuasive effects. Numerous studies have shown that the presence of touch produces more compliance during petition drives, requests for charity, and requests from strangers for change for a parking meter, along with higher tips for waiters and waitresses (Andersen, 2008). Of course, some areas of the body are open and accessible to touch for nearly everyone. The hands are often used for greetings, and the handshake is an important form of introductory communication; a handshake that is too strong or too weak conveys very negative impressions. The shoulders are generally a safe zone of touch, but the thighs, chest, crotch, and buttocks are generally taboo zones except between people who have very intimate relationships. Types of touch also differ greatly; strokes are sensual or sexual and pats tend to be friendly, whereas squeezes are ambiguous.

Vocalics (Paralinguistic Communication): Speech is the primary form of verbal communication, but speech is frequently unclear and uninterpretable without nonverbal, vocal inflections that can totally change the meaning of words. In our nonverbal communication class, we conduct an exercise in which we see how many ways we can say the single word "yes." Depending on one's **vocalics**, or vocal inflections, the word "yes" can signal agreement, affirmation, reluctance, hostility, confusion, intimacy, boredom, seduction, affection, impatience, and a multitude of other messages. Vocal qualities such as pitch, rhythm, tempo, resonance, control, and accent nonverbally modify the spoken word. The study of these nonverbal elements of the voice is called *vocalics* or *paralinguistics*. Throughout human history, even before and during the evolution of language, the voice, and music as well, provided instant emotional communication between people (Juslin & Laukka, 2003). Researchers in the area also examine other vocal characteristics such as laughing, screaming, inhaling or exhaling, sighing, yawning, groaning, and crying, as well as vocal segregates such as "uh-huh," "uh-uh," "ah," and "um" (Trager, 1958), as well as singing (Andersen et al., 1979). Moreover, every person has a unique voice. A person's vocal signature is as distinctive as a fingerprint. No two voices are identical; each has its distinct combination of pitch, regional accent, volume, resonance, and other vocal qualities. Vocalics may be one of the most important forms of nonverbal communication because it provides the context for everything we say. Bateson (1972) stated that "paralanguage has blossomed side by side with verbal communication … [our] vocal intonation far exceeds anything that any other animal is known to produce" (p. 412).

Box 2.1 Ethical Issues

The NCA Credo for Ethical Communication presented in Box 1.1 covers a broad range of communication ethics issues. It is important to note that ethical communication includes both verbal and nonverbal communication. Makau (2009) asserts that ethical communication involves attending to "one's intentions, the means used to fulfill these ends, and the likely consequences of one's choices" (p. 437). Three broad ethical issues are described here to foster discussion about communication choices we make:

- **The "Golden Rule"**

  Several religious and philosophical traditions provide the foundation for what is commonly called the "Golden Rule": Do unto others as you would have them do unto you. Some version of this instruction for treating other people can be found in various ancient spiritual texts and reflects multiple cultural perspectives. Although the Golden Rule is not specific to communication, our communication messages and behavior fall within the realm of "doing." Accordingly, one general ethical issue within the domain of communication is to apply in principle the criterion that action is moral to the extent that you would be willing for others to act in accordance with the same principle.

- **Intentional Ambiguity**

  Because communication occurs across the spectrum of human experience and contexts, ambiguity is an inevitable feature of communication processes in which we engage (Johannesen, Valde, & Whedbee, 2008). However, intentionally ambiguous communication should also be approached with caution. Ambiguous language is open to multiple interpretations, such as informing a visitor that you are "not available." Sometimes ambiguity benefits involved parties. Messages are ethically suspect when ambiguity is used to intentionally confuse others or avoid developing common understanding that is required in particular situations. For example, in a decision-making situation involving sharing facts, experiences, and other information, intentional ambiguity may contribute to poor decision-making and a lack of full understanding of critical issues. Such ambiguity could lead to consequential mistakes in relationships, organizations, municipalities, and entire nations.

- **Ethics in Nonverbal Communication**

  As noted in this chapter, nonverbal communication uses different codes than verbal communication. Furthermore, some degree of our nonverbal communication is involuntary such that it seems almost outside of the realm of ethics. However, nonverbal communication also involves a degree of choice, and accordingly involves many of the same ethical considerations as verbal communication. One domain of nonverbal communication is *visual communication*, such as communication with photographic images. Photographic images involve choice of subject, frame, angle, what is left out, what is left in, etc. All of these choices influence what is communicated by the image, and accordingly influence the impact on people who view the image (Johannesen et al., 2008).

People tend to think they are better looking than their peers think those people are (Hitsch, Hortaçsu, & Ariely 2010a, 2010b; Pozzebon, Vissner, & Bogaert, 2012). Students tend to report higher grades and test scores than they actually have (Ehrlinger, Johnson, Banner, Dunning, & Kruger, 2008; Kuncel, Credé, & Thomas, 2005). Students tend to view themselves above average in cooperativeness, leadership ability, public speaking ability, self-confidence, understanding others, writing ability, tolerance regarding those with divergent beliefs, openness to challenges to one's own views, ability to negotiate sensitive or controversial issues, and ability to cooperate well with diverse others (Higher Education Research Institute [HERI], 2009, 2010). Even though most people know that about half of all marriages end in divorce, almost no individuals expect in advance that their own marriage will fail (Baker & Emery, 1993). Yet, evidence indicates that college students today are as much as 30% more narcissistic (Twenge, Konrath, Foster, Campbell, & Bushman, 2008) and 30% less empathic (Konrath, O'Brien, & Hsing, 2011) than they were only 30 years ago. Thus, despite evidence of sharply declining rates of empathy and perspective-taking abilities among college students in the United States, students think of themselves as overwhelmingly empathic and skilled at perspective taking. Perhaps the most insidious aspect of these findings is that distorted views of self are themselves an indicator of communicative incompetence; communicators with inflated self-perceptions are more likely to be those who are most lacking in communication competence (Dunning, Heath, & Suls, 2004; Karl & Kopf, 1994; Kruger & Dunning, 1999; Mattern, Burrus, & Shaw, 2010). Because they cannot accurately monitor the reactions of others, they are unaware of their own incompetence, which further distorts their ability to know what skills to modify and improve. None of this is helped by the findings of research by Microsoft (Gausby, 2015), which concluded that workers' average attention span of 12 seconds in 2000 had by 2013 dropped to 8 seconds, about the same as a goldfish.

Thus, if the longest journey begins with a single and first step, the first and most important first step is to recognize that regardless of how skilled a communicator you are, there is substantial room for improvement, and such improvement can only occur by first recognizing the need for such improvement. As a senior and a communication major, you may feel at the height of your communicative competence, and you may well be. But there is still more to be done, more to learn, and more to achieve.

We talk, converse, socialize, and communicate every day of our lives, and yet we are generally only vaguely aware of the enormous complexity underlying this remarkable process. The axioms, features, and explanations of the nature of verbal and nonverbal communication are intended to draw attention to this complexity. With an appreciation of the nature and scope of verbal and nonverbal communication, it is now possible to examine the major ways in which this phenomenon is studied.

Conclusion

In general, people assume that people tell the truth and therefore that communication tends to be a relatively accurate representation of the world (Levine, 2014; Makau, 1991; Mieth, 1997). In general, people also do not consider themselves in particular need of education or improvement when it comes to their general attractiveness or personal communication abilities. Most able-bodied people walk every day and do not consider themselves in need of training in walking. Likewise, people communicate every day and generally do not consider themselves in need of greater expertise in talking. This is often referred to as the "**Wobegon**," "self-enhancement," or "better-than-average" effect, where all individuals believe themselves to be "above average" (Alicke & Govorun, 2005; Kruger, 1999; Sedikides, Gaertner, & Toguchi, 2003). It is also related to the "illusion of transparency" (the spotlight effect), in which people assume greater clarity and accuracy in communication because their primary frame of reference is an assessment of their own mental clarity in forming their messages (Fay, Page, & Serfaty, 2010; Gilovich & Savitsky, 1999). These self-serving biases in perception show up in a wide variety of contexts (Simons, 2013). It is relevant to point out in regard to these biases that that within 5 to 10 minutes of engaging in a conversation, a college student accurately recalls only about 10 to 15% of that conversation in any detail (Samp & Humphreys, 2007; Stafford & Daly, 1984).

Credit

FIG. 2.1: Dan Dediu and Stephen C. Levinson, from "On the Antiquity of Language: The Reinterpretation of Neandertal Linguistic Capacities and Its Consequences," *Frontiers in Psychology*, vol. 4, no. 397. Copyright © 2013 by Dan Dediu and Stephen C. Levinson (CC BY 3.0).

PART II

Knowing How We Know What We (Claim to) Know
Research Paradigms

CHAPTER 3

Knowing What We Don't Know Yet
Major Paradigms of Knowing

Brian H. Spitzberg

LEARNING OBJECTIVES

After reading this chapter, you should be able to do the following:

- Explain how research paradigms are like cultures.

- Articulate the rationale for, and against, the dichotomies of quantitative versus qualitative and humanistic versus scientific perspectives.

- Identify and differentiate the elements of the argumentative rationale underlying different methodological paradigms in the field of communication (i.e., claims, data, and warrants).

- Identify and differentiate the contents of the methodological paradigm arguments (i.e., theory, critical, interpretive/ethnographic, performative, conversation analytic, and quantitative/experimental).

- Identify the correct usage of the term "paradigm" in social scientific and humanistic usage.

- Specify the role of values in the structure of arguments.

- Identify the implications of viewing different methodological paradigms as distinct magisteria.

Scholarly Spaces:
An Ethnological Analogue

The diaspora of our forebears involved treacherous journeys into unknown areas and uncertain futures. The trek out of Africa and into uncharted territories occurred when, according to the best available historical records, our species possessed only the most rudimentary tools and artifacts. Yet, even as far back as 500,000 years ago, people may have experimented with working with artifacts with some aesthetic motivation, and obviously artistic artifacts emerged around 30,000 years ago. When aesthetic motives intersected with the much older ability of tool use, among the innovations that arose was basketry—the art of weaving baskets.

Using a wide variety of indigenous plant-based materials, various forms of basketry were developed, using grasses (coiled basketry), wide palms and yucca plants (plaiting basketry), roots and tree barks (twining basketry), and reed and cane (wicker or splint basketry). Each technique involves the complex interlacing of horizontal lines (weft) and vertical lines (warps), and each technique often begins at different places in the making of the basket and employs design methods and aesthetic elaboration often distinct to the maker or to the tribe or culture of the maker. Thus, as with so many artifacts, *baskets represent a signature* of a particular person's craft, and this craft reflects a form of knowledge and ability that other people apprenticed through instruction. Baskets are a tool, a form of art, and a signal of cultural distinction. Over time, basketry became a tradition of certain cultures, and traditions constitute elements of culture taught and apprenticed to each successive generation. As such, tracing particular basketry forms provides one way of tracing how knowledge of methods is transmitted both within and across geographic regions, tribes, and cultures over time (Ellen, 2009; Jordan & Shennan, 2003; Thulman, 2014). In short, weaving a particular style of basket represents a method of doing something and a way of seeing one's culture manifested in a product of that culture. A careful study of such crafts offers a window into the particular culture they represent—they also represent a type of language specific to their respective cultures. To learn such a language or craft is time-consuming, but once learned, offers a type of deep insight into the ways that culture both shares and differs in elements from one's own culture.

Scholarship also has its form of weaving tools and aesthetics. Scholars do not simply "know things." Scholars *learn* methods, their crafts, which reflect their different cultural orientations to seeing and making sense of the world. As with any craft, it tends to be learned over time, generally through the apprenticeship of a mentor who methodically shows and guides a student to master the craft. Naturally, mistakes are made, corrected, and taught to students who eventually can become autonomous and even creative of new techniques in their method.

Because it is so time-consuming, such craftsmanship often makes it difficult for someone to learn more than one simple method of basketry. Going about the business of discovery and knowledge production, it is difficult to take time out to engage the arduous task of learning an entirely new approach to crafting artifacts. Furthermore, to do so often appears as a type of cultural betrayal—leaving behind a cultural tradition and emblems of one's cultural heritage. Thus, once a tradition is learned, an alternative tradition is often difficult to master. In this sense, particular basket styles become distinctive representations of one's tribe or culture.

Scholarly ways of knowing provide many parallels with basketry. Although scholarly traditions might not have developed until relatively modern times, clearly the search for understanding the world around us would have begun at least with the development of language itself. The ability to ask questions would have entailed the ability to wonder why things happen the way they do. Accordingly, by the dawn of modern history the ancient African and Mediterranean rhetorical traditions were already centuries old. Over the next two millennia, the search for greater and more valid insights into the world in which we live led to various cultures and crafts of artistry and methodology, each with its own way of making sense of the world.

These scholarly traditions and cultures coalesced into various academic tribes, represented to varying degrees in different academic departments, disciplines, colleges, associations, and, occasionally, even hallways and faculty room tables. Tribes often would tout their aesthetic approach, their method of basketry, as superior to those of other academic tribes. Wars would sometimes be fought among those who sought to represent their own techniques and methods as the most sophisticated or traditional or useful or insightful. In other academic contexts, however, the multiplicity of crafts would be valued, and artists would seek collaborations in which multiple techniques and aesthetics would be applied, mixed, or combined by multiple creators to achieve new visions of how the warp and weft of knowledge could be expressed.

Scholars have developed different methodological idioms of systematic inquiry in somewhat the same way that different tribes or cultures have developed different modes of basketry. These methodological idioms represent distinct cultures, sometimes cooperating, but more often competing, to claim the larger territory of wisdom in both the humanities and social sciences. Even when representatives of distinct cultures publicly claim the importance of "getting along," in private conversations with people in their own tribes, the conversation often turns defensive, resentful, and even incendiary of other people's intrusions into territories more "righteously" reserved for one's own chosen endeavors.

Competition for the sake of competition may have reached the limits of its evolutionary value. Two millennia have helped hone an array of methodological tribes. Productive progress in the future may well require more than a mere mutual tolerance. Instead, academic tribalism may need a common bill of rights, a common sense of collective purpose, and a common recognition of multiple forms of knowledge production. Unfortunately, such a revolution is not in the immediate offing. Before such a revolution can occur, conversation must be established across tribal boundaries. In an effort to facilitate mutual collaboration and regard for multiple forms of weaving knowledge, this textbook seeks to locate the nature of methods in the nature of argument, and, second, to represent the broader scope of methods currently employed by the communication discipline.

Theories and Methods as Arguments

In making a basket, a person needs the raw materials—the raw "data" of his or her craft. How those materials are assembled, the warp and weft of their weaving, reflects the skill of the weaver. Similarly, scholarship involves a craft of taking the raw materials of experience and observation and weaving them into articles, books, scripts, sculptures, and works of art. Each of these ventures can be viewed as a form of **argument**—a form of consensus-seeking discourse—through which the scholar converses with audiences and convinces them of a particular point of view. Instead of plant-based materials and weaving techniques, scholars rely on their methods for observing and interpreting the world, and each of these methods represents a unique argument for seeing the world. Understanding these varying arguments resembles understanding how different types of baskets represent different tribes or cultures. Each type of argument is an emblem of an underlying **logic**—a fundamental form of reasoning about the world.

Despite a multitude of different tribes and aesthetics, all basketry has certain elements in common; so, too, all scholarly traditions have certain basic elements in common. All baskets can be understood as a product of a limited number of forms and structures. Scholarly traditions, despite their variability, can also be understood as a product of a certain set of logical elements.

No matter what else a scholarly method attempts to accomplish, it must rely on argument to establish the validity of its elements. Every method guides the production, collection, and analysis of **data**, the amount of which is vast in the discipline of communication. Such data consist of observations, literature, artifacts, cases, examples, responses, and so on. However, data alone prove nothing. Data are always open to multiple interpretations of their meaning and implications. Data only become meaningful in the crucible of argument, which makes those data sensible through their warrants to claims. **Warrants** are the reasons, rationale, or answers to the question, "Why is this claim reasonable—why does it make sense?" The **claim** is the conclusion or the particular proposition the argument seeks the observer to believe (e.g., interpretation, hypothesis, value judgment, belief statement, etc.). The claim, once established, may then graduate to become a warrant for later arguments. Warrants construct the bridges between data and claim, and claims, so established, serve as the bases for more arguments.

Artists and craftspeople often take pride in their handiwork. Scholars also tend to produce their craft with a sense of pride. As such, scholars tend to produce their arguments with a sense that their claims are privileged or perhaps "right." This privilege is sometimes treated as a claim to "truth," and, at other times, simply a claim of reasonableness or legitimacy—an argument that deserves recognition and acceptance. Such claims of privilege derive not only from the specialized methods learned through the long and hard efforts of apprenticeship (i.e., a college education), but also from learning the logic and reasoning underlying that methodology. The method *is a type of logic*. One implication of this logic is that scholars claim to know things distinct from layperson's ways of knowing.

Many elements exist where the methods of scholarly knowing can be traced. A traditional, if generally misleading, distinction occurs between **quantitative** and **qualitative** methods (Burrell & Gross, 2017), which also is often mistakenly viewed as parallel to **scientific** versus **humanistic** perspectives. This distinction is useful in understanding certain cultures of scholarship (Snow, 1959), but it is also misleading in many senses. Many humanistic scholars employ quantitative methods, and many scientific scholars use humanistic motivations and subjective interpretations in their work.

Instead of conflating the humanistic/qualitative with the scientific/quantitative distinction, this text primarily examines six illustrative tribal cultures in the communication discipline. These tribal cultures are referred to as paradigms. As explained in more detail in Chapter 4, a **paradigm** involves a collective set of practices and beliefs shared by a group of scholars (Kuhn, 1970). The paradigms examined in this text include: (a) theory as a way of knowing, (b) critical and rhetorical ways of knowing, (c) interpretive and ethnographic ways of knowing, (d) performative ways of knowing, (e) conversation analytic ways of knowing, and (f) quantitative and experimental ways of knowing. These paradigms will be elaborated more extensively in subsequent chapters. These six are relatively common but not exhaustive, as there are other paradigms beyond these (e.g., observational, content analytic, big data, social network, etc.), and different communication programs may emphasize their own particular methodological craft.

"You cannot know what needs to be done until you know what has been done." These sage words from one of my graduate professors, Walter R. Fisher, resonated with my background in intercollegiate debate. Before you know what your theory is, before you know which paradigms are best to pursue as a perspective toward a subject, it is important to engage in background research to find out what scholarly research has already realized about the topic (Chapter 4). Without conducting serious background research, you risk "reinventing the wheel," and you are more likely to speak from ignorance and sound ignorant, especially to an audience that may know the difference between informed and uninformed claims.

Theories and the methods of theory construction provide frameworks that suggest how information and data should be comprehended in a single sense-making explanatory perspective (see Chapter. 5). **Critical methods** assume that reality is always influenced by underlying systems of often-hidden influence and power. Also, such structures must be interrogated through an evaluative perspective that reveals these hidden forces, thereby presenting opportunities for pursuing more idealistic

FIGURE 3.1: Diagramming the Underlying Arguments of Different Ways of Knowing

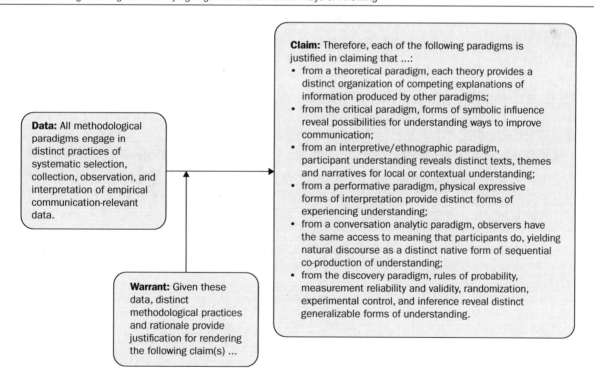

Data: All methodological paradigms engage in distinct practices of systematic selection, collection, observation, and interpretation of empirical communication-relevant data.

Warrant: Given these data, distinct methodological practices and rationale provide justification for rendering the following claim(s) ...

Claim: Therefore, each of the following paradigms is justified in claiming that ...:
- from a theoretical paradigm, each theory provides a distinct organization of competing explanations of information produced by other paradigms;
- from the critical paradigm, forms of symbolic influence reveal possibilities for understanding ways to improve communication;
- from an interpretive/ethnographic paradigm, participant understanding reveals distinct texts, themes and narratives for local or contextual understanding;
- from a performative paradigm, physical expressive forms of interpretation provide distinct forms of experiencing understanding;
- from a conversation analytic paradigm, observers have the same access to meaning that participants do, yielding natural discourse as a distinct native form of sequential co-production of understanding;
- from the discovery paradigm, rules of probability, measurement reliability and validity, randomization, experimental control, and inference reveal distinct generalizable forms of understanding.

or practical ends (see Chapter 6). **Interpretive and ethnographic methods** assume that reality is socially constructed—that there are as many realities as there are people experiencing such perceptions through their interactions (see Chapter 7). **Performative methods** seek visceral and active engagement of audiences with the knowledge produced by interpretive and ethnographic means—by actual enactment of voice in and through performance settings in forms that variously involve audiences in their collaborative construction (see Chapter 8). **Conversation analytic methods** assume that because communicators accomplish everyday life exclusively through their specific communication behaviors, researchers can understand the functioning of these behaviors through meticulous observation and analysis of such naturally occurring activities (see Chapter 9). **Quantitative** and **experimental methods** assume that a singular objective reality is discoverable through attention to measurement, control, and probability. Although no method can reveal objective truth in the social world, quantitative and experimental methods use various procedures of objectification, including experiments, control, and quantification in an attempt to inch ever closer to that reality (see Chapters 10 and 11). If these paradigms are analyzed through the lenses of the rationales they rely on, they might look something like the arguments in **Figure 3.1**.

Methodological Rationales

Theories as Ways of Knowing

Each paradigm or method can be further elaborated into its own particular rationale. Before considering methodology, there is the question of how a scholar's theoretical perspective influences that scholar's ability to make sense of the data available or the data to be collected. Theories influence how ideas, concepts, and relationships, including cause and effect, are understood. Theory tends to influence what a scholar chooses to observe and how the scholar understands what has been observed. For example, affection can be explained by a cognitive theory (focusing on the viewpoints of those engaging in affectionate behavior), a dialectical theory (focusing on how bipolar tensions occur in motives and interpretations in a relationship), or a communicobiological theory (focusing on connections between affectionate behaviors and their physiological indicators). These three different theoretical types rely on different forms of observation and focus. Thus, *theory as a way of knowing* can be understood by its underlying argument, as **Figure 3.2** shows.

Critical and Rhetorical Ways of Knowing

The oldest extensively articulated paradigm in communication can be traced back to ancient Greece and Rome,

FIGURE 3.2: An Underlying Argument of Theory as a Way of Knowing

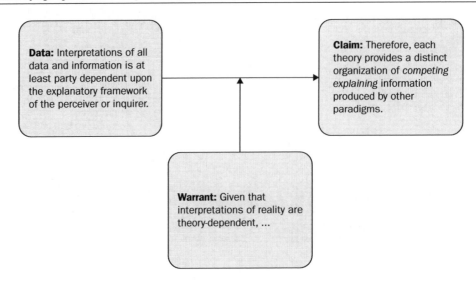

in which scholars engaged in dialectic discourses of argument and counterargument and critique and conjecture about how to improve the uses of rhetoric in society. These methods are referred to contemporaneously as critical methods and/or rhetorical criticism. The world may reveal disparities and distortions that imply underlying forces at work, which sustain themselves through power, deception, manipulation, and bias. Such forces are often masked and require critics to expose them and to provide an evaluative standard against which such exploitative practices might be revealed, and thereby the victims of such distortions may be liberated to empower their own interests. For example, a rhetorical scholar might be curious about whether the *absence* of rhetoric on a particular topic, if occurring in a powerful rhetorical office, might influence the outcomes of public policy. Perez and Dionisoupolis (1995) proposed that President Reagan's refusal to even mention the growing AIDS crisis during his presidency may have muted the movement of the public policy agenda needed to address the early stages of this public health crisis. They concluded that by refusing to place AIDS on the national agenda through presidential rhetoric and communication, probably due to its association with stigmatized groups (i.e., intravenous drug users, gays, etc.), that vital scientific progress was also muted, potentially resulting in untold suffering and death of future generations of AIDS patients. An argument model of this critical and rhetorical way of knowing is displayed in **Figure 3.3**.

Interpretive and Ethnographic Ways of Knowing

Interpretive and ethnographic ways of knowing represent a more recent approach to studying communication. These methods value the careful building of expertise through interviews, analysis of artifacts and documents, and penetrating interrogation of the observer's own insights into sense-making in regard to some particular individual(s) or group(s) or context(s). For example, Geist-Martin, Bollinger, Wiechert, Plump, and Sharf (2016) engaged in intensive observation and interviewing of 14 physicians who practice integrative medicine (IM), a more holistic person-centered approach to health care. These scholars hoped to develop a deeper understanding of the challenges that such IM faces when practitioners try to collaborate with more traditional Western-style healthcare practices and institutions. Across the interview transcripts and notes, they selectively interpreted four challenges faced by IM practitioners: challenges to (1) collaboration, (2) legitimacy, (3) consistency, and (4) unification. This allowed the researchers to recommend changes in education and policy that might facilitate future collaboration and true integration of healthcare practices. The underlying argument of such is displayed in **Figure 3.4**.

FIGURE 3.3: An Underlying Argument of Critical and Rhetorical Ways of Knowing

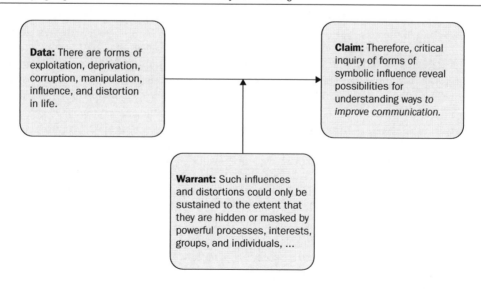

FIGURE 3.4: An Underlying Argument of Interpretive and Ethnographic Ways of Knowing

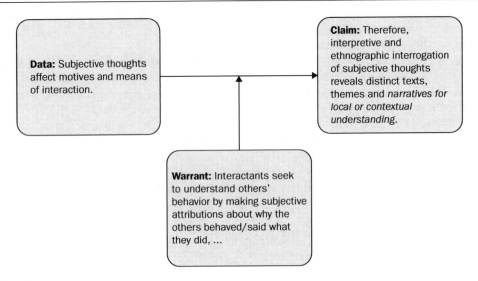

Performative Ways of Knowing

Ethnographic methods are often extended into an additional process of expressing or giving voice to the people who are interviewed. Performative ways of knowing reflect a recognition that a difference exists in the way that consumers of scholarly knowledge experience understanding by reading a report versus coexperiencing a performative representation of that knowledge. Somewhat analogous to the difference between reading a play and attending a play, and the difference between passively watching a play and being interacted with by a character in that play, performance studies involve not only interpretation, but also the selective enacting of the voices and lessons of interpretive and ethnographic research. By seeking to engage audiences at a more visceral level, the scholar's intent is to generate a more empathic and felt experience of understanding. For example, Lindemann (2011) experienced and analyzed a disabled student's performance of a personal narrative and interviewed various performers in that student's academic life, including the campus's Disabled Student Services office, the student's family, and the student. Lindemann identified a variety of tensions, forms of identity management, and aspects of differing notions of (dis)ability. The results of such research can then be woven into a presentation of these themes, including enactments of character voices gleaned from the interviews and observations. Thus, performative ways of

knowing reflect an argumentative rationale, as displayed in **Figure 3.5**.

Conversation Analytic Ways of Knowing

Much of the research paradigms examined thus far either rely on the observer's interpretations of the experiences of others, or on others' recollections and interpretations of their own experiences. Conversation analytic ways of knowing are instead focused on naturally occurring talk and embodied behaviors - interactions that occur whether or not a recording is being made. Such recorded natural interactions are then methodically transcribed, preserving detailed nuances of everyday conversations. By meticulously analyzing everyday conversation, a highly complex process through which people achieve social life is revealed. That is, apologies, compliments, requests, and the "events" of everyday life are accomplished through a subtle choreography of sequential, coconstructed moves and countermoves of behavior. In such a dance, thoughts, values, and beliefs become irrelevant to uncovering the structure of such accomplishments. Interactants cannot peer into each other's mind during a conversation; instead, they recognize interactional functions through the structure of the behavior observed. Therefore, such behavior is also observable to a researcher. The data of everyday accomplishments exist in behavior. If this is accurate, then it seems

FIGURE 3.5: An Underlying Argument of Performative Ways of Knowing

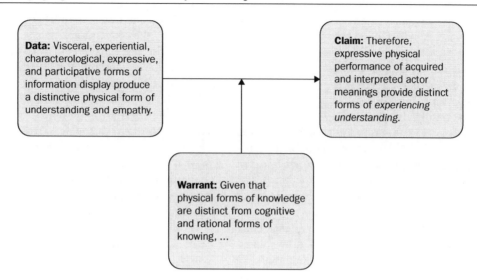

reasonable that all inferences about what conversationalists are attempting to achieve through interaction is exclusively "available" to others through their behavior. For example, Beach and Dozier (2015) recorded interactions among cancer patients and their oncologists or physicians. Intensive analysis of the resulting videotapes and transcripts revealed, among many things, that new cancer patients raise their concerns in indirect rather than direct ways, and with minimal emotional expressiveness. Doctors, in turn, respond to those concerns quickly but with less emotional content. Such emotional disengagement may diminish the sense of human connection in such crucial encounters. Several arguments could be derived from this rationale, but consider the argument in **Figure 3.6**.

FIGURE 3.6: An Underlying Argument of Conversation Analytic Ways of Knowing

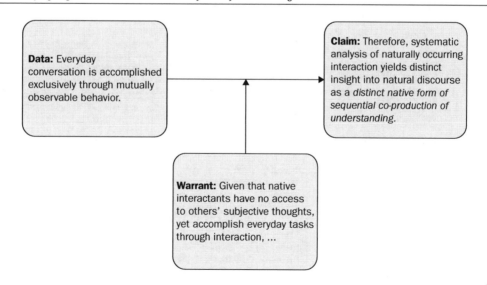

Quantitative and Experimental Ways of Knowing

Quantitative and experimental ways of knowing are sometimes referred to as a *discovery paradigm* because they presume that there is a single objective reality awaiting discovery rather than multiple equally legitimate realities reflected in the differing subjective perceptions of people. The quantitative and experimental way of knowing presupposes that in any given process a set of causes and effects exist. Also, methods properly designed to manage or control for researcher subjectivity, along with translating observations into quantifiable measurements, can reveal something about such causal connections. For example, Fleischmann, Spitzberg, Andersen, and Roesch (2005) proposed a model that certain goals in a relationship predict certain strategies enacted to intentionally make one's romantic partner jealous. They also explored how intentional attempts to make a partner jealous predict certain outcomes for the relationship. They developed a survey to measure various goals of jealousy induction, tactics of jealousy induction, and outcomes of jealousy induction. They found that, for the most part, when people intentionally try to make their partner jealous, the relationship is perceived to improve. Such a nonintuitive finding might escape people who do not search for causal associations with data collection and quantitative analysis. This approach to knowing implies an argument such as that displayed in **Figure 3.7**.

These various arguments lead to very different claims (i.e., methods) of understanding social interaction. For example, to the conversation analyst, only people's naturally occurring behaviors count as data, whereas in ethnographic or interpretive methods both thoughts and behaviors count as data. Rhetorical critics generally only use existing texts and rarely interact with the actual persons whom their analyses examine. Discovery researchers often experiment with people, whereas interpretive and conversation analytic researchers take people's behavior for what it is, or was, and generally do not seek to introduce new stimuli to the investigation context. Further, what counts as a theory can differ substantially across these paradigms. In one, behavior explains behavior, whereas in another, perceptions and feelings explain behavior. Each "tribe" uses its own vernacular and aesthetic for weaving its baskets—from each tribal perspective, only certain types of baskets "make sense" to make.

So it is with *all* methodological arguments; they constitute how we know, the ways in which we represent what we know, and the ways we choose to know that often seem to preclude other ways of knowing. Collective practices and vocabularies of scholars represent what Kuhn (1970) referred to as paradigms, and he believed them to be incommensurable (i.e., not comparable or consistent). That is, a paradigm answers all the questions it needs to, in much the same way a religion is meant to do; consequently,

FIGURE 3.7: An Underlying Argument of Quantitative and Experimental Ways of Knowing

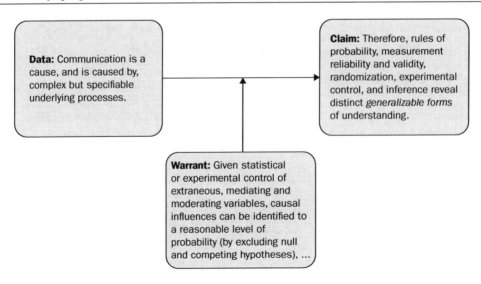

no need exists to borrow from another paradigm, just as most people find no need to borrow religious beliefs from another religion to supplement their own.

Methodological Pluralism

One can differentiate the tribes in which these researchers work and play by the arguments they make. But maybe, just maybe, if they recognize this fact, they can begin to understand *why* their crafts differ in the first place. Maybe they can begin to see how their crafts, their arguments, relate to each other, and thereby begin a dialogue through cooperation rather than conflict (Craig, 1999). Perhaps they can learn to talk each other's language (Kuhn, 1970) and thereby better understand their differences. Perhaps they can recognize the value of **methodological pluralism**, or the integration of multiple methodologies, just as many developed societies have begun to recognize the value of cultural pluralism. This textbook, by examining the underlying basis of these differences, lays the initial bridges (and warrants) for this dialogue to begin.

This dialogue is facilitated to the extent that the various tribes and their customs are known. Arguments are most competent when adapted to their audiences, including those with whom we argue as well as other interested parties (e.g., granting agencies, foundations, the media, etc.). A fair representation of the domain of the discipline provides another strength of this text. Few survey textbooks, for example, do justice to conversation analysis or performance studies, or only give shallow consideration of critical and rhetorical methods. In contrast, this textbook sees the legitimacy of these methods as equivalent because their endeavors are predicated on the same discourse structure of argument. As Walter Fisher (1978) claimed, the foundations of underlying values ultimately compose all arguments, and "no analytically grounded hierarchy of values will ever claim universal adherence" (p. 377). Nevertheless, the more we understand the multiple cultures of values wherein we can seek congress, the better the dialogue can become in the service of that understanding.

Nowhere is this dialogue more important than in the initial enculturation of students, beginning their intrepid voyages into the often-turbulent waters of the communication discipline. Just as it is easier developmentally to learn multiple languages early in the process of language learning, so it is easier to accept multiple methodologies before any mentors fortify a single methodological argument with its armaments and defenses against other scholarly cultures with which it competes. Distinct cultural groups need not engage in similar practices to reap the benefits of mutual understanding and cooperation.

The potential competition among tribes of inquiry reflects an old concern. Scholars have suggested that key differences lie in the questions that each culture seeks to answer. The types of questions asked can be important frames for arguments—such as determining what kind of argument represents a sensible response. People suggest, for example, that no need for competition occurs between religion and science (Gould, 1999) or science and humanities (Gould, 2003; Miller, 1975) because these **magisteria**, or distinct domains of interest, activity and inquiry, ask different types of questions and thereby avoid encroaching on each other's territories. Others, however, suggest that the differences between religion and science, for example, go far deeper than only the questions asked. They point to issues such as their orientations to skepticism, openness to new knowledge and discovery, and the degree to which their faith resides in preserving the past versus accumulating, revising, correcting, and accumulating past knowledge (Fuchs, 2001).

In the case of the arguments posed for the methods encountered in this text, for the most part, the big questions addressed remain the same: Why do people communicate the ways they do, and how does such communication affect the human condition? Instead, the major differences in the paradigms of inquiry examined in this text have to do with *ways* of answering questions, and with different methods, representing different kinds of arguments for pursuing understanding in addressing these "why" and "how" questions.

The journey is not an easy one. Forging relations with strange cultures and tribes seldom is. There are many barriers that even the most motivated and capable among us face in forging paths through and across the historical and geographical boundaries of these methodological divides (Bryman, 2007). On the other hand, great benefits usually derive in developing an acquaintance and ongoing relationship with these cultures. Eventually, with enough trade, commerce, and experience in multiple cultures of research, scholars may become truly multilingual and multicultural, appreciating their indigenous culture, yet fully appreciating and engaging other cultures as well.

People can taste and experience many fruits of knowledge and experiences, which can only derive from encounters with people beyond the borders of our own comfortable domains.

Conclusion

All scholarship and research represents an argument. It is an argument that certain knowledge claims derive from a particular theoretical orientation and related methodologies. But a methodology itself adopts a logic—a rationale—that accounts for the frailties of our experiences, perceptions, biases, and intuitions. Personal experience is highly trusted as a route to knowledge and understanding, but experience alone is fraught with error, bias, and inconsistencies. Scholars have developed a number of paradigms for attempting to grapple with these frailties, from trying to control for such errors and distortions, to identifying such potential biases and incorporating them into their research. In the chapters to follow, you will be introduced to some of the major methodological arguments made in the communication discipline. These different academic tribes sometimes trade freely across their techniques and reasoning, and at other times compete for credibility by criticizing one another and touting the superiority of their own perspectives. Ultimately, the importance of understanding the full panoply of paradigms is twofold. First, an artist is liberated to make better aesthetic choices to the extent that more artistic techniques are understood—having more tools in the toolbox allows for better choices of which tools work best for any given task. Second, the chances for intertribal cooperation are enhanced when more understanding of the underlying cultural logics of such tribes occurs. There are many ways of weaving the knowledge of the communication field, each of which expresses its own aesthetic and reflects the orientations of its tribe.

Chapter 4

Knowing What We Already Know
The Process of Background Research

Brian H. Spitzberg

LEARNING OBJECTIVES

After reading this chapter, you should be able to do the following:

- Identify and differentiate intuitive from scholarly ways of knowing.
- Identify examples of ways in which political, social, cultural, and personal beliefs influence knowledge relative to evidence.
- Differentiate sources from scholarly books, chapters in scholarly edited books, and scholarly journals, based only on references.
- Specify the typical steps and strategies involved in developing a topic.
- Articulate the definition and principles of plagiarism.
- Correctly identify instances of secondary citations.
- Correctly identify instances of plagiarism.
- Specify the rationale for mastering a professional style guide for writing research.

Box 4.1 A Life Well-Researched and Well-Lived

Sean started noticing some things that seemed odd about Samira's behavior. They had only been dating for a few months, but she seemed to have somewhat vague explanations for canceling some recent plans for a couple of dates, and she had casually mentioned her ex-boyfriend a few of times. More noticeably, however, he noticed that she was particularly friendly when conversing with an attractive guy at a party the other night. He wondered if she was having an affair. He considered simply confronting her, but that might start an argument, because he had little real reason to suspect her, and she might take it as his being jealous at a delicate stage of the relationship. He liked her a lot and did not want to mess things up. Still, he wanted to know.

Being a university student, he wondered if the research skills he had been using to research his papers for his professors might be useful in figuring out the best approach to manage the situation. Maybe communication research offered something practical. He logged into *Communication and Mass Media Complete*, added *PsycINFO*, and conducted a search for "jealousy" AND "affair" OR "infidelity." He found more than 1,000 hits, so he restricted it to scholarly peer-reviewed articles. There were still hundreds of hits. He recalled that one of his professors had conducted research on the topic, so he opened a fourth search term window and added "Spitzberg," whereupon a couple of articles showed up—one on communicative strategies for dealing with jealousy, and one on jealousy-induction tactics. In reading these articles, he found that (1) jealous partners often engage in "counterinduction" jealousy, that is, people experiencing jealousy attempting to make their partner jealous in return; (2) partners often try to make their partners jealous as a way of getting their attention and testing the relationship; and (3) there were a lot more words used to describe infidelity than he realized (e.g., affair, cheating, extramarital relations, extra-pair or extra-dyadic sex/copulation/intercourse, and, of course, cuckoldry). He then went back to the original search that was restricted to scholarly articles, and he found research by Shackelford and colleagues that had developed a list of cues that people use to determine if their partner is cheating, and Samira only displayed a couple of them. Sean decided that Samira was simply trying to test him and get his attention. So, Sean made a variety of efforts to pay more attention to her, and a few months later he told her he had wondered, and she admitted that she occasionally "teased" new partners to check to see how jealous they were because she had had bad luck with jealous boyfriends in the past. Sean came to realize that research is not merely a technical requirement that professors assign, but that research involves investigating things that could make a difference in life—things that might have more credibility than the typical *GQ* or *Cosmo* article.

Précis: Scholarly vs. Intuitive Ways of Knowing

Consider, for a moment, some of the following points:

- Approximately 38% of Americans believe that "God created man in present form" (Swift, 2017).

- Republicans (48%) *increasingly* do not believe in evolution compared to Democrats (27%) or Independents (28%) (Pew Research Center, 2013).

- Approximately 38% of Americans believe that "God created human beings pretty much in their present form at one time within the last 10,000 years or so" (Gallup, 2019).

- 60% of Texans either agree that (30%) or do not know whether (30%) "humans and dinosaurs lived at the same time" (Ramsay, 2010). More conservatively, around 12 to 17% of U.S. adults definitely "believe that dinosaurs and humans once lived on the planet at the same time," but another quarter believe they "probably" coexisted (YouGov, 2015), despite the extinction of dinosaurs approximately 65 million years ago, and modern humans evolving less than 500,000 years ago.

- Of 20 policy issues, "dealing with global warming" is 18th in terms of Americans' priorities (38% rating it a top priority (Pew Research Center, 2017).

- Despite extensive scientific evidence of global warming, "just one-in-ten conservative Republicans say the Earth is warming due to human activity. By contrast, fully 78% of liberal Democrats hold this view" (Pew

Research Center, 2015b, p. 16). By another estimate, 74% of Republicans believe news about global warming is "generally exaggerated," compared to 50% of Independents and 15% of Democrats (Newport & Dugan, 2015).

- Out of 11,944 climate-related abstracts in the scientific literature, among those that expressed an opinion, 97.1% concluded that climate change is primarily anthropogenic (i.e., human caused) (Cook et al., 2013).

- Approximately 40% of college students believe in astrology or that "the positions of the planets affect everyday life; a similar percentage thinks some people have psychic powers, and about 1 in 6 think aliens visited ancient civilizations" (Impey, 2013, p. 173). By a more recent survey, 40% "strongly agree" (8%) or "somewhat agree" (32%) "that someone's astrological sign (e.g., Aquarius, Pisces, Aries, etc.) accurately describes their character and personality traits" (YouGov, 2017).

- "More generally 80% [of students] take the anti-rationalist stance that there are phenomena that science cannot explain" (Impey, 2013, p. 173).

Granted, many disagree with these claims or believe that they are merely the biased products of a "liberal academic conspiracy." Such persons are in the company of almost half of Americans in believing at least one kind of conspiracy theory (Oliver & Wood, 2014). The people who believe such conspiracy theories are also more likely to believe that devils, angels, ghosts, and ESP exist, and that we are living in biblically prophesied end times.

Research supplies most of what a scholarly, and sometimes professional, field claims to know, but it is also a *way* of knowing. Sources referenced throughout this *CITE* textbook, and particularly Chapters 5 through 11, represent the most common *ways of knowing* in the communication discipline. One of the most important ways of knowing for scholars and practitioners is to be able to conduct research to see *what is already known*. A wise professor, Walter R. Fisher, once opined that "you can't know what *needs* to be done until you know what *has* been done" (personal communication). Learning how to use the library and to take a scholarly approach to a research a topic are among the most fundamental competencies that every graduate of a university should know. Just as important is knowing why Google, or even Google Scholar or *Academic Search Premier,* is most assuredly *not* a sufficient search

tool; there is an art to the science of library research. This chapter provides an overview of this process, along with a variety of tips for how to engage the process more strategically, and what to do with the results. This chapter is only introductory, and it should serve as a springboard for further and more advanced explorations of the vast toolbox that is available to the modern researcher, such as those covered in Chapters 5 through 11.

A study in 2014 examined the U.S. public's beliefs in a variety of common conspiracy theories (as of 2011), along with some factors that might explain why people believe in narratives that have almost no evidence for their validity and considerable evidence contradicting their validity (Oliver & Wood, 2014). The results are displayed in **Table 4.1**. In all, approximately half of Americans believe in at least one of these conspiracy theories.

Interestingly, such beliefs do not appear to be particularly connected to liberal or conservative belief ideologies, education level, or ignorance, but they are correlated to paranoid and supernatural beliefs, such as the belief in the "end times" (i.e., "We are currently living in end times as foretold by Biblical prophecy"), "Manichean" (i.e., "Much of what happens in the world today is decided by a small and secretive group of individuals"), "supernatural" (e.g., the Devil, angels), and "paranormal" (e.g., ghosts, ESP) and similar belief systems. The resilience of such beliefs illustrates that people often come to "know" things without, and in spite of, evidence or research. Further, it suggests that people can believe almost anything as long as it makes a good story. Furthermore, research on social media indicate that *false information tends to travel faster and farther than true information* (Vosoughi, Roy, & Aral, 2018), indicating that the spread of misinformation and miscommunication may be one of the defining challenges of the 21st century.

For the most part, people learn and know ideas based on a variety of what might be broadly considered **intuitive ways**. Furthermore, as the statistics examined thus far indicate, it is clear that people form beliefs about what is and what is not true based, in part, on their political, cultural, and personal values. Finally, despite being informed of alternative approaches to knowing, "what constitutes 'research' for most students today has come to mean 'Googling'" (Pew Research Center's Internet & American Life Project, 2012, p. 3). Turnitin (2012) examined 37 million higher and secondary student papers and concluded the following:

TABLE 4.1: Percentage of Americans Agreeing With Various Conspiracy Theories: 2011 ($n = 1,935$)

Conspiratorial Narrative	Heard Before?	Strongly Agree or Agree	Neither Agree nor Disagree	Strongly Disagree or Disagree
Iraq war: "The U.S. invasion of Iraq was not part of a campaign to fight terrorism, but was driven by oil companies and Jews in the United States and Israel."	44%	19%	33%	49%
Truther: "Certain U.S. government officials planned the attacks of September 11, 2001, because they wanted the United States to go to war in the Middle East."	67%	19%	22%	59%
Birther: "President Barack Obama was not really born in the United States and does not have an authentic Hawaiian birth certificate."	94%	24%	24%	52%
Financial crisis: "The current financial crisis was secretly orchestrated by a small group of Wall Street bankers to extend the power of the Federal Reserve and further their control of the world's economy."	47%	25%	38%	37%
Chemical trails: "Vapor trails left by aircraft are actually chemical agents deliberately sprayed in a clandestine program directed by government officials."	17%	9%	28%	69%
Soros: "Billionaire George Soros is behind a hidden plot to destabilize the American government, take control of the media, and put the world under his control."	31%	19%	44%	37%
CFLB: "The U.S. government is mandating the switch to compact fluorescent light bulbs because such lights make people more obedient and easier to control."	17%	11%	24%	65%

Source: Cooperative Congressional Election Surveys; adapted from Oliver & Wood (2014), p. 956.

- Students appear to value immediacy over quality in online research,
- Students often use cheat sites and paper mills as sources,
- There is an overreliance on the "wisdom of the crowd" (i.e., crowd-sourced content),
- Student "research" is synonymous with "search," and
- Existing student source choices warrant a need for better search skills (p. 5).

We are born genetically knowing certain emotional expressions and sensory abilities, and many of our basic communication dispositions have substantial genetic roots (Beatty et al., 2002), including being hardwired to acquire language (Dediu & Levinson, 2013). We learn, through direct reinforcement processes, things that seem to work or do not work in achieving our goals (rewards) or in harming us (punishments). "An appropriately programmed perceptual mechanism has survival value" (Kuhn, 1970, p. 161), such that we collectively have the ability to discern certain properties of the world that surrounds us through our experiences of that world. Initially, such experiences might result from direct experience, such as touching a hot stove and realizing that glowing hot things hurt skin. We can also learn through social reinforcement if we reach toward the hot stove and a parent screams at us to stop before we do and then explains the rule involved. But, people develop many other beliefs, behaviors and norms through social modeling in which we observe what works and what does not work, what is normal, and what is punished in our interactions with our family, our peers, and our culture.

Before long, we come to believe in concepts that we cannot directly observe, such as our parents' love, angels, the devil, ghosts, UFOs, or gravity (we see the *effects* of gravity, but not gravity itself). As we grow more sophisticated in our ability to engage in sense-making, we combine these concepts into broader narratives. So, for example, up to half of the U.S. adult population believes at least one conspiracy theory, which involves using certain pieces of information about observed things in the world, but constructing an elaborate set of presumed beliefs about what accounts for these observed things. Once established in a person's mind, such beliefs tend to resist counterevidence, counterargument, and other forms of reasoning. Other belief and value systems, such as most formal religious systems, represent broadly based beliefs and forms of faith about the nature of the world, where it came from, and what it means. Most standard religions have canonical and foundational texts that are considered sacred and beyond reproach as guideposts for their group (Fuchs, 2001).

In contrast to these forms of belief and knowledge, **scholarly ways of knowing** approach knowledge quite differently. Of course, scholars cannot completely escape their own intuitions, but they have developed methodologies (i.e., systematic rule-based forms of knowledge formulation) that can regulate their acquisition of knowledge (see Chapter 3). Scholars are fundamentally *skeptical* of intuitive forms of knowledge and tend to approach all knowledge claims as tentative and based on increasing accumulative revision and progress. That is, scholars view all propositions from a perspective that is constantly renewing itself, looking to improve on, add to, and provide new perspectives or discoveries about the topic of interest. All responsible scholarship, including science, is foundationally skeptical of even its own knowledge claims. To a large degree, scholars start with the presumption that their conjectures are *wrong* and seek evidence to demonstrate that those ideas are wrong. In the process, the scholarly view both builds on what has been claimed as knowledge in the past and is fundamentally restless—presuming that such knowledge is incomplete and in need of correction, revision, or expansion. No other philosophy or approach to knowing in society is naturally self-skeptical in this sense. Self-skepticism differentiates scholarly from other ways of knowing.

Most layperson approaches to knowledge start from the assumption that their approach to knowledge is secure. For example, when something is "known" from a religious perspective, it tends to be taken on faith rather than tested or critically re-examined and is foundationally grounded in a particular past or history. Its approach to the past is that of a sacred past—a past that cannot be revised or doubted. It also tends not to assume that there are substantial unknowns waiting to be discovered that would contradict what has been previously taken on faith (Fuchs, 2001). Such an orientation may explain the small but statistically significant negative correlation between religiosity and intelligence (Zuckerman, Silberman, & Hall, 2013). The scholarly approach to knowledge is also distinct from everyday (e.g., intuitive or practice-based) approaches to knowing. These ways of knowing assume that knowledge and expertise can improve based on accumulated personal experiences, which are naturally biased by the particular exposure, experience, culture, and insight of the knower. Scholarly approaches, in contrast, attempt to control for such biases or limitations or explicitly account for and incorporate their influence in explicit ways. That is, they either try to limit their biases (as in experimental and quantitative studies), or they explicitly address and apply their biases (as in interpretive and critical studies). Across all scholarly approaches to knowledge, however, students are responsible to know previous investigations so that a clearer path forward may be charted. Only by building on the past can scholars hope to avoid reinventing the wheel, and to ascertain most efficiently the value of new information and complement what has been done in the past.

One of the first considerations in determining what we know is to ask, *"What is my perspective toward understanding the world?"* To some, this question may seem nonsensical—do we not all experience the same world? It turns out that we do, and we do not. We all do live in the same world, and in a broad sense, we have to work our way through and around this world in similar ways. We also, however, interpret this world in widely varying ways. Consider some of the differences between Democrat and Republican views of information about climate change, for example. One common traditional way of distinguishing different ways of understanding reflects in many of the departments and majors in higher education: the *sciences* and the *humanities*. The initial seeds of these differences emerged early in human history. At the same time that humans were speculating on the mechanics of

TABLE 4.2: Traditional Dualities Typically Differentiating the Humanities and Sciences

Humanities	Sciences
The textual exploration of the myriad meanings and implications of personal and human existence and possibilities.	The systematic application of method and observation in the pursuit of discovery and testing of reasoned conjectures regarding the description and explanation of worldly phenomena; or, the systematic search for explicable and replicable pattern(s).
Procedural Concerns	
• Imaginative (mentalistic) • The possible (the imaginable) • *Bricolage* (using whatever is available) • Progressively distinctive	• *Empirical* (interobservability) • The testable and observable (predictable) • Systematic (*deduction*, *induction*, probability) • Progressively corrective and cumulative
Ethical Concerns	
• Private (audience of the self) • Openness to experience • Self-examining/reflective • Adopting critical stance	• Public (audience of the peers and the world) • Skeptical of experience and the known • Self-correcting • Risks being incorrect (i.e., falsificationist)
Philosophical Concerns	
• Embrace *self-reflexivity* • Reflexively interdependent • *Idiosyncratic*/"local" • *Ideological* (*axiological*) • Celebration of *ineffability*	• Control self-reflexivity • Reflexively independent • *Generalizable* • Theoretical • Reduction of ineffability

the cosmos, they were also creating great art, poetry, and dramatic representations of the role of humans in these same cosmos.

The division between the **sciences** and the **humanities** offers an imperfect distinction between ways of knowing. There are many ways in which they interact, overlap, and reflect the intrinsic synergies of their relationships. Nevertheless, these distinctions do reflect both substantive and "political" differences that are still evident in the legacies of contemporary higher education and scholarship. These differences are summarized in **Table 4.2**. A simple way of thinking about these differences is to ask, "To what extent is human communication best understood and appreciated by its regularities or the things that make it unique?" This difference is illustrated pointedly by Prior (1962):

Granting the existence of a discernible regularity in the phenomena being studied, it is conceivable, too, that someday the gravitational formula would have been discovered even if it had escaped Newton. None of this can be said of a sonata of Beethoven's or a play of Shakespeare's, or for that matter, of a history of Thucydides. These possess a uniqueness not characteristics of the discoveries of science. (p. 16)

The sciences tend to seek the regularities, whereas the humanities seek to query the creative and unique aspects of human communication.

Finding Out What We Already Know

If indeed every journey begins with a single step, then the first practical step in researching a topic is to have some topic or question in mind. Numerous strategies exist for coming up with and developing a topic for inquiry, including, but not limited to, the following:

1. Is there a topic, issue, problem, or interest the inquirer has that is personally engaging, relevant, or important? Sean wanted to know if his partner was cheating and what to do about it.

2. Does a topic relate to career or professional objectives? A student might want to go into sports contract negotiations, so searching topics and terms related to this profession could allow the student to begin pursuing such objectives.

3. Do topics listed in the course textbook table of contents or subject index, or mentioned in lecture, sound interesting?

4. Do topics the instructor is particularly interested in interest the inquirer as well? A professor who researches the rhetoric of labor movements, or stalking, may represent an opportunity for the inquirer to pursue topics of interest to the instructor as well.

5. Are there topics that reflect the specialization that the program or major is most recognized for by reputation? A program that offers a degree in health communication suggests a variety of topics in doctor–patient interaction, support group dynamics, health or persuasive campaign effectiveness, intimate partner violence, the process of disease outbreaks through social media analysis, and interaction processes that facilitate health in personal relationships, such as stress hormone reactivity during interpersonal conflicts.

6. An inquirer may be interested in subsequent education plans, such as topics that might provide good preparation for an intended graduate degree.

7. A simple process of brainstorming can be conducted to generate ideas for search.

8. People often discover topics when researching another topic. So, for instance, an initial search on the topic of infidelity might lead a student to the related search terms and topics of jealousy, divorce, conflict, or intimate partner violence. Following those topics might lead to a more interesting topic or a more sophisticated way of articulating a thesis or research question.

Sean wanted to know how to recognize a partner's cheating and what to do about it. This allowed him to use a fairly broad net to see what scholarly fish might be caught. This form of **exploratory research** seeks to see what kinds of research have been done on a topic. It is useful when an inquirer begins with relatively little knowledge of "what's out there" in the ocean of research. Sometimes a number of exploratory ventures in different search engines might be necessary to discover if the topic selected is too broad (too many hits are returned by the search terms), too narrow (too few useful hits are returned), or simply irrelevant (returned hits are in unrelated fields or on overly technical or tangential topics).

Search Engines (Other Than Google)

Students are increasingly likely to begin (and unfortunately, often end) their research with Google (Purcell et al., 2012). Furthermore, by some estimates, about three-quarters of all global search engine searches are through Google (NetMarketShare.com, 2019), over 80% of all searches end on the first page of results, and over 95% of all clicks occur on the first page of results (Internet Marketing Ninjas, 2017). Google, it turns out, tends not to be very adroit with thesis topics. In contrast, once Sean started examining the research on the topic of infidelity, he decided to write the paper on the topic of "identifying and managing communication in response to partner infidelity." This narrowing of a topic term into a topic statement or title facilitates **focused research**, in which particular research studies are sought. For example, when this chapter was written, April 20, 2019, the search using the two search engines *PsycINFO* and *Communication and Mass Media Complete* showed 1,880 publications available on the topic of "infidelity." When this was limited to "scholarly peer-reviewed journal articles," this return list was reduced to 1,285 publications. When a second search term was added, "cues," this was reduced to 36. This adding of a search term could have required that the search commence either for the article to have both terms "infidelity" *and* "cues," or it could have searched for articles that had either "infidelity" *or* "cues." These are referred to as **Boolean** conditions, and they can either delimit or expand the search net. When the search term "cues" was replaced by "intimacy," it revealed 60 journal articles mentioning both terms somewhere in the article title, abstract, or key terms list. Because the term "intimacy" takes multiple forms, a *cheat* symbol was then used: "intima*"; this asterisk allows all forms of ending to be included, such as either "intimacy" or "intimate." This expansion of the net returned more than double the articles ($n = 161$). When all of those articles were glanced at for interest, the following sources were checked in the "save manager" and downloaded in American Psychological Association (APA, 6th ed.) style format:

Bohner, G., & Wänke, M. (2004). Psychological gender mediates sex differences in jealousy. *Journal of Cultural and Evolutionary Psychology, 2*, 213–229. doi:10.1556/JCEP.2.2004.3-4.3

Buss, D. M., Shackelford, T. K., Kirkpatrick, L. A., Choe, J. C., Lim, H. K., Hasegawa, M., & … Bennett, K. (1999). Jealousy and the nature of beliefs about infidelity: Tests of competing hypotheses about sex differences in the United States, Korea, and Japan. *Personal Relationships, 6*, 125–150. doi:10.1111/j.1475-6811.1999.tb00215.x

de Visser, R., & McDonald, D. (2007). Swings and round-abouts: Management of jealousy in heterosexual swinging couples. *British Journal of Social Psychology, 46*, 459–476. doi:10.1348/014466606X143153

Drigotas, S. M., Safstrom, C., & Gentilia, T. (1999). An investment model prediction of dating infidelity. *Journal of Personality and Social Psychology, 77*, 509–524. doi:10.1037/0022-3514.77.3.509

Lewandowski, G. R., & Ackerman, R. A. (2006). Something's missing: Need fulfillment and self-expansion as predictors of susceptibility to infidelity. *The Journal of Social Psychology, 146*, 389–403. doi:10.3200/SOCP.146.4.389-403

Millner, V. S. (2008). Internet infidelity: A case of intimacy with detachment. *The Family Journal, 16*, 78–82. doi:10.1177/1066480707308918

Nemeth, J. M., Bonomi, A. E., Lee, M. A., & Ludwin, J. M. (2012). Sexual infidelity as trigger for intimate partner violence. *Journal of Women's Health, 21*, 942–949.

Pauley, P. M., & Emmers-Sommer, T. M. (2007). The impact of internet technologies on primary and secondary romantic relationship development. *Communication Studies, 58*, 411–427. doi:10.1080/10510970701648616

Wilkins, A. C., & Dalessandro, C. (2013). Monogamy lite: Cheating, college, and women. *Gender & Society, 27*, 728–751. doi:10.1177/0891243213483878

Williams, S. S., & Payne, G. (2002). Perceptions of own sexual lies influenced by characteristics of liar, sex partner, and lie itself. *Journal of Sex & Marital Therapy, 28*, 257–267. doi:10.1080/009262302760328299

The save and formatting tools of most search engines are flawed, and most of these sources had to be visually inspected and edited to make them entirely correct according to APA style, but the citation manager still did most of the formatting work. It is also important to remember that this was basically only one search combination. Additional Boolean searches could have been added to "infidelity," and multiple synonyms for infidelity could have been investigated (as suggested earlier).

These software programs are fallible, and they often make mistakes that may cost an author if the author has not directly examined the original document to confirm that the information is correct. For example, in searching *PsycINFO* and *Communication and Mass Media Complete* for the search term of "argument," a researcher could find an article by D. Canary and colleagues. The following citation results from the option to download the APA format of the citation:

Canary, D. J., Brossmann, J. E., & Weger, H. (1995). Toward a theory of minimally rational argument: Analyses of episode-specific effects of argument structures. *Communication Monographs, 62*, 183–212. doi:10.1080/03637759509376357

Any student or scholar who did not click on the PDF file and examine the article, however, would not realize that the engine left out one of the four authors completely, and that it implies that Harry Wegner Junior's father authored the article because it leaves off the "Jr." designation:

Canary, D. J., Brossmann, J. E., Brossmann, B. G., & Weger, H., Jr. (1995). Toward a theory of minimally rational argument: Analyses of episode-specific effects of argument structures. *Communication Monographs, 62*, 183–212. doi:10.1080/03637759509376357

Search engines are enormously helpful, but they should never be the sole crutch on which search and reference formatting are based. This is why in the search engine used for this chapter whenever a citation is downloaded in a particular format, a warning is offered, even if seldom heeded by students: "NOTE: Review the instructions at http://support.ebsco.com/help/?int=ehost&lang=&feature_id=APA and make any necessary corrections before using. Pay special attention to personal names, capitalization, and dates. Always consult your library resources for the exact formatting and punctuation guidelines."

Scholarly vs. Nonscholarly Sources

The search illustrated in the previous section used a parameter that most search engines permit, which is to restrict the search exclusively to "scholarly peer-reviewed journal articles." Some combination of these terms may be used to describe the gold standard of scholarly research. Before differentiating these two classes of scholarly publication, a little background is in order.

The landscape of collective knowledge is evolving rapidly. Google began as a college research project in 1996 and did not begin its substantial diffusion until around 2000, about the same time that Wikipedia began. The widescale availability and convenience of these search engines and information sources have substantially changed the way college students approach research (see, e.g., Judd & Kennedy, 2011; Schweitzer, 2008; Shen, Cheung, & Lee, 2013). But, it is important to recognize that Google is a search engine that operates by certain algorithms and is designed to cast a broad net to bring back popular cultural references that are, for the most part, publicly accessible. In contrast, scholarly search engines are focused on expert publications that are generally only available through the library, subscription, or membership in a professional academic association.

Why is scholarly research more credible, in general, than popular cultural published products? The simple answer is that scholarly research occurs in a context of **peer review** and criticism that helps to vet the quality of claims being made. For this to make sense, it is important to describe the prototypical approach to publishing a scholarly article. First, an author finds out what has been done before because the review process will hold the scholar accountable to prior knowledge. This also provides the scholar with a fuller historical context for how knowledge on a topic has evolved over time. Second, the author writes a manuscript, often with certain presentation and publication outlets in mind. Sources are cited throughout the manuscript to demonstrate awareness and understanding of what has been done before on the topic. Third, the manuscript typically is submitted to an academic conference of a professional association. In this step, the paper is read and evaluated typically by two to four experts whose responsibility it is to only accept high-quality manuscripts to be presented to students and peer scholars as the vital, state-of-the-art knowledge of the field or discipline. At this step, conferences often have rejection rates of approximately 50 to 70%; that is, half to two-thirds or more of all papers submitted to a conference are rejected by the readers as inadequate to represent the knowledge of the field. If accepted, the author presents the key ideas of the paper to an audience of peers at the conference, where it is common for the paper to be further responded to in front of that audience by an expert critic.

Taking the feedback from the readers, critic, and audience into account, the author then may decide to submit the paper to a journal for publication review. **Scholarly journals**, whether established as standard "hardcopy" publications or "online" publications, have an editor who puts together a highly selective editorial board of experts in the areas covered by the journal. When authors submit their papers for publication, the editor may make a "desk" decision to reject the manuscript prior to full review. If deemed relevant and of sufficient quality to review, the editor sends a submission to two to four reviewers on the editorial board who are technically *blind* to the authorship of the manuscript (to avoid bias). Expert advice from area expert "guest" reviewers is also sometimes sought. The sole job of these reviewers is to tear the manuscript apart, or, more precisely, to conduct a few tasks:

1. Provide feedback to the author(s) that can improve the manuscript, or subsequent work in the area.

2. Maintain the quality of research published in the journal.

3. Provide a rationale for a recommendation to the editor whether to:
   a. Publish as is,
   b. Publish with minor revisions,
   c. Publish with major revisions,
   d. Reject, with recommendation to submit to a more topically appropriate journal, or
   e. Reject outright.

This review process may go through several rounds, at several subsequent journals, and take months or years to complete by the time a manuscript comes out as a published article. Across this complex process, most credible scholarly journals maintain *rejection rates above 90%!*

Thus, the vast majority of higher education instructors understandably never attempt to publish in a scholarly journal—the task is too great. Of scholars who do, between rejection rates at conferences and the rejection rates at journals, average scholars who do publish have only one publication in their career. By the time a scholar has 5 to 10 journal articles, that scholar is above the 90th percentile of all published authors in a field such as communication (Stephen, 2008; Stephen & Geel, 2007). That is, the vast majority of the scholarship of a typical academic discipline is authored by a very small minority of the most expert, experienced, and productive scholars of that discipline. The effect of all these processes is that scholarly, **blind peer-reviewed** journal articles represent the gold standard of scholarship. This does not mean that such research is infallible. It simply means that it has passed far more methodical efforts at quality control than the average form of knowledge claim.

Given the many protections against bias, favoritism, and poor quality in peer-reviewed journals, they tend to be valued by professors who value credible backing and sourcing of arguments in their assignments for student papers. Search engines tend to provide simple parameter icons for restricting searches to scholarly peer-reviewed journals. It is also possible, and advisable, to know the difference between scholarly and nonscholarly articles by their presentation and content. **Table 4.3** presents a set of comparisons between scholarly and nonscholarly articles. Collectively, these differences reveal a scholarly culture that seeks to manage its biases through careful self-reflection, self-criticism, evidence-based claims, consistency of application, and rigor in approach.

TABLE 4.3: Differentiating Scholarly Journals From Popular Periodicals

Features	Popular Periodicals	Scholarly Journals
Authorship	Author, typically a staff writer or journalist; credentials often not provided.	Author(s) typically expert(s) or specialist(s) in field, from recognized academic institution, with "terminal academic degrees."
Editors	Articles are not evaluated by experts in the field, but by the staff editors.	Articles usually reviewed and critically evaluated by a board of experts in the field (i.e., refereed or peer reviewed); statement of article submission procedures provided. The gold standard: blind peer review.
Credits/ citations	A reference list is typically not provided, although names of reports or references may be listed for "suggested reading."	A reference list (works cited) and/or footnotes are always provided to ground the article in the existing research literature.
Language/ audience	Written in nontechnical language for anyone to understand; written for broad appeal.	Written in the technical or theoretical jargon of the field for scholarly readers (e.g., professors, researchers, students, etc.).
Format/ structure	Articles often do not follow a specific format or structure.	Articles typically more structured; may include "boilerplate" sections (e.g., abstract, literature review, method, results, conclusion, references or bibliography).
Length	Shorter articles, providing broader overviews of topics.	Longer articles, providing in-depth analysis.
Special features	Illustrations with glossy or color photographs; typically include advertisements between articles.	Illustrations that support the text such as tables of statistics, graphs, maps, or photographs, labeled numerically as Table 1, Table 2, etc.
Serialization	Each new issue begins with page 1, and individual issues are most likely referred to by "month" and/or day/date rather than volume (issue) numbers.	Typically, volume and issue numbers are identified, and pagination of the articles is continuous from one issue to the next within a volume or year.
Scholarly books vs. textbooks	Scholarly books and scholarly edited books are written for other scholars and tend to be heavily referenced throughout.	Textbooks, particularly undergraduate textbooks, are written for students—not for scholars. They are *not* acceptable for citation in proposition paper assignments.

Source: Adapted from a San Diego State University library handout.

Being Responsible for What We (Claim to) Know

Scholars are responsible for knowing what has gone on before—to know what has already been done in order to know what needs to be done. This responsibility carries with it another responsibility—the responsibility to give credit where credit is due. Throughout almost all domains of life, artists, businesspersons, inventors, writers, and the like get to protect their own intellectual property—the fruits of their individual labors. So it is with scholars. The primary legacy that scholars leave to their future generations *as scholars* is their ideas, and their ideas are expressed in language, sound, and image. When these ideas are stolen or appropriated by others without due credit it is a type of theft. It steals the scholar's identity, property, and legacy.

Identifying Plagiarism

In 2016, on the first night of the Republican National Convention, in the primetime keynote speech, Melania Trump gave what most, at the time, considered a highly polished and professional presentation introducing her husband to the nation as an ideal candidate for the presidency. Hidden within the speech was a problem, however; several sentences were either word for word, or in mosaic form, spoken by Michele Obama when introducing her husband 8 years previously to the Democratic National Convention. None of the other content of the speech mattered at this point; the news cycle now focused only on the plagiarism, and not the RNC or Melania's excellent delivery. Republican apologists and campaign proxies went about their business of attempting denial at first, and then rhetorical repair (e.g., Chris Christie defiantly claimed that only 7% of the speech had been plagiarized!), and eventually it was admitted that Melania had (1) relied on a professional speechwriter, who (2) had taken notes from Melania who mentioned passages from previous convention speeches, Michelle Obama's included, which got inserted into her speechwriter's notes, and thus, Melania's speech, which obviously never got sourced (Rasnic, 2016). Furthermore, in attempting to blame the speechwriter, the Trump campaign attempted to ignore Melania's role in the process:

> It was Melania who sought out Michelle Obama's speech for inspiration. It was Melania who plucked passages that she admired from the 2008 speech. It was Melania who gave those passages to her speechwriter. How could Melania not recognize those exact lines when she received the final draft? (Lizza, 2016)

In short, Melania stole, then the speechwriter stole, and then the Trump campaign apologists lied about the theft. It was a daunting rhetorical car wreck on the opening night of one of the most visible rhetorical events of every 4 years. Such is merely one potential damage from plagiarism. Plagiarism is not limited to political speech or academic writing either. For example, Shakira, Robin Thicke, Pharrell Williams, Mark Ronson, William and Chris Brown, the Black Eyed Peas, Led Zeppelin, and Radiohead have all been successfully sued for damages due to replicating but not attributing features of their music or songs to other artists.

In 2015 the late-night comic and headlining show host Conan O'Brien and his broadcast company were sued by a person claiming that O'Brien had used several one- or two-line jokes that were stolen from his blog and Twitter feed. O'Brien and his legal team vehemently denied any awareness or theft of this person's blog or Twitter account. Nevertheless, they decided to settle out of court to avoid the extended legal fees and publicity. O'Brien and his legal team attributed the coincidence to the fact that jokes often emerge in very similar ways because people think and find humor in similar ways. Concurrent with the settlement, O'Brien (2019) opined that:

> Short of murder, stealing material is the worst thing any comic can be accused of, and I have devoted 34 years in show business striving for originality. Had I, for one second, thought that any of my writers took material from someone else I would have fired that writer immediately, personally apologized, and made financial reparations.

Even the appearance of plagiarism was the subject of expensive legal fees, professional reputations, and people's careers put at risk. In contexts in which the artistically formed image, or the written, spoken, or sung word or sounds are the coins of the realm, authenticity of source and originality are preeminent.

Box 4.2 Academic Dishonesty

Cheating is defined as the act of obtaining or attempting to obtain credit for academic work by the use of dishonest, deceptive, or fraudulent means. Examples of cheating include, but are not limited to

- Copying, in part or in whole, from another's test or other examination;
- Discussing answers or ideas relating to the answers on a test or other examination without the permission of the instructor;
- Obtaining copies of a test, an examination, or other course material without the permission of the instructor;
- Using notes, cheat sheets, or other devices considered inappropriate under the prescribed testing condition;
- Collaborating with another or others in work to be presented without the permission of the instructor;
- Falsifying records, laboratory work, or other course data;
- Submitting work previously presented in another course, if contrary to the rules of the course;
- Altering or interfering with the grading procedures;
- Plagiarizing, as defined; and
- Knowingly and intentionally assisting another student in any of the above.

Plagiarism is defined as the act of incorporating ideas, words, or specific substance of another, whether purchased, borrowed, or otherwise obtained, and submitting same to the university as one's own work to fulfill academic requirements without giving credit to the appropriate source. Plagiarism shall include but not be limited to:

- Submitting work, either in part or in whole, completed by another;
- Omitting footnotes for ideas, statements, facts, or conclusions that belong to another;
- Omitting quotation marks when quoting directly from another, whether it be a paragraph, sentence, or part thereof;
- Close and lengthy paraphrasing of the writings of another;
- Submitting another person's artistic works, such as musical compositions, photographs, paintings, drawings, or sculptures; and
- Submitting as one's own work papers purchased from research companies.

Source: Cheating and plagiarism. (2012–2013). San Diego State University. Retrieved from: http://go.sdsu.edu/student_affairs/srr/cheating-plagiarism.aspx

Plagiarism is a form of cheating. Students often practice some form of "double-dipping," in which they write on a given topic across more than one course assignment. In general, there is nothing wrong with double-dipping *topics* or *sources*, but there is a problem with double-dipping *exact and redundant text*. It is common for scholars to write on the same topic across many publication outlets; this is part of developing expertise and the reputation of being a scholar on a topic. Scholars, however, are not permitted to *repeat exact text* across papers or publications except when noted and attributed because this wastes precious intellectual space with repetition and does a disservice to the particular source of original presentation by "diluting" the value of the original presentation. Any time a writer simply "cuts-and-pastes" exact text from former papers into a new paper, it is a form of **self-plagiarism**. Consequently, a given paper should never be turned in to multiple classes. Entire paragraphs, or even sentences, should not be repeated word for word across course assignments. Each new writing and speech assignment is precisely that—a new writing or presentation assignment—requiring new composition on the student's part.

Secondary Citations

Secondary citation is not strictly a form of plagiarism, but, in blatant forms, it can present similar ethical challenges. A **secondary citation** is citing source A, which, in turn, cites source B, but it is source B's ideas or content that provide the unique basis for the claims the student intends to make in the assignment. For example, assume there is an article by Jones (2006) in the student's hands, in which there is a discussion or quotation of an article by Smith (1998). Assume further that what Smith seems to be saying is very important to the student's analysis. In such a situation, the student should always try to locate the original Smith source. *In general, if an idea is important enough to discuss in an assignment, it is important enough to locate and cite the original source for that idea.* These policies are important for several reasons: (a) authors sometimes commit citation errors, which might be replicated without knowing it; (b) authors sometimes make interpretation errors, which might be ignorantly reinforced; (c) therefore, reliability of scholarly activity is made more difficult to assure and enforce; (d) by relying on only a few sources of review, the learning process is short-circuited, and the student's own research competencies are diminished, which are integral to any liberal education; (e) by masking the actual sources of ideas, readers must second guess which sources come from which citations, making the readers' own research more difficult; (f) by masking the origin of the information, the actual source of ideas is misrepresented. The only reasonable exceptions are if the original source is simply not available (e.g., through interlibrary loan, expense, historically no longer available, etc.).

The following are some suggestions that assist with this principle:

- When the ideas Jones discusses are clearly attributed to or unique to Smith, then find the Smith source and citation.

- When the ideas Jones presents are historically associated more with Smith than with Jones, then find the Smith source and citation.

- In contrast, Jones is sometimes merely using Smith to back up what Jones is saying and believes, and is independently qualified to claim whether Smith would have also said it; in such a case, citing Jones is sufficient.

Never simply copy a series of citations at the end of a statement by Jones and reproduce the reference list without actually going to look up what those references report; the only guarantee that claims are valid is for a student to read the original sources of those claims.

The age of "cut-and-paste," mashup art forms, sampling, and Internet memes has ushered in an unprecedented potential for reproducing another person's creations and intellectual property (see **Figure 4.1**). Scholars are not immune. In a study of 100 doctoral dissertations, 46% had a low level of plagiarism, 22% had a medium level, and 3% had a high level (Ison, 2012). In one study, 23% of students did not know that even when writing in their own words they have a responsibility to cite authors who influenced their thinking, 48% did not know it is possible to plagiarize themselves, and 38% did not know that plagiarism extends beyond a failure to cite and reference (Voelker, Love, & Pentina, 2012). In another study of college students, 24 to 30% admitted to copying text without citation, and 8 to 10% had requested or purchased a paper to hand in (Scanlon & Neumann, 2002). A newer study of **contract cheating** (i.e., contracting with another person or agent to provide a paper) indicated that almost 16% of college students have engaged in this process (Newton, 2018). Indeed, even in fields in which society can ill-afford graduates with insufficient knowledge of their subjects, one study found that over 90% of medical students plagiarized to some degree (Bilić-Zulle, Frković, Turk, Ažman, & Petrovečki, 2005). Furthermore, emphases in education and business on team-oriented work and collaborative innovation makes it harder and harder to isolate the individual creation of individual creators. Nevertheless, ideas, words, and images are intellectual property, and almost everyone understands the concept of theft and fraud, in which one party's property is stolen or misrepresented. Whether it reduces that party's profits, worth, or historical legacy, it is still theft and fraud. Furthermore, it fundamentally erodes the entire process of assessment of competence, whereby an institution of higher learning attempts to certify that an individual student "knows" what the student and university claims the student knows. As such, plagiarism devalues the validity of all student degrees. Tools such as Turnitin are increasingly being used to shore up the university's defenses against such erosion. As such, students will generally face dire consequences if they are caught plagiarizing.

FIGURE 4.1: Empirically Derived Types of Plagiarism (Adapted from: https://www.turnitin.com/static/plagiarism-spectrum/)

#1. CLONE
Submitting another's work, word-for-word, as one's own (including "contract" cheating)

#2. CTRL-C
Contains significant portions of text from a single source without alterations

#3. FIND-&-REPLACE
Changing key words & phrases but retaining the essential content of the source

#4. REMIX
Paraphrases from multiple sources, made to fit together

#5. RECYCLE (Self-Plagiarism)
Borrows generously from the writer's previous work without citation

#6. HYBRID
Combines perfectly cited sources with copied passages without citation

#7. MASHUP
Mixes copied material from multiple sources

#8. 404 ERROR
Includes citations to non-existent or inaccurate information about sources

#9. AGGREGATOR
Includes proper citation to sources but the paper contains almost no original work

#10. RE-TWEET
Includes proper citation, but relies too closely on the text's original wording &/or structure

Voicing What We Know

Scholars seek to leave a legacy for their domain of expertise; their work, creative achievements, manuscripts, equations, theories, and studies are intended to contribute to the ongoing course of knowledge in a given field. In order for such contributions to be made, scholars tend to do so in a fishbowl of other academics and scholars who work in similar ways on similar problems. Like almost all domains of professionals, scholars tend to associate in such fishbowls in the form of professional associations. Professional associations exist to maintain, promote, protect, and facilitate work in that profession. As one of the ways in which professional associations maintain their discipline, they formulate and develop style guides that specify consistent ways in which the knowledge of that field should be comprised and shared.

One of the many tools professions use to preserve their legacy is a writing style guide. A **style guide** is a document that articulates in as full and detailed a way as possible the ways in which scholars should write and format their manuscripts or creative representations of their work and ideas. Such guides are essential touchstones for the discipline because they organize almost all intellectual products of a discipline, including journal articles, chapters, books, posters, and papers, as well as statistical, figural, and tabular representations. They provide multiple advantages for the discipline.

First, style guides provide consistency so that readers, graders, and students all know what to expect, where to find it in an intellectual product, and how to arrange and display it. Such consistency allows a similar professional appearance in presenting the products of that profession to its own audiences, as well as to audiences outside of the discipline. Second, style guides help provide a certain linguistic and visual "voice," which, like any language, allows "natives" to know who is a visitor and who is a native. That is, a style guide helps educate the student into the voice of the profession, and, like any language learning, it takes a while to master that language to the point of sounding like a native.

Third, style guides help answer questions about how to present complex information. Despite an infinite potential number of intellectual and artistic ideas that might be presented, a style guide seeks to anticipate such ideas and how they might be formatted into a common linguistic format. Throughout such a range of varying types of information, any given author may seek guidance from the style guide regarding the formatting and composition of such information. An example of a common style guide used by scholars in the communication discipline can be examined in the **Appendix**.

Conclusion

There may be a vague sense in which there are so many rules and guidelines for scholarly writing that it is difficult for authors to find their own individual voices. The many requirements and expectations of scholarly voices, to some degree, make it all the more important for the scholar to find his or her own voice, style, and idiom for composition. Authors may introduce their own tropes and their own poetry in their prose, and seek out their inner imaginations. A finite vocabulary can nevertheless produce an infinite number of sentences and expressions. Out of that infinity, authors have an opportunity, and a responsibility, to create an identity in the words and images to which they give birth in their own caldrons of creation.

Athol Fugard (1990) writes, in the words of a character in one of his plays, *My Children! My Africa!,*

> Be careful! Be careful! Don't scorn words. They are sacred! Magical! Yes they are, … . Stones and petrol bombs can't get inside … police armored cars. Words can. They can do something even more devastating than that; they can get inside the heads of those inside those armored cars. I speak to you like this because if I have faith in anything, it is faith in the power of the word. (p. 51)

Appendix: A Brief Overview of a Professional Style Guide: APA Basics

One of the more common style guides in the social sciences is the *American Psychological Association Style Guide* (APA; 6th ed., 2010). Reflecting changes in language and professional publishing, the APA style guide is in transition to a 7th edition. Although there are thousands of issues regulated and recommended by the style guide, a few are selected here regarding some of the more common needs for students and expectations by professors: heading levels, in-text citation basics, common reference formats, indents, and selected writing basics (e.g., contractions, underlining, italicization, etc.).

Headings are a presentational way of demonstrating that an idea is complex, can be divided into subcomponent themes, and can be organized in sequential and hierarchical ways. Such organization illustrates depth of insight into a topic, along with an ability to outline an idea in ways that advance a rationale or argument. The APA style guide recognizes five levels of organization for composing ideas in a manuscript (see **Table 4.4**). Not all manuscripts will need all five levels of heading, but most manuscripts can benefit from at least two to three levels of organization.

Using in-text citations is one of the fundamental ways in which evidence is introduced to provide backing for claims. Citations reference a source by its author (or title, if there is no author noted for the information). Citations tend to refer to either the exact source of the information or to sources that provide support or agreement with the claim being made. All direct quotations require a single citation from which the quotation is extracted, as well as a page number if a particular page can be identified in the original source. Citations can be integrated into the text in several ways.

For example, Spitzberg and Cupach (2011) argued that "ordinarily, we take notice of our own, or someone else's, interpersonal skills when they are exceptionally bad, exceptionally good, or simply not at all what we expected" (p. 481). Note that the direct quotation required a page number. This quotation could have been paraphrased thusly: Most people only notice everyday interpersonal communication when it is peculiarly good, bad, or unexpected (Spitzberg & Cupach, 2011). In this instance, two things occurred. First, the *idea* was raised in emphasis, as the citation was subordinated. This helps the idea to flow with the text of the prose. Second, that the idea was paraphrased rather than quoted allowed the citation not to include the page number.

For most collegiate papers in communication, three types of scholarly sources are common, each with its own citation format. There are scholarly books, chapters in scholarly edited books, and journal articles. Scholarly books are listed in the "References" list according to the basic format:

Author, F. I. (year of publication). *Italicized title of work: Capital letter of first word beginning sections of title.* Location: Publisher.

An example of this follows:

Spitzberg, B. H., & Cupach, W. R. (2014). *The dark side of relationship pursuit: From attraction to obsession and stalking* (2nd ed.). New York, NY: Routledge.

Edited books tend to involve one or more editors who propose a book to a publisher with selected, invited authors to write chapters according to those authors' areas of expertise. The basic format of such a chapter follows:

Author, F. I. (year of publication). Unitalicized title of chapter: Capital letter of first word beginning sections of chapter title. In F. I. Editor & F. I. Editor (Eds.), *Italicized title of book: Capitalized first word of each title section* (inclusive page numbers of chapter). Location: Publisher.

An example of such a source was cited earlier:

Spitzberg, B. H., & Cupach, W. R. (2011). Interpersonal skills. In M. L. Knapp & J. A. Daly (Eds.), *Handbook of interpersonal communication* (4th ed., pp. 481–524). Thousand Oaks, CA: SAGE.

Scholarly journal articles, discussed earlier as the gold standard of scholarly publications, take the following basic form:

Author, F. I., Author, F. I., & Author, F. I. (year). Unitalicized title of article: First letter of major sections of title capitalized. *Italicized Journal Title, Volume* #(issue #), inclusive pages. doi (digital object identifier):

It should be noted that the digital object identifier is a relatively recent addition to the citation requirements in the APA style guide. Following tradition of many textbooks, the "doi:" number is not included in the *CITE* textbook's own reference lists, but the APA guidelines recognize that any given publisher or course may make exceptions to certain style guide rules. Any writer or author should always confirm and abide by the exact expectations of a given course, publisher, or outlet.

An example of a journal article follows:

Spitzberg, B. H., Tsou, M-H., An, L., Gupta, D. K., & Gawron, J. M. (2013). The map is not which territory?: Speculating on the geo-spatial diffusion of ideas in the Arab Spring of 2011. *Studies in Media and Communication, 1*(1), 101–115. doi: 10.11114/smc.vli1.64

There are several additional general rules about listing such sources in the reference list. First, the overall list is alphabetized by the first author of each source. Second, authorship order *within* any given citation matters. In general, the first author gets to be the first author by virtue of having done the most work, or most important work, on the manuscript. Thus, although the *list* is alphabetized, the authorship *within* each source is set by the authors in the way they are listed in the original work. Third, only

TABLE 4.4: APA Heading Levels (Sixth Edition)

Level	Format
1	**Centered, Boldface, Uppercase and Lowercase Headings.**
2	**Left-aligned, Boldface, Uppercase and Lowercase Headings.**
3	**Indented, boldface, lowercase heading with a period.** Body of text begins after the period.
4	***Indented, boldface, italicized, lowercase heading with a period.*** *Body of text begins after the period.*
5	*Indented, italicized, lowercase heading with a period.* Body of text begins after the period.

Source: American Psychological Association (2010).

sources that are cited in the manuscript are listed. Otherwise, it would be a bibliography rather than a references cited list. Fourth, and in general throughout APA style, first names are not used; only initials. Finally, a "hanging indentation" is utilized for the reference list.

Citing sources is a way of demonstrating that scholars have done their homework and know what has been done before, where ideas have come from, and how to provide evidence for their claims. They are fundamental to the process of scholarly argumentation and to the credibility of scholarly writing. They contextualize a set of ideas in a larger history of related ideas, and exemplify the scholarly responsibility to situate ideas in that history.

Credit

FIG. 4.1: Adapted from https://www.turnitin.com/static/plagiarism-spectrum/.

CHAPTER 5

Knowing What We Think We Know
Theorizing as a Way of Knowing

Brian H. Spitzberg

LEARNING OBJECTIVES

After reading this chapter, you should be able to do the following:

- Identify and differentiate a theory from a paradigm.
- Identify and differentiate humanistic (or interpretive) paradigms from scientific paradigms.
- Identify and differentiate scholarly paradigms based on empirical/analytic and foundational/reflexive dimensions.
- Analyze how induction and deduction fail to prove claims (and identify the principle on which they permit falsification).
- Identify and differentiate the components of the Toulmin argument model (i.e., backing, warrant, claim, and rebuttal/qualifier).
- Extract and analyze the flaws of different types of argument in text (i.e., syllogism, Toulmin argument, etc.)
- Develop logically sound deductive syllogisms reflecting theoretical hypotheses.
- Identify and differentiate definitions from hypotheses.
- Identify and differentiate distal and proximal variables from outcome variables.
- Identify and differentiate a moderating from a mediating variable.
- Identify and differentiate simple from complex hypotheses and concepts.
- Identify and differentiate which criteria are being used in criticizing or evaluating a theory or model.

The Nature of Theories and Paradigms

"It is the theory which decides what we can observe."
—Albert Einstein (as cited in Heisenberg, 1971, p. 77)

"The most incomprehensible thing about the world is that it is comprehensible."
—Albert Einstein (as cited in Hoffmann, 1972, p. 18)

The word "theory" is much misused and abused. People sometimes say things such as, "I have a theory about that," "In theory, this should work," or "I need results, not theory." There are even people who dismiss something such as evolution as "only a theory." We also sometimes hear someone say, "We need a paradigm change" or "That's an old paradigm." So, colloquially, theories are not very useful, but paradigms are. In contrast, as Kurt Lewin (1943, p. 118) opined, "there is nothing so practical as a good theory" (see Bedeian, 2016, p. 237). Einstein similarly proposed that "the most practical solution is a good theory" (as cited in Zeidler, 1995). We employ theories and paradigms in our everyday processes of enacting and cocreating practical achievements, and we express the summaries of those theories and paradigms in our everyday speech. Yet, most people cannot articulate or define the precise nature of these concepts. This chapter seeks to specify the nature of theory, the ways in which theories can be evaluated, the nature and role of paradigms in relation to theories, and some of the basic processes involved in developing theories or theoretical models. Specifically, this chapter is about theory as a way of knowing.

Defining Theory

A **theory** is a verifiable conceptual system of interrelated propositions explaining conditionship among a set of phenomena. Such propositions may be formal (e.g., axiomatic theories or causal models) or informal (e.g., elaborate metaphors or narratives). These propositions may be explicit (e.g., mathematical formulae) or implicit (e.g., a diagrammatic model or narrative description of how a process occurred or proceeds). The essence of a theory is that *it explains* an event, a process, or a set of phenomena. The concept of explanation may be understood in a primitive sense as the offering of an account or narrative that renders an event, set of events, phenomenon, or process comprehensible. Comprehension, in turn, is ordinarily, and perhaps necessarily, tied to notions of causality, structure, and function (Corrigan & Denton, 1996; Pavitt, 2000). **Conditionship** refers to how various relations among concepts in the theory are specified; that is, under what conditions does one concept result in the more or less likelihood of another concept occurring.

People have simplistic informal theories that they use every day. Consider the following conversation:

Sandy: What's wrong?

Lance: My girlfriend just broke up with me last night.

Sandy: That's awful, Lance, but I have to say, I'm not surprised.

Lance: Really? Why not?

Sandy: Well, recently when I've seen you two together, I just got the feeling that she was probably seeing someone else.

Lance: You think she's seeing someone else! Why?

Sandy: She seemed distracted, a little reserved or distant, and she seemed to avoid discussing personal things. I think people withdraw a little when they are thinking about getting out of a relationship.

In this conversation, Sandy has an informal theory about infidelity and relationships. She associates certain communication behaviors as indicating something about internal cognition and emotion and believes that certain communication cues indicate a disinterest in a primary relationship partner, along with a greater interest in another person. Such an informal theory could be made more formal by translating the explanation into propositions (P's), such as the following examples:

P_1: As attraction to a primary partner wanes relative to a new prospective partner, the communication of interest in the primary partner will decrease.

P_2: People engaging in infidelity display less personal disclosure than people in exclusive relationships.

P_3: People engaging in infidelity display fewer verbal and nonverbal interest cues in their primary partner than people in exclusive relationships.

Consider another conversational example:

Sandy: I see you're playing *Call of Duty* again.

Lance: I enjoy playing *CoD*. Why, what's wrong with it?

Sandy: Well, I just think that shooting people all the time has a bad effect on people when they spend all their time doing it.

Lance: Oh, so you think I'm going to become a serial killer some day?

Sandy: No, but I think over time it probably makes a person less sensitive to violence. When spread across everyone in society, playing such games push people just a little bit along the continuum of accepting violence as normal.

Here, Sandy displays another informal theory—that playing violent first-person shooter video games desensitizes players to the harms of violence in everyday life and in society. Underlying her beliefs is a view of how people's minds and emotions work and how experience serves as a model for learning and emotional development. This informal theory could also be formalized in the form of propositions (you are encouraged to try to formulate these propositions on your own).

Scholars use everyday informal theories just like everyone else, but scholars are expected to translate their informal theories into more formal models and propositions, constrained by the best evidence available (Turner, 1985, 1990, 1991). The exact nature of such models and propositions will vary across disciplines and paradigms. One of the key ways in which such models and propositions differ is based on whether the scholar pursues a more humanistic or a more scientific approach to understanding communication. The humanities and the sciences represent two of the fundamental paradigms of scholarly activity (Gould, 2003).

Paradigms

Many people use the term "paradigm," yet few use it as it was originally intended. Kuhn (1970) broadly defined a **paradigm** as a collective set of practices among a group of scholars. These collective practices indicate that certain professionals tend to share similar grounding assumptions and beliefs, similar language, similar explanatory metaphors, and similar methodological tools and procedures for pursuing their knowledge claims. Paradigms tend to house theories (i.e., a scholar pursuing the testing of a theory generally is doing so within a paradigm that houses the kinds of questions and study that best facilitate understanding and testing of the theory). Paradigms tend to change only when a better paradigm is demonstrated to do most of what the prior paradigm did but accomplishes something more and reorganizes what went before. One classic example is the Copernican revolution, when the Sun became the center of our cosmos rather than the Earth. People's observations of the planets and stars did not change—but their understanding of their relationship to one another changed radically.

At some level, scientific revolutions are progressive, but not in the sense that they increasingly achieve "truth" status. Rather, they are **progressive** in the sense that theories become better at solving puzzles that previous theories seem incapable of solving (Lakatos, 1970). Kuhn (1970) clearly recognizes that paradigms are not entirely subjective. He confesses that "scientific development is … a unidirectional and irreversible process. Later scientific theories are better than earlier ones for solving puzzles … , and it displays the sense in which I am a convinced believer in scientific progress" (p. 169). Whether all paradigms of higher learning and scholarship are progressive depends on which paradigm is being considered. Two widely recognized paradigms in higher education are the humanities and the sciences.

Theory in the Humanistic (Interpretive) and the Scientific Paradigms

One of the broadest distinctions across various disciplines of higher learning is between the humanities and the sciences. Communication bridges both these approaches, which are sometimes described as if they were mutually exclusive domains of intellectual pursuit. Some disciplines, such as literary criticism (in the humanities paradigm), seem a distant process from computational linguistics (in the sciences paradigm), yet clearly they appear to be interested in the nature and function of language and symbols.

Miller (1975) suggested a relatively elegant distinction between the humanities and the sciences. If a scholar seeks to make "factual generalizations about similar phenomena not encompassed by the observations that have been made," then it is science (Miller, 1975, p. 232). In contrast, if a scholar is seeking to arrive "at ethical or aesthetic judgments about the phenomena themselves, or about the event, or events, with which the phenomena are associated," it is a form of humanistic, or "interpretive" endeavor (Miller, 1975, p. 235). From this perspective, the distinction is not the type of method used to study the world, but the kind of questions asked of that world.

Both paradigms serve essential functions in higher education and society. "It would be possible to describe absolutely everything scientifically, but it would make no sense. It would be without meaning, as if you described a Beethoven symphony as a variation of wave pressure" (attributed to Albert Einstein, as cited in Clark, 1984). Similarly, Prior (1962) argues that had Newton or Einstein never been born, someone eventually would have discovered the laws of gravity because these things exist in the universe and are there to be discovered. In contrast, had Beethoven never been born, the Ninth Symphony would never have been composed, and had Shakespeare never been born, *Hamlet* would never have been written. Newton did not create the laws of gravity, but Van Gogh created a sky like no one had known before. **Humanities**, therefore, represent the exploration of the myriad meanings of personal and human existence and its possibilities, typically using analytic, critical, or speculative methods. In contrast, the **sciences** represent the systematic application of method and observation in the pursuit of discovery and testing of reasoned conjectures regarding the description and explanation of worldly phenomena (or the systematic search for explicable patterns).

Varieties of Paradigms

The distinction between science and religion (Fuchs, 2001), science and pseudoscience (Popper, 1980), science and ideology (Martindale, 1979), and science and humanities (Miller, 1975) represent fairly fundamental distinctions (Hoyningen-Huene, 2008). Yet, the distinctions between these perspectives should be understood as continua, not mutually exclusive divisions (Geertz, 1980). All scientists create, as well as discover, and all humanists seek their own forms of universal connection with their audiences. Furthermore, it is possible to view paradigms both as distinct *views* of the world, as well as distinct *methods* of viewing. As *views*, paradigms refer to differing theories that serve as different lenses through which the world is

perceived. As *methods*, paradigms refer to different sets of methodologies for studying, observing, interpreting, and commenting on the world. A religion can be a set of beliefs about the world, and a set of practices of observing adherence to those beliefs. Similarly, paradigms can be understood as a selection of a particular set of beliefs about the world, as well as a set of methods for reaching, reinforcing, and reinventing those beliefs through observation.

Many maps of these paradigms exist (for a selection, see, e.g., Anderson, 1996; Craig, 1999, 2007; Smith, 1988), each of which tends to emphasize certain distinctions among paradigms. One conceptual map that provides considerable complexity, but also is relatively comprehensible, is provided by Anderson and Baym (2004). They argue that communication scholarship can be identified by its position on two dimensions: an empirical/analytic dimension, and a foundational/reflexive dimension. Basically, the **empirical/analytic dimension** refers to the degree to which a scholar believes evidence is primarily located in the observed and measured world (empirical), or in the mental categories and judgments our mind uses to make sense of the world (analytic). The former scholar is more scientific, and the latter is more humanist. The **foundational/reflexive dimension** refers to the degree to which a scholar believes reality exists independent of the observer and abides by causal principles (foundational) or is cocreated by social actors and the observer participant (reflexive). These dimensions, when crossed, create the map displayed in **Figure 5.1**.

Each quadrant, or corner, represents a paradigm that provides answers to the most essential questions with which a scholar is concerned: What kinds of theory and methods are legitimate approaches to understanding communication? What kinds of arguments are valid in justifying such theories and methods? What is the ultimate goal of scholarship? What is the nature of reality? In the context of this map, then, both theories and methods combine to illustrate that the nature of theory influences the nature of the methods that are considered appropriate or valid, and the nature of methods have implications for what kinds of theories can be formulated.

The Status of Proof and Disproof

Many people believe it is possible to prove things, and that it is the distinctive province of science to provide such proofs. Even Einstein (1919) admitted that "the truth of a

FIGURE 5.1: Paradigm Map of Significant Tensions in Communication Scholarship

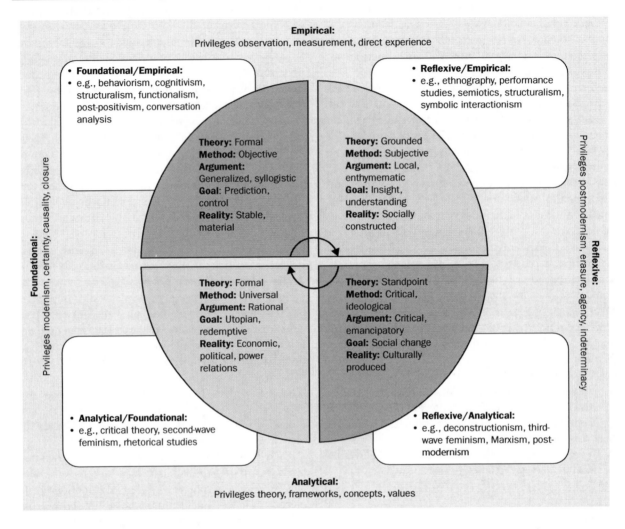

theory can never be proven. For one never knows if future experience will contradict its conclusion; and furthermore there are always other conceptual systems imaginable which might coordinate the very same facts" (p. 109). This latter view exemplifies the philosophy of Sir Karl Popper (1959), who sought to distinguish science from pseudo-science. Science, he claimed, must make falsifiable claims.

To understand this **demarcation criterion** between science and nonscience, it is necessary to go into a simple example. Suppose a theory about marital conflict makes the claim (i.e., proposition, or hypothesis) that marital conflict decreases marital satisfaction and increases the probability of divorce. Popper would point out that no

such claim can ever be proven. No matter how many marriages and how many conflicts within those marriages are observed, it is impossible to verify that every marriage with conflict experiences lower satisfaction and eventually ends in divorce. It is impossible to observe every marriage, every conflict, for all time (as we know, some couples like to argue). Even if millions of couples were observed, and all of them demonstrated this pattern, there is no way of knowing if the *next* couple observed does not fit the pattern. Thus, it is impossible to prove a social scientific claim or proposition in any universal sense, but it is relatively straightforward to **falsify** such a claim. A single example of a couple that experiences conflict but also increases in satisfaction (or does not decline in satisfaction) and does not increase the likelihood of divorce would falsify the claim that marital conflict decreases marital satisfaction and causes divorce. The typical way in which such falsifications occur is through induction.

Research could, for example, observe some number of marriages, ask the marital partners about their conflicts, commitment, and satisfaction with their relationship, and analyze whether there is a relationship between conflict and propensity to divorce. This approach to research involves induction. **Induction** is the process of observing many specific instances or cases of something and drawing a general conclusion about what these instances have in common (e.g., the more conflicts married couples in a particular study sample report, the more dissatisfied they are). Induction is generally distinguished from **deduction**, which involves drawing a conclusion that is entailed by prior premises. Its classic formal form is found in a **syllogism**. There are many forms of syllogism in logic and mathematics, but, in general, social science syllogisms take the (modal) form: P_1: As X occurs, Y tends to occur. P_2: As Y occurs, Z tends to occur. Therefore ($\therefore$), as X occurs, Z is likely to occur. Unfortunately, deduction cannot prove claims either because its premises lack proof and may be illogically connected.

An important historical example of a flawed syllogism is Aristotle's (1994–2009) axiom in *Physics* that heavier objects fall faster than lighter objects. This *seems* as if it *must* be true, and if it is true, it is possible to deduce other things, such as in the following:

P_1: Heavier objects fall faster than lighter objects.

P_2: An iron cannonball is heavier than a wooden cannonball.

$\therefore P_3$: Therefore, the iron cannonball will fall faster than a wooden cannonball.

The problem is that it simply is not true. It is, in fact, fundamentally false. It was not until Galileo actually designed experiments on how fast objects of different weights roll down ramps that he found that objects of varying weights roll at precisely the same speed. That is, Galileo *falsified* Aristotle's deductive claim by demonstrating empirical instances in which Aristotle's claim does not hold. Galileo, in this sense, became the putative "father" of modern science. Much later, Newtonian and Einsteinian theories

of gravity conceptualized how gravity works on all objects similarly. The point is, inductive logic cannot prove propositions because it is always incomplete, and deductive logic cannot prove propositions because it depends on the truth of its own premises, which themselves are not proven.

If neither induction nor deduction can prove anything, how is scholarship to advance? Popper (1980) realized that although there is no guaranteed way of proving a proposition, it is entirely possible to *disprove* propositions. Observing a single relationship in which conflicts are experienced as satisfying and in which divorce never occurs falsifies the claim that conflicts always cause dissatisfaction and divorce. The basic logic of falsification does not change with more probability or modal-based claims. If a hypothesis predicts that a positive association exists between conflict and the likelihood of divorce, and research consistently shows that this relationship is not observed when research investigates it, then the hypothesis is disconfirmed. Popper concludes, therefore, the following:

1. It is easy to obtain confirmations, or verifications, for nearly every theory—if we look for confirmations

2. Confirmations should count only if they are the result of risky predictions …

3. Every "good" scientific theory is a prohibition: it forbids certain things to happen. The more a theory forbids, the better it is

4. A theory which is not refutable by any conceivable event is nonscientific. Irrefutability is not a virtue of theory (as people often think) but a vice

5. Every genuine test of a theory is an attempt to falsify it, or to refute it. Testability is falsifiability … One can sum up all this by saying that *the criterion of the scientific status of a theory is its **falsifiability**, or refutability, or testability*. (Popper, 1980, pp. 22–23, italics in original)

Thus, science makes models, claims, hypotheses, predictions, and propositions that can be disproven *if* they are indeed false. The more precise the predictions (i.e., conditionship) about the way the world must be, the more scientific the scholarly perspective. Conceptual systems such as astrology, religion, and Freudian theory are considered *pseudo*scientific because they make no claims that when confronted by contradictory evidence they lead to the forfeiture of belief in the conceptual system itself. Any theory that is impervious to empirical contradiction or makes no claims that *can be* empirically contradicted in the event they are false claims is not scientific. The criterion of scientific status is the positing of predictions that are at *risk* if they are, in fact, empirically untrue.

From this perspective, **science** is cumulatively progressive. Unlike religion, which is fundamentally conservative in holding to tradition, belief, and faith, science is radical in its ongoing pursuit of newer, better understandings (Fuchs, 2001). Religious institutions may occasionally mimic science (e.g., when declaring sections of a text as apocryphal), but such mimicry is predicated less on external evidence than on consistency with prior beliefs or ideologies. Science never forgets the past (so that it neither repeats its mistakes nor forgets to benefit from its previous discoveries), but it is fundamentally forward looking toward what is yet unknown. It cannot rest on its foundations nor accept any article of faith without test or observation. Science begins most research trying to disprove its hypotheses, which makes it fundamentally self-critical and revisionist in nature. It must continuously build on, evolve, expand, refine, and innovate new ways and contents of understanding—no text is without potential error, and no text or article of faith is beyond doubt. Thus, the past is mere prelude to the present, and the present is always geared toward a future that renders the present partially inadequate. It is in this sense that traditional religion seeks to reify its past as the strictures of the present—to accept that what once was known must be cherished as inviolate in the present. Science, in contrast, views the past as something to constantly revise and grow beyond.

The **humanities**, in contrast to science and religion, work toward different types of claims, envisioning the ways in which human activities and endeavors *mean things* for us, *empower or liberate* us, or *should or should not be pursued* by us. It follows that the role of theory is somewhat different in the sciences (to explain, predict, and control) than in the humanities (to interpret and intellectually enrich). In order to appreciate the ways in which theories can be evaluated, criteria for evaluation must be established.

Evaluating Theory

Criteria are standards for evaluating beliefs and behaviors. The most fundamental criterion for theory evaluation is **quality**. A theory is higher in quality to the extent it more adequately accounts for or explains a phenomenon (Pavitt, 2000) compared to competing accounts, and thus to the extent that it advances accumulation of knowledge over time. There are many more specific ways of evaluating quality. A list of criteria is provided in **Table 5.1** and is organized into four categories: necessary, desirable, comparative, and critical standards.

Necessary qualities are those functions a theory must fulfill in order to even be considered a theory (versus a primitive metaphor, a story, a description, a taxonomy, etc.). **Desirable theoretical qualities** are those features of the theory that connote generally higher general quality; the more of these characteristics (e.g., parsimony) the theory possesses, the more desirable it is. **Comparative theoretical qualities** are those characteristics of the theory that are advantageous compared to other potentially competing theories. Finally, **critical theoretical qualities** are those characteristics of a theory that provide better directions or guidelines for pursuing future action.

Necessary Qualities

A theory must explain a process, event, or phenomenon (**explanatory power**). To do so, a basic understanding must be provided of the concepts relevant to this explanation, along with their interrelationship. These interrelationships among the concepts must be articulated as clearly and reasonably as possible (**conditionship specification**). This explanation must be more abstract than the referent, but the limits and applicability of the theory to other phenomena or contexts must be specified (**boundary specification**). Within the contexts to which the theory does apply, it should apply throughout that entire context; otherwise, the theoretical boundaries need to be respecified (**intraboundary generality**). Within those boundaries, the theory cannot contradict itself (**internal consistency**). That is, a theory's claims must also avoid direct contradiction. A theory cannot claim, for example, that in context C, stimulus S produces both platonic love (X) and sexual attraction (Y) simultaneously, if X and Y are defined in by the theory as mutually exclusive states or experiences. Further, the theory cannot contradict what is empirically known (**external consistency**), and some portion of the theory must be observable and falsifiable, at least potentially.

TABLE 5.1: Criteria for Evaluating Theories

I. **Necessary conditions:**

- **Explanatory power**: The theory must provide a sensible account of the phenomena of concern.
- **Construct and conditionship specification**: The theory must indicate the nature of the constructs and the relationships among these constructs (i.e., necessity, sufficiency, parameters, function form, generality, etc.).
- **Boundary specification**: The theory must indicate the domain of its legitimate scope and relevance.
- **Intraboundary generality**: The theory must provide statements of relationship that hold across all phenomena of concern.
- **Internal consistency**: The theory must maintain logical consistency of all statements of conditionship, assumptions, and units.
- **External consistency**: The theory must avoid contradiction of "known" data.
- **Verifiability/falsifiability**: A theory's components need to be observable and testable.

II. **Desirable conditions:**

- **Precision**: The more the theory allows prediction of phenomena, the better the theory.
- **Parsimony**: The more elegant and simple the theory, the better the theory.
- **Correspondence with observables**: The more of the theory units that are observable, the better the theory.
- **Breadth**: The broader the scope or range of the theory, the better the theory (i.e., verisimilitude).
- **Control**: The greater the potential for strategic manipulation of the phenomena, the better the theory.
- **Synthesis**: The more the theory facilitates the organization and inclusion of existing ideas and information, the better the theory.

III. **Relative conditions:**

- **Heurism**: The more the theory suggests new scholarly questions and endeavors, the better the theory. The more the theory explains new facts or counterintuitive facts, the better the theory.
- **Competition principle**: Theories should compete favorably vis-à-vis their rivals.
- **Money-in-the-bank principle**: "We are warranted in continuing to conjecture that a theory has high verisimilitude when it has accumulated 'money in the bank' by passing several stiff tests" (Meehl, 1990, p. 115).
- **Damn strange coincidences principle**: "The main way a theory gets money in the bank is by predicting facts that, absent the theory, would be antecedently improbable" (Meehl, 1990, p. 115).

IV. **Critical conditions:**

- **Aesthetics**: The higher the narrative fidelity, aesthetic satisfaction, and/or perceiver interest in the theory, the better the theory.
- **Generative capacity**: "[T]he capacity to challenge the guiding assumptions of the culture, to raise fundamental questions regarding contemporary social life, to foster reconsideration of that which is 'taken for granted,' and thereby to generate fresh alternatives for social action" (Gergen, 1994, p. 109).
- **Countersuggestiveness**: "What we need here is an education that makes people contrary, counter-suggestive, without making them incapable of devoting themselves to the elaboration of any single view" (Feyerabend, 1970, p. 63).

Desirable Qualities

Generally speaking, the more specific a theory is in specifying its propositions, the better it is (**precision**). Prediction is a desirable but not necessary aspect of propositions. For example, Darwin's theory of evolution is highly explanatory but lacks predictive power in a number of senses. For example, it predicts that organisms will evolve based on their local environments, but it cannot specify in advance the specific direction or form of these evolutionary changes because it cannot specify the types of environmental changes that will occur or the epigenetic interrelationships of all the organism's form. Communication is an extremely complex process, with equifinality and multifinality (see Chapter 2), making precise prediction particularly challenging.

If predictions are to be useful, at least some of the theory's concepts need to be observable. The more observable the content of the theory is, the easier it should be to assess the verisimilitude of the theory (**correspondence with observables**). Theories that subsume more concepts are generally considered preferable to those that subsume fewer (*synthesis*). Theories that provide guidance on how to intervene or alter phenomena (*control*), and apply to broader domains of interest (**breadth**), are more desirable. Simple and "elegant" theories, however, are generally preferable to those that are overly complex (**parsimony**). These latter two criteria often produce tension, but they are not logically incompatible. At its core, for example, $E = mc^2$ is simultaneously universal in scope, is specific, and is parsimonious. In contrast, formulae such as $B = f P \times E$ (i.e., behavior is a function of person times environment) are universal and parsimonious, but far from specific in their empirical content and operationalization.

Comparative Qualities

Theories are generally viewed as more desirable to the extent that they generate new ideas and new scholarly questions or research pursuits (**heurism**). Sometimes good theories are not valid but highly suggestive of new directions in which better theories may be developed. The better any given theory is at explaining a phenomenon compared to its direct competitors (**competition principle**), the more desirable the theory is. Scholars want theories that provide unique insights, explain more, and suggest more than other available theories.

Scholars may not have access to *the* truth as a reference point from which to evaluate theories. Groups of scholars, however, can nevertheless collectively make theoretical predictions that are supported and replicated. Theories can accumulate credibility (Meehl, 1990) by putting research "money in the bank" by repeatedly avoiding disconfirmation (*ongoing empirical success*), in which the coin of the realm consists of "damn strange coincidences" (i.e., **empirical novelty**). That is, theories are often most credible when they predict something that could not be, or had not previously been, predicted through any other line of reasoning or observation. The classic example is Einstein's theory that predicts that a star would appear to be somewhere it is not because of the light-bending lensing effect of a large gravitational object such as the Sun.

Critical Qualities

Humanists, in particular, tend to seek more out of their theories than just explanation. They seek to understand and enhance the human experience and its creative possibilities through deeper insights into the meanings of human activities. As such, humanists often establish particular standards of beauty or artistry, such as the extent to which the theory fits with existing narratives, is aesthetically satisfying, or evokes perceiver interest (**aesthetics**). Theories tend to be viewed as better, to the extent that they reflect the core metaphorical images of self that culture upholds and to the extent they fit the contemporary aesthetic preferences of that culture. As Weick (1989) explained:

> A good theory is a plausible theory, and a theory is judged to be more plausible and of higher quality if it is interesting rather than obvious, irrelevant or absurd, obvious in novel ways, a source of unexpected connections, high in narrative rationality, aesthetically pleasing, or correspondent with presumed realities. (p. 517)

Humanists also seek theories that are enabling, either by giving people new choices and capabilities to recognize and enact such choices (**generative capacity**), or by identifying ways of seeing and understanding things in ways that are contrary or alternative to existing ways of comprehending the world (**counterrsuggestiveness**).

Other approaches to theory do not fit neatly into the humanistic and scientific paradigms. For example, ethnographers seek theories that preserve the narrative voices of those observed and interviewed (**multivocality**) but also respect the necessity of communicating the textural and textual details of the world that those people inhabit (i.e., **thick description**). Conversation analysts extract micro theories of conversational pragmatics—how people accomplish "avoiding blame," "expressing hope," or "holding a speaking turn." Such theories may not meet many of the traditional criteria for theory evaluation, but they do tend to operate as distinct types of explanations within their own paradigms (Soulliere, Britt, & Maines, 2001; Shields, 2000).

The Process of Modeling

Modeling is one of the zeniths of scientific reasoning. It incorporates analytic reasoning (breaking wholes into parts), synthetic reasoning ([re]assembling parts into wholes), abstract reasoning (recognizing similar things across levels of abstraction and concreteness), **abductive** reasoning (hypothetical conjecturing and refinement), and theoretical reasoning (explaining how and why phenomena happen the way they do). As such, models serve various functions in science and in everyday life.

A **model** is a visual (and sometimes mathematical) simplification of concepts that exist in both a hypothesized conceptual form and an actual or potential observed form. Most models of social behavior explain the process or event as a product of four possible factors. First, there may be factors in the deep past of a person, group, institution, society, or culture that influence the process. These are **distal factors** because they occurred in the distant past. Second, proximal process factors represent the things that occur in the immediate context that influence the phenomenon of interest. It is in this proximal context that communication processes are almost always involved. Conceptually, theories can usually be thought of as explanations of why things have become, and/or why they continue to become, what they become. As such, theories are about some form of causation, and some form of change. Thus, to some degree or another, theories are about **variables**—any concept that can be viewed as taking on different values (see Chapters 10 and 11).

Third, at almost any point of a social process, moderating or mediating factors might occur. Basically, moderating factors resemble a lens that either moves a process into one direction or another, or it magnifies or reduces a relationship (Hefner, 2017). That is, a **moderating variable** influences the direction and/or strength of a relationship between two or more factors. For example, if it is theorized that exposure to images of models and celebrities in television, movies, magazines, and the Internet lead people to develop distorted body images, good reason exists to consider biological sex to be a moderating variable; this effect seems much stronger for women than for men. In contrast, a **mediating variable** accounts for the relationship between two variables (Hefner, 2017). For example, when research found that people of color were much more likely to engage in violent crime than whites, laypersons often concluded that this represented an indication that some races are more aggressive than others. Instead, scholars theorized that because people of color face more discrimination, they are more likely to be lower in socioeconomic status (SES). When SES and related variables are controlled for, the relationship between race and violent crime tends to disappear (Brown & Males, 2011; De Coster, Heimer, & Wittrock, 2006; Kaufman, 2005). That is, it is the poverty and educational limitations that account for criminal activity, not "race."

The final standard component of models specifies the outcome(s), or the result(s), of the process being explained. Any given social process is likely to be complex enough to generate numerous **outcomes** or effects, only some of which will interest the theorist. For example, a simple attempt at modeling Aristotle's theory of rhetoric might look something like **Figure 5.2**. In the model, the rhetorical canon of memory facilitates discovery, arrangement, style, and delivery. Discovery of persuasive techniques, when moderated by rhetorically competent arrangement, style, and delivery, tend to predict successful persuasion. Each rhetorical competency enables the next.

As another example, a scholar might seek to develop a theory of what makes for a successful romantic relationship. One approach is to deduce certain basic principles by which relationships operate. So, for example, it might be assumed that individuals who are more similar in values and beliefs (homophily) are more likely to succeed in their relationships. An alternative approach is to review the existing research and begin assembling a model of factors that influence relationship outcomes, according to prior research. Another approach is to use some metaphor to help orient an understanding of a phenomenon—what if we view people as computers, or as lay scientists, or as primarily a biological product of evolution?

FIGURE 5.2: Adaptation of Aristotle's Core Concepts of Rhetoric

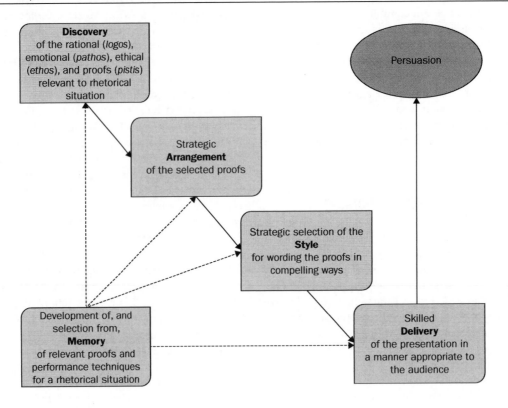

Using a basic model, it is relatively simple to start asking additional questions, such as how biology (e.g., sex, age, etc.), culture (e.g., ethnicity, regional identification, etc.), context (e.g., socioeconomic status, intact family status, etc.), personal background (e.g., attachment disorder, relational history, etc.), or dispositions (e.g., self-esteem, attribution style, etc.) influence various components or relationships of the model.

Most models follow some relatively simple rules:

1. Some components lead to other components, commonly displayed by moving from left to right visually.

2. Every conceptual component is measurable or observable.

3. Every arrow represents a direct effect of one concept on another or relationship between concepts. These do not have to be causal relationships, but often imply such an influence.

4. Concepts are simple (unidimensional) or complex (comprising multiple dimensions or factors), and are grouped according to larger components (multiple indicators of a single concept; e.g., social skills above might be further explained by coordination, expressiveness, attentiveness, and composure skills).

5. When a complex variable is connected to other variables, each of the dimensions or factors that comprise that concept has potential separate hypotheses connecting it to other variables.

An additional aspect of most modeling of social processes is that such processes are often accounted for by some combination of certain types of variables. First, **independent variables** precede and influence subsequent variables. The subsequent variables are referred to as **dependent variables**. A common way of thinking about independent variables is as causes, and the dependent variables as effects of these causes. Your biological sex (independent variable) is likely to influence how teachers react to you (dependent variable) in the classroom, or your experience of childhood trauma (independent variable) is likely to influence the degree to which you trust others (dependent variable). Furthermore, independent variables can be more **distal** (in the distant past) or more **proximal** (more recent or immediate in experience). For example, your biological sex tends to be distal, whereas the amount of stress in your life right now is more proximal. Because our interest is in explaining communication and its effects, most communication models will examine some combination of distal and proximal variables that explain communication behaviors, which then result in certain dependent variables. These variables are connected by arrows to show relationships between and among them, and the organization of these variables and their arrows determine the nature of the explanation, and thus the theory being developed. The arrows usually imply hypotheses.

Hypothesizing

A **hypothesis** is *a verbal or symbolic statement of relationship between two or more variables*; it describes how changes in one concept correspond to changes in another concept (e.g., self-esteem is positively related to self-disclosure). A **variable** is *any construct or concept that can be observed to take on different values* (e.g., age, gender, anxiety, selfdisclosure, assertiveness, etc.). It takes the form of $X = fY$. A hypothesis differs from a definition. A **definition** (e.g., self-esteem is the degree to which self is perceived positively) characterizes the nature of a variable. It takes the form of $X = Y$.

All this is just a fancy way of saying that hypotheses are formal ways of describing how two or more things relate to one another (Shin & Lu, 2017). The "things" are theoretical concepts, and scholars are responsible for providing clear conceptual definitions of these concepts. A conceptual definition is similar to a dictionary definition, except scholars tend to identify the specific features that constitute their particular conceptualization. In particular, for the purposes of this chapter, a **conceptual definition** is a statement formally specifying the requisite features that characterize a component of a theory or model. The concepts, once defined, become easier for scholars to measure and to compare across researchers.

For example, it matters if "aggression" is defined as any behavior intended to harm someone physically, or if it is defined as any behavior that harms someone physically, emotionally, or psychologically. These are substantially different definitions, and each has extensive implications for how they might be observed, measured, or studied. Conceptual definitions are therefore very important and require careful background research (how has this concept been defined previously?), thought, and articulation.

Many hypotheses may be articulated in the existing research literature, and they may be derived from conceptual models or may be products of creativity and imagination. Hypotheses cannot stand on their own. They always require additional explanation and a justificatory argument—that is, a set of statements, narrative, or description that provide a justification and an explanation of the hypothesis—that answer the "why" question (i.e., why is X related to Y this way?).

To explain a hypothesis means to make sensible how and why things are related the way they are. A Toulmin-based model of argumentation (Toulmin, 1958) clarifies how explanatory arguments can develop a hypothesis (Reed & Rowe, 2005; Whithaus, 2012). Arguments consist minimally of explicit or implicit evidence (**backing**), reasons (**warrants**), and intended consequences in the hearer(s) (**claim**). Sometimes there is additional evidence for any of these elements of arguments (backing). Theories make claims about the world, and have an underlying set of observations or evidence, and reasons why such evidence leads to the theory's predictions or claims. Some arguments also include consideration of their own limitations (**rebuttal/qualifier**). In brief, theories are sets of conceptual links among hypotheses. For example, a person may want to explain the hypothesis, "As jealousy increases, the likelihood of relational violence increases." Guided by an understanding of argument, this hypothesis could be justified and explained thusly:

> Jealousy is a complex blend of emotions based on the perception that a person's valued relationship is threatened by a third party or rival [backing]. Retzinger (1991) has reviewed evidence [grounds] that violence is likely to result from a combination of anger and shame, but neither alone [backing]. Because [warrant] anger creates an inner sense of expressive frustration and arousal, and shame provides a target for this expression (i.e., the partner and/or the rival), the jealous person is much more likely to engage in violence than non-jealous persons

[claim]. This hypothesis may not apply to contexts in which strong moral, religious, or public restraints are in place (e.g., even jealous persons tend not to be overtly violent in public places) [rebuttal/qualifier]. The rebuttal is not necessary, but sometimes illustrates the relative objectivity and openness of the author.

Types of Hypotheses

What follows is a series of hypotheses to illustrate different types of propositions. These hypotheses may seem overly sophisticated or technical right now. Once research of a topic has begun, however, hypothetical relations will begin to emerge either stated explicitly (i.e., in the form of hypotheses being tested) or implicitly (i.e., implied by the explanation and discussion of the concepts).

The simplest, and weakest, form of a hypothesis is a *nondirectional* statement of relationship. See the following example:

H$_1$: Self-esteem is related to communication competence.

Although this is a hypothesis, it provides minimal information regarding the conditioning of the relationship. A more precise form is as follows:

H$_2$: Self-esteem is *positively* related to interpersonal communication competence.

Note that this statement can be reworded as, "Persons high in self-esteem are significantly higher in communication competence than persons low in self-esteem." Hypotheses can also vary by the form (or shape) of the relationship:

H$_3$: Talkativeness is curvilinear to perceived communication competence.

That is, talk time in a conversation is positively related up to a moderately high range of perceived competence, after which higher values lead to lower perceived competence. In other words, talking too much decreases people's impressions of your competence.

Finally, deductive construction allows the development of stronger and more tightly controlled theoretical arguments as the following examples show:

H$_4$: As [X: TV exposure] increases, [Y: verbal skills] decrease.

H$_5$: As [Y: verbal skills] decrease, use of [Z: physical violence] in conflict increases.

H$_6$: As [X: TV exposure] increases, use of [Z: physical violence] in conflict increases.

Thus, having the first two hypotheses allows the deduction of the third hypothesis, assuming there is a logical explanation for the connections among the concepts.

On the Art of Explanation

Explanation implies the identification of some "bridge" (i.e., warrant, "because … ," etc.) that serves as an account of why one concept is related to another concept. It is an "animating mechanism" that gives life to a concept. For example, one popular concept is that exposure to violence in the media causes violence in society. The natural question is *why*. Answering the "why" question gets at the concept of explanation. Even though seeing or hearing the equation "Media violence causes societal violence" seems like an explanation, it is not. It is missing the bridge, animating mechanism, or explanation.

To illustrate, consider a few "nonexplanations." It is not an explanation to say media violence causes societal violence because (a) media depictions of violence are increasing; (b) societal violence is increasing; (c) some people have engaged in crimes they saw on TV ("copycat crimes"); (d) people believe what they see on TV; and (e) research shows media violence is positively related to levels of societal violence. Each of these merely suggests correlation (rather than causation) repeats the original assertion, or simply provides backing for an explanation that is itself missing. In contrast, to illustrate legitimate explanations, consider the following:

- *Cultivation.* Social learning theory claims that people learn both by direct experience (e.g., touching a hot stove) and observation of others (e.g., observing one's sister touch a hot stove). Because we cannot or do not always directly experience things (e.g., robbing a bank), we look to real and imaginative role models (e.g., media figures and narratives). Thus, the crime and violence in the media provide models—and rewarding ones at that—for us that we otherwise would not have had.

- *Disinhibition.* Growing up in a culture is largely about learning what one cannot or is not supposed to do. The very nature of culture is conformity and normative action within a given body of beliefs and behaviors. Exposure to violence in the media may make violence appear more normative than it is; thus, engaging in violence seems less deviant. In essence, the media do not make violence seem more rewarding (cultivation) or available, but they make the violence within a person seem more acceptable.

- *Desensitization.* One of the reasons people avoid violence is that it hurts others. When violence is everywhere in the media, however, it can numb one's sensibilities and lower one's ability to empathize. Further, the more cartoonish the violence, the more it seems it does not really hurt anyone. Such exposure to violence may take the "brakes" off, making violence seem less hurtful and less costly to use.

- *Excitation.* Violence is a thrill. Through 5 million years of evolution, we have come to find violence a potential threat, a potential path to victory, and therefore arousing. Thus, seeing violence in the media is itself arousing, and this arousal stimulates our own arousal. Our arousal (adrenaline, muscular tension, etc.) needs to find an outlet and is expressed in violence.

- *Peer-group mediation.* Research on sexual violence indicates that people who engage in sexual violence are much more likely to have friends who approve of, and have engaged in, sexual violence. The suggestion is that peer groups mediate the transfer of violence. That is, if a peer group watches violence in the media, this peer group may then become self-reinforcing through its interaction, thereby serving as the proximal stimulus to its members' violence.

- *Cultural chaos.* Violence in the media may reflect the very breakdown of society, norms, and culture. If everyone is violent to everyone in the media, then this communicates a sense of despair, hopelessness, alienation, and angst to the viewing public. This has the effects of both (a) inciting some to exploit the lawlessness (e.g., looting during natural disasters), (b) joining the crowd (e.g., mob violence during the L.A. riots), and (c) bystander apathy providing a permissive environment for violence.

Each of these explanations offers slightly and sometimes strongly distinct sources of causation. For example, fantasy fulfillment, excitation, and disinhibition tend to assume that we are by nature violent and all that is needed is something in the media to take the restraints of society away. Cultivation argues that media instill violence in us.

Peer-group mediation and cultural chaos tend to view media as having an effect on society at large, which only then affects our individual behavior.

In all these examples, concepts are elaborated to make sensible the link between violence in the media and in society. Co-occurrence makes no sense without an explanation, and it matters *which* explanation is offered. A "theory" cannot be evaluated until its explanatory rationale has been specified, and the brief examples listed illustrate how significant and distinct such explanations can be.

Building a Model (of Dysfunctional Relationships)

One of the beautiful features about theories is their ability to account for variations. For example, every species is different, but a single theory of evolution explains those differences. That is, the nature of theory is to *explain* unique differences, not gloss over them. Romantic relationships form for any number of reasons and develop in any number of directions. Yet, extensive research and theories have attempted to explain why some relationships last and some do not, and why some relationships are dysfunctional and others are not. What follows is a model built of a particular form of a typically dysfunctional relationship.

Most relationships die before the individuals in those relationships die. Romantic relationship breakup is a process that most people experience at some point. But, some people do not learn to let go so easily after a breakup. Theory and research on relationships have proposed a theoretical model of why some people persist in pursuing intimacy from someone who does not want to reciprocate that intimacy. The theory is referred to as relational goal pursuit (Cupach, Spitzberg, Bolingbroke & Tellitocci, 2011; Spitzberg & Cupach, 2014; Spitzberg, Cupach, Hannawa, & Crowley, 2014).

The theory first assumes that people enter relationships as individuals, with individual histories. Some people have more self-esteem and are more secure in their attachment relationships, whereas others may have experienced challenging relationships with their parents or previous relationships, such that they become anxious or desperate for intimacy but do not trust others to be reliable intimate partners. Other people may have personalities that predispose them to react negatively to rejection (narcissism), to exploit others (Machiavellianism), or with a general inability to empathize with others (psychopathy). These "dark triad" traits are relatively enduring personality traits, generally formed over time. Thus, people who are insecurely attached, sensitive to rejection, manipulative, and lacking in empathy are more likely to take a relationship breakup badly, especially when that breakup is initiated by the other person. These are distal independent variables in the relational goal theory—they do not guarantee that such a person high in these characteristics will engage in unwanted relationship pursuit. But they increase the likelihood of such behavior. In particular, these traits increase the likelihood of such behavior under certain proximal circumstances.

A person thinking of a relationship partner as vital to his or her life happiness is engaged in goal-linking. It is illustrated by statements such as, "I don't know what I'll do without you" or "But you are the only person for me." In the context of a relationship breakup, such goal-linking can initiate a process of continuous and involuntary anguish (affective rumination) and mental (cognitive rumination) thinking about the other person and the relationship. Eventually, such rumination and constant reflection on the relationship leads the person to contemplate trying to get back with the person, or, worse, seeking revenge on the person through a campaign of

harassment. But, such contemplation is unlikely to result in such behavior unless the person perceives that such behavior might work to change the relationship for the better. That is, self-efficacy is a mediator of initiating unwanted pursuit or harassment of the lost relationship partner. Assuming the person believes that such behavior might work, the determination to persist in continued pursuit of the ex-partner ensues (self-efficacy), resulting in a process referred to as obsessive relational intrusion. Such intrusion can take many behavioral forms, each of which is identified in the model (see Spitzberg & Cupach, 2014). Thus, the relational goal pursuit theory can be modeled as illustrated in **Figure 5.3**. Models allow the verbal to become visual.

Models begin on a blank conceptual canvas. The model any student builds from the available theories and literature for any given topic will develop based on the student's own creativity, imagination, and research skills. Like a conceptual Lego set, investigating any given topic will reveal a broad array of conceptual pieces that can be used in constructing a particular puzzle that allows a process to be better understood. Once the basic skills of building models are practiced, modeling becomes a fundamental way of looking at the world and helps organize information in a particularly useful way. "During his Zurich stay

FIGURE 5.3: Model Components Illustrating Relational Goal Pursuit Theory

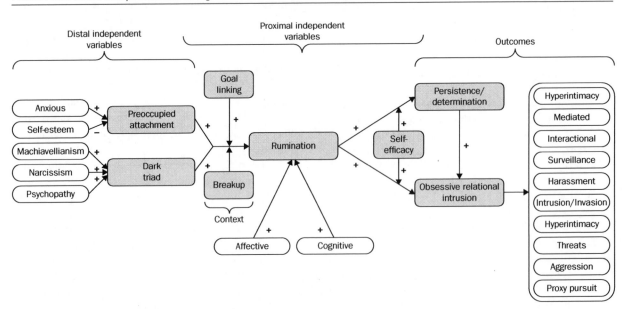

… Paulette Brubacher asked the whereabouts of [Einstein's] laboratory. With a smile he took a fountain pen out of his breast pocket and said: 'here'" (Seelig, 1956, p. 154). In an intriguing contrast, Pirsig (1991) notes that "Phaedrus had written on one of his slips, 'The pencil is mightier than the pen'" (p. 222). Every configuration of a model implies a potentially new theory, and every new theory offers some potential for scholarly advancement.

Conclusion

Understanding and explaining ultimately rely on some underlying concept of causation, whether viewed in narrative, idiographic, historical, or analytical ways. Causation, in turn, always reflects an argument, represented by propositions, whether formal (e.g., X is positively related to Y) or informal (e.g., X happened because Y and Z happened in context C). Theories are the conceptual tools, and modeling a basic toolbox permits such explanations to be formalized and tested in the crucible of social science, interpretive methods, and academic disciplines. If a theory is poorly conceptualized and constructed, it cannot be tested adequately or criticized adequately. Such a theory thereby provides signposts to paths down which scholarly inquiry should not continue. Until the field becomes more schooled in and adept at theory construction, however, such errant crusades are likely to continue. Theories work in often mysterious ways; when they work well, they seem to end the mystery and, at the same time, create new wonder in the mystery itself. Pirsig (1991) muses about "the mark of a high quality theory: It doesn't just answer the question in some complex roundabout way. It dissolves the question, so you wonder why you ever asked it" (p. 161).

Credit

FIG. 5.1: Adapted from J. A. Anderson and G. Baym, "Philosophies and Philosophic Issues in Communication, 1995–2004," *Journal of Communication*, vol. 54, no. 4. Copyright © 2006 by John Wiley & Sons, Inc.

CHAPTER 6

Critical and Rhetorical Ways of Knowing

Joshua S. Hanan & Christopher N. Gamble

LEARNING OBJECTIVES

After reading this chapter, you should be able to do the following:

- Specify the key differences between rhetorical knowledge and foundationalist philosophical knowledge.

- Define and differentiate between the little rhetoric and big rhetoric perspectives.

- Identify some of the modern historical and intellectual contexts that enabled a big rhetoric perspective to become increasingly prominent.

- Specify the defining features of rhetoric as a constitutive practice.

- Identify the key assumptions and implications of viewing rhetoric from a dramatistic perspective.

- Define and differentiate terministic screens, god terms, and identification.

- Specify big rhetoric's contribution to conceptualizing argumentation as a practical and context-specific mode of reasoning.

- Specify the interrelationships among rhetoric, knowledge, and power.

- Identify the six exemplary ways of approaching big rhetoric from a critical perspective (i.e., feminist, economic, critical race, queer, disability, environmental), and how each one illustrates the role of a rhetorical perspective in critiquing power relationships.

IN POPULAR DISCOURSE, *RHETORIC* HAS A decidedly dubious reputation. Indeed, most of us likely first encounter this word in the routine denunciations of political speech as either "all rhetoric, no action" or "all rhetoric, no substance." When opposed to "action," rhetoric simply means "speech," or "words," albeit with the negative implication that talk is cheap because words presumably do not, in and of themselves, count as physical actions in the world. When opposed to "substance," meanwhile, rhetoric designates the purely stylistic devices or flourishes someone uses to make what he or she says appear more credible than it really is (or, conversely, to make counterarguments seem less credible). In short, in popular usage, rhetoric refers to the mild to strongly unethical use of speech to mislead or manipulate—basically the art of deception through words.

Given the prominence of this negative but popular portrayal of rhetoric, it may be surprising to learn that, within academic scholarship today, rhetoric is defined in much more positive terms. As an established subdiscipline and methodology of communication studies, rhetoric is studied as a critical dimension of *all* human communication. The modern rhetorical discipline has therefore also taken on a much broader scope than its popular counterpart, now encompassing research on the persuasive character not only of speech and language, but also of images (Biesecker, 2002; DeLuca, 2012; Goehring, Renegar, & Puhl, 2017; Gries, 2015; Lucaites & Hariman, 2001), affect (Hawhee, 2015; Rice, 2008; Winslow, 2017), and communication media (Rufo, 2009; Towns, 2015). Rhetoric's increased scope and standing within academia is a relatively recent development, however, and has gone hand in hand with an increased appreciation of the ways in which truth and knowledge are themselves fundamentally rhetorical in nature.

The primary aim of this chapter, then, is to tell the story of how modern scholarship has increasingly learned to stop worrying and love rhetorical ways of knowing. More specifically, and against the popular view that portrays knowledge and rhetoric as fundamentally incompatible, modern scholarship has developed an understanding of rhetoric that treats human (and, increasingly, also nonhuman) meaning and communication as deeply contextual, contingent, and influenced by power-laden processes that are social, cultural, and historical. In telling this story, we have organized this chapter into the three main sections.

In the first section, we show how the roots of the popular–academic divide over rhetoric can be traced to an old and pivotal debate that centers on a conflict between "little rhetoric" and "big rhetoric." In that debate, which originates in ancient, classical Greece, the philosophers Plato and Aristotle each advanced their own version of a **little rhetoric** view in which, at best, rhetoric acts in the service of a philosophical understanding of knowledge and truth. Against them, the Sophists, who were the intellectual rivals of Plato and Aristotle, advanced a **big rhetoric** view in which knowledge and truth are themselves fundamentally rhetorical. In the second section, we show how modern rhetorical scholarship in many ways marks a return to and further development of a Sophistic big rhetoric view. Focusing especially on the important transitional work of Kenneth Burke, we show how the modern big rhetoric approach supports an understanding of all human communication (including rational argumentation) as inherently rhetorical. In the third section, we explore how a big rhetoric view has influenced the development of critical rhetoric. As we discuss, one of big rhetoric's most important contributions to the communication discipline is to show how power relations shape and structure the material and symbolic construction of meaning.

Little Rhetoric vs. Big Rhetoric

According to the view that has dominated the Western, Greco-Roman tradition from its classical roots up into the Renaissance era of the Scientific Revolution, truth and reality reside somehow beyond the physical, material world of sensory-based appearances. Those appearances, this view maintains, are always changing. Gaining real knowledge thus requires the use of a purely intellectual capacity for abstract reasoning and logical deduction for accessing truths alleged to be absolutely nonphysical and unchanging.

One of the first and most influential thinkers to make this argument was the Greek philosopher Plato. Plato often describes the nonphysical realm of truth and the uniquely human ability to access it by way of comparison with mathematics. To illustrate, we can consider the famous Pythagorean theorem, known already in Plato's time and which, as middle-school geometry classes continue to teach even today, states that the squared sum of a triangle's two smaller sides is equal to the square of that triangle's hypotenuse (i.e., $a^2 + b^2 = c^2$). The significance of such a theorem for Plato's philosophy is that it exemplifies the human discovery of a preexisting, eternal, nonphysical truth through the use of logic and reason. Once discovered, moreover, humans can then use further deductive reasoning to discover a host of related and equally unchanging mathematical principles as well.

In much the same way, Plato says philosophy relies on reason and deduction to discover the eternal, nonphysical truths of human nature, a process he calls the ***dialectical method***. Plato demonstrates this method in action throughout his written works, or "dialogues," generally through conversations between his somewhat fictionalized version of Socrates and those with whom Socrates engages on philosophical topics.

In attempting to persuade his fellow Greek citizens of their merits, Plato formulated his philosophy and dialectical method in direct opposition to the teachings of a diverse group of prominent intellectuals of his time known as the Sophists. The **Sophists** can be characterized as some of the world's first professional public speaking instructors. For a fee, the Sophists would teach Greek citizens how to communicate effectively and win arguments, an especially valuable skill to have in the young Greek democracy (Brummett, 2000; Fredal, 2008). Memorably capturing their view of truth and knowledge, a famous Sophistic maxim says that "humanity is the measure of all things." In other words, whatever a given society decides through speech and debate—which the Sophists considered the defining characteristics of humanity—to be true or lawful at a given moment is therefore the highest truth there is. In spite of how such a view may sound to us, however, the Sophists did not in fact reject morality, ethics, or standards of truth. For the Sophists, rather, and in sharp contrast to Plato, no one could attain a god's-eye, objective perspective on truth because all truth, for them, was both context specific and contestable.

Box 6.1 Ethical Issues

Ethical implications of rhetoric have been theorized and discussed since the earliest conceptions of rhetoric were articulated. Three issues tend to span multiple approaches to rhetoric:

- **Freedom vs. Responsibility Tension**

  In the process of rhetorically constructing human understanding and experiences, an ever-present tension exists between having freedom to express oneself fully and having responsibility to consider implications of that expression. Especially in the United States, where there is a constitutional protection of freedom of speech and press, "each of us also has the responsibility to exercise that freedom in an ethical manner" (Johannesen et al., 2008, p. 6). According to Johannesen et al., "the responsible communicator reflectively analyzes claims, soundly assesses probable consequences, and conscientiously considers relevant values" (pp. 7–8).

- **Habermas's Communication Assumptions**

  Philosopher Jürgen Habermas asserts that participants in communication situations assume that four expectations are met. Rhetorical situations may be evaluated using the following "tests" (adapted from Johannesen et al., 2008, p. 41):

  - Test of comprehensibility: Statements made are capable of being understood.
  - Test of truth: Statements made are true representations of existing, agreed-upon, factual states of affairs.
  - Test of sincerity: Statements sincerely and accurately reflect the actual intentions of others.
  - Test of appropriateness: Statements are appropriate.

- **Epistemic Ethic**

  Robert Scott (1967, 1976), among the first contemporary rhetorical scholars to argue for an epistemic view of rhetoric, offered three ethical guidelines for communication:

  - Tolerate divergence of viewpoints and the right to self-expression.
  - Strive for maximum participation in the communication situation.
  - Strive to achieve good consequences.

Whereas the Sophists saw themselves as teaching citizens how to speak effectively, Plato rather unfairly portrayed them as moral relativists driven not by the pursuit of philosophical truth but by profit and power. This characterization of them is the very source of the pejorative term "sophistry," which still refers to the use of fallacious or deceptive arguments. In both the *Gorgias* and *Phaedrus* Plato offers what is likely the earliest technical treatments of the art of rhetoric (see Schiappa, 1990). Ironically, however, Plato advances what is likely the first explicit definition of this art not in order to promote or to define it in a fair way but, rather, to critique and condemn it.

For instance, in the *Gorgias* (Plato, 1998a), Plato casts rhetoric in a harshly negative light as, essentially, an irredeemably toxic force in society. Centered largely on a debate between Socrates and Gorgias, who was a famous actual Sophist of the day, this dialogue leaves little room even for a respectable "little" kind of rhetoric. That is, unlike philosophy or other more valued arts of the time such as medicine, which Socrates says are based on real knowledge of the timeless principles of nature and reason, rhetoric, he argues, is not rooted in any real knowledge or truth at all. Instead, says Socrates, rhetoric is merely an experientially acquired "knack" for making any given topic or position *feel* or *sound* true even when it is not. Rhetoric therefore merely targets opinions (**doxa**) rather than real truth or knowledge (**episteme**). And on this basis, Socrates denounces rhetoric as a poison to society, given that skillful rhetoricians can lead fellow citizens to adopt false opinions, often for corrupt or nefarious purposes. As the antidote to this "poison," Socrates proposes his own philosophy. That is, through the use of the dialectical method, he claims humans can transcend the dangerous physical world of deceptive opinion, or *doxa*, and thereby access the nonphysical, real, or *epistemic* truths. Today, we call such a conception of philosophy—in which truth and knowledge are defined as eternal and unchanging—a **foundationalist view**.

In *Phaedrus* (1998b), a dialogue Plato composed well after *Gorgias*, Plato revisits the topic of rhetoric and presents a somewhat modified view that amounts to the first version of a little rhetoric perspective. To be sure, Socrates once again portrays rhetoric in an overall negative light as inherently dangerous and deceptive. And yet, in this later dialogue, Socrates also expresses an openness to rhetoric playing a positive role in society—so long as it

works fully in the service of a foundationalist philosophy. Specifically, Socrates says a philosopher must first acquire knowledge of the transcendent, eternal principles of human nature and ethics, including how to most effectively persuade each kind of human mind on any given topic. Once acquired, the philosopher can then use that knowledge to persuade no less effectively than any Sophist and yet, unlike the Sophists, will do so only in the service of real truth rather than mere opinion. In this way, the best possible function of rhetoric for Plato is for it to act as a servant or "handmaiden" to real, philosophical truth and knowledge.

A generation later, Plato's most famous student, Aristotle, advanced a "little rhetoric" view in his influential work, *On Rhetoric* (2006). The first systematic, book-length treatment of the "art" of rhetoric, *On Rhetoric* should be understood largely as a response to Plato's depictions of rhetoric. Characterizing it as the "counterpart to dialectic" (p. 263), Aristotle grants rhetoric its own rightful yet limited domain of practice in the civic and political arena. Given that this arena—in which laws were passed, amended, and enforced—was full of vigorous debate on ever-shifting topics by citizens who, for the most part, were not trained as philosophers and who were therefore prone to logical errors and contradiction, Aristotle argued that, in this domain at least, rhetoric is in fact better suited than dialectic to achieving moral and just outcomes. For these reasons, Aristotle characterizes rhetoric as an art concerned with **endoxa**, or informed opinion, and offers the now classic definition of rhetoric as the "ability, in each [particular] case, to see the available means of persuasion" (Aristotle, 2006, p. 37). Importantly, then, in Aristotle's view, rhetoric is a practice that concerns the "live," partly improvisational discovery of the most effective way to persuade a *particular* audience on a *particular* topic in a *particular* historical situation or setting. In this way, Aristotle saw rhetoric as the art of discovering *context-specific* principles of persuasion. As with Plato, however, Aristotle continued to see the ultimate *purpose* of persuasion as always about leading fellow citizens toward eternal truths. In short, then, both Plato and Aristotle saw rhetoric, at best, as an inferior servant of foundationalist philosophy. And yet, for Aristotle, rhetoric also refers to a distinct kind of situated knowledge that is the best option in what is an important yet limited societal context.

In sharp contrast, however, the Sophists promoted what can be called a "big rhetoric" perspective. Plato condemned what he characterized as Sophistic rhetoric for operating only in the *doxastic* realm of deceptive appearances, feelings, and opinions, which he claimed his own foundationalist philosophy transcended. In contrast, however, the Sophistic perspective viewed truth and knowledge themselves as inescapably rhetorical (see Ballif, 2001; Consigny, 2001; Poulakos, 1983; Vitanza, 1997). For the Sophists, there is simply no nonphysical domain of eternal principles that somehow remains totally unchanged by the changing events of the physical world. According to the Sophists, then, through speech and debate we do not simply attempt *to discover* preexisting eternal truths, as Plato argued, nor even *to persuade* others of those same eternal truths in context-specific ways, as Aristotle argued. For the Sophists, rather, truth itself is context-specific and thus speech and debate always involve partly discovering and partly *producing* truth and knowledge.

The modern and present-day orientations to rhetoric in the remainder of this chapter share much in common with the Sophistic big rhetoric perspective. Like the Sophistic approach, more recent big rhetoric perspectives challenge a foundationalist view of reality and argue that our encounters with truth and reality are always negotiated in and through language and communication, which today is called a *constitutive perspective*.

Foundational Scholarship on Big Rhetoric

Having explored the tension between little rhetoric and big rhetoric perspectives, we are now in a position to examine conceptualizations of big rhetoric in communication studies. Before turning to this scholarship, it is important to emphasize that contemporary approaches to big rhetoric are *modern* inventions and cannot be decoupled from the prevailing mathematical, scientific, and political developments of the 19th and 20th centuries. The modern conception of big rhetoric has been influenced, for example, by the discovery of statistics, non-Euclidean geometry, and a liberal-democratic culture that seeks to represent the diverse interests of all members of society.

An important motivating factor for the modern conception of big rhetoric is also a very different understanding of language than the one shared by Plato and Aristotle. Plato and Aristotle adhered to a **mimetic conception of language**—where the goal of words, as symbols, was to accurately and objectively represent preexisting truth and reality. In contrast, modern approaches to language start from the premise that symbols *always* have an intersubjective dimension that is greatly influenced by human history and culture (Brummett, 1976). This modern **constructivist conception of language**, which has roots in the late 19th-century writings of French linguist Ferdinand de Saussure, asserts that symbols always acquire their meaning in historically specific ways as part of larger cultural webs of symbolic relations. Thus, as those symbolic webs change across history, so, too, does the meaning of any individual symbol. The modern constructivist view is therefore inherently rhetorical because it treats meaning as an imperfect accomplishment that is always shaped by human history and social convention, rather than as something objective, universal, and ahistorical, which symbols can ideally capture and accurately represent.

For modern scholars of rhetoric, then, communication is never a neutral process of exchange or "meeting of minds" (Peters, 2001, p. 20). Instead it is shaped by historically shifting values of particular cultures and their interactions with one another. On this view, moreover, language can always be challenged and contested, in culturally and historically specific ways, precisely because its meaning is never objective or eternal.

Kenneth Burke

Although thousands of scholars have published important big rhetoric scholarship since the official founding of the communication discipline in 1917, here we provide a concrete example through the works of Kenneth Burke. Through his highly influential articles and books on rhetoric from the late 1930s to early 1970s—especially, *Language and as Symbolic Action* (1966), *The Rhetoric of Motives* (1969a), and *The Grammar of Motives* (1969b)—Burke advanced a wide range of rhetorical concepts that play a profound role in shaping how rhetorical scholars now analyze symbols.

In appreciating Burke's contributions to rhetoric, we begin by considering the **dramatistic approach** to rhetoric that he developed. Rather than treat rhetoric as merely one important aspect of human life among others, Burke, much like the ancient Sophists, saw humans as fundamentally rhetorical beings. According to Burke, this is because, unlike plants and nonhuman animals who are determined by their biology, humans have a unique capacity for symbolic language that enables them to construct their identities through cultural stories that transcend their genes or physical environments. For much of Western history, for example, human stories centered largely on an omnipotent God who created the cosmos and occasionally intervened into the world of human affairs. Following the 18th-century Enlightenment, however, competing stories emerged emphasizing human "progress" through secular developments of science and technology. For Burke, the primary significance of all such narratives is not how objectively accurate they may or may not be, but that they all demonstrate how humans create and inhabit a domain of **symbolic action**, that is, a domain in which humans define themselves in culturally specific ways as the primary actors in grand stories of cosmic significance.

From this dramatistic vantage, then, Burke sees humans as creating and performing meaning in everyday life much the way actors do on the stage or in a play. Such an approach, moreover, leads Burke to define rhetoric as "the use of language as a symbolic means of inducing cooperation in beings that by nature respond to symbols" (1969a, p. 41). In other words, rhetoric for Burke refers to the ongoing use of language to establish, perform, or contest shared symbolic meaning. Clearly, then, a standard political speech delivered by a politician would count as rhetorical. And yet for Burke, symbolic meaning is not limited to words but can also be projected onto and evoked by images, monuments, art, or even natural objects. Through language, for example, humans can agree to assign particular symbolic meaning to trees, monuments, or land areas that they encode in laws, a practice that dictates how these entities can and cannot be treated (e.g., you can cut down a tree in your own backyard but not in your neighbors' yard or in a national park).

Terministic Screens

One of the most important concepts Burke advanced to convey the essentially rhetorical character of language and symbols is his notion of **terministic screens**. In defining this notion, Burke (1966) famously wrote, "Even if any given terminology is a *reflection* of reality, by its very nature as a terminology it must be a *selection* of reality; and to this extent it must function also a *deflection* of reality" (p. 45). For Burke, language never functions simply as a neutral, objective mirror that reflects reality as it really

is, but functions instead as a kind of symbolic filter that always selects some aspects of reality while deflecting or excluding others. In this way, all words function similarly to the way different color filters on a camera lens (or, today, in our smartphone apps) reveal "notable distinctions in texture, and even in form" (Burke, 1966, p. 45) of the same object.

Terministic screens are often adopted and deployed quite strategically. Consider, for example, Donald Trump's strategic use of language, both before and during his political career. Whether referring to his venture into mail-order meat with the sales slogan of "the world's *greatest* steaks," or references to his 2016 campaign opponents Jeb Bush as "a very low-energy kind of guy," Marco Rubio as "little Rubio," or Hillary Clinton as "crooked Hillary," he used terministic screens to frame himself, his products, and his opponents in strategic ways. Thus, for Burke, the use of symbols to create and share meaning is inherently rhetorical because it always depicts reality in a particular, limited way to the exclusion of others. In doing so, certain values, beliefs, and attitudes are privileged that themselves, as we examine next, evoke larger cultural stories and networks of meaning more broadly.

God and Devil Terms

Another concept Burke (1969b; 1970) emphasized that influenced how rhetoricians understand symbols are what he called *god terms* (see also Weaver, 1953/1995). **God terms** are symbols that encapsulate a particular society's ultimate, overarching ideals. Given the central importance of such ideals, other less dominant symbols even acquire much of their own meaning insofar as they resemble or deviate from god terms. An example of a god term in modern society is "democracy." Since the establishment of the United States in 1776, democracy has been a defining, and a very selectively applied, national ideal that officially informs all aspects of society, from civil to political and legal institutions. Democracy is thus not a neutral concept but an ideal that defines much of the very fabric of the United States as a society. This ideal is connected, moreover, to a shared Western history that generally traces its origins to the invention of democracy in ancient Greece.

A clear illustration of how democracy operates as a god term is the period of the Cold War (1947–1991), when the United States was involved in a global nuclear arms race with the Soviet Union. During that time, democracy was the primary ideal continually touted in opposition to Soviet communism. In President Ronald Reagan's famous "Evil Empire" speech delivered to the National Association of Evangelicals in 1983, for example, he pits the "good" or virtuous "American experiment in democracy" directly against the "evil empire" of the Soviet Union that he says is ruled by tyranny and oppression. In doing so, Reagan also explicitly linked the democracy = good/communism = evil opposition to religion and God. That is, the U.S. democracy is "good," he said, in large part due to its embrace of Judeo-Christian values, while the communist empire was evil due largely to its renunciation of such a belief.

Burke's notion of god terms needs to be understood in relation not only to positive ideals, but also to its own negative counterpart: **devil terms**. Coined by Richard Weaver (1953/1995)—devil terms refer to just what their name suggests, namely, to that which a given society considers to be most evil and that therefore stands in opposition to its god terms. "Communism" and the "evil empire," for example, functioned as devil terms in Reagan's characterization of the Soviet Union against the good and virtuous American democracy.

A final brief comment about god and devil terms is warranted. As we see with the rise of the word "terrorism" as a post–Cold War replacement for "communism," prevailing god and devil terms shift and change across history. Were we to travel back even further in time, we could also find long periods when "monarchy" or "royalty" were god terms and "democracy" was a devil term. Thus, despite their dominance in a particular era, the fact that even god terms are always historically situated and changeable underscores Burke's view that symbolic meaning is inherently partial, limited, and always based on certain inclusions and exclusions.

Identification

The final key Burkean concept we will discuss is identification. **Identification** captures most directly just *how* rhetoric works. That is, identification maintains that rhetoric persuades to the extent that we are able to see ourselves reflected in a given rhetor through the symbols he or she uses. The god terms, for example, can all be thought of as rhetorical symbols that promote identification by uniting diverse groups under an umbrella of shared ideals. At the same time, it is important to recognize that just as terministic screens not only *select*—but

also always deflect—certain aspects of reality, Burke's notion of identification likewise always implies *dis*identification. Thus, part of what enables the identification with democracy or the American dream is in fact the implied disidentification with or rejection of their opposites: communism, tyranny, monarchy, or any other social structure that prevents social mobility no matter how hard you work.

As Burke knew, the double-sided process of identification and disidentification can and—sadly, all too often has—played a central role in horrific events in human history. In an influential essay examining Adolf Hitler's fascist use of rhetoric, for example, Burke (1939) shows how the Nazi party's success derived in large part from its ability to cultivate a sense of identification among the majority of Germans as members of the so-called "Aryan race" through disidentification with Jews and other minorities. A crucial part of this process involved Nazis dehumanization of Jews by portraying them as a national "virus" responsible for Germany's economic instability following World War I. In this and other ways, German Jews were thereby transformed into a racial figure of disidentification that played a central role in producing the symbolic unification of German "Aryans."

To summarize our discussion of Burke, terministic screens, god terms, and identification form a small but important sample of the concepts Burke developed. In particular, they provide a sense of how Burke's work helped guide the communication discipline toward a much greater appreciation of the fundamentally rhetorical character of its object of study. At the core of what prompted this shift is Burke's view that symbolic meaning is inherently rhetorical because it always selects and privileges certain aspects of reality while ignoring or excluding others.

Argumentation and Rhetoric

As we saw in the first section of this chapter, argument and debate have enjoyed a privileged position in the West going back to ancient Greece. The most influential treatments of argumentation were provided by Plato and Aristotle, who, in light of their foundationalist philosophies, attempted to identify and define what they believed to be the eternal principles of logic underlying rational argumentation. Additionally, they argued that rational arguments must move from general to specific premises, as Aristotle's notion of the syllogism illustrates. Like a mathematical axiom, a **syllogism** defines the key elements of an argument and arranges those elements in a logically coherent and deductive way (see also Chapter 13). For example: "All men are mortal, Socrates is a man; therefore, Socrates is mortal." By abstracting from this example, we can see the syllogism's formal, mathematical-like character: if a = b and b = c, then a = c.

While the views of Plato and Aristotle long dominated how argumentation was understood, in the 20th century the foundationalist assumptions on which those views rested came to be increasingly seen as culturally relative and historically contingent. One of the most helpful scholars in promoting this nonabsolute conceptualization of argumentation was the British argumentation scholar Stephen Toulmin. Toulmin is famous for developing a model of practical reasoning that made explicit the implicit assumptions of syllogistic arguments (see also Chapters 3 and 13). This argument model particularizes the universal character of all syllogistic arguments. According to **Toulmin's** (1958) **model of practical reasoning**, no syllogism can ever be constructed in a truly universal way and must instead always be appreciated as situated, contextual, and provisional. Toulmin's model accomplishes this task by adding to the Aristotelian conception of the syllogism terms such as "qualifier" and "rebuttal." A **qualifier** brings attention to the probabilistic character of all syllogisms (e.g., it is *likely* that Socrates will die), and a **rebuttal** specifies the conditions under which a syllogism could fail (e.g., it is likely that Socrates will die *unless* we figure out before his death how to download our brains onto computers). In this way, Toulmin's model not only made the argumentation framework more precise, but also brought attention to the fundamentally rhetorical character of all arguments.

Two other scholars who have greatly expanded and enriched our understanding of argumentation during the 20th century are Chaim Perelman and Lucy Olbrechts-Tyteca, with their influential book, *The New Rhetoric: A Treatise on Argumentation* (1958). At the center of their rethinking of argumentation was a new rhetorical theory of audiences. Against those like Plato and Aristotle who assumed audiences had an innate underlying human nature that was timeless and ahistorical, Perelman and Olbrechts-Tyteca challenged this perspective by showing how rhetoric is always directed toward particular audiences who have historically shifting attitudes about

what counts as legitimate facts, beliefs, or values. Effective argumentation, including through syllogisms, must therefore begin from the premise that audiences are always historically specific entities. In order to avoid an entirely relativistic perspective, however, Perelman and Olbrechts-Tyteca also developed the concept of a universal audience. The **universal audience** is an imagined audience—comprising a diverse population—that adheres to a general conception of "reasonableness." This conception of reasonableness varies with history, however, and therefore preserves the fundamentally rhetorical nature of their theory of argumentation and its key difference from classical conceptions of argumentation rooted in absolute, unchanging principles of logic.

Another scholar whose work transformed our understanding of argumentation during the 20th century is Walter Fisher. Developing an anthropological conception of rhetoric with strong parallels to Burke, Fisher argues that humans are fundamentally "storytelling animals." For Fisher, this means that effective persuasion always takes place as part of larger, compelling stories and that rhetors who try and isolate formal or deductive argumentation apart from these stories are fundamentally misguided. In his book, *Human Communication as Narration: Toward a Philosophy of Reason, Value, and Action* (1989), Fisher put forward two key concepts for assessing the effectiveness of arguments: narrative coherence and narrative fidelity.

Narrative coherence refers to how consistent the speaker's values are with the story he or she tells, or how well the two things "hang together." For example, if you saw your humble authors of this chapter deliver a speech about how urgent we think it is to combat climate change, after which you saw us roar away from the speech in a Hummer that gets about 10 miles to the gallon, you would likely think our speech lacked narrative coherence. **Narrative fidelity**, on the other hand, centers on the audience in a rhetorical interaction and asks whether the story being told rings true to their particular experiences. Trump's proposal to build a border wall to protect America from the "criminals, drug dealers, [and] rapists" he says are flooding into United States from Mexico, for example, has resonated much more with White American families who have lost jobs due to globalization than, say, with Mexican or Latin American families.

What Toulmin, Perelman and Olbrechts-Tyecha, and Fisher all share in common, then, is a rhetorical approach to argumentation. In their own ways, that is, each of them helped to illuminate how there is no way to ever present a perfectly rational or objective argument and how arguments are always influenced by history and culture. One major benefit of such a rhetorical approach is that it encourages us to be sensitive to arguments that sound very different from our own worldviews and to recognize that our own accustomed way of seeing things is not necessarily the only or best perspective. Thus, a crucial connection exists between rhetoric and ethics.

The exemplars selected for review illustrate a variety of distinctions across paradigms of rhetorical theory and criticism. Some of the key distinctions are summarized in **Table 6.1**.

TABLE 6.1: Contrasting Paradigms of Rhetoric

Characteristic	Big Rhetoric	Little Rhetoric: Plato	Little Rhetoric: Aristotle
Reality: Rhetoric is …	… constitutive of reality	… at its best, the art of persuading souls based on timeless, ahistorical principles, about the true, unchanging nature of reality discovered by philosophy.	… at its best, the art of persuading reason-deficient citizens in the public sphere based on context-specific principles about the true, unchanging nature of reality discovered by philosophy.
Truth: Truth is …	… produced and contested by citizens in a community through speech and debate.	… universal across all contexts, discoverable by philosophy, something rhetoric can clarify or distort.	… universal across all contexts, discoverable by philosophy, something rhetoric can clarify or distort.
Function: Rhetoric is best suited for …	… establishing and contesting truth, facilitating civic participation and action.	… acting as a servant or "handmaiden" of dialectical philosophy's search for transcendent, context-independent truths.	… acting as a context-specific compliment or "counterpart" to dialectical philosophy's search for transcendent, context-independent truths.
Operation: Rhetoric acts mainly through …	… speech and dialogue.	… *doxa* (opinion) rather than *episteme* (truth).	… *endoxa* (informed opinion).
Context: Rhetoric is …	… context specific and partly context creating.	… contextual only in that it targets particular kinds of souls in particular ways.	… capable of discovering and employing context-specific principles of persuasion, especially in speech and debate about topics of public concern.
Ethics: Rhetoric is …	… moral and ethical when it serves the greater good in context-specific ways.	… moral and ethical when fully subordinated to philosophy; otherwise dangerous and toxic.	… capable of promoting an ethical and just society when acting as a complement or counterpart to philosophy.
Evaluative stance: Rhetoric is characterized as …	… teaching communication skills to citizens to improve their station in life and strengthen society.	… good when it leads souls toward immaterial, eternal truths; otherwise, a toxic danger.	… good when it helps persuade nonphilosophical citizens about philosophical truths.

Critical Approaches to Big Rhetoric

In the previous section, we explored how a big rhetoric perspective supports an understanding of human communication that is always historical, social, and cultural. Indeed, in addition to promoting an understanding of language and argumentation as always provisional and context specific, the big rhetoric approach has also shone a critical light on the complex workings of power that impact communicative practices. Whereas the communication ideal that was inherited in large part from Plato and Aristotle was long held to be the *neutral* use of language to capture and represent preexisting truths, a big rhetoric perspective illuminates how communication is *never* a neutral process. Systems of power always subtly (or not so subtly) infiltrate the language we use and so play a role in shaping what we mean, even when it comes to seemingly power-neutral terms such as "nature," "humanity," or "society." Indeed, what most defines a **critical approach to rhetoric** is that it seeks to expose or make explicit just what these systems of power are and just how they seek to normalize or "naturalize" what are in fact historically and culturally produced disparities, such as those based on race, class, sexuality, ability, or between humans and nonhumans. In "denaturalizing" them in this way, critical rhetoric scholars help to illuminate how such disparities are in fact contestable and changeable. In other words, critical approaches to rhetoric seek to expose and counter the prevailing commonsense or taken-for-granted claims that serve to privilege and protect certain bodies or groups over others.

A critical big rhetoric perspective is generally considered to formally begin with the work of Raymie McKerrow in the late 1980s. In his touchstone essay, "Critical Rhetoric: Theory and Praxis," McKerrow (1989) builds on the insights of critical theory to develop an approach to rhetorical analysis that seeks to reveal the role of power in shaping human communication. In pursuing such a task, McKerrow also sought to challenge the assumption that rhetorical scholars could themselves ever stand outside of the systems of power they were critiquing. Whereas previously rhetoricians tended to assume they could critique power from a detached and objective position, McKerrow argued that the act of studying and analyzing rhetorical practices is itself also influenced by systems of power, and therefore an inescapably rhetorical process.

Not only are all claims about truth or reality rhetorical, according to McKerrow, but rhetoricians are themselves also always caught up in a web of historical and cultural assumptions that will lead them to privilege certain power relations over others, however unintentionally. The best a critical scholar can and should do, then, is to be as reflective and reflexive about those power relations as possible by critiquing not only rhetorics of domination (such as discourses that advocate for white supremacy and racism) but also the emancipatory rhetorics that are explicitly or implicitly affirmed (such as discourses that advocate for social justice, worker's rights, and universal suffrage).

McKerrow's critical rhetoric perspective thus supports an approach to critical rhetorical analysis that is always imperfect and incomplete. For McKerrow, an ideal method for conducting rhetorical criticism does not exist because what appears as a set of universally shared values and beliefs is actually always historically specific and contingent upon the lived experience of particular rhetorical critics. As an illustrative example, we can consider how feminism has continually rethought the relationship between rhetoric, freedom, and domination. When the feminist movement first formally emerged in the United States in the late 19th century, women were, at best, second-class citizens. Not only did women then lack the basic right to vote, they also enjoyed little to no educational or professional opportunities, inadequate health care, and by law could not refuse sex with or divorce their husbands. Such extreme inequalities had long been justified and normalized on the basis of alleged "natural" differences between men and women. And yet, the particular historical context of that moment—including the successful abolitionist movement to end slavery and the Quaker belief in husband and wife equality—encouraged a more critical examination of and response to inequalities than before. Due in part to **first-wave feminists'** successes such as winning the right to vote in 1920, and partly to other factors like the need for women to join the workforce during World War II, it became increasingly possible to identify and challenge other sex-based disparities as well, and feminist goals were revised accordingly. For example, with more career opportunities but the same expectations of (unpaid) household work, "the personal is political" became a major rallying cry for **second-wave feminists**. Second-wave successes and shortcomings, in turn, contributed to the rise of **third-wave feminism** in the 1980s, which has continued to expose and challenge gender- and sex-based norms even further. For example, in seeking to counter the ways many White second-wave feminists tended to erase important differences *among* women, an important part of third-wave feminism has been an appreciation of how identity always involves multiple dimensions—such as race, class, sexuality, and ability—at once. In this way, third-wave feminists have again exposed disparities and injustices, in this case by privileging the lived experiences of particular rhetorical agents. And finally, from a critical, pragmatic perspective, there is no doubt that this latest wave will also be critiqued and further developed as new feminist goals and movements emerge in the future.

Feminist Rhetoric

The primary aim of feminist rhetoric is to critique the field's longstanding male-centric biases in order to develop rhetorical theories and practices that are sex and gender equitable. The roots of such biases certainly run deep and, historically, women have often been excluded from practicing rhetoric altogether. Indeed, when it first emerged as a formal practice in the political sphere of ancient Greece, rhetoric was strictly reserved for adult male property-owning citizens. Barred from citizenship status, women could not participate in public deliberation and by law were even required to have a designated man speak on their behalf in court. It was also almost entirely men who theorized rhetoric well into the mid-20th century when, for the first time, women entered universities and began studying rhetoric in significant numbers. In this section, we briefly examine three specific strategies feminist rhetoric scholars have employed, which roughly parallel feminism's three (overlapping) waves, to counter male biases: inclusion, pluralistic inclusion, and transformative approaches.

Understandably, early feminist rhetorical scholars focused largely on fairly straightforward *inclusion* efforts. Those scholars, that is, closely examined historical records to identify and introduce noteworthy but neglected women rhetors into the discipline's official history books. An exemplary product of such efforts is the two-volume collection, *Man Cannot Speak for Her*, in which Karlyn Kohrs Campbell (1989) examines rhetorical contributions of numerous public speeches and writings by leading female abolitionists, reformers, and suffragists of the 19th and early 20th centuries. Through such

inclusion-driven work, rhetorical theory and history have been broadened and enriched with powerful, previously excluded examples of women acting as political agents of change through the use of rhetorical skill and eloquence rivaling those of any man.

While affirming the necessity and value of inclusion-oriented work, feminist rhetoric scholars in the 1980s began to consider its limitations as well. The main problem, they found, is that early inclusion work tended to judge the rhetoric of women against criteria established by men, thereby either erasing women's own distinctive ways of communicating or casting them as deficient and inferior (for two important survey papers advancing such a critique, see Foss & Foss, 1983; Spitzack & Carter, 1987). In response, these scholars argue for a **pluralistic inclusion** approach that seeks to recognize and value the unique and varied communication strategies of women and other marginalized groups.

More recently still, scholars have critiqued prevailing rhetorical norms even further. Whereas a pluralistic inclusion approach enabled greater appreciation of the distinctive ways women and other marginalized groups communicate, it also continued to reinforce more fundamental assumptions about rhetoric and its role in society. From its Greek origins on, for example, rhetoric has overwhelmingly been defined as a practice enacted by individual citizens acting in the public domain in the service of their states. Drawing on poststructuralist work, some have critiqued rhetoric's privileging of individuals and argued for attention to "collective rhetoric" instead (Biesecker, 1992), whereas others have critiqued the privileging of citizenship and argued for also affirming the rhetorical practices of noncitizens, non-Westerners, and indigenous communities (Chávez, 2015). In doing so, such scholars demonstrate a **transformative approach** that seeks to develop fundamentally new theories of rhetoric and identity that are truly sensitive to non-normative, alternative ways of communicating.

Economic Rhetoric

A key aim of **economic rhetoric** is to show how economic power influences human communication at both the micro and macro levels of society. According to Karl Marx (1867/1992), the founder of this tradition, economics is a way of organizing society that privileges certain classes over others. In Ancient Greece, for example, the male, property-owning household heads were able to participate in democracy in large part because of the unpaid labor of women, children, and slaves. Likewise, under feudalism (9th- to 15th-century Europe), the lord who ruled over a particular political territory was able to experience significant freedom only by heavily taxing the serfs who harvested agriculture and produced craft goods. Marx argues that under capitalism the situation becomes more complex because labor comes to be understood as a universal quality that all human beings have to control or sell if they so choose. He argues that the majority of the population in capitalist societies continues to be exploited, however, due to a division between one class that owns the land and controls the instruments needed to produce commodities (the **bourgeoisie**), and another class that works for the bourgeoisie (the **proletariat**). In addition, Marx argued that the bourgeoisie maintain their power by subtly controlling how humans communicate in various civic and private spaces believed to external to the workplace (which, following Adam Smith, he characterized as civil society). From our participation in mainstream social institutions such as schools and spaces of religious worship, to our engagement in more particular cultural activities such as reading a favorite book, watching TV on Netflix, or hanging out with friends at a shopping mall, Marx maintained that a subtle rhetorical campaign is constantly being waged by the bourgeoisie to convince the working class that capitalism is the only option and that if they do not succeed or profit in society it is due to their own personal failings (see Cloud, 1998).

Since the 1990s, a large body of Marxist-influenced analyses has emerged in rhetorical studies. These works range from more traditional Marxist approaches that emphasize the role of class power in shaping human consciousness (e.g., Aune, 1994; Cloud, 1994), to neo-Marxist approaches that attempt to rethink economic rhetoric in a postindustrial society where labor, class, and exploitation take on new and more expansive meanings (e.g., Bost & Greene, 2011; Chaput, 2010; Greene, 2004; Hanan, 2010; May, 2009). While the scholarship is diverse, what unifies the economic rhetoric conversation is a concern for how economic power shapes human meaning, as well as how humans instrumentalize nature for profit or other ethically dubious and unsustainable ends. Through a vast range of case studies from television shows to public speeches and cultural forms, Marxist-influenced

scholars seek to illuminate how humans are shaped by economic-driven agendas and biases in both implicit and explicit ways.

Critical Race Rhetoric

A central aim of **critical race rhetoric** conversations is to critique how Whiteness has become a privileged norm and cultural ideal in today's increasingly cosmopolitan and globally interdependent world. As Thomas Nakayama and Robert Krizek (1995) argue, **Whiteness** has become a cultural norm today not so much in the form of overt racism and bigotry (although this still exists as well), but by subtly permeating nearly every facet of modern society. In many countries across the globe, Whiteness has come to be the default or neutral standard of human identity when, in fact, it is itself a particular racial construct with a particular history. Critical race scholars seek to expose this history in order to make explicit the nonconscious racial biases that serve to devalue people of color and maintain a White norm. Critical race scholars also seek to bring greater attention to the complex colonial history underlying modern racial discourses and how those discourses are deeply rooted in xenophobia that can be traced all the way back to ancient Greeks and their belief that they were culturally and intellectually superior to other civilizations (see, e.g., Chávez, 2015; Nakayama & Krizek, 1995; Wanzer, 2012).

In recent decades, rhetoric scholars have produced a large body of literature on the topic of race and critical rhetoric. This scholarship explores, for example, the symbolic negotiation of race among Asian American identities (e.g., Ono & Pham, 2009), Chicano/a identities (e.g., Flores, 2003), African American identities (e.g., McPhail, 1998; Wilson, 1999), and Native American identities (e.g., Kelly, 2011; Lake, 1991). Critical race scholars also increasingly incorporate an **intersectional** perspective that considers how race always intersects or interacts with other social dimensions, such as class and gender, to collectively and variably produce particular subjective experiences. This research, for example, explores how experiences of Black men in the United States differ in important ways from those of Black women, as well as how their experiences are impacted by social class, sexual orientation, or ability (hooks, 2004). Although a major focus of critical race scholarship is to expose the ways that racial norms are constructed through a systemic process that grants certain bodies greater economic and cultural privileges than others, such scholars also explore how rhetoric can be used to *resist* and *counter* such processes through myriad everyday cultural practices and rhetorics (e.g., Ono & Sloop, 1995, 2002).

A present-day example of critical race rhetoric can be appreciated in relation to the Black Lives Matter social movement. Black Lives Matter can be understood on a rhetorical level as a campaign that encourages the public to confront how, in the 21st century, Black lives often continue to be treated as less valuable than White lives. Against the postracial narrative in which racism, slavery, and discrimination are mere relics of the past, Black Lives Matter exposes the ways that Black lives continue to suffer from higher rates of police brutality and homicide, incarceration, and general economic hardship and exploitation. The public reception of the Black Lives Matter movement has clearly been deeply mixed and divided. Many activists on the political left have embraced the movement and see it as an heir to the Black Power tradition of the 1960s and 1970s. Many conservatives, on the other hand, widely dismiss the need for such a movement in the first place, with some going so far as to propose modified slogans of their own such as, "All Lives Matter." To critical race scholars, such a slogan reasserts a color-blind ideal by erasing the ongoing violence and injustices that Americans of color continue to experience (see Biesecker, 2017).

Queer Rhetoric

An important task of the queer rhetoric conversation is to expose the symbolic forces that perpetuate heteronormativity. Building on the highly influential work of Michel Foucault (1990a, 1990b) and Judith Butler (1990, 1993), this conversation promotes what has come to be known as a performative understanding of human identity. From a performative perspective (see also Chapter 8), human sexuality, for example, cannot be reduced to biological factors rooted in human genes or sex chromosomes but must be understood, instead, as an always unstable discursive process maintained through heteronormative language, symbols, institutions, and other cultural practices. Conceived in this way, **heteronormativity** is a discursive construction that normalizes heterosexuality to the exclusion of all other sexual orientations. At the same time, because it is discursive and not genetically

determined, heteronormativity is an unstable and historically rooted construction that can always be changed through rhetoric. The recent federal legalization of same-sex marriage in the United States in 2015, for example, is, in large part, the result of many years of activism to counter heteronormativity and affirm a diverse range of sexual orientations and identities as equally normal and legitimate. Likewise, the mainstreaming of the acronym LGBTQI—for lesbian, gay, bisexual, transgender, queer, or intersex—is another example of the successfulness of queer activist movements to alter prevailing language in ways that challenge and disrupt heteronormativity.

In the communication studies discipline, a significant body of queer rhetoric scholarship seeks to define rhetoric in queer terms. Paralleling the feminist and critical race scholarship on which this research builds, queer rhetoricians contend that queer rhetorical perspectives and practices have always existed and that the conventional narrative of rhetoric violently limits how rhetoric can be conceptualized. Consequently, a queer rhetoric perspective illuminates how dominant, normative notions of rhetoric are always entangled with the nonnormative rhetorical performances that they exclude.

A good example of this approach to queer rhetoric is the "queer public address" perspective popularized by Charles Morris (2007). One of the most influential approaches to queer rhetoric in the discipline, this perspective takes up particular historical figures, such as Abraham Lincoln, in order to show how the success of their public rhetoric was in fact influenced by queer experiences that society has attempted to ignore or erase. There is much evidence, for example, that Lincoln was bisexual and that this sexual orientation influenced his style as a great American orator. Such evidence, however, has been largely excluded from official history and Lincoln biographies, which a queer public address perspective seeks to recognize and affirm (Morris, 2009). Queer rhetoric scholars also study and contribute to queer activist movements, which can be seen, for example, in the work of Daniel Brouwer (2001) and Erin Rand (2012) on the ACT UP movement that sought to bring an end to the AIDS pandemic.

Disability Rhetoric

A primary goal of disability rhetoric is to expose the centrality of **ableism** in Western society and culture. While there is increased discussion of "inclusive excellence," "diversity," and "disability accommodation," this is a very recent development. Throughout the majority of Western history, society has strongly discriminated against and at times even killed people with disabilities. In the ancient world, for example, the Spartans practiced state-sanctioned infanticide that only allowed those babies to survive who were perceived to be free from disabilities. In similar ways, Plato and Aristotle portrayed women, slaves, and foreigners as mentally deficient versions of men, which, in turn, justified excluding them from politics or practicing rhetoric in the public sphere (Wilson & Lewiecki-Wilson, 2001). The modern Nazi Party combined the ableism of the ancient world with a modern practice known as *eugenics*. Rooted in sham scientific knowledge, eugenics is a racially motivated set of beliefs and practices, often overseen by state and/or nonstate institutions, that promotes the segregation or, in extreme cases, even the murder of human populations believed to be physically, biologically, and/or cognitively inferior, undesirable, or disabled. In the case of the Nazi Party, eugenics motivated the mass extermination of all Jewish people and the confinement of the state's disabled citizens to psychiatric wards or concentration camps. While today eugenics does not exist in the socially acceptable form that it did for the Nazi Party, some argue that subtler expressions continue to be practiced against people with disabilities. In many countries, for example, procedures are available that enable pregnant women to screen for factors suggesting a risk of various genetic diseases, such as Down syndrome, which, when found, may even influence the decision to have an abortion.

As the common thread in dominant Western discourse linking together the disparagement and marginalization of *all* human nonnormative groups, disability rhetoric scholars have also been able to seize on rhetoric as a particularly powerful means of developing and advancing an intersectional understanding of identity in general. In his recent book, *Disability Rhetoric*, for example, Jay Dolmage (2014) argues that an understanding of knowledge as inherently rhetorical rather than philosophical enables an understanding of differences among humans as generative and valuable rather than treating differences as deficits measured against a single, dominant norm. Dolmage also develops his argument through critical analyses of prevailing disability **tropes** (i.e., common figurative or metaphorical expressions

or representations of a group or other topic) in popular films and other media.

Disability has become an increasingly widespread topic of conversation in the 21st century. With more disabilities diagnosed than ever before the question over what constitutes a disability has increasingly come to the fore. Consider, for example, attention deficit disorder and attention deficit hyperactivity disorder, referred to, together, as AD(H)D. As a learning difference that is said to afflict more than 10% of the American population, AD(H)D has become a veritable pandemic in recent years (Schwarz, 2013). Yet whether AD(H)D is actually a disability or not has become the topic of heated debate and contestation. For example, some argue that AD(H)D is not a disability at all but rather the product of living in a hypermediated environment that inundates people with a nonstop flow of information (Carr, 2011). Others have argued that AD(H)D is a rhetorical technology of selfhood that results from living in a capitalist society whose highest ideals are productivity and efficiency (Hanan, 2019). Still others have argued, from a very different angle, that AD(H)D gives an unfair advantage to diagnosed individuals because the medications that get prescribed for treatment are the cognitive equivalent of steroids (Hirneise, 2016). Thus, whether AD(H)D is a disability or not remains the subject of contestation and speaks to the historical, environmental, and social conditions that underpin disability diagnoses.

Environmental Rhetoric

A central aim of the environmental rhetoric conversation is to show how human interactions with the nonhuman environment are influenced by the symbols they use in the public sphere to communicate about the environment (see Pezzullo & Cox, 2017). The historical roots of this conversation can be found in the conservationist movements of the 19th century that were pushed in new directions by later environmentalist movements that emerged in the second half of the 20th century. Many argue that the mainstreaming of words like "green," "organic," and "sustainability" provides compelling evidence of the environmental movement's successes and progress. Others, however, see the recent popularity of such terms merely as an example of savvy marketers coopting environmentalist language in the service of promoting the fundamentally unsustainable system of capitalism (for a discussion of these tensions see Hanan, 2013; Kendall, 2008).

In recent decades, environmental communication has grown into an established subdiscipline of communication studies. Whereas not all environmental communication scholars employ only rhetorical methods, they all analyze the important role played by symbols in shaping how humans interact with their environment and ecology. One of the most important developments of the environmental communication subdiscipline has been a discussion of the way nature is negotiated rhetorically. These scholars argue, for example, that nature is not a passive backdrop against which the saga of human history unfolds, but a dynamic and shifting web of ecological relations (see, for example, Stormer & McGreavy, 2017). Rhetoric scholars have also highlighted the centrality of rhetoric to the political framing of climate change. For example, Chris Russill (2008) argued for the rhetorical usefulness of the "tipping points" frame for conveying the severity and urgency of global warming (e.g., if enough Artic ice melts it will eventually expose so much sunlight-absorbing dark water that a "tipping point" will be crossed, resulting in rapid melting of the rest of the ice). Finally, environmental communication scholars have brought attention to the role of rhetoric in resisting organizations and corporations that are bent on environmental exploitation. Kevin DeLuca (2012), for example, brings our attention to the importance of images, or visual rhetoric, for resisting environmentally harmful and inhumane practices such as whale harpooning.

Rhetorical scholars have investigated many genres and contexts. The genres selected for review here have provided

TABLE 6.2: Contrasting Critical Approaches to Modern Rhetorical Theory and Criticism

Critical Approach	Critiques	Affirms	Function(s) of Rhetoric
Feminist rhetoric	Patriarchy and sexism	Differences in rhetorical practices across sex and gender as equally valid and effective	Inclusion; pluralistic inclusion; promoting social transformation
Economic rhetoric	Economic power and class exploitation	Economic freedom and equality for all	Ideology critique; class mobilization
Critical race rhetoric	Colonialism; White supremacy; the pervasive ideology of Whiteness	Decolonization; conceptualizing race as a historically mutable social construct	Transforming symbols that naturalize racial difference; decentering Whiteness
Queer rhetoric	Heteronormativity	Gender nonconforming identities; equal dignity, rights, and freedoms for LGBTQI populations	The means through which sexual identity is performed and negotiated; queer public address
Disability rhetoric	Ableism; eugenics	Equal dignity, rights, and freedoms for people living with physical and mental disabilities; an understanding of disability (and ability) as historically, socially, and politically produced	Critically examining how tropes and the designs of physical places perpetuate ability and disability norms; practices that symbolically influence the role and image of disability in all human communication
Environmental rhetoric	Human exceptionalism; environmental destruction	An active rather than passive conception of nature and ecology; sustainable human–nature relations	Visual images; frames; other symbolic vehicles for resisting environmental exploitation

exemplars of how rhetoric has approached uses of rhetoric in society. Some of the key features of these arenas of rhetorical inquiry are summarized in **Table 6.2**.

Conclusion

In this chapter, we have provided an introduction to the broad and exciting world of rhetorical scholarship in the communication discipline. A core argument we have advanced is that in contemporary academic thought, rhetoric is central to generating knowledge about the world. As the Sophists first argued, rhetoric plays an active role in producing our shared sense of reality through a wide range of symbolic practices that are always influenced by society and culture. Rhetoric is not merely a form of flattery or manipulation that distorts our sense of an ideal, unchanging truth. Rather, as we present it here, rhetoric refers to the historical, symbolic, and material conditions out of which conceptions of truth and knowledge emerge in the first place. From this perspective, all of the areas of communication studies discussed in this textbook can be said to have rhetorical dimensions.

Another argument emphasized in this chapter is that modern rhetorical scholarship supports a reflexive critical process that continually challenges dominant cultural norms. Because a big rhetoric orientation assumes that there is never a predetermined goal or end point to rhetoric, it promotes a climate that thrives on the continual questioning of reality and reorientation of ourselves in relation to that reality. In our view, rhetoric is valuable not because it moves us toward an idealized end point, or *telos*, but because it challenges the very existence of such a telos. Rhetoric, that is, encourages us to be humble and to acknowledge that the universe and world that we inhabit will always exceed our historical, finite ability to control or master it.

On this note, we conclude by mentioning briefly one of the most recent and important developments in rhetorical scholarship today, which is the growing appreciation that, contrary to what has long been presumed, humans do not in fact enjoy any sort of monopoly on rhetoric. Some scholars, for example, have demonstrated how even plants and animals should be understood as rhetorical beings as well (see for example, Davis, 2011; Hawhee, 2011; Keeling, 2017; Kennedy, 1992; Pfister, 2015). Others have argued that human rhetoric, language, and symbolic meaning are always partly constituted through particular entanglements with surrounding nonhuman physical environments (see Rickert, 2013; Stormer & McGreavy, 2017), or even that the material cosmos should itself be understood as a meaningful, performative, rhetorical actor whose physical movement produced humans (Gamble & Hanan, 2016). In this spirit, then, we conclude this chapter not by settling on a preferred notion of what we think "true" rhetoric really is or always has been. Instead, we conclude by arguing that, as an expression of the material world in which we live, rhetoric is a shape-shifter that is always in flux and that takes on (relatively and temporary) stable forms and meanings only in relation to and as part of particular, shifting contexts.

CHAPTER 7

Interpretive and Ethnographic
Ways of Knowing

Patricia Geist-Martin & Kurt Lindemann

LEARNING OBJECTIVES

After reading this chapter, you should be able to do the following:

- Articulate the historical origins of ethnography.
- Identify the main components of ethnographic research.
- Identify the main methods of conducting field work.
- Practice effective field note writing techniques.
- Identify the main steps of conducting interview research.
- Distinguish types of interview questions commonly used.
- Distinguish focus group research from other types of ethnographic research.
- Distinguish autoethnographic writing from other types of ethnographic writing.
- Define the various steps of data analysis in ethnography.
- Articulate the ways ethnographic researchers ensure sound data analysis.
- Understand how ethnographers address issues of validity and reliability.

Starting From Where You Are

The ethnographic adventure begins with you! In ethnography you "start from where you are" by choosing a context to study that you are passionate about or that has touched your life in some way (Lofland & Lofland, 1995). For example, imagine that you play pick-up basketball every week; you would not miss it. Studying something like this that you are passionate about allows you to get inside the story of what it means to jam with new people (Eisenberg, 1990), to gear up for competition (Lindemann, 2008; Lindemann & Cherney, 2008), or to improvise when rules are violated and people disagree (Hook & Geist-Martin, 2018). Even more, these weekly games become essential to stress relief when demands are coming at you from so many different directions. In this way, it becomes possible to interweave work and play, and research and fun, and it is something you already do anyway. The same could be said for other passions such as yoga, dance, hockey, music, running, and attending concerts. These are joyful, passionate, and fun activities that take place in diverse contexts where we can learn about the history, the culture, the politics, and, most important, the communication that is part of the day-to-day experience of these forms of interaction.

At the same time, "starting from where you are" can mean something entirely different. Let us say you or a family member have been through or are currently experiencing a life challenge related to illness, divorce, return from military service, birth of a new family member, a move to a new city, death in the family, or any other type of unexpected life change. How we communicate and live through these challenges can depend on many things covered in other chapters of this book, for example: our cultures, gender, race, ethnicity, religion, as discussed in Chapters 11 and 17; degrees of closeness or distance in our family relationships, the communities we live in, as discussed in Chapter 12; and the organizations that support us or deny us the support we need, as discussed in Chapter 16. Our research adventures may lead us to study particular organizations (e.g., hospice care facilities, sports arenas, schools, nursing homes, veterans' organizations) or to contexts or communities where people gather to communicate with others (e.g., playgrounds, hair salons, barber shops, support groups, coffee shops, and other places where people congregate).

Once we decide on a context to study, we must gain permission to study that context, spend time, weekly, observing and taking field notes of our interactions there, interview people who move in and out of that context to gain their views of the experience of being there, and seek out any other forms of knowledge that might shed light on the complexities of communicating in that context, including its history, culture, and politics. There might be documents or websites we can look at, along with photos, graffiti, newsletters, uniforms, and just about anything that might offer insight on the goings on and communication in that context. We may find that going to that context in the morning is very different than going in the afternoon or at night. We may find that people of certain ages feel more comfortable going there on weekends, but not during the week. We may learn that there has been a lot of turnover in staff that has changed the whole experience of being there for everyone.

The ethnographic adventure can be likened to a mystery, in which you are the detective who must find and follow the clues that help you solve the puzzle or mystery that you find most fascinating about a certain context (Goodall, 1991). Bud Goodall wrote a book called *Living in the Rock and Roll Mystery,* and in the first chapter he describes what he sees as the ethnographic *mystery* that guides his research:

> Mystery begins in a feeling, something deep, poetic, and sweet.
>
> You get caught up in it. You get caught up in it fast. Little raptures of being alive ripple down the back of your neck, trickle like ice crystals doing an unknown, familiar dance across the constant heat of your spine. This is what it is like, this is where it all begins. Mystery is like a seductive voice deep into the way cool and hot of the music that you suddenly discover is singing to you, directly to you, only to you, breaking you away from what you thought you were, which until that very moment you thought was the whole and substance of your life. Mystery changes all of that because mystery changes you. Mystery defines you in the casting of its spell, in something as simple as the enchantment of a voice, a voice inviting you to dance, a dance that promises something you will always remember, or, maybe, that you will never forget. (p. xi)

Goodall describes well the feeling of what it means to be immersed in an ethnographic adventure and to become that detective, passionate about unearthing clues and following them until the shape and color of the mystery begin to materialize.

Researchers have explored this mystery for over 200 years. Ethnography has a rich tradition of rigorous investigation that predates communication studies. From the Greek root words *ethno* meaning "culture" and *graphy* meaning "writing or representing," ethnography, literally, means writing of culture. Before the ease of widespread travel, anthropologists went long distances through dangerous terrain, immersed themselves in a particular culture, and wrote vivid accounts of those rituals, norms, and lifestyles for those who couldn't themselves witness it. This **thick description**, a term coined by Clifford Geertz (1983) while studying the ritual of cockfighting among the Balinese people, allowed readers to place themselves in the settings and among the people being written about. Many of the practices of ethnography, including fieldwork, an emphasis on writing, and a focus on understanding (rather than predicting and controlling), remain vital components of the way ethnography is conducted in communication studies.

In general, **ethnography** consists of fieldwork, reflexivity, interviews, and document analysis. In general, a **field** is the collection of places and spaces in which a particular topic or phenomenon might occur. **Fieldwork** can be described as physically going to a **scene** (i.e., a particular geospatial location), or going online (Kozinets, 2015), and recording what the researcher sees, smells, feels, hears, and/or otherwise observes. These **observations**, commonly called **field notes**, are usually written down but may be video or audio recorded depending on the permission given to the researcher. **Reflexivity** asks us as researchers to "work the hyphen" (Fine, 1994) between self and other in ways that "we probe how we are in relation to the contexts we study" (p. 71), and that entails "taking seriously the self's location(s) in culture and scholarship … to make research and cultural life *better* and *more meaningful*" (Berry, 2013, p. 212). **Interviews** are simply asking questions of another person familiar with the topic or phenomenon being studied. Sometimes interviews are conducted formally, with a specific set of questions. Other times, interviews are conducted more informally, with one or two broad questions meant to spur a conversation. *Document analysis* can consist of reading and rereading an organization's policies and procedures manual, the rulebook of a sport, or even emails sent between participants in a particular group or setting. **Reflexivity**, something practiced throughout the ethnographic process, occurs when researchers reflect on the ways they gather data, how they interpret that data, and the conclusions they make. As we explain next, however, reflexivity can play an even more crucial and explicit role in the ethnographic research process.

In this chapter, we want to immerse you in the meanings and doings of ethnography. We will begin in a typical way that ethnography begins—in the middle of things—where life is ongoing, and we will step into that stream of activity and observe, ask questions, participate, and do anything we can to make sense of it all. First, we will present some field notes from past ethnographic projects to illustrate the ways observation, description, and reflection on interactions in the ethnographic scene function in the gathering of data. Next, we will provide some examples and best practices of interviewing in the course of conducting ethnographic research. We will then discuss autoethnography and its role in conducting and writing research. We will conclude with a brief discussion of data analysis and the options researchers have in presenting their analysis to readers.

Observation and Thick Description

The phrase "seeing is believing" is a common sentiment. Indeed, witnessing something happen has power in solidifying our own beliefs and in persuading others. In a courtroom, for example, witnesses are just as important as any argument a lawyer may make. And, before technology allowed us to explore remote corners of the world, the next best thing to being there was reading the words of someone who was there. It is here where the roots of ethnography lie. It is important to note that ethnographers do not go into the field and draw conclusions after a few minutes of observations or based on a few conversations. The more occurrences of some phenomenon researchers conducting ethnography see, the more those researchers come to believe that those patterned occurrences are not random, but they are instead indicative of larger meanings.

Field Notes and Writing

Getting access to a group of people, organization, or another place you want to observe may require you to get permission from a *gatekeeper*, or the person (or people) who controls entry. Some places or groups may be open to the public and not require permission per se, though it is good practice to let people know you are a researcher when talking to them.

Once you have entered the scene or setting (which is simply a circumscribed physical place within the entirety of where you believe your topic or phenomenon is occurring), you will likely find that one thing separating field notes from other types of data you might gather (e.g., surveys, audio recordings, and other data collection strategies) is that researchers' writing constitutes both data and part of the analysis. This writing may first occur in researchers' **scratch notes**, or brief jottings made in the field. Scratch notes may contain short phrases, bullet points, matter-of-fact recordings of the setting, what people are wearing, and what they are doing. If researchers are unable to take notes during interactions in the field, they can make mental notes. These are often called **head notes** and should be turned into scratch notes as soon as the researcher can find time to jot down his or her thoughts (Emerson, Fretz, & Shaw, 2011). No more than 24 hours after jotting down scratch notes researchers should write **field notes**, which are elaborated versions of scratch notes, using complete sentences, paragraphs, and sometimes even dialogue. Field notes do not have to include chronologically arranged observations; they can shift around to tell a story that captures the experience of the researcher in the field.

As you can gather from this explanation, ethnographers generally believe that people cannot record what they observe objectively, without their filters or points of view. On the contrary, ethnographers recognize that the writing of field notes can both *capture* what the researcher observes as well as *shape* understandings through the use of language. In fact, an essential aspect of ethnographic writing is describing researchers' **positionality**, which includes their stance in relation to the relevant social, cultural, and political dimensions of the context of research (Rowe, 2014).

Researchers may use metaphors, imagery, figures of speech, and other descriptive language in their field notes. Consider this when reading the excerpt that follows from one of Kurt's published ethnographies. Kurt spent close to 2 years and over 100 hours observing and interacting with wheelchair rugby players, friends, family, and referees (for more on the sport of wheelchair rugby, or "Murderball," see also the Oscar-nominated documentary *Murderball*; Mandel, Shapiro, & Rubin, 2005). True to what we wrote in the introduction about starting from where you are, Kurt grew up in a culture of disability from the age of 7 when his father became disabled in a motorcycle accident. Kurt became even more immersed in this culture when his father became a wheelchair athlete, competing in a variety of sports. His father's disability complicated their family life in various ways and shaped Kurt in profound and long-lasting ways (Lindemann, 2010a, 2012). For Kurt, the

mystery surrounding disability, family, sport, and communication was a compelling one. So, the sport of wheelchair rugby, although his father did not compete in the sport, was a natural choice for a long-term investigation.

The sport, as with any organized competitive sport, consists of rules and regulations. Wheelchair rugby, however, is not only an ultracompetitive Paralympic sport; it is often recommended by doctors for men and women as rehabilitation. In other words, the sport can help quadriplegic persons regain some degree of motor function, strength, and even self-esteem and a network of friends who understand their experience. This tension between competitiveness and rehabilitation, though, creates a tension in the sport of wheelchair rugby (Cherney, Lindemann, & Hardin, 2015). The rules of this sport say a team has to have a mix of more and less severely disabled players (depending on the degree of motor function, torso mobility, and strength) on the court at any given time. This means some players will "fake" or pretend to have a more severe disability so they can be on the court with other skilled and more mobile players, making their team more competitive (Lindemann, 2008).

Because of these rules, coaches and players will often watch competitors from the sidelines to try and determine if another player is faking. Given this phenomenon, it was important for Kurt to try and capture what it was like watching skilled and mobile players play the game. Practicing the "thick description" and imagery we discussed earlier, Kurt wrote the following field note:

> A player, "Philly," cruises along the court toward an easy score. His hands are more like fins as his fingers are singed together at the ends of his shortened but muscular arms. Both legs are amputated above the knees. As he reaches the goal line, a player from the opposing team hits his chair and Philly rolls onto his two right wheels. Gravity is too much for him, however, and he tips over. Instead of stopping, though, he immediately pushes himself upright, spring-boarding onto his wheels in a somersault fashion. Players on the sidelines laugh and applaud, while others look on incredulously. (Lindemann, 2008, p. 108)

Notice the use of descriptive terms and metaphors meant to place the reader in the scene. The use of such terms is also important because these antics on the court are just the sort of thing others might use to accuse someone of "faking" a more severe disability.

Field notes are not restricted to passive observations. By immersing themselves in the scene, ethnographers have the opportunity to interact with others, talk with them informally, and get their reactions and opinions to whatever is going on in the scene. Kurt took this opportunity to wander the sidelines and strike up conversations about this particular player. He then wrote the conversation and his thoughts about it in his field notes:

> I'm sitting with Alan and Bill watching the fast kid play. He weaves in and out of players like he's gliding on ice. He reminds me of the Roadrunner cartoon character, and I half-expect to see a cloud of dust behind him every time he whizzes down the court. We're sitting at one end, and he comes right toward us to score a goal. Instead of turning before reaching the edge of the 3" raised court, which he could easily do, he "hops" onto the cement, tips himself over, and does something resembling a barrel roll back onto the court.
>
> Researcher: He's pretty mobile.
>
> Bill: Yeah [a little sarcastic].
>
> Alan: A little too mobile. (Lindemann, 2008, pp. 108–109)

This field note shows the skepticism that Alan and Bill communicate about the level of Philly's injury. It not only has the descriptive terms the previous note did, but it also includes dialogue that sheds a bit more light onto how others view this kind of on-court performance of disability. The more you do fieldwork, the more skilled you will become at remembering what was said. In this example, Kurt engaged in this conversation, then immediately sat down in a remote corner of the gym and recorded what was said. Remember that your field notes are your data, so it is important to be as thorough and complete in your recordings as you can. Remembering your interactions and writing them down are a big part of taking good field notes, but they are not the only important parts. Now we are going to introduce a term that we will come back to later in this chapter: reflexivity.

Reflexivity

Reflexivity can be loosely defined as the quality of being thoughtful about the research process as you are conducting research. Although researchers in any methodological tradition should be reflexive, ethnographic research requires researchers to reflect not only on their data and the way they gathered them, but also on the ways their interactions might shape what they notice and how they write about them. Consider the following scene, which took place in an airport as Kurt was waiting for a plane with the athletes he was observing:

> Waiting in line at the airport with the team, Steve offers me a piece of Starburst candy. I take it and thank him, unwrapping the piece quickly. Watching me intently, Steve says, shaking his head, "Look at that. Do you have any idea how hard that it is for me, something as simple as that? You need to do it like we do it." Steve illustrates the way quads have to unwrap Starburst candy: holding the piece on the flat palm of their hand (as flat as they can make it) and only using their mouth. Pretty soon, the team is racing each other to see how fast they can unwrap pieces of candy with our mouths. Jokes abound about the guys' oral sex "technique" as evidenced in the unwrapping. (Lindemann & Cherney, 2008, p. 119)

Notice the reflexivity about an important moment in Kurt's field research. He seemingly missed an important, yet taken-for-granted difference between the quadriplegic athletes and the researcher: the full use of hands to perform otherwise ordinary, mundane tasks. This confessional excerpt is face-threatening to Kurt, the researcher, because: (a) he totally missed an obvious and crucial difference between himself and his participants, (b) he was "called out" on his obliviousness, and (c) the interaction morphed into a risqué, potentially embarrassing performance of identity by the group of participants. Nonetheless, this scene communicates to readers the embodied nature of disability and its material consequences in everyday life. The jarring nature of how Kurt came to make this observation is captured in this reflexive field note in order to jar readers into the same realization.

Similarly, in her research, Patricia and her coauthors Summer and Katherine found intense value in reflecting on "feelings of helplessness, embarrassment, and anger, as well as gratitude, joy, and enlightenment" (Geist-Martin, Carnett, & Slauta, 2008, p. 401) as they immersed themselves in Costa Rican culture to study holistic health care. In fact, their reflexivity is what allowed them "to count what counts" in each step of the way as they adjusted to a new culture and a new language to make small steps every day in conducting their field observations and interviews. So, in this sense, the writing we do in ethnography is not simply recounting events, but our writing tells the story of a process of coconstructing events with one another in a particular context. On their return to the United States, Patricia and her coauthors read and reread their field notes and the transcripts of their interviews and became more mindful, reflecting about the moments in time when they doubted themselves. Upon reflection, they discovered truths about the challenges they faced in the 6 months they lived in Costa Rica and the accomplishments they made that were difficult to see when they were living in that context. As they listened more carefully to their own voices, reflecting on what they learned that they did not know before, they coconstructed truths about the ways they embraced change and uncertainty and accomplished more than they could have imagined. Geist-Martin and Dreyer (2001) state:

> It is our goal to explicate and understand the effects and responsibilities in the interview process … [and to recognize] that the storied construction of reality has less to do with facts and more to do with the meaning created from the context of explanation in which it is situated. (pp. 125, 139)

For Geist and Dreyer (2001), reflexivity means recognizing the ways a person's reality or worldview might be created through interaction. This recognition is important because it informs the ways the researchers not only conduct their interviews, but also the ways in which they analyze their interview data.

As you can tell from these excerpts, reflexivity can come in many different forms. It can be used to reveal mistakes and missteps the researcher makes in the field. It can also help researchers assess the ways they conduct their research and derive meanings from their data. Reflexivity is particularly important when interacting with others, be it in the field or in interviews. The next section elaborates the significant considerations for ethnographers as they conduct interviews as part of their research design.

Interviewing in Ethnographic Research

One predominant area of Patricia's research has been holistic health (Geist-Martin, Becker, Carnett, & Slauta,

2008; Geist-Martin & Bell, 2009; Geist-Martin, Bollinger, Wiechert, Plump, & Sharf, 2016; Geist-Martin, Carnett, & Slauta, 2008; Geist-Martin, Sharf, & Jeha, 2008; Hook, Plump, & Geist-Martin, 2018; Plump & Geist-Martin, 2013; Sharf & Geist-Martin, 2014; Sharf, Geist-Martin, Cosgriff-Hernandez, & Moore, 2012; Sharf, Geist-Martin, & Moore, 2012). She has traveled to Guatemala, Costa Rica, Cuba, and Hawaii to study holistic health practices such as acupuncture, meditation, yoga, nutrition, visualization, massage therapy, and a wide array of other indigenous health practices. The focus of many of these research projects is to understand how holistic practitioners communicate with their patients and what they see as the health benefits of these health practices. Patricia lived in Oahu, Hawaii, for 3 years and conducted research on the island of Hawaii. Often referred to as "the Big Island" or "the Healing Island," it is the most ethnically diverse area of the United States (Census Scope, 2000). She begins one of her publications about her work in Hawaii in this way:

> This island is world-renowned for its active volcano, beaches comprised of white, black, and green sand, as well as its world-class resorts and spas (Sims, 2004). To many it is also known as "The Healing Island." In fact, the College of Chinese Medicine describes Hawaii as "long recognized as having produced a land of gentle and healing energies" (http://www.tcmch.edu/). Additionally, a center that trains practitioners in Native Hawaiian Healing invites participants to attend educational programs that emphasize personal healing "within the rejuvenating environment of the healing island of Hawaii" where they can "absorb the mana (spiritual power) each day, each hour, with each breath" (http://www.haleola.com). Moreover, alliances are being built between practitioners of complementary and alternative medicine and conventional medicine through the efforts of organizations such as the Hawaii Integrative Healthcare Consortium (http://www.hawaiiconsortium. com/site/371/about_us.aspx). The Consortium states that its vision is helping the people of Hawaii to "enjoy increased and timely access to all forms of health care that may be of benefit, including traditional systems of healing." Part of its strategy is to place "a high priority on embracing and supporting the native Hawaiian healing community." Hawaii's diversity in ethnicity and in complementary and alternative medicines translates to varied interpretations of healing, health, and health care

practices (Crites & Crites, 2003). The call to Hawaii is a call to a place where spirituality is a way of life based on: (a) aloha (love, affection, and kindness); (b) ohana (family solidarity); (c) mana (life force); and (d) aloha 'āina (deep connection to nature and ecological stability) (Freitas & Dixon 1997; Handy & Pukui 1977; Kanahele, 1986; Mokuau & Browne 1994). Thus, healing and medicine in Hawaii are based on a spirituality of balancing these key values. Because Hawaii is a spiritual, healing locale, a significant research endeavor would aim to investigate the perspectives of holistic health providers practicing there, examining the values they describe as inherent in their identity and their communication with patients. To that end, our intention is to identify the communicative practices of a healing encounter as described by holistic providers in Hawaii. (Geist-Martin et al., 2008, pp. 133–134)

The context under study was not only one organization or one specific place per se, but the island of Hawaii. Although it was not possible to know everything there is to know about the island's healing practices or to travel every area of the island, her coauthor, Catherine Becker, had lived on the Big Island for 10 years and, as a professor at the University of Hawaii, Hilo, had developed a wide range of connections with healers and healing places. Patricia and Catherine became collaborators, collecting the data over a 1-month period, driving all over the island, observing and participating in healing sites and interviewing over 20 healers.

The fieldwork and field notes conducted for this study offer a picture of healers working within a healing environment that draws on nature or is constructed in alignment with the natural surroundings of Hawaii, including natural hot springs, bamboo forests, and all the myths and rituals that surround gods and goddess. For example, Pele, the goddess of volcanoes, is known on the Big Island as both a destroyer and creator. Health retreats have been connected to Pele in that the fire of the goddess is viewed as the divine, creative spark within us (e.g., http://fireofthegoddess.com/fire).

Intensive interviews were conducted with 20 healers who utilize different healing modalities in their practice. The results revealed a pattern that indicated four practices that healers perceive as central to their communication with clients: (a) *reciprocity*—a mutual action or exchange in which both the practitioner and patient are equal partners in the healing process; (b) *responsibility*—the idea that, ultimately, people must heal themselves; (c) *forgiveness*—the notion that healing cannot progress if a person holds the burden of anger and pain; and (d) *balance*—the idea that it is possible to bring like and unlike things together in unity and Harmony (Geist-Martin et al., 2008).

They learned a great deal in this research, which become lessons for conducting interviews. Although some of these lessons may be specific to their study—its focus and location—more often these are essentials that might guide any of you in the process of conducting interviews for your research.

Box 7.1 Ethical Issues

The research process is fraught with ethical issues and implications. Each chapter in this section of *CITE* discusses a different research approach, and many ethical issues apply across methodological approaches. One such issue is the ethical obligation to *benefit* people, not *harm* them.

- **Potential Benefits of Research (Berg, 1998):** Among the many possible risks and benefits of engaging in scholarship are the following considerations, each of which may imply ethical tradeoffs or dilemmas:
  - Valuable relationships
  - Knowledge or education
  - Material resources
  - Training, employment, opportunity for advancement
  - Opportunity to do good and to receive the esteem of others
  - Empowerment
  - Scientific/clinical outcomes

- **Interpretive Trustworthiness**

  As noted in this chapter, issues of validity, reliability, and generalizability are handled differently in ethnographic and interpretive methods than they are in quantitative social science. Altheide and Johnson (2011) note that researchers using this way of knowing share the ethical obligation of all researchers "to make public their claims, to show the reader, audience, or consumer why they should be trusted as faithful accounts of some phenomenon" (p. 584). One way to demonstrate interpretive trustworthiness is to engage in *member checks* with participants as part of the final analysis and representation stages. Member checks involve presenting preliminary interpretations and findings to participants who provided the raw data for those findings. This can be achieved through face-to-face interviews, email exchanges, phone calls, or other ways that best allow participants to provide their reactions about analysis. These responses can then be used to refine, and perhaps revise, final presentations of results, making the research more accountable to the concerns and interests of the participants.

- **Feminist Communitarian Ethics**

  Norman Denzin (1997) coined the term *feminist communitarianism* to describe an ethical paradigm for ethnographic research. From this perspective, the goal of social science research is community transformation (Christians, 2011). Accordingly, researchers have an ethical obligation to include participants in the design, conduct, and dissemination of research studies. According to Christians (2011, p. 71), three ethical conditions exist for "interpretive sufficiency," which address the cultural complexity and the multiple interpretations at stake by:

  - Representing multiple voices

  - Enhancing moral discernment

  - Promoting social transformation

Field Work Comes First

Ethnographers know that context is rich and complicated. Although it is essential to read thoroughly about the context (e.g., the healing community in Hawaii) and the topic of study (e.g., holistic medicine, healing, and communication), it is not until researchers engage in fieldwork—observing and conversing with the people in the context—that ethnographers begin to more narrowly focus their topic of study. This iterative process of moving back and forth between time in the field—observing, writing, and reflecting—and reading scholarly articles about the narrower focus of study is essential in the evolutionary process of conducting ethnographic research.

Investigate the Historical and Political Background of the Context

Although it is clear in their ethnographic research that Patricia and Catherine's project required them to know the history of the Healing Island and how it gained the name and reputation, including learning about legends, myths, rituals, and the diversity of healing practices, history is *always* essential. In the write-up of your research, you can appear as if you have not done your homework (by asking obvious questions) if you do not gain as much knowledge as possible about your context and the history and politics of what has occurred in that context. For example, it was critical for Patricia and Catherine to know the politics surrounding holistic health and the ways that biomedicine is often privileged over other types of healing (e.g., massage, acupuncture, meditation, etc.). Learning that the Healing Island faces less of this stigma or marginalization because of the ways in which the culture and history of the island do more to promote rather than stigmatize holistic health was an example of essential knowledge of history, politics, and culture in conducting interviews and field observations.

Interviewing in Context

Interviews most often occur in the context under study. They may be formal in the sense that they are set up in advance to occur at a specific time and place, and that you use an interview guide with a clear set of questions designed to explore the theoretical concepts being studied. Interviews may also occur informally and spontaneously in conversations in context; this type of interview is referred to as an unstructured or ethnographic interview. Tracy (2013) tells us that the **unstructured interview** is "more flexible and organic in nature … [including] flexible questions and probes" (p. 139). By conducting interviews in context, the ethnographer can observe participants in situations that are typical of the context or that might stimulate dialogue. Sometimes, participants might request to conduct an interview outside of the context under study, especially if the interview focuses on topics that they believe are sensitive or confidential.

Clarifying and Narrowing the Focus of the Interview

It is essential to be prepared with an opening to the interview that tells interviewees about its focus. Furthermore, it is essential to narrow the set of questions that you plan to ask about a focused topic. No more than but probably fewer than 10 questions are all that you need. For example, Patricia and Catherine decided on six primary questions that focused on the following:

> Specific questions asked providers to discuss their cultural affiliation(s), education/training/background, philosophy and definition of health and healing, recount their history with Hawaii, and indicate their experience with health care and healing in Hawaii County and stories of the role they believe communication plays in the process of providing care to their patients. They were also asked to recall their most profound healing encounter and describe it in detail, elaborating on the communicative process. The final question of the interview asked the respondents to identify community members or practitioners they recommended that we interview to gain more insight into issues of health care, healing, and communication in Hawaii County. (Geist-Martin et al., 2008, p. 136)

In both the structured and unstructured interview, however, no matter what questions you plan to ask, it is critical for you to feel free to *engage* in casual and free-flowing conversation in ways that encourage your participant to kick back with you and dialogue. Often, they learn as much about you as you do about them.

Recognizing Activism and Advocacy Experienced Through Interviewing

One of the many advantages of conducting interviews is that the dialogue between researcher and interviewee may lead to new insights for both participants. It is not unusual for interview participants to tell the researcher how profound and insightful the interviewing process was for them. For example, in Patricia and Catherine's study, this was the way they described the activism experienced by many participants:

> The interview data from this research as well as comments from health care practitioners, community members, and researchers confirm that when individuals talk about healing, opportunities increase for health activism and citizenry. According to the statements offered by many of the practitioners, the process of participating in the interviews has helped many of them experience a renewed sense of energy, clarity about their practice, motivation, and inspiration. … In the words of one of our participants, healing is "living the question … [life] is following that question … and letting it lead to the next, and to the next, and to the next [question]." Healing is described more as a cyclical process that continues over the course of people's lives and one that moves them from an articulated discomfort to a philosophy of living a "mindfulness." In this way, holistic healing for these providers is an ongoing process of mind-body medicine treating the whole person, including the spiritual and emotional issues that are integrally related to people's bodies. (p. 140)

Although much more exists to learn about the process of conducting interviews in ethnographic research, these five lessons offer a basic guide for engaging in this important aspect of data collection. And, even when the primary focus of your field work, reflexivity, and interviewing is learning as much as you can about others, there is always an autoethnographic component to any ethnographic research. All ethnographic research is "highly particular and hauntingly personal" (Van Maanen, 1988, p. xv). Clearly, reflexivity is essential in conducting and writing ethnographic research for fieldwork and interviewing. For most ethnographic researchers, reflexivity and passion for a topic is what leads them to choose their research site and the focus of the research.

Patricia has been an avid proponent of holistic therapies; practicing yoga, meditation, and visualization, as well as utilizing acupuncturists, chiropractors, massage therapists, and energy healers in her own health care. So, her program of research focusing on holistic and integrative medicine (medicine that combines and integrates biomedicine and holistic therapies) started from where she was and was a natural extension of her own life experiences, philosophy of preventative health care, and utilization of integrative medicine for any of her pain or injuries. When the researcher's positionality in the research is central, and he or she is the main character of the story told, however, then the project is defined as autoethnographic.

Autoethnography

Earlier in this chapter, we traced the Greek roots of the word ethnography: *ethno*, meaning "culture," and *graphy*, meaning "writing." As you can probably guess, *auto*ethnography means the writing of self in culture. Although some scholars might use the terms "narrative ethnography" and "autoethnography" more or less interchangeably, others are careful to point out that **autoethnography** involves the process of drawing on ongoing ethnographic research (fieldwork and interviews, in particular) to excavate researchers' personal stories in relation to what is being studied, as opposed to sitting in a room and writing about a remembered experience (Lindemann, 2010b). Regardless of how a researcher approaches the practice of autoethnography, that researcher will find that it definitely has some commonalities with ethnography.

All autoethnographers write about their personal experiences as a way of examining or critiquing cultural experience (Holman Jones, Adams, & Ellis, 2013). There are four characteristics that define autoethnography:

> First, autoethnographers intentionally highlight the relationship of their experiences and stories to culture and cultural practices. … Second, autoethnographic texts demonstrate knowledge of past research on a topic they seek to contribute to this research. … Third, autoethnographic works present an intentionally vulnerable subject. … Fourth, autoethnography actively seeks a reciprocal relationship with audiences—one marked by mutual responsibility and participation—in order to compel a response. (Holman Jones et al., 2013, pp. 22–24)

Goodall (1996) characterizes autoethnographic research as "the study of the self as the other" (p. 9). This relationship is captured in the following excerpt, in which

Kurt writes about his struggle to write about his rocky relationship with his disabled father:

> As I write this, I look over to my bookshelf and the photograph of the three-year-old boy sitting on my father's lap. My father is grabbing the boy's tiny elbow in his large hands, as if teaching the boy to punch, as if training the boy in the "manly" poses he thinks necessary to get along in life. He is smiling. So is the boy. (Lindemann, 2010a, p. 30)

In this excerpt, the self is literally the other as Kurt examines a photograph of himself as a boy. Given that he (an able-bodied researcher) is studying the ways disabled athletes communicate masculinity in the context of a wheelchair sport, a reflexive consideration of the ways his disabled father shaped his own understanding of what it means to "be a man" was necessary. Such a consideration, favorable to his self-image or not, helps him analyze his interactions with disabled male wheelchair athletes.

This vulnerability is often a hallmark of autoethnography. In his autoethnographic research of his experience as a victim of bullying, Keith Berry (2013) writes:

> Autoethnographically exploring bullying and our responses to the problem illustrates a relation space of heightened complexity, curiosity, and concern. Mindfully and reflexively engaging the issue immerses and implicates us within an emotional and thoughtful context of vulnerable selves who negotiate relationships, identity, care, and awareness. (p. 22)

We know the power of connecting with others through relationships, as noted in Chapter 12. Similarly, Berry's hope is that writing his own stories of being bullied will direct our attention to the issue of bullying and "provoke more open and connected ways of relating to/with ourselves and others" (pp. 23–24). Elissa Foster (2010) writes of a similarly powerful motivation in the story of her experience as a woman who has postponed motherhood, attempting to conceive when she states that "many competing discourse clamor in the arena of infertility" (p. 155). Foster (2010) tells us that in the writing of her story of "delayed conception, miscarriage, and failure to conceive for twelve months following the loss of the pregnancy," she faces the limits of critical thinking when "biology and biography meet biomedicine" (pp. 153–154). In both these autoethnographic studies, we witness researchers' pain and identity struggles as they work to seek meaningful answers to difficult, complicated questions and to implore readers to consider how communication can be more caring and compassionate, and to ask us to "touch down on these sentiments with [them] as a testament that hope can take many forms and can offer us a story we can live with" (Foster, 2010, p. 156).

Most research begins as either ethnographic or autoethnographic, but there are times that what began as an ethnographic project shifts to an autoethnographic investigation. The same goal presides—to describe, critique, and be reflexive about culture and cultural practices. Every ethnographic project demands the reflexivity that tips toward autoethnographic research. And every autoethnographic research demands the same critical attention to the taken-for-grantedness about communication, inviting all of us to be reflexive about our complicity in communicating in ways that can be painful, marginalizing, and stigmatizing and, at the same time, to be activists

for communicating understanding, caring, and compassion. This diagram from Pitard (2017) illustrates the ways our reflexivity influences not only how we understand our relationship to our research, but how that understanding fits into the ways of knowing discussed in Chapter 3 (see **Figure 7.1**).

It may seem, from this brief explanation, that all autoethnographies are about painful experiences. Although this is not necessarily true, it may be the case more often than not. This is because it is often the ineffable experiences that are the most difficult to represent with and within scholarly research. Nonetheless, these difficult-to-capture experiences are often crucial to understanding the communication phenomenon being studied. Indeed, in ethnographic research, the **representation** of a researcher and his or her participants' experiences are just as important as how that data were gathered in the first place. In the following section, we discuss the ways ethnographic data is analyzed and represented.

FIGURE 7.1: Philosophical Assumptions of Ethnographic Methods

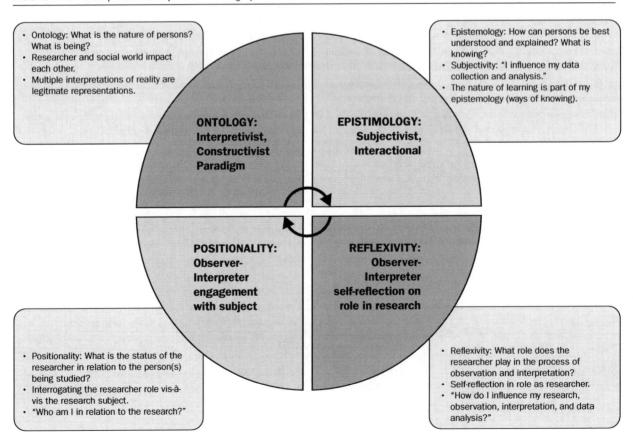

Data Analysis and Representation

Data analysis is the process whereby ethnographers read over and review the data they have collected and written (e.g., field notes, transcripts, documents, photos, reflexivity, and any other form of data) to determine what they now know that they did not know before they started the research. Ellingson (2017) tells us that this data analytic process may involve "coding with an established set of codes, inductively deriving a typology of categories or narrative schemas, reading data through a theoretical lens, or reflecting on field notes in order to construct an ethnographic story or poem" (p. 150). At its core, then, data analysis is the process whereby ethnographers read and reread their field notes, interview transcriptions, and relevant documents to determine if any patterns of communication or common themes emerge (often called *emic* coding) or if there are any "negative cases" that do not fit these patterns or themes and/or to apply existing theoretical constructs to the raw data (usually referred to as *etic* coding). This is all accomplished with the goal of better understanding what is going on in the scene and identifying and clarifying the meanings participants construct through their communicative interaction.

Asides, Commentaries, and Memos

Often, writing can be a form of data analysis. This can occur on multiple levels. First, when reading and rereading the data, researchers may write or (if doing analysis on a computer) type comments within the field notes and interview transcriptions. Sarah Tracy (2013) provides a helpful explanation of this process. Short notations designed to help the researcher think about the data or pin a particular thought for later consideration are usually called **asides**. Longer asides that may follow through on a tentative speculation, deduction, or conclusion are called *commentaries*. It is often helpful to flesh out these musings captured in asides and commentaries in lengthier, formal writing as well. These **memos** (Tracy, 2013) can actually become part of a paper's analysis and conclusion section if written with care and a serious consideration of the ways relevant theory and literature informed the researcher's analysis.

For ethnographers, data analysis is a continuous process from the very first visit to the research site. As we mentioned earlier, ethnographers read scholarly literature to focus on concepts that seem relevant to their research interests and to what they have learned from researching the history and politics of the site. Even after that first visit, however, observing, writing field notes, and even possibly conducting unstructured interviews provide ethnographers with data they can review and analyze to better understand their contexts and to narrow the focuses of their studies. That is why it is important to realize that ethnographers work inductively and creatively to analyze their data and represent their findings. Some would say that the writing we do as ethnographers is *not* a representation of our findings, but is instead a process of inquiry in which we write to find out what we know (Richardson, 2000). Richardson suggests that writing as a method of inquiry allows us to investigate, reflect on, and write "how we construct the world, ourselves, and others, and how standard objectifying practices of social science unnecessarily limit us" (p. 924). Writing as a form of inquiry allows for magic, imagination, creativity, and a nurturing of writers to discover new and often provocative insights about themselves and others.

Accuracy and "Reliability"

As you are reading this, you may be wondering about the rigor of ethnographic analysis. How do we know it is accurate? How do we know it is reliable? Well, in qualitative research, and in ethnography in particular, we do not discuss the rigor of such research in exactly those terms. Sure, we want our research to be accurate, but we do not necessarily refer to it as "validity." Instead, ethnographers strive for "triangulation" (Tracy, 2013). In **triangulation**, ethnographers gather data from multiple sources. We have already discussed these sources earlier in this chapter: field observations, interviews, and document analysis. With this in mind, think of triangulation as "pinging" a cell phone. When someone wants to locate a phone signal, that person might send a "ping" to several cell phone towers in a particular area. The signals bounce off each other, and the phone is presumed to be somewhere in between those towers that were pinged, similar to GPS tracking. In ethnography, researchers use multiple data sources to accurately ping the meanings of participants. While these meanings may not be similar, they offer layers of understanding about the phenomenon under study. In terms of external validity—commonly called generalizability—it is sometimes difficult to argue that the in-depth study of group can be applied to other groups. One way ethnographers address this issue is to argue for what is called **naturalistic generalizations** (Stake & Trumbull, 1982). This concept refers to the ability of ethnographic writing to engender in readers the same feelings participants and/or researchers described and experienced in the research. In this way, the findings—encapsulated as they are in the writing of ethnography—are generalized to readers.

Reliability is a little more difficult to transfer to qualitative research because researchers bring their own identity into the field with them and are supposed to practice reflexivity regarding how that identity informs data gathering and analysis. The idea that another person with different identity markers could go into the same scene and settings as you and find the same things in the same ways is a little suspect. As Sarah Tracy (2010) explains, the most researchers can do is to establish credibility through the use of thick description, triangulation, and **member checking,** which is simply asking participants to comment on your initial analysis to get their thoughts as to its accuracy. So, while other researchers may not be able to "test" your findings by attempting to replicate your study, they (and readers) can hopefully trust that you did everything in your power to ensure the accuracy of your analysis.

Of course, the writing of ethnographic research is also important in determining how to present the study to readers. It is probably evident from our earlier discussion that interrelated with data analysis is the decision that ethnographers make about representation, which is the form that ethnographers choose to tell the story of what they have learned through data analysis. Referring to this process as "the art and magic of interpretation," Tracy (2013) offers seven ways of analyzing/representing data, including exemplars and vignettes, typologies, dramatistic approaches, metaphor analyses, visual data displays, explanation and causality, and discourse tracing. Clearly, data analysis and representation influence one another; as ethnographers discover insights in data analysis, they realize that these key insights might be best understood by representing the insights as one of the types offered by Tracy (2013) or some other creative invention that makes sense. No matter what form of data analysis/representation the ethnographer chooses, the data adds up to a tellable story that has a beginning, middle, and an end, with all forms of data woven together and not separated by type(s) of data.

Conclusion

The ethnographic adventure may begin with you, but by now it should be clear that it involves much more than simply writing about yourself and your own experiences. We discussed the process of entering a scene or setting within a field, writing field notes, and the role reflexivity plays in conducting observations and writing field notes. We have also discussed the process of interviewing individuals and groups and some things to keep in mind when conducting interviews. We briefly covered what autoethnography is, how it relates to more traditional ethnographic research, and when and why a researcher might choose to write an autoethnography. Finally, we covered the basics of data analysis and some options researchers have when considering how to present that analysis to readers. The iterative process of moving back and forth from the field to the scholarly literature helps you to refine your focus, conduct your research, and represent your new knowledge about the context you have immersed yourself in. In doing all this, we hope we have kept the allure of the mystery of ethnographic research while demystifying some of the when, why, and how.

Overall, it is important to remember that *ethnographic research is an inductive process.* When we do ethnography, we are not testing or proving theory, though we may frame our analyses with theory to better understand them. And although we may study a similar topic, group, or organization as another researcher, we are not attempting to replicate someone else's study. When you are your research instrument, such notions of replication are impossible to apply. We are all so very different in what we focus on for our studies, what we observe, the questions we might ask, and the ways we reflect in and out of the contexts we are studying. Of course, none of this should be taken to mean that ethnography is not a rigorous research method. In fact, you may find that it is actually a lot of work. And, for some, it is especially difficult because of the freedom, creativity, and imagination that is required in context and throughout the writing process. The payoff comes in the form of an in-depth understanding of the people, group, or organization you are studying. Do not be surprised, though, if you still have more to investigate and more to say after you have completed your study. If you are passionate about your topic, the ethnographic adventure may continue as long and far as you are willing to take it!

CHAPTER 8

Performative Ways of Knowing

Kurt Lindemann

LEARNING OBJECTIVES

After reading this chapter, you should be able to do the following:

- Identify the historical tensions that led to performance studies being situated in communication departments.

- Identify the reasons why performance studies is often called an "essentially contested concept," as opposed to a "widely accepted concept."

- Distinguish performative writing from other types of scholarly writing.

- Identify the ways in which performance is a "way of knowing."

- Distinguish the formal defining features of performance.

- Distinguish the terms "performance" and "performative."

- Identify and distinguish the dramaturgical, cultural, and language approaches to understanding performance in communication.

- Distinguish the major theories of performance most often applied in communication research.

- Recognize the real-world applications of performance in the public and private sector.

- Identify the interconnections between performance and other areas of communication study.

S ITTING AT MY DESK, MY EYES DRIFTED FROM the computer screen to falling dust motes momentarily captured in the sunlight pouring through the windows. I know what I want to say, but I'm not yet sure how to say it. Here's the difficulty: Performance studies is both theory and method—an embodied way of knowing that views communication as constitutive and epistemic. Yet, it also encompasses the competent display of skills for a particular audience to understand—a message that may take place on stage (Carlson, 2004) or in everyday life

(Goffman, 1959). Do I start with a scholarly definition in an attempt to provide some sort of initial grounding—a temporary location on a scholarly roadmap? I'm stuck. Most writers, scholarly and otherwise, have sat here, like me, staring at a blank page and wondering how to begin.

***

My narrative exemplifies only one type of communication research on a broad continuum, ranging from applying performance theory to studying communication, to actually performing a text in front of an audience. My narrative is a type of writing you might encounter in performance studies research: performative writing. This form of writing, similar to a personal style of writing practiced in some ethnographic research, is called **performative** because it attempts to create a kind of performance on the page for the reader (Pollock, 1998). We'll revisit this term later in this chapter and distinguish it from *performance*. First, I'll discuss the concept of performance by providing an extended definition.

Defining Performance

Performance, as an academic study and practice, owns a rich and varied history in the communication discipline, with its history rooted in the speech communication classroom, in the theatre, and, much earlier, in English classrooms and training in oratory and elocution (Jackson, 2004). As discussed in Chapter 1, this outgrowth mirrors the development of communication as a discipline. Perhaps for this reason, people often refer to performance studies as an "essentially contested concept" (Strine, Long, & Hopkins, 1991, p. 183). These *rhizomatic* origins of performance studies make it tricky to understand how and why the practice and study of performance is necessary for a fuller understanding of the communication discipline, but this chapter seeks to provide just such an argument. We'll briefly explore the historical tracings of performance studies and how it has come to be, in many universities, associated with communication. Through this kind of academic archeology, we'll have a clearer view of why it is so difficult to point to one definition of performance, let alone the ways scholars might study it.

Many definitions of performance have been forwarded by theorists associated with communication and related disciplines such as anthropology, sociology, and linguistics. Erving Goffman (1959) defines performance as all activity enacted by a person designed to persuade observers, which he likens to audience members. By persuasion, he simply means activity intended to make others believe something or adopt the actor's particular point of view. Others have indicated that performance must be marked as somehow out of the ordinary and adhere to a specific set of criteria (Bauman, 1977). And still others have posited that performance is simply twice-behaved behavior (Schechner, 2003), or the conscious recreation, for an audience, of everyday behaviors we do less consciously. For the purposes of this chapter, we adopt the following definition: *Performance is the aesthetically-shaped display of verbal, nonverbal, and mediated communication within a frame of meaning established by a communicator and intended to be shared with an audience.* I unpack this definition in the next section.

Understanding Key Concepts

The definition I've provided may be a bit clunky, but by this point in your academic career you have probably realized the lengths to which some scholars will go to provide as specific a definition as possible. For understanding performance, though, such thoughtfulness is especially important. Let us consider some key concepts in our definition because each will play an important role in understanding the major approaches to conceptualizing performance, along with its study.

Displays

"Display" is an important term because scholars, although they may draw from philosophical theorists, are often interested in how communication behaviors are aesthetically shaped to achieve an effect on an audience (i.e., convey an emotion or idea, present a desired self, etc.). Verbal and nonverbal communication are discussed in-depth in Chapter 2. In the case of performance, this "aesthetic shaping" is another way of saying that we make choices about our gestures, vocal intonation, dress, body posture, etc. Using the term "display" implies some level of decision-making on the part of the communicator about what others see and why. Granted, some decisions are more conscious than others, but we at least choose how much thought and effort go into our displays. Consider merchandise on a store shelf: Certain displays may attract buyers, whereas others may not. In each case, however, someone decided how much effort to put into the display of items. These communicative displays may happen verbally, nonverbally, and/or via mediated communication, which in this definition simply means communication in a medium other than verbal or nonverbal displays, such as an image.

In sum, **displays** represent a variety of ways exists in which we might express, enact, or perform something, as well as a number of things we might display. For example, we might display clothing choices to communicate gender. We might speak a certain way to display our education, class, or race. And, each of these display choices may vary in our level of awareness and intention. The most successful displays, however, will not just communicate something to an audience; such displays will also communicate *how* they should be understood by those audiences. This is called **framing**, and when discussing performance, framing can mean the difference between an audience viewing a performance as "good" or as "bad."

Framing

Framing is a concept theorized in depth by Goffman (1986); we'll address his ideas in more depth later in this chapter. In short, though, we can think of a frame like a literal picture frame around a photograph or painting. When audience members see this frame, they are supposed to think, "This picture is important enough that someone took the time to highlight it with this frame." In fact, some conceptual visual artists might put a frame around a scribble or doodle and call it "art," prompting the audience to question the very meaning of "art" itself. As

such, frames are *metacommunicative* in that they communicate to audiences how to think about the communication inside the frame. With that in mind, an audience will usually view that picture differently than if a photograph were just in a shoebox in the closet.

Establishing a frame isn't possible without others' cooperation. Someone may try to communicate a frame that highlights his or her communication as a performance but fail to gain the cooperation of others. In theatre, the audience members are sometimes asked to "suspend their disbelief"—in other words, to momentarily forget they are watching actors on stage or in a performance and instead focus on what is being said and done by the actors. Of course, sometimes audience members do not do this and instead focus on all the unrealistic aspects of the theatrical performance. This can also happen in communication, resulting in a misalignment of frames (Goffman, 1986), a misunderstanding between communicators, and a relatively unsuccessful performance.

Audience

"Audience" is a term readily associated with performance. Audiences can be thought of on a continuum. Pelias and VanOosting (1987) explain that audience participation and activity can range from inactive receivers to proactive producers of content (see **Table 8.1**).

Audience, then, is an important concept in considering how communication is a performance. The term "audience" is meant to encompass people in nontheatrical happenings, like a team in the locker room listening to a coach's story or company employees engaging in a ritual at work.

TABLE 8.1: Levels of Audience Participation

Receiver	Respondent	Coproducer	Producer
Clearly defined audience role, common response expected (silence during funerals, weddings, etc.).	Clearly defined audience role, taking into account individual variations in response (applause for a concert, laughter at parts of a play or film, etc.).	Audience and performer roles not clearly distinguished; performance dependent on individual response (interactive theatre, improv, etc.).	All participants assume performer roles in a community-wide performance (Mardi Gras, etc.).
Inactive	Active	Interactive	Proactive

Source: Adapted from Pelias & VanOosting (1987).

Putting It All Together

People can view everyday communication events as performances of identity, of cultural affiliation, and as an attempt to persuade, or to accomplish understanding, among other goals. In general, understanding communication as a performance allows us to focus on things about the communication process we may not be able to see using another lens (e.g., as a biological process or a system). We are able to view company picnics as more than simply a gathering of employees; instead, we might see them as cultural rituals that communicate meaning to those in attendance through the use of signs and symbols. We can view gender, for example, as a series of display choices designed to communicate a desired self to an audience, much like an actor tries to convince an audience that he or she *is* the character.

We can think about performer and audience in several ways. Sometimes an audience can be part of the performance, as in cultural rituals such as weddings, Mardi Gras, and quinceañeras. We can also view performance on a continuum, from the everyday to the extraordinary (i.e., not ordinary). We can also view performance on a continuum—ranging from its roots in cultural rituals, traditions, and roles, to performances more aesthetically shaped and polished, like a theatrical production. Additionally, performances might involve individuals or collectives of people, and sometimes might even draw from a written text. All these types of performances may intersect with one another. Stern and Henderson (1993) encapsulate these types of performances (see **Table 8.2**).

Performance and the Performative

With understanding a definition of performance, it is necessary to distinguish it from the term "performative." The British language philosopher J. L. Austin (1975) brought the term "performative" into scholarly usage in his recorded lectures (eventually published as the book *How to Do Things With Words*). He called *performative utterances* sentences that do not describe things, but instead perform an action (e.g., promising someone something or saying "I do" in a marriage ceremony). As you can see, these are not displays of skill in the way we've defined performance. Instead, this communication creates an action through its use. Although this difference may seem a bit confusing now, we'll revisit the idea of the performative later in this chapter.

Whereas a multitude of definitions might frustrate students just learning about performance, these myriad definitions allow a variety of approaches to conceptualizing and studying communication. After examining why we've come to talk about performance studies in the context of a communication capstone review, I briefly address three approaches, roughly dividing scholars' theorizing in several thematic groupings: dramaturgical, cultural, and language. Naturally, these categories are not necessarily mutually exclusive; instead, they offer an initial avenue to understanding performing as communication.

Historical Tracings: Communicating (in) the Past and Performance in the Present

One overriding belief in the mid-20th century was that teachers should be good public speakers. Oral interpretation and elocution were generally practiced by females who were training to be teachers themselves, but not by the male academics who were professors in the university classroom. Soon, oral interpretation came to be viewed as an outmoded and ineffective way of understanding literature. In accordance with a decrease in the market value of literature, the practice of oral interpretation was shuffled

TABLE 8.2: Performance Continuum

Ordinary Everyday Experiences	Blended or Intermediate Experiences	Extraordinary Experiences
Individual	⟵————————⟶	Collective
Server at a restaurant (cultural)	Theatrical events and concerts (aesthetic)	Mardi Gras and other festivals
Children playing (cultural)	Performance art (cultural/aesthetic hybrid)	Cultural rituals (weddings, etc.) (cultural/aesthetic hybrid)

Source: Adapted from Stern & Henderson (1993).

from English classrooms to education classrooms, and eventually to communication departments. This development was discussed in Chapter 1. Already, though, the roots of performance and communication were intertwined. Jackson (2004) provides another parallel tracing of the development of performance studies.

One parallel to "speech" teachers leaving English academic societies at the start of the 20th century involves the infusion of theatre with the study of culture. Jackson (2004) explains that, in a time of a great upheaval in English departments regarding the conceptualization and teaching of literary theory, George Pierce Baker approached his chair at Harvard about the teaching of drama. Baker found himself teaching an applied discipline in an age where classroom discussion of theories and texts was considered the pinnacle of academic achievement. The "cultural turn" in drama studies, whereby scholars and practitioners began to use theatre to study cultural rituals and practices written about by anthropologists and sociologists, dovetails with literary critics and philosophers such as Roland Barthes and Michel Foucault, whose work was just coming to bear in the United States. These French thinkers provided a readily available way of thinking about cultures as texts—something the anthropologist Clifford Geertz (cf. Jackson, 2004) was advocating at the time. So, performance studies not only has interdisciplinary tensions with both English and theatre in the age-old practice-versus-theory debate, but it is also shaped by anthropologists and sociologists as a way of understanding culture as dynamic and unstable.

These early incarnations of performance studies were regarded by many academics as practical and applied, and therefore "inferior" to other areas of scholarly study in English and communication. Nonetheless, scholars from literary criticism, sociology, anthropology, theatre, cultural studies, and communication (especially rhetoric, intercultural, organizational, and media scholars) continued to adapt and apply performance theory to their own needs. And it is because of this continual redefinition and reapplication that we come to call "performance studies" an essentially contested concept.

On a basic level, however, both performance studies and communication examine the verbal and nonverbal behaviors that constitute human communication. Moreover, performance studies employs aesthetically shaped verbal and nonverbal communication in its findings. Just as communication has embraced both the cultural and narrative turns in the social sciences, performance studies partly examines communication texts writ large—cultural scripts and human behavior—and highlights the ways people shape understandings of each other through stories we tell. Because of its pedagogical roots and applications, performance studies exist nicely in the classroom alongside what may seem like the paradigm of postpositivism; even teachers of scientific communication see the benefits of "hands-on" learning in the form of, say, role-playing scenarios. So, performance studies is in communication departments not because it cannot find a home anywhere else, but because communication scholars have brought it here and made this its home.

Approaches to Understanding Communication as Performance

With a historical understanding of why performance studies is sometimes called an "essentially contested concept" and why it is so often situated in communication departments, let us move to a discussion of how we study it. Next, I cover three main thematic approaches to the study of performance, each with its own distinct definition of performance. Within each of these approaches are several theories commonly employed. We begin with the most common approach and the one most familiar to communication students: the dramaturgical approach.

Dramaturgical Approach: Burke and Goffman

This approach views communication as one would a stage performance, with social "actors" who each share a front stage (and sometimes a backstage) and deliver (usually unwritten) social scripts for audiences to achieve a desired effect. The scholar most commonly cited here is Erving Goffman, who developed his concept based, in part, on Kenneth Burke's (1945) notion of dramatism. Burke and his approach to communication are discussed at length in Chapter 6. For Burke, life is drama and, as characters in a play, people have (often hidden) motives for what they do. These motives may become apparent from their actions and their discourse (use of language) by asking certain questions about them. By foregrounding certain aspects of the situation—act, scene, agent, agency, and purpose—we may better understand someone's motives.

One reason Goffman is readily used in analyzing communication as a performance is that, unlike Burke, Goffman focuses on interactions. Burke's approach is very much a macro-level view of a communication situation; Goffman, however, zeroes in on specific interactions and how a social actor may seek to align frames with an audience (sometimes made up of one person) or break that frame for a specific purpose. We can take many important concepts from Goffman to understand how communication might be a performance. I address the most salient ones next.

Backstage, Front Stage, Roles, and Scripts

While Goffman used Burke's notion of dramatism as an inspiration for his own work, Goffman's focus on everyday interactions allowed him to incorporate many more concepts closely associated with the theatre. At its core, Goffman's (1959) notion of performance lies in the ability of a social actor to convince an audience of one or more people, in a particular situation and over an extended period of time, to view the social actor as he or she wants to be viewed—as a good person, a "normal" person, a competent person, etc. This process resembles how an actor in a play convinces a theatre audience that he or she is the character being portrayed. Three very important and easy-to-understand concepts involved in this process are backstage, front stage, and roles.

To put it simply, as with actors, all people have **backstage** spaces in which they prepare to portray certain *roles* to an audience in **front stage** spaces. Actors in a play have dressing rooms and other offstage spaces to change into costumes and to prepare themselves to convince audience members that the actors are the characters they are playing. We utilize our everyday spaces in similar ways. For example, we might prepare to play the *role* of an employee in numerous *backstage* areas; in our closets and bedrooms, we carefully (or not so carefully) choose what we wear (our costumes). In our bathrooms, we make sure we look appropriate for work (some with hair and makeup, among other things). We might prepare notes for a meeting in any of these spaces, or maybe even in our cars or our offices (which may become backstage spaces if we close the doors); a backstage space can be anywhere in which an audience is not present. Ready or not, we make our way to the front stage space (e.g., the office, the meeting, etc.) to play the role of a competent employee.

We cannot forget the idea of *scripts*. Each character in a play has a set of lines. Similarly, the roles we play in our everyday lives come with scripts. Unlike in a play, however, our scripts are mostly informal and unwritten, though sometimes no less ritualized. For example, we know the standard script for greeting someone at work, and that a deviation from that script could damage our audiences' perceptions of us; we may want to be seen as "good" coworkers, but not following the standard greeting script (i.e., "Hi, how are you?" "Fine, thanks") may cause our coworkers to question whether we are good in terms of being friendly, pleasant, easy to work with, etc.

Obviously, a successful performance requires the cooperation of an audience. In the theatre, a common saying is an audience must engage in a "willing suspension of disbelief," which means audience members must willingly forget that they are in a theatre, that the actors on stage are speaking louder than people do in real life, that the set behind them is not actually a house, office, and so forth. For our everyday performances, a similar level of cooperation is required from audiences, whose members are, of course, engaging in their own performances at the same time. This cooperation, often called *facework,* is a crucial part of *impression management* and the *presentation of self* (Goffman, 1959). I explore this concept in more detail in the next section.

Presentation of Self

This concept of the presentation of self is, for the most part, contained in the previous section. To review, we are like actors on a stage; we play roles—each with its own variation of costume—and we prepare to play these roles in backstage spaces. One crucial addition I will address here will set the stage (pun intended) for the next several concepts: cooperation with an audience. We can perform desired selves for others all we want, but if no one believes us, then we have to ask ourselves, "What is unbelievable about our performances and why?" The *impressions* we *manage*, then, are sustained with the help of others, and these impressions are part of our overall presentations of self.

But, how do we arrive at these selves we present? According to Goffman (1959), a person's motives include the achievement of personal goals, the presentation of consistent and positive self to others, and conforming to social norms. You might say that all these motives represent aspects of our "true" selves that we reflexively choose to showcase, highlight, and display (i.e., perform). For Goffman, however, no "real" self or one "true" self exists. Rather, he argues, people are a multiplicity of all the selves that they perform for others. One critique often leveled at Goffman, then, is the question, "If there is no "real" self, then who or what chooses the self we present to others?" This lingering question makes Goffman's theory of self-presentation interesting for those studying communication. Goffman is more successful in providing an understanding of interaction rather than of the self, and one such understanding of communication interaction as performance is framing.

Frames and Framing

As noted earlier in this chapter, a **frame** refers to an imaginary picture frame a communicator may draw around an interaction, designed to tell the other person or persons: "Hey, everything that occurs in this particular frame should be looked at as 'special.'" Most works of art hanging in museums and galleries have frames around them, of course. But take away the frames, and some works may seem puzzling, or even ordinary (e.g., sketches on napkins by famous artists). On a different note, consider the sport of ice hockey. Players may get into fights, employing tactics that they might use were they to get into a fight on the street (e.g., punching, pushing another player down, etc.). Although hockey contains penalties for fighting, it is tolerated and sometimes even encouraged. Why? Because although such fighting is real in the sense that it is really happening, it is not a "real" fight; it's framed as part of the sport.

So, what separates a piece of paper with a drawing on it from a work of art? What separates fighting in the hockey rink from fighting in real life? Perhaps obviously, it is the *context*. But the metacommunicative aspects of a museum or gallery (e.g., the lights, the space, etc.) or the sport (e.g., the arena or stage, the uniforms or costumes, etc.) establish a frame. For art, the interpretive frame established for visitors is, "These are important and should be evaluated and appreciated as such." For hockey, the frame around the fighting says to others, "This is real fighting behavior, but not a 'real' fight'" (Lindemann, 2008). In our definition of performance, this concept of framing functions in the same way—to highlight communication as a performance.

Play

Framing represents an integral element of "play." If you are thinking of kids playing a game, you are not too far from the mark. In fact, that sort of playing can teach us a lot about the power of communication to frame activities. But, before we get to human interaction, let us examine dogs playing. When dogs play together, they may bark, get in a crouched position, jump on each other, and do other actions they might actually do in a fight. For people who have never seen this before, it can be scary because it may look and sound like actual dogs fighting; but they're not fighting. In fact, some behavior, such as tail wagging, signals that, while what they are doing is *like* fighting, it isn't *real* fighting. The tail wagging *keys* a *play* frame around what they are doing.

Now, imagine two children playing at sword fighting with plastic swords. The two kids may be doing what they've seen in the movies, but they have established a play frame in some way, maybe by saying, "You be this person, and I'll be this person, and we'll have a sword fight." Maybe they wear costumes. Maybe they fight in slow motion. And, it follows that if the play frame can be communicatively keyed, or activated, it can be broken using communication. Consider the power of the words "time out." The two children could be in the heat of battle, and if one yells "time out," the action is usually halted without question. Those two words break the frame of play.

What about everyday adult interaction? Does play factor into our communication? And, is this performance? The answer to all questions is yes, it can and does in a variety of ways. When thinking about conversation, we can find many instances of framing to separate out conversation as play. One instance is teasing. Often, sarcasm and other teasing insults are separated from everyday conversation by the tone of voice and maybe even a facial gesture. These nonverbal displays are one form of metacommunication (talk about talk is also metacommunicative); they key the play frame around the conversation and communicate to both parties what is being said. The words themselves could be uttered as insults, but the frame directs the impact and should be understood within the play frame.

Of course, keying, framing, and play do not always work that smoothly; there is not always *frame alignment* among participants. Sometimes there is *frame misalignment*. For example, someone may not understand the sarcastic tone of voice. There may also be *frame breakage* on the part of one or more participants in the interaction.

TABLE 8.3: Experiences and Audience in the Dramaturgical Approach

Ordinary Everyday Experiences	Blended or Intermediate Experiences		Extraordinary Experiences
Individual	← →		Collective
Server at a restaurant	Theatrical events and concerts	Mardi Gras and other festivals	
Children playing	Performance art	Cultural rituals (weddings, etc.)	
Receiver	Respondent	Coproducer	Producer
Clearly defined audience role, common response expected (silence during funerals, weddings, etc.).	Clearly defined audience role, taking into account individual variations in response (applause for a concert, laughter at parts of a play or film, etc.).	Audience and performer roles not clearly distinguished and performance dependent on individual response (interactive theatre and improv, etc.).	All participants assume performer roles in a community-wide performance (Mardi Gras, etc.).
Inactive	Active	Interactive	Proactive

Source: Adapted from Pelias & VanOosting (1987).

Someone may understand the play frame but choose to break the frame by drawing attention to the frame and questioning its utility or desirability, or by critiquing someone's attempt to play.

As fully as the dramaturgical approach explains how self-presentation occurs in these interactions (see **Table 8.3**), this approach doesn't fully account for the manner in which people create and sustain culture.

Granted, these performances may include cultural norms, but the dramaturgical approach doesn't attempt to examine culture to any greater degree. By "culture," I mean the values and beliefs of a community of people shared through communication. Race and ethnicity can certainly be a part of this community, and this is explored in-depth in Chapter 17, but race and ethnicity don't necessarily have to define the community. Performance studies offers several ways to think about communication and culture. I delineate some distinctions of this approach next.

Cultural Approach: Bauman, Schechner, and Turner

Unlike the dramaturgical approach, which includes the theorists commonly covered in communication courses—Burke and Goffman—the cultural approach to performance as communication evokes scholars not usually taught in communication courses. Nonetheless, their collective theories and approaches have impacted

the way performance studies scholars think about performance in an academic sense. Coming from the areas of folklore, theatre, and anthropology, the cultural approach provides an interesting avenue in which to enter this rich discussion of performance and communication. We'll begin this section with a summary of the contributions of folklorist Richard Bauman.

Verbal Art as Performance

Richard Bauman's main contribution to our understanding of communication as performance is rooted in his notion of *verbal art as performance*. He borrows the concepts of **keying** and framing from Goffman (1986) for his discussion of folklore. Folklore and fairy tales, although written down in books, are based on an orality that existed before books. Folk tales, fairy tales, and allegories, which often teach the audience a lesson, were passed down orally by performing these stories for others. In many of these instances, the speaker spoke (or performed) and the audience listened.

But, how would audience members know what they were listening to? They didn't have a book cover that read *Popular Fairy Tales From Eastern Europe*. Instead, Bauman (1977) argues, tellers keyed an audience's interpretive frame by employing any number of communication strategies, each of which is culturally bound. For example, when most of us hear the phrase: "Once upon a time," we know that we are going to be hearing a fairy tale, most likely involving a princess and/or prince, or some human or animal that has a wish to be granted. Bauman calls the phrase "once upon a time," a code or **formula** that signals to the audience or keys their interpretive frame: "Hey, you are about to hear a special story, and you can expect certain features in this story." These codes or formulae are metacommunicative in that they communicate to an audience *about* the communication from the speaker.

Bauman also mentions that other textual markers exist, including the nonverbal aspects of voice, tempo, tone, and pitch. Imagine, for example, that relative who, at family reunions, tells slightly off-color jokes or stories. Maybe these stories always involve the same cast of characters, such as his or her childhood friends. We know such a story is about to start because that person—let's say he's a crazy uncle—may physically gather himself up, puff out his chest, look around, and start speaking with a loud voice: "You know, that reminds me of this time Shorty and I drove down to Florida in his VW bus." When we see and hear him start this way, we know what to expect. His verbal and nonverbal communication key a frame, and we know to expect a certain kind of storytelling performance and a certain kind of story. As you may also guess, some people are simply good storytellers. These people mastered the art of verbal performance, and are likely well aware of these kinds of special codes, formulae, and verbal and nonverbal keys. Following this example, we can consider another culturally bound type of verbal performance: the telling of jokes. We know the use of keys (e.g., certain language, verbal, and nonverbal cues, etc.) is often what makes a joke successful; we all know there's a certain way to set up a punchline.

This invocation of special codes, formulae, verbal and nonverbal cues, and other textual markers encapsulates Bauman's notion of verbal art as performance. In many ways, Bauman's conceptualization of verbal art as performance is similar to Goffman's, but it differs from Goffman's in several important ways. First, whereas it draws on some of Goffman's concepts, such as keys and framing, it also offers specific ways a performance might be keyed. Importantly, Bauman argues that these metacommunicative keys are culturally bound as they might differ from cultural to culture. Finally, Bauman argues that the invocation and utilization of textual markers are *aesthetic*. Simply, more artistic and less artistic ways exist to tell a story or tell a joke. What makes a performance

good is the way the speaker artistically employs these textual marker, such as timing, tempo, and figurative language used—again, all of which may be culturally bound. Harkening back to our tables at the beginning of the chapter, we see that these performances are often *aesthetic/cultural hybrids with an active audience responding at appropriate moments.*

Schechner's "Twice-Behaved Behavior"

A large part of performance studies entails actually performing. One of the reasons performance studies offers an "essentially contested concept" (Strine et al., 1991) is that performance studies is a process and product—a method of inquiry and a means of reporting that inquiry. Just as performative writing—exemplified at the very beginning of this chapter—is a way of exploring theories, concepts, and reporting that analysis to an audience, performing itself is also a way to do the same thing.

For example, instead of interviewing people about a communication concept and analyzing those interviews for a paper, a performance scholar may *perform* those interviews, indicating in his or her verbal and nonverbal communication the very analysis he or she might otherwise put on paper. The scholar's performance may illustrate his or her struggles, passion, anger, sadness, and whatever else he or she thinks relevant to communication analysis. In this sense, the performer also needs artistic and aesthetic competence when performing research, although this doesn't mean she has to become the next Meryl Streep.

Theatre and anthropology scholar Schechner (2002, 2003) helps us think about performance in a "nonacting" way. Although Schechner is affiliated with the NYU School of Performance Studies, which is based more in theatre theory and practice than in communication concepts, his approach to performance still offers an insightful way to conceptualize communication as performance. When I teach performance studies, often to students with little or no performance experience, I usually have to reassure them that they don't have to aspire to be great actors when performing. Schechner's (Schechner & Appel, 1990) notion of **twice-behaved behavior** helps students understand this.

Simply put, Schechner argues that *all* behavior is twice behaved in the sense that it is not necessarily original. We have observed others behave in certain contexts in order to better understand how to behave in those contexts. Children observe and model parents' behavior at a dinner party, students observe other students' behavior in the classroom, and so on. When performing, then, all we're really doing is enacting behaviors we have already observed in our daily lives. One can "never step in the same river twice" (the river keeps flowing and so the very water we might step in one day is different from the next day) (Schechner, 2002), however, so each behavior is new and unique in that we can never *reperform* something exactly as it had been performed previously.

What does all this have to do with culture and performance? A few things. Schechner (Schechner & Appel, 1990), often in collaboration with the anthropologist Turner, staged rituals of other cultures to study them and to bring a better understanding of culture to audiences. Schechner also saw many similarities between theatre and anthropology, including the following: Rituals studied by anthropologists are performances with audience–performer interactions, and the transmission of cultural knowledge is embodied, experiential, and performative. All notions of audience and aesthetics from our previous table are encompassed in this broad view of performance.

Liminality, Communitas, and Social Drama

Not surprisingly, the next theorist we cover is Schechner's frequent collaborator—anthropologist Victor Turner. Turner has contributed much to our current understanding and application of performance theory in everyday life. This section briefly covers three of the most important concepts: liminality, communitas, and social drama.

Liminality

The first concept is something a lot of students, once they understand it, seem to relate to on an intimate level: the concept of **liminality**. From Latin, a *limen* is a threshold, like a door frame, that may also be a beginning and an end. In some uses of the word, this threshold may be imperceptible. Developed from Turner's (2002) study of rites of passage in many cultures, liminality represents the in-between state felt by those going through a rite of passage. In tribal cultures, this may be a boy leaving for a hunt and coming back a "man." The time on the hunt is liminal; the boy is no longer a boy because he left his village. He may not, however, yet be considered a man in the eyes of the villagers because he may need to return safely, kill an animal, or complete some other task.

In modern societies, the liminal may not be as clearly defined, but it is nonetheless present. Rites of passage, such as a graduation, a wedding ceremony, a quinceañera, a bar mitzvah, and so forth, may all involve the person crossing an imaginary threshold by which the person leaves one cultural role and assumes another. The in-between, Turner argues, is the state one is in during this "crossing." Such a concept is important for understanding performance because we may not only have to enact certain rituals during a state of liminality, but we may also have to learn new cultural performances to enact in order to take on the new role (e.g., adult, spouse, etc.) convincingly.

Communitas

Liminality is sometimes experienced by more than one person. For example, fans at a sporting event may experience liminality in that the stadium is contained within particular cultural practices (e.g., orderly lines, paying for food, etc.), but it also constitutes its own space separate from that culture. During some moments in the communal liminal spaces, people may experience what is called **communitas**, or spontaneous community. Think about European football (soccer) matches in which the entire stadium breaks into song. Such feelings of community may also happen during protests or demonstrations, such as the Occupy Wall Street movement, in which an unstructured and diverse group of people is transformed into a relatively structured community with espoused values of togetherness and egalitarianism.

These performances of spontaneous community—deemed so because the communication usually involves some kind of public display of rituals such as chanting, call and response, singing, or marching—occur precisely because of the liminal space. Separated from the structure of "outside" society, literally (e.g., the Occupy Wall Street encampments or the soccer stadium) or figuratively (e.g., a civil rights march on city streets), participants may feel more free to draw from certain rituals, such as singing songs, while interacting in ways they may not normally.

Social Drama

One of Turner's (1982) most important contributions concerns the way communities deal with conflict. Taking his cue from elements of stage plays, similar to the dramaturgical approach, Turner provides a way to understand macro-level societal communication as a type of **social drama** involving breach, crisis, redress, reintegration, and schism.

Any play must have conflict, and this conflict is usually spurred by competing goals or motivations. Likewise, societal conflicts often occur from a perceived *breach* in social norms. For example, a community might debate a proposed highway through a residential area. Although this proposal may seem like a conflict, nothing has been decided, and the community plans a series of open forums to weigh its options. One night, however, some of the construction equipment is vandalized. Decorum has been breached. And a crisis (with the accompanying questions, e.g., "Who is to blame?" "How should the community proceed?" and "If the proposal is passed will there be more severe vandalism?") is created. The parties involved can redress the crisis in any number of ways. The city council can pursue the vandal as a criminal; the council can seek criminal charges but also interpret the graffiti as a sign of dissatisfaction in the community and hold more open forums. This redress, however communicated, might result in one of two outcomes.

A successful redress allows for a *reintegration* of the maligned parties into a communal whole, while an unsuccessful redress might result in a *schism* in a community or society—one that might never be repaired. This drama plays out in public, and the communication in each of these stages functions *performatively* in that the communication enacted brings into being a particular state between the parties involved. As Austin (1975) explained, some speech acts in this redress might promise something, thereby creating a relationship of obligation that, nonetheless, sustains the relationship. Similarly, a schism may sever a relationship. In each case, the communication brings the state of the relationship into being.

Table 8.2, a blending of the two tables from Pelias and VanOosting (1987) and Stern and Henderson (1993), might look quite different from its form in the dramaturgical approach to performance studies. So, let's break the table down even further to separate each type of cultural approach covered in this section (see **Table 8.4**).

TABLE 8.4: Experiences and Audience in the Cultural Approach

Verbal Art as Performance		Twice-Behaved Behavior, Theatrical Events, and Concerts			Liminality, Social Drama, Communitas	
----------		----------			----------	
Storytelling on a stage or storytelling conversations		Performance ethnography			e.g., Mardi Gras and other festivals or cultural rituals (weddings, etc.)	
Individual		Individual and Group			Collective	
Receiver	Respondent	Receiver	Respondent	Coproducer	Coproducer	Producer
Clearly defined audience role, common response expected (silence during funerals, weddings, etc.).	Clearly defined audience role, taking into account individual variations in response (applause for a concert, laughter at parts of a play or film, etc.).	Clearly defined audience role, common response expected (silence during funerals, weddings, etc.).	Clearly defined audience role, taking into account individual variations in response (applause for a concert, laughter at parts of a play or film, etc.).	Audience and performer roles not clearly distinguished and performance dependent on individual response (interactive theatre and improv, etc.).	Audience and performer roles not clearly distinguished and performance dependent on individual response (interactive theatre and improv, etc.).	All participants assume performer roles in a community-wide performance (Mardi Gras, etc.).
Inactive	Active	Inactive	Active	Interactive	Interactive	Proactive

Source: Adapted from Pelias & VanOosting (1987).

The cultural approach to performance studies spans every type of performance and audience role in the table. Does this mean that the cultural approach is the best? Not really, but it illustrates that performance is an inextricable part of sustaining and understanding culture. Although Turner (1990) didn't necessarily view speech acts and performativity as integral to his theory of social drama, bringing up Austin again helps us transition nicely into the final approach to communication as performance covered in this chapter: the language approach.

Language Approach: Derrida and Butler

We already covered part of this approach when we discussed Austin and speech acts earlier in the chapter. Although speech act theory is not commonly taught in many communication classes anymore, it does provide a foundation for thinking about *performativity*. Often confused with *performance*, the two are conceptualized very differently. This section is called a "language approach" because both theorists covered came to a theory of performativity via Austin's notion of performative utterances and a focus on the "text." Before exploring their contributions to performance studies, let's distinguish a few important differences between the two terms.

Of course, performance is related to performativity, but the distinction lies primarily in the conceptualizations of the two terms. "Performance" is a fairly common term, bringing to mind everything from performance reviews at the workplace to athletic performance on the field. For Pacanowsky and O'Donnell-Trujillo (1983), this is entirely accurate because the term "perform" comes from the French *parfournir*, which means "to accomplish." Certainly, the notion that conversations accomplish something is not unique to performance, as evidenced in Chapter 9. In this case, however, performance can not only mean to act on stage, but to act to completeness in everyday life.

Performativity refers to the quality of communication to fulfill such completeness, so performativity does not necessarily mean to literally perform, but instead the capacity of language to complete an action as if it were a performance. Our two theorists in this section initially focused on applying performativity to better understand written texts. We will also think of "text" more broadly to refer to a discourse of written and spoken behavior. If this all seems confusing to you, you're not alone. Exploring the major theorists whose thinking about performativity has influenced communication and performance studies will help clear up this confusion.

Derrida and Citationality

The concept of citationality is similar to the citations you might do for a class paper. You make an argument and, in essence, cite another article as support, essentially telling the reader, "This is my argument, but to fully understand it you need to read this article." This process of one text referencing, or *citing*, another text is the basis of Jacques Derrida's notion of **citationality**. Derrida is known for his famous phrase, "There is no outside-text" (Derrida, 1978, p. 158). In short, to read and interpret a text, whether it's a novel, a poem, an article online, or a scholarly journal article, one must necessarily draw on other texts for help. In this sense, the text is performative because it can be thought about as creating a web of interrelated references, all of which become part of the text.

Consider a simple online article critiquing the *Star Wars* movie franchise. In order to understand the article, a reader would need to know about the films being referenced. But, all the films are connected, so is it possible to understand any one film without having seen the others? And to better understand this simple article, does the reader have to have seen *all* the films? The article also provides a link to a YouTube video parodying some of the *Star Wars* characters. These videos are integral to the argument of the article, but the parodies draw on the actual films. Suddenly, one text (i.e., the original online article) becomes a multitude of texts—including films, other articles written about the films, shared conversations about the films, memories of seeing the films, etc. It's easy to see, then, why Derrida might argue that there is nothing that is outside of any particular text.

So, how does citationality pertain to human communication and, more specifically, to performance? Next, we'll explore how another figure important to understanding performance has taken this concept of citationality and has applied it to how we enact gender in our everyday lives.

Butler and the Performativity of Gender

In communication, and particularly in performance studies, theorist and literary critic Judith Butler is most well-known for her conceptualization of gender as performative. Taking up Austin's idea of illocutionary acts as performative, or as accomplishing something through their utterances, she argues that our enactments of gender in our everyday lives are similarly performative (Butler, 1990, 1998). In short, she contends that there is nothing "natural" about gender (that masculinity requires a man to walk and sit in a certain way, that women wear a more feminine style of clothing, etc.). Instead, we've come to accept such things as taken-for-granted characteristics. What makes such events *seem* natural is that we've created all the characteristics of gender through our everyday enactments; as performative utterances, Butler argues, gender itself is performative, or brought into being through its enactment. You can read more about the ways we communicatively construct gender in Chapter 11.

You may be wondering if someone can merely declare, "Well, I won't perform my gender in these expected ways, then"; not so fast, Butler might contend. Drawing on Derrida's notion of citationality, she claims our enactments necessarily cite previous enactments of gender whether we know it or not. This citationality is so strongly embedded in our everyday behavior that we cannot simply choose *not* to perform our gender. We necessarily cite the historical context in which we communicate, thereby citing others' understandings and enactments of gender (in the media, in the workplace, in our family, etc.). In short, a man cannot simply wear a dress and claim to be enacting a different gender.

As we enact our preferred gender in our everyday lives, though, we necessarily enact gender *failures*. Why do we fail at gender? Because there's an impossible ideal that's been engrained into us from an early age. This ideal, perpetuated by the media, family, authority figures, fashion designers, etc., exists only in concept or theory. Like most ideals, it is ultimately unattainable; none of us can ever be "perfect." It is in these gender failures, Butler argues, that we can also find room to resist constrictive gender expectations. So, while a celebrity going without makeup

in an Instagram selfie may seem trivial, it may, indeed, prompt audiences to critically think about gender expectations and our conformity to them.

Given the complexity of these concepts, it is difficult to provide a table as I have with previous sections. We are certainly performers of gender in our everyday lives, though often unknowingly because we accept gender characteristics as "natural." It is difficult, though not impossible, to resist ideal gender expectations. Often, staged performances that are able to invoke critical distance in audiences can best accomplish this resistance.

Applications of Performance Theory

As far back as the 1980s, organizational communication scholars were embracing concepts from performance studies to illustrate facets of organizational life. Performance studies scholars were making connections between what performers study and do, and what managers do (Trujillo, 1985). Some of these managerial parallels include the ability to tell a compelling story to achieve a desired effect in an audience, practicing self-reflexivity in one's performance, and being comfortable speaking in front of audiences of varying size (and adjusting one's communication accordingly) (Palmer, 1988). Understanding the business meeting as a ritual enables a performance studies scholar to advise change agents in organizations to facilitate meetings in particular ways, which may include asking employees to perform or "step into the shoes" of another (client, colleague, or other stakeholder) and encouraging self-reflection about one's own self-performance (see the dramaturgical approach in this chapter) (Wimmer, 2002). Similarly, Dishman (2002) found that engineers designed more user-friendly products when engineers "performed" as customers interacting with prototypes of tech products, including embodying the confusion and frustration that customers who know nothing about technology might experience.

Box 8.1 Ethical Issues

As with other methods of inquiry, communication scholars using performative ways of knowing face ethical issues in their work. Dwight Conquergood (1985) describes four ethically problematic performative stances in research, placed along axes of Identity-Difference and Detachment-Commitment. He proposes one ethical stance that avoids the extremes of the other four stances by being centered between the poles of the two axes.

- **The Custodian's Rip-Off:** This stance is motivated by selfishness and what the researcher can "get" from the other being performed. At its extreme, it is at the same time detached from the other and taking on the identity of the other. This is similar to plagiarism, in that it takes genuine performances and passes them off as products of the inauthentic researcher.

- **The Enthusiast's Infatuation:** This stance superficially engages the other, jumping to quick and easy points of connection between researcher and the other. At its extreme, it is both committed to and identified with the other. This stance downplays critical differences in lived experiences, values, and purposes for the sake of superficial identification between self and other.

- **The Curator's Exhibitionism:** This stance is motivated by sensationalism. At its extreme, this stance amplifies difference while also representing commitment to the other. The performative researcher seeks to display shocking and exotic curiosities that treat the other as a nonhuman artifact.

- **The Skeptic's Cop Out:** This stance is marked by detachment and difference. Researchers with this approach to performance argue that accessing others' experiences and cultures through performance is impossible. They refuse to engage in critical dialogues of discovery, for themselves or for others.

- **Dialogical Performance:** To ameliorate the unethical extremes of the other four stances, Conquergood offers this stance as genuine dialogue. This approach to performance research recognizes that tensions exist for self and other and does not try to resolve those tensions. Rather, dialogic performance "is more like a hyphen than a period" (Conquergood, 1985, p. 9).

As the reader might guess, performance studies contains many intuitive intersections with several areas of communication, including areas that often utilize a qualitative methodological approach. I have discussed many of the overlaps with organizational culture in preceding sections, but there are others as well. Rhetoric, given our discussion of Burke earlier, is a natural fit with performance studies. In fact, a whole issue of the preeminent performance studies journal, *Text and Performance Quarterly*, was recently devoted to this intersection (Fenske & Goltz, 2013). Such applications may focus on both staged performance—for example, the political humor of stand-up comics—and artifacts, such as the photos and discourse surrounding lynching murders in the South. As several of the sections in this chapter indicate, intercultural communication is another area with rich crossovers with performance studies. Several critical-cultural scholars working in this area have explored the performance of race (Calafell & Moreman, 2009), African American narratives of oppression and discrimination (Davis, 2007), and performances of cultural rituals (Conquergood, 1991; Turner, 1990). Finally, media and communication hold great promise for applications of performance studies theory, from analyzing celebrity "performances" on reality shows (Fox, 2013), to social media (Lindemann, 2005), to examining the ways memes go viral (Johnson, 2013). And these scholars are only a small representation of the myriad intersections performance studies shares with other communication areas.

Conclusion

Can I capture this feeling? I wonder. I'm torn between talking about performance in the everyday, as a presentation of a desired identity (Goffman, 1959, 1963) and as a literal performance as a way of understanding some concept (Carlson, 2004; Schechner, 2003; Schehner & Appel, 1990). The specks of dust floating in front of me seem to rearrange themselves into patterns. I realize, perhaps this feeling is indicative of performance studies itself, straddling, as it does, theatre, social sciences, and the humanities. Perhaps performatively writing about my struggle in a way that Pollock (1998) says is evocative, is self-consciously partial, and moves among the genres of creative nonfiction and scholarly citations, is as good an introduction to performance studies as I can provide. I turn back to the screen and begin to write.

***

When thinking about performance studies as a lens through which to examine human communication, several important considerations occur. In each of the three major approaches covered—dramaturgical, cultural, and language—the performer(s), audience, and context are all important. First, who is doing the performing? Is it one person or a group? Second, what is the role of audience members? Are they inactive viewers of the performance, interactive participants, or somewhere in between? And, finally, what is the context for this performance—a traditional stage, a cultural ritual, or everyday interaction? And, obviously, none of these questions is either-or; rather, each points to a continuum on which we might place performances. This multitude of potentiality is one of the reasons performance studies is referred as "an essentially contested concept" (Strine et al., 1991, p. 183). The ability of performance to be both a theory and method constitutes it as a "way of knowing."

CHAPTER 9

Conversation Analytic Ways of Knowing

Wayne A. Beach

LEARNING OBJECTIVES

After reading this chapter, you should be able to do the following:

- Identify four basic activities involved when doing conversation analysis (CA).
- Explain why audio and/or video recordings, in unison with carefully produced transcriptions, are necessary for conducting CA research.
- Compare and contrast five basic assumptions of CA research.
- Identify how and why conversations are "sequentially organized."
- Identify validity, reliability, and generalizability as verification procedures for conducting and evaluating CA research.
- Define and provide examples of assessments in ordinary conversations.
- Summarize how agreements and disagreements can be identified in ordinary conversations.
- Summarize what research on assessments has revealed about human communication.
- Summarize what the two listening/analysis exercises reveal about human communication.
- Identify and discuss needed CA research projects and possible implications for addressing social problems in contemporary society.

THE PRIMARY FOCUS OF *CONVERSATION analysis (CA)* is to understand how persons involved in social interactions produce and manage together a wide variety of social actions that comprise everyday living. Doing CA research involves a series of activities:

- Recording and transcribing naturally occurring interactions.

- Conducting repeated listening/data sessions in unison with transcriptions.

- Generating written findings that carefully exemplify and describe how everyday interactions are accomplished.

- Elaborating the implications of understanding ordinary conversations (e.g., Lerner, 2004; Sacks, 1992; Sacks, Schegloff, & Jefferson, 1974; Schegloff, 2007) and, when relevant, developing possibilities for improving interactions that construct institutional settings (Drew & Heritage, 1992). Examples include clinical encounters between patients and providers, courtroom interrogation and testimony, and counseling/therapy sessions.

Recordings are not the events themselves but they provide the best and repeatable access to how speakers, first for them and in just those ways made available for analysts, rely on communication to organize their daily lives. Each time a recording is played, researchers can access the same real-time interactions that do not change over time. What changes become increasingly detailed and compelling explanations about how ordinary conversations, and a wide variety of institutional encounters (e.g., medical clinics, courtrooms, classrooms), get audibly and noticeably done in the first instance? Using CA effectively, understandings about communication become more sophisticated, and realistic, with repeated listenings in unison with examinations of carefully produced transcriptions designed to capture not only what speakers say but how and when speakers offer utterances.

Speakers collaborate to produce a wide array of sequentially organized social actions (e.g., greeting, asking, answering, agreeing, disagreeing, arguing, interrogating, avoiding, challenging). These and many other activities are not random but precisely patterned. CA researchers seek to document how there is "order at all points" (Sacks, 1984a, p. 22), actions making possible the very existence of a social order that is often taken for granted and misunderstood. Close and systematic examinations of naturally occurring interactions reveal how the social, inherently communicative world, gets organized by and for participants who rely on language and social interaction to navigate the complexities of everyday living during phone calls, face-to-face communication, and a variety of mediated interactions (e.g., Skype, Zoom, teleconferencing, and telemedicine).

Fundamental Assumptions and Verification Procedures for Conversation Analysis

One way to introduce CA and this chapter to readers would involve reading and discussing fundamental assumptions and verification procedures of CA (Beach, 2009):

1. CA data must consist of naturally occurring talk and embodied activities.

2. Interaction is **sequentially organized**.

3. The validity of CA claims derives from grounded and unmotivated analyses.

4. The reliability of CA claims derives from the discovery and rendering of consensually accessible interactional orders.

5. CA claims are generalizable in the sense that the structure and function of interactional order is universally available, and discoverable, in naturally occurring talk and embodied action.

These assumptions and verification procedures are elaborated in **Tables 9.1** and **9.2**.

Talking about CA is different than inviting readers to participate in actually doing CA, however, and the following sections include transcribed instances for inspection. These data provide opportunities to be drawn into how CA reveals otherwise unnoticed features of interactions that are routinely produced yet little understood. A reflexive exercise is proposed addressing these primary questions:

- How can CA be demonstrated as a way of knowing by examining speakers' practices and methods for claiming to know (or not know) what they are talking about?

- Rather than thinking of ways of knowing as a research method, or knowledge as what individuals possess (i.e., cognitively), on what occasions does knowing/not knowing become interactionally relevant for managing daily activities?

- How is knowing/not knowing relevant for ordinary conversations (e.g., assessing, agreeing, and disagreeing; claiming insufficient knowledge), courtroom interrogation and testimony, and family conversations about health and illness (e.g., bulimia and cancer)?

TABLE 9.1: Two Fundamental Assumptions of Conversation Analysis (CA)

Data are naturally occurring talk and embodied activities.

- CA involves the direct examination of recordings and transcriptions of naturally occurring verbal, **embodied activities** (e.g., gaze, gesture, touch, and the use of instruments or objects), and nonvocal communication activities—interactions that would be occurring whether or not a recording device was present (Beach, 1990a). These activities are *naturally occurring* in the sense that they would have occurred whether or not the observer were there to record the conversation.

- Observations about interactional phenomena are anchored in contingently organized features of diverse ordinary conversations and institutional encounters involving bureaucratic representatives (e.g., in medical, legal, educational, and corporate settings).

- Researchers do not prompt the commencement or content of the talk, nor do they need to be present when interactions are being recorded.

- Data are not idealized or hypothetical constructions of communication but records of actual interactional involvements (see Atkinson & Heritage, 1984, pp. 2–5; Heritage, 1984, pp. 234–238).

- Systematic collection and analysis of interactional data may be complemented with intensive fieldwork, enacted to better understand how interaction is employed in-situ as a resource for participants as they collaborate in organizing natural environments. However, researchers' field observations, notes, and/or interviews are not treated as primary data about interaction.

- Giving priority to recorded and interactional data is fundamental: The detailed contingencies comprising interactional events, and more generally the circumstances addressed through speakers' actions, cannot be intuited, anticipated in advance, nor fully reconstructed following the occurrence of any given interaction or series of involvements. Such embedded temporal and spatial features are impossible to capture by means of self-reported information.

Interaction is sequentially organized.

- During communication, participants continually reveal their orientations to and understandings of moment-by-moment interactional involvements. In the precise ways speakers construct and respond to turns at talk and related embodied actions, they demonstrate, first for one another (and subsequently for analysts' inspections), their real-time and practical understandings of evolving conduct in interaction. Exactly what gets achieved in communication is thus a result of how speakers construct and make available to one another their understandings of the local environment of which they are an integral part (see Beach, 1990a, 1990b, 1991b, 1993, 1995; Jefferson, 1981; Schegloff, 2006, 2007).

- A speaker's current turn at talk is an *action projection*; it projects the relevance of a next turn, since "talk amounts to actions" and "action projects relevance" (Schegloff, 1991, p. 46; Schegloff, 2006, 2007). Not just any response will normally suffice, because speakers project the relevance of some (not just any) range of appropriate and next actions.

- The range of possible activities, accomplished by the second speaker, display variations of responsiveness: Talk is sensitive to *recipient design* as next actions reveal how speakers hear, and orient to, specific and local social actions comprising prior speakers' utterances. Talk involves *conditional relevance*: Speakers design their talk for specific recipients and project the relevance of some (not just any) range of appropriate and next actions.

- Talk is context shaping and renewing. By describing and explaining the precise ways participants organize and thereby shape their interactions, evidence is provided about the inherent consequentiality of communication. And, because *context* is not treated as external to or removed from communication (see Beach, 1990b; Duranti & Goodwin, 1992; Mandelbaum, 1991; Schegloff, 1996b, 1997), but achieved through interaction, social actions are both context shaping, as speakers tailor them to prior and immediate circumstances, and context renewing, as speakers contribute to evolving and subsequent actions.

Source: Adapted from Beach (2009).

TABLE 9.2: Verification Procedures for Conversation Analysis

Validity

- CA is capable of identifying real instances of interaction behavior achieving real functions; that is, it is a *valid* observational method. Recordings and carefully produced transcriptions allow for examinations of actual communication—as noted, not idealized, hypothetically derived, self-reported, and/or reconstructed choices and actions driven by participants' motives, needs, or other observer imposed phenomena (see Atkinson & Heritage, 1984, pp. 2–5; Heritage, 1984, pp. 234–238). No details of interaction are prematurely dismissed as disorderly, accidental, or irrelevant (Heritage, 1984).

- This allows for what is commonly referred to as "unmotivated" analysis: as best as possible, working to (a) avoid predetermining what is meaningful in interactional data and (b) minimize bringing social problems to analysis, but rather allowing such problems (and their possible resolutions) to emerge from systematic inspections of speakers' practices for organizing actual communication events and activities.

- Thus, in the ways that empirical findings are grounded within and exemplified through close inspections of interactional materials, rather than preselected categories or abstract assumptions about communication practices, CA can be understood as a science for discovering and verifying the social organization of everyday life.

Reliability

- Despite the apparent idiosyncrasy of any given conversation, CA is capable of uncovering considerable consistency or **reliability** in how it observes and interprets such behavior, and in the types of activity patterns uncovered. However random naturally occurring conversations and institutional interactions might initially appear, a considerable amount of evidence supports a central tenet of social interaction studies: There is **order at all points** (Sacks, 1984a; 1992), much of which awaits examination by analysts, and all of which was produced in the first instance as meaningful and thus in meaningful ways by participants.

- Recordings and transcriptions of these real-time communication involvements allow for repeated re-hearings, reviewings, and reinspections of "actual and determinate" (Schegloff, 1986) social events and activities. While neither recordings nor transcriptions are conversations in and of themselves (Beach, 1990a, 1993, 1995; Zimmerman, 1988), they nevertheless preserve and embody the integrity and distinctiveness of many conversational activities.

- Moreover, as selected fragments of transcriptions are made available for readers' critical inspections, attention is drawn to specific details of actions rather than glossed versions of what might or could have happened (i.e., idealized, intuited, and/or recollected data).

- It is also a central tenet of CA to make data available for public inspection, for example, to provide readers with the opportunity to agree and/or disagree with claims being advanced. Transcriptions are published with findings, and (as noted, when possible) recordings of the phenomena being investigated are disseminated for listening and inspection. Most recently, various web sites can be accessed that provide opportunities to repeatedly hear digitized interactional materials (e.g., see www.sscnet.ucla.edu/soc/faculty/schegloff/index.html).

Generalizability

- CA inquiry begins with a single case study in order to form a grounded basis for developing **generalizable** descriptions of communication phenomena; descriptions of activities that are universally available to natural language speakers (Beach & Dixson, 2001; Hopper, 1989; Pomerantz, 1990; Schegloff, 1987; 2006).

- Once the foundation is laid with a single case, analysts employ a procedure of constant comparison to examine how larger collections of instances reflect generalized actions and patterns across diverse settings, speakers, topics, and cultures (e.g., see Atkinson & Drew, 1979; Haakana, 2001; Jefferson, 1980a, 1984a, 1984b, 2004; Lerner, 2003, 2004; Maynard, 2003; Pomerantz, 1984, Robinson, 2004, 2006; Schegloff, 1968).

- The recurrence of communication events, balanced with how actions are determined to be relevant and significant, can be examined to determine whether and how same, similar, or deviant patterns of interaction occur across a wide array of data (e.g., see Maynard, 2003; Schegloff, 1968).

- Working simultaneously with single cases and collections can yield warrantable claims (rather than underspecified assumptions) about social order (Beach, 2009).

Source: Adapted from Beach (2009).

Following analyses of these social actions across multiple speakers and settings, readers are encouraged to engage in a second exercise: Produce your own descriptions and explanations of selected moments and social actions. Two transcriptions are provided later, including linked, digital audio recordings of these conversations, which will allow readers to listen to, analyze, and discuss these examples.

This chapter concludes with a stocktaking of what has been learned, not only about CA as a way of knowing, but as an increasingly viable mode of scientific inquiry for conducting basic research extending well beyond data previewed in this chapter. The potential for CA to yield valuable knowledge, with the potential to change and improve how communication gets achieved in everyday life, will also be discussed.

How Does "Knowing" Get Accomplished in Social Interaction?

A long history of CA studies reveal that managing how "knowing" gets organized in everyday social interactions involves a wide array of practices for achieving important social actions: agreeing and disagreeing, telling and receiving stories, proposing to know more about how best to resolve a problem, or establishing authority and the "right to know" as patients and doctors diagnose health problems (e.g., Beach, 2000, 2013b; Heritage, 2012; Pomerantz, 1984; Sidnell & Stivers, 2013). These and many more knowing activities are omnipresent, and thus omnirelevant, because they shape (and are shaped by) how knowledge about the world gets interwoven into the conversational and institutional encounters we participate in on a daily basis. Relying on, invoking, and attributing knowledge is, in all cases, finely grained, patterned, and often highly consequential for understanding how conduct unfolds and social relationships get negotiated.

Before examining actual transcribed instances, it is important to note that, over time, a transcription notation system has been refined and adapted from Gail Jefferson's work (Atkinson & Heritage, 1984, pp. ix–xvi; Sidnell & Stivers, 2013). These symbols are universally employed by CA researchers who examine casual/ordinary and institutional interactions across diverse languages, contexts, and cultures. The symbols are listed and described in **Table 9.3**.

Box 9.1 Ethical Issues

Conversation analysis poses unique ethical issues due to the nature of the method, naturally occurring talk (Speer, 2014). Three issues are commonly addressed:

- **Participant Identification**

  CA is strongly committed to full and informed consent for all recordings used for research and analysis. Recordings should never be made without the informed consent of those being recorded. Names and other personal identifications are masked before any distribution or presentation of findings. Exceptions to this de-identification occur when data include video recordings or photos of participants. Accordingly, CA researchers have an ethical obligation to obtain consent from participants for all possible ways their conversational data may be used, including if their voices or images might be made public.

- **Manipulation or Undue Influence**

  The knowledge gained from close analysis of interactional conduct (e.g., claiming knowledge, teasing, blaming) could provide readers with information that could be used to manipulate others and/or behave at their expense. Having recordings and transcripts of naturally occurring talk means that careful analysis can reveal patterns, functions, and meaning of that talk that may not be immediately apparent to the interactants. It is an ethical decision to not use research knowledge to exert undue influence on others.

- **Private Information**

  Personally private information gained through research, such as studies of patient–provider oncology interviews, could be inappropriately shared with others or somehow used in ways that might harm patients, family members, or healthcare providers (e.g., damaging reputations). This information might include diagnoses, prognoses, family dynamics, and a wide range of other information participants would not want publicly known. Protection of privacy is violated when information about patients is used beyond the scope of research specified in the informed consent process.

TABLE 9.3: CA Transcription Notation Symbols and Descriptions

Symbol	Meaning
:	**Colon(s):** Extended or stretched sound, syllable, or word
---	**Underlining:** Vocalic emphasis
(.)	**Micropause:** Brief pause of less than (0.2)
(1.2)	**Timed pause:** Intervals occurring within and between same or different speaker's utterance
(( ))	**Double parentheses:** Scenic details
( )	**Single parentheses:** Transcriptionist doubt
.	**Period:** Falling vocal pitch
?	**Question marks:** Rising vocal pitch
– ‡	**Arrows:** Pitch resets; marked rising and falling shifts in intonation
° °	**Degree signs:** A passage of talk noticeably softer than surrounding talk
=	**Equal signs:** Latching of contiguous utterances, with no interval or overlap
[ ]	**Brackets:** Speech overlap
[[	**Double brackets:** Simultaneous speech orientations to prior turn
!	**Exclamation points:** Animated speech tone
-	**Hyphens:** Halting, abrupt cut-off of sound or word
> <	**Less-than/greater-than signs:** Portions of an utterance delivered at a pace noticeably quicker than surrounding talk
CAPS	Extreme loudness compared with surrounding talk
hhh hhh	**H's:** Audible outbreaths, possibly laughter. The more h's, the longer the aspiration. Aspirations with periods indicate audible inbreaths (e.g., hhh). H's within parentheses (e.g., ye(hh)s) mark within-speech aspirations, possible laughter
Lip smack:	Often preceding an inbreath
Laugh syllable	Relative closed or open position of laughter (hah, heh, hoh)

Source: Adapted from Beach (2009), p. 30.

Assessing, Agreeing, and Disagreeing

Analysis begins with an overview of one of the classic studies in the history of CA research. Pomerantz (1984) lays bare how speakers provide, agree, and disagree with **assessments** when "a speaker claims knowledge of that which he or she is assessing" (p. 57). A series of excerpts from this article appear next. Note that headings for Excerpt 1, and all subsequent excerpts, are provided by the original authors cited in introducing the dialogue (in this example, Pomerantz, 1984). In what follows, "VIYMC" is the source and identification code of the recorded data assigned by the original author, "1" is the recording number," and "4" is the transcription page this

excerpt was drawn from. The "[p. 57]" identifies the page number where this excerpt appeared in the Pomerantz (1984) publication (and thus where this excerpt was copied from).

In this first excerpt, a critical foundation is laid for understanding that displays of knowledge are grounded in personal experience and shared participation:

1. (VIYMC 1:4) [p. 57]

   J: Let's feel the water. Oh it. …

   R: It's wonderful. It's just right. It's like bathtub water.

When J suggests they "feel the water," R next completes what J's "Oh it …" only previews. This "collaborative completion" (Lerner, 1989) by R emerges as a series of assessments, claims about the water R can only make because he or she is actually experiencing how it feels. Knowledge is rooted in experience, which yields the ability to assess what one claims to know. When there is insufficient knowledge, a speaker can decline to assess what prior speaker has addressed:

2. (SBL: 2.2.-2) [p.57]

    A: An how's the <u>dresses</u> coming along. How d' they <u>look</u>.

→ B: Well uh I haven't been uh by there-…

B does not claim the ability to assess progress with the dresses, simply because he or she had not been "there" and thus cannot (or does not attempt to) provide an update.

From Excerpts 1 and 2, it is clear that assessments are not only individuals' statements about what they know, but actions positioned in sequential environments created through shared participation between speakers. Individual speakers make reference to an occasion or event [1] they experienced; [2] they or others can assess that experience (especially if it is shared) as good or bad; and

3. (JS: II :61) (J and L are husband and wife) [p. 59]

    J: [1] We saw Midnight Cowboy yesterday –or [suh- Friday

    E: [Oh?

    L: Didju s- <u>you</u> saw that, [2] it's really good.

Claiming knowledge about and assessing something as good or bad often occurs as adjacently positioned first (A_1) and second (A_2) assessments:

4. (NB: IV.7.-44) [p. 59]

    A_1 A: Adeline's such a swell [gal

    A_2 P: [Oh god,

                    <u>wha</u>dda gal

5. (JS: II: 28) [p.59]

    A_1 J: T's = tshuh beautiful day out isn't it?

    A_2 P: Yeh it's jus' gorgeous …

In both cases, the first speaker proffers positive assessments as invitations for the second speaker to agree. And, in each instance, the second speaker agrees with a second assessment. In Excerpt 5, however, P's "jus' gorgeous" could also be heard as an upgrade of J's "beautiful day," one example of how agreements can be offered yet modified to encapsulate speakers' claims of knowledge about persons (Excerpt 4), weather (Excerpt 5), and a plethora of other referents, topics, and events.

In contrast, however, downgrades and disagreements can and frequently do occur. In the following example, a "fox" is relegated with "pretty girl":

6. (GJ: 1) [p. 68]

    A: She's a fox!

→ L: Yeah, she's a pretty girl.

Both speakers must know the person being assessed, or the knowledge to characterize his or her appearance would not be available as a resource for proffering and downgrading an assessment. Responses to assessments can also disagree by taking alternative stances:

7. (SPC: 144) [p. 74]

    R: … well never mind. It's not important.

→ D: Well, it is important.

Like agreements, disagreements can be weaker or stronger. But, in all cases, speakers take alternative stances that do not align fully with prior speakers' assertions. The knowledge they possess prompts displays of differing thoughts, opinions, or positions. Consider the following instance, drawn from my field notes:

8. [Movie field notes]

    W: That was a great movie, wasn't it?

→   (1.0)

→ S: Well (0.2) I don't think so. I've seen a lot better.

One way of marking disagreement is to pause following a prior speaker's assessment, which invites agreement. The silence can preview an "as yet unstated disagreement" (Pomerantz, 1984, p. 76). As is common, and evident in Excerpts 8 and 9, pausing is also followed by a turn beginning with "Well"—a "pre-disagreement preface" (p. 99) setting up the next-positioned disagreement:

9. (MC: 1.-30)
    L: Maybe it was just ez <u>well</u> you don't know.
 →   (2.0)
 → W: Well, uh, I say it's sus<u>pic</u>ious it could be
        something <u>good</u>
        [too
    L: [Mmhm mmhm
 →   (1.0)
 → W: Well--I can't think it would be too good …

To summarize, Pomerantz (1984) provides convincing evidence for the existence of several canonical structures of social action: (a) Speakers rely on their experiences to claim (or not claim) knowledge; (b) what speakers know, the actions they initiate, and the positions they construct shape the sequential production of assessments; (c) assessments invite agreement, which may be provided by the next speaker or withheld as disagreement (and combinations thereof); and (d) agreements are preferred, and disagreements are not, in most circumstances of everyday living. And, as evident in Excerpts 1–7, agreements often occur immediately, whereas disagreements (Excerpts 8 and 9) can be marked with delay. Delivering and receiving good and bad news reflects similar patterns: Good news tends to be announced instantly, whereas bad news gets suspended with actions such as foreshadowing and stalling the news (see Beach, 2009; Maynard, 1996, 1997, 2003). When disagreeing and bad news are delayed, it may well be a reflection of more cautious management of difficult matters.

The impacts of these early findings by Pomerantz (1984), an extension of Harvey Sack's (her dissertation advisor) pioneering work that led to the creation of CA, are cumulative and considerable. A growing body of research examines how speakers develop closeness with one another, while also creating relationships where participants are "independently capable of experiencing, knowing, and thus assessing" issues, topics, and priorities (Beach, 2009, p. 211). Research on *epistemic authority* focuses squarely on what speakers experience and know, who claims to know more or less about relevant concerns, and how "territorial preserves" of knowledge and action are defended and violated (Heritage & Raymond, 2005,

p. 47; Heritage, 2012). On occasions when speakers face problems navigating delicacies associated with closeness/dependence and distance/independence, the human social condition is fraught with "a basic dilemma of self-other relations" (Raymond & Heritage, 2006, pp. 47–48). For example, agreements and subordination can occur too frequently and in dysfunctional ways. Disagreements can be fruitful (e.g., agreeing to disagree) but can also escalate into hurtful arguments. Unresolved conflicts can trigger disputes and altercations resulting in separation, alienation, and even harassment, physical/sexual abuse, and violence. Conflict talk (e.g., see Grimshaw, 1990) occurs throughout these alternative modes of conduct and relational outcomes, behaviors anchored in different and at times opposing orientations to experience, knowledge, and social action.

The following material offers brief overviews of a series of studies, including transcribed excerpts, further exploring how "knowing/not knowing" are central to communication across multiple settings and activities: courtrooms, ordinary conversations, and family discussions about health (bulimia and cancer).

Claiming Insufficient Knowledge

As previously noted (Excerpt 2), speakers may *claim insufficient knowledge* to assess what prior speakers had raised. Such claims can create numerous problems during courtroom cross-examinations, which are inherently adversarial interrogations designed to challenge and undermine the credibility of opposing/unfriendly witnesses (see Atkinson & Drew, 1979). Lawyers routinely ask questions to solicit witnesses' answers, and testimonies are relied on to reconstruct details about earlier events relevant to a case or trial. A witness who claims that he or she "doesn't know," or "can't remember" can be treated by opposing attorneys as techniques for avoiding confirmation—or perhaps even purposeful evasion—of alleged wrongdoings, which can be tantamount to "producing alternative versions of the 'truth' and often incompatible constructions of past 'realities'" (Metzger & Beach, 1996, p. 750).

During one alleged rape trial, a defendant's attorney tries to establish an ongoing relationship by documenting numerous phone calls between his client and the woman/witness claiming rape. This normalcy of contact is designed to establish that the defendant was innocent of harmful sexual intentions:

10.   (Da: Ou: 1: 6; Drew, 1992, pp. 482–483)

   (A = Attorney; W = Witness; arrows added)

   A: How many ph<u>o</u>ne ca:lls would you say that you (.) had received from the defendant, between (0.6) February and' June twenny ninth:,

   (1.1)

→ W: Ah don't know

   (0.7)

   W: Ah didn't answer all of them.

   (0.8)

   A: 'Scuse me?

→ W: Ah <u>don't</u> re<u>mem</u>ber,=<u>I</u> didn't answer all of them.

The witness reports not knowing or remembering how many calls had been received and not answering "all of them," actions which cast doubt on how significant these calls were to her. If the details the attorney was asking were not important to the witness, it is possible for her to maintain her own position of innocence by maintaining that she was/is a victim of unwanted sexual activity.

Another example is drawn from the now infamous "Broderick trial," which was fully broadcast nationwide by Court TV. A well-known San Diego attorney and his current wife were murdered by the attorney's former wife. She admitted to both murders but claimed self-defense. Prior to this excerpt, the opposing attorney raised a series of topics suggesting that the defendant had a temper and violent tendencies:

11.   SDCL: (California vs. Broderick, 10: 13–21)

   A: (Well) do you remember ripping the- the wrappers off the <u>presents</u> =

→ W: = I'm <u>sorry</u> I <u>don't</u>. =

   A: = Do you remember <u>testi</u>fying the <u>la:st</u> time > when you <u>testi</u>fied that you re<u>mem</u>bered doing that. < =

→ W: = I <u>could</u>'ve done that. (.) I <u>could</u>'ve done that. = I mean that's: not some[thing real <u>vi::olent</u>.]

   A: [So you could have] done a <u>lot</u> of these things but you're not re<u>mem</u>bering them now.

Although "ripping the wrappers" off presents is something most all persons do, in this context such an action can contribute to building the case for the defendant's violence. Even though the witness politely states an inability to remember, she is held accountable by previous testimony that contradicts her current lack of knowledge and memory. Only then does the witness admit she "<u>could</u>'ve done that," but it's "not something real <u>vi::olent</u>." Rather than further addressing violence, notice that the attorney next exploits this moment as an opportunity to raise the possibility that events raised by the attorney, though not remembered by the witness, could nevertheless have occurred.

Behaviors in institutional settings, such as courtrooms, are adapted from ordinary conversations and tailored to specific bureaucratic constraints—such as rules for asking and answering questions and appropriate/inappropriate conduct, during interrogation and testimony. After studying actions that entailed not knowing/remembering during courtroom interactions, we returned to a collection of ordinary conversations to identify sequential environments when speakers claimed insufficient knowledge (Beach & Metzger, 1997). In particular, "I don't know" (and variants thereof) can achieve a range of actions such as qualifying guesses and opinions, providing instructions for how others should hear and respond to speakers' concerns (e.g., troubles they are experiencing), or even delaying and rejecting others' invitations:

12.   (SDCL: Allergies, 12: 145–150)

   L: Any:way (0.4) .hh anyway >when=er you go::nna come by?<

→ S: Well I don't know. I'm going te=to school tomorrow be:cuz Suzanne and John are taking me to lunch?

   L: .hh Are they really?

Prefaced with "I don't know," S announces a plan making him or her less available to visit L. In this way, S "neatly avoids a direct acceptance or rejection of the invitation by offering a response that leaves for the recipient the work of deriving the upshot of S's upcoming plans and impacts on visiting L" (Drew, 1992, p. 576). Rather than accepting invitations, or making commitments in everyday life, speakers can invoke not knowing as a viable resource for avoiding nonpreferred events for good reasons, creating legitimacy rather than getting them in trouble (and/or hurting others' feelings) for not doing what others would like them to.

The Difference "Knowing" Makes in Families and Health

Analysis thus far only begins to reveal how "knowing" is woven into social interactions. Conversations between family members provide unique environments for understanding how experience and knowledge are, literally, "brought to life." When communication occurs between persons sharing extensive relational backgrounds, especially when matters of health and well-being are at stake, what is known and not known about illness and disease receive considerable attention.

Following are two cases studies focusing on very different health problems—bulimia and family cancer—yet both make clear how knowing about the disease is a constant concern prompting action to resolve health problems.

Pursuing and Avoiding Bulimia as Wrongdoing

One central feature of family life is determining not only what other family members know about an individual's actions, but making decisions and motivating a change in behaviors that may be harmful (e.g., smoking, unhealthy eating, excessive drinking, lack of exercise). Making decisions about what is known, by what parties, and agreeing/disagreeing about appropriate next steps to manage disease creates ongoing challenges for family relationships.

The following excerpt is drawn from a longer conversation involving Gramma and Sissy, her granddaughter (see Beach, 1996). Gramma is a registered nurse (RN) who suspects that her granddaughter, Sissy, is binging and purging her food and thus bulimic. Throughout, Gramma relies on her medical knowledge as an RN, but also what she observes daily when living with Sissy, to surmise that Sissy is engaging in unhealthy behaviors. These moments begin as Gramma frames the alleged problem as a concern that can be confronted together (1→, "let's ↑ face it no:w"):

13. (SDCL: Gramma/Sissy)

1→ Gramma: We:ll Sissy, (0.8) let's ↑ face it no:w. (.) **You kno:w** .hh that ch'u are so: e::ager: (.) to be thin: (0.2) that you sometimes go in the bathroom (0.2) and throw up your

2→ food. **I kno:w it's tr[ue!]**

3→ Sissy: [GR]AMMA YOU ARE SO:: FULL O(F) SHIT!

I am so: su:r[e.]

Gramma: [(S]i::ssy stop) - sa:ying such a thing as tha[t.]

Sissy: [-W]E:LL: I can't believe > that ch'u would even say something like tha:t. <

4→ Gramma: Well it's true isn't it?

(0.4)

5→ Gramma: **You know I:? know more about this than you ↑ think I know.**

(0.5)

6→ Sissy: Gra:mma, you are so we::ird (.hh aghhh).

Though a problem to be faced together, with "Yo:u kno:w" Gramma next attributes to Sissy knowledge and awareness of an eagerness to be thin. As Gramma constructs the problem, Sissy is motivated to "sometimes" throw her food up in the bathroom. Similar to courtroom interrogation, not only is a motive identified that yields wrongful behavior, but a stance is taken that Sissy knowingly vomits her food: These actions are intentional and premeditated. And, in 2→, to enforce that her stance is not a figment of imagination, Gramma boldly claims "I kno:w it's true!" In these ways, Gramma initiates a sensitive topic by alleging that Sissy's intentional and unhealthy vomiting is not a secret, but known and now a family problem to be openly discussed and remedied. She does not, at this moment, describe "how she knows" (Jefferson, 1984b), but throughout the entire conversation these claims and observations are disclosed (e.g., Sissy's bad breath, postvomiting odors in the bathroom, moody behaviors).

These actions are, as evidenced in Sissy's vehement response (3→), not only presumptuous, but they treat Gramma's position as faulty and easily cast aside with disbelief. Notice that Sissy does not directly deny vomiting her food (e.g., "I've never done that"), but instead challenges Gramma as a credible and knowing source. That Gramma is "SO:: FULL OF SHIT" is particularly interesting, not only as an novel and potentially disrespectful way to address a grandparent, but also an utterance with potential "poetic" significance: As odd and gross as this may sound, it is not a claim that Sissy is in any way aware she has produced. The very nature of poetics is not to assume that speakers' language is purposeful, but that at times talk can capture and mirror the very situations speakers are themselves caught up within and preoccupied with. The very possibility of poetic language, and how CA may be used to reveal poetic possibilities, obviously involves a longer discussion that cannot be fully addressed herein (Beach, 1996; Jefferson, 1996; Sacks, 1992).

Returning to Excerpt 13, Gramma treats Sissy's "SHIT" reference as inappropriate, and Sissy replies with further disbelief that Gramma "would even say something like tha:t." In 4→, when Gramma counters with "Well it's true isn't it?," it is significant that the following (0.4) pause—Sissy's opportunity to confirm or deny Gramma's "true" assertion—is passed by. One way that pauses can be meaningful involves the noticeable absence of response, as in this instance when Sissy does not refute what Gramma knows and claims as "true." Perhaps not surprisingly, Gramma's next "You know I:? know more about this than you ↑ think I know" in 5→ further establishes Gramma as a knowing source. Her comparison of what she "knows," with what Sissy "thinks she knows," further establishes Gramma as an authoritative yet concerned family member. What one can see, then, is a pattern of pursuit and avoidance that evolves across the entire and longer Gramma/Sissy conversation.

Claiming Epistemic Authority in the Midst of Family Cancer

Earlier it was noted that when speakers claim epistemic authority they accomplish at least two primary social actions. First, they are establishing who knows more and are thus in the best position to speak with authority about a given topic, concern, or event. Second, balancing being together yet being capable of independent thought and

action are basic tensions whenever speakers claim "territorial preserves" (Heritage & Raymond, 2005, p. 34). These actions set the boundaries for determining the rights for claiming knowledge based on experience—and the responsibilities that come with knowing more than others.

The excerpts that follow are drawn from a collection (61 phone calls over 13 months) of actual phone calls between family members traveling through cancer together (Beach, 2009). These interactions are the first natural, recorded history of a family's cancer journey from diagnosis through death of a loved one (mom/wife/sister). Unlike the previously examined Gramma/Sissy conversation, these family interactions do not necessarily reflect family conflicts. But, they do exemplify how a cancer diagnosis understandably triggers tensions, and ways that differing types of knowing are made apparent as conversations unfold.

For example, in the following instance it can be seen that the patient (Mom) has the right to know simply because she is the person who has been diagnosed and is undergoing treatment. When Mom reports that she will be undergoing radiation and chemotherapy, and following an extended (1.4) pause, Son's "Oh bo:y?" provides a response cry (Goffman, 1981) revealing that he did not know and is surprised by this news:

14. (SDCL: Malignancy #2:3)

    Son: .hh hhh (.) Whadda you <u>do:</u> with this kind of thing. I mean-

          (.)

    Mom: >Radiation <u>chemo</u>therapy.<

    →   **(1.4)**

    → Son: **Oh bo:y?**

    → Mom: **Yeah.**

Son's "Oh bo:y?" also acknowledges the seriousness of the diagnosis, while displaying realization that Mom will have to undergo such treatment regimens. A concerned son certainly has the right to claim such surprise and concern, simply because he is impacted by this news about a mom he loves. However, Mom's next "Yeah" is more than an agreement: She also "claims the superiority of her right to know. As the person whose body and experiences are intertwined, her "Yeah." simply (and elegantly) stakes out a territory of knowledge that son cannot bring into play" (Beach, 2009, p. 212). Though both family members are impacted, a notable difference thus exists between caring for a loved one who has been diagnosed, and actually being the patient whose body cancer is growing within. If Son's "Oh bo:y." is merited, how much more is Mom justified for claiming access to the embodied cancer experience?

A similar instance appears next. As the husband and father, Dad is also entitled to claim impact. But his epistemic entitlement far exceeds the roles he assumes. In this case, Dad is living with Mom (Son is not), going to every clinical encounter with her, and privy to otherwise private discussions with doctors and medical staff. In what follows, Dad provides Son with an update of cancer type, growth, and treatment. He also states several additional sources of uncertainty:

15. (SDCL: Malignancy #1:7-8)

    Dad: [But] ya know it's a very <u>slo::</u>w growing thing. So if it is sti:ll in <u>tha:t</u> fa:mily of

→   (.) of cancer then ya say >well okay.< **It's <u>un</u>likely it's anyplace <u>else</u>.** = They can

→   just treat these two bu-pt .hh (0.3) .hhh But °that **we won't know**° ah- at least

→   'til tomorrow and may not have the results of the bo:ne scan back til

→   Monday. = >I don'(t) know how long it takes ta get that back.<

→ Son: °Hm:.° pt .hhh Oh <u>bo:y</u>.

→ Dad: **A::hh ye:ah: hhhhh** (.) <u>But</u> she seemed to be doing (.) as I said pt .hh at this point it was mostly (0.2) <u>co:n</u>firmation and resignation.

From Dad's experience talking with medical experts and Mom (wife) in the clinic, he is able to inform son that it is not yet known whether the cancer has spread or not, when they might find out, and how long it might take to get the "bo:ne scan" results back. Collectively, these are critical pieces of information that Son was not knowledgeable about and thus aware of. In response, Son's "°Hm:.° pt .hhh Oh <u>bo:y</u>." response unfolds as quietly reflective and a big in breath, plus "Oh bo:y"—another response cry marking surprise, and at least some recognition, of

what Mom and the family are confronted with. As with Mom, Dad's "A::hh ye:ah: <u>hhhhh</u>" claims a knowing that son neither has nor is asserted by him. The "A::hh ye:ah:" not just agrees with Son, but upgrades the ability to know how difficult these events have been (and will be). Followed with "<u>hhhhh</u>," an emphasized and aspirated outbreath of frustration, Dad makes his case with few words and optimal impact. This utterance also foreshadows bad future news and the troubles such news might have on both Mom and the family.

In both Excerpts 14 and 15, then, all family members display some knowledge and impact from Mom's cancer circumstances. Son's twice stated "Oh bo:y" situates him as a concerned news recipient that is authentic yet, in comparison, less informed and directly impacted than Mom or Dad.

Exercises for Listening to and Analyzing Conversations

Thoughtful considerations of the data, and analyses previously provided, should bring readers much closer to understanding CA as a way of knowing about a social world shaped by what speakers know and do not know. An introduction to CA, however, can be further refined through repeated listening/data sessions. Two longer excerpts are provided next, one from Gramma/Sissy and another from the Malignancy/family cancer phone calls.

With the benefit of the audio or videotape, a conversation analyst would engage in the following steps:

1. Listen repeatedly to each recording (and return to recordings when needed).

2. Take increasingly detailed notes on the transcriptions.

3. Draw attention to specific line numbers, portions of utterances, and the social actions that appear to be occurring.

4. Identify moments when knowing and not knowing are apparent (and other relevant/interesting moments). Describe how these actions get managed and are consequential.

5. Working in small groups, discuss these moments/actions and continue to refine the transcription notes.

6. When ready, write up the emerging findings. When completed, share these drafts with group members and continue to discuss and refine positions taken.

7. If the writings are developed further, read and integrate relevant citations and quotes to further substantiate claims.

8. In the end, make sure to have thoughtful final discussions (talking and/or in writing) addressing the "So what?" question: Why are these insights meaningful? How might they be employed to better understand and improve family conversations about health and illness?

Even without the benefit of the audio recordings, the following conversations, which have been previously and methodically transcribed from such recordings, will nevertheless give you some exposure to the complex structure and nature of interactions.

Gramma and Sissy: "It could ruin your whole life"

17. (Gramma/Sissy, 105–150)

```
1   Gramma: We:ll Sissy, (0.8) let's ↑ face it no:w. (.) Yo:u kno:w .hh
2           that ch'u are so: e::ager: (.) to be thin: (0.2) that you
3           sometimes go in the bathroom (0.2) and throw up your
4           food. I kno:w it's tr[ue!]
5   Sissy:                       [GR ]AMMA YOU ARE SO:: FULL
6           O(F) SHIT! I am so: su:r[e.]
7   Gramma:                         [(S]i::ssy stop) ↑ sa:ying such a
8           thing as tha[ t. ]
9   Sissy:             [-W]E:LL: I can't believe > that ch'u would
10          even say something like tha:t. <
11  Gramma: Well it's true isn't it?
12          (0.4)
13  Gramma: You know I:? know more about this than you ↑ think I
14          know.
15          (0.5)
16  Sissy:  Gra:mma, you are so we::ird (.hh aghhh).
17          (1.0)
18  Gramma: °Sissy I wanna tell you something.°
19          (0.8)
20  Gramma: I: ↑ know:, (0.8) that ch'u are throwing up your food
21          purposely. (.) .hh > And do you realize that this is a (.)
22          ill:ness?<
23          (0.4)
24  Gramma: And the m:ore > you do it (up) <
25          [(if) you don't stop right now- ]
```

26 Sissy: [↑ You'r::e so: FUNNY GRAMMA!]
27   .hh this is an ill:ness I can't believe you're throwing up your
28   food. ((mimmick voice))
29 Gramma: Well you ar:e?
30   (1.2)
31 Gramma: And- you know something (0.4) it's gonna gro:w and gro:w
32   > and you know what it can- do (t[o) you.]
33 Sissy: [Gram] ma I'm
34   no[t even gonna (s:t-)]
35 Gramma: [it could ruin your wh]ole life. > Don't tell me that now.
36   You just better stop < (.) [denyin(g).]
37 Sissy: [Gra:mma] I've ↑ o:nly done that
38   a couple a ti:m:es
39 Gramma: ↑ ° A couple[of times.°]
40 Sissy: [It's not? Th]at big of a deal. My friends used
41   to do it in the sorority £all the t(h)i:me.£ <
42   (1.0)
43 Gramma: °Well listen?° your friends used to do a lot of things in the
44   sorority that you didn't have to pattern after I'm quite
45   sure?

Mom and Son: "My only hope- I mean (.) my only choice"

17. (SDCL: Malignancy #2: 2)

1	Mom:	No there's nothing to say. >You just-< .hh I'll- I'll wait to
2		talk to Dr. Leedon today = he's the cancer man and =
3	Son:	= Um hmm.
4	Mom:	See what he has to say, and (0.4) just keep goin' forward.
5		I mean- (.) I might be real lucky in five years. It might just
6		be six months.
7		(0.4)
8	Son:	Yeah.
9	Mom:	°Who knows. °
10	Son:	pt .hhh Phew::.
11	Mom:	↑Yeah.
12	Son:	.hh hhh (.) Whadda you do: with this kind of thing.
13		I mean- (.)
14	Mom:	>Radiation chemotherapy.<
15		(1.4)
16	Son:	Oh bo:y?
17	Mom:	Yeah.
18		(0.5)
19	Mom:	My only hope- I mean (.) my only choice.
20	Son:	Yeah.
21	Mom:	It's either that or just lay here and let it kill me.
22		(1.0)
23	Mom:	And that's not the human condition.
24	Son:	No. (1.0) I guess [not.]
25	Mom:	[No.] (.) So that's all I can tell you
26		(°sweetie°).
27		(0.8)
28	Son:	.hhh HHHUM.
29		(0.8)
30	Mom:	°Yeah I'm sorry.°
31	Son:	$Well::$ I should think yeah um- (0.2) Me too.
32	Mom:	°Yeah°.

Conclusion

A growing and considerable momentum for utilizing CA research methods has occurred within the communication discipline and across the social and medical sciences (e.g., Beach, 2009; Peräkylä & Sorjonen, 2012; Sidnell & Stivers, 2013). Researchers want to know how naturally occurring interactions are organized, and CA offers a very rigorous method for identifying, describing, and explaining the practices employed by speakers (in talk and the body) to accomplish a wide array of everyday conversations and institutional encounters (Streeck, Goodwin, & LeBaron, 2011). A more detailed chronology of how CA became prominent within the communication and related disciplines can be found elsewhere (Beach, 2013a; Sidnell & Stivers, 2013). Suffice it to say that the gradual but cumulative emergence of CA has been triggered by the growing need for, and value of, CA as a powerful resource for laying bare how real people, in real time, rely on language and social interactions to accomplish "the social order" (e.g., in health communication, family communication, and mass media). Research on gender, for example, reveals valuable insights about "doing being" men and women (e.g., Beach, 2000; Hopper & LeBaron, 1988; Speer & Stokoe, 2011).

Little has been said in this chapter about how CA is being used to investigate patient–provider relationships (but see Chapter 16). Building on extensive prior research (e.g., Heath, 1986, 2002; Heritage & Maynard, 2006), ongoing studies (e.g., see Beach, 2013b) identify numerous social actions which CA has examined during clinical encounters, including how patients raise and doctors respond (or not) to biomedical symptoms, as well as emotional and psychosocial concerns about life, illness, and disease; the organization of diagnosis and treatment recommendations; complex relationships between empathy, sympathy, and compassion throughout phases of care; and a wide variety of delicate moments (e.g., laughing, crying, fears, uncertainties, and hopes about healing and dying), accomplished through talk and simultaneously displayed in bodies (e.g., gaze, gesture, touching, using medical records and computers). Related research is being initiated on communication during genetic counseling sessions and following clinical visitations on how patients and family members in home environments attempt to understand and make decisions about the promises and risks of genetic screening.

Taken together, these and other studies on health communication can yield "best" and "less effective" practices for managing inevitable challenges with illness and disease, information which can be invaluable when developing innovative materials for medical education designed to advance the public good. For example, *When Cancer Calls* ... (e.g., see Beach, Buller, Dozier, Buller, & Gutzmer, 2014; Beach, Dozier, & Buller et al., 2016) is a professional theatrical production adapted from the set of family cancer phone calls examined herein. This performance includes only verbatim language from the actual calls, and provides powerful opportunities for patients, family members, survivors, and medical professionals to view and discuss the importance of communication throughout cancer journeys. A related media project is *A Journey Through Breast Cancer* (Beach & Powell, 2019), which emerged from CA research on oncology interviews. Over nearly 2 years, this documentary film traces the communication involved as a patient and her husband interact with medical staff, family, and friends/acquaintances from diagnosis through surgery, chemotherapy, breast reconstruction, and eventual recovery. Research has shown that these kinds of innovations trigger important discussions about the prominence and power of communication, raising key implications for enhancing social relationships and thus quality of everyday living.

Credits

TABLE 9.1: Wayne A. Beach, "Two Fundamental Assumptions of Conversation Analysis," *A Natural History of Family Cancer: Interactional Resources for Managing Illness.* Copyright © 2009 by Hampton Press, Inc. Reprinted with permission.

TABLE 9.2: Wayne A. Beach, "Verification Procedures for Conversation Analysis," *A Natural History of Family Cancer: Interactional Resources for Managing Illness.* Copyright © 2009 by Hampton Press, Inc. Reprinted with permission.

TABLE 9.3: Wayne A. Beach, "CA Transcription Notation Symbols and Descriptions," *A Natural History of Family Cancer: Interactional Resources for Managing Illness.* Copyright © 2009 by Hampton Press, Inc. Reprinted with permission.

CHAPTER 10

Quantitative Ways of Knowing, Part I
Key Principles

Lourdes S. Martinez, Rachael A. Record, & Brian H. Spitzberg

LEARNING OBJECTIVES

After reading this chapter, you should be able to do the following:

- Identify the ideal steps or features of the scientific process and its aims in the context of communication research.
- Differentiate between different theoretical types of variables and their possible interrelationship types.
- Articulate criteria for attributing research findings to a causal process.
- Differentiate between population and sample.
- Articulate and identify the reasons and applications for using probability versus nonprobability sampling procedures.
- Define and articulate differences between conceptualization and operationalization.
- Identify and differentiate between various levels of measurement.
- Specify the relationships and differences between reliability and validity.
- Define and interpret applied examples of measures of central tendency and dispersion.
- Distinguish between statistics that summarize or describe distributions of variables and statistics that infer relationships between variables.
- Articulate the role of probability for hypothesis testing.

QUANTITATIVE METHODS CONSTITUTE important research approaches in the field of communication. Through the use of quantitative methods, communication theories can be tested, and communication processes can be quantified, explained, and predicted.

These approaches rely on the logic of the scientific method and have played an important role in communication research since the modern founding of the field. Quantitative methods continue to significantly shape our present-day understanding of communication and its processes.

This chapter introduces quantitative methods in communication research. The chapter begins with a discussion of why quantitative research methods are necessary in communication research and their foundation in the scientific method. Key aspects of quantitative methods, including sampling, measurement, and the role of probability in hypothesis testing, are also discussed. As analogized in Chapter 3, there are four distinct skillsets or languages of quantitative basket-weaving, each of which complements the others to allow a valid methodological artifact to be created. Chapters 10 and 11 will therefore be, at best, a broad overview of these languages of inquiry. Chapter 10 overviews the key principles of quantitative research: languages and logics of hypothesis testing, design, measurement, and probability (statistics). Chapter 11 focuses on four popular methods in the communication field that employ these logics in distinct empirical ways. Specifically, Chapter 11 surveys survey, content analysis, experimental, and observational designs in communication research, with focus on the unique features of each design.

Conducting Quantitative Research

Quantitative research is useful for answering a variety of questions posed by communication scholars. In order to perform quantitative research in a correct and ethical manner, however, researchers must take into account a number of considerations. This section examines the primary purpose of conducting quantitative research in the communication discipline, how these methods differ from other methods of research, and the ideal process by which researchers perform quantitative research. A deep understanding of the quantitative research culture involves mastering four languages: research or experimental design, measurement theory, probability theory, and hypothesis-formation and testing. This chapter can only scratch the surface of the first three languages, and much of the latter was covered in Chapter 5.

Much communication research is concerned with answering questions that seek to uncover causes, effects, and processes of communication. These questions try to focus efforts to discover patterns and scientific explanations for what we observe in the real world. Communication can be studied through the lens of social science, which seeks to predict, explain, and understand social processes (Wrench, Thomas-Maddox, Richmond, & McCrosky, 2015). *Social science* has several defining features, which are summarized in **Table 10.1**. Because the aims of quantitative methods are closely aligned with the goals of social science

TABLE 10.1: Defining Features of Social Science

Feature	Properties
Logical	The study of social science is based on formal logic and reason.
Deterministic	Social science posits that there is a reason, or cause(s), for every event that happens.
General	Social science seeks to explain why an event occurs—explanations that apply to other events are preferred.
Parsimonious	The goal of social science is to maximize understanding while using the smallest number of variables.
Specific	Social science needs to provide specific definitions of concepts and ways to measure them.
Empirically verifiable	Social science examines questions and theories that can be tested in the real world.
Intersubjective	Social scientific studies need to be described with enough detail for other investigators to replicate.
Progressiveness	Existing social science theories need to be open to improvement or expansion based on new evidence.

Source: Adapted from Babbie (1973) and Sparks (2013).

research, quantitative methods are most effectively applied to answering questions posed within a scientific framework. **Quantitative methods** can be defined as research approaches that answer questions by using numbers to quantify a phenomenon (Bryant, Thompson, and Finklea, 2012). How widespread is gossip in the workplace? Or, what are the causes and effects of gossip in the work environment? These are examples of communication questions that can be addressed using quantitative methods.

The scientific method (depicted in **Figure 10.1**) starts with a theory, or theories, that provide(s) guidance for the research. A **theory** is a set of statements that explain or predict a phenomenon (Bryant et al., 2012; see also Chapter 3). In order for an idea to be considered a scientific theory, it must (a) include more than one statement, and (b) these statements must define the key concepts of the theory and how they relate to each other (Sparks, 2013). Well-specified theories are useful in guiding predictions and the formation of testable hypotheses; this comprises the second step of the scientific method. At this point, a researcher develops predictions or hypotheses about the phenomenon under study based on what is already known about the variables involved. A *variable* is anything that can assume more than one value (e.g., age, sex, number of hours spent on social media in a week, self-esteem, etc.), while a *hypothesis* is a proposal or statement regarding the relationship between variables (e.g., age is positively associated with the number of hours a person spends on social media in a week; compared to males, the more females consume media as teens, the lower their self-esteem) that can be tested by empirical observation (Bryant et al., 2012; LeFebvre, 2017a, 2017b).

FIGURE 10.1: A Simplistic Scientific Method Visualization

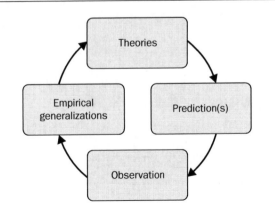

In the third step of the scientific method, a researcher tests the hypothesis using care to be as objective and empirical as possible (Warner, 2017; Wrench et al., 2015). In other words, researchers go to great lengths to ensure that their opinions and emotions do not influence their observations and that the phenomena they wish to study can be observed in replicable ways. Researchers also strive to eliminate alternative explanations (i.e., rival hypotheses) for what is observed in a study by controlling conditions while a phenomenon is being observed. Quantitative methods vary in the degree to which they can control study conditions. These differences are covered in greater detail in subsequent sections of this chapter (see "Surveys and Experiments").

The next step of the scientific method requires moving from observations to empirical generalizations. In order to draw empirical generalizations, researchers have to place the observations within the context of what is already known about the phenomenon under study. Sometimes a study will not generate observations that support the hypothesis, or will generate observations that diverge from what previous research suggests should be expected. In such cases, observations that do not support or that contradict what is already conventionally understood about a phenomenon can still be informative for the research community and warrant discussion when publishing a study. At this stage, it is also important for researchers to be up front about the limitations of their study in an effort to avoid overgeneralizing or applying findings to situations or populations for which the evidence is insufficient.

Empirical generalizations can help researchers refine or learn more about a theory. This advancement of understanding of theory is the final step in the scientific method. The implications that empirical generalizations have for extending what is known about how and why a theory works are important for moving the field forward in future cycles of the scientific method. Thus, the outcomes of empirical generalizations feed into theory refinement, development, and expansion, spurring subsequent cycles of the scientific method application.

Communication researchers use quantitative methods to study a range of questions relevant to the communication field. The proper and ethical use of these methods, however, requires careful thought regarding several factors. These factors include understanding the principal objectives quantitative methods can achieve in research, the strengths and limitations of quantitative methods in relation to other types of research methods, the standard process by which quantitative methods are effectively executed, and the ways in which research involving quantitative methods can be conducted in an ethical manner.

Formulating Research Questions and Hypotheses

Communication scholars using quantitative methods begin their research first by developing research questions and hypotheses that are both testable and important to the field. Sometimes these questions seek to examine different types of attributes or elements of communication and how they are related to each other. This section introduces what makes a research question or hypothesis testable, different types of theoretical elements or variables, how these variables relate to each other, and the criteria for determining causal processes (see also: Chapter 5).

In the earliest days of human inquiry, events were observed in nature, and people began to speculate, and to theorize, explanations of those events. Over time, however, these speculations and theories became more specific and better conformed to accurate knowledge of nature. Thus, in current times, instead of beginning with observations, the scientific method typically begins with received or refined theory, guiding the development of predictions or hypotheses. Still, these hypotheses must be at least potentially testable through observation. Without a way to observe the phenomenon under study, it is difficult to accept, reject, or adjust theories that move science forward (Sparks, 2013).

In order to be testable, a hypothesis must be *falsifiable* (Popper, 1959), meaning it can be tested empirically and shown to be false or incorrect (West & Turner, 2006). With a falsifiable hypothesis, it is "possible to specify ahead of time what sort of data, if observed, would make the hypothesis false" (Sparks, 2013, p. 11). This is one of the most fundamental criteria for the scientific status of an idea or approach, and it is among the least understood by the general public.

Science is prized for its "certainty," but, in practice, science begins its approach to understanding from an entirely *critical* role; its entire approach to research is to try to falsify its theories, not to confirm them. Only when a theory survives multiple attempts to falsify it can the theory begin to be accepted as valid. This is what makes

conspiracy theories nonscientific: Their adherents only look for confirming evidence of their theories, and they are unable to hypothesize (or accept the possibility of) evidence, if any, that would invalidate their theories. Scientists seek to begin and end every research project by taking the chance that they are wrong in their theory, and they must accept the results if the results disagree with the theory they proposed (see also Chapter 3). Falsifiability is key to the idea of scientific ethos and is a litmus test of what qualifies as "scientific."

When developing a hypothesis, one should consider the variables under study and how they might relate to one another. A variable represents an element that can assume more than one value. A hypothesis often proposes to study the relationship between independent and dependent variables. An **independent variable** is examined in relation to how it affects a **dependent variable**. Although independent variables can be altered or manipulated, dependent variables are only measured for changes as a result of variations in independent variables. For example, a researcher wants to know how voting behavior changes in response to varying levels of exposure to political campaign ads by proposing a hypothesis that tests the effects of exposure to political campaign ads on patterns of voting behavior. In this case, exposure to political campaign ads acts as the independent variable, while voting behavior represents the dependent variable.

The relationship between independent and dependent variables may be influenced by other types of variables. Studies often test **intervening variables**, which can explain the effect of an independent variable on a dependent variable. If exposure to political campaign ads affects voting behavior because it shapes voters' attitude toward political issues, then attitude is an intervening variable because it helps explain in part how the independent variable (exposure to political campaign ads) influences the dependent variable (voting behavior). Antecedent variables can also impact the relationship between independent and dependent variables, but, unlike intervening variables, **antecedent variables** come before both independent and dependent variables. One example of an antecedent variable is political party affiliation. If individuals affiliate prior to an election, their affiliations can influence both their exposure to political campaign ads and their voting behavior.

In addition to looking at different types of variables, hypotheses may also test various kinds of relationships

FIGURE 10.2: Types of Relationships Between Variables

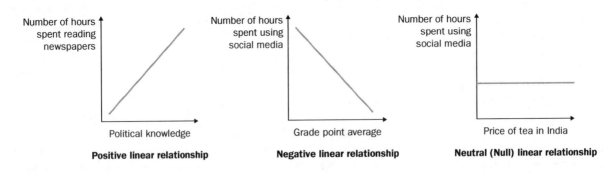

between variables. The concept of a **relationship** denotes a connection or link between variables (Wrench et al., 2015). Although relationships are usually classified as positive, negative, or neutral, they can also be classified as curvilinear. **Figures 10.2** and **10.3** display these relationships.

Positive relationships occur when a change in one variable creates a change in the same direction for the other variable. The relationship between years of education and yearly income is an example of a positive relationship. In general, levels of an individual's education tend to be positively associated with yearly income. Conversely, we also consider a relationship to be positive if a decrease in one variable generates a decrease in the other. As years of education decrease, so does yearly income. **Negative relationships**, on the other hand, arise when a change in one variable produces a change in the opposite direction for the other variable. For example, we might find that the more time an individual spends consuming violent media, the less sensitive he or she is to depictions of violence.

FIGURE 10.3: Curvilinear Relationships Between Fear Messages and Behavior

Sometimes, however, a change in one variable does not lead to a change in the other variable under study. When this occurs, it is considered a **neutral relationship**. An example of two variables that are likely to share a neutral relationship is the relationship between daily general media use (or how much time an individual typically spends using various forms of media) and daily fruit consumption.

There are instances in which a relationship may start out as positive or negative but may reverse direction after crossing a certain threshold. When two variables relate to each other in this manner, they exhibit a **curvilinear relationship** (see **Figure 10.3**) Research on the use of fear appeals to persuade individuals in order to adopt healthy behaviors represents an area of study where we may see examples of curvilinear relationships (Tannenbaum et al., 2015; Witte, 1992). More specifically, a certain level of threat needs to be included in a fear message in order for individuals to become motivated to perform self-protective behaviors, but a threat that is too strong can lead some individuals to reject the message and engage in maladaptive coping such as denial or discounting of the message.

A relationship between two variables *does not* necessarily imply **causation**—meaning that one variable is a cause of the other. It is not appropriate to assume that the presence of a relationship signifies causation, because this can lead researchers to arrive at the wrong conclusions. For example, we might see a positive association between the number of schools in a geographical area and the number of crimes. It might be tempting to assume that schools lead to crime, but this is likely an incorrect conclusion when we consider the possibility of a third variable, or *confounder*, that explains both the presumed independent variable (schools) and dependent variable (crime) in this scenario.

On closer examination, we might find that population density is acting as a confounder because it may lead to both a greater number of schools and crimes in a given geographical area. Indeed, actual research shows that the correlation between race (African Americans) and violent crime essentially disappears once socioeconomic status (Akins, 2009) and racial segregation are accounted for (Stolzenberg, Eitle, & D'Alessio, 2006). There are many correlations between variables that bear no causal relationship between one another (see www.tylervigen.com/spurious-correlations). An important aspect of science is to account for these confounding variables and rival hypotheses in ongoing research.

To arrive at a claim of causation, three criteria must be met (Sparks, 2013). First, a relationship between the independent and dependent variables must be present. If a neutral relationship exists, it is not possible to conclude that one variable is the cause of the other. Second, the two variables must have a logical time order. This requires that the independent variable precede the dependent variable and indicates that if the independent variable occurs after the dependent variable, it logically cannot be the cause of the dependent variable. The third condition is that the relationship between the independent and dependent variables must not be caused by an unmeasured third variable. A researcher must try to eliminate potential explanations for the observed relationship that may be caused by an unmeasured third variable. It should be noted that many variables likely relate in reciprocally causal ways. For example, self-disclosure of positive information may

Box 10.1 Ethical Issues

Research of all types must be conducted ethically and responsibly. The U.S. Congress passed the National Research Act in 1974 that provided the basis for current research ethics guidelines and procedures followed by universities and other research institutions. Many countries adopt versions of the U.S. guidelines for research conducted in their countries and require their researchers to take online research ethics courses sponsored by the U.S.-based Collaborative Institutional Training Initiative.

Four general principles are widely recognized as foundational for conducting ethical research:

- **Treat people with respect.** Researchers should make every effort to respect the autonomy of all human participants, and act as accountable and responsible agents in research activities. Part of this responsibility calls on researchers to ensure that participants are sufficiently informed about the research process (including the study's purpose, risks, and voluntary nature) and able to make an informed choice free from coercion (Wrench et al., 2015).

- **Provide study participants free choice.** Informed consent or a "person's voluntary agreement, based upon adequate knowledge and understanding of relevant information, to participate in research" (National Institutes of Health [NIH], 2002, p. 64) is essential for the protection of human participants, and extremely important for studies using children or adolescents, which require parental permission for participants under the age of 18.

- **Protect participants' right to privacy.** Many times communication researchers collect data from human participants that is sensitive in nature, the public release of which could bring personal or professional harm to participants. In order to prevent this, researchers must take precautions to protect the anonymity and confidentiality of the participants. Anonymity relates to situations in which the researcher does not know who participated or with data corresponds to which participant in a study (NIH, 2002). In contrast, confidentiality refers to situations where although sensitive participant information could potentially be linked back to participants, the expectation is that "it will not, without permission, be divulged to others in ways that are inconsistent with the understanding of the original disclosures" (NIH, 2002, p. 24).

- **Benefit, not harm, participants.** As a basis for performing ethical research, good studies should seek to answer questions that impact positively society and improve the lives of others. This is especially true for participants in research, who should benefit from the research in which they participate (Wrench et al., 2015). In addition, researchers are required to provide strong justification for the need to perform a study which poses potential harm to participants, even when this risk to participants is minimal. If a study poses more than minimal potential harm or discomfort to participants, questions regarding the ethicality of the research are raised by institutional review boards, which serve to protect rights and welfare of participants recruited into research efforts.

prompt positive feedback, which causes a slight increase in self-esteem. Feeling higher self-esteem may then cause future positive self-disclosures, which then continue this cycle of mutual causation.

Research using quantitative methods starts with the development of testable research questions and hypotheses that are recognized as important for pushing the discipline forward. Some of the most pressing questions for the field involve testing different communication variables and their relationships to one another. Such questions often revolve around understanding whether variables are part of a causal process and disentangling which variables represent causes and effects (see Chapter 3).

Design

Sampling

One of the primary goals of quantitative research is to collect and analyze samples of data with the aim of drawing conclusions about a greater population. The purpose of this section is to review the procedures required to achieve this goal. First, understanding the difference between a population and a sample provides the necessary framework for accurately making generalizations. Next, an understanding of different types of sampling designs is critical for conducting accurate research. Finally, a working knowledge of the impact of sample size on data is essential in planning and executing quantitative research.

The key to understanding how to generalize data from a sample to a population lies in an understanding of the difference between a population and a sample. A **population** refers to the entire set of people, objects, observations, or scores that have a characteristic in common (Wrench et al., 2015). For example, all U.S. adults age 18 or older would constitute a population with a common characteristic of "age." Given the difficulty in reaching, in this case, all U.S. adults age 18 or older, scholars use samples in order to provide estimates of the population. A **sample** refers to the group of selected people, objects, observations, or scores to be included in an actual research study. In the rare opportunities to collect data from the entire population, or, in other words, to conduct a *census*,

the analysis of those data provides **parameters** that give mathematical estimates related to the actual population. When analyzing the data collected from a sample, **statistics** are used to provide mathematical estimates of the population parameters. The following paragraphs review standard sampling procedures, including the benefits and drawbacks of different types of sampling.

There is a series of steps for determining the best sampling procedure for any given quantitative research project. **Figure 10.4** displays these steps. These steps begin with an assessment of the population. The first step is to pretend that we live in an ideal world where we would have access to anyone without restriction. For example, if a researcher were interested in how adults communicate stress to their spouses, the desired, or **theoretical population**, is all married adults—regardless of citizenship, length of relationship, or partner sex. Obviously, reaching every single person that fits this criterion is not feasible. So, the next question becomes, "What is the feasible population?" Most often, the feasible population is narrowed down to accessible participants, such as citizens of the same country, residents of the state, or students at the funding university. After outlining the feasible population, the researcher can create a sampling frame. A **sampling frame** is a list of all potential participants within the feasible population. This list can take the form of resident addresses, email addresses of enrolled students, lists of employees, and so on. Once there is a clear list, selecting the actual participants to be part of the sample can be done through one of a number of sampling designs.

FIGURE 10.4: Steps of Sampling Procedures

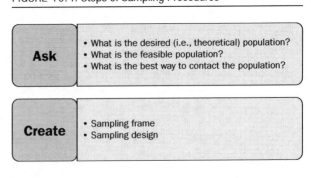

All sampling designs can be categorized as either **probability** (i.e., randomly selected) or **nonprobability** (i.e., not randomly selected) samples. **Random** means that each member of the population has an equal chance of being selected for the sample. Ensuring an equal chance of selection reduces **sampling bias**. Probability sampling is the most ideal because it provides the most confidence that the sample is representative of the population. Because probability sampling is not always feasible, however, nonprobability sampling is often used. Regardless of the sampling deign, the sample size (i.e., the number of participants included in the sample) is an important factor related to the generalizability of the data. Typically, the larger the sample size, the more generalizable the data. Too large of a sample can be unnecessary, however, because at a certain point no additional information is being contributed.

In sum, following appropriate sampling procedures is essential to collecting sample data that can be generalized to the population. This section reviewed the purpose of sampling, different types of sampling designs, and the impact of sample size. With sampling procedures understood, determining variable measures is the next focus of designing a quantitative research study.

Measurement

Quantitative research relies on the numerical measurement of variables. **Measurement** is "the process of systematic observation and assignment of numbers to phenomena according to rules" (Wrench et al., 2015, p. 165). The purpose of this section is to review (a) the distinctions between conceptualizing and operationalizing variables, (b) the four different ways to measure a variable, and (c) what makes measures reliable and valid.

So far in this chapter we have reviewed different variable functions (independent and dependent) and different ways variables can relate to each other (positive/negative/ neutral relationship, intervening, antecedent, and confounding). But regardless of function and relationship, all variables need to be independently conceptualized and operationalized. **Conceptualization** refers to the explanation—or definition—of a variable. Most variables can be conceptualized in numerous ways. To demonstrate, **Table 10.2** provides five different conceptualizations of the variable *television viewing*. While reviewing the conceptualizations in the table, the essential question is, "Which is the best definition of the variable of *television viewing*?" Each conceptualization varies slightly but importantly. For instance, Option A doesn't specify that television programming must be watched, just that the television set must be on. Similarly, in Option B it is unclear what type of programming or device counts as television viewing. Is it any content viewed on a television set? If yes, then streaming from a laptop to your television might count. Or, does watching Netflix on your tablet count? Each conceptualization in **Table 10.2** has different strengths and weaknesses regarding the description of *television viewing*. The answer to the question regarding which is the best conceptualization of *television viewing* depends on the hypothesis or the interests of the research study.

As with conceptualizing variables, numerous ways exist to operationalize variables. **Operationalization** refers to the techniques used to observe or measure the variable given its conceptualization. For example, if heart health is conceptualized as a product of the amount of the stress hormone cortisol, then swabbing saliva and using a chemical test that measures cortisol is the operationalization. In studies that use survey research, there are two steps in operationalizing a variable. The first step is selecting the

TABLE 10.2: Example Conceptualizations of Television Viewing

Concept	Exemplar
A	The amount of time the television is turned on
B	The amount of time one spends watching television
C	The amount of TV series programming viewed
D	The amount of cable-based programming viewed from a television
E	The amount of programming watched, regardless of TV series, movie, device, or network

TABLE 10.3: Example Operationalizations of Television Viewing

Concept	Exemplar
A	On average, how much do you watch movies or television each week?
B	• During your average week, how many hours of programming on Netflix, Hulu, or Amazon do you watch? • During your average week, how many hours of programming on cable TV do you watch? • During your average week, how many hours do you spend watching programming on YouTube?

best questions to ask. Going back to the variable of *television viewing*, **Table 10.3** presents two different ways to operationalize the variable of television viewing, assuming the conceptualization was determined to be "the amount of programming watched, regardless of TV series, movie, device, or network." Option A presents a direct and concise operationalization of television viewing; however, Option B provides the researcher with a more accurate estimation of the variable of interest.

The second step in operationalizing a variable is determining the appropriate type of variable measure. There are four different types of variables: nominal, ordinal, interval, and ratio. Each of these types represents an increasingly precise representation of some concept, feature, characteristic, or attribute. To understand the variable types, it

is essential to understand variable ***attributes***—the options participants can choose from when answering questions. The attributes of a variable are what determine the variable type. **Table 10.4** presents descriptions and examples of each variable type.

After careful conceptualization and operationalization, variables need to be assessed in regard to their reliability and validity. **Reliability** refers to how consistently a variable measure will produce the same results. There are three ways to confirm reliability. The first way compares two measures of a variable from samples that should produce statistically similar results, such as one sample completing measures at different points in time, or two random samples from the same population. The second way uses statistics, such as Cronbach's alpha, which assesses how

TABLE 10.4: Descriptions and Examples of Variable Types

Variable Type	Description	Examples
Nominal	• Categorical attributes • No category is necessarily more or less of some attribute than another (i.e., cannot be put in any pre-established order of importance or amount) • No set common difference between categories	• Sex/gender • Ethnicity • Political affiliation
Ordinal	• Categorical attributes • Rank ordered (i.e., categories follow a logical order regarding amount of attribute) • Groups are balanced, with an equal difference between each category	• Education level • Letter grade • Military rank
Interval	• Numerical attributes • Logical order that represents equal distance between each successive level and the next (i.e., integers) • No absolute zero value	• Likert scale • Fahrenheit temperature • SAT score
Ratio	• Numerical attributes • Logical order that represents equal distance between levels • Absolute zero value, representing total absence of the attribute	• Celsius temperature • Distance • Talk time

responses to each item in a measure correspond to other items in the measure intended to measure the same concept. The third way is to assess reliability across observers, coders, or raters (i.e., intercoder or interrater reliability) using the same categories or items evaluating the same concept or subject.

In contrast, *validity* refers to how accurately a measure assesses the intended variable. There are several ways to support the validity of a measure. **Table 10.5** presents the three most commonly used ways to confirm validity. Thus, if television viewing is conceptualized using definition E in **Table 10.2**, and operationalized using option B in **Table 10.3**, and, assuming that the item is reliably measured, then the measure is valid if support is provided through content, criterion, and construct validity.

One of the most essential principles of reliability and validity is their asymmetric relationship to each other. A measure must be reliable in order to be valid, but just because a measure is reliable does not make it a valid measure. For example, a bathroom weight scale that gives the same person a different measure every time the person stands on it is unreliable, and it is impossible to know which reading is the valid measure of the person's weight. But, a perfectly reliable weight scale is an invalid measure of IQ. A measure needs to provide consistent representations of the concept being measured, but just because it is consistent does not mean it measures what it is intended to measure; it may be measuring something else altogether. There is a lot of debate, for example, about the theoretical relationship of the 2D:4D finger digit ratio in males to aggressiveness (Pratt, Turanovic, & Cullen, 2016; Turanovic, Pratt, & Piquero, 2017), and the waist-to-hip ratio in females and attractiveness (Kościński, 2014), but obviously these measures can be obtained in highly reliable and objective ways.

In sum, this section reviewed (a) the distinctions between conceptualizing and operationalizing variables, (b) the four different ways to measure a variable, and (c) what makes measures reliable and valid.

Basic Statistics for Quantitative Research

Statistics represent an essential element of quantitative methods because they help researchers summarize and describe data, develop predictions, and gain a greater understanding of the world. A statistic uses data—information gathered, recorded, or observed—from a sample to make an estimation about what we can expect to occur in a population. In this section, we discuss important aspects of statistics and how researchers can use them to summarize, describe, and infer aspects about variables under study.

Researchers use two types of statistics: descriptive and inferential. **Descriptive statistics** are usually used in early stages of data analysis to summarize or describe data. In contrast, **inferential statistics** are typically calculated at more advanced stages of data analysis in order to infer or draw conclusions about a population based on the sample used in the study. Both types of statistics, however, use samples to draw conclusions about the

TABLE 10.5: Ways to Confirm Measurement Validity

Type	Description
Content	Based on face value, the measures should assess the intended variable (i.e., the content of the measure shares intuitive, obvious shared meaning with the concept being measured). For example, a measure of affectionate communication is likely to have at least one item in it such as "I like to show my affections to those I like."
Criterion	Relationships with other variables are as research expects (i.e., a measure of affectionate communication should be correlated with relationship length).
Construct	Relationships with other variables are as theoretically expected (i.e., given the theory of self-esteem, a measure of affectionate communication should be positively related to attachment security and relationship satisfaction, negatively related to communication anxiety and conflict and unrelated to intelligence).

populations they are intended to represent. **Probability theory** helps explain how this is possible. According to this theory, the score appearing most frequently in the sample will coincide with the score most frequently observed in the population. Also implicit in probability theory is the assumption that larger samples will more probably represent the population than will smaller samples.

In order to describe and make inferences from a sample, researchers examine central tendency and dispersion. Measures of central tendency gauge the middle score in a sample and can be captured using the mean, median, and mode. These measures are often visualized using **frequency distributions** (displayed as a histogram in **Figure 10.5**). Frequency distributions are useful for examining the shape and symmetry of the distribution of a variable's values and can help researchers identify **outliers**—extreme scores that can potentially influence results of an analysis. The desired shape of a curve for most (but not all) statistical analyses is a normal distribution.

The **mean**, or average, is calculated by adding all the values of a variable together and dividing this sum by the total number of values. The **median,** or middle value, represents the 50th percentile of the data—the point at which half of the values fall below or above—and can be computed by first sorting all values by increasing order and determining if there is an even or odd number of values. If the number of values is odd, the middle value is simply selected. If the number of values is even, however, then the average of the two middle values represents the median. To calculate the **mode**, or the most frequently occurring value for a variable, a list of all values is first generated; then the number of times each value appears in the data is counted. The value with the highest tally is the mode. Sometimes data can have more than one mode. When this happens, researchers describe the data as being bimodal (two modes) or multimodal (more than two modes). **Figure 10.6** depicts the frequency distribution (displayed as a histogram) of bimodal data, with each peak denoting a mode within the distribution.

At times, data are not symmetrically distributed, and in such cases researchers examine the data for the presence of skewness and kurtosis. Evidence of **skewness** in a curve appears when values of a variable tend to cluster to one side of the distribution. The direction of skewness can be positive or negative, as displayed in **Figure 10.7**. **Kurtosis** refers to the degree to which a distribution is peaked or

FIGURE 10.5: Frequency Distribution for a Normal Distribution

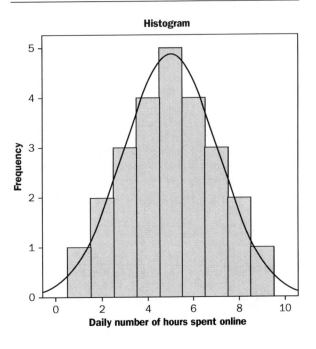

FIGURE 10.6: Frequency Distribution for Bimodal Data

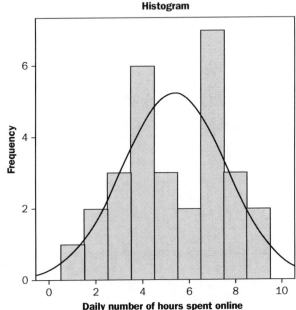

FIGURE 10.7: Distribution of Data with Positive (Left) and Negative (Right) Skew

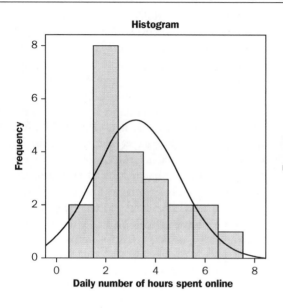
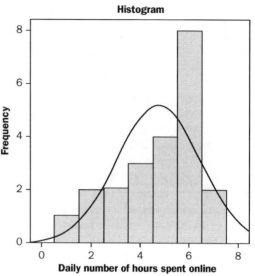

flat. When compared to a normal distribution, positive kurtosis is more peaked, while negative kurtosis is more flat. **Figure 10.7** shows the different shapes of these distributions in relation to a normal distribution. Skewness and kurtosis equal zero in a normal distribution.

In describing distributions in a sample, researchers also need to discuss the amount of variability between the values of a variable. **Measures of dispersion** are designed to capture the variability, or how close or far away each value is from the mean score; these measures include range, variance, and standard deviation. The **range** of a distribution represents the distance between the highest and lowest value and can be computed by subtracting the lowest value from the highest value. The range does not, however, provide any information regarding how much each value differs from the mean value. **Variance** tells us about the distribution's spread—the average distance between the values in a variable from the mean value. Distributions with greater distances across values have higher variance, while shorter distances between values have lower variance. **Standard deviation** is related to variance in that it also examines the distance of each value or observation from the mean value, but differs in that it indicates, on average, how much each value differs from the mean value.

When using measures of either central tendency or dispersion, it is important for researchers to choose appropriate statistics for the level of measurement of the variable they wish to summarize. For interval or ratio variables, all the measures of central tendency and dispersion introduced in this chapter (e.g., mean, median, mode, range, and standard deviation) can be used. For ordinal variables, however, only the median, mode, and range are appropriate. Nominal variables should only be described using the mode and the frequencies or percentages within each category.

In addition to summarizing individual variables, statistics can be used to infer relationships or differences between variables. Recall that a relationship implies a link between variables, while a **difference** signifies the extent to which an individual or group of individuals differs or diverges from another. It may be interesting, for example, if researchers investigating whether men and women differ in their use of social media conducted a study to observe the presence of gender differences. A difference test would be appropriate in this case because researchers could measure time spent using social media and calculate the averages or means for both groups. These means could then be compared to see if, on average, one group engaged in greater use of social media than the other.

In some situations, it would not be appropriate for a researcher to conduct a difference test as part of an analysis. Although difference tests are excellent tools for analyzing differences between nominal variables, one important case in which they are not appropriate to use is when a researcher wishes to look at the relationship between two interval/ratio variables. Instead, running a correlation analysis would be the proper approach. A **correlation** provides a measure for the degree to which two variables are associated with each other. In the context of the possible types of relationships previously discussed in this chapter, a correlation between two variables can range from zero to one (denoting a positive relationship) or negative one to zero (indicating a negative relationship). Stronger relationships are represented by correlations that approach one or negative one, while correlations closer to zero are considered weaker.

Although a relationship or difference may exist between two variables, whether it is meaningful represents another issue with which researchers must contend. A meaningful finding is one that a researcher can feel very confidently did not occur simply by *chance*. To test whether a relationship or difference was observed in a study due to chance, a process of significance testing is needed, which represents an important aspect of hypothesis testing. **Hypothesis testing** involves the use of inferential statistics to help a researcher arrive at a decision about whether to accept or reject the null hypothesis. A **null hypothesis** almost always proposes that no difference or relationship exists between two variables (Levine, Weber, Park & Hullett, 2008; Levine, Weber, Hullett, Park & Lindsey, 2008). For example, if a researcher hypothesizes that exposure to violent movies increases aggressive behavior, the null hypothesis would propose that no relationship exists between exposure to violent movies and aggressive behavior.

Generally, in social science research, the null hypothesis is assumed to be true unless a researcher can demonstrate evidence showing otherwise. This is one of the distinguishing features of scientific method; it begins with the assumption that it is wrong about something, and its methods are focused on disproving that it is wrong. What is being tested is not the research hypothesis, but the null hypothesis. But, if the null hypothesis is rejected, it lends probability to the research hypothesis. This may sound convoluted, but it reflects a simple problem of logic. Consider the following theoretical research hypothesis: As

media consumption of depictions of violence increases, aggression perpetration increases. Proof of this research hypothesis would require observation of *all instances* of viewing media violence. This is obviously impractical. Thus, the research hypothesis cannot be proven. But, the null hypothesis can be disproven: There is no relationship between media consumption of violence and viewer aggression perpetration. If a study is conducted in which participants report on how much TV violence they recall viewing in the past month, and it is observed that as reported media violence consumption increases so does the number of self-reported acts of aggression, then there is evidence that these variables are not unrelated and the null hypothesis is logically rejected. Rejection of the null adds probability or credibility to the research hypothesis. It is in this sense that scientists actually do not believe that anything can be "proven" in a deep philosophical sense, but that many conjectures can be easily *disproven*.

One way a researcher can gather convincing evidence to reject the null hypothesis is through **significance testing**, which puts the null hypothesis to test. Significance testing involves a statistical equation for a particular type of test (e.g., a *t*-test for difference between two nominal groups, and an *r* coefficient for a correlation between two interval-level measures). These equations each have a distribution of the test statistic that would be expected by chance. That is, if random sets of numbers were plugged into the equation hundreds of thousands of separate times, what is the likelihood that a particular value of the statistic would occur? Just like a roll of the dice, there is some chance, based on random probability, that five 12s (i.e., five instances of both dice coming up six) would be rolled in a consecutive sequence. It is a very, very, small likelihood, but if the dice were rolled a million times in a row, at some point there would probably be a few instances of five throws in a row coming up 12. Similarly, there is some probability that any two things may be correlated at a certain level. In general, however, things are strongly correlated not because of chance, but because they are causally connected to one another. Significance testing is a way of comparing the statistical test or result of a given study to the probability that a particular result would occur by chance alone. This comparison is always made as a statement of probability: What is the probability that this particular statistical result would occur by chance?

To use significance testing, a researcher must first select a confidence level for rejecting the null hypothesis. The level of confidence (or confidence interval) used to reject the null hypothesis (e.g., no relationship or difference) is set by the **probability level**, which can be calculated by taking the percentile of the desired confidence level (for example 95%), and subtracting it from one (e.g., 1 − .95 = .05). Another word for the probability level is the **probability value** or *p*-value. Standard practice in research sets the probability level at 95% and probability value at .05, which means that we reject the null hypothesis (i.e., there is no relationship between exposure to violent movies and aggressive behavior) with a *p*-value less than .05, with 95% confidence. In other words, we are 95% confident that if we observe a finding that suggests exposure to violent movies increases aggressive behavior, it did not occur by chance. If, however, the *p*-value is greater than .05, we cannot rule out the possibility that the result was a product of chance.

A researcher might reject a null hypothesis when it should be accepted or accepts a null hypothesis when it should be rejected. Incorrectly accepting or rejecting a null hypothesis represents two specific types of errors: type I (alpha) errors and type II (beta) errors. **Figure 10.8** summarizes the differences between these errors and their origins. A **type I error** happens when a researcher rejects a null hypothesis when it should have been accepted. For example, a researcher conducting a study on exposure to media violence and aggressive behavior may observe a relationship in the sample of the study that does not exist in the population in the real world. Based on this, the researcher may incorrectly reject the null hypothesis and commit a type I error. Conversely, a researcher may not observe a relationship between these variables in the study's sample, but the relationship may exist in the population. In this type of error—**type II**—a researcher incorrectly accepts the null hypothesis in concluding that there is no relationship. Investigators may not be aware when they make these errors, but they have ways of estimating the likelihood that they have made such errors, and they generally try to strike a balance between

FIGURE 10.8: Type I Errors vs. Type II Errors

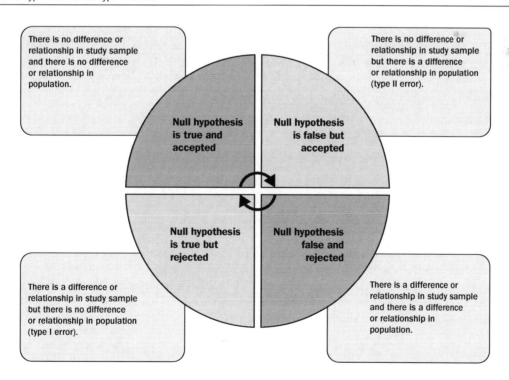

the two, depending on the importance of the error given what is being studied. Studying a lifesaving drug requires balancing the error of missing its curative effects against the error of concluding it works when it actually does not, thereby potentially leading to premature mortality in comparison to other more effective drugs.

Quantitative methods rely on the use of statistics to help researchers summarize and describe data and draw inferences about relationships between variables. Capturing data that is directly representative of entire study populations is usually very expensive and is generally not feasible. Statistics allow researchers to make statements about populations while bypassing the need to collect data from every member of the study populations by using samples to approximate what is likely to occur at the population level.

Conclusion

Throughout this chapter, we discussed the most commonly used approaches to quantitative research in communication (i.e., content analysis, survey, and experimental designs), different aspects of quantitative methods relevant to sampling and measurement, and the use of probability for hypothesis testing. Using the scientific method, researchers can employ quantitative methods to extend the boundaries of communication theory and research. The question, however, of whether to use quantitative methods or another research approach, should rest squarely on the nature of the question posed by a researcher. Quantitative methods are particularly ideal for answering any question related to quantifying, explaining, or predicting a communication phenomenon.

CHAPTER 11

Quantitative Ways of Knowing, Part II
Four Research Methods in Communication

Lourdes S. Martinez, Rachael A. Record, & Daniel J. Canary

LEARNING OBJECTIVES

After reading this chapter, you should be able to do the following:

- Given a description of a study, identify which design (survey, experimental, content analysis, observational) is being applied.
- Compare and contrast types of survey designs (cross-sectional, longitudinal, trend, panel).
- Distinguish between internal and external forms of validity.
- Identify and differentiate the key elements of experimental designs (e.g., manipulation, confederate, debriefing, etc.).
- Explain the role of random assignment in experimental knowledge claims.
- Specify features of content analysis and its limitations.
- Specify the steps involved in selecting and defining content categories and units of analysis.
- Exemplify and articulate the implications of the process of unitizing in a study.
- Describe the observational analysis method.
- Define two phases of observational research—collecting and coding.

SEVERAL CHAPTERS IN THIS VOLUME describe various methods of qualitative research. In this chapter, we attempt to depict four different quantitative methods. As the reader will discover, quantitative methods vary immensely, as Chapter 10 indicates. Quantitative methods involve the use of numbers to help find answers to research questions. Numbers provide enormous help in keeping track of people's group membership (e.g., male or female), values (e.g., liberalism vs. conservativism), attitudes (e.g., whether a particular artist is good or bad), beliefs (e.g., how sure one is that the government tells the truth), intentions to behave (e.g., get a measles shot), perceptions of partners' behavior (e.g., how supportive the partner was in a specific situation), and past behavior (e.g., how much one self-disclosed). In a word, numbers are a tool that can give powerful, flexible, and interpretable ways to analyze various phenomena in the social sciences as well as the hard sciences. And researchers often use numbers to help solve riddles regarding human communication behavior. As with any research method, quantitative methods are limited; they cannot answer, for instance, questions concerning one's understanding of implicit cultural rules, of sexual preference, of national-level oppression, and so forth as other chapters in this anthology argue. But numbers can make the research process more precise regarding the questions and hypotheses they test.

This chapter extends Chapter 10 by discussing four distinct quantitative methods that communication researchers often use. First, we summarize perhaps the most commonly used quantitative method—the *survey method*. Following that, we discuss how communication scholars use *experiments* to assess differences between groups in controlled settings. Third, *content analysis*, is discussed, which has proven very effective especially in exploring mass media content. Finally, the chapter concludes with a brief analysis of *observational research*, where people's conversations are recorded, transcribed, coded for specific behaviors, and analyzed. Importantly as well, researchers can combine different methods to approach different facets of a research issue or sets of issues. Of course, other quantitative methods exist. However, the four method types that we discuss clearly represent quantitative research methods generally, and they reflect the study of human communication very specifically.

Choosing a method of doing research should be guided by one's theoretical framework (Burgoon, Dunbar, & Elkins, 2017; Margolin et al., 1998). Simply adopting a particular method for method's sake severely handicaps understanding the idea under investigation. And quantitative researchers should not engage in some study because they think they know how to do it, or it can be tamed within the confines of a particular method, or it has never been done before, or one can gain access to interesting data, and so on. Running correlations between variables can provide knowledge (even with less than 5% of the time knowledge dictated by chance). But making sense of those correlations requires a theoretical model. And as the above sentences imply, no one method is inherently superior to another. Instead, the value of a particular method is fundamentally based on whether it can help the researcher answer theoretically derived questions. At this point, we begin our review with the survey method.

The Survey Method

The survey constitutes one of the most commonly used quantitative methodologies in communication research. A **survey** offers a method used in social science research that seeks to learn more about individuals or groups by directly asking participants questions about their perceptions, attitudes, beliefs, and behaviors (Wrench et al., 2015). In this section, we discuss specific features of survey, their strengths and limitations, various designs of survey studies, and the difference between internal and external validity.

Surveys can be administered by the researcher or self-administered by participants. If administered by the researcher, the survey typically occurs through face-to-face interviewing or by telephone. Face-to-face interviewing has several advantages because interviewers can evoke trust and clarify any confusion over questions in person, keep participants more engaged, and administer surveys that are longer in length. This form of survey dissemination, however, tends to be more expensive than other forms, and the face-to-face format may affect how respondents answer questions. Telephone interviewing shares some of the same advantages as face-to-face interviewing but is not limited to geographical location. The disadvantages of telephone interviewing, however, include the need to administer shorter surveys, the recognition that the format may affect how participants may respond to questions, and the need to ensure that certain groups of people are not left out of the study because they cannot be easily reached by telephone or because they rely exclusively on cell phones.

When surveys are self-administered, participants receive and complete the survey on their own, without an interviewer. Self-administered surveys can be received by participants in person, through the mail, or online. Self-administered surveys tend to be much more affordable in terms of costs and speeds for collecting data from a many participants when compared to researcher-administered surveys. But they do not, however, provide participants with an easy way to gain clarification regarding questions that may be confusing. Additionally, it is difficult to gauge participants' level of engagement (e.g., whether they answer questions thoughtfully or not) until after data collection is complete.

Researchers also must decide on selecting a survey research design. Two broad categories of survey research designs are cross-sectional surveys and longitudinal surveys (Fowler, 1993). A **cross-sectional survey** is a research design that allows researchers to take a cross-section or snapshot of a group of individuals at one time point. This type of research design helps explore associations between/among variables but does not provide any information about how individuals may change over time.

In contrast, a **longitudinal survey** permits researchers to examine how individuals change over time, and it can be designed in two ways. The first is a **trend design**, which follows different groups of individuals over time. The Health Information National Trends Survey (HINTS: hints.cancer.gov) exemplifies a well-known trend design that targets different individuals to track information gathering trends about a variety of health topics changes over time. A longitudinal study can also be constructed using a panel design. A **panel design** resembles a trend design, with the difference that it follows the same group of individuals over time. In a study that sought to determine the effectiveness of relational maintenance strategies (such as being positive and assuring) on important relational features (e.g., marital satisfaction, commitment), Canary, Stafford, and Semic (2002) followed the same sample of married couples at three data points spread a month apart from the others. They found that, when measured at the same time, relational maintenance strategies were strongly associated with relational characteristics, such as commitment. Over time, the effect due to maintenance strategies almost disappeared, implying that partners need to offer maintenance strategies continually to keep their relationships satisfying.

Although widely used by researchers, the survey as a methodological approach contains some limitations that deserve discussion. After data collection is complete, researchers check to confirm that a sufficient number of respondents invited into the study actually submitted the survey, and that those submitting the survey actually

completed it and without excess bias (e.g., answering all "three" or all "seven," answering only in ways that make the respondent "look good," etc.). The percentage of participants who return a survey in relation to the percentage invited to participate is called the **response rate**.

Results of a survey can be greatly affected by low response rate because a low response rate can reduce generalizability and introduce a **nonresponse bias**. Nonresponse bias arises when the participants who do not answer a specific question or set of questions differ in important ways from the participants who did answer. For instance, student evaluations of teachers can easily trend toward the negative if only a handful of students criticize the teacher and many of the other students do not complete the teacher's evaluations. In a class of 30 people, for instance, only 5 students are needed to trash an instructor's teaching reputation if only 15 of the 25 remaining students who did like the teacher actually respond. Depending on the level of bias, results could be very different if everyone had answered the question(s). Although no way exists to prevent nonresponse completely, researchers can improve response rates by creating surveys that are shorter in length, easier to complete, offer options for participation (e.g., via mail, online, telephone, etc.), make multiple contacts with potential participants, include a convincing cover letter, and provide a self-addressed envelope for mail surveys (Wrench et al., 2015).

Another limitation of research using surveys relates to the internal validity of the study. **Internal validity** refers to the extent a researcher can be confident in the cause-effect relationship within a study. In general, surveys tend to have lower internal validity than other quantitative methods such as experiments. Recall that three criteria are required to posit a cause–effect relationship. Although surveys can be useful in observing relationships between variables (and meeting the first requirement of causation), they are limited in their ability to tell researchers about whether the independent variable (presumed cause) is responsible for producing changes in the dependent variable (presumed effect) because cross-sectional surveys may not sufficiently address the second or third requirements of causation.

Cross-sectional surveys are the most commonly used design in survey research, given their relatively low costs and their ability to quickly gather data corresponding to a large sample. Because cross-sectional surveys collect data at only one point in time, however, and simultaneously measure independent and dependent variables, researchers are unable to fairly determine the time order of the variables, which would be necessary to meet the second requirement of causation. For example, if you take a survey asking the degree to which you perceive yourself to be communicatively anxious and communicatively competent, one cannot know if the correlation between these variables means that anxiety makes you less competent, or if your lower competence leads to social rejection, which causes you to feel anxious. It should be noted that because panel studies follow the same individuals over time and collect multiple data points, researchers can use such **longitudinal surveys** to determine if the independent variable in fact precedes the dependent variable and to establish if the second requirement of causation is fulfilled.

Last, neither cross-sectional nor longitudinal surveys can completely eliminate other potential variables as alternative explanations for observed associations. Researchers can and often do measure potential third variables, however, as part of a survey study in order to include them in an analysis as control variables. A **control variable** is a variable that accounts for changes in the dependent variable that are not accounted for by the independent variable and can help researchers eliminate third variables as potential explanations for observed relationships. For example, Hornik and colleagues recognized that, in addition to information seeking, general health status can help explain behavioral changes among cancer patients (see Lewis et al., 2012). For this reason, these researchers measured general health status as a control variable for analyses examining potential effects of cancer patients' information. Because it is impossible to measure all possible third variables and include them in an analysis as control variables, however, surveys are rather limited in their ability to fulfill this last condition for causation.

Despite these limitations, surveys most often contain external validity. **External validity** regards the extent to which a researcher is able to generalize the findings of a study to a population and to situations not directly examined as part of the research. Surveys tend to have higher external validity than other quantitative methods, such as experiments, because they usually occur in more natural settings reflective of the real world. Surveys are a widely used quantitative method that allows communication

scholars to ask participants directly about their attitudes, beliefs, and behaviors. The unique features of surveys allow them to be designed in a variety of ways. These features, however, can present limitations and strengths in terms of validity and need to be considered when weighing different quantitative approaches.

The Experimental Method

Another often used quantitative methodology in communication research is the experiment. Communication scholars often rely on experiments to leverage their strengths in testing causal links between variables. This section briefly discusses characteristics of experiments, different types of experimental research designs, strengths and limitations associated with experimental research, and threats to validity that are commonly encountered when performing experiments.

An **experiment** is a quantitative method that manipulates an independent variable in order to see its effects on a dependent variable (Wrench et al., 2015, Chapter 10). **Manipulation** simply means altering important features or levels of an independent variable between/among groups and measuring a dependent variable for any changes that result from that manipulation. Experiments can be designed to manipulate several independent variables, or just one. A **factorial experiment** is an experiment where the researcher manipulates more than one independent variable, or factor. A researcher interested in testing the effects of social setting and exposure to alcohol advertising on college students' attitudes about consuming alcohol might consider manipulating the social setting (e.g., in a room alone vs. with a group of friends) in addition to manipulating ad exposure (e.g., zero ads, one ad, two ads, or three ads). Factorial experiments are described according to the number and level of independent variables manipulated. In this example, we have two independent variables (i.e., setting and number of ads). Furthermore, the social setting variable has two levels (i.e., in a room alone or with a group), while the ad exposure variable has four (i.e., zero, one, two, or three ads). Hence, we designate this as a two-by-four factorial experimental design.

Successful manipulation of an independent variable can be achieved in a few ways. A researcher can assign one group of participants to a stimulus or phenomenon and leave another group without it or give an unrelated task. In this scenario, the first group is considered the **experimental group**, and the second represents the **control group**. Another option is to use confederates as part of the experimental manipulation. A **confederate** is trained by the researcher and, unbeknownst to the participants, is also a part of the study. The confederate will be instructed by the researcher to behave in certain ways, depending on the manipulation, which will expose participants in one group to behavior that is different from behavior participants are exposed to in the other group(s). Researchers also can create hypothetical scenarios or engaging in role-playing activities and measuring participants' responses.

Regardless of how a researcher decides to manipulate the independent variable(s), the manipulation needs to be strong enough to produce changes in the dependent variable. If the manipulation is insufficient or weak, changes in the dependent variable that would have occurred with a stronger manipulation will not be detected. One way to assess whether the manipulation needs to be strengthened is through the use of a manipulation check. A **manipulation check** is a procedure that allows a researcher to see if participants are in fact receiving the correct stimulus and/or the intended level of exposure to stimulus. Researchers can accomplish this by asking participants to recall elements of the manipulated stimulus to ensure the participants experienced the manipulation as intended. For example, in a study testing the effects of health messages using statistics, researchers might ask participants exposed to statistical messages if they recalled seeing numbers in the messages.

Researchers also have to make decisions about how to measure the dependent variable. Two commonly used approaches to measuring the dependent variable are questionnaires and observation (see the last section of this chapter). If using a questionnaire, the researcher can administer it to participants in a control group (if part of the study), and to those in an experimental group, but only after they have been exposed to the manipulation of the independent variable. Similarly, researchers can also administer a questionnaire before and after participants in an experimental group have been exposed to the manipulation of the independent variable. This allows researchers to compare changes in scores before and after the manipulation. Using observation to measure the dependent variable, researchers directly observe what happens after participants in an experimental group are exposed to the manipulation of the independent variable and compare these observations with those observed in the control group. Likewise, researchers can also take observations of participants prior to and after an experimental manipulation and examine any changes before and after the manipulation.

In addition to choosing how to manipulate and measure key variables, researchers need to consider other aspects of a study when designing an experiment. First, researchers can provide participants with a debriefing, especially if any deception was used as part of the manipulation. **Debriefing** represents a process by which researchers correct any deception introduced through the experiment, restate the purpose and value of the study, and thank the respondents for their participation. This process is important from an ethical perspective and helpful from a methodological perspective because it can provide an opportunity for participants to disclose any factors that may have influenced the way they behaved and/or how they completed questionnaires. Researchers can take note of these factors for explaining their research to the broader scholarly community as well as improving future research in the area of study.

Among the most crucial decisions to make when creating an experimental design concerns how the researcher decides if participants are assigned to an experimental condition (and if there are multiple experimental conditions, which participants are assigned to which one), or if they are assigned a control condition. One of the advantages of experimental design rests with the possibility of using random assignment. **Random assignment**, which includes all procedures for assigning participants to various conditions in an experiment study, is the single most powerful form of experimental control because it guarantees that each participant in the study has an equal chance of being assigned to any condition. In this way, random assignment helps researchers increase the comparability of conditions while addressing concerns of unmeasured third variables and sources of potential bias that can affect research results. Random assignment, which can be easily achieved through random means (e.g., coin flip, random number generator, lottery, etc.), also represents the defining feature between true experimental design and quasi-experimental design.

For example, a researcher might investigate whether exposure to a rape education video decreases belief in rape myths among college students (e.g., we had been dating a long time). The researcher gains access to a pool of 100 college students from an introductory communication course. The hypothesis states that the rape education video will reveal a significant decrease in endorsing rape myths for the experimental group only. The researcher then randomly selects 50 students to be in the treatment group, who see the rape education video; the other 50 students serve as a control group to view an unrelated video about the history of the United States. A measure of belief in rape myths will be administered before and after exposure to the video. The hypothesis that the rape education video will reveal a significant decrease in endorsing rape myths for the experimental group only. Some chance exists that among these 100 students that 5 to 10 males who have indeed engaged in date rape at some point. At the same time, there might be another 5 to 10 females who are rape victims. If all the rape victims ended up in the rape education (experimental) group, and all the rapists end up in the control condition, the hypothesis might fail to show any effect because these variables were not controlled for across the conditions of the experiment. Hundreds of other variables could affect the findings (e.g., victimization or perpetration, religious beliefs, culture, media consumption, social skills, etc.) that could alter the effects of exposure to a rape education video.

Random assignment to different treatment and control groups distributes *all these other possible variables in a random way* to the two conditions of the experiment, so that *all other potential spurious factors are relatively equal across conditions except for the experimental stimulus.* Thus, if changes occur in the experimental group that are not observed in the control group, one can conclude that the *only* variable that could have accounted for that difference between the groups is the stimulus (i.e., exposure to the video). This is why "true" experiments—defined as those that use random selection or assignment—presents the only method that can claim to observe causation. **Quasi-experimental designs** refer to studies where the structure of experimental designs are used but does not use random assignment to assign participants to different group conditions (Cook & Campbell, 1979). A **true experimental design** always randomly assigns to different experimental groups and control groups.

True experimental designs constitute the gold standard for building theory and theory testing because they fulfill all requirements for causation. Showing if an independent and dependent variable have an association while controlling the time order of the independent and dependent variables, and using random assignment to address issues of potential unmeasured third variables, true experimental designs tend to demonstrate very high internal validity. In contrast to surveys alone, the properties of true experimental designs give researchers a great degree of control over the research environment and the confidence that any change observed in the dependent variable is a result of manipulating the independent variable. Without the benefit of random assignment, quasi-experimental designs can only meet the first two conditions for causation because they cannot completely eliminate threats from unmeasured third variables. They can, however, demonstrate if a relationship exists between the independent and dependent variables, along with the time order of the variables.

Despite these strengths, experimental designs suffer from a few weaknesses. In general, experimental designs have a lower level of external validity and are less generalizable compared to surveys. First, experiments often occur in laboratory settings, and it is possible that the way participants behave as part of a study is inconsistent with their behavior in their natural environments. As a result, experiments tend to introduce a level of artificiality that may not reflect the real world. Second, researchers are limited in the number of variables, relationships, and populations they can examine within an experiment before the design becomes too complicated. This simplification can leave out key factors, and this can also reduce the researcher's ability to generalize a study's findings. (However, random assignment limits any systematic bias due to other factors).

Experiments can be powerful research designs for testing causal processes and building theory. To perform an experiment properly, researchers must consider which type of experimental design to use, strengths and limitations of the selected design, and whether the experiment will involve random assignments of participants (not intact groups, such as classrooms) to treatment versus control groups. In addition, researchers need to remain cognizant of different validity threats inherent in various types of study designs.

The Content Analysis Method

Content analysis refers to the "systematic, objective, quantitative analysis of message characteristics" (Neuendorf, 2016, p. 1). This section elaborates on the methodology of content analysis, including strengths and weaknesses of the approach. The necessary steps for performing content analysis will be briefly discussed, and exemplars will be presented.

Elaborated from the previously stated definition, content analysis presents a methodology that follows structured guidelines (i.e., systematic) that foster unbiased data analysis (i.e., objective) resulting in numerical estimations (i.e., quantitative) of the specified content. Unlike survey and experimental methodologies, content analysis does not involve collecting data from human participants. Instead, data are collected through preexisting communication content, which can take the form of verbal (e.g., comparing speeches of different presidents), nonverbal (e.g., exploring differences in gestures of children with and without autism), visual (e.g., examining culture of graffiti in bathroom bars), and mediated (e.g., assessing political communication in non-political forums online) content.

Instead of analyzing responses from participants, researchers using a content analysis design analyze **units of analysis**, or the data points selected for coding. Units of analysis are unique to each content analysis (and observational) project—much as a sample of participants is unique to each survey or experimental study. **Table 11.1** provides some examples of such "unitizing" in content analyses. To insure reliability and validity, best practices for conducting a content analysis require at least two coders to code each unit of analysis. The comparison of coder responses is essential for confirming **intercoder reliability**—the consistency of responses between coders. Without high levels of intercoder reliability, the data cannot be argued as objective, and thus are irrelevant (Neuendorf, 2016). Intercoder reliability is increased through clearly written conceptualizations and operationalizations of the variables of interest, clear and valid units of analysis, and consistent training or management of coders' ability to code the content correctly.

Nine essential steps exist for conducting a content analysis (Neuendorf, 2016; Wrench et al., 2015). **Table 11.2** presents and briefly explains each step. The first three steps and step five are standard practice for quantitative research and have already been reviewed in this chapter. The remaining five steps are unique to content analysis. Steps six through nine regard coding, intercoder reliability, and statistics (Chapter 10). Step four requires additional elaboration. Step four is the creation of a **coding scheme** (also see section on observational methods, below), which includes two parts: a codebook and a coding form. A **codebook** stipulates the coding rules. For example, a codebook will (at minimum) explain how to identify the unit of analysis (a speaker turn? a thought turn?), provide the conceptualizations of all variables, and attribute explanations for each variable. With a clearly written codebook in hand, coders are able to consistently complete a **coding form**, which is the sheet of items, paper or electronic, that each coder completes for each unit of analysis. The goal of a clear coding scheme is to eliminate individual differences in coder responses (Neuendorf, 2016).

TABLE 11.1: Example Units of Analysis for Content Analysis

Author(s)	Description of the Unit of Analysis
Matthews & Weaver (2013)	A single play (in a research lab) of one of the two best-selling M-rated games during the time of data collection (i.e., *Call of Duty: World at War*, and *Grand Theft Auto IV*).
Record, Staricek, & Pavelek (2014, November)	Individual graffiti drawings in the bathrooms of randomly selected bars.
Oleinik (2015)	Each paragraph of the presidential speeches given in four countries across 19 years.
Parrott & Parrott (2015)	An episode randomly selected from the crime-based dramas from the 2010–2013 seasons of U.S. basic cable television programming.

TABLE 11.2: Nine Steps to Conducting a Quantitative Content Analysis

Step	Description
1. Theory and rationale	Theoretical expectations and past research findings are the foundation for writing hypotheses and research questions.
2. Conceptualization	The definition of all variables being explored in the study.
3. Operationalization	The measurement tool for all variables being explored in the study.
4. Coding schemes	Creation of a codebook and coding form for study.
5. Sampling	Determining the content population and following appropriate sampling procedures to ensure a generalizable sample.
6. Training and pilot reliability	Randomly selecting a few or subsample of units from the sampled data to test the codebook and coding form with coders to ensure high intercoder reliability.
7. Coding	After making any necessary changes learned in step six, coding all the remaining data with the final codebook and coding form.
8. Final reliability	Using statistics to test intercoder reliability.
9. Tabulation and reporting	Using statistics to analyze the data in order to answer the hypotheses/research questions.

As with all methods, content analysis contains important limitations that should be acknowledged. First, findings from content analysis data cannot make assessments about media effects or whatever domain of behavior is being studied. For example, just because a study finds that stalking crime scenes in movies portray stalkers as more mentally ill or more likely to commit murder than in real life, it does not mean that people in society believe that stalkers tend to be mentally ill and more likely to commit a crime (Schultz, Moore, & Spitzberg, 2014); further survey or experimental research would be needed to explore such media effect relationships.

Second, content analysis findings are limited to the data explored. For example, if portrayals of illness are analyzed on *Grey's Anatomy* and *ER* (Ye & Ward, 2010), claims cannot be made about *Private Practice* or other shows not included in the analysis. Finally, different researchers define variables differently; therefore, drawing claims across studies is difficult. The discussion of conceptualization and examples provided in **Table 11.2** demonstrate this challenge.

The Observational Method

People observe other people much of the time. We notice the manner in which people look at us, how they look, how loud or soft they talk, what their different tactics are to persuade others, whether they are polite, how they engage in conflict, how well they back up their claims, and much more. The issue is to make our observations systematic; that is, we must identify and use valid concrete steps to ensure the credibility of our findings.

Observational analysis focuses on the actual interaction of people discussing various topics, whereas content analysis emphasizes features of content. It should be stressed at the outset that observational methods require an extraordinary amount of time, effort, and resources (e.g., creating or using a "lab," pay for research assistants). Beyond the dedication required, observational analysis has other features.

Features of Observational Research

First, if communication is a process, then it is important to represent that process. Observational methods provide researchers the ability to probe interactive communication as a process (VanLear, 2017). People cannot see or hear themselves communicating to another person, because their *field of vision* is external to them; but people's *field of experience* is internal to them in terms of thoughts, feelings, and reactions (Storms, 1973). However, very little connection exists between how people actually communicate and how they perceive their own communication and their partners' communication (Sillars, Roberts, Leonard, & Dunn, 2000). Humbad et al. (2011) summarized, "individuals interpret their partner's actions through either a generally positive or a generally negative perceptual filter, more or less regardless of the partner's objective behaviors" (p. 759).

A second feature of observational methods concerns its ability to analyze **patterns of interaction** as they occur in real time (VanLear, 2017). Margolin et al. (1998) argued that "observational data uniquely offer a means to study how behavior fluctuates as a function of the ongoing context and how behavioral sequences unfold across time" (p. 196). Researchers can observe the ebb and flow of communication of partners as they respond to each other beyond a single moment (Burgoon et al., 2017). Examples of various positive and negative communicative patterns are reported in **Table 11.3.**

Third, observational analysis can connect important relational outcomes to communication. For example, Woodin (2011) analyzed 64 studies that used 21 different observational coding systems. Her main goal examined the link between relational satisfaction and conflict strategies. Woodin's analysis revealed five conflict strategies: *hostility* (e.g., hard negative emotions, attacking, dominating), *withdrawal* (e.g., avoidance, detachment), *distress* (e.g., vulnerability, distress, hurt), *problem-solving* (constructive communication & neutral emotions), and *intimacy* (messages of closeness, statements of understanding the partner). Marital satisfaction was positively associated with intimacy and problem-solving communication behaviors, but satisfaction was negatively associated with hostility and distress.

Fourth, observational analysis can identify the ways in which communication behavior affects individuals' mental and physical health. For example, observations of actual interaction associate in various ways with hurt, depression, cardiovascular reactivity, immunological functioning, and other issues (e.g., Denes, Afifi, & Hesse, 2017).

Next, observational methods are needed to investigate nonverbal communication. Burgoon et al. (2017) illustrated how a simple smile may not be all that simple:

Smiles can be "authentic" or "false." The former are known as Duchenne smiles; these universal, naturally arising and spontaneous expressions associated with joy and happiness have a quick onset and offset and activate muscles around the mouth and eyes. … The "fake" smile, a deliberate,

learned expression with a slower onset and offset and longer duration than the Duchenne smile, may only activate muscles around the mouth. …

Burgoon et al. (2017) also summarized questions that one should consider before collecting data:

(a) Are the behaviors of interest better *conceptualized* as analogic or digital? (b) Are they better *measured* as analogic or digital signals? (c) What functions do they serve? (d) Are they subject to mutual influence and therefore better measured and analyzed dyadically? (e) Are the temporal fluctuations in their presentation sufficiently stable to justify a static measurement approach or should a longitudinal approach be adopted? (f) How small or large should the units of analysis be? (g) Should behaviors be measured objectively or subjectively? (h) Should observation be conducted by humans or machines? (p. 37)

In addition to these questions, Burgoon et al. posed challenges for five major components of a nonverbal study, one of which concern facilities needed. **Table 11.4** reports questions regarding this one issue.

Although variations of observational methods contain various procedures, one critical phases regard how interaction data are collected and then coded (Margolin et al., 1998). Margolin et al. also underscore the necessity of using one's research purpose as the primary criterion when using observational methods. The following sections raise only a few of several challenges that observational researchers face.

Observational Data Collection

Communication Task. Researchers must consider what communication behavior they want to observe. One critical task concerns the topic of conversation. Johnson (2002), for example, found that how people managed conflict varies by public versus private topics: arguments were less satisfying and more ego-involving when discussing private issues about the relationship (vs. public issues such as politics). Margolin et al. advised: "Faced with an infinite array of options regarding tasks, the investigator first needs to determine which task would optimize the likelihood of capturing specific behaviors and affects of interest" (pp. 197–198).

TABLE 11.3: Examples of Positive and Negative Interactive Patterns

Positive Interaction Patterns

1. **Validation** (argument exchange): Comment followed by another that offers consent.

2. **Contracting**: Direct modification of one's own point of view to bargain with partner's previous statement.

3. **Supportiveness–Supportiveness**: Genuine information seeking and information giving are reciprocated.

4. **Cajoling** (coaxing–coaxing): Mutually oriented communication that attempts to make the partner feel good about himself/herself before flattering other, appealing to other, joking.

5. **Metacommunication–Metacommunication** (with positive feelings): Brief statements about the constructive process of communication.

6. **Socioemotional** (description–question): Descriptive statements concerning one's feelings, followed by statements regarding the affective state of the partner.

7. **Task oriented** (question–description): Statements that ask for factual information or request further elaboration of task-oriented points, followed by issue-oriented factual statements concerning the past, present, or future.

8. **Mind-reading** (said with neutral or positive emotion): Attributing emotions, opinions, states of mind, etc., to a partner with neutral or positive affect, which is responded to as if it was a question about feelings.

9. **Summarizing** (one person or both): Any statement by the other speaker that summarizes a previous statement by the other person and/or a statement that prevents a review of the conversation.

10. **Confirm–Agree**: Reveals one's understanding of the situation and offers acknowledgment, empathy and/or acceptance of partner's feelings/ideas, which is followed by the partner's agreement and/or compliance.

Negative Patterns

1. **Demand–Withdraw**: One person attempts to discuss an issue, often in a negative manner; the other person refuses to engage in discussion, denies the problem exists, and/or deflects the issue.

2. **Complaint–Countercomplaint**: A complaint by one person is followed by a complaint by the partner.

3. **Proposal–Counterproposal**: a proposal from one person is met by a proposal from the partner.

4. **Disagreement–Disagreement**: Disagreement is reciprocated and/or is faced with challenges to the other person's points.

5. **Defensiveness–Defensiveness** (indifference): Behaviors that are threatening or punishing to others that produce defensive behaviors in return.

6. **Attack–Counterattack**: Exchange of contempt/criticism between partners.

7. **Metacomuunication–Metacommunication** (with negative emotion): The reciprocation of negative statements about the process of communication.

8. **Mind-reading** (with negative affect): Attributing emotions, ideas, etc. that is responded to as if it was a criticism; it is then disagreed with by the second person.

9. **Summarizing self**: A statement by one partner, followed by a statement from the other partner that evaluates the speaker's previous statements.

10. **Complain–Justification**: Individual-oriented blaming that discloses discontentment and resentment indirectly, followed by the other's individual-oriented act that persists in clarifying one's own position regardless of other's feelings/idea.

Source: Adapted from Cupach, Canary, & Spitzberg (2010).

TABLE 11.4: Burgoon et al.'s Questions Regarding Facilities

Questions Regarding Facilities and Arrangements
1. Will the recording be in a laboratory or a natural field environment? If you have access to a laboratory, that provides you with more control over your environment and can ensure the proper placement of your recording equipment. Recording people in their natural environments, such as children in their classrooms or families at home, can encourage more natural behavior but makes the placement of recording equipment and furniture a challenge.
2. What kinesics are you trying to capture? If you want to examine minute facial expressions, then you will need close-ups of the face.
3. What type of furniture is used? This may seem like a trivial issue, and it may be tempting to just grab the available furniture from a nearby office space. But the furniture can have a major effect on the kinesics you can observe.
4. Are you examining individuals or dyads as the focus of your recording? If you are recording individuals, you can position the cameras and microphones near each individual, but if you are recording a dyad, you must consider how you will capture both individuals.

Source: Burgoon et al. (2017).

Instructions. Observational researchers need to plan what instructions they will give to participants. Instructions must yield behaviors of interest. In the area of conflict communication, researchers have created various tasks that elicit targeted communication behaviors (Canary, 2017). In several studies, the researcher has asked partners to discuss a list of conflict topics. Giving participants lists of topics requires that the items on the list are relevant to the participants. For instance, Zietlow and Sillars (1988) presented participants with 10 salient topics to discuss. A second way to generate talk is to instruct partners to (separately) volunteer what they consider are important problem areas in their marriage and then to take turns talking about whose issue is discussed.

Setting. Another question to ask before collecting data regards the setting for the observations. Observational methods have been used in many different kinds of settings, including the researcher's lab or natural settings (e.g., home or school, Burgoon et al., 2017; Margolin et al., 1998). One reason to collect data at home concerns whether the task encourages people to behave naturally. A simple procedure to acquire interaction behavior would be to ask participants to record themselves and return their recordings to the researcher (e.g., Canary, Brossmann, Brossmann, & Weger, 1995). More complex procedures exist. For instance, Sillars et al. (2000) funded research assistants to answer telephone calls 24/7 from married partners who were instructed to call when a conflict between began. A research team drove a van loaded with audiovisual equipment to the participants' homes. After the research team set up their equipment, then the couples would resume their interaction while being recorded.

The advantage of using a lab to collect data is that it offers the researcher a certain amount of control. In brief, having a lab allows the researcher to guarantee higher-quality recordings that can detect variations in communicative behavior (Margolin et al., 1998). **Figure 11.1** represents how cameras can be positioned in a lab setting to maximize observations.

Although naturalistic settings might appear attractive, they are harder to control and record. Also, labs can be made to resemble living spaces by being furnished with couches, a kitchen table, or any other prop to increase representational validity. In a very ambitious effort, Gottman (1996) built an apartment on the University of Washington campus where participants would live for a full day. This apartment contained audiovisual devices that could detect and record couples' interaction. Our experience has been that people will behave in ways that they know how to behave. Relational dynamics that partners have built over time will emerge even in a lab setting.

Unitizing. As with content analysts, observational researchers must decide in advance what counts as a unit of behavior. In observational studies, unitizing most often concerns how to frame the interaction for *micro-level* analyses. Researchers use milliseconds, 30 seconds, 1 minute, 3 minutes or more to unitize communication. Others rely on speaker turns, or who holds the floor, such

FIGURE 11.1: Example Placement of Cameras in a Lab Setting

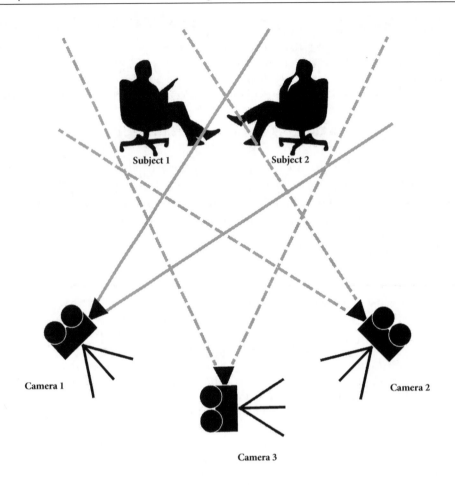

that the unit focuses on the speaker more than time. A third approach is the "thought turn." A *thought turn* is the "smallest semantic unit" (Notarius, Markman, & Gottman, 1983, p. 119) that can be observed, for example, in independent clauses, one word responses, and nonverbal behaviors that carry an idea (e.g., "Geez!" can mean "no"). Of course, the selection of the unit of analysis depends on the researcher's purpose.

Once observations of interaction are collected and adequately recorded they can be used for the present study and for future research purposes that require interaction data. Although this point is not unique to observational analysis, it does suggest that the researcher's immense time and effort in collecting observational data can look at different features of interaction.

Observational Data Coding

What Coding Entails. Coding conversations can be exhausting yet interesting, and it represents a most critical phase of observational research. Coding data involves providing each unit of analysis of the interaction a "code" (e.g., word or number) that represents the topic of interest. For example, if a unit of behavior (e.g., speaker turn) is a "disagreement" then one might record it as a *DGMT*; if the behavior functions to interrupt the other in a domineering way, then it would receive the code *INPT-*; and if the interruption helps the partner develop his or her ideas, then such interruptions would be coded as *INPT+*.

If you use such labels to code, then you would assign numbers to all codes, which can be entered into a computer software package. For instance, a *DGMT* (disagreement) could be assigned the number "1" and *INTP-* (negative interruption) could be designated as a "2," and *INPT+* (positive interruption) could be designated a "3," whenever these behaviors occur. (The reader may recall from Chapter 10 that such numbers are *nominal* level data, where the numbers represent names more than real numbers.) Once codes are assigned numbers, they are entered into the computer.

The Coding System. Researchers have developed many different coding systems (Woodin, 2011). A "coding system" simply refers to instructions one gives coders, including definition of terms, how individual codes can be combined, decision rules that explain what code to use, etc. For example, should disagreements, interruptions, and swearing automatically be combined into a more general category of "negative behavior"? Does one need to assess positive and negative emotions to determine what are negative behaviors and what are not?

Coder Training. Coders must become experts in using the coding manual, else all the data collected are meaningless (Margolin et al., 1998). A coding system should offer the coders a precise document that two or more coders can use with little disagreement between/among them. Disagreement about definitions and applications about how to apply codes will also render the data meaningless. Why? The reason is that one would not know what not to trust—the individual coders' work, some combination of the coders' backgrounds, the instruction manual, the instructor/researcher's work, a weak setting, equipment problems, or any other unforeseen error. To assess inter-coder reliability, several statistical formulae are readily available, and intercoder reliability must be checked before and should be calculated at intervals during the coding period (e. g., once a week, once a month).

Because coding observational data requires patience as well as intelligence, the selection of who will serve as coders should be carefully made (Margolin et al., 1998). From experience, graduate research assistants are probably the most competent at coding, and they should be rewarded financially and/or with recognition (e.g., as coauthor). However, we have also known graduate RA's who question the research, the units of analysis, the other

coders' decisions, and even the coding system itself. Margolin et al. (1998) suggest the following procedure for training coders:

> (a) Coders read the coding manual on their own; (b) once the coders are familiar with the code definitions, the investigator reviews each individual code and highlights distinctions between codes; (c) together the coding group reviews examples of codes on pilot tapes; and (d) the investigator explains any applicable decision trees and hierarchy of codes. During these initial sessions, it is important to encourage the coders to ask questions and point out any sources of confusion in the coding system or manual. Based on this feedback, it is not unusual to refine or clarify various aspects of the coding system. (p. 205)

As stated, once the data are coded (and checked for reliability), they can be uploaded into a computer software package (e.g., Excel) or even directly into one of several statistical packages.

If the codes have been carefully applied and if they use a small unit of analysis, then the researcher can combine the microscopic codes into larger categories. For example, Gottman, Markman, and Notarius (1977) used the eight codes to compare unhappy to happy couples. They also coded positive and negative affect in the face, voice, and body movement of each participant. Turn taking was the unit of analysis. Each turn reflecting positive affect was coded, and each turn involving negative affect was coded. They combined *proposing a solution, problem information, mind-reading (positive),* and *agreement* into a more *macroscopic* category of "positive" behaviors. They also combined *mind-reading (negative)* and *disagreement* to operationalize "negative" behaviors. *Communication talk, summarizing other,* and *summarizing self* were combined into a "neutral" category. Note that one can only combine more specific codes if those codes represent small, microscopic behaviors. One cannot disentangle abstract codes into smaller units if the data were not also coded at a specific level.

Once communication behaviors are coded, numbered, and entered into the computer, then one can engage in various quantitative analyses. The codes thus serve as compasses to find various domains and sequences of interaction. That is, one can first find when couples use different sequences, and then connect the occurrence of those patterns with other important variables, such as health and relational satisfaction. Again, one's research question (and hypotheses, if made) should guide the selection of the proper statistical analysis to use.

Although we did not cover all different phases of observational research, we hope the reader acquired a solid idea about the findings one can obtain about communication through observational method. The observational method often means time-intensive work, yet it gives us a precise view of communication processes as they unfold in actual interaction. In summary, observational research provides an excellent method for statistically analyzing actual interaction. For fuller treatments of the ins and outs of observational research in communication, see: Burgoon et al. (2017), Gottman (1994), Margolin et al. (1998), Sillars and Overall (2017), and VanLear and Canary (2017).

Conclusion

We live in an age of metrics. Much of our everyday life is increasingly recorded and measured, from our walking, our health indicators, our faces, our academic abilities and achievements, our work performance, and even our daily moods. At the same time, we are inundated by self-help advice about how to alter our behaviors and our environments to observe the outcomes we can achieve from such interventions. That is, we live in an age in which of quantitative and experimental methods have moved from the more exclusive domains of trained scientists, and into our everyday realms of experience. The more we understand the logics and languages of such methods, the better served we can be in applying the fruits of such methods in our lives.

Credits

FIG. 11.1A: Source: https://pixabay.com/illustrations/interview-conversation-sitting-2071228/.

FIG. 11.1B: Source: https://pixabay.com/illustrations/video-camera-filming-media-1872963/.

PART III

Knowing Where We Are and What Our Communication Is Doing
Functions and Contexts of Communication

CHAPTER 12

Gender in Communication

Julie L. Taylor

LEARNING OBJECTIVES

After reading this chapter, you should be able to do the following:

- Describe the historical, social, and U.S. cultural perspectives of communication and gender.

- Analyze communication and gender in everyday life, popular media, and other mediated discourse.

- Identify key theoretical perspectives used in researching gender in communication.

- Articulate core principles of consideration in gender in communication.

- Compare and contrast various benefits and challenges involved in intersections between gender and particular interactions, identities, institutions, texts, events, and power structures.

- Analyze how gender is communicated as well as how communication shapes gender.

- Identify your own implicit assumptions about gender and reflect on how they affect your or others communication.

I F YOU PAY ATTENTION TO CONVERSATIONS around you, inferences about gender and communication are plentiful. However, connections are often implicit. Throughout this chapter we examine how to discern the gendered message and make the implicit explicit. In fact, typically at the conclusion of my gender and communication course, students often proclaim, "I see gender everywhere!" Yes! That's the point.

Gender is everywhere, and my task is to make you astutely aware and critical consumers of gender in your everyday lives.

Chances are, at some point in your life you have been asked to fill out a form requiring you identify your gender (as male or female). If you are already a critical consumer of gender, you know that in fact what the survey regards biological sex, not gender. **Sex** refers to biological or genetic designations. West and Zimmerman (1987) defined sex as "a determination made through the application of socially agreed upon biological criteria for classifying persons" (p. 127). **Gender**, however, "refers to the social expectations attached to how particular bodies should act and appear and, thus, is socially constructed" (Palczewski, DeFrancisco, & McGeough, 2019, p. 10). Although in everyday discourse sex and gender may be used interchangeably, the concepts are not one in the same.

At a very basic notion, our communication is gendered but also our gender communicates (often through performance). Take for instance, the terms "masculine" and "feminine." Some readers may imagine male and female bodies respectively; whereas, other readers may take the terms for what they are—qualifiers or descriptors of behaviors (see **Figure 12.1**). This very reality makes studying gender in a communication context nuanced and bountiful. In other words, certain bodies may choose to align with assumed gendered behaviors (i.e., **cisgender**) but that certainly is not mandatory. In 1974, psychologist Sandra Bem coined the term "androgyny" through combining Greek words *andros* (male) and *gyne* (female). In alignment with such terms, Bem created the Sex Role Inventory (SRI) to identify a person's gender orientation. The scale measured highly masculine to low masculine, highly feminine to low feminine, and then androgynous to undifferentiated.

Because communication is dynamic, gender is dynamic. We are all born into a gendered world, and through social construction either conform or challenge the systems in place that might affect us. In this chapter, I move beyond simple constructions and reductionist bipolar models to approach gender as something individuals *do* and

FIGURE 12.1: Stereotypical Gender Expression Continuum

Feminine	Androgynous	Masculine
Soft		Assertive
Nurturing		Powerful
Focus on Appearance		Direct
Weak		Strong

communicate in everyday life, rather than something that individuals *are*. In order to make sense of this claim, this chapter outlines major theoretical assumptions gender and communication scholars use. The second section details key assumptions and fundamental considerations that should be considered and examined by scholarship. The final section highlights a few exemplars of gender in practice.

Theoretical Approaches

Theories are a perspective used to make sense of the world. Although theories may often feel abstract in nature (see Chapter 4), gender scholars typically adopt a theoretical perspective to situate their conversation and findings. For instance, even the very basic identification of gender/sex is predicated on theoretical underpinnings. In this section, I will highlight three of the most prominent theoretical approaches used in gender and communication research. As an overview, **Table 12.1** identifies the approaches with key assumptions and sample phrases often used that reify perspectives.

TABLE 12.1: Theories of Gender

Theoretical Perspective	Assumptions	Sample Phrases
Biological	• Gender is intrinsic. • Gender is decided by sex (biological characteristics). • Sex differences are inherent and uncontested. • Gender is binary (male or female).	• "Boys will be boys." • "She's a pretty princess."
Psychological	• Gender is formed by most immediate/present guardians. • Gender is learned through social interactions. • Studies often focus on interpersonal dynamics.	• "Boys don't cry." • "Little girls don't act like that."
Critical/cultural	• Gender is socially constructed by a multitude of influences. • Gender differences are saturated in power dynamics. • Language (and thus reality) are not gender neutral.	• "Generic man(kind)." • First years vs. freshmen.

The Biological Perspective

Messages congruent with biological theory are often at the forefront of conversations regarding differences and similarities between sexes. Think about the number of times you have heard "boys will be boys," or "young ladies don't act like that." These very statements (re)produce the assumption that gender is innate. That is, sex and gender are one in the same, insofar as sex determines gender. **Biological theories** rely on findings about distinctive hormones, brain structures, and genitalia to classify sexes. More important, the concept of gender binary—a category of two options for sex/gender—is founded in biological messaging about sex differences (i.e., male or female).

Sex organs are often at the center of the gender binary, which are based on chromosomal differences. Most commonly, people have 23 sets of chromosomes and one of those determines a person's sex. More often than not, people who are biologically female have an XX set and people who are biologically male have an XY set. This scientific pattern is what often leads people to believe that sex differences are innate. However, Blackless, Charuvastra, Derryek, Fausto-Sterling, Lauzanne, and Lee (2000) found alternate genetic makeups of XO, XXX, XXY, or XYY sets. The mere presence of alternative sex chromosome combinations challenges the binary, chromosome-based typology.

Another common assumption within biological theory is that of hormonal distinctions. For instance, think about conversations that have described "too much testosterone" as a citation of men's anger or ego; or the opposite, "estrogen" as too many "leaky emotions" for women. Testosterone is often associated with aggression, risk-taking, and violent behaviors (McAndrew, 2009). Although more testosterone is typically present in male bodies, all bodies contain some level of testosterone. Both estrogen and testosterone appear in all human bodies. Fausto-Sterling (2000), a biology professor, claimed that "social belief systems weave themselves into the daily practice of science in ways that are often invisible to the working scientist" (p. 194). That is, people are both creating and (re)creating cultural assumptions through their work, which means that more productive questions would engage the role of hormone levels in all bodies rather than simply attributing hormone levels to maleness or femaleness.

The Psychological Perspective

Psychological theories represent a broad and diverse range of perspectives toward gender. Theoretical perspectives housed in the psychological tradition are often predicated on interpersonal relational dynamics. Think, for instance, about the role parents and siblings play in helping one establish their gender identity. The people who surround us while we are growing up and negotiating what it means to be "us" shape the various reactions we have to gender. One of the more widely cited theories in this perspective is social learning theory, which was developed by Walter Mischel (1966) and Albert Bandura (2002; Bandura & Walters, 1963). According to social learning theory, parents and primary caregivers are the most influential parties in a child's development. Central to this perspective are the communicative responses of rewards and punishments regarding what others deem as appropriate or inappropriate gendered behaviors. Girls are typically rewarded for imitating traditionally feminine behaviors such as being polite, kind, caring, nurturing, and attentive to their physical appearance. Boys are usually rewarded for masculine behaviors such as independent play, roughness, aggression, being emotionally controlled, and being physically active.

When children perform outside of these stereotypes, they often are punished for their behaviors. In other words, they are told "little girls don't act like that," or "boys don't cry." But gender roles are more flexible than that. In her study on parent's responses to gender nonconformity, Kane (2006) found that parents seemed to be more tolerant of their girls being masculine than vice-versa. Parents explained that they wanted their girls to be independent and athletic. For instance, "I never wanted a girl who was a little princess, who was so fragile … I want her to take on more masculine characteristics" (p. 157). When it came to boys, parents were less accepting of emulating feminine behaviors. The most commonly cited reason for disapproval was an assumption that communicating in a more feminine way would directly impact one's sexual preference. The following example reflects this common justification: "If he was acting feminine, I would ask and get concerned on whether or not, you know, I would try and get involved and make sure he's not gay;" and "if [he] were to be gay, it would not make me happy at all. I would probably see that as a failure as a dad … as a failure because I'm raising him to be a boy, a man" (pp. 162–163). Parents also contended that it was reasonable for boys to occasionally hold a doll or play with a kitchen set because one day they may need to feed a child or make food for themselves (Kane, 2006). That is, life skills are considered acceptable to practice if only for a brief moment.

Social learning theory can also be applied more broadly to the way media or peer groups socialize gender conformity. Advertisements inundate our everyday media consumption. Beauty advertisements comment on something that is wrong (i.e., "short eyelashes got you down?") and then they solve your problems (i.e., "wearing our mascara will get you the dream job, guy, and life you want"). In Kimmel's (2008) book *Guyland: The Perilous World where Boys Become Men*, "guyland" is synonymous with **hegemonic masculinity**. Kimmel talks about social pressure to not only play in guyland, but to reproduce guyland—something that both guys and gals are responsible for (re)creating. In one section he comments on a sorority ritual called "circle the fat" or "bikini weigh in." Women must get into bikinis in order to identify their so-called problem areas. If the members are "too heavy" they are ejected from the sorority. In this context, women are being rewarded for being thin and punished for not conforming to traditional standards of femininity/beauty.

Critical/Cultural Theories

Theoretical considerations for critical/cultural scholars really beg the question of "what came first the chicken or the egg?" Fundamentally, culture is both produced and (re)produced through communication, and thus the **critical/cultural** scholar critically examines the (re)production(s). Specific questions within gender and communication scholarship draw into light an examination of power and social inequities. For instance, Simone de Beauvoir's *The Second Sex* put into print explicit discussions of "what is woman?" The very presence of this article illuminated the one-sided nature of conversation about gender. In other words, "men" or even the "generic man(kind)" had been used as a placeholder for all people. Linguistically, the erasure of women is materially consequential, and as de Beauvoir (1952) would put it "One is not born, but rather becomes, woman … It is civilization as a whole that elaborates [what] is called feminine. Only the meditation of another can constitute an individual as an *Other*" (p. 283). Clearly, the social construction of gender norms was called into question.

Similarly, scholars like Dale Spender (1985) emphasized the reality that "language is *not* neutral" (p. 139). Spender argued that language constructs reality, and so (in this case) "if women are to begin to make their own world, it is necessary that they understand some of the ways in which such *creation* is accomplished" (p. 138). Spender said that if women, or we could even argue, all people, want to be acknowledged they must first be linguistically present. For if the foundation of language rests on the generic "he" or "man" then both linguistically and as a subsequent material consequence there is room for no more. Whereas, if the language structure is modified then spaces emerge for more to be in conversation with rather than as the "other."

Scholars often cite standpoint as an ideal starting or sticking point for critical gender scholarship. The traditions for standpoint theory date back to Hegel (1770–1831) and Marx (1818–1883). Importantly, **standpoint theory** begins with an acknowledgment that different groups that constitute society. Each group has a differing level of access to power and privilege. Standpoint theory focuses on how membership in groups (i.e., gender, race, class, and sexual identity) informs how one experiences the world. Standpoint theory claims: (1) all perspectives on social life are partial; (2) some perspectives are more limited than others; and (3) a standpoint is earned, in part, by reflecting on multiple perspectives (Wood & Fixmer-Oraiz, 2017). Reflection is a vital component of standpoint theory. In other words, simply because a person is a part of a group does not mean that this person fully identifies with what it means to be a part of that group both socially and historically. For example, outsiders may assume that all women are feminists; of course, not all women identify with being feminists.

A final point of consideration are key tenants to critical thought: power and hegemony. According to critical scholars, systems of **power** are always in play and it is up to the scholar to reveal not only the power systems but also the subsequent social inequities. Feminist poststructural scholar Weedon (1997) claimed **feminism** is a politics "directed at changing existing power relations between women and men in society" (p. 1). Weedon continued to explain, "we need[ed] a theory which can explain how and why people oppress each other … which can account for the relationship between the individual and the social" (p. 3). The need for feminism was and is apparent for critical scholars due to socially constructed power inequities.

Perhaps one of the most prominent scholars to discuss power is the French Philosopher, Michel Foucault. Although some scholars have criticized pairing his work with feminism, the utility of his work supersedes the critique. Diamond and Quinby (1988) elucidated four points of convergence for feminist thought and Foucault's articulation of power: (1) both identify the body as a site of power, (2) both concepts point to the local and intimate operations of power rather than focusing exclusively on the supreme power of the state, (3) both bring to fore the crucial role of discourse in its capacity to produce and sustain hegemonic power and emphasize the challenges contained within marginalized and/or unrecognized discourses, and (4) both criticize the ways in which Western humanism has privileged the experience of the Western masculine elite as it proclaims universals about truth, freedom, and human nature (p. x). Using discourse as the site of power, Foucault (1994) established that negotiations of power are constant. Moreover, power is negotiated at various levels, interpersonally, culturally, socially, and/or institutionally.

The concept of **hegemony** represents a form of covert power. Hegemony was originally developed by Gramsci (1971) and refers to an organizing process whereby a dominant group leads others to accept subordination as normative, as status quo. Critical organizational communication scholar Dennis Mumby (2001) argued "Hegemony does not refer to simple domination, but rather involves attempts by various groups to articulate meaning systems that are actively taken up by other groups" (p. 587). That is, people willingly adopt the dominate power structure and then reinforce it through their actions.

Two examples of hegemonic power in gender studies concern patriarchy and hegemonic masculinity. **Patriarchy** is a "hegemonic system that exercises hegemonic control wherein men are privileged over women, and some men are privileged over men … [people] accept it because such an ordering appears to make sense" (Palczewski, DeFrancisco, & McGeough, 2019, p. 46). Often patriarchy is conflated with being a man, and this is inherently wrong. Canadian author, Justine Musk (2014) wrote in her blog "The enemy of feminism isn't men. It's patriarchy. And patriarchy is not men. It is a system." Similar to patriarchy, is a concept coined by Sociologist R. W. Connell (1982) called hegemonic masculinity. Hegemonic masculinity acknowledges multiple types of masculinity; however, one is often privileged over others (white, upper middle class, heterosexual). Gender scholar and creator of Mentors in Violence Prevention (MVP) group Jackson Katz (2013) said that men should call on other men to re-normalize a different type of masculinity. Katz imagines a masculinity that is more supportive of all people and less detrimental to men-on-men violence and men-on-women violence.

The Multiracial Approach. In the beginning, feminism was critiqued for being a white woman's fight. In other words, the issues that were taken up and the way that scenarios were framed were centered on framing from one perspective. It was not until the "second wave" of feminism that a more **multiracial feminism** developed, in which there were more voices and perspectives considered in the movement (Frye, 2000). From a critical perspective, it is important to remember that not one single definition or perspective encompasses "woman." Perhaps more important is the reality that one characteristic (in this case race), does not define a person's experience.

Queer Theory. At the heart of **queer theory** is the desire to disrupt and call into question identity categories. More specific to gender discussion, queer theorists challenge simplistic (and reductionistic) applications of binary categories (e.g., masculine/feminine, male/female, homosexual/heterosexual). Queer theorists "context and deconstruct identity categories by conceptualizing identities as multiple, fluid, unstable, changeable, and constantly evolving" (McDonald, 2015, p. 319). Overall, queer theorists challenge heteronormative categories of sex (male/female) and gender. The next section addresses issues that are fundamental to discussions about gender.

Fundamental Considerations of Gender

The following fundamental considerations operate as key principles within gender and communication scholarship. That is, in order to truly understand the interconnected nature of gender and communication of how people construct, (re)construct, perform, and discipline gendered behaviors the following considerations must be taken into reflection.

Interdisciplinarity

Genuinely, a very exciting reality of conducting research in gender studies is the interdisciplinary nature of investigation. Research on gender is explored from a variety of paradigmatic perspectives. Scholars pull from a multitude of research traditions in order to examine gender and gender constructs in varying capacities. In other words, quantitative, qualitative, rhetorical, critical, and even opinion pieces often found online inform how we see and experience studies of gender. Even if you think about the courses you have taken along your collegiate journey, you may recall that discussions of gender were infused into course lectures, reading, examples, and/or assignments.

Why then, is this discussion important to consider? As a student and participant in the world around you, it is important to remember the interdisciplinarity of gendered studies and perspectives. This reality invites us, as life-long learners, to see a concept examined with varying findings and implications. For instance, in a study that examined a few layers of interdiciplinarity, Kedrowicz and Taylor (2019) looked at responses to gendered bodies. Their study was situated in an interdisciplinary program where doctoral students from the College of Humanities taught undergraduate classes in the College of Engineering. First, the authors noted the interdisciplinary culture clash that was the two colleges. They explained that colleges have their own ideological ways of doing, being, and knowing. In this case, the College of Humanities is known as the "soft" or feminine ways of doing and being; whereas, the College of Engineering embodied traditional masculinity. Results highlighted the interdisciplinary variable of "gendered knowledge" as an initial barrier to students learning. Students struggled between the utilitarian nature of needing communication to secure a job and potential promotion with their common misconception that communication is "easy."

A second layering involved the interdisciplinary presentation of faculty bodies. In all, they examined 42 sets of evaluations over 14 courses with 16 different instructors (10F; 6M). Kedrowicz and Taylor (2019) noted that the comments about physical form were much more prevalent in the female instructor's feedback than in males. The following are examples: "She's hot," "She's really pretty," and "I would like to learn how to communicate orally in bed." In a similar context, Taylor (2013) maintained that, "sexualization devalues the female body as a way of making sense of her [otherness]" (p. 8). In the end, the authors argued that the gendered responses to knowledge and bodies were part of the enculturation that manifests itself in disciplinary settings. However, importantly, this example provides space to problematize the silo effect of collegiate experiences because workplaces are also interdisciplinary spaces.

Intersectionality

The concept of intersectionality is to recognize that gender and sex cannot be studied in isolation. **Intersectionality** refers to a conceptual recognition that identities are multiple rather than singular. That is, identity markers are additive insofar that they make us more complex beings. Intersections such as ethnicity, class, sex, sexual orientation, religion, biological markers, gender, and even citizenship status inform one's identity and social relations. Theoretically, intersectionality is an approach that examines identity and oppression. Gender scholar May (2015) explained that intersectionality "approaches lived identities as interlaced and systems of oppression as enmeshed and mutually reinforcing" (p. 3). Feminist scholar Curry-Johnson (2001) explained her negotiation of intersectionality as an "identity tapestry." She wrote, "As an educated, married, monogamous, feminist, Christian, African American mother, I suffer from an acute case of multiplicity … each identity defines me; each is responsible for elements of my character; from each I derive some sustenance for my soul" (pp. 51–52). Throughout her article, Curry-Johnson talks about how each component of her identity is equally as important as the next. Moreover, she must not only intrapersonal negotiate her identities, but also socially negotiate her roles, for instance, qualifying how she is both an attentive mother and a committed academic.

Feminism

It may seem peculiar that it has taken until now to address feminism explicitly as a component of gender studies. At its very foundation, feminism is a theory of political, economic, and social equality for all sexes. Feminism is often considered a dirty word, or the "other F word" in many social settings. Images of feminists often conjure up assumptions of man hating, bra burning, angry women. Germinal scholar bell hooks (2000) offered the following definition, "Feminism is a movement to end sexism, sexist exploitation, and oppression" (p 1). Put in simpler terms, feminism has changed cultural and social responses of gender and sex. Frye (2000) wrote, "Such theory is distinguished from non-feminist thinking about women or gender by its general respect for women's own perspectives and authority, and its persistent attention to the workings of power structures which privilege men" (p. 195).

Notably, both women's and men's movements emerged out of feminism. First, we will take a look at women's movements and explore the rhetorical efforts used to garner support feminist ideologies. Women's movements are often described as "waves"—first, second, and third. The wave metaphor allows scholars to situate within a specific time frame and ideological preference; however, some scholars critique the metaphor as being inaccurate and overly simplistic (e.g., Nicholson, 2013). Nonetheless, waves are used to thematically organize feminism, and to organize, waves will be employed in this discussion.

Although the first wave of feminism is estimated to be from 1848–1920, the term "feminism" was not discussed in popular discourse until the 1910s (Nicholson, 2013). The women's rights movement emerged in the 1850s "advocated a single sexual standard for men and women, (primarily within marriage), dress reform, equal property and other legal rights, and higher education for women, especially in professions such as medicine and law" (Frye, 2000, p. 208). Although many women came together, clearly there were ideological differences that came to the surface through the first wave. Thus, the second wave of feminism emerged.

The 1960s were an important time in history, a time advocating for change and diversity in many ways. Important texts such as Simone de Beauvoir's *The Second Sex* (1952), and Betty Friedan's (1963) *The Feminine Mystique* characterized the transition into the second wave. de Beauvoir (1952) claimed "one is not born a woman, one becomes one," inspired important conversations around what it means culturally and socially to be the second sex. Friedan (2001) articulated the frustrations felt by many middle-class women who felt isolated and dissatisfied with domestic life. Similarly, Valerie Solanas (1967), who is often the characterization of radical feminism (see, e.g., Fahs, 2008; Haut, 2007; Lusty, 2009; Rowe, 2013; Third, 2006), wrote the *S.C.U.M. Manifesto*. To summarize in polite company, her document details how men are ruining the world and how women are the only option to save both the world and future generations. Meaningfully, out of the second wave many types of feminisms were born. To

name a few, womanism feminism, multiracial feminism, ecofeminism, separatism, etc.

Perhaps lesser known, men's movements were also established during the time of the second wave. Until that point, men were described in what I call "one note." That is, all men are the same, have the same issues, and believe the same way. Obviously, the establishment of men's movements shatters these assumptions. One type were profeminist movements, which were established for two reasons: (1) to support women's battles for equitable treatment and increase women's rights, and (2) to increase men's emotional development and capacities (Wood & Fixmer-Oraiz, 2017). Examples of profeminist groups are: NOMAS, ACT UP, the White Ribbon Campaign, Walk a Mile in Her Shoes, and Mentors in Violence Prevention (MVP). Another type of men's movements involve masculinist men's groups. These groups maintain that men and women are inherently different and that difference is so fundamental it should remain as such in practices and sometimes policies. Men's rights activists wish to restore traditional roles and views of masculinity. Father's rights groups take on issues of custody with their children and believe that fathers should be awarded 50% custody (not assumed as secondary parent). Other men's groups are mythopoetic men, Promise Keepers, and the Million Man March (Wood & Fixmer-Oraiz, 2017). Today, there is a continual pushback on traditional displays of masculinity, groups such as The Good Man Project are challenging roles of masculinity in society. For instance, on today's college campuses we see #*itsonus* as a social movement and men keeping other men accountable around sexual assault and prevention.

Conversely to how the first and second wave of feminism had women joining to support larger issues, the third wave of feminism is focused more on the individual. In fact, people who are more connected to organizing and ideology of the first two waves critique third wavers for being unorganized, vague, and consumer focused. Think for instance, about shirts you may have seen that state, "This is what a feminist looks like." This is an example of third-wave feminist rhetoric at work. Third-wave feminists push the boundaries of sexuality, expressions of femininity, and gender performance under the umbrella of being a feminist. Frye (2000) noted, "One feature of third-wave feminism is the centrality of anger, used as a mechanism to provide voice to girls *[sic]* who had been silenced in society and within feminism" (p. 474).

Organized examples of these over the past few years are the *#metoo* movement, *#timesup*, and *#askhermore*. Each of these hashtag movements center on gender pay and work inequality, sexual assault, and the theoretically systemic silences that pervade male dominated spaces (see Taylor & Canary, 2017). Hashtag trends are a way of organizing social movements. Communication scholars Chávez and Griffin (2014) explained that gender studies is "a field of study that emerges from activist efforts and grassroots social movements" (p. 262). I think we need to pay particular attention to the way that digital media is providing a "newer" platform for organizing.

Gender as Performed

Theoretically, the notion that gender is performed comes from a social constructionist perspective. That is, how we perform who we are is socially constructed or (re) produced learned behaviors. The interesting thing about gender, is that the process often starts before we are born. For instance, some people choose to find out the sex of their baby before it is born and the subsequently host a "gender reveal party." Although exciting to have everyone celebrate, critical scholars would question the need for such a party when the child really has yet to perform gender. Rather, the party is a "sex reveal party," based on biological markers that an ultrasound technician discovered. Moreover, discovering the sex of the baby often elucidates how people began to treat, think about, and talk to the baby even while in utero. For example, if we hear she's a girl perhaps we will soften our tone and we will talk about how pretty she will be; whereas, if he is a boy our tone will deepen, and we will note his physical strength. These communicative patters continue when the baby is born and only heighten as people around the baby continue to produce and (re)produce social structures of gendering (recall the theories discussed earlier).

When discussing gender as performed, few central scholars advocate this argument. In 1987, West and Zimmerman coined the term "doing gender." They noted that gender is not a noun, or something stagnant, rather it is a verb and a continual process and performance one makes in relation to their sex. Queer scholar Judith Butler (1990) problematized the a priori assumptions of gender performance and then the reproductions of those assumptions. She wrote, "On one hand, *representation* serves as

the operative term within a political process that seeks to extend visibility and legitimacy to women as political subjects; on the other hand, representation is a normative function of a language which is said either to reveal or to distort what is assumed to be true about the category of woman" (emphasis in original, p. 2). In other words, Butler questioned the controversial connection between representation and politics. Here, she specifically identified women, but ultimately asked for the queering of all performances as a political positive.

Another application of looking at the role of gender as performance could be explored through the method of discourse tracing (LeGreco & Tracy, 2009). Although it has not been used yet, its applicability is clear. According to LeGreco and Tracy (2009) "discourse tracing analyzes the formation, interpretation, and appropriation of discursive practices across micro, meso, and macro levels. In doing so, the method provides a language for studying social processes" (p. 1516). According to **gender performance**, and scaling up, microlevel discourses could be individual performances of gender. That is, on a daily basis one ponders what performances do people enact or resist. Mesolevel discourse could be explored in relation to family and friend groups, in other words, examining what influence these social groups have on individual performances. Last, macrolevel discourses contain the cultural and ideological presumptions of gender performance. For instance, consider the role dress codes have in (re)producing appropriateness of gender dress. Men are typically not told to wear dresses "below the knee" because the assumption is that men wear pants and not dresses in U.S. American culture.

Gender Diversity vs. Binary

Although stereotypes are often used to contextualize examples and to start with a foundation of understanding, it is imperative to break though the stereotypes to establish more complex ways of knowing. Gender studies often use the communicative markers of masculine and feminine. The extremes of both masculinity and femininity are commonly used in order to establish the binary of either/or. Although helpful in setting an initial foundation, **gender binary** is being problematized and its continued use challenged by scholars. In her article about the linguistic consequence of binary pronouns, Wayne (2005) situated the need to look at grammar as it denotes women secondary "*via-a-vis* men" (p. 85). For instance (s)he only exists in relation to he, and (s)he cannot be a Mr(s) without he(r) Mr. Even more progressive is the role that the binary pronoun system has in excluding queer voices. Wayne (2005) explained pronouns are "regulatory instruments to be assigned only when and where authorities deem the existence of a properly-sexed body or culturally acceptable lie … thus people who do not conform to a rigid two-sex system are relegated to the discursive purgatory and non-signification" (p. 87). The binary system is present and deeply rooted in grammar and is materially consequential.

Think, for instance, about how often a binary materially governs daily actions. If you are in a public space and need to use the restroom, you are often required to identify by using the male, female, or (if available) family restroom. In their study of trans* bodies in airport security Currah and Mulqueen (2011) talked about the assumptions and (in)security of gender presentation at the airport. They address the role that identification has in a two-sexed system—male or female. They wrote "the gender marker on a piece of state-issued ID can be troublesome: a transgender woman presenting herself as female at the airport, might, unlike other woman, have an M on her passport" (p. 560). In this case the assumption of gender presentation does not match how the person is performing their gender, and thus the individual is forced to either identify as trans* or miss their flight.

Masculinity

Often, when people hear "gender" they think the sole focus will be on women or expressions of femininity. Similarly, when people hear "race" they think of anything but Caucasian, and "sexual orientation" is anything but heterosexual. It is important to ascertain why this happens. Or, we should question why this is our auto response and then open our minds to gender being many forms. This is a form of silencing or privilege experienced by the dominant group. Katz (2012) in his TED Talk explained, "This is one of the ways that dominant systems maintain and reproduce themselves … because that's one of the key characteristics of power and privilege, the ability to go unexamined." Katz, who is also the creator of the MVP group has been a champion over the past few decades in asking men to get involved in gender issues and conversations.

Similar to Katz, I believe it is imperative to include everyone in conversations about gender. If you have a chance, watch the documentary *The Mask You Live In*. In this film, boys and men are asked to talk about what it means to be **masculine**. Statements such as "don't cry," "don't be a sissy," "stand up for yourself," and "be a man" qualify masculinity. In short, being a man is being anything but feminine. In this sense, feminine is what Trethewey (1999) deems "leaky emotions" because men have "disciplined bodies." Although her study is set in a workplace, the applicability can be at the societal level. Masculinity is about being strong, composed, aggressive, and independent. Therefore, there is not space for the "other" ways of being, knowing, and communicating. You may be asking why or if this is all by chance. Communication scholars would argue, no! These are socially constructed and learned behaviors.

Think back to when you were little and playing with different toys, which are typically gendered. The toys that you were given when you were little encouraged a certain type of play and communicative opportunities. Toys that are stereotypically given to girls are items such as dolls, play kitchens, and other items that encourage pretending. The goal at the end of playtime? It is collaboration through communication. In other words, no one really wins at playing dolls or making pretend breakfast, communication occurred about how to collaboratively have everyone work together to enjoy the experience. For this scene you can picture the all too popular movie scene where the little girl is sitting in her pink room, at a mini-table, surrounded by her stuffed animals having a tea party. She speaks to the animals as if they are speaking back to her.

On the other hand, we have what are typically identified as "boys' toys." Toys in this realm are typically Legos, race cars, and sporting gear. The ultimate goal at the end it to build something the tallest, to drive the fastest, or to win an event. Therefore, communication patterns learned through this type of play center on independence and winning. In 1976, Sattel wrote an article entitled "The Inexpressive Male: Tragedy or Sexual Politics?" If you pick up this article, the content is still as tangible today as it was in 1976. Sattel comments on silence as a cornerstone of masculine power, especially in the workplace. However, he notes that silence then becomes problematic in heteronormative intimate relationships. He explains that women typically expect more communicative feedback in their day-to-day than men are socialized to give. Thus, highlighting tensions of not only the gender binary, but also socializing masculinity in one way.

Violence

Similar to the term "masculinity," the term "violence" often elicits thoughts about men-on-men or men-on-women bodies (see also: Chapter 15). To put it another way, violence is a problem that male bodies perpetuate. I do think that it is important to give time and validate the situations described above; however, it is also important to examine critically the reality of those scenarios. Let us continue our conversation around masculinity. What has already been established is that masculinity is about strength and winning. As such, one could argue that the way we train boys to communicate in relation to and with

---

Box 12.1 Ethical Issues

Feminist communication scholars have offered several approaches to ethics that are intended to provide more inclusive sets of ethical principles for guiding behavior and decisions than those viewed as reflective of traditional male, hetero-normative perspectives. Johannesen et al. (2008) note, "feminist ethicists question the privileging of rationality over emotion, of universality and detachment over particularity and engagement, of the public sphere of discourse over the private sphere, and of individualism over relationship" (p. 203). We highlight three such approaches below.

- **An Ethic of Care**

  Carol Gilligan (1982) introduced an ethic of care in her critique of moral development stage models that she argued were based on male-dominated research that inadequately addressed unique values priorities and experiences of women. She contrasted an ethic of care with an ethic of justice, which she claimed marginalized relational principles in favor of autonomy and independence. Gilligan's assertions have been widely debated, as well as empirically investigated, since her original publication. Many ethicists argue that she set up a false dichotomy and that her assertions actually reify inaccurate gender assumptions. Nevertheless, proposing an ethic of care opened the scholarly conversation about inclusive ethical principles, valuing the role of relationships in ethics, and considering how diverse life experiences impact people's ethics.

- **Telling It Slant**

  "Telling it slant" is the term used by some feminist communication scholars to describe the practice of not being entirely truthful out of necessity. The phrase is taken from an Emily Dickinson poem. According to Gillian Michell (1984), this is a form of lying that is ethical and justifiable because women must use it when they function in male-dominated, sexist contexts. For example, a woman might excuse herself from a meeting to "deal with an emergency," although the "emergency" is actually her need to pump breast milk for her child due to leaking breasts. Breast pumping scheduling is not truthfully what one would consider an "emergency." However, in a professional context with predominantly male colleagues, a woman might feel that describing her need to leave a meeting for a length of time can only be justified by an "emergency," rather than her biological and relational role as a mother who provides breast milk to her child. As gender ethics have developed to account for nonbinary approaches to gender, telling it slant likely describes a diverse array of messages that people use to avoid disclosing their personal situations that do not conform with expectations.

- **Feminist Ethics for Journalists**

  Sandra Davidson Scott (1993) proposes four ethical guidelines for journalists:

  - Listen to one's emotions.
  - Quit rationalizing.
  - See situations with moral imagination from viewpoint of victims, families, and audience.
  - Trust emotions.

  These guidelines align with an ethic of care that prioritizes relationships, experience, and emotion over universal principles and autonomous decision-making.

---

others encourages violence (albeit a slippery slope). For instance, if being masculine is about being strong and not weak, in a situation of violence then masculinity is about upholding appearances of strength.

On the other hand, and what I think is a more theoretically engaging conversation is to think about the statistics of reporting. Is it that male bodies really commit more crimes than female bodies? Or, are men in male bodies socialized to report less than female bodies? Imagine for instance a man went to his friends and said, "my wife or girlfriend beat me up." Whenever I play out this scenario in my classroom, this is when the class typically laughs. They laugh not because violence is funny. Rather, they laugh because they cannot envision a woman beating up a man. I posit that it is this social response that keeps our statistics one-sided in reporting. In other words, being a "victim" is feminine and perpetrator is masculine.

Moreover, to take the conversation out of bodies and into the gendering of communication, violence in this sense is engendered. For instance, when I was conducting my dissertation research, I was looking at the organizing of sex for sale (i.e., sex trafficking and prostitution) through both policy-as-written and policy-as-practice. Important to discuss here is the fact that the policy-as-written did not specifically identify a particular sexed body with regard to sex selling, sex buying, or sex brokering. However, when people talked about sex for sale, they almost exclusively talked about sex sellers as women and sex buyers as men. Thus, one finding was that sex for sale is a woman's problem. When I asked if men sell sex and if that is considered prostitution, I was typically met with a hard "no" or a reframing of the issue. For instance, male sex for sale was often termed "male lewdness" for two reasons: (1) in a same sex situation, the exchange was seen as consensual because "all men want sex," and (2) police officers did not want to have to go undercover in order to catch men trying to sell sex. Importantly, "johns stings," which is where female undercover officers are used to catch men in solicitations are common across the country. To return to engendering violence, sex for sale, through the way that criminalization is carried out, is a woman's issue.

Another important consideration around violence expands to experiences of LGBT (lesbian-gay-bisexual-trans*) persons. Nearly 40% of homeless youth identify as LGBT. Furthermore, "half of gay teens report a negative reaction from their family, and 26 percent of them are actually kicked out of their house" (Houston, 2009, p. 17). In other words, gender/sex nonconforming leads to potential violence from others. Even instances of cyber-bullying are considered violent.

Gender in Communication Praxis

The scope of this chapter was not meant to be exhaustive, rather to highlight exemplary work, theories, and methods used in gender and communication research. The following section highlights particularly salient topics where gender research is being conducted.

Family

Conceivably, the first place we learn about gender and gender roles is through our families. As an aside, the structures that often define family (e.g., single parent, step-families, extended, etc.) are not going to be take up here. By family I mean the people who surround you during formative years. In other words, we learn how to be "us" through the people we are predominantly surrounded by. Within gender and communication research, studies of family communication often include who is performing what labor in and out of the house.

In her satirical essay, Syfers (2000) wrote, "As I thought about him while I was ironing one evening, it suddenly occurred to me that I, too, would like to have a wife" (p. 387). Syfers details the many support roles played by women in the home and in the end proclaimed, "My God, who *wouldn't* want a wife?" (emphasis in original, p. 389). Although satirical, this piece highlights traditional expectations of division of labor in the home according to gender roles. Often, domestic labor (housework, support work, and childcare) are relegated to female bodies in the home (Hochschild, 2003). Increasingly, more families have dual-incomes and often the domestic labor roles still fall to the woman in a heteronormative relationship (Parker & Livingston, 2016).

Some may argue that the role of childcare is assigned to women because of the biological realty that female bodies can carry babies, whereas, male bodies of course cannot. This argument aside, it's important to ask do domestic labor tasks still unfold in the same way under situations of adoption or foster care when neither body physically labored a baby. Furthermore, the exercise of family leave policies. It was not until recently that family leave was just that, "family leave." This type of leave was solely identified as maternity leave. The policy then materializes the assumptions that only female bodies can take time to be with babies after delivery. Peterson and Albrecht (1999) explained, "First, although a pregnancy—the actual reason for maternity leave—involves at least three parties (i.e., mother-father-child), the policy focuses on only one part of this triad, the female employee, or mother" (p. 176). In this sense, individuals are articulated as gendered subjects. Cheney and Tompkins (1988) wrote, "Names and titles given to textual subjects are 'important as condensed symbols for the essences of things … [they] tell us not only who people are but also how we should act toward them" (p. 467). In this sense, outside institutional structures often inform how we can or cannot organize our family structures.

Education

The topic of education can be explored in a few ways. Scholars could explore educational structures such as programmatic outcomes or dress codes. Scholars could also explore historical accounts of educational knowledge and hidden curricula. Scholars can also explore interpersonal interaction in the classroom and potential bullying or harassment that can also be linked back to gender. The following are exemplars.

First, is the role gender socialization plays in our educational journeys. At some point along the way girls were told that "boys are better at math" and boys were encouraged to be better at math. For instance, all through my educational journey I just assumed I was "bad at math" because my older brother, who is now an engineer, was always better than me. However, it was not until recently where I reflected on the fact that I was always placed in the honors and advanced math classes. I can conclude that it was not necessarily that I am not good at math, just perhaps not as interested in math as I was in other subjects. A more critical view would examine the discourse along my route to determine if I was ushered into humanities over sciences. Importantly, I was not alone in this experience. Scholars who study engineering highlight the extreme culture of masculinity in their collegiate experience (Faulkner, 2000; Godfrey & Parker, 2010; Taylor, 2013). At this point, you should be asking whether we choose our educational outcomes or whether we are the subjects of social preference.

Work

Ashcraft (2005) stated "organizations are fundamentally gendered social formations, and gender is a constitutive principle of organizing" (p. 148). In other words, organizations are gendered, and gender organizes. To explore this concept in a more tangible way, we can look at workplaces. Work is an interesting concept. Often when we meet people for the first time, we ask their name followed by "what do you do?" What follows an answering of the question is a snap judgment made the interested party on how much or in what ways are they contributing to society. Connecting to the earlier consideration of education, people are socialized into career paths. For instance, think about spotlighting gender in occupations: male–nurse, female–doctor, male–nanny, female–police officer. Spotlighting gender assumes that something is out of the ordinary within the structure.

In a nuanced study, Ashcraft (2007) looked at the roles of identity and gender as axes for organizational divisions of work. Ashcraft articulates her nod toward and appreciation for discourse as materially consequential (citing poststructural thought). Her study examines the multifaceted discursive identities of airline pilots. Of importance here is the juxtaposition of where pilots do their work (cockpit) and being a female airline pilot. The work of discourse examined how pilots experienced their work. She wrote, "The eventually triumphant claim that an airline pilot's work is 'naturally' manly and professional was staked upon a particular form of white masculinity … and the image overhaul generated tangible effects" (p. 18). Ashcraft describes the relegation of female pilots from cockpit to cabin as the tangible effect of airline pilot discourse. Thus, the social construction of masculinity reigns supreme in the skies.

Conclusion

One of the exciting realties about studying gender in communication is that the communicative landscape is always changing. The way that we talk about gender is constantly shifting and thus our understandings about the way that people experience and perform gender are expanding. Our gender performances exist in relation to the larger social systems that are in play. At first glance, you may assume you identify one way or another, but I hope after a critical glance you realize that we are all a bit androgywnous in our communication patterns. In sum, gender/sex is about real people and real-life experiences. The material consequences of our gendered worlds are apparent in our educational systems, families, and work-spaces. We must be critical evaluators in what and how we are (re)producing gendered spaces.

CHAPTER 13

Interpersonal and Relational Communication

Perry M. Pauley, Colter D. Ray, Brian H. Spitzberg, & Matthew Savage

---

LEARNING OBJECTIVES

After reading this chapter, you should be able to do the following:

- Identify and differentiate interpersonal communication from other contexts and levels of communication study (e.g., public, mass, group).

- Identify and differentiate proximal and distal factors influencing interpersonal communication.

- Specify how personality and individual traits influence individuals' approaches to interpersonal communication.

- Apply assumptions associated with norms (derived from cultural and gendered expectations) to specify how they lead to interpersonal communication challenges.

- Understand how contextual factors, such as emotion and environment, influence interpersonal communication.

- Identify and differentiate elements of attachment theory and how they influence interpersonal communication and relationships.

- Specify the different implications of attachment theory, social support, affection exchange theory, and uncertainty reduction theory for relationship development.

- Identify the pathways whereby interpersonal communication can facilitate positive psychological and physical health outcomes.

- Specify the rationale underlying the view of communication competence as an impression rather than an ability.

- Identify and differentiate appropriateness and effectiveness as criteria of competent communication.

- Identify and differentiate the components of the interpersonal communication competence model and their interrelationships with relationship outcomes.

THINK FOR A MOMENT ABOUT MOST OF THE INTER-
action you have during any given day. You might start out your day by sending a text message to a friend to see what he or she is doing. Next, you might go to school because you need to discuss a difficult assignment with one of your professors. After school, you might go to work for your latest performance review with your boss. After work, you might go out on a date with someone you care about. Even though the contexts—and undoubtedly the contents—of these interactions are quite different, there is one thing that they all have in common: These are all interactions that take place *between people*. In other words, these are all instances of something we call interpersonal communication.

Defining Interpersonal Communication

It sounds fairly obvious to say that communication occurs between people, so what distinguishes *interpersonal* communication from other forms of communication? One of the main features is the number of people involved, often referred to as the **levels perspective** toward communication (see **Table 13.1**). Differences in levels or quantities of communicators influence the nature of the communication and the types of relationships possible. You might have noticed that all the hypothetical examples focus on you (as a hypothetical student) and one other person, and this distinction is appropriate with how most scholars define interpersonal communication: interactions involving two people. Even though many of the same principles

of communication are at play in many encounters (e.g., the goal of interaction is the transmission of meaning; communicators encode and decode messages), the addition of just one person to a dyad can significantly alter the dynamic of the interaction (Beebe & Masterson, 2000). Interactions within families provide an excellent example. Within each family unit, the individual members of the family maintain interpersonal relationships with one another (e.g., sibling–sibling, father–daughter, and parent–parent relationships), but the family is not merely the sum of these individual relationships. When all the family members are together, the interaction takes on a group communication dynamic that is very different from the kinds of communication that take place within the individual dyads. This observation—that a family is simultaneously a collection of individual interpersonal relationships and a unique collective with its own group dynamic—is one of the underlying premises of family systems theory (see Noller & Fitzpatrick, 1993).

Interpersonal communication is also different from the kinds of communication that take place in groups with larger numbers of people such as, for example, public communication and mass communication. As anyone who has ever taken a speech class can attest, public speaking is very different in both content and character from private speech. Public speaking is generally defined as one individual addressing a group of 12 or more people, although it is worth noting that the number of people is generally less important than the roles assigned to communicators. Most public speaking opportunities typically involve a clear distinction between one (or more)

TABLE 13.1: Definitions of Interpersonal Communication

Author(s)	Definition
Weaver (1949)	"The word *communication* will be used here in a very broad sense to include all of the procedures by which one mind may affect another." (p. 95)
Canary, Cody, & Manusov (2008)	"The exchange of symbols used, at least in part, in the joint pursuit of interpersonal goals." (p. 4)
Floyd (2011)	"Communication that occurs between two people within the context of their relationship and that, as it evolves, helps them to negotiate and define their relationship." (p. 21)
Pearson & Spitzberg (1990)	"The process of transaction between people from which meaning is mutually derived." (p. 7)
Watzlawick, Beavin, & Jackson (1967)	"Two or more communicants in the process of, or at the level of, defining the nature of their relationship." (p. 121, about an *interactional system*)

communicator(s) who is a designated speaker and another group of communicators who are the audience. Over the last several decades, several scholars have examined the role that communication apprehension plays in public speaking scenarios. Sawyer and Behnke (2009) detailed the progression of this research over the course of the last 70 years. Starting in the 1950s, instructors in public speaking courses began to develop systematic techniques to assess how students felt, both objectively (through physiological indices such as heart rate and hormone fluctuation) and subjectively (primarily through self-report measures of nervousness and tension) over the duration of a public speaking course. Results from this line of research have revealed that most students—including those who are relatively comfortable engaging in personal or small group conversations—experience some degree of anxiety while speaking publicly. Although this anxiety tends to decrease with time and exposure to public speaking opportunities (a process known as systematic desensitization), even professional speakers occasionally experience communication apprehension.

Mass communication is both different from and similar to aspects of public and interpersonal communication. First, in terms of public communication, mass communication is intended for a large audience; think of the number of mass media outlets that boast large national or international audiences. The structure of mass communication is also similar to the flow of information in public communication settings insofar as there is a clear "speaker" (or message source) and a clear audience (the media consumers). Unlike in public communication contexts, in mass communication contexts the members of the audience are geographically dispersed (e.g., people often read books or blogs or watch television shows by themselves). As a result, audience members sometimes feel like they are having private conversations with authors, television personalities, or even fictional characters because of the ways in which these forms of communication are typically consumed. The perceived closeness of these interactions can lead to something known as a parasocial interaction—the belief, on the part of the audience member, that he or she has gained the kind of personal knowledge about the originator of the message that would be typical in an interpersonal relationship (Rumpf, 2012). Although this perception is usually harmless (e.g., viewers might really feel like they can "trust" one newscaster and will exclusively watch the news when she or he is

on air), it can lead to very negative outcomes in some cases. Robin Roberts, coanchor of the ABC news program *Good Morning America*, was threatened by a stalker right outside of the studio, a man who was apparently upset over something Roberts had said or done while on the air (Rosenberg, 2014).

Most forms of communication have some defining features in common with interpersonal communication, but interpersonal communication remains distinct from other forms of interaction. Thus far, interpersonal communication has been identified primarily by what it is *not; the only identifying feature of interaction that essentially defines interpersonal communication is that it occurs between two people.* This conceptual ambiguity is owed to two underlying factors. First, there is not critical consensus within the scholarly community about the real meaning of the phrase "interpersonal communication"; in fact, some scholars have even argued that the two-person distinction is unnecessary (see Knapp & Daly, 2011, for review). As can be seen in **Table 13.1**, the definitions of interpersonal communication that exist vary widely. The second reason for the conceptual ambiguity surrounding interpersonal communication is that it is difficult, in some cases, to separate interpersonal communication from relational communication. For the purpose of this chapter, **interpersonal communication** will be defined as *the process of interaction,* and *relationships (or relational communication)* will be defined as *the product of interpersonal interaction—the coconstruction of a relational identity.* Toward that end, the sections in this chapter will detail several factors that influence the process by which individuals interact with each other in a variety of contexts; the sections will then examine how relationships take shape. This discussion begins with the individual communicator, along with the distal and proximal factors that influence the ways that individual approaches interaction.

The Communicator: Distal and Proximal Influences on Communication Behaviors

Although there are countless factors that influence the ways individuals approach interpersonal interaction, many can be classified according to their relative duration (see Cupach & Canary, 2007). Some factors, such as personality traits or cultural beliefs, tend to be relatively stable over long periods of time and lead to consistent (i.e., predictable) outcomes. These kinds of long-term influences can be classified as **distal influences**. Conversely, some factors, such as the physical context for an interaction or an individual's mood, change relatively frequently and produce effects that are time limited. These factors can be thought of as **proximal influences**. In the following sections, each of these influences will be reviewed, in turn.

Distal Factors

Personality Traits

Understanding the basis of human personality traits has been a goal of researchers in the social sciences, particularly in psychology, for the last several decades. **Traits** are relatively enduring individual differences or characteristics. Although countless personality typologies have been proposed, one has gained the greatest traction in communication studies. The traits within this typology, known as "**the Big Five**" (Fleeson & Gallagher, 2009; Goldberg, 1993; Liu & Campbell, 2017), include *openness* (particularly to new ideas and experiences), *conscientiousness* (being orderly, dependable, and goal-oriented), *extraversion* (possessing a friendly and outgoing demeanor), *agreeableness* (being trustworthy, empathic, and sincere), and *neuroticism* (being nervous/anxious, self-conscious, and sometimes hostile). Daly (2011b) notes that some of the earliest social scientific studies in the field of communication (i.e., the aforementioned studies about communication apprehension—the public speaking studies), were based, in part, on understanding how personality affects communication. Since that time, however, personality's role in human interaction has received comparatively less attention from communication scholars. This is surprising, particularly given the role that personality and personality compatibility play in forming relationships. When people seek long-term romantic partners, personality is one of the leading characteristics on which people base their decisions. Dating websites such as eHarmony.com, Match.com, and Chemistry.com are all acutely aware of the importance of personality in terms of interpersonal compatibility; as anyone who has ever used one of these dating resources will tell you, all have lengthy personality profiles that users are required to complete before they can begin meeting potential partners online. But what does all this personality data mean?

Helen Fisher, a cultural anthropologist and the scientific consultant for the websites Match.com and Chemistry.com, set out to explore the underpinnings of personality and the influence of personality traits on interpersonal compatibility with a group of her colleagues (Brown, Acevedo, & Fisher, 2013). Using data from over 34,000 Chemistry.com users' personality profiles as the starting point for their research, the members of the team were able to determine that four key personality traits—factors they labeled curious/energetic, cautious/compliant, analytical/tough-minded, and prosocial/empathic—successfully discriminated between participants' personality types. Although this finding was noteworthy by itself, it was not novel; personality inventories (like the aforementioned Big Five) have existed for more than a century, and researchers from across the social sciences have utilized them to classify individuals into personality groups with a high degree of consistency (for an excellent review and comparison of scientific personality measures, see Zuckerman, Kuhlman, Joireman, Teta, & Kraft, 1993). Instead, the novel aspect of Brown et al.'s (2013) research was the underlying hypothesis that various biological systems contribute to the development and manifestation of each of these personality types. In a pair of follow-up studies that used fMRI brain-scanning technology, the researchers were able to partially confirm what Fisher (the creator of the personality inventory) had long suspected: Curious/energetic individuals demonstrate greater sensitivity to dopamine (a neurotransmitter associated with reward/reinforcement), and prosocial/empathic individuals demonstrate greater sensitivity in the activation of **mirror neurons** (one of the key neural pathways by which humans identify with the pain or distress of others, the ability underlying empathy). Results from this particular study add to a growing number of studies that have explored the link between biological processes and personality traits.

Although it might seem obvious that personality characteristics are influenced by biological processes, the claim that biology influences personality has been a source of debate in communication studies for nearly 20 years. This difficulty was influenced, in part, by the introduction of the communibiological paradigm (Beatty & McCroskey, 2000; Hazel, Karst, Saezkleriga, Wongprasert, & Ayres, 2017). The **communibiological paradigm** starts with the premise that communication behaviors are influenced by personality traits and further claims that personality characteristics are heritable given their biological underpinnings. To this point, these claims are certainly not controversial and are consistent with much of the research about personality traits from other disciplines. The final claim of communibiology, the one that caused most communication scholars to balk at the paradigm (or to reject the notion of biological influence at all), is that personality traits (and their corresponding biological mechanisms) account for 80% of communication behaviors, although many meta-analyses suggest rates closer to 40 to 50%. As McCroskey and Beatty (2000) note, much of the communication research done throughout the 20th century was based on social learning models of interaction, such as Bandura's (1998) **social cognitive theory**, which presumes that behavior is mediated by mental appraisals and environmentally learned behaviors. Social cognitive studies assume that communication behavior is primarily learned by observing how others deal with similar kinds of relationships and/or situations. Among the communication behaviors that people learn through observation are cultural norms and gendered expectations for communication (and more about those sociocultural attributes will be provided later).

This discussion gets at one of the most fundamental debates in the social sciences over the last several decades: the question of nature versus nurture (a term widely attributed to Sir Francis Galton, 1875). Communibiology then would stand on the nature side of this issue with its claim that biologically linked personality traits account for as much as 80% of behavior. Social learning theories would stand on the other side of the debate with the claims that humans acquire behavior by observing the actions of others (although it should be noted here that many social learning theorists do not assume that people are born *tabula rasa*). Here is how the claims work in reality. Studies of newlyweds' conflict styles reveal that newly married individuals tend to engage in the same kinds of conflict behaviors they witnessed in their families of origin (Amato, 1996; Dennison, Koerner, & Segrin, 2014). Unfortunately, this **intergenerational transmission hypothesis** seems to be stronger for negative, as opposed to positive, conflict behaviors. From a biology/personality perspective, this similarity in conflict styles could be attributed to heritable biological systems that reinforce certain personality characteristics—those that, in this case, lead to negative and/or hostile conflict episodes. From a social learning perspective, it could be argued that newlyweds acquire these negative conflict skills by observing their parents' dysfunctional conflict styles during their childhood. Which perspective is correct, then?

The current thinking on this question is that the old **nature versus nurture paradigm** is outdated and that human behavior is actually a combination of both biologically linked personality characteristics and observational learning (Condit, 2000a, 2000b). In fact, the idea of a gene-by-environment interaction has received a great deal of empirical attention lately (Floyd & Denes, 2015; see also Condit, 2000b). According to this perspective, individuals are indeed born with a biological predisposition toward certain traits, but environmental factors can either exacerbate or attenuate these genetic predilections. Research on the oxytocin receptor gene by Floyd and Denes (2015) provides an excellent example of this logic. Results from that study revealed that some individuals have a greater sensitivity to **oxytocin**—a neurotransmitter that has been implicated in feelings of interpersonal closeness and intimacy—because of the presence of a specific gene in their DNA. As might be expected, individuals with this specific oxytocin receptor gene were also generally rated as more affectionate, but the link between genetics and behavior is moderated by environmental factors. Among all participants with enhanced oxytocin receptivity (as determined by their genes), those who were raised in an environment that fostered a secure attachment style (more about that later) were the most affectionate in the entire study. Results from this study support the nature *and* nurture perspective; biological traits certainly influence personality and behavior, but these factors are not deterministic. Instead, it takes the combination of genetic and environmental (i.e., learned) factors to really understand interpersonal interaction. With that in mind, we will turn our attention to culture and gender—two learned systems that have been investigated widely in the field of interpersonal communication.

Culture and Gender

Studies linking gender to interpersonal interaction are not nearly as consistent as those that have investigated cultural influences. Whereas most scholars tend to agree that culture affects interpersonal communication, the influence of gender is debated. On one hand, some scholars (using primarily linguistic analyses) have concluded that men's and women's approaches to communication are pretty different (e.g., Tannen, 1990; Wood, 1997). Scholars advocating this perspective have even asserted that men and women use different forms of language—sometimes called **genderlects** (a portmanteau of *gender* and *dialect*)—when communicating (Tannen, 1990). The claim that gender produces profound differences in the ways that individuals communicate has a fair amount in common with the various approaches to understanding culture mentioned earlier; men and women represent different cultural communities, each with different expectations for behavior, including appropriate forms of speech (Wood, 1997).

Not surprisingly, the "different cultures" approach to communication has generated a fair amount of discussion within the scholarly community (Metts, 1997). At least a portion of this ongoing discussion can be attributed to the publication of John Gray's (commercially successful but largely baseless) book *Men Are From Mars, Women Are From Venus* in 1992. In this particular book, Gray greatly exaggerates the different cultures notion, arriving at the conclusion that these differences between men and women are so great that they might as well be from different planets. Of course, this is not what credible communication scholars such as Wood (2002) had in mind when arguing in favor of the different cultures approach. Different cultures might have different customs, different norms for interaction, and different systems of belief, but a person from Japan would never logically be considered a different species than a person from Argentina. Even though they might show it in different ways, Japanese and Argentine people experience the same basic human emotions, have the same underlying desires for happiness, and seek relationships with others with whom they share important similarities.

As Wood (2002) notes, there are indeed differences in the things that men and women want from relationships, and there are even differences in the ways that men and women communicate. In terms of magnitude, most of these differences are relatively small. As Dindia (2006) put it, "Men are from North Dakota, Women are from South Dakota." At the end of the day, both men and women seek secure, satisfying, and emotionally supportive relationships. Although research has shown that men and women sometimes think about these constructs slightly differently (e.g., men typically consider tangible assistance as the best form of social support whereas women typically prefer esteem support; Burleson, 2003), the same basic desires guide how men and women engage in interpersonal communication.

Proximal Factors

Emotion

Communicators' relatively stable characteristics are not the only influences on interpersonal interactions. In addition to individual traits, several factors of the situation also influence the ways that people approach interaction. Without question, emotion is one such factor that has received a great deal of empirical attention. According to Richard Lazarus (1991), an **emotional state** is "a transient reaction to specific encounters with the environment, one that comes and goes depending on particular situations" (p. 47). Emotions have four main characteristics according to Lazarus: *action tendencies* (the private behaviors that emotions stimulate), *physiological reactions* (changes in blood pressure, skin temperature, or sweat that accompany emotions such as anger or sadness), *subjective experience* (the labels that people give to the emotions they experience), and *environmental context* (the ways that individuals process and react to emotional stimuli based on social factors).

The experience of a particular emotion can have a profound experience on an individual's communication skills and abilities. Perhaps not surprisingly, positive emotions, such as happiness and contentment, have been associated with prosocial behavior and a desire to expand one's social circle, whereas negative emotions, like anger and hostility, have been associated with increases in egotism, selfish individualism, and ultimately relational negativism (Hamilton, Buck, Chory, Beatty, & Patrylak, 2009). Other studies have determined that jealousy, a negative emotion that includes feelings of anger, sadness, and fear, significantly affects communication in relationships. In a series of studies, Guerrero and Andersen (1998) determined that jealousy tends to motivate individuals to engage in a host of negative communicative behaviors, including surveillance and restriction, avoidance of the partner, negative communication toward or about the rival, violent or threatening (both verbally and physically) behavior, verbal aggression, and even counterjealousy inductions. The overarching message of studies examining how emotion affects communication is relatively straightforward: As anyone who has ever felt his or her face flush with intense anger or feelings of jealousy can likely attest, emotions are extremely powerful and can motivate individuals to engage in behaviors, both positive and negative, that can have lasting repercussions in their personal relationships.

Context/Environment

As with emotion, the physical environment in which an interaction occurs is a transient factor that tends to affect the approach people have to an interaction. Even though you might not have considered the effect that the physical environment has on interaction, the study of specific environments—including the emotions they evoke and the kinds of interaction they foster—is an established area of investigation for communication scholars. Consider the example of Las Vegas casinos: Everything inside of a major casino is specifically engineered to achieve a certain effect. Psychologist Mark Griffiths, director of the international gaming research unit at Nottingham Trent University, has spent most of his career studying the environmental cues that designers employ to lure—and keep—gamblers in casinos. Most people are familiar with some of the more obvious physical cues within casinos such as, for example, the conspicuous lack of natural light and clocks. Griffiths's (2013) research has revealed much more than those factors, though. The darkness of casinos does not only conceal the time of day from gamblers; it also highlights the amount of light that gaming machines generate. Gaming machines are designed so that jackpots are very loud; in addition to the sound of coins hitting a metal pan, most machines now include sirens and flashing lights. Why is that, you might ask?—so that potential gamblers walking through casinos on a busy night are overwhelmed with the sound of winning everywhere. Just walking through a casino is part of its psychology; casinos are intentionally laid out like mazes, and non-gaming attractions such as restaurants and theaters are often buried deep within the labyrinth so that patrons can be lured into the casino by row after row of shiny, noisy machines. Griffiths has found that even the *scent* of the machine can have an effect on gamblers' psychology; machines that have been designed to emit pleasant odors generate more revenue than machines that are not equipped with scent technology.

Even though most of our personal spaces are not designed with the same level of scrutiny and precision that casinos are, there is no denying that physical environments affect both mood and interaction. Think about environments that you would associate with each of the following adjectives: peaceful, romantic, serious, exciting. The truth is that some environments are very useful for facilitating interaction, and others are intentionally designed to discourage it. When you picture a romantic environment, for example, you likely picture a place where you could sit side by side or face to face with your romantic partner and have an intimate conversation. Spaces like these are called **sociopetal space** because they are designed to facilitate interaction (Sommer, 1967). Now recall the place you think of when you imagine a serious spot. There is a chance you might have thought of a place like a classroom or a religious site, even though those spaces serve different purposes. They have many features in common: People generally sit in rows and face away from one another and toward a speaker in the front of the room. Environments like these are generally called **sociofugal space** because they are designed to discourage interaction (Sommer, 1967). Of course, the arrangement of physical objects is not the only environmental factor that affects communication; factors such as noise, degree of crowding, and temperature all affect how people feel about a place, the likelihood they will feel comfortable conversing, and the length of time they will stay.

An alternative way of thinking of contextual proximal factors that affect personal relationships is how people find one another when seeking romance or attraction. At present, as much as a third of U.S. married adults met originally online (Cacioppo, Cacioppo, Gonzaga, Ogburn, & VanderWeele, 2013). Some research indicates that those who meet online are more satisfied and less likely to break up (Cacioppo et al., 2013) and other research indicates that those who meet first online are more likely to break up (Paul, 2014). Technologically mediated contexts of interaction affect how we communicate immediacy and how we hope to develop intimacy (Spitzberg, 2006).

Relational Communication

If interpersonal communication helps us understand the skills we need to be successful communicators, then relationships are the product of successful interpersonal communication. Not all relationships are the same, though; Berscheid and Peplau (1983) have classified personal relationships by the degree of **interdependence** that individuals within those relationships share—that is, by the degree to which one person's goals or outcomes depend on the actions of another person or persons. Following this typology, the most basic, and least personal, relationships are known as role relationships. **Role relationships** are generally defined by the social roles that people play in certain situations, or the degree to which the role is relatively common and generic within a society. For example, customers and cashiers rely on each other to fulfill their roles, but there is generally nothing that makes a customer–cashier pairing unique. Most students engage their professors from a role relationship—that is, their behavior is relatively rule and role scripted by the nature of the institutional context: raising a hand to speak, speaking on curricular topics, avoiding disruptive or inattentive behaviors, and so forth. The second classification of relationships, **interpersonal relationships**, consists of relationships that are more intimate than role relationships. Interpersonal relationships involve repeated interactions, a feeling of uniqueness about the relationship, and some degree of personal (as opposed to just role) interdependence. Finally, **personal relationships** are the most intimate and significant relationships that people typically develop throughout their lifetimes. Personal relationships are highly interdependent, and the parties involved in those relationships see one another as irreplaceable (Guerrero, Andersen, & Afifi, 2011).

Recent scholarly attention has focused on the importance of personal relationships in people's day-to-day lives. Some scholars (Cohen, Gottlieb, & Underwood, 2000) have suggested that Émile Durkheim's observation—that Industrial Revolution–era factory workers with few social ties were more likely to end their own lives than workers with large social networks—began the shift in thinking that has come to define the modern study of personal relationships. Nearly 50 years later, Harry Harlow's observations of rhesus monkeys refined the field even further. In those studies, Harlow separated infant monkeys from their mothers and substituted two different surrogate "mothers." Both of these mother mannequins were simple wire frames, but the things they offered to the babies were very different. One mannequin had a bottle of milk attached to the chest so that the baby monkeys could nurse. The other mannequin was covered in layers of soft terrycloth and was available for snuggling and comfort only. Without exception, the baby monkeys would spend only as much time as they needed to eat with the bottle-only mannequin, and as soon as they were full, they would run to the cloth-covered mannequin to seek comfort and shelter. The baby monkeys seemed to bond with the cloth-covered mannequin who was unable to nurse them and meet their physical needs. To Harlow and his research team, the baby monkeys' tendency to spend more time with the "mother" who met their emotional needs suggested that the comfort and nurturance a mother provides was even more significant to the babies than the provision of food.

The current thinking on human relationships is deeply rooted in the observations of those earlier studies. From Harlow's time until the present, the thinking about personal relationships is that they constitute a fundamental human need; this is a claim that is reflected in the need-to-belong perspective (Baumeister & Leary, 1995). This perspective argues that humans, like Harlow's monkeys, have an innate need to form attachments with others. This need for personal connection is carried throughout the lifespan and translates into a series of behaviors designed to facilitate and maintain significant personal connections with other humans. In the following sections, we will review significant theories and constructs that have helped to understand how and why relationships leave an indelible mark on us all.

Lifespan Attachments

Early Childhood Relationships: Attachment

John Bowlby, a contemporary of Harry Harlow, developed a very influential theoretic perspective that continues to influence how scholars from across the social sciences think about relationships between infants and their caregivers. Attachment theory (Bowlby, 1969/1981) begins with the infant–caregiver relationship, but the reach of theory extends far beyond that single relational context. The premise of the theory is that children, beginning in infancy, develop internal working models of both themselves and the people around them. These internal working models are based, in large part, on caregivers' responses to infants' distress. When distress is met with consistent care and nurture, infants begin to internalize positive notions of both self and other; in other words, children believe that they are worthy of others' love and attention, and they begin to trust others to help them when they face a challenge. When infants experience distress and receive either no comfort or inconsistent levels of comfort, they begin to develop negative internal models of self and other. According to attachment theory, these internal working models together lead to the development of one of three attachment styles: secure, avoidant, and anxious-ambivalent.

Although attachment theory was originally proposed as a way to explain child-caregiver relationships, several researchers, including Hazan and Shaver (1987) and Bartholomew and Horowitz (1991), have extended the basic principles of the attachment process into adult relationships. From the adult relationships perspective, an individual's **attachment style** begins to emerge during childhood in accordance with the processes outlined by Bowlby. Experiences during adolescence and adulthood can still, however, influence (specifically through reinforcement or change) adult attachment styles. The infant learns from its caretaker(s) what counts as intimacy and connection. This learning forms over time what can be considered **mental models**, which are cognitive conceptions about self and other.

These mental models can be considered as holistically reflecting positive or negative ideas about interacting with others: Are people, and the relationships we form with them, basically rewarding or basically punishing? Caretakers who are relatively distant or negligent may instill a mental model in an infant that relationships cannot be counted on, thereby reinforcing a *dismissive style*, in which the developing adolescent, teen, and adult increasingly learns to be independent of others. Caretakers who are punishing, abusive, or who model angry and painful interactions may reinforce a mental model in the infant that he or she is to blame, and that human relationships offer no solace or comfort. This infant is likely to develop an *avoidant attachment* style, insecure in approaching intimacy at all. Caretakers who are inconsistent, sometimes demonstrating nurturance and love, and at other times being unavailable or aggressive, instill an ambivalence in the infant—a person who has glimpsed what intimacy can be, but not trusting it to be stable and real. Such persons develop a *preoccupied or ambivalent attachment style*, in which they become desperate to find intimacy but distrust it and often unconsciously sabotage their relationships. In contrast, some infants are raised with consistently caring and nurturing caretakers, who mature into secure attachment models. These *securely attached* individuals desire intimacy, are able to move in and out of relationships, and are confident that they can achieve intimacy but are respectful of the rewards it offers and are willing and capable of maintaining such relationships over time (see **Figure 13.1**).

Numerous studies have confirmed that attachment styles affect a host of relationship outcomes, ranging

FIGURE 13.1: Attachment Styles

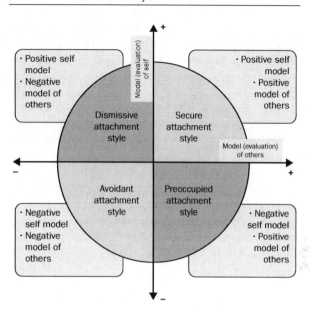

from liking to trust, to sexual satisfaction (for review, see Shaver & Mikulincer, 2006). A new set of studies has extended this line of research to demonstrate that individuals' attachment styles also affect how their *partners* experience their relationships (e.g., Kane et al., 2007). Extensive research has demonstrated the effects of early attachment experiences on adult relationships (Bolen, 2000; Colonnesi et al., 2011; Fraley, 2002; Hadden, Smith, & Webster, 2014; Levy, Ellison, Scott, & Bernecker, 2011; Pallini, Baiocco, Schneider, Madigan, & Atkinson, 2014; Verhage et al., 2016).

Adult Relationships: Relationship Development

The first professional organizations dedicated to the study of personal relationships were founded in the early 1970s (Knapp & Daly, 2011), and in the years that followed, scholars within the emerging field introduced a slew of new theories devoted to various relationship phenomena. Several of those theories focused on the process of relationship initiation and development, proposing that a few central constructs drive the processes of initiation and escalation. Altman and Taylor's (1973) social penetration theory was one such theory that was introduced into the field very early. **Social penetration theory (SPT)** is a stage theory that proposes that the development of personal relationships happens in a specific sequence that can be identified according to the kind of interaction that takes place in each stage. SPT is a **social exchange model**, viewing people in relationships (or, in the case of SPT, in developing relationships) in terms of the rewards and costs associated with the relationship (Taylor & Altman, 1987). SPT is perhaps most well-known for its claim that the development of relationships is analogous to peeling back the layers of an onion; as such, the "layers" of a relationship, in order from broadest and most superficial to most intimate, are *orientation* (the period of initial interaction), *exploratory affective exchange* (the period of experimentation with more personal topics), *affective exchange* (a personal relationship with the discussion of numerous personal topics), and *stable exchange* (arriving at the psychosocial core of the other). The catalyst for this progression in intimacy is the process of self-disclosure. According to SPT, self-disclosure in developing relationships can be classified according to its breadth (i.e., the range of topics one is willing to discuss) and depth (i.e., the level of intimacy associated with each disclosure). As individuals in relationships move from superficial to intimate communication, the breadth of self-disclosure tends to decrease while the depth of self-disclosure increases.

Knapp and Vangelisti (2005; see also Knapp, 1978) draw on a social penetration perspective to describe a staircase model of relationship development (and deterioration) as a function of verbal and nonverbal communication between partners. The stages of coming together and coming apart they describe are often referred to as a stage theory, but Mongeau and Henningsen (2008) caution that the process they describe is a model rather than a theory because it provides descriptions without clear predictions. Based in SPT, the stage model illustrates that partners work through stages of communication that escalate their relationship where messages increase in intimacy. The five stages of coming together include initiating (e.g., "Hi, how are you?"), experimenting (e.g., "What are your hobbies?"), intensifying (e.g., "I love you"), integrating (e.g., "I feel like our lives are intertwined"), and bonding (e.g., "Yes, I will marry you!"). On the other hand, the five stages of coming apart are differentiating (e.g., "I don't enjoy that shared hobby"), circumscribing (e.g., "Did you have fun on your trip?"), stagnating (e.g., "Do we have to keep arguing about this?"), avoiding (e.g., "I don't know when I will be able to see you again"), and terminating (e.g., "I'm leaving you"). Knapp and Vangelisti (2005) assert that movement

through stages is generally systematic and sequential, but that movement can be slow or fast, forward or backward, and is always to be a new place based on the tensions present in the relationship. This model was created in a heterosexual context and, as the simple example dialogue suggests, this model favors idealized views of marriage, which was an unavailable right to gay and lesbian couples at the time the model was created.

One of the first theories to tackle the process of relationship development from the communication discipline was Berger and Calabrese's (1975) uncertainty reduction theory. As the name suggests, **uncertainty reduction theory** (URT) posits that uncertainty—individuals' lack of "predictability about the behavior of both themselves and others in the interaction" (Berger & Calabrese, 1975, p. 100)—is the force that drives relationships forward. As such, people engage in a series of communicative behaviors—specifically, verbal communication, nonverbal pleasantness, information seeking, and (reciprocal) self-disclosure—in order to reduce the uncertainty they experience in new relationships. Relationship outcomes, such as liking and intimacy, are then influenced by both the presence of uncertainty and the enactment of the various communication behaviors. Like SPT, URT includes a series of *possible* (emphasis in original) stages that people might follow during the process of relationship initiation and uncertainty reduction that include the *entry phase* (socially normed initial interaction), the *personal phase* (beginning to talk about attitudes, opinions, beliefs, problems, etc.), and the *exit phase* (interactants decide about future plans). Unlike SPT, URT is not a social exchange theory; Berger and Calabrese (1975) are rather direct in their assertion that uncertainty is a more useful construct for predicting relationship behaviors, whereas cost–reward analysis might be useful for examining relationship outcomes (like satisfaction or stability).

Although URT has been an extremely heuristic theory, one of the most notable critiques (and extensions) of the theory was published about 10 years after URT. Sunnafrank (1986) noted that several of the proposed relationships within URT are based on the assumption that uncertainty reduction always results in *favorable* outcomes. For example, URT argues that lower levels of uncertainty lead to greater conversational fluidity and more liking. The problem is that less uncertainty is not always a better thing; sometimes relational partners disclose things that are shocking or unpleasant—the kinds of things that would probably *not* lead to smooth interactions and more liking. To address this limitation, Sunnafrank proposed a new formulation of URT that he called predicted outcome value theory (POV). Borrowing heavily from both URT and social exchange perspectives, POV asserts that individuals make forecasts about the potential future of a relationship based on the things they learn during the process of uncertainty reduction. When predicted outcome values are high, as would be the case if you were talking to an attractive potential romantic partner or your new boss, the process of uncertainty reduction and the relationship itself is likely to continue. When predicted outcome values are low, as might be the case if someone says something distasteful or you find that you just do not have anything in common, the process of uncertainty reduction and the future of the relationship is in doubt. Theory and research has significantly extended and refined uncertainty reduction theories to incorporate varied goals and thresholds of motivation (e.g., Afifi & Weiner, 2004; Fowler, Gasiorek, & Afifi, 2018; Lancaster, Dillow, Ball, Borchert, & Tyler, 2016; Tian, Schrodt, & Carr, 2016).

Adult Relationships: Relationship Maintenance

Steve Duck (1988) famously remarked that, although much scholarship had been devoted to the ways in which people begin relationships, the "real skills" (p. 87) required for a successful relationship—that is, the things that people do to keep existing relationships going—had received somewhat scant attention. Human tendency, according to Duck, is to ignore things that are running well and instead focus our attention elsewhere—on things that are novel or in need of repair. In the decades that have passed since that claim, several new lines of research have emerged that are designed to examine what Duck claimed the field lacked: a thoughtful examination of the things that partners do to keep their relationships going.

One of the first approaches to studying the day-to-day processes of ongoing relationships coined the term "relational maintenance behaviors." Introduced by Stafford and Canary (1991), **relational maintenance behaviors** (RMBs) were defined as "actions and activities used to sustain desired relational definitions" (Canary & Stafford, 1994, p. 5). The original typology of RMBs included five strategies, but recent work by Stafford (2011) has expanded the typology to seven discrete behaviors. Those behaviors

are positivity (having a cheerful and upbeat demeanor), understanding, self-disclosure, engaging in relationship talk, providing assurances (e.g., remembering the relationship or planning for the future together), sharing tasks (primarily domestic duties), and sharing social networks. Studies examining the effects of these RMBs on personal relationships have been plentiful. To offer a *very* brief summary, RMBs have been associated with perceptions of equity (i.e., an even distribution of rewards and costs; see Walster, Berscheid, & Walster, 1973) in the relationship (Canary & Stafford, 1992; Stafford & Canary, 2006). RMBs have been shown to affect relational outcomes, such as satisfaction and stability (Dainton & Stafford, 2000; Weigel & Ballard-Reisch, 1999), and have also been shown to disrupt the negative effects of stressful events (such as deployment; Merolla, 2010) or antisocial personality traits (such as alexithymia; Hesse, Pauley, & Frye-Cox, 2015) on personal relationships.

Social support behaviors constitute another feature of close personal relationships that has received a great deal of recent attention in relational research. Although several definitions of social support exist, the one that has perhaps gained the most traction in the communication field comes from Brant Burleson: "verbal and nonverbal behavior produced with the intention of providing assistance to others perceived as needing that aid" (Burleson & MacGeorge, 2002, p. 374). To date, much of the analysis of social support has utilized a five-category typology to classify the kinds of support that people provide to one another (Cutrona & Suhr, 1992). Those behaviors include **emotional support** (enhancing the recipient's emotional state), **esteem support** (helping the recipient feel better about himself or herself), *tangible support* (meeting a "real," or physical, need), **informational support** (providing guidance, advice, or instructions), and **social network support** (linking the recipient to other network members who might be of assistance).

Recent theoretic developments in the field of communication have focused attention on the *process* involved in the exchange of social support. Goldsmith's (2004) model of enacted support is one such perspective that has received a fair amount of recent discussion. According to this perspective, conversations of social support are best conceptualized as mutually beneficial transactions, a contrast to earlier models that had conceptualized supportive conversations as having a clear sender (supporter) and receiver (recipient). Through conversation, people work together to support one another; in fact, Goldsmith contends that partners take turns disclosing their fears or concerns and offering each other hope in the majority of supportive interactions. This is particularly true when the stress one individual faces is shared by the other, a phenomenon Goldsmith calls **communal coping**. When thinking about significant challenges or transitions, this perspective makes great intuitive sense; it is easy to imagine siblings engaging in this kind of conversation after the death of a parent or to envision romantic partners having a similar interaction when discussing the loss of one partner's job.

Another aspect of close personal relationships that has received a great deal of research in recent years is the exchange of affection. Guided by **affection exchange theory** (Floyd, 2006), this research has examined outcomes that are both familiar, such as psychological health or relationship satisfaction (Floyd, 2002; Floyd et al., 2005), and relatively novel, such as physiological markers of stress (Floyd, Pauley, & Hesse, 2010) or assessments of immune health (Floyd et al., 2014), within the communication discipline. Regardless of the outcome, the conclusion of these studies is consistent: Engaging in affectionate communication with others is beneficial for one's health.

The breadth of outcomes examined under the auspices of affection exchange theory (AET) is owed in part to its formulation. AET is a neo-Darwinian theory and situates the fundamental human need for relationships (a perspective shared with the aforementioned need to belong perspective; Baumeister & Leary, 1995) within the larger evolutionary drives of survival and procreation that influence all species. For humans, then, affection is an evolutionarily adaptive behavior that helps them achieve these goals. Affectionate individuals are more likely than less affectionate peers to live in communities that will share resources and offer mutual protection, and affectionate individuals will also experience greater reproductive success because others will be inclined to form romantic partnerships with them. Because these behaviors are rewarding in the long term, AET posits that the body rewards affection in the short term through improvements to physical health—with some important caveats. One of the first caveats is that the expression of affection needs to be desired; according to theory, individuals have a range of **optimal tolerance** for affection, and behaviors that fall within this parameter are the most beneficial. When people receive either too little or too much affection (including the receipt of undesired affectionate gestures), they begin to experience stress that might result in long-term decrements to health. Another caveat is that affectionate feelings and affectionate expression do not always coincide with one another. Indeed, some people have learned to manipulate expressions of affection, displaying either more or less affection than they actually feel for someone else in order to manipulate the situation or relationship (Floyd & Pauley, 2011). Affection is optimal, then, when it coincides with genuine feelings and falls within the recipient's desired range of affectionate behaviors.

Adult Relationships: Relationship Termination

No one begins a new relationship thinking about how it will end, but the reality is that most relationships end because of conscious or subconscious efforts on the part of the involved parties. For example, friendships often end because of physical separation (i.e., moving away from friends), but that is not the only reason; people sometimes grow to dislike friends and sometimes other relationships—including new romantic relationships—and take away the time needed to maintain such a relationship (Rose, 1984). The reasons why *romantic* relationships end are a little more complex, and they have justifiably received a little more empirical attention. Although many people (mistakenly) assume that romantic relationships usually come to a dramatic end, research has shown the opposite to be true. John Gottman (1999) might have said it best when he wrote, "[M]ost [relationships] end with a whimper, the result of people gradually drifting apart and not feeling liked, loved, and respected" (p. 24). What are some of the reasons that cause people to drift apart in their relationships?

If your first thought was that most relationships end because of conflict, you would not be wrong, per se. Gottman's (1994) extensive research on the subject has indeed determined that certain aspects of conflict can be quite corrosive and lead to relationship termination. From a series of observational studies, Gottman concluded that there are two broad types of couples. He refers to the first set of couples as *regulated*, and what is remarkable about these couples is that they average about five acts of positive communication for every negative act of communication—even when they are engaged in conflict. The second type of couple, **nonregulated**, has a positivity to negativity ratio that is closer to one to one. These couples are more likely to experience something that Gottman calls emotional flooding—that is, becoming so overwhelmed with negative emotion that you are no longer able to engage with your partner. In fact, when people become flooded emotionally, their natural inclination is to withdraw from the interaction (and possibly the presence of the partner as well) completely. This repeated cycle of negative affect expression, emotional flooding, and withdrawal eventually drives partners to experience what Gottman calls the distance and isolation cascade. At this point in the relationship, romantic partners start to feel lonely, they might intentionally avoid interaction, and they are likely to start leading parallel lives (Gottman, 1994). Thinking back to Gottman's earlier quote, then, it is not that relationships are likely to end right after an explosive argument; it is rather that a series of unresolved arguments leads partners to become emotionally distant from each other until they reach a point of loneliness and isolation. To outsiders, their relationship might look tranquil at this point because the constant bickering has ended, but the reality of the situation is that the affection and positive emotion that held the relationship together—those five positive acts for every negative act—have ended as well.

Although conflict certainly contributes to the dissolution of many relationships, it is not the only factor that drives relationships apart. In some cases, relationships end simply because relationship partners become disillusioned with one another. This problem is often exacerbated by something known as fatal attraction (Felmlee, 1995). **Fatal attraction** occurs when the characteristic(s) that makes someone else seem like an attractive partner ends up being the thing that drives the relationship apart. So, the person who is initially "the life of the party" ends up being "the person who never wants to have a quiet evening at home," or the person who is "so funny" ends up being the person who "can't take anything seriously." Fatal attraction is often, but not always, related to another important issue in close personal relationships: homophily. Generally speaking, most people find relationships with others who are like themselves easier to maintain and more enjoyable; this is representative of the "birds-of-a-feather-flock-together" mentality. The other perspective that "opposites attract" is often true, but research suggests that, unless the differences are complementary, that they can end up becoming sore spots in the relationship (Bohns et al., 2013).

Putting It Together: Interpersonal Communication Competence

A relatively simple syllogistic exercise suggests the importance of communication to relationships:

A_1: Communication constitutes relationships.

A_2: Relationships are vital to quality (and quantity—i.e., longevity) of life.

Therefore,

A_3: communication is vital to quality (and quantity) of life.

Further, given that,

A_4: the greater the quality (i.e., competence) of communication, the greater the quality of relationships, and

A_5: the greater the quality of relationships, the greater the quality of life.

Therefore,

A_6: the greater the quality of communication, the greater the quality of life. (Spitzberg, 2013a)

Indeed, extensive research demonstrates the importance of quality relationships to everyday life. The quality and durability of marriage are best predicted by the quality of interaction, particularly during conflict, but also in the ways in which affection is communicated (Proulx, Helms, & Buehler, 2007; Robles, Slatcher, Trombellow, & McGinn, 2013). Meta-analytic research, for example, indicates that lacking quality and quantity of social support and social capital, which are entirely constituted of communication and relational processes, are more predictive of mortality than smoking, alcohol consumption, not getting a flu vaccine, engaging in less physical activity, gaining weight, avoiding treatment for hypertension, or being exposed to air pollution (Holt-Lunstad, Smith, & Layton, 2010; Holt-Lunstad, Smith, Baker, Harris, & Stephenson, 2015). Similar results arise from the study of social capital (see Gilbert, Quinn, Goodman, Butler, & Wallace, 2013), although this is apparently based on actual, rather than merely perceived (Nyqvist, Pape, Pellfolk, Forsman, & Wahlbeck, 2016) or purely social media-based, social capital (Valenzuela, Halpern, & Katz, 2014).

If our relationships are constituted by communication, and the quality of communication determines the quality of those relationships, then the concept of quality needs to be specified. At the most basic and intuitive level, quality refers to how well a person or message communicates. How *well* someone communicates begs the question, how well for *what*? What is the communication *for*? If giving directions, communication needs to be clear and understood. If interviewing, communication needs to reduce uncertainty and evaluate fitness for employment. If delivering health care, communication needs to be accurate and compassionate. There are many potential purposes to which communication is put, but, in general, communicators tend to seek to achieve whatever functions, objectives, or goals they prefer, but, whenever possible, to do so in a manner that is perceived to be legitimate and acceptable by others. In short, communicators seek to be appropriate and effective. These are inherently subjective judgments. They are demonstrably subjective for several reasons.

First, judgments of communication appropriateness and effectiveness vary by context. Laughing at a party or in response to a joke is viewed differently than laughing at a funeral or when being reprimanded. Second, research

Box 13.1 Ethical Issues

Numerous ethical issues pervade interpersonal and relational communication processes. Below are three examples of ethical considerations in this context.

- **Ethics of Lying**

  Although there is a widespread negative attitude toward lying, ethicists provide more nuanced considerations of lying and deception. Deception is an evolved adaptive strategy, and even most ethicists envision specific situations when it is justified by higher-order moral concerns. For example, Sissela Bok (1979) asserts that while there should always be a preference for the truth, there are certain circumstances in which lying could be considered ethical: lying to protect confidentiality, lying to people who are dying, lying for the welfare of others, and other situations. On the other hand, philosopher Charles Fried (1978) argues that lying is always wrong because it removes others from making rational, free, and intentional choices. Bok notes that lying increases the power of the liar and decreases the power of those deceived by altering their choices. Considering the NCA Credo for Ethical Communication and principles discussed in this chapter, it is clear that lying is a communication act that deserves due consideration and scrutiny.

- ***Prima Facie* Duties**

  Philosopher W. D. Ross proposed moral duties in our significant relationships (i.e., family members, friends, neighbors, etc.) that he regards as reasonable and obvious on their face (*prima facie*). They can be summarized as follows (adapted from Johannesen et al., 2008, pp. 145–146):

  - Fidelity: Keeping promises and telling the truth.
  - Reparation: Compensating for wrongs we have done to others.
  - Gratitude: Expressing appreciation for good things others have done for us.
  - Justice: Equitably distributing pleasure and happiness based on merit.
  - Beneficence: Improving conditions of others.
  - Self-improvement: Improving ourselves in terms of wisdom and ethics.
  - Nonmaleficence: Avoiding doing harm to others.

- **Privacy**

  Sharing private information about oneself or others, often referred to as *disclosure*, is rife with ethical implications. For example, disclosure of private information might result in an undue burden and stress on the other, disclosure might be used as a form of interpersonal influence or compliance-gaining, or even further, as a form of coercion or manipulation. Another ethical implication of disclosing private information is that it could be a form of impression management by only disclosing selected information to shape perceptions of oneself. Sandra Petronio's (2002) communication privacy management theory is often used to study the relational impact of disclosure, including cultural and relational rules used to guide expectations of acceptable and unacceptable disclosure.

indicates that communication is often ambivalent in function and evaluation. For example, argumentative but verbally nonaggressive communication tends to be viewed as highly competent, but nonargumentative and verbally aggressive and argumentative and nonaggressive communication are viewed as very incompetent, but argumentative and verbally aggressive communication is viewed as very effective but not appropriate (Nicotera, Steele, Catalani, & Simpson, 2012). Third, too much of a good thing can be bad. Think of any communication skill (e.g., eye contact, asking questions, arguing, gesturing, etc.). Any one of these skills gets evaluated differently depending on whether it is used infrequently, occasionally, frequently, or constantly. Communication skills tend to be curvilinear to judgments of competence (Bolotova, 2012). Too little or too much of a behavior is evaluated very differently than moderate levels of the skill.

Fourth, there are well-demonstrated biases in judging communication, especially in judging one's own communication skills. Actors' self-rated competence tends to be higher than others' views of that actor—reflecting a better-than-average, or Wobegon, bias. This is consistent with the finding that people think they are better drivers than they actually are, believe themselves more physically attractive than they are viewed by their friends, and believe they will never get divorced even when they know that 40 to 50% of marriages end in divorce (Peck, 1993).

Finally, consistent with the principles of equifinality and multifinality (see Chapter 2), engaging in any given skill or communication behavior may work sometimes and not others. A behavior that fails in one context may work in another. A skill that achieves a given outcome in a variety of episodes may achieve a very different outcome in any given episode. A pickup line may work on one person but not another. A joke told very similarly in one situation may work but not in another.

The implication of all these claims is that *the mere ability to enact a particular behavior does not guarantee that this behavior will be judged as appropriate, that it will be effective, or that it will be viewed as competent.* Thus, **communication competence** is a judgment, not an ability or skill. An **ability** is the capacity for goal-driven, repeatable behavior. A **skill** is an ability internalized to some degree of efficiency, stability, or other criterion of quality. So, a person may be able to drive a car, a person may be

very *skilled* in this ability, and others may evaluate this person as a "good" driver—that is, a competent driver. If abilities and skills are the behaviors, and competence is the judgment of the appropriateness and effectiveness of such behaviors, then the interesting question becomes, "Which skills tend to be viewed as competent, and in which types of contexts?"

While judgments of competence may be based on any number or type of evaluative criteria, appropriateness and effectiveness are the most generalizable and useful criteria. **Appropriateness** is the judgment that behavior is legitimate or acceptable in a given context. **Effectiveness** is the judgment that behavior has achieved relatively preferred outcomes or functions in a given context. To the extent that a communicator is evaluated by others across a wide variety of contexts, that communicator tends to be judged as a "competent" communicator. An inappropriate and ineffective communicator is engaging in a *minimizing* style—failing to achieve preferred outcomes, perhaps because of inappropriate behavior. An appropriate but ineffective communicator is *sufficing*, in that behavior is not particularly wrong, but neither does it accomplish anything. A communicator who is effective but inappropriate is likely to be engaging in coercive or manipulative behavior that accomplishes preferred outcomes at the expense of others' sense of propriety. Clearly the most competent communicator is *both* appropriate *and* effective, suggesting four possible **competence styles** (see **Figure 13.2**).

FIGURE 13.2: A Communication (In)Competence Typology

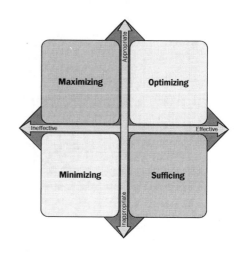

If competence is a judgment, then the question arises, "How do communicators achieve that judgment from self and others?" Consider an analogous question: What makes a great actor or acting performance? To give a competent acting performance, an actor needs to first be motivated to give a great performance. Such motivation is likely to activate such behaviors as studying the script, interrogating the author's and director's intent, analyzing the likely audience, learning the setting, props, lighting, and so forth. Further, it helps if the actor has studied the acting craft. That is, being motivated is not enough; an actor needs to have acting knowledge. Even an actor who is motivated and knowledgeable may still not enact an award-worthy performance. If motivation and knowledge alone enabled great acting, then Kevin James, Adam Sandler, Mila Kunis, and Dakota Johnson would have Academy Awards; it is also necessary to have acting skills. *In general, the more motivated, knowledgeable, and skilled a communicator is, the more likely the communicator is to be viewed as appropriate and effective—that is, competent.*

What communication skills are most important? When research across hundreds of studies is summarized, across several hundred types of skills, four tend to represent most of these skills (Spitzberg, 2000, 2006, 2007, 2011, 2013a, 2014, 2015a, 2015b, 2015d). **Attentiveness** refers to the ability to demonstrate attention to, interest in, and concern for others in a conversation. Showing eye contact, mirroring nonverbal behavior, asking questions, and following up on the topics of others all reflect attentive skills. **Composure** refers to the ability to demonstrate confidence, calmness, comfort, spontaneity, appropriate assertiveness, self-control, and directedness of behavior. Avoiding nervous twitches and nonfluencies and demonstrating intention and self-control in communication behavior reflect such composure. **Coordination** represents the ability to manage timing, ebb and flow, and the initiation and ending of speaking turns, conversations, episodes, and sequences of interaction. Managing interruptions, initiating speaking turns and conversations, and enacting smooth departure from interactions all represent forms of composure. Finally, **expressiveness** represents animation and variability of behavior, especially in regard to affect, emotion expression, vocabulary, imagery, narrative, humor, and vivacity of enactment. *Collectively, in general, the more moderately attentive, composed, coordinated, and expressive a communicator is, the more likely the communicator is to be viewed by self and others as competent.*

There are numerous implications to this model of competence (see **Figure 13.3**). First, the impression or judgment of competence mediates the effect of communication behavior on other interactants. *Mediation* in this usage means that the effect of a behavior on a person is mostly or entirely based on a mediating factor—in this

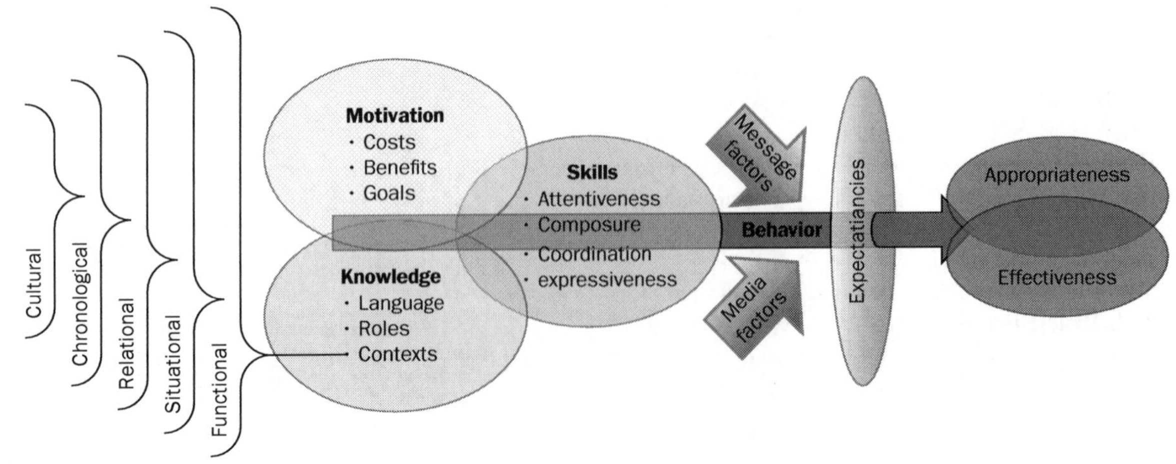

FIGURE 13.3: The Model of Interpersonal Communication Competence

case, the evaluation of competence. So, for example, a person may engage in aggressive behavior, which typically is viewed as incompetent, thereby resulting in diminished relational satisfaction. If, in a particular encounter, Asher thinks that Olivia's angry yelling was the appropriate and effective way of getting his attention in a conflict, then Asher is likely to feel more satisfied with the encounter and his relationship. So, it is not the behavior that determines his relationship satisfaction, but his impression of the competence of that behavior (Karazsia, Berlin, Armstrong, Janicke, & Darling, 2014).

Second, people rarely encounter any conversation that is entirely unlike any other encounter they have experienced. Thus, people typically have expectancies about how a given encounter will unfold. Intuitively, people might think that competent interactants seek to fulfill the expectancies of other interactants. This intuition ignores that some expectancies are negative. If a professor ends a lecture by singling out a student by saying "Jared, you need to see me in my office after class," Jared may well imagine all manner of terrible outcomes that such a request might suggest. If the professor informs Jared that he has been awarded "Outstanding Major" and will receive the award at the graduation ceremony, Jared's negative expectancies will be violated, but in a manner that is likely to lead Jared to think his professor was a very competent communicator. Thus, *in general, judgments of competence are more likely to the degree that positive expectancies are fulfilled and negative expectancies appropriately violated.*

Third, as already suggested, a curvilinearity principle proposes that too little or too much of any given behavior or communication skill is likely to be evaluated as incompetent. This may seem obvious, but it contradicts the implicit kinds of advice that popular press books and friends may suggest, such as "You should make eye contact," "Give a firm handshake when you meet someone," or, "You need to talk about what the other person is interested in." Clearly, a person can make too much eye contact, give too firm a handshake, talk too little about self, and too much about the other person.

Fourth, much communication advice is premised on another piece of advice—think before you speak. It turns out that this is not necessarily sound advice. One of the hallmarks of many experts and professionals is that they have *overlearned* their skills. Commuters, for example, often find that they have driven home, made changes in their speed, braking, lane changes, and so forth, with no specific memory of how they got from point A to point B. Many communication processes are enacted with relatively little conscious forethought. As a simple example, try typing your name on a keyboard, and then on flat surface that is not a keyboard. Then try typing your name backwards. Having to think about something you do not ordinarily think about significantly disrupts your ability to engage in that behavior. The principle is that *due to mindfulness, when learning new skills, competence decreases temporarily before it can increase with practice and feedback* (Donner & Hardy, 2015).

The final implication of this competence model is the diagnostic principle: *When a communication encounter does not go well, it is likely due to one or more of the following issues: motivation, knowledge, skill, context, medium, message, expectancies, or evaluative criteria.* This provides a relatively simple heuristic checklist for analyzing communication problems and for providing some insight into possible approaches to improving the communication and relationship.

Conclusion

Personal relationships, and the interpersonal skills that form their foundation, can be complex and confusing. Although we have learned a lot about both in the last several decades, there is still much to learn. The effort is worth it, though. Personal relationships are often our greatest sources of joy and frustration, so, to the extent that we can maximize the former and minimize the latter, we can work toward making our personal relationships more satisfying and rewarding for the good of all involved.

CHAPTER 14

Argument, Persuasion, and Influence

Rachael A. Record, Lourdes Martinez, & Brian H. Spitzberg

LEARNING OBJECTIVES

After reading this chapter, you should be able to do the following:

- Identify and differentiate deductive, inductive, abductive, and warranting approaches to argument.
- Identify the key defining features of persuasion.
- Differentiate between persuasion and propaganda.
- Articulate the definition of attitude.
- Distinguish principles of the relationship of attitudes to persuasion.
- Distinguish the relationship between attitude and behavior.
- Compare and contrast the tenets and key variables of social judgment, elaboration likelihood, cognitive dissonance, and reasoned action models of persuasion.
- Summarize and analyze interpersonal research findings related to persuasion.
- Specify relevant small-group research findings related to persuasion.
- Summarize and analyze social-norms research findings related to persuasion.

THE FIELD OF COMMUNICATION WAS ORIGI-nally founded as the study of the processes surrounding argumentation and persuasion as the primary means through which a democratic society can be sustained. The study of rhetoric, or the available means of persuasion, originated with a focus on the nature of argument in discourse in all its forms, including the use of logic (*logos*), the use of emotion (*pathos*), and the use of credibility (*ethos*). From a social scientific perspective, the study of persuasion examines the persuasive processes through the constructs of

196

attitude and behavior change. This chapter presents theoretical and practical understandings of argumentation and the process of persuasion. In particular, three categorizations of argument formation are reviewed (deductive, inductive, abductive), as well as theoretical understandings of the persuasive process as it appears generally, interpersonally, and socially. Although mass mediated communication is also essential to understanding persuasive processes, the role of media for persuasive processes (referred to as media effects) is examined in the media chapter.

Argumentation

Some days it can feel like the sole purpose of communication is to argue. Everyone wants something, and almost everything seems to seek to influence. In the contemporary media environment, people are inundated by text, smell, sound, touch, image, and social forms of influence. This is not surprising; control over one's environment is a fundamental survival advantage and reflects an intrinsic tendency. One of the most elemental discursive approaches we use to influence others is that of argument (see also: Chapters 3 and 4). *Arguments* are forms of convergence-seeking discourse that refer to "communicative attempts to reach accord with the minds or behavior of another person" or persons (Canary & Seibold, 2010, p. 12). Thus, argument is inherently an attempt to seek agreement—attempts that often share similarities across contexts. There are at least four primary forms in which arguments are structured: deductive, inductive, abductive, and warrantable.

Deduction

Ancient philosophers were greatly concerned with seeking some form of argument that produced more reliable claims to truth. In speculating on the need for an ethical approach to influence, they formalized a way of thinking that has come to be known as deduction. *Deduction* is a form of reasoning from general to particulars. Its idealized structure is summarized by the *syllogism* (Hacking, 2013). Deduction is involved in the form of a highly flexible structural template. For example, consider the following deductive chain of hypotheses:

Major premise (MjP): Communication majors are more rhetorically competent than other college majors.

Minor premise (MnP): Rhetorical competence is positively related to career success.

Conclusion (Cncl): Therefore, communication majors will have greater career success than other majors.

There are many derivations of such syllogisms that represent causal schemata or informal ways of thinking (Khemlani, Barbey, & Johnson-Laird, 2014). See the following example:

MjP: A causes B (e.g., recessions cause unemployment).

MnP: B prevents C (e.g., lowering taxes produces economic recovery).

Cncl: Therefore, A prevents C. (e.g., we should lower taxes to reduce unemployment).

Aristotle recognized the challenges of example and syllogism as forms of persuasion and formulated an alternative form of persuasion he named **enthymeme**, which is a syllogism with one or more suppressed propositions that is filled in by the audience. Suppose a presidential candidate says, "My opponent still has not released his tax returns, so what is he hiding?" The implication of this statement is for audience members to think, "Why would anyone refuse to release his or her taxes? It must be because that person is hiding something incriminating." At no point did the candidate's statement explicitly say, "My opponent is a criminal." But, it is assumed that the audience is likely to *think* this, and, consequently, it does not need to be expressly stated. Many advertisements operate using an enthymematic structure. An ad for men's fragrance that shows beautiful women leaping to caress a man after he sprays on the fragrance is essentially making an enthymeme:

MjP: Absent this fragrance, the character in the commercial was alone.

MnP: Having sprayed this fragrance, the character in the commercial attracted women.

Cncl: If I buy and use this fragrance, I will attract women.

There are at least two attractive features to this form of argument. First, by not making all the claims of the argument explicit, it is harder for an audience to criticize the exact logic underlying it. Second, because the audience members essentially help complete the argument, they are more likely to feel convinced because their own thought processes are what fit the pieces together. Who is more credible than oneself?

Induction

Induction is a form of reasoning from particulars (specific cases or examples) to generalizations. For instance, in the earliest days of what became the AIDS epidemic in the United States, the Centers for Disease Control and Prevention, among other organizations, had relatively little to tie the disparate cases together other than the discovery that most of the people contracting these odd diseases that are associated with compromised immune function were either gay, intravenous drug users, or people who

had received a blood transfusion. The examination of such cases led to several potential generalizations, including that there was a "gay disease" or "gay cancer" and that whatever the underlying cause, it seemed to be involved in the transfer of bodily fluids. The second generalization was largely accurate, but the idea that it was a "gay disease" was not. For example, most AIDS cases in Africa are heterosexually transmitted.

Induction is the foundation of almost all scientific research, in which the observation of many instances of an experiment, or of survey responses, provides a basis for generalizing from those instances. As with the **evidence tests** (see **Table 14.1**), however, the generalization of results from looking at many instances of something is only as valid as the representativeness and adequacy of that sample of examples. One of the reasons that scientific research does not always replicate exactly—why what "science" believed 20 years ago is not believed now—is

TABLE 14.1: Tests of Evidence and Examples

Evidence Test	Principle (Fallacious Example)
Recency	The timeliness of the evidence (e.g., citing medical evidence from the 1950s is likely to be less accurate than current research).
Relevance	The logical, practical, and reasonable connection to the claim being made (e.g., citing that you know a good security guard is not relevant to the argument of racial bias in police stops of African Americans).
Internal consistency	The coherence of the evidence (e.g., citing an example of your parent who smoked all his/her life but did not die of lung cancer to argue the safety of smoking when your parent did die of esophageal cancer).
External consistency	The degree to which the evidence is representative of the domain/population of external phenomena to which it is applied (e.g., citing that you believe in God because you experienced a transformative experience may not seem sensible to those who have not had such an experience).
Sufficiency	The degree to which there is adequate quantity and quality of evidence to generalize (e.g., citing that your first two cars were Fiats and they were lousy may seem sufficient to you, but hardly disqualifies the entire carmaker).
Comparative quality	The degree to which the evidence is the best available (e.g., citing a single study based on a small sample is likely to be questionable compared to a meta-analysis of hundreds of studies).
Ethos	The credibility or expertise of the source of the evidence (e.g., citing an unattributed Internet blog instead of a blind-reviewed scientific report).
Accessibility	The degree to which the evidence can be verified, observed, authenticated, and inspected by others (e.g., citing that space aliens have visited because you were abducted by them when you were 3 and returned).

that even large-scale studies involving tens of thousands of people are still situated in a particular culture, time, and place. Nevertheless, statistical inference, which underlies most of modern scientific research, is basically an inductive logic that is founded on the odds that one set of observed cases differs from what would be expected by chance (see chapters 10–11).

Abduction

Given the limitations of deduction and induction, scholars have tried to develop better insights into the logical foundations of argument and proof and better understandings of the nature of everyday rationality and discursive influence. One approach to a better foundation was formulated as an alternative to deduction and induction. Originally formalized by Pierce (1839–1914), **abduction** is generally viewed as a form of reasoning in which various reasonable explanations for a surprising or unexpected observation are compared (Velázquez-Quesada, 2015). The process has been proposed as a series of steps, in which (a) a phenomenon is detected, (b) some causal mechanism is inferred or deduced, (c) a causal model is formulated, (d) the causal model is evaluated or tested, and (e) theory is formulated (Mirza, Akhtar-Danesh, Noesgaard, Martin, & Staples, 2014).

Warranting (Toulmin) Argument Model

In the 1950s, Stephen Toulmin (1958) sought to merge a more pragmatic language use perspective with traditional interests in the logic of argumentative discourse. In attempting to model how people actually argue, he formulated the **warranting model** of argument, often referred to as the "Toulmin model" (see also: Chapters 3 and 4). The Toulmin model indicates that to be considered an argument at all, discourse must articulate, or at least imply, a *claim*. The claim is the thing a person wants others to believe, think, or do as a result of the argument. Toulmin (1958) argued that claims are predicated on some form of empirical experience, observation, research, or example(s), which is referred to as *data*. But, data never unequivocally justify a particular claim. For example, even when everyone agrees that the data show that the world is unequivocally getting hotter, the implication of these data is not obvious. These data may lead to the claim that we need to decrease our use of fossil fuels, or that we need to invest in better infrastructure to manage the effects of such temperature trends.

In order to connect the data to the claim, arguers express or imply one or more warrants. *Warrants* are reasons that bridge the relevance of the data to the claim in a way that formulates a coherent narrative structure. Furthermore, any component of this model may involve further evidence or warrants, which could be considered forms of *backing*. Backing may involve statements providing further evidence (quantity), credibility substantiation (quality), durability of evidence (consistency), and so forth. Finally, to the extent that an arguer is contemplative, critical, and self-reflexive, counterarguments will be considered. To the extent that counterarguments are included in an argument, they are considered a *rebuttal* and require that a *qualifier* moderate the degree of confidence or certainty expressed in the claim.

These components are displayed in **Figure 14.1** in their template form, and in **Figure 14.2** using an analysis of a policy argument exemplar regarding the decriminalization and deinstitutionalization of prisoners having violated marijuana laws. Arguments will generally not explicitly reveal all components. In particular, "unlike all other components of the warranting model, warrants usually remain implicit in an argument; they are the unspoken assumptions that bind together claims and data" (Warren, 2010, p. 42).

Persuasion

Persuasion has two branches of research. The first is in the field of rhetoric, in which the origins of persuasion can be traced back to Aristotle, as discussed through the lens of logic and argumentation in this chapter, and as a method of interrogating persuasive texts in Chapter 6. The rhetorical criticism approach to persuasion tends to focus on "the political or civic contexts of persuasion, and an overriding emphasis on ethical concerns" (Hogan, 2013, p. 2). The second branch of persuasion is in social scientific research, in which persuasion processes are explored through the constructs of attitude and behavior change. From this perspective, O'Keefe (2016) defines **persuasion** as "a successful intentional effort at influencing another's mental state through communication in a circumstance in which the persuadee has some measure of freedom" (p. 4). This definition consists of five key features, each of which is expanded next.

FIGURE 14.1: Conceptual Components of a Warranting Model of Argument

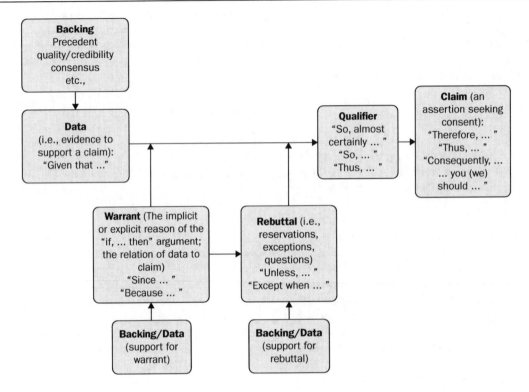

Adapted from Kneupper (1978)

Success

Successful influence. The first feature of persuasion is that it is a successful attempt to influence. When we say that one person has persuaded another, success is inherent in the statement. As O'Keefe (2016) puts it, you cannot say "I persuaded him but failed" (p. 2). Although we can attempt to persuade someone unsuccessfully, to say "I persuaded someone" implies a successful attempt.

Intention. Second, persuasion requires a specific intention to influence an individual. When we make statements such as, "I persuaded her to go there," the implication is that you wanted that outcome to occur. Although we can make claims about accidently persuading someone, our need to make those claims in the first place stems from the assumption that persuasion is intentional.

Freedom. The third feature is the freedom of individuals *not* to be persuaded. This freedom refers to free will, free choice, and voluntary action. For instance, if you got pushed off a diving board, you were not persuaded

to jump. Of all the features of persuasion, this one is the least black and white. For example, if someone is threatening to hurt you unless you do what they ask, is that true freedom? Technically, you have a choice. Most individuals, however, would categorize this instance as coercion. Similarly, brainwashing and Stockholm syndrome also push the line of freedom. Although individuals in those situations can feel like they are making a sincere choice, most people would argue that their perceived freedom was compromised. Thus, with the exception of extreme circumstances, persuasion is the result of a freely made choice.

Communication. Fourth, persuasive effects are achieved through a communicative process. The communicative process can take an intrapersonal, interpersonal, large group, or mediated form, but it cannot take a physical form. Similar to the diving board example, to physically push someone off a cliff into the water below is very different than using a strong argument, such as, "It's thrilling!"

FIGURE 14.2: An Exemplar of the Warranting Model of Argument

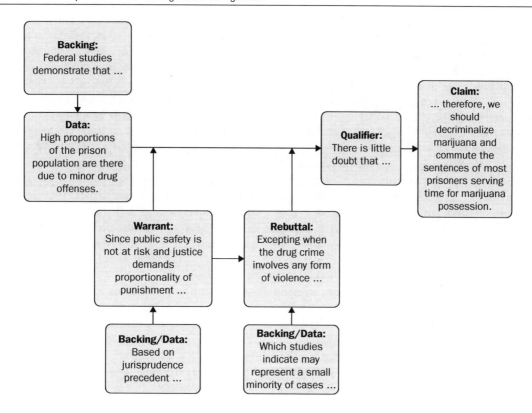

and "No one has ever died jumping off this cliff," in order to talk him or her into jumping off the cliff. The persuasive process occurs solely through a communicative channel.

Mental change. Finally, persuasion requires a change in the mental state of the persuadee. This follows one of two approaches. The first is a direct change in mental state, such as changing attitudes toward a topic. The second is a change in mental state as an indirect or intermediate step toward a change in behavior. For example, if you are hoping to persuade someone to donate money to a cause, then it is logical to assume that if you improve his or her attitude toward the cause, then he or she is more likely to be persuaded to donate to the cause. Thus, regardless of the persuasion goal (i.e., attitude change or behavior change), a change in mental state will result.

When you are thinking about persuasion, the term propaganda likely comes to mind. All propaganda is a form of persuasion, but not all persuasion is propaganda. Jowett and O'Donnell (2014) defined **propaganda** as "the deliberate, systematic attempt to shape perceptions, manipulate cognitions, and direct behavior to achieve a response that furthers the desired intent of the propagandist" (p. 7). Propaganda carries a negative connotation in our society and is typically only associated with persuasion efforts being employed by large institutions, most commonly the government, to influence the masses for the sake of a gain that directly benefits that institution. For example, much of the propaganda literature looks at the U.S. government's efforts to garner support for World War I. The use of mass media to persuade American citizens to support the war directly benefited the government's goals of continuing the war. Persuasion, on the other hand, does not carry those same restrictions. For example, an individual can attempt to persuade another individual and gain nothing from achieving the goal, such as a friend encouraging another friend to go to college. Thus, although propaganda is a type of persuasion, the persuasive process is larger and more complex than just propaganda.

Attitudes and Behavior

Social scientific scholars study the persuasion process through the constructs of attitude and behavior. Although not required in the persuasive process, behavior change is often the desired goal of the persuader. For example, your instructors attempt to persuade you to study, your parents try to persuade you to eat your vegetables, and your friends persuade you to spend time with them. Thus, your positive evaluation of school, vegetables, and socializing is desired, but your behavior change is the end goal. The importance of attitudes to the persuasive process stems from the relationship between attitudes and behaviors (Rhodes & Ewoldsen, 2013). **Attitude** refers to a person's evaluation of an object, with object being used in the broadest sense of the term, such as person, event, product, policy, etc. (O'Keefe, 2016). In order to successfully persuade someone, you must change his or her attitude in the desired direction. For example, if you want your friend to believe that *Game of Thrones* is the best television show of all time, then you will employ strategies, such as making him or her watch the programs, discussing your favorite qualities, and articulating your rationale, in order to change his or her evaluation (i.e., attitude) of the program. Thus, by changing attitudes, you might increase the chances of changing behavior (i.e., your friend watching *Game of Thrones*).

Attitudes usually serve a specific function. Katz (1960) suggested that attitudes can serve one of four specific functions. Each function is discussed in **Table 14.2**.

Understanding different attitude functions can also help facilitate the persuasion process (i.e., attitude change). Furthermore, attitudes are complex constructs made up of multiple evaluations. For example, someone's attitude toward a course likely consists of an evaluation of the instructor, classmates, and content, among other things. In research, when variables cannot be directly measured with one question, they are referred to as *latent variables* (see Chapters 10 and 11). Attitude is a latent construct that requires a broad understanding in order to change. For example, if someone does not like a NFL team, you will not change that person's opinion by simply stating, "You should like that team." Instead, you need to focus on the factors that contribute to the overall attitude, such as team record for the decade, current record for the season, and skill level of players. Thus, attitude change occurs by changing evaluations of the related elements.

Changing attitudes is not as simple as learning the evaluation of related elements and the functions they are serving and then changing those evaluations. Individual attitudes are most often constructed over years of exposure to, and processing of, relevant information. Our attitudes are rarely changed through immediate exposure to information. Instead, attitude change requires specific targeting of elements and repeated exposure to information. The best approaches for effectively changing attitudes can be found in theoretical frameworks of persuasion.

TABLE 14.2: Functions of Attitude

Function	Explanation	Example
Utilitarian	Attitudes that help people maximize benefit and minimize cost	Individuals who win trophies will enjoy the activity/sport more than individuals who do not win trophies.
Ego-defensive	Attitudes that defend one's self-image	Putting down another individual to enhance the image of oneself.
Value-expressive	Attitudes that reflect central values and self-images	Individuals attending a university will support resources and policies that benefit that university.
Knowledge	Attitudes that organize and process information and events	Based on information at hand, categorizing people into "good" and "evil."

Central Theories

Theoretical foundations are essential to social scientific research, and studies regarding the persuasive process are no exception. There are numerous persuasion theories in the social sciences. The most commonly cited persuasion theories include social judgment theory, the elaboration likelihood model, cognitive dissonance theory, and reasoned action approaches. Each of these theoretical frameworks will be reviewed in the following paragraphs.

Social Judgment Theory

Social judgment theory (Sherif & Hovland, 1961; Sherif, Sherif, & Nebergall, 1965) postulates that persuasive messages are evaluated (i.e., judged) based on preexisting attitudes. According to **social judgment theory**, our overall evaluation of each attitude dimension will determine whether a persuasive attempt is successful. Attitudes can have one of three types of evaluations, known as judgmental *latitudes*. To demonstrate, complete the survey in **Table 14.3** regarding recycling programs. These latitudes are acceptance, rejection, and noncommitment. Subject positions that an individual finds acceptable fall into the **latitude of acceptance** (e.g., the items you marked with either a + or ++ in **Table 14.3**). Similarly, subject positions that an individual finds unacceptable fall into the **latitude of rejection** (e.g., the items you marked with either a X or XX). Finally, a subject position that an individual does not have an opinion on falls into the **latitude of noncommitment** (e.g., the items you left blank). For any given attitude, our latitudes depend on our ego involvement. In other words, the more *ego-involved* we are (i.e., the more we care about a topic), the larger our latitude of rejection will be and the smaller our latitude of noncommitment will be (O'Keefe, 2016). Your survey responses represent what social judgment theory refers to as your judgmental latitude regarding recycling programs. For example, if you are confident that recycling programs are more costly than they are worth for the return to environmental preservation and energy use, then you are likely to reject evaluations that favor recycling, and you will be neutral on most arguments that promote recycling.

With these tenets in mind, social judgment theory suggests that in order to persuade individuals, we need to first be aware of their attitude evaluations and their existing judgmental latitude. With that information in hand, this theory suggests that attitude change is most likely to occur

TABLE 14.3: Evaluation of College Recycling Programs

Read each statement that follows. Put a ++ next to the statement you agree with the most, put a + next to all other statements you agree with, put a XX next to the statement you agree with the least, put a x next to all other statements you disagree with, and leave blank all statements with which you neither agree nor disagree.

	Despite the environmental benefits of recycling programs, they are too expensive.
	Despite the environmental benefits of recycling programs, they might not be worth the cost.
	Despite the environmental benefits of recycling programs, the cost-efficiency of other environmental programs should be evaluated.
	Although there are environmental benefits of recycling programs, the cost-effectiveness of those programs is unclear.
	The environmental benefits of recycling programs are worth the cost, regardless of the cost-efficiency of other environmental programs.
	The environmental benefits of recycling programs might be worth the cost.
	The environmental benefits of recycling programs are worth the expenses.

Table notes: Measures of social judgment theory require the items to be in a balanced order with the most pro statement on one end and the most con statement on the other end. The middle should represent neutral ground.

with arguments that fall into an individual's latitude of acceptance or latitude of noncommitment. When an argument falls into the latitude of rejection, this theory expects no attitude change to result. In addition, arguments that fall in to the latitude of rejection may even provoke boomerang effects, such as strengthening the initial position. This helps explain why trying to persuade a person about religion or politics may actually lead that person to believe more fervently in their own viewpoint. Thus, according to social judgment theory, persuasion occurs through an individual's evaluation of his or her preexisting attitudes.

Elaboration Likelihood Model

The **elaboration likelihood model** (ELM; Carpenter, 2015; Petty & Cacioppo, 1986) explores persuasion as a function of information processing. The ELM is a dual process model, suggesting that people will predominantly process information through one of two routes—either the central or the peripheral route. Which route the information is processed through depends on how much someone thinks about, or elaborates on, the information. Examples of elaborating on information include, but are not limited to, paying attention to the content, thinking about the message, and critically evaluating the perspective. When elaboration of information is high, an individual is processing through the **central route**. When elaboration is low, an individual is processing through the **peripheral route**.

When we process information through the central route, we are typically thinking closely and critically about the information at hand. For example, think about the last time you heard that a political candidate was proposing a new policy plan. Did you consider how that plan could impact your daily life? Did you think about how the new plan would change life for the average citizen? Maybe you compared the policy plan to that of another candidate. If you engaged in any of that sort of thinking then, according

to the ELM, you were processing the information through the central route. If not, you processed the information through the peripheral route using heuristics (i.e., mental shortcuts). Through this route, you might have evaluated the plan based on whether you already supported the candidate, on which political party the candidate represented, or on how your friends and family felt about the plan. Or, perhaps you pay primary attention to how credible (Wilson & Sherrell, 1993) or attractive you find the source (Hornik, Ofir, & Rachamim, 2016), your mood (Hullett, 2005), or whether or not the message uses humor (Walter, Cody, Xu, & Murphy, 2018), or evokes fear (Hornik et al., 2016) or anger (Walter, Tukachinsky, Pelled, & Nabi, 2018). But which route results in a more persuasive outcome?

Persuasive messages can look differently along the two processing routes. For the central route, messages are most persuasive when they are in the direction of pre-existing beliefs (e.g., going back to the previous example, if we were looking forward to a new policy plan) and when they exhibit a strong argument quality (O'Keefe, 2013). For the peripheral route, messages are most persuasive when they employ heuristic strategies, such as featuring credible information, likeable sources, and demonstrating that other people like the message (O'Keefe, 2013). Overall, research has found that when we process information through the central route, our attitudes are more stable, are more predictive of our behaviors, and are more resistant to counterarguments (see O'Keefe, 2016). Thus, persuasion is dependent on how individuals process information.

Cognitive Dissonance Theory

Festinger (1957) proposed cognitive dissonance theory as a way to examine the relationships between cognitive elements (e.g., beliefs, opinions, attitudes, and knowledge). According to this theory, cognitive elements can have one of three relationships, which are displayed in **Table 14.4**.

TABLE 14.4: Relationship Types Among Cognitive Elements

Type	Definition	Example
Irrelevant	The two elements do not relate to each other.	I like my college classes, and I like dogs.
Consonant	The belief in both elements represents a consistent perspective.	I like dogs, and I donate money to the local humane society.
Dissonant	The belief in both elements represents an inconsistent perspective.	I like my college classes, and I do not attend class.

Cognitive dissonance theory proposes that a consonant message will strengthen the pre-existing perspective, whereas a dissonant message will put the receiver in a potential position for change.

When we are exposed to a dissonant message (i.e., a message that is inconsistent with our preexisting perspective or behavior), we are said to be experiencing **cognitive dissonance**. When we are in these situations, we attempt to reduce dissonance and, ideally, create a consonant relationship. For example, the student who likes his or her college classes but does not attend class may decide either that attending class has nothing to do with liking class or that maybe he or she does not actually like his or her classes. Thus, messages are thought to be the most persuasive if they create a small degree of cognitive dissonance. For example, if exposed to the message, "One way to show you enjoy a course is to attend class," then individuals may not feel a lot of pressure to attend and may take the time to consider attending and maybe eventually attend. On the other side, if exposed to the message, "Attending class is the only way to show you enjoy a course," then individuals may create a reason why that cognitive element is false, such as deciding that plenty of students who attend class do not enjoy class and that, therefore, class attendance has nothing to do with demonstrating enjoyment of a class. A particular form of persuasion occurring through the drive for consistency is a process called counterattitudinal advocacy, in which a person who is conscious of having a belief or attitude, who is then involved in doing, writing or saying something that is contradictory to that belief or attitude tends to change their attitude or behavior toward the contrary position (Kim, Allen, Preiss, & Peterson, 2014). Thus, cognitive dissonance theory provides a framework for creating attitude change.

Reasoned Action Approaches

The reasoned action approach to behavior change is a broad field of study that includes multiple theoretical perspectives, such as the theory of reasoned action (Fishbein & Ajzen, 1975), the theory of planned behavior (Ajzen, 1985), the integrative model of behavioral prediction (Fishbein, 2000), and the reasoned action theory (Fishbein & Ajzen, 2010). All **reasoned action** approaches expect behavior change to be determined by a series of beliefs and perspectives related to a particular behavior. Although these theories differ slightly in their specific predictions of what variables affect behavior, they share foundational assumptions and some overlap in their key variables.

These theories assume that humans are reasonable, even if not always rational, beings. For example, if you tell a human that performing a behavior will kill him or her, then, following reason, he or she will make the decision to not perform that behavior. In this example, the individual is also being rational. Being rational, however, is not always a requirement of these perspectives. For example, someone with a fear of spiders may spray pesticides daily to prevent spiders from entering the home. Individuals not afraid of spiders may look at that behavior and describe it as irrational.

All the reasoned action models are extensions of the theory of reasoned action, which includes four key variables. The first is a measure of *attitude*, to evaluate current beliefs related to the behavior, and the second is *subjective norm*, to evaluate social pressures and perspectives related to the behavior. The theory postulates that these two variables predict the third variable—intention to perform a behavior. Finally, this **behavioral intention** predicts actual *behavior*. For example, an individual who uses hookah may consider not using hookah anymore (a) when provided with information in order to change his or her attitude about hookah use (e.g., regular use of a hookah is associated with an increased risk of a heart attack) and (b) with a perception that hookah use is socially unacceptable (e.g., only 5% of college students use a hookah regularly). This information is expected to influence that individual's future intention to use a hookah, which is expected to result in an actual reduction in hookah use.

The other three reasoned action approaches build on this framework, with the inclusion of additional variables (see **Figure 14.3**). Under the assumption that the intent of a health message or campaign is to alter relevant behavior (e.g., to diet), then the need is to change people's intentions to engage in that behavior. The theory of planned behavior includes **perceived behavioral control** (i.e., perceived capability of performing the behavior; e.g., disciplining eating habits), which is a function of a person's **self-efficacy** (i.e., the belief in one's own ability to engage in a behavior; e.g., making healthier choices) and **controllability** (i.e., the belief that making better choices is within one's own control, as opposed to dependent on the choices of other people). Further, behavior is partly a function of the **normative beliefs** of others (i.e., the degree

FIGURE 14.3: Theory of Reasoned Action

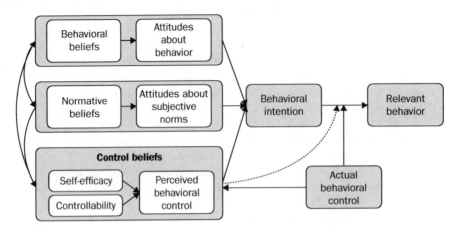

to which others pressure someone to behave in certain ways; e.g., others frequently trying to get someone to try unhealthy foods) and **subjective norms** (i.e., the perception of others' views of performing or not performing a behavior; e.g., someone's perception that his or her friends and family think people should eat what they want). These control and normative beliefs interact with *behavioral beliefs* (e.g., beliefs about whether dieting is healthy) and *behavioral attitudes* (e.g., that the results of dieting will be desirable). To the extent that you believe dieting is healthy and will make you look and feel better, to the extent that your social network believes that dieting is a good idea for you, to the extent that you perceive their beliefs accurately, and to the extent that you believe you can discipline your dietary choices and obtain healthier foods, you are more likely to intend to diet.

Finally, whether your behavioral intention actually results in dieting depends on contextual constraints. For example, if you live and work in an area where there is little access to healthy foods, or if you do not have sufficient money to spend on healthier foods that cost more, then your best intentions may not produce any behavior change. Only when all elements are in sync are you likely to engage in dieting. Each one of these components is open to particular persuasive messages.

Social judgment theory, the elaboration likelihood model, cognitive dissonance theory, and reasoned action approaches are all important frameworks for understanding and influencing the persuasive process. The theoretical perspectives reviewed here all explore the persuasive process for individuals. Not all persuasive processes, however, occur as strictly individual experiences. Persuasion is also a function of social and mediated influences. As we review social and mediated influences, specific theoretical frameworks within these approaches will be examined.

Box 14.1 Ethical Issues

Few topics in the field of communication immediately evoke concerns about ethics as persuasion. Issues of manipulation, deception, coercion, exploitation, disinformation, fake news, guile, cheating, and fraud tend to be evoked when discussing the process of persuasion. Below are three examples of ethical considerations in this context.

- **Professional Ethics**

  Many communicators will find themselves representing others in their construction and delivery of messages. These communicators will therefore often be bound by professional or organizational codes of conduct. For example, the Public Relations Society of America (PRSA) has an ethical code (www.prsa.org). The PRSA handbook proposes eight questions that should be asked before acting:

- Am I going to violate any laws?
- Am I going to violate any core ethical values such as honesty, fairness, and civility?
- Do I have all the facts I need?
- Could I live in a world where everybody did what I am about to do?
- How would I feel if what I am about to do was featured on the first page of tomorrow's paper?
- How would I feel if someone did to me what I am about to do to others?
- What would my mother say or think?
- Am I already thinking about a justification or an excuse for what I am about to do? (Whitman & Guthrie, n.d., p. 10)

The handbook also specifies some practical warning signs of unethical conduct. If you find yourself saying something along the lines of any of the following, you may be about to breach professional ethics:

- "Do what it takes."
- "Everybody does it."
- "Nobody will ever know."
- "It is OK because it is legal."
- "There is no other way, you have no other choice."
- "Just follow orders." (Whitman & Guthrie, n.d., p. 10)

- **Functions vs. Ethics**

Many theorists and practitioners implicitly or explicitly take a systems theory approach to their communication practices—communication is viewed simply as a part of a functioning system. Fawkes (2007) argues that this perspective does not adequately account for the ethical complexities of communication. Simply viewing communication in regard to how it functions, effectively or ineffectively, tends to overlook the moral implications of that communication. After reviewing several models of ethical consideration in public relations and other persuasive professional contexts, Fawkes (2007) proposes a model that integrates the communicator's personal ethics, the audience's ethics, the media's ethics, socially accepted or normative ethics, the team's and organization's ethics, and the profession's ethical code, all in the context of power asymmetry between these parties.

- **Doxastic vs. Evidential Persuasion**

People tend to cherish their own beliefs as uniquely representative of their own identity and sense of self. As such, when others seek to coerce our beliefs or behaviors through threat or force (i.e., doxastic influence), it seems particularly unfair—we each have rights to define our own identity. In contrast, when communicators attempt to persuade us by presenting evidence for a position, it seems more fair and ethical, as it leaves the choice of decision to our own sense of self-relevance (Fârte, 2016). People tend toward truth; that is, they tend to believe that their own beliefs represent a propositionally true or accurate picture of the world as it actually is. Evidence, therefore, represents the backing of propositional claims about the world. Ethical argument and persuasion, therefore, links the best available evidence to the decision preferences being espoused by a communicator. Fârte (2016) argues that persuaders should seek to follow a few rules of interaction with their audiences (pp. 74–45):

1. People should be aware of their feelings toward empirical evidence.

2. The persuader should help people establish personally logical relationships between certain evidence and certain doxastic states [i.e., people need to learn that their view of the world is subjective as well as objective].

3. The persuader should help people internalize the principle of closure [i.e., we need to help people develop valid logical principles of deduction to more efficiently retain valid beliefs and devalue invalid beliefs].

Social Influence Theories

Scholars of interpersonal communication have long known that the process of persuasion can often be observed in routine and ordinary social settings—what is more commonly referred to as **social influence**. Individuals are continuously persuading and being persuaded by close others (Rule, Bisanz, & Kohn, 1985). This process of persuasion can occur interpersonally between two or more individuals, in a group setting, or as a result of social or cultural conventions. In the following section, we discuss the research findings related to persuasion that occur at the interpersonal, group, and normative levels.

Interpersonal-Level Social Influence

Interpersonal communication occurs when two individuals engage in the exchange of information (Roloff, 1981). As part of this information exchange, it is not unusual for an individual to attempt to influence the behavior of another by using persuasive strategies. This is called **compliance-gaining**. Marwell and Schmitt (1967) identified five broad approaches to compliance-gaining, derived from 16 tactics they uncovered during the course of their research. More recent research has expanded these to include as many as 64 strategies (see Kellermann & Cole, 1994). A full taxonomy of the 16 tactics is presented in **Table 14.5.** The five broad approaches are rewarding, punishing, using expertise, and appealing to both impersonal and personal commitments. *Rewarding* involves implying that the recipient will benefit by complying and be satisfied with a choice, and *punishing* denotes that the recipient will experience a negative outcome or forfeit a benefit by failing to comply, which will ultimately leave the recipient unsatisfied with a choice. *Expertise* conveyed by the communicator to the recipient may cause the recipient to believe he or she possesses privileged information that places him or her at an advantage for making the correct decision. Last, appealing to *impersonal commitments* results in activating a sense of internalized commitments to oneself, and appealing to *personal commitments* involves activating the recipient's commitments toward others.

The tactics identified by Marwell and Schmidtt (1967) represent a range of approaches a communicator may use to increase compliance-gaining and to persuade a recipient to engage in a desirable activity. Additionally, a communicator who perceives that certain tactics are more socially or relationally appropriate (e.g., positive expertise, liking, altruism, etc.) will be more likely to launch these tactics for compliance-gaining (Burleson et al., 1988; Wiseman & Schenck-Hamlin, 1981).

Identifying the relevant contextual aspects of a situation that may influence compliance-gaining requires a working definition of what comprises a situation. Previous scholars have defined a situation "by who is involved, what is going on, and where the action is taking place" (Pervin, 1978, pp. 79–80), and outlined six situational dimensions to consider (Cody & McLaughlin, 1980). These six dimensions include (a) intimacy (the closeness between communicator and recipient), (b) dominance (the presence of a power differential between communicator and recipient), (c) personal benefit a communicator stands to gain from persuading a recipient to comply with a request, (d) whether the consequence of making a persuasive attempt is short- or long-term in nature, (e) rights to engage in a particular behavior based on honesty and justice, and (f) resistance to the communicator's attempts to gain compliance that curtail or infringe on the recipient's personal freedom. We will discuss resistance in greater detail later in this chapter.

Compliance-gaining as a one-shot attempt to persuade, however, may not be sufficient to convince the recipient to change a behavior. Instead, "interpersonal influence often proceeds in stages, each of which establishes the foundation for further changes in beliefs or behavior. Individuals slowly come to embrace new opinions, and actors often seduce others to gradually comply with target requests" (Seibold, Cantrill, & Meyers, 1985, pp. 583–584). Techniques that involve a series of persuasion tactics to convince a recipient to alter a behavior are known as **sequential influence strategies**.

One commonly studied sequential influence strategy is known as the **foot-in-the-door effect**. If a communicator can successfully convince a recipient to comply with a small initial request, the recipient will be more likely to comply with a second larger request. For example, if a fundraiser is able to convince a potential donor to make a nominal donation now, the donor will be more likely to comply with a larger request for a donation in the future. This strategy can be very effective if the request is associated with a prosocial issue (Dillard, Hunter, & Burgoon, 1984), is of ample size to activate commitment but not too large to trigger refusal (Seligman, Bush, & Kirsch, 1976),

TABLE 14.5: Sixteen Tactics for Compliance-gaining

Tactic	Definition	Example
1. Promise	A reward is offered in exchange for changing behavior.	"If you take advantage of this special offer today, you get an additional 50% off."
2. Threat	A punishment or undesirable outcome is assured if behavior is not changed.	"If you do not take advantage of this special offer today, you will not get an additional 50% off."
3. Positive expertise	Providing expert view on desirable outcomes of changing behavior. Outcomes are beyond control of the communicator and receiver.	"If you take advantage of this special offer today, you lock in the price at a discounted rate and get an additional 50% off."
4. Negative expertise	Providing expert view on undesirable outcomes of failing to alter behavior. Outcomes are beyond control of the communicator and receiver.	"If you do not take advantage of this special offer today, you can't lock in the price at a discounted rate and you will not get an additional 50% off."
5. Liking	Behaving friendly in order to elicit a sense of obligation and reciprocity.	"Are you feeling overwhelmed with choice? We can help."
6. Pregiving	Offering a gift to create a sense of obligation and reciprocity.	"Please help yourself to complimentary cookies."
7. Debt	Recalling past favors to imply an obligation already exists.	"We have put in a lot of effort to get this deal for you; now it's your turn to show up."
8. Aversion stimulation	Inflicting punishments or undesirable acts in order to elicit concession.	"Every minute that passes by without a decision, you risk seeing an increase in price."
9. Moral appeal	Suggesting changing behavior is morally correct and failing to is immoral.	"Opening an account with us today is the right thing to do."
10. Positive self-feeling	Implying that changing behavior will increase good feelings about self due to taking action in doing what is right.	"Wouldn't it be nice to take this home and enjoy it today?"
11. Negative self-feeling	Implying that changing behavior will increase negative feelings about self due to not taking action in doing what is right.	"Wouldn't it be sad to let go of this opportunity today and let someone else enjoy it?"
12. Positive altercasting	Indicating that individuals with positive attributes are likely to change their behavior.	"Anyone with two eyes can see this is a good deal."
13. Negative altercasting	Indicating that individuals with negative attributes are likely to refuse to change their behavior.	"You would have to be blind not see this great opportunity."
14. Altruism	Suggesting action would benefit the communicator or others.	"If you let me make this sale today, I will get to keep my job."
15. Positive esteem of others	Implying being held in higher esteem by others as a result of changing behavior.	"If you take this home today, your family will be thrilled."
16. Negative esteem of others	Implying being held in lower esteem by others as a result of refusing to change behavior.	"If you don't take this home today, your family will be sad and disappointed."

Adapted from: Kellermann & Cole (1994), Marwell & Schmitt (1967), and Miller, Boster, Roloff, & Seibold (1977).

and prompts internal motivations instead of external ones to comply (Uranowitz, 1975).

In direct contrast to the foot-in-the-door effect, the **door-in-the-face effect** is that a recipient is more likely to comply with a smaller request after refusing an initial larger request. Here, the communicator begins with a large request and, after the recipient rejects the initial request, the communicator returns with a smaller request, which is actually the one desired from the onset. For example, a student may ask a course instructor to move the due date for a large project knowing that the request is too large for course instructor to honor. After the instructor refuses the request, the student may return with a smaller request for the course instructor to devote more class time to the project. This technique works particularly well for prosocial issues in which the same communicator is making the requests (Cialdini et al., 1975).

Persuasion is a routine and ordinary practice in social settings. Through an interpersonal lens, persuasive processes can be identified and studied as way to best understand how interpersonal influence results in attitudinal and behavior change. This line of research, studying compliance-gaining, focuses on the explicit interpersonal attempt to influence another person through persuasive strategies. Within this realm of research, sequential influence strategies, such as foot in the door and door in the face, are studied in way to understand the extent to which they can effectively move individual attitudes and behaviors.

Group-Level Social Influence

Persuasion can also be observed beyond the individual level and occur at the group level. A predominant form of social influence is conformity. **Conformity** describes the process by which a person alters his or her behavior in an effort to correspond or match responses of other individuals (Cialdini & Goldstein, 2004). At times, when we desire to seek social approval from others or to behave correctly by observing how others behave, we may be persuaded to change our behaviors based on how we may expect people around us to respond to them (Cialdini & Trost 1999; Deutsch & Gerard, 1955). Although several theories of social influence relevant to group-level effects have been offered, the groupthink model is examined in the group's chapter (Chapter 16), and the spiral of silence

theory is also relevant here, but explored in the media chapter (Chapter 22).

Influence Through Social Norms

Social and cultural norms can also be powerful agents of persuasion and social influence on individuals and the choices they make about how to behave (Yanovitzky & Rimal, 2006). *Social norms* represent "rules and standards that are understood by members of a group, and that guide and/or constrain social behavior without the force of laws" (Cialdini & Trost, 1999, p. 152). Social norms can be categorized in a couple of distinct ways. Norms that refer to what is socially approved or disapproved are known as **injunctive norms**, while norms that reference what is typically done are **descriptive norms** (Cialdini, Reno, & Kallgren, 1990). For example, in the context of normative behavior for recycling on college campuses, one injunctive norm may be that individuals should recycle aluminum cans on college campuses, and receptacles full of such cans could be evidence of a descriptive norm related to this behavior.

Social norms can influence the persuasive process a number of ways. Social normative influence can be understood through a number of key theories. Some of the most studied theories include the focus theory of normative conduct and the theory of normative social behavior. Both theories will be reviewed in the following paragraphs.

Focus Theory of Normative Conduct

The concepts of injunctive and descriptive norms fall under the **focus theory of normative conduct** (Cialdini, Kallgren, & Reno, 1991). This theory states that in order to influence behavior, a norm must be in focus (i.e., relevant in the mind of the individual) prior to acting (Kallgren, Reno, & Cialdini, 2000). For example, if you do not perceive recycling to be an important behavior, then you will not find other people recycling to influence your recycling behaviors. In addition, effects of norms may be enhanced when injunctive and descriptive norms are consistent (e.g., most students approve of recycling aluminum cans and the majority of students do recycle aluminum cans), and when norms are closely aligned with social situations (e.g., the majority of students *on this campus* do recycle aluminum cans; Goldstein, Cialdini, & Griskevicius, 2008). Other factors, such as whether the behavior is performed while being observed with others, may also impact the influence of social norms on behavior (Lewis, 2013). For example, seeing full recycling cans on campus will not be as persuasive as seeing a fellow student in the process of recycling. Thus, according to the focus theory of normative conduct, social norms are most persuasive when the context is important to us.

Theory of Normative Social Behavior

Although the focus theory of normative conduct tells us when a norm is likely to influence behavior, the theory of normative social behavior helps us understand why norms have an impact in the first place. According to this theory, a norm's influence on behavior can be explained by the desired level of social approval (e.g., strength of injunctive directives), the perceived benefits of performing the behavior (e.g., outcome expectancies), and the degree to which an individual aspires to be similar to the group endorsing the norm (e.g., group identity; Rimal & Real, 2005). Hence, norms are likely to exert the greatest effects on behaviors that appear to offer attractive outcomes and are strongly endorsed by a group with which individuals strongly identify. These effects may be increased in the presence of a strong descriptive norm. For example, research has shown that undergraduate students desire to fit into their college community (i.e., group identity), perceive social benefits of alcohol consumption (i.e., outcome expectancy), and overestimate the rate of alcohol consumption among their peers (i.e., strong injunctive directive). Thus, according to the theory of normative social behavior, this combination of perceptions influences students to have increased alcohol-related behaviors (Neighbors et al., 2007; Rimal & Real, 2005).

Conclusion

The purpose of this chapter was to examine the theoretical and practical understandings of argumentation and the process of persuasion. The three most common categorizations of argument formation were reviewed (i.e., deductive, inductive, abductive). In addition, theoretical understandings of the persuasive process as it appears generally, interpersonally, and socially. As the foundation of the field of communication, argumentation and persuasion is relevant to all facets of the discipline. As theory and research continue to advance our understanding of the processes, we, as a society, will better be able to understand each other and make decision on the basis of valid evidence.

Credits

FIG. 14.1: Adapted from Charles W. Kneupper, "Teaching Argument: An Introduction to the Toulmin Model." *College Composition and Communication*, vol. 29, no. 3. Copyright © 1978 by National Council of Teachers of English (NCTE).

FIG. 14.2: Adapted from Stephen Toulmin, The Uses of Argument. Copyright © 1958 by Cambridge University Press.

CHAPTER 15

Conflict Management Communication

Brian H. Spitzberg & Daniel J. Canary

LEARNING OBJECTIVES

After reading this chapter, you should be able to do the following:

- Identify the reasons why it matters more how conflict is managed rather than if it occurs.
- Identify and differentiate the key features of competent communication.
- Distinguish the key elements of the definition of conflict.
- Differentiate conflict from related concepts and processes (e.g., fights, aggression, arguments, etc.).
- Exemplify the concepts of conflict styles, strategies, and tactics.
- Articulate the dimensions, styles, and strategies in the dual concern model.
- Illustrate the dimensions, styles, and strategies in the strategic choice typology.
- Identify, differentiate, and exemplify reciprocal and complementary conflict patterns.
- Identify and differentiate the stages of the "four horsemen" pattern of conflict management.
- Classify and distinguish examples of major account types (e.g., justifications, excuses, and apologies), and their relative position on the aggravation–mitigation continuum.
- Identify key variables and their role in the PAIN model of aggression escalation.
- Correctly identify key propositions of the PAIN model of aggression escalation.

The Importance of Conflict

In interpersonal contexts alone, such as in marital, dating, family, and friendship contexts, how conflict is managed is the *single most important predictor of the success or failure of the relationship*. Indeed, by examining conflict in married couples, Gottman (1994) can predict with almost

95% accuracy which couples will divorce and which will not. Given a 50% chance accuracy in such a prediction, such a massive enhancement of predictability is astonishing. Some research indicates that managers spend 15 to 20% of their time at work managing employee and staff conflicts (Acuna, 2013; Bolden-Barrett, 2017; Half, 2011), and half to two-thirds of employees attribute at least some employee turnover to conflicts at work (CIPD, 2008). Moreover, conflict is often credited as a major source of failure in politics, diplomacy, societal development, and relationships.

Importantly, however, such failures are *not, absolutely not,* due to conflict per se. How conflict is managed, not *the mere existence of* conflict, is what makes the critical difference in people's relationship as well as their own well-being (Canary & Lakey, 2013). People in happy relationships experience conflict, as do partners in abusive relationships. What differentiates happy from unhappy (and abusive) relationships is how partners *manage* their conflicts. For example, Gottman (1994) found a five-to-one rule in characterizing one of the key differences between satisfied and dissatisfied marriages: Unhappy couples "balance" their negative comments with only one positive comment. That is, dissatisfied partners offer only one positive comment for each negative comment to maintain their unhappy relationships. But, happy couples engage in approximately five positive comments to "balance" each negative comment. Competent conflict management, it turns out, makes all the difference in how relationships among parties develop and continue (Spitzberg, Canary, & Cupach, 1994).

Competence is an evaluation of the quality of a performance. Competent communication is of high quality and judged on a continuum, from low to high competence. Many criteria exist for assessing someone's competence, such as clarity, accuracy, understandability, efficiency, and so forth. In contrast, Spitzberg and Cupach (2011) propose that these various criteria are subordinate to appropriateness and effectiveness (see also: Chapter 13). Competent communication is appropriate and effective in a given context. Appropriateness refers to the degree to which a person's communication is viewed as legitimate and acceptable in a given context. Effectiveness concerns the degree to which people use communication to achieve preferable outcomes or goals in an encounter. Note that communication can be inappropriate *and* ineffective (i.e., minimizing), inappropriate *but* effective (i.e., sufficing),

or appropriate *but* ineffective (i.e., maximizing), but is most competent when it achieves relatively preferred outcomes in a manner that is perceived to sustain the relational integrity of the context (i.e., appropriate *and* effective, or optimizing). Conflict encounters inherently complicate competence (Canary & Spitzberg, 1987, 1989). Because conflicts involve one party pursuing a goal that the other party perceives as obstructing, most conflicts involve either ineffectiveness or inappropriateness, or both. In fact, research reveals that perceptions of appropriateness and effectiveness are positively associated during conflict. That is, when people are appropriate, they also tend to succeed at obtaining their goals that they believe the other person is blocking. In brief, learning to engage conflict competently is intrinsically challenging and potentially rewarding.

Definitions, Differences, and Distinctions

Conflict is an engine of change. Indeed, in the grand scheme of things, conflict might constitute the most important engine of change. The theory of evolution, for example, reliant as it is on self-generating deviations in DNA and cooperative processes such as mating, still requires such changes to be molded and regulated by the conflict of natural selection and a nature that is "red in tooth and claw" (Alfred Lord Tennyson, *In Memoriam A. H. H.,* 1850). In human affairs, conflict presents the process by which differences between and among people are negotiated and managed. As such, conflict can be a source of terrorism and tragedy, and it can be one of the only sources of peace, political and cultural progress, and relationship growth. Conflict, therefore, is normal rather than abnormal. All social systems (e.g., personal relationships, families, organizations, societies, and cultures) experience conflict, but they also *need* to experience conflict if they are to adapt and survive. Again, the question is not *whether* conflict will occur, but *how* it will be managed.

Conflict takes many forms, often believed to include bargaining and negotiation, on the more formal end of a continuum, and fighting and aggression, on the opposite end of the continuum. In its essence, **conflict** can be defined as any expressed struggle between two or more parties. In general, at least one person will perceive some degree of interdependence with the other party, perceive obstruction from the other party about one's desired goal(s), and perceive a scarcity of resources and preferred outcomes ("My roommate won't clean his/her dishes and I really want a clean place to live") (Cupach, Canary, & Spitzberg, 2010). The qualifier "expressed" means that conflicts only exist when they are somehow shared in social behavior or communication (see section on styles and strategies). Sometimes conflict is focused more on specific goals, tasks or objectives, and at other times it is focused more on the relationship between interactants or the process or means by which those objectives the relationship is managed (O'Neill, Allen, & Hastings, 2013). In general, conflicts, whether in a dyad or a group, will ebb and flow across these facets of task, relationship, and process.

If only one person perceives a problem, it is not conflict. For example, simply disliking someone is not conflict. But, dislike becomes conflict when it is communicated, and resisted, by the disliked person. The qualifier *perceived* in the previous paragraph means that conflicts might occur in cases in which a party blames the wrong individual for a transgression or as standing in the way of a desired outcome. A boss may engage an employee in conflict about a failure to obtain a new contract with a buyer but believe mistakenly that it was the employee's fault. The qualifier *parties* means that conflicts sometimes occur between individuals, and at other times between or among agents and actors of groups, institutions, countries, or associations. The term **interdependence** means that one party's objectives, goals, preferences, and/or behaviors, to some degree, rely on the other party's actions, or are at least they are perceived to be interdependent on those actions. That these objectives, goals, preferences, or behaviors are perceived to be *scarce* means that a potential exists of not achieving preferred processes or outcomes because they are not infinitely available through one's own autonomous actions. That is, something party A wants, or wants to do or say, can only be accomplished with party B's compliance or cooperation. If such preferred processes or outcomes were available through autonomous action by A, then there would be no need for conflict with B.

Terms such as *preferred outcomes, interdependence,* and *obstruction* often suggest that conflict always concerns tangible things such as money, natural resources, and retribution (e.g., the proverbial "eye for an eye and tooth for a tooth" for past losses). Importantly, however, much, if not most, conflict regards intangible things as much, if not more, than tangible things. One of the most damning but intangible sources of conflict is disrespect of a person's **face** (often called *identity management* or *self-presentation;* see also: Chapter 8). Face concerns reflect the identity or impression a person wants to make on others. Face is the respect or deference an interactant claims and attempts to maintain in the eyes of others (Ho, 1976). For example, bar fights and relational violence are often triggered by challenges to face when one perceives verbal slights, criticisms, insults, flirtatious glances, perceived transgressions, jealousies, envies, and so forth (Spitzberg, 2010a, 2010b). The face we present to others may well be entirely authentic rather than a role we are "playing at." According to one conceptualization (Lim & Bowers, 1991, for example, we sometimes seek to be included (belonging face), to be respected (competence face), or not to be imposed upon or restricted in our actions (autonomy face),

Hypothetically, self-esteem is an infinite resource; a person *can choose* to perceive his- or herself as positively as he or she chooses. Yet, a perceived slight or rejection by another person often lies at the heart of conflicts. Furthermore, conflict is not always about outcomes (e.g., a salary increase or joint custody of children). It is often about process or procedure, such as when students have a conflict about what topic to pursue for a final group project, or when members of a workgroup disagree about whether parliamentary procedures are getting in the way of progress on the meeting's agenda. Other dimensional representations have been identified (e.g., Ma, Yang, Wang, & Li, 2017; Weymouth, Buehler, Zhou, & Henson, 2016), but a common perspective envisions conflict that can be about **identity** (how self or face is perceived or evaluated), *procedure* (how to achieve goals), **instrumental** objectives (what goals to achieve), and/or *interpersonal* desires (how a relationship is defined or is unfolding).

A **fight** represents a particularly intense conflict. **Violence** is a conflict involving physical contact, restraint (e.g., kidnapping or imprisonment), and the potential for physical injury. Similarly, **aggression** is conflict motivated to hurt another person psychologically, relationally, and/or physically, using any combination of verbal and physical means. Not all conflict intends harm, and, therefore, not all conflict is aggression, but *all aggression is a form of conflict.*

Negotiation is any conflict in which all parties involved begin the interaction with a presumption of potential mutual benefit. Negotiations, therefore, tend to follow more cooperative and rule-regulated forms of interaction and are often moderated or mediated by third parties who have an interest in the outcomes of the negotiations. **Arbitration** is a form of negotiation in which a third party (e.g., a judge, an arbitrator) has some degree of authority to make an enforceable decision in resolving the conflict, either on his/her own or with assistance by another person. **Mediation** concerns **alternative dispute resolution (ADR)**, which is a process in which a neutral third-party attempts to facilitate a cooperative communication process through which the conflicting parties can achieve their own enforceable resolution to the conflict. Because mediation involves a process in which the parties generate the resolution themselves, but engage in a process facilitated and guided by an expert third party, mediation tends to result in conflict resolutions that produce greater compliance (e.g., father paying child care) and higher satisfaction than direct conflicts or arbitration (Ocaña, Chamberlain, & Carlson, 2005; Shaw, 2010).

Conflict constitutes a form of communication (Maier & Burrell, 2017). That is, conflict can only occur through communication. Conflict is also studied in research on power and influence. Because conflict is an attempt to alter another party's viewpoints and/or actions, it is an attempt at influence. If conflict is a form of communication and influence, it becomes essential to understand how people communicate during conflict.

Tactics, Strategies, and Styles

Every conflict might seem to possess its own unique characteristics, but it turns out that conflicts are often highly patterned. Various ways exist of characterizing these patterns. Two widely used approaches to conflict patterns are considered here: individual patterns and sequential patterns.

In almost any team sport, it is possible to analyze the game in part through individual plays (a specific set of actions expected from all members of the team), game plans (a general goal for the types of plays to be called during a game), tendencies (a team's proclivity to use certain consistent plays and game plans across games),

and strategies (e.g., how to defend against a particular team). In football, for example, a "bubble screen pass" is a short-yardage pass, used during early downs to set up the long pass or short third-down runs for a first down. The bubble screen is one play, or tactic, in the game plan, whereas the general habit of engaging in these plays and game plans for an entire season is a strategy, and the degree to which tactics and strategies are used consistently over time could be considered a style of play. That is, a specific conflict behavior is a **tactic**. When tactics are bundled toward a particular goal, they can be considered a **strategy** of conflict. When a party uses a particular set of similar tactics and strategies over time and across contexts, it is a **style** of conflict.

Two Models of Conflict Communication

The Dual Concern Model

There are many typologies and approaches to identifying conflict behavior (e.g., Leung & Kim, 2007; Trippe & Baumoel, 2015). Most commonly, however, conflict tactics, strategies, and styles are mapped in two ways—a goals approach or a structural approach. A goals approach represents an analysis of conflict in regard to the primary valued objectives of the individual. An individual can be primarily motivated by, or care about, his or her own goals. In contrast, an individual may care more about the other party's satisfaction than about the issues at stake in the conflict. This contrast represents two dimensions: concern for self versus concern for other (Woodin, 2011). If these two dimensions are crossed, they create what is known as the **dual concern model** (see **Figure 15.1**).

A party who examines a situation and concludes that there is very little worth fighting for in that situation, but who also sees little interest in the other party's goals or objectives, is likely to take an **avoidant** strategic approach to the conflict, preferring not to get involved in the conflict in the first place. If a coworker attempts to involve another employee in a conflict he or she is having with his or her boss, the third party may decide that there is nothing to be gained by getting involved in their conflict. Such an avoidance strategy would result in a preference for avoidance tactics, such as delaying, changing the topic, suggesting the other party take the conflict elsewhere, and so forth.

FIGURE 15.1: The Dual Concern Model

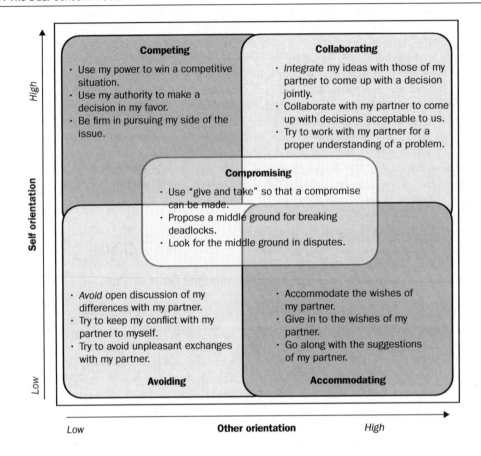

A party who cares little for his or her interest in a particular situation but realizes that it is very important to the other party is likely to take an **accommodating** strategic orientation to the conflict. For example, a husband could attempt to engage his wife in a discussion of landscaping choices between flowering vines versus low shrubs. This may be a topic she cares very little about. After some discussion of their differing viewpoints, the wife may simply accommodate the husband's interests by giving in, agreeing, or otherwise finding ways to allow her husband to get his way.

A party who is greatly self-interested, to such an extent that the perceived interests of the other party mean little, is likely to take a **competitive** strategic orientation to the conflict. This "win-at-all-reasonable-costs" orientation results in tactical choices of persistence, aggressive pursuit of self's positions, and even personal attacks, if needed. An employee with considerable experience at a particular task may argue aggressively when coworkers with far less experience attempt to suggest courses of action.

A party with strong interests, but who recognizes the importance of the other party's interests, is likely to take a more **compromising** strategic orientation to the conflict. Compromise is a blend of win-lose and win-win concerns. It involves tactics such as "tit for tat," reciprocal concessions, and "meeting in the middle" of each party's level of aspiration. A newlywed couple who is engaged in a conflict over whose parents to spend time with during vacation may end up deciding to swap holiday destinations sequentially (e.g., "your parents for Thanksgiving, my parents for Christmas, and our own vacation in the summer").

Box 15.1 Ethical Issues

Conflict is a subset of the study of power. All conflict is an attempt at influencing other parties, and thus issues of power asymmetry constantly elicit concerns about the ethics of using tactics and strategies that exploit such asymmetrical power relationships (Das & Pegu, 2016).

- **Professional Codes of Conduct**

Just as public relations, advertising, and journalism have professional codes of conduct, so too do professional mediators, arbitrators and negotiators of conflict. For example, JAMS (formerly: Judicial Arbitration and Mediation Services, Inc.) adopted the following set of ethical guidelines:

1. A mediator should ensure that all parties are informed about the mediator's role and nature of the mediation process, and that all parties understand the terms of settlement.

2. A mediator should protect the voluntary participation of each party.

3. A mediator should be competent to mediate the particular matter.

4. A mediator should maintain the confidentiality of the process.

5. A mediator should conduct the process impartially.

6. A mediator should refrain from providing legal advice.

7. A mediator should withdraw under certain circumstances [such as might involve illegal conduct, coercive influence of the parties, etc.].

8. A mediator should avoid marketing that is misleading and should not guarantee results (www.jamsadr.com: Mediators Ethics Guidelines).

- **Ethical Decision-Making During Conflicts**

Ness and Connolly (2017) proposed that interpersonal conflict tends to diminish ethical decision-making because of biases in perceiving the causes of conflicts (i.e., we tend to blame the other party), because conflict evokes and favors prior experience over current circumstances, because situational and personal goals tend to overpower deliberative decision-making, and because conflicts tend to push parties to overly simplified positions in complex and ambiguous dilemmas. Indeed, they found that conflict diminishes a person's ability to anticipate consequences, and leads parties to consider their own goals more so than the goals or orientations of the other party. One factor they did not examine was the role of emotions in affecting ethical decision-making. In what ways do you think emotions in conflict situations affect ethical decision-making? Can you think of some situations in your social or work life in which ethical considerations have been short-circuited due to the emotions of one or more of the parties?

- **Information Sharing**

People cannot make sound decisions about their beliefs, values, and behavior choices in conditions of incomplete information. Thus, communicators who possess but do not share relevant information in a situation in which others' choices or decisions are at stake raises ethical issues. Can you make a legitimate decision about your health, your government, your family, or your relationship, if the others involved in such choices have not shared all the relevant information upon which your decision depends? People neurologically tend to weigh the costs and benefits (or rewards, pleasure) of sharing information—when sharing information is expected to be valuable in some way to the communicator or the communicator's relationship with the target of such disclosure, the information tends to be shared (Falk & Scholz, 2017). Ethical and moral concerns often become secondary concerns or easily rationalized when tangible costs and rewards are evaluated. How then can communicators directly draw ethical or moral issues into the subjective utility of their reasoning and negotiations regarding issues of choice, and what role should social norms play a role in such subjective valuations?

A party who recognizes the importance of the interests of both parties in the conflict, especially when the relationship is considered extremely important, is likely to take a **collaborative** strategic orientation to the conflict. Such an orientation promotes efforts to discover the other party's views, elaborate each other's needs and interests, and seriously examine the options available for achieving the best possible "win-win" approach to managing the conflict. A married couple discussing a situation in which one spouse's employer has restructured the business, requiring a transfer to a foreign country for that spouse, is likely to have significant life issues to consider.

The Strategic Choice Model

As noted, the dual concerns model focuses on how people tend to manage their conflicts over time and contexts—that is, their conflict styles. The **strategic choice model**, on the other hand, describes how people create and enact their individual "game plans," or strategies, for managing conflict (for a list of specific tactics for each strategy, see Sillars, Canary, & Tafoya, 2004). The strategic choice model holds that people make two decisions when determining how they will manage a conflict. The first decision concerns the **directness-indirectness** of the strategy to use—that is, whether one should confront or avoid the other person. People who decide to confront typically use direct conflict tactics (see **Table 15.1**), whereas people desiring to avoid the person engage in indirect tactics. Direct strategies tend to go to the heart of the conflict, honestly addressing the core issues, whether they are about identity or are instrumental, procedural, or relational problems (Arazy, Yeo, & Nov, 2013; Keck & Samp, 2007; Qin, Andreychik, Sapp, & Arendt). *Indirect* strategies involve actions or statements that attempt to skirt the issue or camouflage what the underlying issues are.

The second decision that concerns people's strategic choice concerns the valence, or the selection of strategies that differ in their valence. The **valence dimension** represents the emotional tone of the behavior. "Valence" derives from the same root word as "value" and refers to the degree to which the values expressed are positive or negative in nature. *Positively valenced* strategies reflect a respect for the process and the other party and generally pursue an optimistic, cooperative prospect for the conflict. *Negatively valenced* strategies reveal a disregard for the feelings of the other party, competitiveness, getting one's way, and often a more coercive and perhaps aggressive orientation to the conflict.

As **Figure 15.2** shows, the two dimensions of directness and valence can be crossed theoretically to yield a relatively clean typology of four conflict strategies and tactics that institute those strategies (Overall, Fletcher, Simpson, & Sibley, 2009; for other lists, see Sillars, Coletti, Parry, & Rogers, 1982; van de Vliert & Euwema, 1994). First, competitive and direct choices lead to use of "direct fighting" tactics (van de Vliert & Euwema, 1994), which include put-downs, ridicule, sarcasm, accusing the partner, interrupting the partner, and the like. Next, competitive and indirect choices lead to a passive-aggressive game plan that van de Vliert and Euwema (1994) call "indirect fighting." These include invoking guilt, debasing the self, appealing to love, acting hurt, and other emotional appeals. Third, cooperative and direct choices lead to more functional tactics of compromise, showing willingness to manage the problem, accepting blame when needed, honest disclosure, problem solving, and so on. Finally, soft and positive conflict tactics emerge from the decisions to be cooperative and indirect, what van de Vliert and Euwema (1994) called "accommodation tactics." Accommodation can be seen in denying anything is wrong, giving in quickly, changing the topic, and ingratiating the partner, among others.

FIGURE 15.2: The Conflict Strategic Choice Model

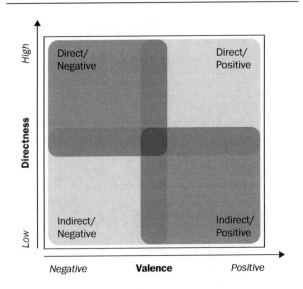

TABLE 15.1: Strategies and Tactics in the Strategic Choice Typology of Conflict

Dimension	Associated Strategies and Tactics
Negative–Direct	**Coercion**
	Derogate partner (e.g., criticize, insult, belittle, ridicule, make fun of in a hurtful way).
	Indicate negative consequences for partner (e.g., threaten punishment, infer that something desired will be withheld) if partner does not conform to desired change.
	Display negative effect (e.g., anger, irritation, displeasure, frustration, yelling, cursing, violence) when partner fails to conform to wishes.
	Accuse and blame partner for discrepancies and/or problems in the relationship.
	Autocracy
	Insist or demand that the partner think, feel, or behave in a certain way.
	Talk from a position of authority and/or assert or imply that self is more of an expert regarding the topic under discussion or is in a superior position to comment on the topic.
	Attempt to exert superiority by trying to make partner feel inferior and/or invalidate partner's point of view (e.g., be patronizing, use sarcasm, be condescending, or reject and invalidate partner's arguments).
	Take a domineering or non-negotiating stance (e.g., not listen to partner's arguments, repeat own point of view, argue until partner agrees, interrupt partner, control the conversation).
Negative–Indirect	**Manipulation**
	Attempt to make partner feel guilty (e.g., remind of past favors or partner transgressions, appeal to obligations, commitments, or fairness).
	Appeal to partner's love and concern.
	Supplication
	Use emotional expression of hurt (e.g., tears, sulking, making sad face, pouting).
	Debase self (e.g., portray self as less capable, worthy, or powerful than partner) and/or present self as needing help.
	Emphasize the negative consequences the situation or partner's behavior has for self.
Positive–Direct	**Rational Reasoning**
	Use and seek factual or accurate information.
	Use logic and rational reasoning (e.g., weigh pros and cons, assess consequences, present arguments in a logical fashion, suggest solutions, outline benefits of particular approaches).
	Explain behavior or point of view (e.g., outlining possible causes) in such a way that the partner would find it reasonable to behave/think that way if the partner were in the same position.
Positive–Indirect	**Soft Positive**
	"Soften" persuasion attempts (e.g., minimize problem, point out good characteristics of partner).
	Encourage partner to explain point of view and express feelings about the issue.
	Be open to, acknowledge, and validate partner's views.
	Be charming and express positive effect (e.g., humor).

Source: Adapted from Overall, Fletcher, Simpson, & Sibley (2009).

Styles, strategies, and tactics reflect the patterns that an individual enacts during conflict, but conflicts are always multiple-party interactions. When tactics are analyzed across individuals in a conflict, the sequential structure of the conflict begins to emerge. There are many patterns that can be identified (Canary & Lakey, 2013), but three prominent and particularly destructive patterns will be identified here.

Conflict Patterns

Tolstoy (1899) opened his novel *Anna Karenina* with an attempt at a deep, penetrating insight: "All happy families resemble one another; every unhappy family is unhappy in its own way" (p. 1). Later, Nabokov (1996) playfully emphasized how Tolstoy's proposition had been transfigured by its translation from the Russian by opening his novel *Ada* with the provocative transposition: "All happy families are more or less dissimilar; all unhappy ones are more or less alike" (p. 7). In this novel contrast, Nabokov turns out to be the more scientifically validated observer of the human condition. Happy families and relationships tend to find a wide variety of ways of managing their conflicts, varying from situation to situation and issue to issue (i.e., they display both multifinality and equifinality; see Chapter 2). In contrast, dissatisfied couples and families tend to find themselves entrapped in relatively rigid, predictable destructive patterns.

Relying solely on observational research of couple conflicts, Gottman (1994) derived a typology of five marriage types. Three of these are functional and coincide with Fitzpatrick's typology of marriage (Fitzpatrick et al., 1984). Functional marriages contain volatile, validator, and avoider types. The dysfunctional include hostile and hostile detached couples. More precisely, *volatile couples* resemble Fitzpatrick's independent marriages, wherein couples are at ease confronting each other, so they often bargain and negotiate. They also eschew traditional sex roles and display a range of emotions to each other. The second functional marriage is the *validator*, who is similar to Fitzpatrick's traditional type. Validators argue only about important issues, show affection, and seek to spend time together. The third functional marriage by Gottman is the *avoider* and is similar to Fitzpatrick's separate category. As the term implies, avoiders attempt to stay apart from each other, and they discourage open communication about any problems on both the emotional level and cognitive level.

Gottman's two dysfunctional couples are so named due to their "nonregulated" conflict management behaviors; that is, their negative communication outweighed their positive communication. The *hostile* couple is characterized by direct engagement, high accusations, and high defensiveness. The *hostile detached couples* are emotionally divorced from each other, though they engage in "brief episodes of reciprocated attacks and defensiveness" (Gottman, 1994, p. 216). At this point, we elaborate more on what is meant by conflict patterns. The first of these is simply *reciprocity*.

Reciprocity

The first, and most fundamental, pattern is **reciprocity**, the matching of one party's actions with a similar response. To respond in kind to the actions of others is a universal tendency; so much so that the tendency is referred to as the *norm of reciprocity* (Keysar, Converse, Wang, & Epley, 2008), and may be one of the evolved adaptive traits that underlie almost all higher cultural developments of the human species (Nagy et al., 2010). Reciprocal actions are often conceptualized as a two-turn unit of analysis called an **interact**—one party's action responded to by another party's action. For example, reciprocal actions in conflicts are often referred to as a "tit-for-tat" situation. Reciprocity itself can be understood in a variety of ways, but the most common understanding is **symmetry**, in which a party simply responds with the same behavior as the other party. If each statement or action of a party can be considered from a perspective of attempts to assert, or attempts to submit, then behavior can be coded as either a "one-up" (↑) or a "one-down" (↓) move. If conflict interaction is then divided into one party's act, followed by the other party's act (forming an *interact*), then symmetrical reciprocity takes the form of either two one-ups, or two one-downs in sequence (↑↑; ↓↓). Such reciprocity generally reveals a competitive struggle. The first pattern (↑↑) illustrates an assertive struggle for dominance, whereas the second pattern (↓↓) reveals a submissiveness struggle. One of the most destructive patterns predicting relationship deterioration is **negative affect reciprocity**, in which there is a high rate of responding to one person's negative comments or criticisms with one's own criticisms or insults (Carrère & Gottman, 1999; Gottman & Levenson, 2000). This is one example of how unhappy families are more predictable; happy families are more capable of responding to negative or one-up moves with something other than an identical response.

In contrast, **complementary interactions** reflect responses that move in a manner that fit or harmonize with the prior party's action. An assertion (e.g., "You shouldn't bother getting a flu vaccine; they don't work": ⬆) followed by an agreement (e.g., "You're probably right": ⬇), and a question (e.g., "Where would you like to eat tonight?": ⬇) followed by an assertion (e.g., "Let's try that new fusion place": ⬆) represent complementary sequences. These patterns are more typical of communication accommodation, which is somewhat more typical of competent interactions.

Several scholars have discussed positive versus negative patterns (Cupach, Canary, & Spitzberg, 2010). Positive patterns include *supportiveness–supportiveness,* which indicates both people positively acknowledge each other as well as each other's statements; *positive metacommunication,* where one partner favorably comments on the other partner's communication behavior; *problem–solution,* which concerns a joint effort to solve issues; *validation,* where partners agree to behave a particular way in the future, and *convergence,* which are statements indicating that the discussion is on an acceptable path; among others. Negative conflict patterns include *demand–withdraw,* where one partner demands attention and discussion and the other partner ignores, evades, and eventually withdraws or stonewalls; *defensiveness–defensiveness,* where both parties respond as if the partner has or will criticize or otherwise attempt to hurt them; *negative metacommunication,* which refers to partners making negative evaluations of each other's messages; and *proposal–counterproposal,* which concerns how one suggestion by one partner is met with disagreement and suggestion to do something different. As one can ascertain, negative conflict patterns can continue for several minutes—or even days—and critically damage one's relational satisfaction and stability. Not all conflict behaviors yield the same effect. Gottman (1994) identified four conflict tactics that appear especially corrosive. The following section takes a brief look at these four tactics.

The Four Horsemen

A second common pattern that tends to occur over time is the **four horsemen of the apocalypse pattern**, so-named by Gottman (1994), typical of couples likely to divorce. This pattern (displayed in **Figure 15.3**) occurs when one party in a conflict initiates a *complaint or criticism*, which is a general term for a one-up action that implies the other party did something wrong. This complaint/criticism may take the form of an accusation, a negative evaluation of the partner's person/personality, or simply an expectation (e.g., "I see the trash still hasn't been taken out": ⬆). Next, either partner feels and shows *disgust or* **contempt**, which is a specific emotional state indicating nonverbal revulsion, direct frustration, and resentment for having the original demand so disregarded and contested (e.g., "I can't stand it that you always try to get out of *anything* you don't want to do": ⬆). Third, one or both parties engage in **defensiveness** (see also: Chapter 16), which is a communicative attempt to deny responsibility or fault, in a way that generally either criticizes the accuser as being unjust, or simply denying the accuser's position (e.g., "Why am I suddenly the only one responsible for the trash?": ⬆). This disgust or contempt is then responded to by *withdrawal,* or what Gottman refers to as stonewalling, in which an effort is made to avoid further conflict (e.g., "Fine. Think what you want to think, but I'm busy so leave me alone about it": ⬆). This sequence does not necessarily occur only in four turns by two people, but may reflect key markers or actions in any expanded sequence of events. To the extent that these landmarks are apparent in expanded sequences of interactions between conflicting parties, the more dissatisfied the relationships, the more likely the relationships will deteriorate.

Although many scholars have accepted Gottman's four horsemen pattern, other research indicates that not all four horsemen are necessary. For example, Holman and Jarvis (2003) conducted a factor analysis on 82 items that measured the four tactics. The result was three factors, not four. These factors were criticism, contempt/defensiveness, and withdrawal (stonewalling). Also, Gottman, Coan, Carrere, and Swanson (1998) added *belligerence* to Gottman's four horsemen, claiming it represents a kind of four horsemen behavior. They found that the combination of belligerence, defensiveness, and contempt predicted divorce. Although belligerence, defensiveness, and contempt predicted divorce, these factors did not discriminate between happy couples and unhappy couples.

FIGURE 15.3: Gottman's (1994) "Four Horsemen of the Apocalypse"

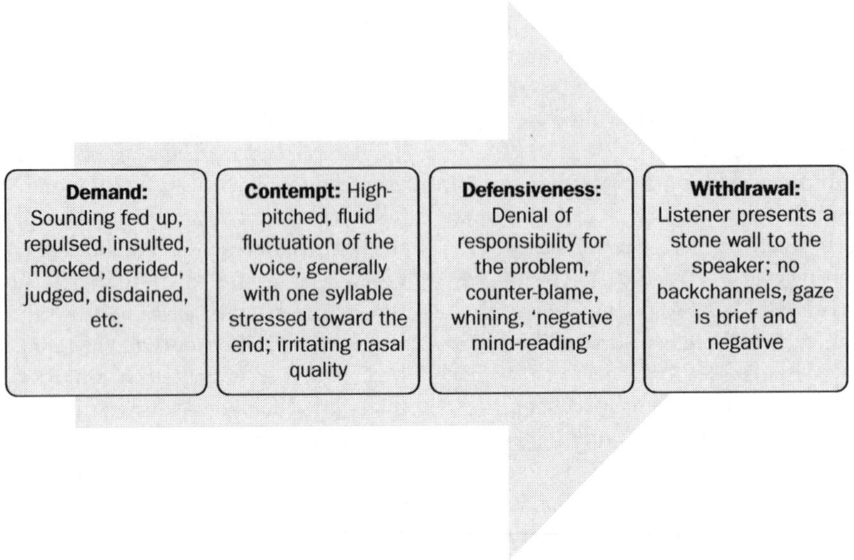

Demand:	Contempt:	Defensiveness:	Withdrawal:
Sounding fed up, repulsed, insulted, mocked, derided, judged, disdained, etc.	High-pitched, fluid fluctuation of the voice, generally with one syllable stressed toward the end; irritating nasal quality	Denial of responsibility for the problem, counter-blame, whining, 'negative mind-reading'	Listener presents a stone wall to the speaker; no backchannels, gaze is brief and negative

The PAIN Model

The final pattern is even more destructive, and is considered typical of interactions that lead to abuse or aggression. Spitzberg's (2010a) abbreviated personal affect and identity negotiation (PAIN) model begins where the four horsemen sequence begins—with perceived transgressions that elicit a demand or reproach of that perceived transgression (see **Figure 15.4**). The defensiveness response is understood not as defensiveness per se, but as an account.

Accounts represent a repertoire of tactics intended to explain, manage, or repair a perceived or accused transgression. Common accounting tactics include refusals or denials, excuses, justifications, concessions, remorse, and apology (Benoit, 1995; Fritsche, 2002; Schönbach, 1980). The most common and relevant to the study of conflict include excuses (along with apologies) and justifications. **Excuses** are statements or actions that attempt to diminish the transgressor's responsibility, typically by either externalizing the cause of a transgression (e.g., "I had a terrible day at work") or attributing the cause to an uncontrollable source, such as an accident (e.g., "I didn't mean to throw the plate at you; I thought I was throwing at the wall") or disinhibiting factor (e.g., "I was too drunk to know what I was doing"). **Apologies** may be used as part of, or independently of, excuses, but they usually imply some degree of responsibility along with regret or sympathy for the victim of the transgression. **Justifications**, in contrast, accept responsibility, but attempt to provide a rationale for the legitimacy of the transgression (e.g., "You had it coming to you for flirting with that person").

Accounts can be understood pragmatically as ranging along an **aggravation–mitigation continuum**, which roughly represents the degree to which the account functions to deescalate or escalate the intensity or negativity of the encounter. Justifications tend to be more aggravating because they imply the "aggrieved party" has no basis for complaint. Such a denial of claim tends to further threaten the face of the person, increasing defensiveness and the already escalating affect cycle. Excuses tend to be further along the continuum toward mitigation by implying some ownership of causation ("Yes, I threw the plate …") and yet diminishing blameworthiness ("… but I didn't mean to hit you with it"). Apologies are likely to be furthest along the mitigation end of the continuum in that they legitimate the aggrieved party's complaint and offer a degree of supplication or relational repair (Barlett, 2013; Fehr, Gelfand, & Nag, 2010; Slocum, Allan, & Allan, 2011).

Impressions of sincerity, genuineness, spontaneity, honesty, and openness are likely to affect the perceived appropriateness and effectiveness of accounts (Exline, Deshea, & Holeman, 2007; Risen & Gilovich, 2007). Apologies, in particular, have been found to have significant

FIGURE 15.4: Abbreviated Personal Affect and Identity Negotiation (PAIN) Model

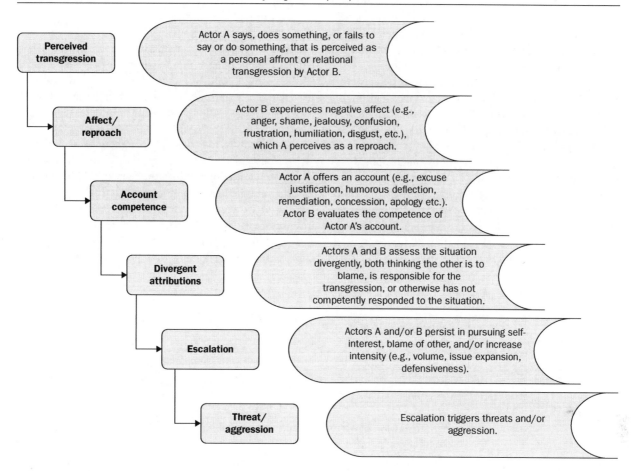

transformative effects on conflicts, both in their own right and because they facilitate forgiveness, which also has its own transformative effects. Apologies generally have an enactment token (i.e., a performance of an admission; e.g., "I'm sorry" or "I apologize"). Apologies may also involve a statement of personal responsibility (e.g., "It's my fault"), remorse (e.g., "I regret my actions," or "I feel really bad"), account (i.e., an explanation of how the event in question occurred), offer of reparation (e.g., "I'll make it up to you"), and future forbearance (e.g., "I promise I won't do this again"). Furthermore, in general, apologies are viewed as more competent to the extent that they not only have more of these elements, but also are viewed as proportional to the severity of the transgression and as sincerely enacted (i.e., the person is *truly* sorry and remorseful).

Any account given in the episode will be evaluated by the receiver in terms of its competence (appropriateness and effectiveness). The competence of the account is, in turn, based in large part on the attributions about its reasonableness. Attributions are perceptions of cause and effect. Social events, such as transgressions, are usually ambiguous in cause. A person's infidelity might be purely opportunistic and selfish or a response to a partner's abuse and inattention. Such abuse often takes the form of **intimate partner violence (IPV)**, which is any behavior intended to harm a person physically in the context of an established personal relationship (Dailey, Lee, & Spitzberg, 2007, 2012). Anger and intimate partner violence (IPV) narratives reveal significant self-serving attributional biases in their interpretation based on victim-versus-perpetrator role (Canary, Spitzberg, & Semic, 1998); perpetrators perceive their anger as isolated and justified, whereas victims tend to perceive it as arbitrary, gratuitous, or incomprehensible (Cavanagh, Dobash, Dobash, & Lewis, 2001; Schütz, 1999). Whether the motive or cause of the transgression is perceived to be selfish or altruistic influences its perceived legitimacy. To the extent the account is viewed as illegitimate, the defensiveness of the offended person is likely to increase, and the conflict is likely to escalate. The PAIN model can be summarized through a series of formal propositions, which are elaborated in **Table 15.2**.

Increasing escalation, fueled further by negative affect reciprocity, leads to divergence of perspectives and positions and amplification of intensity. The negative emotions intensify, which increasingly override executive cognitive control processes and self-reflection, and reinforce "knee-jerk" negative responses. As disinhibition of cognitive control responses increases, the prospect of communicative and physical aggression increases.

The PAIN model anticipates that almost any relationship is capable of experiencing intimate partner violence if the conflict conditions and context develop along a cascade of escalating and divergent intensifications of defensive interpretations and negative emotions (Spitzberg, 2007, 2009a, 2013b). As interactants increasingly defend their respective identities, through both attack and self-protection, conflicts escalate both in intensity and in the layers of incompatibility that emerge in the process of interaction. The frustration of escalating and irresolvable conflict eventually triggers more arousal, which progressively disinhibits cognitive control processes and provokes defensive (and offensive) forms of aggressive communication, which in turn produce a combustible

TABLE 15.2: Formal Propositions of the Personal Affect and Identity Negotiation Model

Transgression management	P_1: Perceived affronts (i.e., rule violations, transgressions) are directly related to face threat.
	P_2: Face threat is directly related to likelihood of verbal conflict.
	P_3: Perceived affronts are directly related to the use of accounts.
Competence evaluation	P_4: The competence of accounts moderates the likelihood of conflict escalation.
	P_5: The attribution of harmful intent or responsibility to face threat moderates the likelihood of conflict escalation.
Negative affect	P_6: Face threat is directly related to the experience of negative arousal.
	P_{6a}: Suspected infidelity is directly related to negative arousal.
	P_{6b}: Relational estrangement is directly related to negative arousal.
Diverging attributions	P_7: Negative arousal is directly related to defensive (i.e., self-biased and divergent) attributions.
	P_8: Negative arousal and defensive attributions are directly related to likelihood of experiencing rage.
Conflict escalation	P_9: Negative arousal in the form of anger, jealousy, and shame moderate (amplify) conflict escalation.
	P_{10}: Verbal conflict with negative arousal is positively related to conflict escalation.
	P_{11}: Conflict escalation is reciprocally related to rage.
Aggression	P_{12}: Rage is directly related to the likelihood of IPV.
	P_{13}: Verbal conflict (escalation) is directly related to the likelihood of IPV.
	P_{14}: Communicative aggression is directly related to likelihood of IPV.

Source: Spitzberg (2010a).

FIGURE 15.5: Elaborated Personal Affect and Identity Negotiation (PAIN) Model

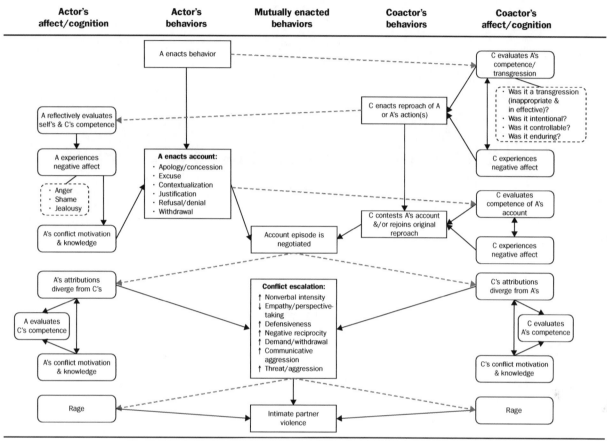

Solid arrows indicate direct causation, dashed arrows indicate indirect causation.

interactional context. The more elaborated form of the PAIN model is displayed in **Figure 15.5**, which illustrates some of the substantial complexity involved in what most people consider a "fight" or an "argument."

there are conflicts, but *how competently* these conflicts are managed. Conflicts are normal, and they are necessary. If they are going to occur, it is vital to learn how to manage them more competently.

Conclusion

Mundane, everyday interaction may constitute the majority of the ebb and flow of activity in any given culture, organization, or relationship. It is conflicts, however, that are likely to be the critical junctures through which the major turning points occur that determine whether these relationships progress or devolve. Quite simply, conflicts are disproportionately important in determining the course and quality of relationships. And, it is not *whether*

Credits

FIG. 15.3: Adapted from J. M. Gottman, What Predicts Divorce? Copyright © 1994 by Lawrence Erlbaum Associates.

FIG. 15.4: Adapted from Brian Spitzberg and Heather Canary, "Intimate Violence," *Competence in Interpersonal Conflict*, ed. W. R. Cupach, D. J. Canary and B. H. Spitzberg. Copyright © 2010 by Waveland Press.

FIG. 15.5: Adapted from Brian Spitzberg and Heather Canary, "Intimate Violence," *Competence in Interpersonal Conflict*, ed. W. R. Cupach, D. J. Canary and B. H. Spitzberg. Copyright © 2010 by Waveland Press.

CHAPTER 16

Small Group Communication and Teams

Kathleen C. Czech

LEARNING OBJECTIVES

After reading this chapter, you should be able to do the following:

- Specify the primary generalizations about small groups.
- Analyze, compare and contrast principles of general systems theory as it applies to the group context.
- Identify the functions of decision-making.
- Conceptualize the interrelationship among components of general systems.
- Differentiate the assumptions and key elements of systems theory, functional theory, structuration theory, and symbolic convergence theory.
- Analyze similarities and differences between descriptive and prescriptive decision-making approaches.
- Identify the key causes and symptoms of groupthink.
- Differentiate examples of defensive and supportive communication climates.
- Compare and contrast status and bases of power in group contexts.
- Compare and contrast groups and teams.
- Specify and exemplify types of professional teams in the applied context of health care.

The Foundations of Small Groups

Small groups have long been a foundation for human survival (Fisher & Ellis, 1992). Learning how to communicate in order to navigate small groups became of pedagogical interest in in the field of communication in the 1950s. Early work in the field of studying small groups was emerging from social psychology as early as the 1930s (Witte & Davis, 1996). However, it was during the 1950s that scholarly scientific inquiry into small group communication began to be present in abundance in the field (Frey, 1999). Several areas of small group communication have emerged over the years. This chapter will take a look at theories of small group communication, communicative characteristics of group members, decision-making, and teamwork.

Theories of Small Group Communication

Several theories of small groups have developed over time, and no one theory has successfully encapsulated small group communication (Poole, 1999). However, most theories seem to agree upon four primary generalizations about small groups (Littlejohn, Foss, & Oetzel, 2017):

1. Groups cannot be separated from the context they take place in.
2. Small groups must develop both task accomplishments and relational goals.
3. Process and structure are interwoven.
4. Effective group work involves communication.

Systems Theory

The first theory we will look at is **systems theory** (see also: Chapter 2) Several small group scholars have used Systems theory to explore small group processes (Mabry, 1999). Bales was a seminal scholar in developing a model that conceptualized groups as social systems and gave a method for observing groups. Systems theory assumed the central idea that communication is an observable phenomenon that brings together parts of the system (Monge, 1977, 1982). Bales's (1950) model was called interaction process analysis, and it paved the way for a method to observe and analyze group communication. This gave rise to the use of systems theory as a metaphor for groups and organizations used by several scholars (Morgan, 1986).

A **system** is defined as a set of interconnected parts. These interconnected elements include a group's input, throughput, output, **feedback**, and the environment (Shafritz & Ott, 2001). A small group is affected by several elements, all which are part of a larger environment that also affects the group. Four basic concepts are essential to

understanding systems theory. All systems have **inputs**, which are all the factors, resources, information, personal characteristics, and abilities and skills that are brought to the group (see also Chapter 17). These inputs can give a group a breadth and depth of interactions. For small groups to reach a goal or complete a task they must engage in throughput. **Throughput** in systems theory is the process and interactions group members go through in reaching their goal. The goal or **output** of the group is the result of their interactions and processes. These three elements are all dependent on the **environment**, the fourth key component of systems theory. A well-functioning group system will systematically monitor **feedback**, or information about how the group is functioning, from its own members, processes, and the environment. Groups cannot exist outside of their environment. The environment can affect how well the group operates and whether or not the group reaches its goal (Katz & Kahn, 1966). Thus groups function like an organic whole and change in one part of the system affects the damage and growth in the entire system (Buckley, 1967). These concepts are illustrated in **Figure 16.1**.

Functional Theory

The **functional approach** to small groups makes communication central to the ability of group members to solve problems and make decisions (Gouran & Hirokawa, 1996). Communication is **instrumental** because it the means by which group members can make decisions to achieve their goals. Groups make a series of small decisions leading to goal accomplishment by using prescriptive questions to reach a rational conclusion.

There are four requisite functions of effective decision-making. These four functions are (1) problem analysis, (2) goal setting, (3) identification of alternatives, and (4) evaluation of positive and negative characteristics of each alternative. This process would lead a group to produce high-quality decisions. Studies that have investigated communication as the function for effective decision-making have found that when group members meet the requisites the group is more successful and produces higher quality decisions (Graham, Papa, & McPherson, 1997).

The functional approach to group decision-making emphasizes the role group members play in communicating with one another. The functional approach assumes groups are goal oriented and that certain communication

228 | Part III: Knowing Where We Are and What Our Communication Is Doing

FIGURE 16.1: An Abstract Representation of General Systems

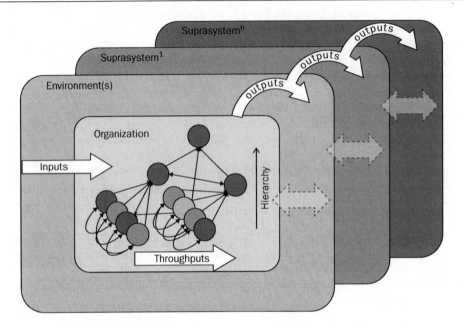

functions need to be performed in order for a group to solve problems effectively. Group members must have the following communication functions happening in the group to be effective: (1) analysis function, (2) idea-generation function, (3) evaluative function, and (4) personal sensitivity function.

Through these key communication functions group members enhance decision-making and achieve goals. In a 2001 meta-analysis of functional theory, Orlitzky and Hirokawa found that the most important process function of group members was the assessment of negative consequences of alternative solutions. Problem analysis was also an important group function, while the function of brainstorming had a much smaller effect on group effectiveness.

Structuration Theory

Structuration theory began as a way to help researchers understand how people behave in groups in the larger society and the inherent structures in society (Giddens, 1983). Structuration theory was further developed by Poole, Seibold, and McPhee (1985) in an attempt to explain how people structure their groups and make use of rules and resources. The theory looks not at the functions of

behaviors but rather the structures and structuring processes that support them (Bastien, McPhee, & Bolton, 1995; Poole, 1999). **Structuration** is the process of producing and reproducing various social systems through the appropriation of rules, and resources (Canary & Tarin, 2017).

Two factors contribute to structuration. The first is concerned with the structures within groups and the relation they have to social institutions such as (a) characteristics of the group, historical structures, and composition; (b) the degree of insight of the members into structures within the system; (c) how power and status is created within the group structure; and (d) the unintended consequences of the groups structures and actions (Poole, 1999; Seyfarth, 2000).

The second set of factors examines the structural dynamics through which groups interact and mediate the structures. Two dynamics are involved in this second set. First, one structure *mediates* another when its production and reproduction involve the reproduction of the other. Essentially this means that group members interact according to particular rules, and those group members also produce those rules through their interactions. Sometimes when groups mediate group structures, structures can come into conflict or contradiction. *Contradiction* is when one social structure undermines or contradicts another social structure already in place (Poole, 1999). This suggests that group members can negotiate group structures, but at the same time, their interactions are constrained by the same or other structures. Contradictions stem from clashes of structural principles and may result in conflicts (McPhee, Poole, & Iverson, 2013).

Structuration theorists have also examined the way group members enact structures and their interactions. Group members affect all kinds of structures, including decision-making structures, problem-solving structures, institutional structures, and appropriated structures. **Appropriated structures** are those structures adopted by groups from larger structures (Seyfarth, 2000).

Structuration theory examines structures in action by focusing on the structuration process. Attention is focused on small group interaction and how group members appropriate, adapt, create, and maintain rules and resources. Researchers must also examine group member communication and how communication enacts structures. Communication structures are examined more closely in Chapter 17.

Symbolic Convergence Theory

Symbolic convergence theory studies the sense-making function of communication. Symbolic convergence theory, often called fantasy-theme analysis, has as the central concern how groups create a common language of shared emotions, motives, and meanings that bring a group into a cohesive unit (Bormann, Cragan, & Shields, 1994). Fantasies or stories are created among group members and create symbolic interaction. These symbolic interactions create and sustain the shared reality of the group (Littlejohn et al., 2017).

Bormann (1972, 1982, 1985) defines a **fantasy** as any message that does not refer to the immediate "here and now" of a group. If a fantasy is picked up and elaborated on by other group members, group members then come to share similar interpretations. Sharing fantasies helps group members create a social reality that indicates who is part of the group and who is not. Sharing fantasy themes increases group cohesiveness as members develop a common interpretation of their experiences. The fantasy themes are the building blocks of the group's reality. Fantasy themes consist of characters, scenes, plot lines, and sanctioning agents. The sanctioning agent is the person who legitimizes the story.

When group members begin to tell a story as a collaborative whole, it is said they are "chaining out" the fantasy theme. In **fantasy chaining** the group can identify actions and "spin out" a common plot to interpret the groups past, its successes, and its failures (Poole, 1999). As group members come to share a number of fantasies and gain a similar understanding of their experiences, group members will begin to develop a rhetorical vision of themselves and the group. A **rhetorical vision** is the composite vision for a group created by its character formations, plots, scene, and sanctioning agents. The drama is the groups' reality as it is played out again and again (Littlejohn et al., 2017). Rhetorical visions tend to fit one of three types: (a) the righteous, (b) the social, and (c) the pragmatic. The visions have at their core privilege and a moral sensibility. The social have a deep structure and depend primarily on social interaction. The pragmatic have a practical logical base as a source of motivation.

Symbolic convergence theory helps us understand how group members interact. This allows groups to identify members and nonmembers, as well as providing a useful framework for examining group identities.

Decision-Making

Many of the theories just discussed also affect the decision-making processes of small groups. This section will look at ineffective and effective models of decision-making that groups use. Models of decision-making are often prescriptive, descriptive, or functional in nature (Gouran & Hirokawa, 1996). Prescriptive models recommend specific agendas and steps to follow. Descriptive models focus and describe how groups solve problems. Functional models identify key task functions that contribute to decision-making (Beebe & Masterson, 2006).

A **descriptive approach** does not offer guidelines or steps; instead, it describes the group process. One popular model developed by Fisher (1980) looks at phases of group life. The life of a group consists of four **phases**: (1) orientation, (2) conflict, (3) emergence, and (4) reinforcement. In the orientation phase, the group's communication is centered on getting to know one another and has a high social dimension. The next phase, conflict, is characterized by persuasive attempts at changing others' positions and negotiating one's own position. The third phase, emergence, is where group members deal with the conflict, usually through task-related communication. The final phase is reinforcement, where the group moves past the struggle and feels unified and positive toward the group (Fisher & Ellis, 1992).

Other descriptive models include the **spiral model** by Scheidel and Crowell (1964; Pavitt & Johnson, 2002). In this model the group does not simply go through the phases in order, but spirals back and forth through the phases in a cyclical pattern. The punctuated equilibrium model by Gersick (1988, 1991) suggests that phases and cycles are not a realistic way to look at groups. Instead, this model suggests groups go through periods of uncertainty and indecision about what to do until they reach a breakthrough that "punctuates" and moves the group to accomplish a task. Finally, the multisequence descriptive model by Poole (1983a, 1983b, 1983c) suggests that groups engage in three types of activities: task-process activities, relational activities, and topical activities. Groups switch from one activity to the other.

A **prescriptive approach** to decision-making utilizes concrete steps and agendas to work through decision-making. John Dewey (1910) developed a rational approach to problem-solving he called reflective thinking. The **reflective thinking technique** is a multistep process groups use to solve problems. The following steps are involved in reflective thinking:

1. Identify the problem.
2. Analyze the problem.
3. Determine the criteria by which decisions will be made.
4. Suggest possible solutions; engage in brainstorming.
5. Evaluate the possible solutions using set criteria.
6. Test and implement the best solution.

According to Dewey (1910), these steps should lead to the best decision possible for a group.

The functional model of decision-making describes the types of communication a group must have to be effective decision-makers. The functional approach centers on key communication functions that must be present in a group if it is to solve a problem. The four communication functions are (1) analysis function, (2) idea generation function, (3) evaluation function, and (4) personal sensitivity function (Hirokawa & Pace, 1983).

Several issues can affect decision-making in small groups. One phenomenon groups must be aware of and deal with is groupthink.

Groupthink

The manner in which information is exchanged can have profound implications for the way a group makes decisions, especially when group members feel socially pressured to voice some opinions and refrain from articulating others. When this happens, groupthink may become problem. **Groupthink** arises when a group embarks on a course of flawed decision-making due to group pressures that undermine "mental efficiency, reality testing, and moral judgment" (Janis, 1972, p. 9).

When groupthink takes over, members are less likely to reflect on alternative courses of action and are more likely to adopt illogical decisions that fail to consider ethical outcomes. In fact, scholars have identified a number of cases in which groupthink likely played a role in events with great historical significance, including, but not limited to, the escalation of the Vietnam War, the United States' lack of preparation for the Japanese attack on Pearl Harbor, the Bay of Pigs invasion, the Cuban Missile Crisis, the Watergate Scandal (Janis, 1972, 1982), and the Challenger space shuttle disaster (Tompkins, 1993). Other case studies have examined more recent events, such as the 2007 financial crisis, which followed years of subprime mortgage lending practices in the U.S. real estate market (Goodhart, 2013). Because the outcomes of groupthink can have deleterious results, Janis and Mann (1977) offer eight symptoms of groupthink that indicate when certain groups are more vulnerable to this form of social influence. These symptoms and their role in groupthink are displayed in full in **Table 16.1**.

Despite the potential issues that may arise from group dynamics, groupthink is preventable. Some precautions group leaders can take for avoiding the emergence of groupthink during key decision-making include (a) designating each group member as a critical evaluator of the process, (b) refraining from making statements about preferences and expectations early in the process, (c) encouraging peer discussions regarding the deliberations of the group at large, (d) inviting outside experts to meetings to challenge group members' opinions, (e) delegating at least one group member to play devil's advocate, and (f) allocating sufficient time to consider warning signs and alternative courses of action (Janis, 1982).

TABLE 16.1: Symptoms of Groupthink

Symptom	Role in Groupthink
Illusion of invulnerability	In a climate of extreme optimism, group members ignore signs of danger and engage in risk-taking actions.
Collective rationalization	Early warnings and signs of danger that run against the prevailing position are discredited or discounted.
Illusion of morality	Group members are convinced their decisions are morally right while ignoring their ethical implications.
Excessive stereotyping	Group members generate or reinforce negative stereotypes of rivals or outgroups.
Pressure to conform	Group members apply strong social pressure against disagreement with the prevailing position.
Self-censorship	Group members with dissenting opinions refrain from opinion expression.
Illusion of unanimity	Group members assume others agree with prevailing position whether expressed or not.
Mind-guarding	In an effort to preserve cohesion and group functioning, some group members may insulate the group from information if it potentially threatens group dynamics.

Source: Adapted from Esser, 1998; Henningsen, Henningsen, Eden, & Cruz, 2006; Janis (1972), & Park (2000).

Box 16.1 Ethical Issues

Ethical issues in small group and team communication overlap with many of the issues presented in earlier chapters. The unique context of groups and teams, however, warrants special consideration of how those ethical issues manifest in small group and team dynamics. We highlight contributions of three group communication scholars regarding ethical issues, which Johannesen et al. (2008) identified as foundational for students of group communication ethics to consider.

- **Political Perspective**

  Ernest Bormann (1981), author of symbolic convergence theory, built on Karl Wallace's four moralities (see **Box 20.2**) to suggest guidelines for ethical group discussion. Those unique to groups include:

  - Participants are enabled to make up their own minds, free from coercion or manipulation.
  - Participants focus conflicts and disagreements on ideas and information rather than on people.
  - Participants present information honestly, fairly, and accurately, and provide the sources of that information.
  - Participants encourage the use of sound reasoning and judgment.

- **Respect for the Other**

  Halbert Gulley (1968) focused his guidelines for ethical group discussion on processes that enhance and nurture individual participants and support the group as a whole. Guidelines offered by Gulley that are not presented above include:

  - Participants should defend decisions of the group when they participate in those decisions. If a participant disagrees with the group decision, that disagreement should be articulated to the group when the decision is reached. It is unethical to participate in a decision process and only communicate dissent when the decision is made public.

- ° Participants should actively seek out all input and perspectives from members, including those that are unpopular.
- ° Participants should reveal their own biases and those of sources they are using for information.
- **Ethical Sensitivity**

  Ethical sensitivity is the ability to be aware of ethical issues relevant to a domain of practice, deliberation, or decisions (Herkert, Wetmore, Canary, & Ellison, 2009). Dennis Gouran (1990) asserted that ethical sensitivity is a shared leadership function in small groups. He noted that discussants should take time during deliberations to consider potential ethical implications of decision alternatives, evaluate their own decision process for any misrepresentations of information, positions, or outcomes, and take stock of whether all members were respected in the process. Johannesen et al. (2008) note, "the ethically sensitive discussant raises questions about the ethical justifiability of ideas and actions" (p. 151).

Groups vs. Teams

There are many different facets of groups, including the formation of groups, the roles of groups, and norms of groups. Furthermore, there are the many outcomes of groups, including production and relationships. Researchers have sought to determine what types of groups are the most effective and satisfied. Research has shown that there is a substantial difference between a group and a team (Guzzo & Dickson, 1996).

A **group** can be defined as three or more individuals interacting for the achievement of some common goal who influence and are influenced by each other (Shaw, 1976). Groups work at two levels: task and team. Task work represents what it is that groups are doing while the teamwork describes how they are doing it. Teamwork has been found to have a higher set of competencies to be effective (McEwan, Ruissen, Eys, Zumbo, & Beauchamp, 2017; La Fasto & Larson, 2001).

Several factors differentiate a team from a group. **Teams** operate at a higher level of interdependence and cohesion. Research has supported a positive relationship between team cohesion and performance. A comprehensive meta-analysis by Mullen and Copper (1994) concluded that cohesion is significantly related to performance in a variety of teams. Teams must have a mix of complementary skills. Katzenbach and Smith (1993) discuss the importance of developing the right mix of skills, which are diverse enough to accomplish the team's task. Teams consist of members with more diverse skills, not identical competencies. Teams have a stronger identity than groups, and teams are more committed in their time and resources than groups (Rothwell, 2016).

La Fasto and Larson (2001), in their analysis of teams, found six distinguishing factors of effective team members (see **Figure 16.2**). These six factors fall into two categories: (1) working knowledge factors and (2) teamwork factors.

FIGURE 16.2: Factors that Distinguish Effective and Ineffective Team Members

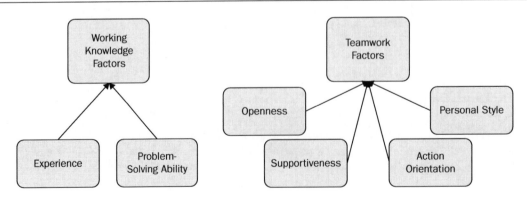

The **working knowledge factors** include experience and problem-solving ability. The **teamwork factors** include openness, personal style, supportiveness, and action orientation. It is interesting to note that the teamwork factors far outweigh the task factors in this model. These teamwork factors are achieved through communication. **Openness** refers to creating an environment open to the promotion and exchange of ideas. This is often referred to as the communication climate. **Supportiveness** is the willingness to help others succeed. This is again accomplished through developing a supportive communication climate in the team. **Action orientation** refers to team members who are willing to do something; making a deliberate effort to make something happen. Finally, **personal style** deals with whether team members display a negative or positive attitude. This trait is again linked to the supportive communication climate.

Jack Gibb (1961) observed groups and their interactions. In an 8-year study of groups he identified specific communication patterns that both increase and decrease defensive communication. A **supportive climate** is communication that engenders trust, which opens communication channels. In contrast, **defensive climates** involve communication that tends to threaten another person's sense of self, thereby evoking and eliciting reactionary, ego-involved behavior that focuses on protecting face and self-esteem. It tends to derail communication and relationships. Gibb described a defensive climate as an atmosphere of mistrust and fear that typically constrains communication. A full typology of Gibb's supportive and defensive climates is provided in **Table 16.2**.

Other elements critical to small group communication include the roles group members' play. Benne and Sheats (1948) compiled a list of possible roles that group members can assume: (1) task roles, (2) group building and maintenance roles, and (3) individual roles. **Task roles** help accomplish the group's goal or task. **Maintenance roles** reinforce and culminate the group's social atmosphere. **Individual roles** are almost always roles that are counterproductive to group processes. As team research points to, a diversity of roles and skills is necessary for effective groups and teams (La Fasto & Larson, 2001).

Another element necessary for groups and teams is norms. Norms are implicit or explicit rules that determine what is appropriate or inappropriate group behavior. Group norms can also affect group member relationships and decision-making outcomes (Postmes, Spears, & Cihangir, 2001). Norms typically develop based on previous group experience. However, most teams work

TABLE 16.2: Defensive Compared to Supportive Communication

Behavioral Dimension	Defensive	Supportive
Evaluative–Descriptive	I use a tone of voice that suggests whether I approve or disapprove of what others have said.	I try to say things in a relatively objective, unbiased manner.
Controlling–Problem-oriented	I say or do things when interacting with others to change their attitudes or behaviors.	I keep communication focused on problems rather than personalities.
Strategic–Spontaneous	I take on certain roles or appearances in order to achieve my goals in interaction.	What people see with me is who I am.
Neutral–Empathic	In an effort to maintain my objectivity, I tend to display a detached attitude in my communication.	I communicate in ways that show I identify with listeners and their problems.
Superior–Egalitarian	I resist other people's attempts to share decision-making power with me.	I avoid drawing attention to distinctions or differences among people in terms of their relative talent, worth, or status.
Certain–Provisional	I am determined to verbally defend my ideas and statements.	I communicate a willingness to change my mind on things.

Source: Adapted from Czech & Forward (2010), Forward, Czech, & Lee (2011), and Gibb (1961).

more efficiently if they produce team *ground rules*, which explicitly state group expectations. Whether group members conform to the norms depends on several factors. Some individual members of the group may not be personally predisposed to following rules. The clarity of the norm and the certainty of punishment for not following it may determine who complies. Still, group members may comply simply because other members have already done so. Finally, the quality of the relationships and the sense of group identification determine compliance to group norms (Beebe & Masterson, 2006).

The final element involved in small groups is power and status. **Power**, in a small group, is an individual's ability to influence or control some other person or decision (Franz, 1998). **Status**, on the other hand, is a person's position or importance in the group. Status can affect power among group members, but it does not always have to. To better understand how group members influence and control one another, French and Raven (1959) identified five power bases in their study of small groups: (1) legitimate power, (2) referent power, (3) expert power, (4) reward power, and (5) coercive power.

Legitimate power is typically the result of a position or title granted by a higher power. Group members feel an obligation to obey the position or given title of a member often regardless of whether they feel they should have to. Legitimate power has been shown to be very effective at getting group members to comply but results in lower satisfaction from group members (Rahim, 2014). **Referent power** is based on a member's ethos or character. Referent power is built from trust and charisma with other group members. When people like or admire other members because of their behavior, they are more likely to be influenced by them. Referent power has a high satisfaction rate among group members (Rahim, 2014). **Expert power** stems from a group members ability to influence others based on their specific knowledge or experience that other group members may not have. If the group finds the members' knowledge credible and important to group processes, expert power has been shown to be very effective with group members in both satisfaction and compliance (Rahim, 2014). **Reward power** is based on the ability of a group member to give rewards to other members. Group members must find the rewards beneficial and satisfying in order for this power base to influence other group members. Reward power has a moderate effect on influence and satisfaction among group members. **Coercive power** is the ability of a group member to punish other group members for their behaviors and actions. The group members must also perceive that the threat or punishment is severe enough and will be carried out. Coercive power much like legitimate power, is effective in compliance but is not one group members are satisfied with when implemented (French & Raven, 1959; Rahim, 2014).

Team Settings

Teams occur in every setting of life. Teams have become a ubiquitous part of today's world (McEwan, et al., 2017). One of the most sought after employment skills is teamwork (see Chapter 24). While teams work in several different settings, one unique setting that is gaining attention is the setting of professional health communication.

Professional Health Communication

Professional health communication is referred to as **interprofessional** health communication, whereby communication is occurring between individuals who identify as healthcare professionals (Real & Buckner, 2015). **Healthcare professionals** are those individuals who work in the business of caring for patients, such as nurses, therapists, dentists, pharmacists, clinicians, paramedics, physicians, and technicians (Villagran & Weathers, 2015). Research attempting to understand and improve interprofessional health communication most often approaches the context through an organizational communication lens. Although interprofessional health communication occurs within the general context of health, jargon and communication styles are unique to the different healthcare subdisciplines.

Ineffective communication among healthcare professionals, which often stems from the various discipline-based communication styles, can have negative consequences on both the quality of patient care and patient safety. The Joint Commission (2012), which is the primary accrediting body for healthcare organizations, found that more than 66% of medical encounters that got unexpectedly worse during the medical visit were related to ineffective or poor communication. Similarly, Kohn, Corrigan, and Donaldson (2000) reported on an Institute of Medicine project that estimated that between 44,000 and 98,000 deaths occur each year in U.S. hospitals due to preventable medical errors. Many of these errors are linked to problems associated with communication. Statistics like these have called attention to the importance of effective interprofessional health communication for ensuring positive patient health outcomes.

Key programs have been developed that strive to improve interprofessional health communication. For instance, detailed and specific checklists have been incorporated to improve interpersonal health communication. Haynes et al. (2009) extensively tested the effectiveness of a thorough surgical room checklist on patient health outcomes. They found that after the checklist was implemented, significant improvements were observed in numerous health outcomes, such as reduced postsurgical complications, in-hospital death rates, and infections. Although checklists can help ensure that communication is not forgotten between healthcare professionals, one of the primary challenges to interprofessional health communication is the perceived hierarchy between different professions—particularly physicians and nonphysicians (Cott, 1997). One of the most well-known programs for breaking down perceived hierarchical barriers to communication, and for providing communication structure within healthcare organizations, is SBAR (Haig, Sutton, & Whittington, 2006), or situation, background, assessment, and recommendation. When adopted by a healthcare organization, SBAR calls for healthcare professionals who are discussing a patient's health to provide information on the patient's current situation, background of the patient's health, assessment of the state of health issue, and recommendation for action. With a requirement to provide these details, as well as a recommendation for care, communication patterns are able to break traditional hierarchical barriers.

Checklists and SBAR are just two examples of communication tools that have successfully improved interprofessional health communication. Given the advanced and complex state of health care in the United States, providers rarely care for a patient without collaboration from other healthcare professionals (Real & Buckner, 2015). More and more frequently, patients receive medical treatment from a team of healthcare professionals rather than an individual.

Healthcare Teams

Healthcare teams are a collaboration of healthcare professionals working together to improve the health of a patient. More specifically, they can be defined as "an intact group of healthcare providers motivated to communicate with each other regarding the care of specific patients" (Real & Poole, 2011, p. 101). Effective communication among healthcare teams is as critical as effective interprofessional health communication—with the same benefits and consequences to patient health outcomes. Through a synthesis of research on various types of healthcare teams, Apker (2012) found three primary indicators of effective healthcare teams: patient care, quality of work life, and health organization functioning. These three factors are critical contributors to effective communication among healthcare teams; by extension, they are critical to improving health outcomes for patients with medical teams.

Members of a healthcare team may frequently work in the same group, such as an operating staff at a hospital, or may come together for a one-time purpose of focusing on a particular patient, such as for a patient with a rare illness (Real & Buckner, 2015). In addition, one healthcare professional may be a member of numerous healthcare teams simultaneously. The type of healthcare team impacts interprofessional health communication. Poole and Real (2003) outlined six different types of healthcare teams:

1. **Ad hoc groups** come together for a restricted time to solve a problem and then cease working together when their goals are met (e.g., to treat a rare illness).

2. **Nominal care teams** provide patient care through the oversight of the primary care physician (e.g., primary care physician recommends appointments with a physical therapist as part of a broader plan of care).

3. **Unidisciplinary groups** are collections of healthcare professionals from the same subfields of medicine (e.g., cardiovascular physicians coming together to propose a new surgical approach).

4. **Multidisciplinary teams** comprise healthcare professionals from various subfields of medicine who work together but function independently (e.g., a health department consisting of health educators, nurses, and board members, all of whom perform required tasks independently).

5. **Interdisciplinary teams** are made of healthcare professionals from various subfields of medicine

who work together at the same time and in the same setting to accomplish patient health goals (e.g., a surgical team that includes a primary surgeon, nurses, and an anesthesiologist).

6. **Transdisciplinary teams** develop when interdisciplinary teams are sufficiently knowledgeable about, and able to provide skills from, the other health fields of the team members (e.g., when a social worker on a hospice team is able to explain a patient's dietary requirements).

Each type of healthcare team experiences different types of communication barriers. For example, ad hoc teams are composed of members who have never worked together before, and who, therefore, will not know how to communicate effectively as a team. Similarly, interdisciplinary team members will work together frequently—often in front of the patient—and will have to learn how to work through each other's differences often. In addition to different types of teams having different communication challenges, communication challenges also exist depending on the patient's health status. For example, end-of-life and hospice care teams are presented with unique communication challenges to interprofessional health communication that may not be present for healthcare teams working with patients who have nonterminal health conditions. Thus, hospice teams are an important point of discussion about interprofessional health communication.

Conclusion

On any given workday in the United States, it has been estimated that there may be as many as 55 million meetings, with managers spending as much as 23 hours a week in meetings, and many spending up to 80% of their time in meetings (Allen, Beck, Scott, & Rogelberg, 2014; Lehmann-Willenbrock, Rogelberg, Allen, & Kello, 2018; Odermatt et al., 2017). Evidence suggests that these trends may be increasing, despite the fact much of this time is unnecessarily wasted (Rogelberg, Shanock, & Scott, 2012), and that a third to almost half of people surveyed have negative views of the effectiveness of their meetings (Geimer, Leach, DeSimone, Rogelberg, & Warr, 2015). It is not the amount of communication in and across meetings, but how competently communication shares and elaborates important task information that most strongly predicts group and team performance (Marlow, Lacerenza, Paoletti, Burke, & Salas, 2018). Being smarter about the purpose and dynamics of meetings will continue to be a vital communication competence to providing better innovation, group performance, and satisfaction (Allen et al., 2012; DeChurch & Mesmer-Magnus, 2010; Gully, Incalcaterra, Joshi, & Beaubien, 2002; Scott, Shanock, & Rogelberg, 2012), especially as meetings become more and more virtual rather than face-to-face in geospatially colocated spaces (De Guinea, Webster, & Staples, 2012; Lin, Standing, & Liu, 2008; Mesmer-Magnus, DeChurch, Jimenez-Rodriguez, Wildman, & Shuffler, 2011).

Credit

FIG. 16.2: Adapted from Frank M. J. LaFasto and Carl Larson, "Factors that Distinguish Effective from Ineffective Team Members," *When Teams Work Best: 6,000 Team Members and Leaders Tell What It Takes to Succeed*. Copyright © 2001 by SAGE Publications.

CHAPTER 17

Organizational Communication and Leadership

Kathleen Czech, Heather E. Canary,

Tiffany A. Dykstra-Devette, & William Snavely

LEARNING OBJECTIVES

After reading this chapter, you should be able to do the following:

- Identify and differentiate the major conceptual features and distinctions (e.g., climate, role of the individual, communication, etc.) among major theories of organizations (i.e., scientific management, human relations, systems, organizational culture, CCO, critical organizational communication theory).

- Identify the major features of organizational culture in general, and strong organizational culture in particular.

- Identify the three schools of thought represented in the communicative constitution of organizations theoretical perspective and identify major differences among them.

- Explain primary assumptions of critical organizational communication theory, and identify three primary concerns of research guided by this theory.

- Identify, differentiate, and arrange the stages of organizational socialization.

- Identify and differentiate theory X and theory Y.

- Identify, differentiate, and analyze the components of expectancy theory as it relates to employee motivation.

- Compare and differentiate management from leadership.

- Compare, contrast, and evaluate major principles and assumptions of two leadership theories.

ORGANIZATIONAL COMMUNICATION HAS EVOLVED over the past century, taking on many theoretical perspectives and issues since the Industrial Revolution (Buzzanell & Stohl, 1999). The Industrial Revolution brought about a need to manage industry and institutions and with it organizational communication. Organizational communication became a serious academic research interest in the 1940s and 1950s (Garner et al., 2016). From the 1950s onward, Charles Redding, whom many consider to be the father of organizational communication, conducted numerous studies about organizational performance and distinctively identified organizational management as a communication phenomenon (Mumby & Stohl, 1996).

A Brief History of Theories

A greater concern for productivity arose from the Industrial Revolution. This gave way to **scientific management**, the first and arguably one of the most influential theories of organizations (Drucker, 1954; Merkle, 1980; Smith, 2017). Scientific management was the first in a long line of theories searching for the most effective means by which to manage people and achieve the goals of organizations.

Scientific Management Theories

Henri Fayol and Fredrick Taylor significantly contributed to the development of scientific management. Scientific management was concerned with the technical elements needed to organize and manage people. The idea was to find the "one best way" to maximize efficiency to increase optimal output (Taylor, 1947). Scientific management studied ideal division of work, authority, responsibility, discipline, subordination, unity of command and direction, and scalar chains. Bureaucracy, as conceived by Max Weber, was a way of increasing efficiency and order. Bureaucracy was highly favored by managers who sought clear lines of communication and clear specifications of authority (Perrow, 1973; Weber, 1946).

Scientific management did little to recognize the rights of the workers or their own satisfaction in their jobs. It was not until Chester Bernard proposed the idea of organizations as cooperative systems that a change in theory began to develop (Perrow, 1973).

Human Relations and Resources Theories

A major contributor to this new school of thought was the Hawthorne studies. The Hawthorne studies were conducted from 1924 to 1933 at the Western Electric Plant in Illinois (Roethlisberger & Dickson, 1939). This set of studies sought to determine the influence of physical, economic, and social variables on employees. This set of extensive studies included the illumination studies, the relay assembly test room studies, the interview program, and the circuit bank wiring observation room study.

The Hawthorne studies first demonstrated the need for organizations to study the social and communication elements of organizing. The *illumination studies* looked at optimal lighting conditions and concluded that productivity increased regardless of what the researchers did to the lighting. The *relay assembly test room studies* isolated a team of workers and altered their compensation, schedules, and rest periods, and found productivity increased as more attention and different supervisory systems were implemented. The *interview program* led researchers to conduct interviews with thousands of employees to discover their attitudes toward working conditions, supervisors, and work in general. The interviews themselves were a way for employees to talk through challenges and improve their attitudes to work. The *circuit bank wiring observation room study* concluded the Hawthorne research and found that employee groups developed an informal system that controlled and regulated the members' behavior and at the same time protected them from outside interference.

The collective implications of these studies demonstrated the importance of communication in management. Not only did these studies focus on the discovery of the importance of informal communication among workers, the studies also gave rise to the need for systematic research into the nature of leadership. For the first time, workers' feelings and satisfaction became a prominent concern of organizations. Shortly after World War II, however, managers found themselves in another crisis, now concerned with how to motivate workers. This gave rise to human resource management.

With workers in secure jobs and no longer desperate for work, managers struggled with ways to motivate and influence their employees in noncoercive ways. Abraham Maslow was one of the first to develop a comprehensive theory of human motivation (Shafritz & Ott, 2001). Major motivational and persuasion theories are discussed later in this chapter.

Systems Theory

Ludwig von Bertalanffy (1951a, 1951b) is considered a founder of general systems theory (Adams, 2013). The perspective was developed to provide a basic vocabulary for integrating concepts of physical, biological, and human systems. We are familiar now with biological systems, ranging from our ecosystem to our circulatory and nervous systems (see also: Chapter 2). **Systems theory** provided an important perspective for modern organizations to understand more complex relationships (Shafritz & Ott, 2001). Systems theory considers organizations and the broader environment within which they must operate and adapt. Systems are like organisms that survive through their interdependence with their environments (Morgan, 1986). Systems are considered open and permeable; that is, they take in and use resources and information from their environments (inputs) and produce products, by-products, and services (outputs). Thus, systems always exist in a hierarchy of subsystems (e.g., organizational members, resources), the system of interest (i.e., the organization), its immediate environment (e.g., supply chains, labor force, etc.) and suprasystems (e.g., regulatory systems, competition, etc.) that interact with one another.

Systems must adjust boundaries to achieve a healthy balance or equilibrium. Major concepts in systems theory include:

- **Interdependence:** System components depend on each other for effective functioning. A change in one component changes all components because they are mutual dependent on each other.

- **Input, throughput, and output:** These are the process variables that contribute to the system (input), formulate decisions and processes within the system (throughput), and the products and byproducts that come out of the system (output).

- **Holism/synergy:** The total outcomes of any system are different than the sum of its parts.

- **Entropy:** The system defaults toward deterioration or decline. Closed systems (e.g. cults) eventually decay, but open systems are able to take in resources and information to adapt and maintain their functioning.

- **Homeostasis:** Like a thermostat, homeostasis is the tendency of systems to maintain balance, maintaining a steady state without excess or dearth.

- **Equifinality:** There are multiple ways or paths to achieve any given outcome.

- **Multifinality:** Any given way or path may result in multiple possible outcomes.

A systems approach to communication was quickly adapted by several scholars (Katz & Kahn, 1966). A systems approach to communication saw all behavior as communicative (Watzlawick et al., 1967). A related theory is **sense-making**, or the ongoing organizational process through which people continually try and make sense of the process they are experiencing—a process constituted in and by communication (Weick, 1979). Weick (2001) asserted that, "organizations are collections of people trying to make sense of what is happening around them" (p. 5). If all behavior is communicative in the system, then we make sense of, and reduce our uncertainty in, organizations through communication. Communication becomes the central process to understanding all organizational behavior.

Organizational Culture Theory

The 1980s saw a shift in organizational thinking. The cultural perspective toward organizations looked at the symbolic behaviors in which people engaged. Immersive interactionally constructed contexts of symbolic behavior can be considered a form of culture (Putnam & Pacanowsky, 1983). Scholars began to study communication phenomenon such as stories, metaphors, and rituals members engaged in to create their realities (Mumby, 2013). Schein (1993) proposed a formal definition of organizational culture that included three levels of culture:

- *Artifacts*: The most visible level of culture and includes the physical and social environments of a culture that are observable.

- *Espoused values*: These are individual values members of the organization hold. Communicated values and individual behaviors often do not match.

- *Basic assumptions*: Uniformly held notions about the world and how it works. Oftentimes, these assumptions are taken for granted.

Organizations with strong cultures tend to be more effective. Deal and Kennedy (1982) identified a number of key components of a strong culture. The components include the following:

- *Values*: These are the shared, basic beliefs of the organization, and they form the core of culture. What does this organization believe in? What is rewarded and encouraged? What is discouraged and unwanted?

- *Heroes*: These are the people in the organization (past and present) who have represented or enacted the values of the organization. They are often high achievers or key individuals that organizational members look up to. When organizational leaders and others communicate stories or news about **heroes**, it serves to reinforce the values and it strengthens the culture.

- *Rites and rituals*: These are public acts that display or reinforce the values of the organization. **Rituals** might include everyday "ways of doing things" in the organization like dress and informal gatherings, while **rites** are more formal events that serve to reinforce the cultural values of the organization. For example, events like awards banquets visibly reinforce the values that are the core of an organizational culture.

- *Communication network*: This is the informal network through which cultural information is shared within the organization. The **communication network** might include the sharing of stories, legends, jokes, or even gossip.

Two approaches characterize the research on organizational culture, the purist and pragmatist approaches (Morgan, 1986). While pragmatists assume management can control and intervene on culture, purists believe that culture is constituted by communication occurring at all levels of the organization.

The cultural approach to organizations continued to develop under many scholars but still left questions unanswered about leadership and organizations. The cultural approach led to scholars theorizing about ways communication creates or *constitutes* organizations. The 21st century ushered in organizational communication theory and research that represents this assumption, known as the communicative constitution of organizations approach.

Communicative Constitution of Organizations

The **communicative constitution of organizations** (or "CCO" as it is commonly called) is the first major organizational theoretical perspective born in the communication discipline. It consists of three schools of thought: (1) the "four flows model," (2) the "Montreal School," and (3) the systems approach. Although all three schools of thought begin with the premise that communication is inherently *organizing*, they differ considerably in how they explain processes involved. Each of these perspectives is based on foundational books or articles that introduced their approach to scholars at the beginning of the 21st century. The four flows model was built upon structuration theory, which focuses on connections between social structure and social actions. This approach includes the following "flows" as constituting organizations: (1) *membership negotiation*, which includes communication that determines whether a person is part of the organization and what that membership involves; (2) *self-structuring*, which includes communication that develops how the organization will function in terms of roles, rules, and the like; (3) *activity coordination*, which is communication people use to get the tasks of the organization accomplished; and (4) *institutional positioning*, which involves communicating the identity of the organization to publics and audiences that are not part of the organization (McPhee & Zaug, 2000).

The Montréal School, in contrast, has a strong link to linguistics and the role of language in constituting organizations (Taylor & Van Every, 2000). This approach asserts that organizing is communicatively constituted in a dynamic process of four translations: (1) *organization as a network of practices and conversations*, which is basically getting things done; (2) *organization as a collective experience* that translates many situated practices into a single collective experience; (3) *organization as authoring through textualization*, which includes codifying practices; and (4) *organization as representation and presentification*, which includes the organization acting on behalf of its members (Brummans, Cooren, Robichaud, & Taylor, 2014).

The systems approach constitutes the third approach to CCO, and it is grounded in cybernetics (Luhmann, 2000). According to this approach, organizations are self-producing social systems that are constituted by communication. Although this view seems completely consistent with the first two CCO views, it is dramatically different in its emphasis that humans are only part of the system, and that communicative processes take precedence over human actors in the production of organizational systems. To summarize, the three approaches agree that organizations are constituted *in* communication and that communication *is* organizing. The approaches differ in how they view humans in the process: (1) the four flows model views humans as having agency within the four flows of communicatively constituting organizations; (2) the Montréal School views human and nonhuman actors (such as computers and policies) as having agency in the communicative constitution of organizations; and (3) the systems approach views *communication* as the only actor in the self-referential process of organizing.

Critical Organizational Communication Theories

Critical organizational communication studies arose out of an interdisciplinary desire to highlight the inequity resulting from systems of meaning that privilege the voices and interests of the organization and management above subordinates. A central assumption is that power is an inevitable and necessary part of organizing and coordinating social action. *Power, ideology,* and *difference* are among the central concepts in critical organizational communication. Unlike scientific management, which focuses on understanding power as a way of increasing efficiency and control, critical organizational studies take an explicitly political approach by *evaluating* communication practices, united by a common commitment to **social justice** (Alvesson & Deetz, 2006). Critical organizational theories look for opportunities to increase democracy, participation, and shared control over decision-making processes.

Critical organizational theories are concerned with a number of questions, including: (1) how do organizations manufacture consent? (2) How are orders and hierarchies naturalized through communication? (3) How are the interests of management represented as the interest of all? And, (4) how do organizations rely on and perpetuate instrumental reasoning (Alvesson & Deetz, 2006)? Although critical theories are extremely diverse in their methods and answers to these questions, three primary concepts used to address these concerns within critical organizational studies include: control and power, ideology, and the communicative construction of difference.

Control and Power. **Power** is the ability to exercise influence and implies some degree of resistance (Fleming & Spicer, 2008). Communication at work consolidates, normalizes, and formalizes systems of control. More recently, organizations such as multilevel marketing and self-managing teams, have experimented with diverse and decentralized structures. Barker's (1993) study of "concertive control" demonstrates the ways that even as organizations impose new structures on employees in an effort to increase motivation and satisfaction, communication processes can recreate potentially more controlling work environments.

Ideology and Naturalization. An **ideology** is a system of beliefs that shape our attitudes and perceptions. Organizations draw on ideological beliefs that inform practices and hierarchies that make them appear natural and normal (Alvesson & Deetz, 2006). For instance, organizations socialize members with particular values and ideologies, in some cases they are hyper-rational, masculine management styles that fail to create space for dissent (Mumby, 1988; Mumby & Putnam, 1992). Similarly, the naturalization of pilots as unerring, gendered, and unquestionably powerful was intervened upon by airlines in the interest of reducing communication problems that resulted in pilot error (Ashcraft, 2005). Beliefs and power dynamics at work have important implications that critical theories address.

Communicative Construction of Difference. From a critical communication approach, difference can be understood as an organizing principle of meaning that categorizes and coordinates work (Ashcraft, 2011). For example, Allen (1996) describes how her experiences as a black woman in a mostly white university organized expectations during the socialization process. Difference impacts "the horizontal division of labor," or how work is allocated, as well as the "vertical division," or how tasks are valued in relation to others (Ashcraft, 2011). Finally, critical organizational theorists use self-reflexivity to identify the ways that even the disciplinary boundaries outlined in this chapter are rooted in studies that historically favor white, corporate workspaces. This has prompted researchers to explore new organizational terrain, including transnational feminist networks and hidden organizations (D'enbeau, 2011; Jensen & Meisenbach, 2015).

Major Concepts in Organizational Communication

Garner et al. (2016) conducted an analysis of 50 years of organizational communication. This study sought to find the most common topics in organizational communication that researchers have studied. It is these topics we now turn our attention to. The top topics studied include: superior–subordinate communication, socialization, job satisfaction, and leadership. While this list is not exhaustive of all organizational communication topics, it offers a reasonable cross-section of the field.

Superior–Subordinate Communication

One of the most common standard forms of interaction in organizations occurs between higher-status and lower-status organization members. This form of dyadic interaction is often referred to as **superior–subordinate interaction**. Numerous researchers have established the significance of superior–subordinate communication as a crucial element in an organization's continuing success (Daniels, Spiker, & Papa, 1997; Kassing, 2008; Lee & Jablin, 1995; Schnake, Dumler, Cochran, & Barnett, 1990; Steele & Plenty, 2015). This is relevant because effective superior–subordinate communication has been linked to a number of positive outcomes, including higher levels of cooperation, employee job satisfaction, organizational trust, and productivity (Madlock, 2008; Thomas, Zolin, & Hartman, 2009).

Early on, researchers linked manager communication style to worker job satisfaction (Clampitt & Downs, 1993; Pincus, 1986). Jablin (1979) and Redding (1972) both conducted studies on supervisory effectiveness that led to the conclusion that morale and satisfaction depend on competent interpersonal communication. Supervisor receptivity to ideas, employee participation in decision-making, and working conditions increase employee satisfaction (Wheeless & Howard, 1984). In one study, when employees agreed with rules and procedures at work, job performance ratings of supervisors and employee satisfaction increased, suggesting the importance of communication and consultation (Eisenberg, Monge, & Farace, 1984).

Employees have been found to respond positively to certain types of communicative behavior. Madlock (2008) found that subordinates are more satisfied when they perceive their supervisor as a competent communicator. Gibb (1961) proposed the idea of supportive versus defensive communication climates. These communication climates resulted in a model that pinpointed specific advantageous communication behaviors for supervisors. This model, while widely discussed, was not tested empirically until recently (Czech & Forward, 2013). Research by Czech and Forward (2013) found that supervisor competence and

relationship satisfaction were diminished by defensive communication and facilitated by supportive communication climate behaviors. Examples of defensive and supportive communication are illustrated in **Table 16.2** in the group communication chapter. The communication between supervisor and subordinate is a critical factor in organizational success and leads to higher overall job satisfaction.

Job Satisfaction

Job satisfaction has been defined as, "a pleasurable or positive emotional state … towards one's job experiences" (Locke, 1976, p. 1297). Steele and Plenty (2015) define job satisfaction as the "enjoyable and or optimistic attitudes of an employee toward his/her job" (p. 298). Job satisfaction is often associated with higher productivity. So what makes an employee satisfied? There are numerous variables; most are related to communication. Studies indicate that subordinates' ratings of job satisfaction are related to both the communication satisfaction and communication competence of their supervisor (Pettit, Goris, & Vaught, 1997; Steele & Plenty, 2015). Low communication satisfaction reported by subordinates, in turn, leads to reduced employee commitment, greater absenteeism, high employee turnover and reduced productivity (Hargie, Tourish, & Wilson, 2002).

Nonverbal immediacy is another communication factor associated with job satisfaction. *Nonverbal immediacy* refers to behaviors that communicate warmth, closeness, intimacy, and openness. There can be positive (e.g., smiling) and negative (e.g., sexual harassment) behaviors. Kelly and Westerman (2014) found that positive immediacy behaviors were linked to positive employee motivation, job satisfaction, and empowerment and negatively related to burnout. Teven (2007) found that when nonverbal immediacy was used positively by supervisors, subordinates reported greater job satisfaction, supervisor liking, and work enjoyment.

A supervisor's temperament and emotional display have also been linked to job satisfaction and employee motivation. In a study by Porter, Wrench, and Hoskinson (2007), temperament variables of extroversion, assertiveness, credibility, and approachability were all positively related to job satisfaction and employee motivation. Additionally, research has found that employee emotional engagement in the workplace motivates workers better than financial incentives such as pay raises (PeopleMetrics, 2011). Even gender can affect job satisfaction. Employees with a female supervisor rather than a male supervisor have reported the female as more communicatively competent, more immediate, and more transformational in their leadership style (Madlock, 2006, 2008; Madlock, Martin, Bogdan, & Ervin, 2007).

Organizational Socialization

Socialization refers to the process by which new members become assimilated into the organization and how they learn and adapt to the organizational culture. Socialization may be planned and formal, but it can also happen in unplanned and sometimes unanticipated ways. Jablin (2001) argued that socialization occurs in three stages:

- **Anticipatory socialization:** This is the stage when new members first begin to think about joining and becoming a part of the organization. One aspect is termed *vocational socialization*, which is the accumulation of expectations throughout an employee's life related to this kind of organization or job. For example, most people's anticipatory vocational socialization begin early on as family and friends may talk about the importance of college, as people read about college, or by watching college sports in the media. The second aspect is *organizational socialization*, which represents more specific expectations related to particular organizations. For example, deciding on one or more potential universities to apply to may involve imagining what each college being considered would be like. A prospective applicant may have done research, may have visited campus, or talked with people who knew each university being considered. Some information may also be gathered unintentionally—what is heard in passing, for example, or news stories. In this stage, the new member tries to imagine what it is like to be a member and expectations begin to form.

- **Organizational encounter:** This stage begins as the individual actually joins the organization—it is essentially the entry phase of socialization. Anticipatory stage expectations come into contact with new realities. New information is presented by the organization in a number of ways. Most organizations have some sort of new member orientation, training programs, and meetings. Many may have either formal or informal mentoring, where senior members of the organization coach new members and help them assimilate into the new organizational culture.

- **Metamorphosis**: In this final stage of socialization, the individual begins to change expectations and behaviors to adapt to and become a vital part of the organizational culture. At this stage, the new member becomes an "insider" and begins to internalize a self-image as an organizational member.

Organizational socialization is essential to the constantly evolving process of forming and reinforcing the organizational culture. Organizations with strong culture tend to think about how to best socialize new members so they contribute to the values the organization wishes to promote and maintain. However, a confluence of factors, including gender, race, and power, significantly influence experiences of socialization processes at work (Allen, 1996).

Organizational Identification

One of the ways that organizations build a better workforce is through the building of organizational identification. According to Burke (1950), organizations are structured in ways that tend to divide people from one another. Similarly, organizational theorists Lawrence and Lorsch (1967) suggested that organizations experience a tension between differentiation ("the difference in cognitive and emotional orientation among managers in different functional departments," p. 11) and integration ("the quality of the state or collaboration that exists among departments that are required to achieve unity of effort," p. 11). In order to function most effectively, a good balance must be established between the two. Organizational communication can serve the purpose of establishing commonality/integration through **organizational identification**. This process is defined by Cheney (1983) as "an active process by which individuals link themselves to elements in the social scene" (p. 342).

What can help establish organizational identity? Organizations may provide workers with an email address, organizational logo objects and clothing, and targeted messages. For example, at Miami University in Oxford, Ohio, faculty and staff are often reminded they are part of the "Miami family." This messaging serves to tie them together, despite a wide variety of differences in job status

Box 17.1 Ethical Issues

Organizations, as communicative systems of people, practices, spaces, and artifacts, are replete with ethical issues and implications. The following are three examples:

- **Whistle-blowing**

  Early in the 21st century egregious conduct by top executives of large corporations mostly headquartered in the United States, and malfeasance by heads of federal agencies, led to a series of "whistle-blowing" acts by employees who could no longer silently witness institutional wrongdoings they knew would harm a large number of stakeholders. Although whistle-blowing (i.e., going outside normal organizational channels to publicly report wrongdoing occurring in an organization) had been around for a long time, the number of organizations involved in scandals during this time period, and the fact that three high-profile whistle-blowers were female executives, increased attention to this communication behavior. Some individuals have negative attitudes toward "tattle tales," whereas others view whistle-blowers as ethical resisters. In the United States laws are in place to protect whistle-blowers from being retaliated against by targeted companies. However, whistle-blowers continue to experience negative repercussions from coworkers and public commentary.

- **Codes of Ethics**

  One practice widely used to prevent unethical behavior by organizational members is the development and distribution of formal codes of ethics or codes of conduct. These formal documents are often included as part of the onboarding process for new members. A review of formal codes across industries and time found that these documents generally reflect "a social system that places ethics within the realm of legal requirements and compliance regulations, promotes company interests, and values formal control of organizational behavior" (Canary & Jennings, 2008, p. 276).

- **Ethical Challenges of Leadership**

  Johnson and Hackman (2018, pp. 362–369) note several ethical challenges leaders routinely encounter:

  - *Information management*: Leaders have access to more information than typical organizational members.

  - *Responsibility*: Leaders are held accountable for others' actions.

  - *Power*: Leaders must decide how to use their power appropriately.

  - *Privilege*: Leaders have privileged access that is easily abused.

  - *Loyalty*: Leaders have multiple obligations and loyalties that may conflict.

  - *Consistency*: Leaders face need to be consistent with being flexible and empathetic.

and function. Other universities and companies may have similar ways of instigating a feeling of identification. According to Cheney (1983), organizational identification is associated with a number of important outcomes, including motivation, job satisfaction, job performance, and lower turnover (among others).

Motivation

One of the key issues in organizational communication involves how managers or leaders construct messages that best motivate other organizational members to maximize their productivity at work. McGregor (1960) was one of the first scholars to try to understand what motivated human behavior. **Theory X** came out of the classical management style which assumed that workers had an inherent dislike for work and they needed to be controlled. However, McGregor proposed Theory Y in contrast to Theory X (1960). **Theory Y** painted a more positive picture of human nature. Theory Y proclaimed that work could be as natural as play and that workers learned under the proper conditions and could show self-direction and control. Theory Y viewed workers as seeking out meaning and responsibility and asserted that individuals are driven and creative in their work. With a concern for finding out exactly what managers could do to propel the self-directed, productive worker, motivation studies began taking center stage.

While there are many theories of motivation in the communication, psychology, and management literature, one of the best supported theories, and the one that will help us construct effective motivational messages, is expectancy theory. Originally elaborated by Vroom (1964), expectancy theory is considered a cognitive theory, which means that it involves attitudes and beliefs, and that these, in turn, will influence individual behavior. The three main variables, or components, of the theory are valence, instrumentality, and expectancy (Bauer, Orvis, Ely & Surface, 2016; Byron & Khazanchi, 2010; Van Eerde & Thierry, 1996). Sometimes, the theory is referred to as VIE theory to represent these variables.

Valence is an individual's attitude, or preference, toward a particular outcome. It is a measure of how much these outcomes are valued—the higher the valence, the more impact the outcome has in motivating performance. An outcome is the incentive, the reward, or whatever might encourage someone to expend effort. For example, students might be motivated to work on a paper if they value the grade they will receive. Workers in a factory might work for their pay or for bonuses. Salespeople often work for commissions. Other potential outcomes might include promotions or even positive words from their leader. A person's valence can be assessed on a scale from −1 to +1, with 0 representing an entirely indifferent or neutral evaluation of an outcome.

A *positive valence* indicates something hoped for or highly preferred. For example, employees may work hard in the hope of receiving a bonus. Students may work for an A, or making the honor roll, or obtaining a scholarship. In these examples, getting a bonus, getting an A in a class, or receiving an honor or award are outcomes with positive valence. The more these outcomes are desired, the closer to +1 the valence becomes.

A *negative valence* indicates something people disprefer or hope to avoid. For example, some people may be motivated to avoid being fired. Students may just want to avoid failing a course. In these examples, being fired and failing the course are outcomes with highly negative valence. The more these outcomes are feared or disliked, the closer to −1 the valence becomes. Generally speaking, motivating to achieve positive valence outcomes is more effective than motivating by avoidance of negative valence outcomes (e.g., the use of threats). People might become motivated to "get even" with the source of a threat of a negatively valenced outcome. Then the outcome of "getting even" becomes a positively valenced outcome.

Some outcomes may have a *zero valence*; this means the outcome is completely irrelevant or unimportant. Clearly, the valence of a particular outcome is an individual assessment. Some people may value promotions, while others would rather stay where they are. Some people may be more driven by monetary rewards than others.

Instrumentality is the belief that a certain level of performance will lead to an outcome. So, in the previous example, instrumentality is the degree to which an individual believes that her work performance will in fact result in a bonus or a promotion. If certain that working the extra hours will result in a monetary bonus, then this is *high instrumentality* for working longer. If a student is not sure whether his writing an A paper will result in a good grade in the class, then his instrumentality would be low. As with valence, a person's instrumentality is assessed on a scale from −1 to +1.

A *positive instrumentality* indicates a belief that performance will lead to (or be instrumental to) achieving the outcome. An employee who is certain that working overtime on a given evening will result in getting overtime pay, then the employee's instrumentality for working late is +1. A *negative instrumentality* is the belief that performance will *prevent* some outcome from occurring. So, a student might be motivated to attend class every day believing that attendance will prevent a failing grade. Employees might choose to wear the company uniform because it will prevent them from being fired for violating the dress code. Perhaps followers are motivated to act in ways that would prevent their leader from being disappointed. The more certain that the action will prevent the outcome, the closer the value is to −1. If we do not see any relationship between our performance and a particular outcome, then we would have *zero instrumentality*.

Expectancy is the belief (a probability from 0 to +1) that effort will lead to a particular performance. This is essentially a measure of self-confidence. If a person is told that she will receive a bonus for producing 100 widgets in an hour, then the expectancy would measure how confident the person is that she could actually produce that many widgets in an hour. If a student believes an A paper will result in a grade of A in the course, expectancy is a measure of whether he believes the completion of the A paper is possible or likely. If the performance is something that has been previously or repeatedly achieved, or something a person is confident about, then expectancy will likely be +1. If the task is something that seems impossible or highly unlikely, then the expectancy would be zero.

Motivation in this theory can be measured by means of a multiplicative function of these three variables. In other words, $M = V \cdot I \cdot E$. And because a person might be motivated by a number of different possible outcomes, the formulas can be summed so that $M = \Sigma(V \cdot I \cdot E)$. For example, suppose a friend wants Joe to steal a sign from a bar. Joe believes he could steal that sign. In that case, Joe's expectancy would be +1. But what outcomes might motivate him to do that (or not)? Outcome 1 might be "Making my friend happy." Outcome 2 might be "Getting arrested for theft." Joe is very sure that stealing the sign would make his friend happy ($I = 1.0$), but he has a moderate valence for that ($V = .50$). So, for this outcome, Motivation = .50 ($M=.5 \cdot 1 \cdot 1$). Joe also feels it is likely he would get caught. In that case, his instrumentality might be $I = .75$. His expectancy is still +1. But what is his valence for getting arrested? Joe wants a clean record, so his valence is −1. So, for this outcome, Motivation = −.75 ($M = .75 \cdot 1 \cdot -1$). When these values are summed, Joe's overall motivation is −.25 (.50 −.75), which indicates that Joe is unlikely to be motivated to steal the sign.

So where does communication come into play? If a manager or leader wants to motivate organizational members (targets) to achieve certain goals, then the leader's messages need to accomplish at least three things:

- The targets need to be convinced that they can accomplish the task. This is expectancy. So leaders need to focus on good training, giving positive feedback when early trials of task behavior are successful, showing targets how to easily do those aspects of the task that seem challenging, and so forth. Messages must be clear and tailored to the individual's situation. They must reinforce the belief that this is a task the person can do.

- The leader needs to identify the outcomes that have high positive valence for a given target. Different people will have different valences, so this is a challenge. These outcomes can then be chosen to be offered in motivational messages as consequences for task achievement.

- The leader needs to construct convincing messages that help the targets bolster their confidence that achieving the task will result in the outcomes they

desire. This implies that follow through on promises made is essential. *Effective leaders never make casual promises*—promises to others should only be made regarding things that can actually be delivered. Leaders need to keep track of the promises made and do everything possible to follow through. Not following through on a promise drastically reduces future instrumentality and followers will no longer be as motivated when given assurances.

Leadership

The process of motivating employees is a typical function expected of leaders and managers. Leadership and management are two very different concepts (e.g., Bennis & Nanus, 1985; Rost, 1991, Zaleznik, 2004). While not always treated as distinct concepts, the human relations movement brought attention to the difference between the two.

Management involves administering the status quo. The concept of management began in 1916 when Fayol identified the functions of management: planning, staffing, organizing, and controlling (Fayol, 1949). Management is about administering the proper rewards and punishments to keep people working toward organizational goals. Thus, management is focused on order, consistency, and stability. People with administrative titles are often engaged primarily in management activities. **Leadership**, in contrast, implies change and innovation. Kotter (1990) identified the functions of leadership as establishing direction (creating vision, setting strategies), aligning people (communicating goals, seeking commitment, building teams and coalitions), and motivating and inspiring (energizing, empowering, meeting needs).

For organizations to be successful, both functions are essential. Both functions may be embodied in one person, or the functions may be split among two or more people. Importantly, both functions are inherently communicative—it is inconceivable to lead or manage except through communication behavior (Hackman & Johnson, 2013).

Trait Perspective

Early attempts at scholarship in the area of leadership focused on the **traits**, the stable characteristics and individual differences, which distinguished between leaders and nonleaders (Stodgill, 1948). After more than a century of research on the topic, the answer is still not clear (Derue, Nahrgang, Wellman, & Humphrey, 2011; Ensari, Riggio, Christian, & Carslaw, 2011; Hoffman, Woehr, Maldagen-Youngjohn, & Lyons, 2011). There is no simple picture of the traits that determine whether a given person will emerge as a leader, take on a leadership role, or even be an effective leader. Some traits (e.g. intelligence, self-confidence, and determination) contribute to leadership but cannot on their own explain leadership (Stodgill, 1974). Even genetic components to leadership have been identified (De Neve, Mikhaylov, Dawes, Christakis, and Fowler, 2013). However, a trait perspective tends to overlook the impact of dyadic and leader–employee interactions and can reinforce gendered, racialized perceptions of leadership. Ultimately, leadership is best viewed as a special type of organizational communication behavior (a state or process). Effective leaders choose message strategies that enable them to meet the functions of leadership noted above (Hackman & Johnson, 2013).

Situational Perspective

Since the trait approach is limited in explaining leadership alone, researchers began to look at the context or situation as a factor in determining leadership. Two situational perspectives that are important for consideration are Fiedler's contingency theory and Hersey and Blanchard's situational leadership.

Fiedler's theory is based on one's view of their least preferred coworker. The idea is that based on how leaders evaluate their **least preferred coworker (LPC)** their own leadership style can be determined. Leaders who rate their LPC positively are more likely to be relationship-oriented leaders. If they rate their LPC negatively, they are more likely to be task-orientated leaders (Fiedler, 1967). Leadership is further based on three factors:

- **Position power**: The leader's ability to either reward or punish members,

- **Task structure**: Whether a task is highly structure or accomplished in a number of different ways.

- **Leader member relations**: The relationship leaders build with their members through interaction.

Fiedler (1967), in turn, plotted all variables and concluded that the most favorable conditions for leaders exist when leader–member relations are good, the task is highly structured, and the leader's position power is strong. The least favorable conditions exist when leader–member relations are poor, the task is not structured, and the leader's position power is weak.

Hersey and Blanchard (1969) looked at the readiness level of followers in each situation to determine the type of leadership that should be used. The model asserts that based on different levels of readiness of the followers a leader should use a different style. The two styles were based on either task or relationship. Hersey and Blanchard developed four levels of readiness with corresponding leadership styles:

- **Directing** (level 1 readiness): Follower needs high directive on task and low supportive/relationship behavior.

- **Coaching** (level 2 readiness): Follower needs high directive on task and high supportive/relationship behavior.

- **Supporting** (level 3 readiness): Follower needs high supportive/relationship behavior and low directive on task.

- **Delegating** (level 4 readiness): follower needs low supportive and low task directive.

Situational leadership has added significantly to the literature and is still studied and practiced (Banks et al., 2014; Martin, Guillaume, Thomas, Lee, & Epitropaki, 2016; Rockstuhl, Dulebohn, Ang, & Shore, 2012; Schriesheim, Tepper, & Tetrault, 1994). However, in the late 1970s a new paradigm for leadership began to emerge.

Transformational Leadership

A particularly influential theory developed by Burns (1978) is transformational leadership. This view of leadership was offered as a way to distinguish transactional leadership from transformational leadership. **Transactional leadership** is similar to the functions of management identified above, whereas **transformational leadership** implies change and transformation of others, much like the definition of leadership itself.

House (1976) constructed a theory of *charismatic leadership*, and it has been considered virtually synonymous with transformational leadership. It specified five behaviors that charismatic leaders utilize. Each of these can be considered communication strategies for effective leadership.

- *Effective leaders set a strong role model.* They model the behavior and values that they expect followers to adopt. Followers can listen to a verbal message, but the enactment of the behaviors in all the leader says and does is the most powerful message.

- *Effective leaders demonstrate competence.* There is a great deal of research in the field of communication on credibility (e.g., Finn et al., 2009; Hellweg & Andersen, 1989), the most important dimension of which is competence. Followers need to feel like they can count on the leader's words as being backed by expertise.

- *Effective leaders articulate ideological goals.* When they speak to followers, they identify the morality or values in which they believe. Martin Luther King Jr.'s speeches were excellent examples of this.

- *Effective leaders communicate high expectations.* Refer back to the section on motivation. Leaders need to communicate to followers a belief in their ability to perform the necessary tasks. They need to build *self-efficacy* in their followers. In motivational terms, they need to build expectancy and demonstrate confidence in the followers' ability to complete the tasks before them.

- *Effective leaders arouse key motives in followers.* By communicating important, high motives, the leader

can improve followers' valence for the outcomes of accomplishing the tasks. President Kennedy's famous "ask not what your country can do for you; ask what you can do for your country" section of his inauguration speech is a good example.

Bass (1985) was the first to provide a full model of transformational leadership based on the works of House (1976) and Burns (1978). Bass saw transformational leadership as the leader's ability to motivate followers to do more than was expected (see **Figure 17.1**). Leaders could accomplish this through getting followers to rise to a higher moral level and transcend their own self-interests (Bass, 1985, 1990).

A meta-analytic review of transformational leadership research by Wang, Oh, Courtright, and Colbert (2011) found that "transformational leadership exhibits a positive relationship with performance across several individual performance criteria" (p. 249). Transformational leadership is positively related to individual follower performance as well as team and organizational performance (Wang et al., 2011). Other studies have found when transformational leadership is used, followers have a more positive perception of the organizational reputation and employees feel more empowered (Men & Stacks, 2013). Czech and Forward (2013) found that transformational leadership is predicated by several supportive communication behaviors and employee job satisfaction. In short, considerable research demonstrates the competence of transformational leadership styles of communication.

FIGURE 17.1: The Additive Effect of Transformational Leadership on Performance Outcomes

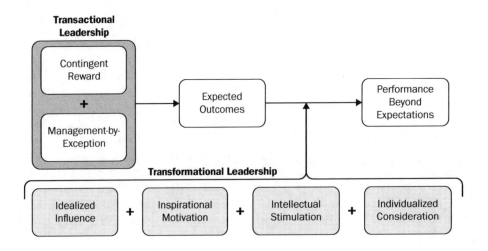

Leadership as Communication

The definitions and theories of leadership have varied over the centuries, but one perspective that is common to all is that leadership is, in its very essence, a communication activity. Clearly, all the theories examined indicate the importance of leader competence in interacting with employees (Rowold, Borgmann, & Diebig, 2015). Northhouse (2013) defines leadership as, "a process whereby an individual influences a group or individuals to achieve a common goal" (p. 5). The only way this can be accomplished is through the art of communication. Leaders use language to tell stories, analyze and evaluate situations, and to present goals and a vision for followers (Hackman & Johnson, 2013). The communicative perspective focuses on the dynamic interplay between organizational members (leaders and followers) involving the sharing of information and an increasing emphasis on the negotiation of meaning (Barge & Fairhurst, 2008).

Conclusion

The subdiscipline of organizational communication has developed over the past several decades from the study of "managerial communication" to the study of how communication *organizes*. Much of a person's life is spent in and with organizations—educational, religious, governmental and civic, corporate, and others. Organizational communication, as a field of theory, research, and practice, will continue to be as central to the discipline of communication as organization is to the human experience.

Credit

FIG 17.1: Adapted from B. M. Bass and B. J. Avolio, "The Implications of Transactional and Transformational Leadership for Individual, Team, and Organizational Development," Research in Organizational Change and Development, vol. 4. Copyright © 1990 by Emerald Insight.

CHAPTER 18

Intercultural Communication

Yea-Wen Chen

LEARNING OBJECTIVES

After reading this chapter, you should be able to do the following:

- Differentiate intercultural communication from cross-cultural communication, international communication, and development communication.
- Articulate key assumptions guiding the study of intercultural communication and what it is about.
- Identify key features that differentiate various conceptual definitions of intercultural communication.
- Trace the core historical roots of the origins of academic study of intercultural communication.
- Characterize key communication challenges in intercultural communication.
- Trace and differentiate core historical eras or periods of intercultural communication research.
- Specify the ways in which the Foreign Service origins of intercultural communication study may have constrained their understanding.
- Analyze cultural dynamics along the dimensions identified by Hofstede.
- Identify exemplary research in the three major approaches to studying intercultural communication.
- Differentiate and interrelate major features of the intercultural praxis model.

A S WITH COMMUNICATION, CULTURE IS A complex, intangible, and emergent concept. Early on, anthropologists Kroeber and Kluckhohn (1952) identified more than 150 concepts and definitions of culture. Today, culture—much like the air we breathe and take for granted—continues to drive, organize, and shape how we live, communicate, and know our selves, others, and the world. In a way, we can approach the study of intercultural communication as answering the charge to understand communication as fundamentally cultural while demonstrating "a passion for culture" in describing and understanding how we communicate (Shuter, 1990, p. 37).

In this chapter, I investigate some of the intricacies of understanding intercultural communication in everyday situations. We begin where it supposedly started, at the Foreign Service Institute in the 1940s and 1950s. Then, I overview three primary approaches to understanding culture and intercultural communication. I conclude with intercultural communication praxis as a model to reimagine what it means to communicate as an intercultural citizen in an increasingly diverse and global world.

Intercultural communication is a diverse and complex subject informed by multiple disciplines, such as (cultural) anthropology, linguistics, sociology, psychology, and cultural studies. The study of intercultural communication (also known as "the study of communication and culture" or "the study of communication between cultures") overlaps and relates to cross-cultural communication, international communication, and development communication. Depending on overarching goals, different groups of scholars approach, understand, and define these terms differently. For our purpose here, we treat these terms as having distinct foci. Generally, **cross-cultural communication** focuses on comparing and contrasting communication patterns within at least two different cultures. As an example, Oetzel and colleagues (2001) surveyed 768 participants across four national cultures (China, Germany, Japan, and the United States) regarding their **face** concerns. Positive face refers to being seen as competent and likeable; negative face concerns having autonomy when wanted. Oetzel et al. found that German participants reported more self- and mutual-face concerns than did Americans, whereas Chinese participants reported more self-face concern than did Japanese participants. **International communication** focuses on examining differences, similarities, and interactions of "mass-mediated communication between two or more countries" at the societal level (Rogers & Hart, 2002, p. 5). For instance, many international communication scholars are critical of the uneven and imbalanced flows of news and entertainment media of one country to other nations, which can lead to cultural domination. **Development communication** (also known as "communication and development" or "developmental communication") examines "social

change brought about by the application of communication research, theory, and technologies" to promote societal evolution (Rogers & Hart, 2002, p. 9). As an illustration, Papa and colleagues (2000) researched the effects of an entertainment-education radio soap opera, *Tinka Tinka Sukh*, on its audience members in one village in India for promoting behavioral and social changes such as family planning practices. For the purpose of this chapter, **culture** is defined broadly as identification with, membership in, acceptance into, or access to resources shared by members of a group based on nationality, race, ethnicity, sex and gender, ability, citizenship, socioeconomic status, profession, sexual orientation, sexuality, immigration status, political affiliation, or others that impact communication. Please note that this definition of culture is intentionally broad and inclusive to encompass all types and levels of cultures, including what otherwise is known as cocultures, subcultures, and microcultures. Later on, we will further examine the concept of culture from different metatheoretical approaches.

To overview the landscape of intercultural communication, various definitions are sampled next. Oetzel (2009) defines **intercultural communication** as "communication that occurs between individuals and entities that are *culturally unalike*" (p. 15). Willis-Rivera (2010) defines it as "communication with or *about* people of different cultural groups," including both interacting with and perceiving/talking about a cultural group in a particular way (p. 7). Taking an identity-based approach to communication, Imahori and Cupach (2005) define intercultural communication as "occurring when people's cultural identities are experienced as salient and *distinct*" as supposed to salient and similar (p. 198). Neuliep (2018) defines intercultural communication as occurring "whenever a minimum of two persons from different cultures or microcultures come together and exchange verbal and nonverbal symbols" (p. 20). Mainstream definitions of intercultural communication like these tend to assume relatively equal exchanges between members of different cultural groups and pay more attention to cultural differences than cultural similarities. Departing from such views, critical intercultural communication scholars aim to challenge and broaden our understanding of intercultural communication. Halualani and Nakayama (2010) reconceptualize "intercultural" as a spatial metaphor to (re)direct attentions to "the intersecting layers of cultural, discursive, and signifying practices that constitute power relations within and around groups" (p. 8). These diverse definitions reflect the complexity of intercultural communication studies. For the purposes of this chapter, **intercultural communication** *is defined as an interactive, dynamic, and negotiated process of communicating one's self with members of different cultural groups and/or representing cultural others to members of one's own cultural group.*

Before moving forward, I would like to establish several key assumptions that guide intercultural communication as an area of inquiry. First, people identify with, belong to, and associate with multiple cultures—or cultural groups (e.g., nationality, race, ethnicity, sex and gender, sexuality, age, socioeconomic status, regional identity, political affiliation, spirituality, (dis)ability, local community, and so on). Thus, it is necessary and critical to embrace the plural and lowercase term "cultures" as opposed to its singular form. Second, studying intercultural communication is very much a process of becoming aware of "the 'out-of-awareness' aspects of [cultural] communication," which can feel uncomfortable especially when the new awareness challenges our unquestioned assumptions about our self, others, and the world around us (Hall, 1959, p. 38). Third, the study of intercultural communication is inherently a political project that seeks to "affirm human interdependence without negating human uniqueness" (Asante, 1980, p. 403). To say that intercultural communication is a "political" project assumes a need to politicize our similar and/or different—if not contested—understandings of communication with or about other cultures and their impacts (e.g., by asking questions such as, "Who benefits?" "Whose voice is heard or silenced?" "Whose interest is served?" "Who is included or excluded?").

Foreign Service Institute and Edward T. Hall

The **early period** of scholarly interest in intercultural communication began with the practical need to train Foreign Service diplomats to serve in their roles representing the United States to other cultures.

> The story of intercultural communication begins at the Foreign Service Institute. In the 1940s many persons recognized that American diplomats were not fully effective abroad, since they often did not speak the language and usually knew little of the host culture. After World War II Americans began to reevaluate their knowledge and understanding of other countries, both in terms of their languages and in terms of their cultural assumptions. (Leeds-Hurwitz, 1990, pp. 262–264)

The need for interdisciplinary approaches to understanding intercultural interactions became apparent across political, professional, and academic contexts. We were sending these diplomats to represent our country and national culture. As conduits between our culture and other cultures, the impressions they made were potentially very consequential.

As a story has many beginnings, the story that we tell about how the study of intercultural communication began can also vary. As Leeds-Hurwitz (1990) indicates, intercultural communication scholars in the United States generally agree on a story about its historical roots and disciplinary beginning. This particular story spotlights Edward (Ned) T. Hall as a founding figure and traces its root back to the Foreign Service Institute of the U.S. Department of State in the 1940s and 1950s. Because Hall did not actively foster the institutionalization of intercultural communication as an academic field, he has been called an "accidental founder" (Rogers, Hart, & Miike, 2002, p. 13). Symbolically, the practical needs for preparation and training Foreign Service diplomats to be effective abroad launched the study of intercultural communication.

Hall (1959) wrote in his groundbreaking book, *The Silent Language*, that "culture is communication and communication is culture" (p. 186). Hall's work shaped and laid the foundation for the study of intercultural communication today. In brief, his influence can be summarized as (a) shifting the focus from a single culture to intercultural interactions; (b) broadening the study of culture to include communication, and thus putting culture and communication together; (c) redefining nonverbal communication as communication not involving words to include proxemics, chronemics, and kinesics; (d) moving from macro-level analysis of culture in general to micro-level analysis of smaller cultural units such as gestures; (e) approaching cultural differences in nonjudgmental ways; (f) establishing participatory and experiential training methods such as critical incidents and case studies; and (g) expanding audiences for intercultural training (Leeds-Hurwitz, 1990; Rogers et al., 2002).

Since Hall's work at the Foreign Service Institute, the field of intercultural communication has grown and diversified. By what could be considered its more **contemporary period**, the first university courses in intercultural communication are believed to have been offered at University of Pittsburgh and Michigan State University in the 1960s (Martin, Nakayama, & Carbaugh, 2012; Rogers et al., 2002). The first professional organization to establish a division of intercultural communication (as its fifth division) was the International Communication Association in 1970. The first publication of an edited book was *Intercultural Communication: A Reader* by Larry Samovar, Emeritus Professor at San Diego State University, and Richard Porter in 1972, which is now in its 14th edition. The first textbook on intercultural communication was published by L. S. Harms at the University of Hawaii in 1973. The first scholarly publication, *International and Intercultural Communication Annuals*, was launched in 1974. As histories are stories that we tell about the past—not necessarily what actually happened, we can contest and debate historical accounts as new information surfaces and becomes available. For instance, Emeritus Professor Michael Prosser at Shanghai International Studies University informally has been advocating the inclusion of Robert Oliver's (1962) book, *Culture and Communication*, as a founding text (Shuter, 2011). Nevertheless, it is important to trace the past as informing the future.

At the same time, remembering the root of intercultural communication as starting with E. T. Hall and the Foreign Service Institute has constrained its inquiry in some ways (Moon, 1996). First, culture narrowly becomes synonymous with "nation-states or national cultures" such as Japanese, German, and American cultures. When equating culture with nationality, this equation has functioned to create an unintended—and false—line between international cultures versus domestic cultures. For the study of intercultural communication, this equation has posed an unproductive tension between whether one should focus on international cultures or domestic cultures. In reality, the either-or tension is false as both international cultures and domestic cultures matter for intercultural communication scholarship.

Also, the line between what is considered "international" or "domestic" is not always clear. Moon (1996) analyzed intercultural communication research published in communication journals and found that scholars studied a diversity of cultures (e.g., race, social class, and

gender) in the 1970s. Yet, scholars in the 1980s narrowly focused on culture as nation-states at a time when intercultural researchers privileged quantitative and objective methods. Second, Hall and his colleagues at the Foreign Service Institute set a pragmatic, applied, and goal-oriented agenda for the study of intercultural communication, which tends to ignore power relations, histories, and politics. A number of scholars have responded by calling attention to those issues. For instance, Collier, Hegde, Lee, Nakayama, and Yep (2002) urged intercultural communication scholars to "create new boundaries and angles from which to view culture and communication" by considering issues of inequality, oppression, social justice, power relations, and social relevance (p. 221). Collectively, they argued that the project of intercultural communication ought to be both highly practical and highly political.

Third, the focus on Hall and the Foreign Service Institute has ignored and neglected other stories, possibilities, and alternatives of how the study of intercultural communication might have begun. If Hall is one of the founding fathers of the field, who are the founding mothers? How did the interdisciplinary study of intercultural communication find its home within the communication discipline? Why has training fallen out of favor in the current intercultural communication scholarship? It is important to know how the study of intercultural communication begun and where it has traveled because it can provide some directions for thinking about the future. The study of intercultural communication today is a diverse, growing, and at times contested area of inquiry.

Why Study Intercultural Communication?

As much as many people pride themselves as open-minded individuals who appreciate and value cultural diversities, being an effective and appropriate intercultural communicator is not as straightforward as it seems. Based on decades of experiences in international education and intercultural training, Barna (1994) identified six communication challenges—or, in her own words, "stumbling blocks"—to competent intercultural communication: (a) assumption of similarities, (b) language differences, (c) nonverbal misinterpretations, (d) preconceptions and stereotypes, (e) tendency to evaluate, and (f) high anxiety. Assumption of similarities becomes a barrier when many people assume sufficient similarities across cultural groups of the world and ignore differences. Not surprisingly, language differences, such as pronunciation, vocabulary, and syntax, are known barriers to cause difficulties. However, most people are less aware of the barrier of nonverbal interpretations that happen when many people are unconscious of how members of different cultures inhabit differing sensory realities in how they see, feel, hear, and smell nonverbal cues that have cultural significance for them. Although preconceptions and stereotypes can help to reduce uncertainty of the unknown, they become unconscious blinders and often inaccurate biases that interfere with objective information processing. Moreover, the deterrent of the tendency to evaluate occurs when persons of different cultural groups are more concerned about approving or disapproving the statements and actions of one another than comprehending as fully as possible the thoughts and feelings expressed by the other(s). The last barrier is the level of stress associated with intercultural and cross-cultural experiences and encounters due to perceptions of uncertainties present.

Despite decades of intercultural communication research, education, and training since Hall's time at the Foreign Service Institute in the 1950s, we have made some but limited progress in overcoming, coping with, or addressing Barna's stumbling blocks (p. 337). Also, recent pronouncements from the U.S. Executive Branch since January 2017 pose additional challenges for intercultural work, such as anti-Muslim and anti-immigrant rhetoric denigrating cultural others. Nevertheless, the ongoing demographic, economic, and geopolitical trends, combined with advancements in communication technology, make studying intercultural communication more relevant, necessary, and urgent than ever.

Recent Movements

For the first time in history, an inaugural Refugee Olympic team competed in the 2016 Summer Olympics in Brazil, composed entirely of 10 refugee athletes. The team represented the presence of millions of refugees around the world, and it symbolized a need for unity and inclusion at a time of great geopolitical uncertainties and sociocultural conflicts. According to the International Organization for Migration (2018), 40.3 million persons were internally displaced, and another 22.5 million were refugees in 2016, and 244 million individuals resided in a country outside their country of birth, the highest number ever recorded. The 2016 Refugee Olympic team represents a global migration trend that challenges traditional understanding about nation-states and national identities.

Within the United States, the Census Bureau's demographic projections highlight a minority-majority nation by *2050 when there will be no racial and ethnical majority groups in U.S. society*. In addition, the Census Bureau reported in 2012 that interracial heterosexual couples increased dramatically, growing from 1% in 1970 to 9.5% in 2010 (U.S. Census Bureau, 2012). When counting interracial unmarried households, the percentage was as high as 18% in 2010. The demographic changes appear here to stay. Yet, many sectors of U.S. society are struggling to keep up the pace with U.S. social demographics, including higher education (e.g., Hendrix & Jackson, 2016).

Besides global and local trends that necessitate intercultural communication studies, the increasing presence of media in our lives presents another opportunity. Media—whether mainstream, traditional, or new media—can both hinder and facilitate intercultural communication. On one hand, media messages tend to perpetuate oversimplified, misleading, and/or inaccurate stereotypes about different cultural groups, especially women, minorities, people of color, and foreigners. On the other hand, media in a global context can become a tool for fighting stereotypes, doing antiracism work, and promoting inclusions.

Teaching at Ohio University, I was fortunate to experience firsthand a 3-year poster campaign (2011–2013) led, designed, and orchestrated by Ohio University's Students Teaching Against Racism in Society (S*T*A*R*S)—a student-led organization with about 10 members. The poster campaign titled "We're a Culture, Not a Costume" was first launched on October 21, 2011, to raise awareness about racially insensitive and culturally insulting Halloween costumes in a small college town that holds an annual and very popular Halloween block party. The posters featured students of various races and ethnicities holding pictures of offensive and insulting costumes such as an Arabian terrorist and a reveler wearing blackface. See two examples in **Figure 18.1**. The posters were distributed across campus, residential halls, and online. The posters were designed as efforts to teach about and fight against everyday racism. To the student organizers' surprise, the campaign instantly went viral on Tumblr and Facebook pages and received national attention from CNN, the *Huffington Post*, and others.

Simmons (2014), applying an ethical analysis examining campaign posters, news articles, and online response comments, identified ethical dilemmas around personal responsibility, community involvement, and use of persuasion. In particular, Simmons (2014) claimed that the S*T*A*R*S campaign raised a coercion dilemma regarding the extent to which "campaign efforts have a right to tell people what to wear and not to wear, as well as how to celebrate" Halloween (p. 108). As indicated previously, intercultural communication research is necessarily political. This case of campaigning against racism illustrates challenges and opportunities—both anticipated and unanticipated—for promoting, facilitating, or engaging in necessary conversations about intercultural communication, cultural appropriation, and everyday racism.

Diverse Approaches to Intercultural Communication

We have a field that springs from personal experience, and responds to metaphors more than models from a dozen disciplines and data from scattered studies. Two different traditions, the humanities and the social sciences, claim to tell us how "we know." I value both, but trust more a different way of knowing. (John C. Condon, as cited in Harris, 2012)

At its core, intercultural communication is about constantly promoting, fostering, and encouraging what Condon calls "different ways of knowing." Condon and Yousef published the second textbook in intercultural

FIGURE 18.1: "We're a Culture, Not a Costume" poster campaign (2011)

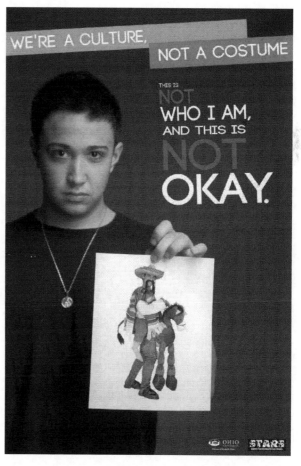

communication, *An Introduction to Intercultural Communication*, in 1975. Jack Condon and Edward Hall were colleagues at Northwestern University and remained close friends. Professionally and personally, Hall and Condon modeled, embodied, and lived a deep sense of valuing experiences of interacting and living with and learning from cultural others. In a way, intercultural communication studies center on seeing, understanding, and reorienting the world through the perspective of communicating and interacting with (other peoples). An intercultural lens means a dual and dynamic process of being, seeing, knowing, and communicating one's self and her, his, or their world through the eyes of the other(s), and vice versa. Next, I will discuss three primary approaches to intercultural communication. For the purpose of this chapter, the finer variations within each primary approach that would be reflected in an entire course on intercultural communication are not elaborated.

Metatheoretical/Research Approach

This refers to the positionality, orientation, or standpoint of researchers and their assumptions about what culture and communication are, how they should be studied, and what counts as useful research. Researcher goals and meta-theoretical assumptions and values about culture and communication guide studies. These metatheoretical approaches inform an overall scholarly standpoint from which to conduct research and guide decisions about how

to approach, design, carry out, and apply the results of a project or investigation.

As with distinct cultural lenses or positions through which to see the world, each approach has its own internal logic about what makes research work. Each approach is governed by its own assumptions about reality, human behavior, research goals, what culture and communication are, how culture relates to communication, how they should be studied, and what counts as useful research. Also, each approach has its own strengths and limitations. See **Table 18.1** for a summary of the three approaches' varying assumptions. As you think through each approach, it is important to keep those assumptions in mind as you consider what each approach reveals and/or hides about different cultural groups and their communication patterns.

The Social Scientific Approach

Broadly, a social scientific approach to intercultural communication strives to explain and predict communicative choices and behaviors based on cultural backgrounds (e.g., nationality, individualism/collectivism, and race). The social scientific approach assumes an external and describable reality that is out there and can be accessed. Positioned as an objective outsider, the **social scientific** (or **functionalist**) assumes that human behavior is predictably patterned. Thus, the social scientist aims to explain and predict human behaviors and make generalizations

TABLE 18.1: Three Approaches to Intercultural Communication

	Social Scientific (or Functionalist)	Interpretive	Critical
Research goal	Explain and predict behavior	Understand lived experiences	Locate oppressions and analyze strategies for resistance
Assumption of reality	External and describable	Subjective	Subjective and material
Assumptions of human behavior	Predictable	Creative and voluntary	Changeable
Culture	A priori group membership	Emergent patterns	Contested societal structured
Relationship of culture and communication	Causal	Reciprocal	Contested

Source: Adapted from Martin and Nakayama (1999, 2013).

through scientific methods such as survey measurements, conducting experiments, and scientific observations (e.g., Spitzberg, 2009b).

The social scientific approach to intercultural communication gained popularity and prominence in the 1980s. Paralleling the broader communication discipline, by the mid-1980s intercultural communication scholarship also shifted to social-psychological and social scientific approaches, away from its interdisciplinary roots in cultural anthropology and linguistics (Martin et al., 2012; Moon, 1996). This shift may have been pressured by desires for credulity and acceptance from fellow communication colleagues (Leeds-Hurwitz, 1990; Moon, 1996). As useful as predictions can be, this approach has been critiqued for not embracing cultures with passion (Shuter, 1990). Shuter (1990) has explained that social scientific approaches often treat "culture as a research lab" for testing and validating existing communication measures rather than showing deep interests in discovering, describing, and understanding nuances of cultural practices (p. 238). Still, it is important to note the prediction is a key strength of the social scientific approaches.

Culture as a Variable

The social scientific approach views culture as a variable (or a comparable factor) that can be measured, quantified, and statistically analyzed. One example of how the social scientific approach defines culture is exemplified by Ting-Toomey (1999) who characterizes culture as "a complex frame of reference that consists of patterns of traditions, beliefs, values, norms, symbols, and meanings that are shared to varying degrees by interacting members of a community" (p. 10). One of the leading researchers in this tradition is Geert Hofstede, a prominent cross-cultural scholar known for conceptualizing culture as "mental programs" or "software of the mind" that people carry to inform and guide their thinking, feeling, and actions. Based on two-time survey results with employees in subsidiaries of IBM in 72 countries around 1968 and 1972, Hofstede's (2001) early work identified five main dimensions that national cultures differ: (a) **power distance**; (b) **uncertainty avoidance**; (c) **individualism** and **collectivism**; (d) **masculinity** and **femininity**; and (e) **long-term** versus **short-term orientation** (see **Table 18.2**). Since then, other cultural dimensions have been identified along with survey measures that can assess cultural variability either at the individual or group level (Spitzberg, 1989, 2015c). To this day, Hofstede's cultural dimensions remain influential and continue to guide and facilitate cross-cultural communication research. To illustrate, Merkin, Taras, and Steel (2014) analyzed 60 empirical studies on the effects of cultural dimensions (e.g., individualism/collectivism and power distance) on communication patterns (e.g., indirectness, self-promotion, and face-saving concerns). Their meta-analysis affirms significant effects of cultural values on communication such as individualism being positively related

TABLE 18.2: Hofstede's Primary Cultural Dimensions

	Definition
Power distance	The extent to which the less powerful members of an organization, institution, or country accept and expect unequal distribution of power.
Uncertainty avoidance	The degree to which a cultural group conditions and controls its members to feel either comfortable or uncomfortable in unstructured situations that are novel or different from usual.
Individualism and collectivism	The extent to which individuals are supposed to look after themselves or remain integrated into groups that they belong to such as the family.
Masculinity and femininity	The degree to which the distribution of emotional roles between the sexes and genders are distinct and specific to gender roles or are allowed to overlap (see also: Chapter 12).
Long-term vs. short-term orientation	The extent to which a cultural group conditions its members to accept or avoid delayed gratification of their materials, social, and emotional needs.

Source: Adapted from Hofstede (2001).

to direct communication and self-promotion but negatively related to sensitivity and face-saving concerns.

As an example of how this approach works, Chen and Nakazawa (2009) sought to understand what factors could affect the development of intercultural and interracial friendships. In particular, they examined how culture might affect self-disclosure patterns when developing intercultural and interracial friendships. They focused on self-disclosure because it has been identified as a key feature of friendship formation and maintenance, both in intercultural and intracultural friendships. They understood **self-disclosure** as the multidimensional process of revealing personal information about oneself to another. They conceptualized and conducted a survey study with 252 participants measuring their (a) cultural orientation (i.e., individualism/collectivism), (b) six topics and five dimensions of self-disclosure patterns (e.g., attitudes and opinions, tastes and interests, positive/negative disclosure, and honesty and accuracy of disclosure), and (c) levels of relational intimacy. Overall, they found that as relational intimacy increased, all six topics and four of five dimensions of self-disclosure also increased. In other words, closer intercultural and interracial friends tended to self-disclose more to each other both in terms of topics and self-disclosure dimensions. Also, reciprocity in self-disclosure was important to developing intercultural and interracial friendships in that friends tended to mirror each other's self-disclosure patterns. Last, they found that relational intimacy had a greater impact on close intercultural and interracial friendships than did cultural orientation. That is, in close and more intimate intercultural and interracial friendships, cultural differences had less impact. One implication from this study is that developing personal relationships plays an important role in overcoming potential challenges posed by cultural differences in intercultural communication.

The Interpretive Approach

In general, an **interpretive approach** to intercultural communication seeks to understand and appreciate how individuals as cultural members come to be, know, experience, enact, or negotiate their everyday communication interactions. The interpretive approach emerged in response to a need to understand a culture deeply and on its own terms. The interpretive approach assumes that humans construct subjective realities and seek to identify multiple truths. Positioned as a subjective participant/observer, the interpretivist assumes that human behavior is creative, voluntary, and resistant to prediction. The interpretivist aims to understand and describe, in depth and with meaningful details, human behavior through qualitative methods such as field studies, participant observations, and oral history interviews.

Culture as a Speech Code

As efforts to embrace culture as "the heart and soul of intercultural research," the interpretive approach gained prominence in the late 1980s (Shuter, 1990, p. 37). One strong tradition of the interpretive approach is called the ethnography of communication. In brief, the **ethnography of communication** is the investigation, discovery, and explication of rules that govern appropriate behavior in a speech community, and a speech community is a cultural group that shares common and functional speech codes based on a specific situation (e.g., a code of honor or a code of silence). **Speech codes**, either in their presence and/or absence, signify deeply held cultural values, beliefs, and attitudes of a community. To ethnographers of communication, culture is a speech code—"a system of socially-constructed symbols and meanings, premises, and rules, pertaining to communication conduct" shared, understood, and practiced by members of a speech community (Philipsen, Coutu, & Covarrubias, 2005, p. 57).

To illustrate the interpretive approach, Houston (2004) examined differing perceptions about conversations between Black/African American women and White women. Houston asked these women to describe their own style of communicating and to discuss how they perceived the communication style of the other racial group. She found that one reason that Black and White women have a difficult time maintaining positive and egalitarian interactions is that each social group pays attention to different aspects of talk. White women in this study focused on language style and described themselves as "correct" or encompassing the standard ways of talking. In juxtaposition, White women often perceived African American/Black women's talk as nonstandard or deviant. On the other hand, Black women in Houston's study described their own talk through interpersonal strategies (such as speaking with confidence), and identified both Black and White women's ways of talk as particular speaking styles (with no single "correct" way to speak). Because of differing expectations about talk, White women may sound "phony" to Black women because they are trying to be appropriate and polite for the situation. Houston's findings led her to caution White women against making statements such as "I never even notice that you're Black" to Black women. She argued that statements such as this were problematic because they ignored an individual's cultural experience, asserted an understanding of what it was like to be Black, or illustrated implicitly the White women's belief that being Black was negative, unusual, or even deviant. In other words, statements such as this deny that blackness should be celebrated.

The Critical Approach

Broadly, a critical approach to intercultural communication aims to critique, challenge, and interrogate existing power relations, macro structures, and ideological forces that (re)produce inequalities, oppressions, and dominations (Halualani & Nakayama, 2010). The **critical approach** assumes subjective and material realities that have varying consequences for different cultural groups. Positioned as a structural critic and intimately engaged outsider, the critical scholar assumes that human behavior, choice, and agency are largely determined within social structures and power relations with possibilities for change. By questioning social and cultural practices that have been taken for granted, normalized, and naturalized, the critical scholar seeks to change the lives and conditions of everyday communicators. The critical scholar aims to promote social change, if not emancipation, through methods such as textual analysis of available public texts (e.g., news, government policies).

Culture as a Site of Power Struggle

The critical approach arose from theoretical and methodological concerns with traditional intercultural communication research that unintentionally reinforces stereotypes and homogenizes cultures (e.g., Collier et al., 2002; Halualani, Mendoza, & Drzewiecka, 2009; Martin et al., 2012). At its core, the critical scholar engages "issues of power, context, and ideology in studying intercultural communication" (Halualani et al., 2009, p. 19). From this standpoint, culture is, in essence, a **conceptual battleground** "where multiple interpretations come together but a dominant force always prevails" (Martin & Nakayama,

2013, p. 67). In other words, culture is "a site of struggle where various communication meanings are contested" (Martin & Nakayama, 1999, p. 8). This definition takes into account the particular and important roles that contexts and power relations play in intercultural communication.

As an example of how the critical approach works, Endres and Gould (2009) investigated whiteness theory in the context of service learning through examining an intercultural communication course they taught together. The authors approached **whiteness** as "strategic rhetoric" in the service of maintaining the racial status quo, particularly focusing on power, privilege, and whiteness. They analyzed student reflections and discourses. They also identified strategies of justifying or denying White privilege, such as conflating "being White" with "whiteness." Such conflation was problematic in at least three ways. First, too much emphasis on the individual made students only see the individual consequences of their racial identities without structural considerations. Second, the focus on being White might allow for the reinforcement of white privilege. Third, the conflation of the two risked the possibility of linking being White with eugenics, leading students toward the ideology of essentialism. Even though students did learn something from the course, being able to distinguish between serving and charity was especially challenging. The authors called for more research on issues of race/ethnicity, power, and identity in instructional communication and communication education.

Defining "Cultural Identity" Across Approaches

Cultural identity is one central and captivating construct, topic, and issue for the study of intercultural communication. Cultural identity is generally understood "as identification with and perceived acceptance into a group that has shared systems of symbols, and meanings as well as norms/rules for conduct" (Collier & Thomas, 1988, p. 113). Its centrality can be evidenced by decades of research and theories of cultural identity across approaches. As a communication construct, cultural identity deals with the static and dynamic processes, negotiations, enactments, and/or contestations of how one communicates one's intersecting sense of the self in relations to cultural groups within and across particular settings. To further demonstrate intercultural communication across approaches, we will examine closely how the concept of cultural identity is defined and conceptualized across the

TABLE 18.3: Defining "Cultural Identity" Across Approaches

	Definition
Social science	Identity is chosen, created, and constructed by the self in relation to cultural groups and group memberships.
Interpretive	Identify is formed and cocreated through communication with in-group and out-group members.
Critical	Identity is shaped and (re)produced by/through social, historical, and political forces.

Source: Adapted from Martin & Nakayama (2013).

social scientific, interpretive, and critical approaches (see **Table 18.3**).

The social scientific approach privileges the role that individual choices, strategies, and actions might play in creating and constructing the self in relations to cultural groups whether one is born into, identifies with, or yearns for.

That is, cultural identity is conceptualized as "a social categorization process" based in part on individual choices and in part on group memberships (Yep, 2004, p. 74). To illustrate, Jameson (2007) defines cultural identity as "an individual's sense of self derived from formal or informal membership in groups" such as nationality, race/ethnicity, and vocation (p. 207). Research following this approach can examine how the degree, or strength, of group identification that one attributes to a particular cultural group membership affects communication strategies and practices.

The interpretive approach emphasizes that cultural identity is a social and cultural construction formed, co-created, and negotiated vis-à-vis communication with in-group and out-group members. To exemplify, Jackson (1999), author of cultural contract theory, defines culture identity as "the sense of belonging to a cultural community that reaffirms self or personhood for the individual and is created by: the people, their interactions, and the context in which they relate" (p. 10). Research reflecting this approach often examines how individuals as cultural groups members come to experience, do, be, or know their sense of self and identities.

The critical approach seeks to expose and/or challenge existing power structures and social forces that (re)produce inequalities based on cultural identities such as race/ethnicity, nationality, sex and gender, sexual orientation, and so forth. To that aim, research subscribing to this approach attend to how cultural identities are shaped and

maintained through social, political, and material forces and conditions as well as how historically marginalized and minoritized identity positions can be reclaimed if not liberated from. To illustrate, Shin and Jackson (2003) define cultural identity as "an ideological construct and representation of power structures (p. 22). Further, they argue to reconceptualize cultural identity as "a rejection of the objectified self that has been dislocated in the terrain of racism, sexism, and classism" (Shin & Jackson, 2003, p. 228).

Ultimately, the varying definitions of cultural identity reminds us that the concept of who we are within intercultural communication is simultaneously an individual and social (if not political) matter. That is, cultural identity is both an individual choice and a social construction (if not group right).

Intercultural Communication Praxis

One of the gravest obstacles to the achievement of liberation is that oppressive reality absorbs those within it and thereby acts to submerge human beings' consciousness. Functionally, oppression is domesticating. To no longer be prey to its force, one must emerge from it and turn upon it. This can be done only by means of the praxis: reflection and action upon the world in order to transform it. (Freire, 1996, p. 33)

Drawing from the work of Paulo Freire, Sorrells and Nakagawa (2008) and Sorrells (2013) theorized a model of intercultural communication praxis. See **Figure 18.2** for a visual representation of intercultural praxis. In essence, **intercultural communication praxis** introduces a critical, reflective, and practical process of being, thinking, feeling, analyzing, and acting in the world as an ethical intercultural communicator for social justice. Broadly speaking, social justice refers to both a process and a goal of promoting fair treatments of all and more equitable distributions of resources As a process-based model, intercultural communication praxis has six interrelated points or ports of entry (i.e., inquiry, framing, positioning, dialogue, reflection, and action) that swirl together in circular loops building on one another. As an entryway into intercultural praxis, **inquiry** refers simultaneously to a willingness and desire to know, ask, and learn about cultural others and also a willingness to have our way of knowing and being be inquired about, challenged, or even changed. **Framing** indicates a range of different perspective-taking lenses, tools, and options that we can learn, acquire, become aware of, or practice in intercultural praxis. It also asks us to consider how local and global contexts frame intercultural communication. Furthermore, it invites us to become aware of our own frames of reference within intercultural moments. **Positioning** considers how and where we are positioned geographically, socially, and politically in society and in the world, and, at the same time, how and where others are positioned in relation to us. How might positioning affect one's voice, silence, agency, and action? With differential cultural frames and positionalities in mind, **dialogue** invites us to stretch, expand, and (re)image our sense of self and our viewpoints and experiences vis-à-vis fuller and more inclusive communication with mutual others. **Reflection**, which is central to the other points of entry into intercultural praxis addressed thus far, describes a growing capacity to learn from introspection, observation, and (re)consideration, whether in response to inquiry, framing, positioning, dialogue, and action. **Action**, as informed by increasing levels of reflecting and thinking, invites us to "join our increased understanding with responsible action to make a difference in the world"

FIGURE 18.2: Intercultural Praxis Model

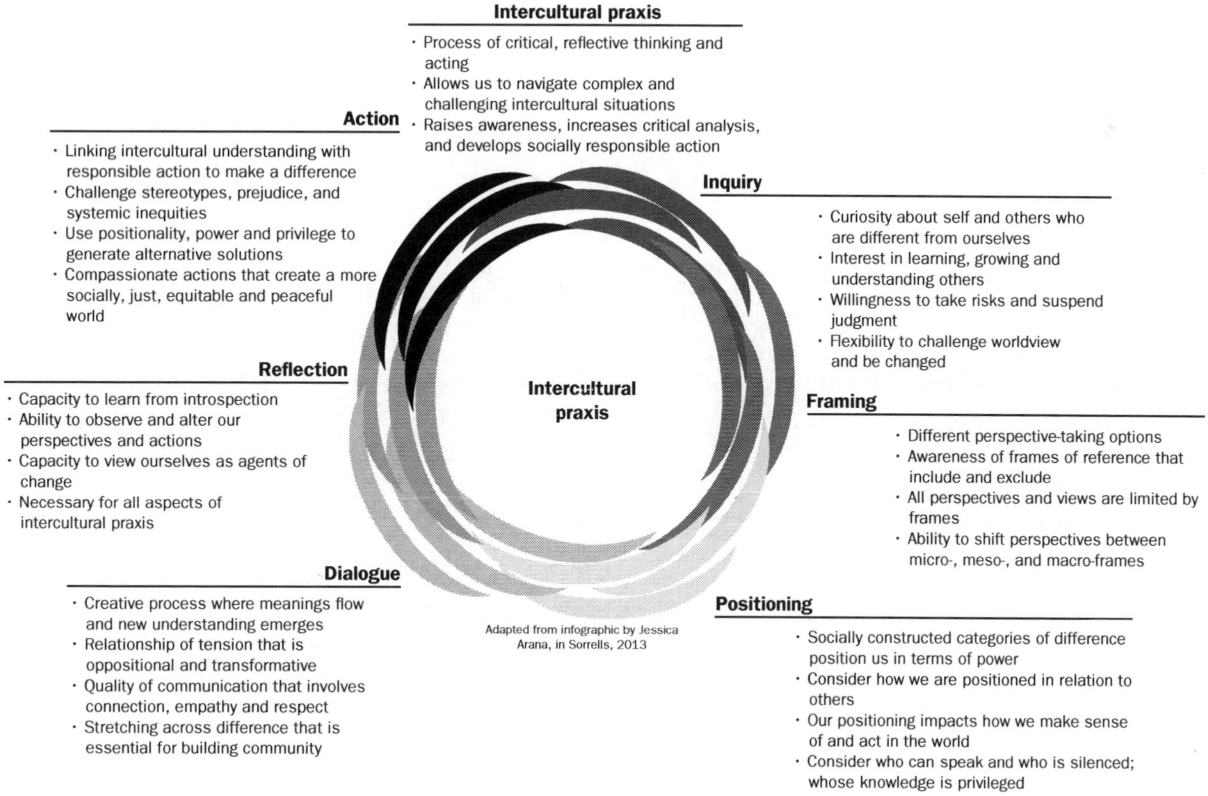

Intercultural praxis
- Process of critical, reflective thinking and acting
- Allows us to navigate complex and challenging intercultural situations
- Raises awareness, increases critical analysis, and develops socially responsible action

Action
- Linking intercultural understanding with responsible action to make a difference
- Challenge stereotypes, prejudice, and systemic inequities
- Use positionality, power and privilege to generate alternative solutions
- Compassionate actions that create a more socially, just, equitable and peaceful world

Inquiry
- Curiosity about self and others who are different from ourselves
- Interest in learning, growing and understanding others
- Willingness to take risks and suspend judgment
- Flexibility to challenge worldview and be changed

Reflection
- Capacity to learn from introspection
- Ability to observe and alter our perspectives and actions
- Capacity to view ourselves as agents of change
- Necessary for all aspects of intercultural praxis

Framing
- Different perspective-taking options
- Awareness of frames of reference that include and exclude
- All perspectives and views are limited by frames
- Ability to shift perspectives between micro-, meso-, and macro-frames

Dialogue
- Creative process where meanings flow and new understanding emerges
- Relationship of tension that is oppositional and transformative
- Quality of communication that involves connection, empathy and respect
- Stretching across difference that is essential for building community

Intercultural praxis

Adapted from infographic by Jessica Arana, in Sorrells, 2013

Positioning
- Socially constructed categories of difference position us in terms of power
- Consider how we are positioned in relation to others
- Our positioning impacts how we make sense of and act in the world
- Consider who can speak and who is silenced; whose knowledge is privileged

(Sorrells, 2013, p. 20). In particular, the intercultural praxis model encourages efforts and actions that can help make the world more just, equitable, inclusive, and peaceful.

As Sorrells (2013) puts it, "[T]he purpose of engaging in intercultural praxis is to raise our awareness, increase our critical analysis, and develop our socially responsible action in regard to our intercultural interactions in the context of globalization" (p. 16). In essence, when approaching intercultural communication from a praxis perspective, the model underscores the complex, nonlinear, and messy nature of engaging in ethical intercultural communication practices for social justice. In other words, no easy answers emerge in ethically navigating the tricky waters of intercultural communication. For instance, right behavior in one cultural context can become wrong in another. Also, popular wisdom, such as "When in Rome, do as the Romans do" and "Treat others as you would like to be treated," might only provide partial answers to solving intercultural communication dilemmas. Consider dilemmas involved in the following controversial case example.

In late 2017, Jenny Niezgoda, a travel blogger, food enthusiast, and self-proclaimed "chic nomad," wanted to bring healthy, plant-based, and vegan food options to Barrio Logan, a historically Chicano/a and Mexican-American neighborhood in San Diego (Zaragoza, 2017). At the time, Barrio Logan was considered a "food desert" with limited food access that requires residents to travel long distances for supermarkets with fresh produce. To appeal to the residents of Barrio Logan, Niezgoda, as a cultural outsider and a racialized White woman, wanted to infuse a modern twist to the cultural tradition of *frutería*—Mexican juice bar. As someone who is new to Barrio Logan, a number of residents have protested Niezgoda's idea of "modern fruteria" as an attempt of **cultural appropriation**. That is, Niezgoda's business idea conjures-up the colonial practice of adopting and adapting cultural practices of minority others (such as Mexican and Mexican American communities in this case) into one's own cultural practices without cultural understanding and often for material and monetary gains. Why do you think this case is controversial? In what ways might her attempt be sound? In what ways might Niezgoda's attempt be problematic? What would you suggest that Niezgoda do differently if she really wants to help make Barrio Logan less of a food desert as an outsider to this community? Consider the intercultural praxis model as shown in **Figure 18.2** as you analyze this case. Read Zaragoza's (2017) analysis if you want to learn more about the case.

Box 18.1 Ethical Issues

Scholars generally agree that culture and ethics are intertwined. Some argue for finding ethical principles that transcend cultural differences. Others argue that there can be no ethics outside of cultural context and understanding. Although consensus on such issues is definitely lacking, some principles provide productive starting points for serious consideration of intercultural communication ethics.

- **Universal Principles of Intercultural Communication Ethics**

  Chen and Starosta (1998) argue that the fundamental interpersonal ethic of reciprocity (cf. Chapter 2, Ethical Issues), in which we communicate with others as we want them to communicate with us, is enacted through four additional principles:

  - *Mutuality*: Search for fullest and clearest possible exchange of ideas.
  - *Nonjudgmentalism*: Recognize and accept different perspectives and ideas.
  - *Honesty*: Communicate under the assumption that information is true.
  - *Respect*: Preserve the dignity of each other.

Johannesen et al. (2008) note that these principles may be difficult to determine in intercultural contexts because interpretations of each may differ between parties from differing cultures.

- **Ethnic Ethics**

  Anthony Cortese (1990), on the other hand, argues for a contradictory position on intercultural ethics. He argues that morality, and moral principles, are bound up with culture and culturally situated relationships. This position negates the need, or desire, for any type of universal communication ethic. Furthermore, Cortese posits that such universal approaches hold up Western ideals and principles as the standard against which all other ethics should be compared.

- **Moral Exclusion**

  Moral exclusion is a term coined by Susan Opotow (1990) for the (often communicative) process in which people are perceived and treated as if they are excluded from moral principles of considerations of fairness. Some examples of communication that creates moral exclusion include:

  - Characterizing others as lower life forms (e.g., "vermin") or inferior beings (e.g., "savages").
  - Denying that others have dignity, feelings, or a right to compassion.
  - Blaming the victim.
  - Misrepresenting cruelty and harm by using neutral, positive, technical, or euphemistic terms to describe them.

  It should be clear from this partial list of strategies Opotow identified as morally exclusionary that these would violate both universal communication ethics and ethnic ethics.

I find this process-based model particularly useful and relevant for intercultural communication for several reasons. First, it highlights social justice as a critical commitment to the study of intercultural communication. Given our current conditions (e.g., widening gaps between the rich and the poor and unequal migration flows), social justice both as a process and a goal is essential for intercultural communication today. Second, it frames intercultural communication in the context of globalization. Sorrells (2013) approaches globalization as simultaneously *contested processes* and *inequitable conditions* of living in our global village. Third, I argue that praxis links the past and the future of intercultural communication. On one hand, intercultural praxis relates to the historical root of training Foreign Service diplomats in that the model addresses practical needs of guiding individuals in better reflecting, thinking, and acting in intercultural situations. On the other hand, intercultural praxis builds on the trajectory of critical intercultural communication research. It offers a new way of reimagining what intercultural communication can, or could, be with all its complexities, diversities, nuances, and contradictions. We need to keep reimagining new ways, possibilities, and lenses.

Conclusion

One of the biggest mysteries about the study of intercultural communication to me concerns how intercultural interactions teach us more about ourselves than about the other(s). Anecdotally, since moving to the United States in the summer of 2004, I have gained insights about my own cultures in ways that I would not have had I never left the island of Taiwan where I was born and raised. I think that the most meaningful moments of intercultural interactions occur when we step outside our cultural bubble and see it from the eyes of the other. In other words, I argue that intercultural communication occurs in contexts of interacting with different others when we can see those others in our self and see our self in those others. Ultimately, the study of intercultural communication centers on seeing, understanding, and reorienting the world through the perspectives and/or positions of communicating and interacting with the other(s). At its core, an intercultural lens means a dual and dynamic process of being, seeing, knowing, and communicating one's self and her, his, or their world through the eyes of the other(s).

Credit

FIG. 18.1: Source: https://www.ohio.edu/orgs/stars/Poster_Campaign.html.

FIG. 18.2: Source: Kathryn Sorrells, Intercultural Communication: Globalization and Social Justice. Copyright © 2013 by SAGE Publications.

CHAPTER 19

Health Communication

Patricia Geist-Martin, Rachael A. Record, Perry Pauley, Wayne Beach,

Lourdes Martinez, & Meghan Bridgid Moran

LEARNING OBJECTIVES

After reading this chapter, you should be able to do the following:

- Differentiate key defining features of health communication.
- Identify the content and scope of the health communication discipline.
- Specify the main conceptualizations of health in Western medicine.
- Distinguish between the elements of the biomedical and biopsychosocial models of health.
- Differentiate between the two main perspectives on social support (main effects/structural vs. stress-buffering/functional).
- Identify and differentiate illness from disease.
- Specify and distinguish among the phases and challenges of medical interview phases.
- Know factors that contribute to illness at work.
- Specify activities and efforts that can assist employees in creating wellness at work.
- Identify significant cultural factors shaping beliefs about health and wellness and implications for health communication.
- Identify and differentiate the theoretical bases for community-level health campaigns and the processes for developing this type of campaign.
- Specify the features of public health communication campaigns.
- Differentiate the tenets of the seven most common theoretical frameworks used in communication campaigns.

HEALTH IS INTIMATELY CONNECTED WITH THE places and times we inhabit. Thomas McKewon (1988) concluded that, in all historical eras, the most common causes of sickness and death were "the prevailing conditions of life" (p. 91). Today, the conditions of our lives continue to significantly impact the diseases we experience. Anorexia nervosa, depression, AIDS, and stroke are all easily recognizable, devastating diseases; yet, none of these diseases was a recognized diagnosis only 100 years ago.

In this chapter, we explore the complexities of communicating health in our day-to-day lives. We begin by defining health communication. The subdiscipline of health communication investigates how communicating about health and illness is a complex but essential part of our lives, impacting our relationships, families, workplaces, and communities, crossing boundaries between states, countries, and continents. The chapter explores conceptions of health and illness and communication health in relationships, families, communities, organizations, societies, health professions, and health campaigns.

Health communication is a diverse area that studies how people communicate about health. The National Communication Association (2018) defines health communication as "[t]he study of communication as it relates to health professionals and health education, including the study of provider-client interaction, as well as the diffusion of health information through public health campaigns." The International Communication Association says, "Health communication is primarily concerned with the role of communication theory, research and practice in health promotion and health care" (ICA Online, 2019). The U.S. Centers for Disease Control (CDC) (2019) define health communication as "[t]he study and use of communication strategies to inform and influence individual decisions that enhance health." Others define it as "[t]he symbolic processes by which people, individually and collectively, understand, shape, and accommodate to health and illness" (Geist-Martin, Ray, & Sharf, 2011, p. 3). These definitions have in common how they conceptualize health communication as interested in how people receive, manage, and use communication to inform and make meaning regarding their health, and how the communication of providers, organizations, and others affect health understanding and outcomes.

Health Communication as a Discipline

Scholars study health communication in many ways. One way to organize this research is to consider many different contexts in which health information is communicated. Our *families* are key people with whom we discuss health issues. Scholarship in this area seeks to understand how families communicate about health and what impact their communication patterns have on the health and well-being of individuals. One study in this area explored how family relationships were essential to cancer survivors' healing processes (Ott Anderson & Geist-Martin, 2003).

Beyond our immediate families, our *communities* include people with whom we communicate and from whom we learn about health. These communities can be bonded through social relationships (e.g., our friends), through places (e.g., our neighbors), through shared identities (e.g., members of a specific cultural or ethnic group), and through shared experiences (e.g., members of a support group). These communities can have significant impact on our health and well-being. For instance, individuals with more social support have lower levels of stress and depression.

Our *places of work* can also affect our health. Farrell and Geist-Martin's (2005) model of working well theorizes that individuals can construct workplace wellness for themselves when messages and feedback communicated to employees coincide with and sustain individuals' health identities.

The larger *society* in which we live also informs a great deal of our health behaviors and understandings. This area seeks to understand how societal structures and institutions, such as the mass media, communicate and influence health. For example, health-related storylines on TV shows have been shown to educate and prompt healthy behavior change among viewers.

Some health communication scholarship also focuses on *public health* (i.e., the health of large populations). Media campaigns are an important public health tool, and a good deal of scholarship investigates the best strategies for persuading people to engage in healthy behaviors. For example, Record (2014) studied the best way to communicate about a college campus's new tobacco-free policy.

Finally, a considerable amount of health communication scholarship studies the ways that health is communicated in *health professions*. Scholarship related to patient–provider communication investigates the ways that healthcare providers and patients interact to create meaning about health and illness and how that meaning affects medical decisions and health outcomes. One example of research in this area analyzed how oncologists use the word "normal" in their conversations with patients (Gutzmer & Beach, 2015).

Wellness and Illness Models

Of the definitions that exist in the literature, one has dominated both scholarly literature and policy discussions since its introduction in 1948. According to the World Health Organization (WHO), "Health is a state of complete physical, mental and social well-being and not merely the absence of disease or infirmity." Even though most people colloquially use the term "healthy" to describe a state in which they are not suffering from any sort of illness, the WHO definition states that such a perspective on health is inadequate; indeed, **health** involves the well-being of the whole person—physically, mentally, emotionally, and socially—and a state of true health requires wholeness in each of these areas.

Although the WHO and other prominent health organizations define health in holistic terms, the standard of medical care (particularly in Western cultures) typically does not involve treating the whole person. Instead, the norm for health care in many industrialized countries adopts the biomedical model of patient care (Roter et al., 1997). Derived primarily from the **illness model**—that is, the assumption that "a specific disease underlies all illness" (Wade & Halligan, 2004, p. 1398)—the **biomedical model** assumes that the human body can be treated like a piece of machinery. The assumptions of the biomedical model contain a number of implications for medical practice. First, given that the healthcare provider plays a similar role to that of a mechanic, the healthcare provider typically dominates healthcare interactions. The communication in biomedical encounters typically revolves around a series of yes-or-no questions posed by the physician to the patient in order to determine the underlying cause of the patient's distress (Roter et al., 1997). Although this method of interaction can be very efficient (du Pré, 2014), it limits the ability and/or willingness of patients to share psychological or emotional concerns that are not directly related to their physical symptoms. The second (and related) problem associated with the biomedical model (and the illness

model on which it is based) assumes that health is merely the absence of disease (Wade & Halligan, 2004). Because health is based on the combination of physical, mental, and social well-being (WHO, 1948), many patients—and a fair number of healthcare practitioners—are dissatisfied with the assumptions of the biomedical model.

Models of care that treat patients holistically have several different names, but the term that has received the greatest scholarly attention is the **biopsychosocial model**. George Engel (1977) introduced the biopsychosocial model into public debate because of inadequacies he observed when applying the biomedical model to the diagnosis and treatment of psychological and social problems. Engel noted that, historically, many of the earliest signs of long-term illness were associated with psychosocial functioning. Several changes associated with long-term illness—such as changes in physical appearance, sudden antisocial behavior, or the inability to perform routine duties such as work—alerted other individuals within the community to the presence of a problem. Biomedical care necessarily discounts all these social and emotional clues to illness because none can be traced to a specific physical problem within the body. As an example, Wade and Halligan (2004) note that many soldiers suffering from what would now be called posttraumatic stress disorder were executed during World War I for faking illness and trying to shirk their duties.

As a response to the biomedical model, the biopsychosocial model takes an integrative approach to health. In this light, emotional and experiential components of illness are as important to health as are physical symptoms (Borrell-Carrió, Suchman, & Epstein, 2004; Engel, 1977). Broadening the scope of medicine beyond the analysis of physical symptoms has significant consequences, particularly when patient health is the primary outcome. For one thing, broadening the boundaries of "illness" allows more people to benefit from the "sick role"; this ability to benefit is a significant factor considering that people are generally not held to the same level of responsibility when they are ill (Wade & Halligan, 2004). Biopsychosocial encounters have also been associated with higher levels of patient satisfaction (Roter et al., 1997). Physician empathy in particular, a hallmark of the biopsychosocial approach, associates with an assortment of enhanced health outcomes that include, but are not limited to, more accurate diagnoses, increased patient compliance, and higher feelings of patient efficacy (Neumann et al., 2012).

Empathy represents the degree to which a person can feel, perceive, or experience the perspective or feelings of another person. Numerous studies have confirmed that provider empathy is one of the most consistent predictors of patients' satisfaction, compliance, and long-term health (Thompson, Robinson, & Brashers, 2011).

Although the biopsychosocial and psychosocial models of health have expanded the ways that patients and health-care providers alike think about the meaning of health, some scholars have argued that these models still do not go far enough to understand patients' contextual realities. Toward that end, several scholars have advocated for the inclusion of spiritual well-being in models of patient health (e.g., Western medical practices should adopt some of the practices from traditional forms of Eastern medicine). Finding balance between various elements in the body, understanding and managing emotions, and being attuned to the flow of energy in the body and the environment exemplify traditional Eastern practices that could be included as an *alternative* (replacement) or *complement* (in addition) to Western medical practices (Chan, Ying Ho, & Chow, 2002). Although the biopsychosocial-spiritual model was proposed primarily for end-of-life care, the ideals that health includes a search for transcendence, a balance of all relationships (including *both* personal relationships and relationships with the physical world), and a feeling of peace and spiritual well-being can be applied in many situations.

Communicating Health in Personal Relationships

Many people intuitively know that meaningful relationships make them "feel" better and that the extent of those feelings includes both emotional and physical aspects. Close relational partners can cheer us up, help us manage difficult problems, give us a different perspective about a troubling situation, and support us during grief or loss. These relationships can provide **social support**, which is the perceived or degree to which a person does or can receive tangible, informational, emotional, or behavioral care or assistance from others in his or her social network(s). The sum of all this social support can be considered a person's **social capital**. Results from a large meta-analysis (including the combined results of nearly 150 studies and more than 300,000 participants)

reveal just how striking the effect of relationships on health can be. Insufficient **social support** and a lack of social integration both present a greater risk to mortality than smoking cigarettes, drinking six or more alcoholic drinks a day, failing to exercise regularly, or being obese (Holt-Lunstad et al., 2010). Although the results from this study are striking in terms of their scope, they are not surprising; social scientists have known for some time that social relationships are vital for both mental and physical health. Relationships do not only make us "feel" better; they actually *make* us better.

Across the lifespan, social support remains as one of the most health-beneficial relational behaviors. Cohen et al. (2000) traced the systematic study of the benefits of supportive interaction to Durkheim's observation (in the late 1800s) that individuals who moved to cities during the Industrial Revolution often experienced tremendous loneliness and higher rates of alcohol dependence and suicide. The idea that social integration is beneficial for our health remains a central idea in the study of social support today. Studies within this vein—often referred to as the **main effects** (Cohen & Wills, 1985) or *structural* (Helgeson, 2003) approaches to social support—investigate how inclusion in social networks positively affects individuals' health. Studies of structural support have revealed some unexpected connections between social network integration and total health. For example, people with large and dense social networks are less likely to develop the common cold, and, when they do, their symptoms tend to be less severe when compared to individuals with smaller social networks (Cohen, Doyle, Alper, & Skoner, 2003).

The other type of social support that has received a great deal of scholarly attention is the **stress-buffering** (Cohen & Wills, 1985) or **functional** (Helgeson, 2003) **model of social support**. This support occurs when people perceive that members of their social network need help, and they work to offer them assistance (Burleson, 2009). Enacting this kind of support can potentially affect specific health-related outcomes through a variety of pathways (Goldsmith & Albrecht, 2011).

Goldsmith (2004) situated this kind of support in something called **troubles talk**, the kinds of conversations people have with family members or close friends when they are facing troubling or uncertain situations. In many situations, troubles talk conversations begin with the disclosure of a problem (e.g., "My doctor thinks I might have skin cancer") or the announcement of a plan (e.g., "I have decided to take better care of myself physically"). Although many scholars have tried to differentiate the roles of support-provider and recipient during supportive conversations, Goldsmith (2004) offers no such distinction. Indeed, conversational partners often work together to *coconstruct* the meaning of a supportive exchange. This conceptualization of support typically involves a high degree of openness, mutual disclosure, and a shared sense of the meaning of the supportive encounter. Mutually supportive conversations that revolve around a shared stressor are called **communal coping** episodes.

Although many situations call for moments of communal coping, death is one of the most ubiquitous shared stressors that people face. Even though death is an inescapable part of life, many people, particularly in Western cultures, often avoid discussions of death because it is a taboo topic (Walter, 1991). Previous studies have revealed that the potential shock of a life-threatening diagnosis such as cancer—whether your own (Pauley, Morman, & Floyd, 2011) or a close loved one's (Beach, 2009)—can be mitigated by supportive communication among close friends and family members. Those studies revealed that the closeness of relationships with romantic partners and/or other family members is often *strengthened* because of the difficult conversations that surround issues related to illness and mortality

Communicating in Patient–Provider Relationships

Although all humans live daily with their own bodies and minds, patients generally cannot recognize how symptoms (e.g., chest pain, difficulty breathing, nausea, & anxiety) might yield an accurate diagnosis (e.g., stroke, heart attack, and/or stress disorder). Even if a correct diagnosis is made, patients most often lack the knowledge, access, and technological sophistication to treat acute medical emergencies or threatening and often-chronic conditions (e.g., diabetes, dementia, or cancer). And, of course, health problems are not limited to physical symptoms, but include a wide variety of biological, social, and psychological conditions. What follows is a brief overview of only a few basic dimensions of interactions between patients and providers (Beach, 2013b, 2013c).

A Basic Framework: Offers, Responses, and the Inadequacy of Biomedicine

A decade before other major contributions to the patient–provider literature, Balint (1957) found that when patients present their symptoms, they do not simply offer physical descriptions, but also make available to doctors their illness circumstances and their impacts on daily living. How doctors respond—by accepting or rejecting these life-world events and experiences—facilitates and/or constrains the ability to address patients' concerns. As Engel (1977) observed 20 years later, medical care needs to abandon the biomedical tendency to avoid patients' mental and emotional concerns.

Illness, Disease, and Treating Patients as Persons

Hippocrates (470–360 BCE)—often described as the "father of medicine"—over 2,000 years ago stated: "I would rather know the person who has the disease than know the disease the person has." This quotation has echoed across the centuries, such as in Cassell's (1985) *Talking with Patients*, which opens with, "Doctors treat patients, not diseases … the spoken language is the most important tool in medicine" (p. 1).

Illnesses express human predicaments, yet doctors are trained to detect disease as symptomatic displays rooted in organic disorders. Symptoms are only signs or indications of potential problems: "Here we encounter the core problem of medical practice. … No matter how hard we try, technology will not help us recognize, understand, or solve human problems in medicine" (Barbour, 1995, p. 12).

It is important to recognize that *illness* refers to patients' life-world circumstances (i.e., affective and emotional experiences influencing sickness and wellness), while *disease* emphasizes how anatomical and physiological symptoms are given priority when determining a patient's overall health condition (see also Mishler, 1984). For example, the American Cancer Society determined that more than one-third of cancer diagnoses could have been prevented with healthier lifestyles. Similarly, a host of medical studies reveals that a striking 80% of problems requiring medical treatment are caused by five troubling health behaviors: lack of exercise, overeating (e.g., obesity) and poor nutritional diets, smoking, excessive drinking, and stress (Deutschman, 2007).

Studying Communication During Medical Interviews

Several prominent areas of research focusing on communication between patients and providers have evolved over time, reflecting a historical movement away from the primacy of doctors' authority (Beach, 2013b; Epstein & Street, 2007; Roter & Hall, 2006). Increasing attention is given to how patients' needs can best be met through relationships promoting partnerships, collaboration, and interactional abilities to heal illnesses, versus curing diseases. This progression might be visualized as shown in **Figure 19.1**.

FIGURE 19.1: Historical Stages of Conceptual Foci in Health Communication

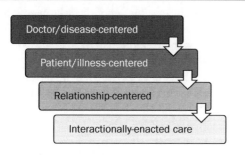

Medical Interviews Unfold in Phases

A **phase** is a distinct or identifiable period of time in which interaction reveals different functions or forms. For example, an extensive investigation of 2,500 primary care encounters identified six distinct phases of interactional activity from openings through closings (Byrne & Long, 1976):

1. Openings during which doctors seek to develop relationships with patients.

2. Patients provide and/or doctors solicit reasons for clinical visitations.

3. Doctors take verbal histories and/or conduct physical examinations.

4. Doctors work alone, and at times in unison with patients, to consider (i.e., diagnose) patients' conditions.

5. Doctors detail further treatments and/or investigations that may be needed.

6. Doctors terminate and thus close consultations.

These activities are frequently associated with eliciting and elaborating on patients' chief complaints, taking medical histories, performing physical examinations, evaluating other investigations, and offering diagnoses and treatment plans. In addition, the interactional difficulties associated with specific activities, such as openings and closings, providing reasons for visits, and prescribing treatment regimens have also received considerable attention (Heritage & Maynard, 2006; Robinson, 2003).

Patient-Initiated Actions and Medical Authority

Doctors routinely regulate and thus control agendas by actions such as asking questions, displaying expert knowledge, using specialized language and jargon (often confusing to patients), adhering to time constraints, and selectively providing and withholding information (Beach, 2015; Heritage, 2005). These *asymmetries* often create delicate imbalances of authority. Interactional problems and dilemmas are continually managed and negotiated throughout care. Consider the following examples:

- Doctors work to make their medical reasoning available to patients, yet invoke evidence to which only they have access and of which only they have sufficient technical background understanding. Doctors invest efforts to convince patients of their authority, yet simultaneously strive to hold themselves accountable for the kinds of authority patients might attribute to them (Peräkylä, 1998, 2002).

- Patients have often been described as *passive* in response to doctors' medical agendas; patients defer and subordinate themselves to medical authority (e.g., Street, Krupat, Bell, Kravitz, & Haidet, 2003). Gill (1998) reported that patients are tentative when explaining their problems, cautious about taking positions on medical issues, and hesitant to draw attention to their varied needs and desires (e.g., expectations, hopes, fears, and uncertainties). Patients' fears about cancer, and other health issues, are often raised indirectly—only hinted at with cues and clues (Beach & Dozier, 2015; Beach, Easter, Good, & Pigeron, 2005).

- Patients are also, however, frequently *proactive*; they initiate a wide range of actions, such as explanations, requests, invitations, offers, or clarifications (Beach, 2013c, 2015). At times, patients and parents also resist or challenge doctors' positions. For example, parents seek antibiotic prescriptions for their children when pediatricians are unwilling to assist (Stivers, 2007), cancer patients disagree that difficulties swallowing are caused by radiation treatments rather than the possible return of cancer (Drew, 2013), and doctors seek specific details of alcohol consumption that patients are unable or unwilling to provide (Beach, 2015; Halkowski, 2013). Patients may also be skeptical that their conditions are as serious as doctors claim they are (Pomerantz, Gill, & Denvir, 2007), at times even justifying their condition when being treated for cancer (Beach, 2013c).

How patients make offers and doctors respond, how doctors perform activities such as not fully attending to patients' full sets of concerns at the outsets of medical histories (Beckman & Frankel, 1984), assessing improvements in soliciting patients' agendas (Marvel, Epstein, Flowers, & Beckman, 1999), and whether female or male doctors are more patient centered (Roter & Hall, 2004) will continue to be central concerns as research moves forward. So, too, will increased attention to topics such as nonvocal and nonverbal actions (e.g., gaze, facial expressions, touch, the use of medical records, etc.).

Communicating Health and Well-Being at Work

Most U.S. adults will spend more of their waking hours at work than at leisure (U.S. Bureau of Labor Statistics, 2014), and, for most people, no concrete boundary exists between their work and home lives. As a result, our wellness and illness travel with us and become part of what we must negotiate at work (Geist-Martin & Scarduzio, 2017). In fact, one particular problem organizations face is **presenteeism**—where employees are present at work but limited in job performance by a health problem (Cancelliere, Cassidy, Ammendolia, & Côté, 2011). Employers recognize this health issue and have spent time and money offering health-based programs for their employees. Today, more companies recognize that enhancing worker productivity and decreasing absenteeism and presenteeism are dependent, to some degree, on what the company offers that might contribute to employees' health and well-being.

Workplace Health Promotion (WHP) and Employee Assistance Programs (EAPs) are designed to address health problems impacted by work, including stress, burnout, and work–life balance. *Stress* refers to a person's psychological and physiological reaction to a potential real or perceived threat. Workplace-related stress is responsible for over 120,000 deaths per year and as much as 5 to 8% of all annual health care costs in the United States (Goh, Pfeffer, & Zenios, 2016). **Burnout** refers to the exhaustion, fatigue, and frustration that result when stress exceeds a person's capacity for withstanding a given level of stress. **Work–life balance**, therefore, represents the degree of homeostasis that permits a person to cope with stress without experiencing dysfunction or trauma. A work–life balance generally means that a worker experiences a physically, emotionally, and psychologically healthy work life. In one study exploring the meanings of good health, participants indicated that good health meant "having good emotional health," "mental well-being," being a "well-rounded person emotionally, spiritually, and physically," having a "balanced life," "not being overly stressed," "feeling good about oneself," and having "strong" family and personal relationships (Mendez-Luck, Bethel, Goins, Schure, & McDermott, 2015). Today's employees want more than attention to their physical health concerns; they want to work in places that are personalized and where they can develop rewarding friendships (Friedman, 2014). A significant piece of this puzzle, for some, is simply being recognized and appreciated at work (Mosley & Irvine, 2015). **Organizational grace**, conceived of as acceptance, forgiveness, awareness, and caring, extends from healthy spirituality in a manner that recognizes, rewards, and respects another person (Geist-Martin & Freiberg, 1992).

Working well is more than simply being free from illness. For many people, working well is about **thriving**. Surviving implies coping but not exceeding the basic well-being requirements of a workplace. In contrast, thriving implies the achievement of positive work–life balance. It is about working in environments that contribute to the quality of life.

One way of thinking about **quality of work life (QWL)** is in terms of four dimensions of health identity: *physical, psychological, social,* and *spiritual health* (see **Figure 19.2**) (Farrell & Geist-Martin, 2005). This model reveals that communication is vital, both in the messages that employers send to employees about the four dimensions of their health identities, and also in terms of the feedback that employees direct toward their managers and supervisors about how they are faring at work. The model also reveals

FIGURE 19.2: Model of Working Well in Organizations

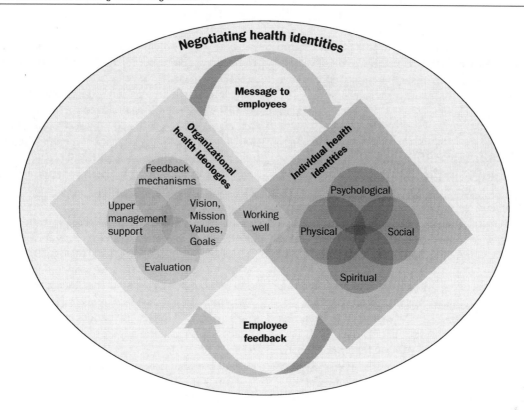

the significant role that an organization's health ideology plays in constructing wellness at work.

All four dimensions are essential for balancing workplace wellness, but most employees see the social dimension as vital (Geist-Martin, Horsley, & Farrell, 2003; Geist-Martin & Scarduzio, 2011; Scarduzio & Geist-Martin, 2015). Employees want quality relationships with others at work and to look forward to going to work and collaborating with others; these relationships facilitate flourishing at work. Aristotle was the first to discuss **flourishing** more than 2,000 years ago (Robinson, 1989). The best life, according to Aristotle, is one where flourishing, happiness, or well-being is valued for its own sake; it becomes the central aim toward which all action is directed (Hursthouse, 1999).

More recently, flourishing refers to overall life well-being or happiness (Dunn & Dogherty, 2008). In this view, to flourish is "to live within an optimal range of human functioning, one that connotes goodness,

generativity, growth, and resilience" (Fredrickson & Losada, 2005, p. 678). Flourishing, or well-being, can be affected by quality-of-life factors such as health status, work–life balance, social connections, civic engagement and governance, and personal security (Giovannini, Hall, Morrone, & Ranuzzi, 2011; Hall, Giovannini, Morrone, & Ranuzzi, 2010). Sarah Tracy, one of the faculty involved in the Arizona State University (n.d.) Transformation Project, focuses her research and teaching on ways to facilitate employees' well-being and happiness. Tracy teaches a course on communication and the art of happiness, which focuses on the communication behaviors related to constructing happiness and well-being in various contexts. One can expect that each of these behaviors contributed in some way to employees flourishing in their workplaces. In fact, some of these same behaviors are integral to the art of positive communication (Mirivel, 2014).

Integral to well-being, of course, is good health, including good mental health. But, given that health is strongly affected by the environments in which we live, our social networks, lack of poverty and social-economic deprivation, and sustainability over time, all have to be addressed if we are to succeed in promoting health and well-being (Organisation for Economic Co-operation and Development, 2011). Communicating happiness and cooperative behaviors through our social networks promote health and well-being.

Communicating Health and Illness in the Community

Variations in concepts of health and illness exist across cultural categories. **Culture** is a broad and encompassing concept but can be understood as all the intergenerational patterns of behavior, belief, value, custom, and ritual of an identifiable group (e.g., nationality, ethnicity, or religion). Some scholars discuss **cocultures** as analogous subgroup patterns (e.g., sexual orientation, transgender, self-selected groups such as goths, tribes, etc.). Cocultures are enduring yet evolving groups identified by shared behaviors, beliefs, and rituals. Cultural variations have the power to alter outcomes of patient–provider communication and health campaigns. This section introduces the vital role that culture plays in shaping perceptions, how communities as microcultures may influence campaign effectiveness, and opportunities for using social support to promote health outcomes and campaign effectiveness.

Cultural Conceptions of Health and Illness

Understanding the way different cultures understand issues related to health and illness is important for promoting effective patient–provider communication. Variations in cultural conceptions of health and illness can affect how individuals explain illness regarding disease progression, and appropriate treatment (Thompson, Whaley, & Stone, 2011). Interpersonal communication in one's social network often helps an individual determine if symptoms warrant healthcare-seeking behavior (Hay, 2008) and provides additional opportunities for defining beliefs surrounding the level of harm posed by a health threat (Aikens, Nease, & Klinkman, 2008). As part of these conversations, **lay ideas** (Leventhal, Leventhal, & Cameron, 2001) about causes and effects of health-related issues are exchanged and used to convey explanations for understanding and managing health threats.

Variations in how individuals explain health and illness can affect access to health care and mortality rates (Furnham & Baguma, 1999). According to Thompson et al. (2011), these factors can influence a healthcare provider's response to a patient's description of his or her health-related experiences and recommendation for a suitable course of action. In addition, such cultural variations often present challenges in patient–provider communication interactions because healthcare providers may hold perspectives on illness and health that differ from how patients explain health-related issues in question. Prior research has shown that when healthcare providers ignore the importance of cultural patterns in conceptualizing health and illness, effective delivery of care and treatment can be compromised (Knibb & Horton, 2008).

Because healthcare decisions often depend on what patients communicate to their healthcare providers about symptoms they experience, ignoring how these experiences are shaped by cultural notions about risk, sensations, and perceptions of the impact of illness on daily routines presents challenges to enhancing quality of care (Garro, 2000). One way to avoid minimizing the role of cultural variations in shaping beliefs about health and illness is to encourage healthcare providers to give patients ample opportunities to describe their symptoms in their own words (Galland, 2005). This allows for patients and healthcare providers to coconstruct explanations for illnesses more effectively (Frosch & Kalpan, 1999).

Community Health Campaigns

Health campaigns, in general, are organized collective communication efforts to facilitate public health-promoting attitudes, values, beliefs, and/or behaviors regarding a particular health-related domain of activity or risk. Health campaigns seeking to promote behavior change encounter challenges among disadvantaged communities in developed and developing countries (Roberto, Murray-Johnson, & Witte, 2011). Scholars have identified a variety of factors that contribute to difficulties in reaching some communities, including stigmatization of certain behaviors and health conditions, marginalization of community members, and shortage of essential resources (Hogan & Palmer, 2005). In such cases, winning support and commitment of community members becomes key for the success of any health campaign. In order to achieve this, a people-centered approach known as community mobilization can be implemented (Dearing, Gaglio, & Rabin, 2011). Community mobilization empowers community members and the target audience as invested **stakeholders** (i.e., any entity or party whose outcomes are affected by the health risk or campaign) and gaining their support for attainment of campaign objectives (e.g., Bigdon & Sachitanandam, 2003).

A few theories help explain how changes can be achieved through community-level interventions. Under the umbrella of **community change theory**, Thompson and Kinne (1999) surveyed studies using change theories across individual, organizational, societal, and environmental levels. Under this framework, the use of individual behavioral change theory to explain population-level phenomena is based on a **systems perspective** of a community (Rice & Foote, 2013). This perspective considers community to be part of a larger dynamic system that is connected to other sectors and organizations. Within such a system, a change in one sector signifies a change in others. Theories explaining human behavior and social advocacy strategies offer another set of models for promoting change within a community. Often, these models work best when used in tandem to promote behavior change in a community. Health campaigns targeting individual-level outcomes, such as lower smoking initiation rates among minors combined with efforts involving greater enforcement of laws penalizing tobacco sales to youth under the age of 18 (Dorfman & Wallack, 2012), can increase likelihood of attaining public health objectives compared to using one approach alone.

Another strategy for developing of community health campaigns is social marketing. **Social marketing** applies marketing techniques developed in the commercial sector to develop campaigns that are prosocial in nature and can promote social good (Lee & Kotler, 2011). These techniques rely on ideas of exchange between the target population and health communication campaign sponsors, ongoing research for understanding the needs of the target population, and marketing mix (Lee & Kotler, 2011). The marketing mix refers to the combination of the four Ps of marketing. The first of the four Ps is the **product**, or the new behavior or idea being "sold," and what benefits it offers the target audience when adopted. The second is **price**, or any barriers to adopting the new behavior or idea. The third is **promotion**, which includes the communication strategy used to convey and publicize the message content. The fourth is the **place** where the target audience can gain access to the product. **Positioning**, or the strategy used to position the product in the context of competitors, although technically not part of the four Ps, is often used in conjunction with them. Community-based prevention programming (CBPM) projects combine social marketing and community-based approaches to achieve desired results. Some recent examples of CBPM campaigns have addressed issues such as alcohol and tobacco use prevention (Bryant et al., 2007) and physical activity promotion among youth (Bryant et al., 2010).

In order to correctly execute the process of launching community-level interventions, a number of steps are required. These steps represent a five-stage process outlined by Bracht, Kingsbury, and Rissel (1999). The first step is to conduct a thorough **community analysis** to provide a profile of important qualities, such as resources, norms, beliefs, and values, that characterize the community. The second step calls for the **design and initiation of campaign activities** that include organizing partnerships with community members, increasing community participation, and laying the framework to launch the campaign to the wider community. The third step involves **implementation** of the campaign, which includes monitoring and refinement of the campaign strategy and coordination with community partners. During the fourth step, the community foundation for **maintaining and consolidating campaign efforts** is established, and campaign elements are incorporated into the community for the long term. **Determining effectiveness** of campaign activities in achieving objectives, identifying lessons learned for improving campaign activities, and revising the community analysis for future campaigns represent the types of activities typically performed at the fifth step. This step also assists with future campaign development.

Box 19.1 Ethical Issues

It should be clear from this chapter that health communication is multifaceted and pervasive. Two broad ethical issues discussed here elaborate on principles presented in this chapter.

- **Paternalism and Therapeutic Privilege**

All new physicians pledge the Hippocratic Oath, originally written about 2,500 years ago. It includes a promise for physicians to use their best ability and judgment on behalf of their patients. For centuries, this was practiced by physicians making treatment decisions "for" patients rather than "with" patients. Many patient advocates and health ethicists now argue that such a paternalistic approach to practicing medicine disrespects patients and their families (du Pré, 2014). The paternalistic model of provider–patient communication privileges the physician's priorities and biomedical knowledge over the patient's priorities and experiential knowledge. Support is increasing for replacing such paternalism with a partnership model that includes multiple perspectives when making health and treatment decisions.

The concept of therapeutic privilege is related to paternalism in that it refers to physicians withholding information from patients if they think disclosing the information would do more harm than good (du Pré, 2014). Therapeutic privilege is more complex than patient–provider communication, however. Family relationships, family communication rules, as well as cultural norms involving health, illness, and death also come into play in how individuals view therapeutic privilege. Sometimes patients' families request that physicians withhold information from patients for the sake of emotional well-being. As an advanced student of communication, it would be an interesting exercise for you to discuss therapeutic privilege with your family members.

- **Health Literacy**

According to the CDC (2019), health literacy is "the degree to which individuals have the capacity to obtain, process, and understand basic health information and services needed to make appropriate health decisions" (p. 3). Health literacy affects how patients and their families understand causes, treatments, and outcomes of health conditions and how they use that understanding to guide their behavior and decisions. Lower health literacy may lead patients to allow others to make their healthcare decisions for them rather than being active participants in their healthcare decisions. The American Medical Association (AMA) encourages patients to ask their healthcare providers three questions:

- What is my main problem?
- What do I need to do?
- Why is it important for me to do this?

You can see the physician privilege in this attempt to address the health literacy gap between patients and providers. How might these questions be revised to account for a partnership model of patient–provider communication?

Some public health and communication researchers encourage the use of "plain language" in written materials about health to account for different levels of health literacy. This includes carefully evaluating the grade level of written materials and how numbers, graphs, and pictures can be used to improve understanding for a wide range of patients and their families.

Communicating Public Health Campaigns

In the study of health communication, health campaigns research is at the intersection of public health and health communication research. The use of the term *communication* in a public health communication campaign indicates that a campaign message is doing more than hoping to improve health. According to Atkin and Rice (2013), *public health communication campaigns* are a "purposive attempt to inform or influence behaviors in large audiences within a specified time period using an organized set of communication activities and featuring an array of mediated messages in multiple channels generally to produce noncommercial benefits to individuals and society" (p. 3). In other words, health communication campaigns have important characteristics of being strategic- (i.e., not accidental), theory- and research-driven efforts that use mediated communication channels to improve health.

Communication campaigns can be an effective strategy for reaching mass audiences. Meta-analytic studies have consistently found support for carefully designed campaigns to improve health behavior (e.g., Derzon & Lipsey, 2002; Snyder & LaCroix, 2013). Campaigns are developed and tested via three stages of campaign evaluation: formative evaluation, process evaluation, and summative evaluation (Atkin & Freimuth, 2013).

The **formative evaluation stage** is the design stage in which campaign planners make critical decisions regarding the theoretical framework, goals, audience, channel(s), and materials (Atkin & Freimuth, 2013). The most common theoretical frameworks used in campaigns are discussed at the end of this section. Successful campaigns are focused on very specific goals. Campaign planners are responsible for understanding the research landscape related to the primary campaign goals, including relevant trends and previous research on the (a) behavior (e.g., stop smoking, eat more vegetables), (b) type of change (e.g., awareness, attitudinal, behavioral), and (c) level of change (e.g., individual, organizational, societal) being sought. When determining a segmented audience to target, a clear group of similar individuals (e.g., adults, youth, ethnic groups, teachers, community members) and the mediated communication channel most likely to reach those individuals should be identified (Atkin & Freimuth, 2013). Few modern campaigns adhere to only one channel; most campaigns use multiple channels, one of which is typically Internet based (Helme, Savage, & Record, 2015). Finally, the campaign materials must be designed. Campaign materials are most often adapted from previous campaigns that were successful. With careful testing and retesting, new materials can also be designed. Regardless of whether materials are adapted or designed from scratch, messages should be tested with focus groups of the target population before implementation (Atkin & Freimuth, 2013). Research has found that thorough formative evaluation processes contribute most significantly to the success of a campaign (Noar, 2006), and that a lack of thorough formative evaluation is a primary reason for an unsuccessful campaign (Smith, 2002).

The *process evaluation stage* occurs when campaign materials are implemented. This stage consists of activities that can confirm that the implementation plan is going forward (Valente & Kwan, 2013). Decisions made during the formative evaluation stage that are relevant here include the channels the message will appear on (e.g., specific stations, papers, websites), the frequency with which the messages will be distributed (e.g., air once an hour, run constantly on a website, placed in 100 locations), and how long the messages will be viewable to audiences (i.e., the amount of time the campaign will run). Activities for confirming that the campaign implementation plan is on track include checking that messages are airing on the chosen channels at the desired time (e.g., on the radio and TV) and periodically visiting locations where messages were placed to confirm that they are still present and undamaged; this includes confirming that Internet-based channels are still operating correctly. The process evaluation stage is critical because if the implementation plan is not being implemented as planned, then campaign effectiveness can be significantly compromised.

The final stage is the **summative evaluation stage**, in which campaign effectiveness is assessed. During this stage, researchers determine whether they have achieved their campaign goals of improving health among their target population (Valente & Kwan, 2013). Effectiveness is primarily determined using quantitative data collected through large-scale quasi-experiments to compare behavioral differences in the target population before, during, and after campaign implementation. Importantly, campaigns do not seek to cause massive amounts of change; a small amount of change can be statistically supported as a significant change in behavior, and thus an effective campaign (Helme et al., 2015). The most important step in this stage is the sharing of results for future campaign planners to learn from. In short, public health communication campaigns are an effective way to change and improve health behavior (Derzon & Lipsey, 2002; Snyder & LaCroix, 2013).

Conclusion

Illness is the night side of life, a more onerous citizenship. Everyone who is born holds dual citizenship, in the kingdom of the well and in the kingdom of the sick. Although we all prefer to use only the good passport, sooner or later each of us is obliged, at least for a spell, to identify ourselves as citizens of that other place. (Sontag, 1977, p. 3)

Managing the dual citizenship of health and illness necessitates adapting our communication and our identities as we move between the kingdom of the well and the kingdom of the sick. We all face challenges and stresses as we navigate our own and others' illness diagnoses, from minor injuries to terminal illnesses, and everything in between. Although most of us strive to maintain healthy bodies and minds, inevitably we must struggle with the personal, cultural, and political circumstances that complicate and constrain our communication with one another (Yamasaki, Geist-Martin, & Sharf, 2016).

We have learned that the process of telling our illness stories by itself is a form of healing. Scholars outside the field of communication have offered insight into the value of illness narratives. For example, Rita Charon, MD, has spearheaded narrative medicine as an essential part of education of physicians, teaching them to honor the stories of illness that their patients tell (Charon, 2006, 2009). For nearly 20 years, James Pennebaker and colleagues have researched and written about the healing power of expressive writing as a path to healing (Pennebaker, 1997, 2000). At the same time that scholarship has inspired people to listen to and engage with the personal illness stories that people tell, the broad landscape of health communication scholarship on narrative reveals that "no story is solely personal, organizational, or public; personal stories cannot escape the constraints of institutional interests, nor are they separate from cultural values, beliefs, and expectations" (Sharf, Harter, Yamasaki, & Haidet, 2011, p. 38). Without a doubt, "storytelling is one of the most potent medicines at our disposal" (Bettencourt, 2015, dedication).

Credit

FIG. 19.2: Adapted from A. Farrell and P. Geist-Martin, *Management Communication Quarterly*, vol. 18, no. 4. Copyright © 2005 by SAGE Publications.

CHAPTER 20

Political Communication, Movements, and Campaigns

Luke Winslow

LEARNING OBJECTIVES

After reading this chapter, you should be able to do the following:

- Identify theories and practices of political communication in the United States.

- Identify and differentiate conditions under which democracy is made better or worse, helped or harmed, by contemporary communication practices and technologies.

- Identify the unique features of the U.S. voter in relation to the contemporary political environment in the United States.

- Identify and differentiate the roles of heuristic shortcuts in navigating the political communication environment in the United States.

- Identify and differentiate the role of symbols, labels, and messaging in navigating the political communication environment in the United States.

- Identify and differentiate the rhetorical strategies that influence the effectiveness of political messaging.

- Identify and differentiate how media change the relationship between politics, governance, and campaign communication.

- Identify and differentiate the roles of narrative in political communication in the United States.

- Identify and differentiate effective political crisis management techniques.

- Identify and differentiate how to become a more engaged political communicator.

- Identify and differentiate the value of a degree in communication for enhancing the health and vitality of political conversation and democratic possibilities.

Political Communication: Movements and Campaigns

This chapter examines the theory and practice of political communication in the United States. Democracy has always depended on open and direct communication between its citizens and those who govern them. In the United States, this has been true since the nation's founding. Political communication is not as important in an autocratic or closed society, such as North Korea or Saudi Arabia. In those countries, political communication plays a limited role in systems of governance because citizens lack *agency*—the ability to control material circumstances and exert influence in avenues of power (Palczewski, Ice, & Fritch, 2012). This is not the case in the United States. Here, it does not matter if you are a rich industrialist, an NFL star, or a first-semester freshman; all our interests are supposed to be equally represented by our elected officials. In an open society like ours, political communication is essential to the health and strength of democracy. A sense of the importance of pursuing such unity through egalitarianism is illustrated by the diversity of the world in which we live; political communication is fundamental to achieving collaborative identities in such a diverse world (see **Table 20.1**).

TABLE 20.1: A Microscope on a Macroworld if It Consisted of 100 People

Characteristic	Approximate Statistics
Gender	50 would be female 50 would be male
Age	26 would be children 74 would be adults, 8 of whom would be 65 and older
Continental origin	60 Asians 15 Africans 14 from the Americas 11 Europeans
Religion	33 Christians 22 Muslims 14 Hindus 7 Buddhists 12 people who practice other religions 12 people not aligned with a religion
Languages	12 would speak Chinese 5 would speak Spanish 5 would speak English 3 would speak Arabic 3 would speak Hindi 3 would speak Bengali 3 would speak Portuguese 2 would speak Russian 2 would speak Japanese 62 would speak other languages
Education/literacy	83 would be able to read and write; 17 would not 7 would have a college degree 22 would own or share a computer

Source: http://www.100people.org/statistics_100stats.php?section=statistics

The goal of this chapter is to explore how contemporary communication practices and technologies impact American democracy. In this chapter, we consider how political communication connects with audiences, the effect of media on political campaigns, the role of narrative in political communication, and effective political crisis management. Ultimately, we use the relationship between voters, politicians, and the media to understand how the principles of political communication can be applied to our own lives.

Applying the principles of political communication is important, even if politics seems beyond your competence or horizon of life relevance. Whether on cable television news or around your Thanksgiving dinner table, conversations about Obamacare, the Middle East, and tax cuts can seem intimidating, overwhelming, or simply uninteresting. For many young people, entering these political conversations is like arriving late to a party. Imagine that scenario: When you walk into the party, you notice several people in a circle having a lively conversation. You have just arrived and do not know what they are talking about, but you can tell by the way they are talking that the topic matters. You would like to understand and maybe contribute to the conversation, but you cannot just barge in. You do not know these people, and you do not know all names and issues they are talking about. In addition, you do not know what was said before you arrived. *Knowledge and interest are prerequisites for entering the conversation.* This is as true at parties as it is in our political communication environment. Although several more specific learning objectives are detailed at the beginning of this chapter, the central purpose of this chapter is to increase your knowledge and interest in political communication so that you can contribute to this conversation, have your voice heard, and use your communication degree to contribute to a healthy and strong U.S. democracy.

In order to fulfil this chapter's central purpose, I begin by defining some key terms. I then detail several foundational assumptions related to the study of political communication. Next, I ground those assumptions in three dimensions: (a) media and campaign communication, (b) narrative in political communication, and (c) political crisis management. Finally, I close by asking you to consider how this chapter's description of our political communication environment can be improved by your own increased interest and knowledge in public conversations about politics.

Defining Key Concepts

Communication

By the time you are taking your capstone course, I am sure you can articulate a basic definition of communication. I have found it helpful, when I need to define communication, to begin with **sense-making**. We all seek to make sense of our interactions with the world and the people in it; to do so, we rely on symbols to create and exchange meaning with other people. The symbolic creation and exchange of meaning is aimed at increasing cooperation, which allows us to exchange ideas, work together to make decisions about matters of shared concern, and act in the world so that things get done, including improving our relationships, our health, and our democracy (Palczewski et al., 2012). **Political communication campaigns** are planned and organized collective communication efforts to pursue political objectives (e.g., election to office, policy change, social movement activation, etc.).

Politics

Unfortunately, the word "politics" is often misused. How many times have you heard others say they were screwed out of jobs because of "office politics"? Or, maybe politics only reminds you of Mayor Quimby from *The Simpsons*, Tina Fey dressed like Sarah Palin, or Hillary Clinton trying to raise more money than Jeb Bush. Instead of all that, a more precise and useful definition of **politics** focuses on how we collectively decide to dispense and withhold goods and resources. For example, politics helps us make sense of resource questions related to who is allowed to work, at what pay, and in what industries. Politics helps us make sense of what we are allowed to purchase and use, including alcohol, cigarettes, cocaine, pornography, and Qualcomm shares. Politics helps us make sense of what we are allowed to sell and make a profit from, including animals, prescription medicine, and a taco truck on the street corner (Hahn, 2003).

Many of these questions concern competing ideas or opinions. If we come to a political decision that allows your neighborhood to get a new road, my neighborhood may not get a new road. We cannot just agree to disagree when it comes to political issues of resource allocation and distribution. Instead, we must come to a shared form of cooperation. To understand how we get there, you must also understand the processes, messaging, and symbols we use to induce cooperation. Our answers to questions such as what people can work, what they can buy, and what they can sell are all essentially political questions because they are sorted out on the terrain of the symbolic, ultimately allowing us to live and act together in a shared system of governance (Hahn, 2003). Put another way, to understand politics, you must understand communication.

Communication and Politics

By putting "communication" together with "politics," we arrive at the study of how we use language and symbols to make sense of how goods and resources are dispensed and withheld. Political science courses tend to be more concerned with the *outcomes* related to resource allocation and distribution: Who won the election? Who voted in it? What legislation will be produced as a result? The communication discipline is more concerned with the *how*, or the processes and the messages that are created and exchanged along the way. Our discipline explores how the polity enacts citizenship, public interactions, and the decision-making processes that influence resource allocation. Citizenship for us is a process of action, not an act.

From a communication perspective, you can begin to see why there is a great deal of political communication in your day-to-day life. Asking a professor to reconsider a grade, returning a new shirt, or asking someone out on a date engages the material covered in this chapter. In each of these situations, you would use symbols to create and exchange meaning in a way that would ensure cooperative resource allocation so that you might earn an A, a new shirt, or a date on Friday night.

It might be wise to anchor our discussion about resources, politics, and communication in a more specific and relevant context. Put bluntly, young people today are being taken advantage of by our political system. Consider how our elected officials approach some of the issues we just raised related to resource allocation. Over the last few decades, the older people who have made most of the decisions about resource allocation have engaged in what can only be described as a series of greedy, ignorant, and selfish public policy decisions. You have grown up and entered the adult world during the years of crony capitalism when powerful officials in Washington have rewritten the rules of the game to favor a few people at the top over everyone else. That collusion has brought devastating results (McGhee, 2012). Just as you are getting ready to enter the job market and begin to settle down and think about buying a home, you will be entering the adult world during the recovery from the worst economic climate since the Great Depression. As a consequence, you will likely be part of the first generation in U.S. history worse off economically than its parents. According to a 2014 survey, the median family income headed by someone under 25 years of age, adjusted for inflation, is 6% less than similar families reported in 1989 (Norris, 2014). Historically, recent generations have enjoyed upward mobility and increased productivity, while still being able to work less and have more time for civic and home life. You will be the first counterexample to the deeply ingrained U.S. story that every generation does better than the one before it (Burstein, 2013). Your elected officials, however, continue to pour resources into public policies that disproportionately benefit older generations.

You know the assumptions about U.S. intergenerational success, but it now seems like older generations are unwilling to reach a hand down to lift you up. The social contract is gone, making it harder for your generation, in particular, to weather the greatest recession since the 1930s, unfunded and catastrophic wars, and environmental problems that threaten the entire planet. You will likely not enjoy the benefits of U.S. economic dominance that characterized the lives of your parents and grandparents, but you will suffer the consequences of short-sighted public policies you had nothing to do with.

How did this happen? How did our systems of governance decide to dispense so much of our resources to older, wealthier people and so little to you? Because we live in a democracy, it is wise to consider these questions from a *political* angle, and because you are a communication major, it would also be wise to consider these questions from a *sense-making* angle. In terms of civic and political participation, older people may argue that you are getting what you deserve. Compared to your parents and grandparents at the same age, young people today are less interested in politics, less likely to be engaged in their communities, less likely to join community groups geared toward solving public problems, less knowledgeable about political life, less likely to participate in electoral politics, less likely to read local or national newspapers, less likely to voice faith in their system, and less likely to express healthy levels of political efficacy (Jarvis, Barberena, & Davis, 2007).

Although the political science major could describe this situation, it is the communication major who can illuminate the processes, messaging, and symbols we use to arrive at some sort of agreement about how resources are allocated and whether that allocation is just. All this reminds us why it is important to think critically about the political words and symbols in our environment.

Assumptions About Political Communication

Three assumptions guide this chapter:

Assumption #1: By International Comparisons, U.S. Voters Display Irrational, Apathetic, and Ignorant Political Attitudes

About half of American voters do not know that each state has two senators, and three-quarters do not know the length of those senators' terms. About 70% cannot say which party controls the Senate. Over half of individuals cannot name their congresspersons, and 40% cannot name either of their senators. Slightly lower percentages know their representatives' party affiliations (Caplan, 2007). More recent surveys suggest that about 30% cannot name the vice president, about 35% cannot assign the proper century to the American Revolution, 6% cannot circle Independence Day on a calendar, and 18% think President Barack Obama is Jewish (only 10% think he is Muslim) (Bruni, 2013).

The causes of this ignorance vary: U.S. voters are said to be overloaded with information, struggle integrating information about their political choices, and lack incentives to seek out the kind of information that will help simplify the political process (Popkin, 1996). The result is a significant number of U.S. citizens who possess underdeveloped political philosophies, uncertain motivations to think carefully about policy issues, and a fragile command of important facts (Entman, 2004).

Assumption #2: U.S. Voters Rely Heavily on Heuristic Shortcuts to Make Political Decisions

The ignorance of the U.S. voter has a profound impact on political decision-making, forcing many to rely heavily on **heuristic shortcuts** to navigate what might otherwise be an unmanageably complex political climate (Caplan, 2007). These shortcuts are increasingly reliant on affect (Entman, 2004; Slovic, Zionts, Woods, Goodman, & Jinks, 2013). Affect does not require the conscious awareness of having gone through the difficult steps of researching public policies or weighing the experience and legislative accomplishments of an elected official. Rather, affect activates the intuitive and automatic thought processes that influence how voters *feel*, not what they cognitively, analytically, and deliberately *know* (see **Box 20.1**).

Very few voters really get to know political candidates or policies. Few individuals have the time, motivation, or knowledge to thoroughly understand how a particular bill might impact their taxes or their schools. The Patriot Act was 342 pages. The Affordable Care Act was 2,400 pages. The U.S. tax code is 13,000 pages. Voters tend to increasingly eschew empirical characteristics—what can be measured—when making decisions about politics. An **empirical description** would include a candidate's educational background or voting record. Instead, the importance of heuristic shortcuts encourages us to rely on **constructed descriptions**—what is adorned through language, adjectives, or buzz. Voters may make political decisions less according to how a candidate's stance on funding education will impact their tuition than whether the candidate can pull off an appearance on *Saturday Night Live*.

Box 20.1 Thinking, Fast and Slow

Daniel Kahneman, a Nobel Prize-winning social psychologist, offers a great illustration of heuristic shortcuts at work in his insightful book *Thinking, Fast and Slow* (2011). He asks readers to consider a simple but revealing question: A bat and ball together cost $1.10. The bat costs one dollar more than the ball. How much does the ball cost?

Most scan the question and quickly arrive at an answer: 10 cents. But that answer is wrong. Read the question again, do the math, and you will see that the correct answer is 5 cents. Kahneman says people who think the answer is 10 cents are often followers of the law of least effort. Furthermore, they may be overconfident, prone to place too much faith in their intuitions, and may find cognitive effort mildly unpleasant and avoid it as much as possible. Failing this test is a matter of insufficient motivation, or not trying hard enough. The U.S. voter very much fits this description.

In turn, our political decisions are increasingly governed by *aesthetic* dimensions, labels, symbols, and messages that operate like blinders on a horse, focusing our attention on some aspects but blinding us to others (Hahn, 2003). The importance of labels, symbols, and messages counter the presumption that politics is governed by some pure form of reason and rationality outside of symbolic interaction. More specifically, we often make decisions about elected officials based on who we would rather have a beer with (see Powell, Richmond, & Cantrell-Williams, 2012). Successful politicians know this, so they work hard to manipulate their hairlines, waistlines, accents, and wardrobes to appeal to the affective heuristics that govern so many voters' decisions. Much of the U.S. political machinery is designed to activate a particular shortcut in the minds of the polity.

Assumption #3: Symbols, Labels, and Messages are Contingent, Struggled Over, and Up for Grabs

The relationship between the peculiar behavior of the U.S. voter and the important role of heuristic shortcuts carves out important space once again for the communication scholar to study politics. The meanings of political labels and symbols used to create those shortcuts shift with time, as meanings become broader or narrower, or change entirely. Labels such as "middle class," "Obamacare," "boots on the ground," "Black Lives Matter," and "yes means yes" not only reflect a reality already existing in the minds of the citizens, but actively create a reality that does not yet come into existence until the language and symbols resonate with enough strength. It is on this shifting terrain that political communication performs its heavy lifting.

The rest of this chapter grounds these definitions and assumptions in three important dimensions of political communication in the United States: media and campaign communication, narrative and political communication, and effective political crisis management.

Box 20.2 Ethical Issues

Because political communication has been the focus of scholarly theorizing and critique for centuries, it is of little surprise that the ethics of political communication represents a vast literature. We present here three scholarly approaches to ethics in the political domain. These are by no means exhaustive; rather, they highlight general ethical issues to consider concerning political communication.

- **Four Moralities**

  Karl Wallace (1955) proposed four ethical guidelines, or moralities, that he asserted are core to fostering a healthy democratic political system. How does recent political discourse stack up according to these moralities?

  - **Habit of Search**: Communicators should have thorough knowledge about the subject they are speaking about and be prepared to answer relevant questions.

  - **Habit of Justice**: Communicators should select and present information and opinions fairly, without concealing relevant information or distorting data. In essence, this morality enables audiences to make fair, informed evaluations of the subject.

  - **Habit of Public Motivations**: Communicators should reveal the sources of their information, along with biases and motivations of those sources.

  - **Habit of Respect for Dissent**: Communicators should allow and encourage expression of diverse arguments, perspectives, and opinions. Compromise and agreement should not be sought at the sacrifice of the expression of opposition.

- **Significant Choice**

  Thomas Nilsen (1974) proposed guidelines for ethical communication in the public sphere that represent both "choice" and "truth." These principles are matters of degree, of course. Nilsen's notion of significant choice concerns how communicators provide contexts with a large degree of free and informed choice for the relevant parties. This is enabled by providing the best information possible, acknowledging alternatives, and expressing diverse views. For Nilsen, "truth" is not an absolute (see Chapter 6); rather, he notes that ethical communicators get as close to the truth as they are aware and they employ rigorous methods to communicate that truth with good intentions.

- **Ideals of Public Discourse**

  Mortimer Sellers (2003) proposed four ideals for public discourse:

  - **Civility**: Includes listening to others' arguments and attempting to understand them, then making reasoned responses.

  - **Sincerity**: Being truly committed to the common good of those involved.

  - **Community**: Public consideration of all members of the involved community.

  - **Toleration**: Overlooking those violations of ideals that are trivial for the purposes of moving forward with public discourse.

Media and Campaign Communication

We begin with the most important and vivid example of all these definitions and assumptions put into practice: media and campaign communication (see also: Chapters 22 and 23). Today, all major political campaigns are media campaigns, dominated by media consultants who serve as an advertising agency for the political campaign (Powell & Cowart, 2013). It is virtually impossible to understand the fundamentals of U.S. politics—including the behaviors of aspiring elected officials, the role of money in the political process, and the outcomes of elections—without also understanding the relationship between media and campaign communication.

Box 20.3 Euphemisms

Consider how the following euphemistic phrases versus the more direct term or phrase change your attitude (see Clark, 2010; Palczewski et al., 2012).

- "Transfer tubes" versus "body bags"
- "Baby" versus "fetus"
- "Invasion" versus "predawn vertical insertion"
- "Special encore presentation" versus "rerun"
- "Janitor" versus "cleaning specialist"
- "Collateral damage" versus "dead, innocent women and children"
- "Illegal alien" versus "illegal immigrant" versus "undocumented worker"
- "Refugee" versus "evacuee"
- "Invasion" versus "incursion" versus "police action"
- "Prisoner of war" versus "enemy combatant"
- "Islamo-facist" versus "jihadist" versus "terrorist" versus "Muslim fanatic" versus "Iraqi insurgent"
- "Defenseless villages bombarded from the air, the inhabitants driven into the countryside, the cattle machine-gunned, the huts set of fire with incendiary bullets" versus "pacification"

Recall the distinctive characteristics of the U.S. voter we just outlined in the previous section: Most voters cannot really get to know candidates or political policies; we are more likely to *feel* politics than to *think* them; there is less room for political potency; and successful campaigners rely on properly activating heuristic shortcuts in the minds of the voters. In turn, **media**—defined in this chapter as electronic communication technologies, such as radio, television, print, and the Internet, whose purpose is to attract audiences by disseminating information—effectively function as the facilitator of that shortcut (see also: Chapter 22). Therefore, given our learning objectives in this chapter, it is worthwhile to consider what happens when political communication is mediated.

Consider what images appear in your mind when you think about media and campaign communication. Some of you may think of Jon Stewart or Stephen Colbert satirizing a Republican politician denying climate change. Others may think of *Fox News* blaring from the television at your grandparent's house. Although these examples certainly fit our definition, it is important to also recognize that while the term "media" is often used to describe a monolithic bloc of electronic channels of communication, it is more useful to think about media as a fragmented, multidimensional set of electronic communities that have become a fundamentally important part of our political ecology. We know this by looking at four functions media serve in campaign communication. The particular word choices we make play a significant role in shaping the way we think about the world (see **Box 20.3**).

Media Educate

The media are our primary sources of political learning. They are the most utilized sources for political and public affairs information. Media make particular topics and individuals more vivid and recognizable. Media can greatly impact the construction of a certain worldview that voters use to navigate a complex political landscape (Weaver, 1994). This is probably quite a departure from your grandparents' day. Your grandparents got their political learning at their Kiwanis club, or through their church or union hall. You are less likely to get your own political learning from any of those sources.

Media Replace

Media have replaced traditional political institutions and traditional sites of learning about politics and civic engagement. Media portray themselves as being able to handle the responsibilities once assumed by families, religious institutions, and political parties. Media attempt to persuade you to agree that they have the capacity to organize voters' alternatives in coherent ways. But, as opposed to traditional sites of political learning, media create a pseudo-community in which citizens feel they are a part of a functioning whole until they try to act on their news-created awareness (Hart, 1999). Today, electronic communities draw citizens together through political spectacles. It would be worthwhile to consider if the media are prepared—emotionally, professionally, and constitutionally—for that role (Hahn, 2003). Jon Stewart and Bill O'Reilly may entertain, but do they inform, engage, or inspire?

Media Filter

Is it not odd that there is always just enough news to fit into a television program's allotted time slot or a newspaper's allotted page limits? Media play such an enormous part in the political communication process because journalists, news directors, and producers get to choose what counts as news and what does not. In this way, media serve what we call an **agenda-setting** function (see also: Chapter 22); that is, by determining what counts as news and what does not, media set the agenda for what viewers should be thinking about in terms of their political lives (Powell & Cowart, 2013). If news is what these agenda setters say it is, then we again must consider the differences between the fundamental purpose of politics in a democracy and the fundamental purpose of a media company such as *Fox News* or the *New York Times*. Mainstream media are designed to attract eyes and ears. If they can do that successfully, they can sell advertising to companies who want to hawk their products to your eyes and ears. And, if the media companies can sell advertising, then they can meet their fundamental responsibility: to make money for their shareholders.

When media cover campaigns or candidates, we need to be reminded that they are in the news *business*, not the business of meeting the needs of a healthy, fully functioning democracy. And because of this, the norms and imperatives of media are not those required for the effective organization of electoral conditions and debate. Journalists' professional values and political values may even be in direct conflict with each other. This surely has a profound impact on both what counts as news and how news stories are covered. Journalists do not reward all candidates and all issues equally. Journalists inevitably filter out candidates who do not fit their story, who do not do as well on television, or who are unwilling to speak in simplistic sound bites that can be easily turned into headlines. Media do not filter in a purely neutral manner. There is plenty of evidence that media are biased in various ways (see **Box 20.4**).

Box 20.4 Newsworthiness

If you have two guys on a stage and one guy says, "I have a solution to the Middle East problem," and the other guy falls into the orchestra pit, who do you think is going to be on the evening news?

—Roger Ailes, founder of Fox News

Media Simplify

One primary goal of media and campaign communication is to transport inherently ambiguous and complicated political issues into a "chunkable" narrative that can be simply told in order to retain the interests of readers or viewers in a way that delivers them to advertisers. Media today encourage us to know candidates as people, not statespersons; media have a harder time depicting abstractions; and media are primarily visual. But, here is the problem: Complex political issues are usually abstract, nonvisual, and sorted out by negotiation and deliberation, not grandstanding and pandering. Because the primary allegiance of the media is to advertisers, the media prefer sound bites, punditry, and manufactured conflict. As **Box 20.5** on media bias indicates, the most powerful influence of media may not be in *persuading* the public, but in *reinforcing* the status quo (Hahn, 2003). This simplification function explains why Ron Burgundy closed his fake news program with a water-skiing squirrel, and why Brian Williams closes his real-life news program with a touching story about a disabled war-veteran volunteering at the old folks' home.

Box 20.5 Media Bias

Are the media biased? Yes, but not in the way we often assume.

1. The media are biased toward what makes money.
2. The media are biased toward the visual.
3. The media are biased in favor of the contemporary and the immediate.
4. The media are biased in support of the status quo.
5. The media are biased in favor of the assumptions of society.
6. The media are biased toward fairness and balance.
7. The media are biased in favor of bad news.
8. The media are biased toward familiar plot lines.

Media Condition and Reward

Media prime us to think of political leaders as campaigners rather than governors. Politicians are increasingly responsible to the perpetual campaign, either in creating mediated spectacles that will draw the coverage of television cameras and online buzz or in raising money for the next election. Elected officials are also influenced by media to fit uncompromisingly into the simplistic categories created during the campaign process. When members of the opposing party—vilified effectively enough that the other party's officials were elected—become the elected party members' governing partners, it is little wonder we are often let down when the promises of elected officials go unfulfilled. Media perpetuate this harmful cycle, reminding us that political promises are *insincere* and that there is no point in mobilizing the electorate, ultimately fostering voter cynicism and mistrust (Hart, 1999).

How might all this relate to you and your life? Even though you may never run for political office, a comprehensive, more accurate understanding of the relationship between campaign communication and media can lend insight into how your communication degree might allow you to influence others, acquire power and resources, and perform more competently in your relationships and career. The media may not be the message, but they have radically altered how we think about our candidates (see **Box 20.6**).

Box 20.6 Mediatized Politics

What happens when political leadership is mediated?

Leadership becomes visual.

Emotion trumps reason.

Audience becomes skeptical.

Narrative and Political Communication

The relationship between politics and communication lends insight into the importance of narrative. There is nothing more important to politicians than their stories. Voters do not want more information. They are up to their eyeballs in information. They want faith—faith in the candidate, and faith in the candidate's vision and experience, and in the story the candidate tells. The same is true for you, for your family, and your future employer (Daly, 2011a).

Our democracy is little more than a collection of stories or **public narratives**—sequences of characters and actions connected by a meaningful thread or through-line. Stories bind our country together by snagging diffuse elements of our symbolic resources into a net of shared meanings. Our stories transform into coherent myths, branch out across generations, and cobble a fragmented symbolic environment into a broader paradigm capable of offering moral instruction and social guidance. The stories of our founding fathers, military heroes, and civil rights leaders constitute a set of shared values. Politicians try to embody the familiar plot line of exceptional people doing exceptional things, offering instruction and guidance within community (Hart, 1997). Stories provide understanding, solve problems, and make sense of the world because they take a diffuse set of actors and actions and create a community of people who can notice and respond to formal plots and storylines featuring "our people" acting in culturally meaningful ways.

Stories can do all that without much cognitive expense. Remember that voters only have a limited amount of what we might call "mental bandwidth." We are all mental minimizers, constantly looking for heuristic shortcuts that allow us to navigate the complex political dimensions of our day-to-day lives without using too much of that bandwidth (Kahneman, 2011; Shafir, 2012). Stories are convenient in this sense. Stories help us reduce a limitless range of individual complexities into mental structures that effortlessly sort people, objects, and situations into categories resonating with our existing individual paradigms and socially shared value systems. For example, there is no "United States" without the stories of George Washington, Abraham Lincoln, and Martin Luther King, Jr.—at least not how "the United States" is widely constituted. The constitution of our community draws boundaries, sets up categories, and calls to certain types of people who must conform to the moral guidance of the story in order to hear and respond to its rhetorical appeal.

Here is where some stories become more politically potent than others. Power is not dispensed and withheld along abstract or objective standards. Social order is never naturally constructed; it only arises from a never-ending contestation over symbolic and material resources (Jameson, 1981). Stories define the parameters within which this contestation is won and lost. Stories can make particular hierarchies of power look empirically present, culturally current, and even necessary and natural. But, in reality, stories are always symbolically constructed in response to a unique political exigency, historical moment, and social situation.

Barack Obama's 2004 speech to the Democratic National Convention illuminates the rhetorical potency of story (**Box 20.7**). To see why (and what you can learn from it) read through it, and look for the ways Obama turned his personal story into one of the most important speeches of the century.

Box 20.7 Political Narrative

Consider how Obama opens the speech:

> Tonight is a particular honor for me because, let's face it, my presence on this stage is pretty unlikely. My father was a foreign student, born and raised in a small village in Kenya. He grew up herding goats, went to school in a tin-roof shack. His father, my grandfather, was a cook, a domestic servant to the British. But my grandfather had larger dreams for his son. Through hard work and perseverance my father got a scholarship to study in a magical place, America, that's shown as a beacon of freedom and opportunity to so many who had come before him.

Because we know that *stories stick*, we can see in Obama's speech how language can be used to embed ideas into the minds of the members of an audience. Newspapers will not reprint the entire speech, and the nightly news will not show more than a few seconds, but by positioning his own story within the familiar arc of the American dream, Obama helped journalists make choices about how his story should be covered and how his political aspirations should be understood in a way that people can understand and remember.

Obama continued:

> While studying here my father met my mother. She was born in a town on the other side of the world, in Kansas. Her father worked on oil rigs and farms through most of the Depression. The day after Pearl Harbor, my grandfather signed up for duty, joined Patton's army, marched across Europe. Back home my grandmother raised a baby and went to work on a bomber assembly line. After the war, they studied on the GI Bill, bought a house through FHA and later moved west, all the way to Hawaii, in search of opportunity.
>
> And they too had big dreams for their daughter, a common dream born of two continents.
>
> My parents shared not only an improbable love; they shared an abiding faith in the possibilities of this nation. They would give me an African name, Barack, or "blessed," believing that in a tolerant America, your name is no barrier to success.
>
> They imagined me going to the best schools in the land, even though they weren't rich, because in a generous America you don't have to be rich to achieve your potential.
>
> They're both passed away now. And yet I know that, on this night, they look down on me with great pride. And I stand

---

here today grateful for the diversity of my heritage, aware that my parents' dreams live on in my two precious daughters.

I stand here knowing that my story is part of the larger American story, that I owe a debt to all of those who came before me, and that in no other country on Earth is my story even possible.

Tonight, we gather to affirm the greatness of our nation not because of the height of our skyscrapers, or the power of our military, or the size of our economy; our pride is based on a very simple premise, summed up in a declaration made over two hundred years ago: "We hold these truths to be self-evident, that all men are created equal, that they are endowed by their Creator with certain inalienable rights, that among these are life, liberty and the pursuit of happiness."

That is the true genius of America, a faith … a faith in simple dreams, an insistence on small miracles; that we can tuck in our children at night and know that they are fed and clothed and safe from harm; that we can say what we think, write what we think, without hearing a sudden knock on the door; that we can have an idea and start our own business without paying a bribe; that we can participate in the political process without fear of retribution; and that our votes will be counted—or at least, most of the time.

Because we know that *stories simplify*, we can see in Obama's speech how complex ideas can be transformed into chunkable messages. We have already discussed how journalists do this. If you are considering going to law school, you should learn how to do this as well. Attorneys often begin their cases with compelling, well-structured stories. As the trial progresses, jurors interpret new information in terms of those stories (Daly, 2011a). In Obama's speech, the complexities of his political philosophies are cloaked in neatly packaged language about "faith in simple dreams" and "insistence on small miracles."

Obama went on:

And fellow Americans, Democrats, Republicans, independents, I say to you, tonight, we have more work to do … more work to do, for the workers I met in Galesburg, Illinois, who are losing their union jobs at the Maytag plant that's moving to Mexico, and now they're having to compete with their own children for jobs that pay 7 bucks an hour; more to do for the father I met who was losing his job and chocking back the tears wondering how he would pay $4,500 a months for the drugs his son needs without the health benefits that he counted on; more to do for the young woman in East St. Louis, and thousands more like her who have the grades, have the drive, have the will, but doesn't have the money to go to college.

This passage is especially effective because, like all good stories, it is instructive. We can see in Obama's speech the power of story as a persuasive tool. You do not need to know much about Obama's (or John Kerry's) plans for the Middle East or reforming health care as long as you believe he can make sure that every child in the United States has a decent shot at life. The specific policies related to Head Start or childhood nutrition programs do not matter that much. We know people find it more difficult to disagree with the notion that "the doors of opportunity should remain open to all" than with the notion that taxes should be raised to pay for better schools.

Finally, Obama said:

Now, don't get me wrong, the people I meet in small towns and big cities and diners and office parks, they don't expect government to solve all of their problems. They know they have to work hard to get ahead. And they want to.

Go into the collar counties around Chicago, and people will tell you: They don't want their tax money wasted by a welfare agency or by the Pentagon.

Go into any inner-city neighborhood, and folks will tell you that government alone can't teach kids to learn.

They know that parents have to teach, that children can't achieve unless we raise their expectations and turn off the television sets and eradicate the slander that says a black youth with a book is acting white. They know those things.

People don't expect—people don't expect government to solve all their problems. But they sense, deep in their bones, that with just a slight change in priorities, we can make sure that every child in America has a decent shot at life and that the doors of opportunity remain open to all. They know we can do better. And they want that choice.

In this election, we offer that choice. Our party has chosen a man to lead us who embodies the best this country has to offer. And that man is John Kerry.

Because we know that *stories build community*, we can see in Obama's speech how fractured and fragmented audiences can be drawn together through references to shared plotlines. Stories explain, in part, why moving to a new school or starting a new job can be so difficult. You do not know the stories. You have to sit around the lunch table and smile meekly while everyone else laughs at a reference you do not get because you do not belong yet (Daly, 2011).

In Obama's speech, references to the immigrant story resonate with so many threads of our nation's collective plotlines in a way that someone from another country would not understand as completely. Obama references his grandfather's hard work and perseverance, the role of education in his upward mobility, and why he signed up for Patton's army. These are all narrative threads Obama's political opponents could not oppose. No one can argue against perseverance, education, or patriotism, and, thus, if Obama can connect his story to those plotlines, a community can be constructed on top of a shared common ground in a way that transcends his legislative inexperience, smoking habits, and Ivy League education.

What can we learn from the relationship between narrative and political communication? Simply put, to get ahead, you cannot be narratively challenged. You have to have a compelling story; you have to be able to tell it well; it has to resonate; and it has to illustrate something of shared value. The most practical application of this important feature of political communication is this: *Go into your next job interview with a set of stories.* Use the prompts in the box that follows as a way to get started (see Box 20.8). Be able to tell a story that connects the qualifications your employer, company, and industry values with your work experience, education, and skill set. Anyone can claim to have "leadership ability" or "analytical thinking skills," but if you can back up such a claim with a cogent and eloquent story about how you organized a 5K run for cancer research or assisted your professor with a research project, you will no doubt make a stronger impression on your interviewer.

Box 20.8 Interview Questions

Go into your next job interview with three or four cogent, eloquent stories that can demonstrate your unique qualifications in the following areas:

- Dealing with crisis
- Handling a tough interpersonal situation
- Juggling many priorities successfully
- Changing course to deal with changed circumstances
- Learning from a mistake
- Working on a team/leading a team
- Going above and beyond expectations

Effective Political Crisis Management

Recall some of the shared features of our political environment, especially the hypermediation of political campaigns, irrational and disengaged voters, and partisan politicians. With all that, we can begin to see why the ability to manage crisis effectively is an important part of political communication competence.

Effective crisis management has never been as important as it is today. After the Bay of Pigs Invasion—a failed CIA-sponsored military invasion of Cuba approved by President John F. Kennedy in 1961—Kennedy did not discuss the event publicly for 10 days. He did not have to. Can you imagine if a major international political event comparable to the failed military invasion of another country happened today and the president simply did not address it? That would never happen. Politicians today must respond to crisis. The individual examples of Ted Kennedy, Gary Hart, Bill Clinton, John Edwards, Elliot Spitzer, Larry Craig, Rod Blagojevich, Chris Christie, and David Petraeus illustrate this point. Our newspaper headlines are filled with contemporary examples of political crisis, including the Abu Ghraib torture and prisoner abuse scandal, the attack on the U.S. embassy in Benghazi, Libya, and the dismal rollout of the Affordable Care Act. Almost every major company deals with crisis, including Johnson & Johnson, Wendy's, Taco Bell, Jack-in-the-Box, PepsiCo, ExxonMobil, BP, Ford, Toyota, and GM.

It is unlikely you will ever be sued by the EPA (BP) or have to explain to the public why a severed human finger was found in a bowl of your chili (Wendy's), but as this chapter has demonstrated, you will face different types of crises. By analyzing the best practice of political actors, we can learn much about how to manage crises effectively when they occur.

Anderson and Spitzberg (2009) define **crisis** as the messages that occur during and immediately after a disaster that attempt to mitigate social harm and disruption. Given this definition and your background as a communication major, you can likely see why the most basic ingredient in any political crisis response is communication. As Anderson and Spitzberg (2009) argue, during a crisis every segment of the public, leadership, and the news media need competent communication and accurate information. Crisis connects a wide variety of people and constituencies and often creates urgent and unique communication problems.

Furthermore, crisis is not something you can avoid. To some degree, crisis is inevitable. Whether it be in your schooling, your relationships, your personal life, your health, or your career, if you are stretching your abilities, it is likely you will encounter some form of crisis. How you handle crisis, not whether it occurs, is what matters. Crisis can test everything about your organization, your community, or your family. Those of you who have been through a divorce, illness, or financial troubles know that crisis can test the seams of a family. Unresolved or ineffectively managed crises can be poisonous to political efficacy as well. Understanding how people deal with a crisis can give you an additional tool for managing it effectively.

First, to properly manage a crisis, *be prepared*. Competent politicians know that, although crises will happen, processes can be put in place to ensure that, when they do, their harmful impacts are limited. We know that during a crisis, emotions are on edge, brains are not fully functioning, and events are occurring so rapidly that drafting a plan at the time of crisis is unthinkable. This is why we should assume crises are going to happen and make a plan to deal with them before they do.

Second, when crises do occur, competent politicians *manage them appropriately*. Competent politicians hang a lantern on their problems. Most people can forgive politicians who are transparent about their behavior, as opposed to being caught. Contain the crisis by telling it all, telling it early, and telling it yourself. Do not lie. Respond quickly and decisively. Try not to let the media, or the Justice Department, or your roommate, find out before you announce the situation yourself. This will allow you to appear transparent in front of the public and frame the situation in an advantageous way.

Third, *take palatable action*. When a crisis occurs, competent politicians know the public want something tangible to be done about it. It is important to gather as much information as possible about the situation before you take action. As soon as possible, accomplish something tangible that ensures the public you are on it. Delays often cause people to be suspicious of your motives and your competence. **Box 20.9** offers a great example (Calmes & Lublin, 2004).

Box 20.9 Motives and Competence

When syringes were discovered in cans of Pepsi diet soda (in some 20 states in 1993), we went public with everything we knew immediately. Craig Weatherup, who was then Pepsi Cola president, made himself available for television interviews. And we made a video of a production line at a diet Pepsi plant, which runs at 2,000 cans a minute. That showed it would have been impossible for someone to have put the syringes in the cans during the production process. We also hooked up immediately with the FDA to establish a cooperative relationship to get to the bottom of the situation.

—Roger Enrico, retired Chairman and CEO of Pepsi

Fourth, *understand the value of symbols* during crisis management. George W. Bush learned this the hard way when he flew over New Orleans in a helicopter after Hurricane Katrina. This decision made practical sense; there is little of nonsymbolic value the president of the United States could have done on the flooded streets of the Ninth Ward. But, the symbolic image of a rich, white, Texas oilman flying over the ravaged city created a symbolic nightmare for the Bush administration.

Fifth, *master the apology.* One of the principle methods for correcting a political crisis is the apology. The competent politician is prepared for a sincere admission that he or she is sorry for whatever happened. We know that when crisis occurs, an individual must be careful about blaming other people. Personal blame usually does not work. For a true crisis, denial and blame are often less effective than emphasizing systemic or technological mistakes (Gass & Sieter, 2014). Jack-in-the-Box learned this the hard way in the early 1990s when *E. coli* was found in some of the company's hamburgers. Several people got sick, and a few young children even died. But, rather than apologize and take palatable action to m ake amends, Jack-in-the-Box blamed its slaughterhouse and meatpackers. What Jack-in-the-Box did not realize was that the public did not want an excuse at that point, but instead wanted reassurance that the problem was going to be solved.

When it is necessary, employ the Four Cs in an effective apology:

1. Confess: Admit it.
2. Contrition: Say you are sorry.
3. Conversion: Promise not to do it again.
4. Consequences: Accept responsibility.

Finally, successful politicians can *use the media* to manage crisis. Media can be a vital tool in a political crisis. Media can be especially helpful if you have established a relationship before the crisis and journalists know and trust you. If the media cannot stand you before the crisis, however, they will hate you after.

When a crisis occurs, be prepared to answer the following questions: What happened? Were there any deaths or injuries? What is the extent of the damage? Is there a danger of future injuries or damage? Why did it happen? Who or what is responsible? What is being done about it? When will it be over? Has it happened before? Were there any warning signs of the problem? A competent politician will be prepared to answer these questions.

Your training as a communication major can assist you greatly in constructing a message that will accomplish your goals with the help of the media. For example, consider employing the following tips from Kathleen Fearn-Banks' book *Crisis Communications: A Casebook Approach* (2011; see **Table 20.2**).

Conclusion

The purpose of this chapter has been to examine the theory and practice of political communication in the United States. Thus, the chapter defined several key terms, described some unique features of the U.S. political system, and detailed the role communication plays in allowing citizens to navigate the political process. The chapter anchored those definitions and assumptions in three specific dimensions: (a) media and campaign communication, (b) narrative and political communication, and (c) effective political crisis management. We hope you have a more complete understanding of how

TABLE 20.2: Recommendations for Communicating With the Media

Do	Do Not
1. Listen to the whole question before answering.	1. Do not be a wimp. Being concerned and empathetic does not mean that you must shake in your boots.
2. Use everyday language, not the jargon of your business or profession. Even if reporters use the jargon, use common vernacular (unless the interviewer is with a professional publication).	2. Do not let the reporter's silence goad you into saying something you do not want to say. Be comfortable with awkward silence.
3. Have a simple, straightforward, core message.	3. Do not answer hypothetical questions.
4. Learn to bridge to that core message.	4. Do not guess or speculate. Either you know or you do not.
5. Have several quotable sound bites beforehand. Short answers are better than long ones.	5. Do not get overly upset about being quoted out of context.
6. Maintain an image that is calm, courteous, responsive, direct, positive, truthful, concerned, and, if necessary, repentant, and apologetic.	6. Do not stick to your story if it has changed just to be consistent.
7. Understand a reporter's job. Respect deadlines and return phone calls promptly.	7. Do not get bogged down with statistics.
8. Treat the reporter as a partner—an ally in maintaining or restoring the politician's positive image.	8. Do not pull your political advertising from a media outlet because reporters are uncooperative.
9. Look the reporter in the eye. In your response, address each reporter by name if possible.	9. Do not consider your news release "golden."
10. Use your crisis communication plan.	10. Do not play favorites with the media.
11. Keep campaign workers informed of the crisis. They may be persuasive volunteer spokespersons.	11. Do not be trapped into predicting the future.
12. Know that there is nothing "off the record."	12. Do not wear sunglasses, smoke, or chew gum.

Source: Adapted from Fearn-Banks (2011).

political communication connects with audiences; the relationship between media, politicians, and citizens; and what your communication degree can contribute to this important conversation.

More practically, we also discussed how (although we may never run for office ourselves) we can learn a lot about how to build our own personal power and enlarge our own personal capacities by paying close attention to how the people who do this for a living accomplish the same objectives. In other words, we discussed what inspires, motivates, and influences political actors, media, and voters, but we also know that many of these same practices inspire, motivate, and influence teachers, romantic partners, and job interviewers.

Finally, if we have described our political environment accurately, we can also use the knowledge we gained about political communication in this chapter to make an *evaluative claim* about the overall health of our democracy. For instance, what does our discussion of affective heuristics, the roles of money and media, and the power of story reveal about larger issues related to the fair allocation of resources, just hierarchies of power, and the ability of every citizen to live a viable and fulfilled life?

Remember that we are represented today by the richest, oldest, most partisan, and least effective politicians in our nation's history. We also know that they have decided to prioritize their special interests, a small group of friends and donors, and their electability above your ability to pay for college, own a home, and get a secure job when you graduate. Hopefully, this decidedly depressing description of our political environment does not paralyze you into dropping out of our political conversations and retreating to the mall or sticking your head into your iPhone. Rather, I hope this characterization of our political environment motivates you to do something about it.

We know that knowledge and interest are prerequisites for entry into the political conversation. It is up to you to gather that knowledge. Read the newspaper, join social organizations, and be alert to forms of political activism on campus that excite you, including advocating against sexual violence, human trafficking, and climate change. Vote! In a country with near universal suffrage you have the power to hold our elected officials accountable at the ballot box. See **Box 20.10** for instructions on how to do so, but also know that voting will not change much by itself. You cannot wait idly for an elected political to save you. You cannot hope that simply stepping into the ballot booth every four years and casting a vote for the most inoffensive personality who can raise the most money and looks the most presidential will solve any of these problems. Young people have always been the primary catalyst for positive social change. If the description of our political environment angers you (as it should), you have a responsibility to do act on it. Do not wait for an old rich white guy to save you. He will not. You have to do it yourself. Hopefully, this chapter has equipped you with some of the skills necessary to do just that.

Box 20.10 Vote!

Register to vote: https://vote.usa.gov/

CHAPTER 21

Public Speaking

Luke Winslow

LEARNING OBJECTIVES

After reading this chapter, you should be able to do the following:

- Identify the best rhetorical practices of great orators.
- Demonstrate an awareness of how public address fosters more engaged citizenship and, in turn, assists in developing both the skills and inspiration to "speak out" yourself.
- Analyze the ways in which public address has influenced our understanding of the discipline of communication studies.
- Demonstrate an understanding of what is means to effectively deliberate, and then display the ability to train people on how to contribute to a more robust and productive democratic deliberation.
- Demonstrate an understanding of the relationship between public address and a healthy democracy by contributing to improved civic and political deliberation.
- Understand the relationship between public speaking and communication competence.
- Recognize the sources of communication apprehension and manage its debilitating effects.
- Organize your public communication for clarity and cogency.
- Recognize and integrate competent communication practices related to verbal and nonverbal delivery in your public communication.
- Recognize and integrate competent communication practices related to your use of PowerPoint in your public communication.
- Recognize and integrate competent communication practices during the question-and-answer sessions of your public communication.

The Central Place of Presentations

You may not give many public presentations in your future career, but when you do, they will likely be incredibly consequential. Presentations become more important the higher you advance professionally; managers and executives give more presentations that matter than lower-level employees. It is possible that much of your professional success will depend on your ability to manage public speaking apprehension, stay organized, speak eloquently, work gracefully with presentation aids, and handle questions and objections with grace and aplomb. Indeed, the third richest person in the world, Warren Buffett, touts skill in public speaking as the single most value-added competence in which a person can invest. He tells his audiences composed of young students, "Right now, I would pay $100,000 for 10% of the future earnings of any

of you. … Now, you can improve your value by 50% just by learning communication skills—public speaking. If that's the case, see me after class and I'll pay you $150,000." Buffett's point is that mastering the art of public speaking is the single greatest skill to boost your career (Gallo, 2017).

It is unlikely you will ever be in the situation described in **Box 21.1**, but you may be asked to deliver a presentation in a situation in which there is a lot on the line. And, you may be smart enough and have enough experience, but your intelligence and expertise may only be evident if you can speak eloquently and cogently. Research supports the Geithner anecdote (see **Box 21.1**) about the importance of public presentations. Cain, in her (2012) book *Quiet*, cites research from Stanford University that found the number one predictor of upward mobility in your future careers is not your technical skills; it is, rather, your ability to communicate orally.

Box 21.1 Presentations are Consequential

Although we make very few presentations, the ones we do make matter a great deal. Timothy Geithner serves as a wonderful example. Geithner had the unenviable job of U.S. treasury secretary when Barack Obama assumed the presidency in 2009 and the U.S. public was questioning the viability of the entire U.S. economy. In one of his first tasks, Geithner was asked to deliver a public presentation assuring the public that the Obama administration had a plan for rescuing the U.S. financial system and assuring U.S. citizens of the safety of their money in their banks. This was quite a task, even for the most poised, experienced, and eloquent speaker. Geithner possessed none of these qualities. He was ill-prepared, staying up late the night before the presentation writing, discarding, and re-writing draft after draft of his speech. When it came time for the presentation, his lack of preparation was obvious; he had not internalized his material, so he had to keep his eyes glued to his speaking notes on the teleprompter. Geithner clearly lacked confidence. By his own admission, he looked like a shoplifter (Geithner, 2014). Even worse, his suit was too big for him; it looked like he snuck into his dad's closet. His voice even cracked at one point, mimicking a 13-year-old boy going through puberty (and not the man who was responsible for saving our economy). When Geithner came to the end, the audience was unsure if it was over. He did not ask for any questions, and instead sheepishly walked off the stage like he just misspelled a word at the spelling bee. And then something amazing happened. The Dow Jones Index dropped 400 points. Think about why that is amazing. Only a select few had access to a paper copy of the plan Geithner was proposing in his presentation, and no one doubted Geithner's intelligence or experience. But that did not matter to the market. There was something about Geithner's inability to speak publicly that led to the loss of billions and billions of dollars.

It is likely that you have taken a public speaking class at some point of your college experience, if not before. Whether a "hybrid" or a public speaking basic course, research indicates that such courses increase self-perceived communication competence and decrease public speaking anxiety (Broeckelman-Post & Pyle, 2017). And,

because repetition is the soul of learning, the purpose of this chapter is to review what you learned and discuss how those skills will make you a more competent employee and active civic participant once you graduate. I begin with a discussion about the history of public speaking, the role of public speaking in a healthy democracy, and the way public speaking can specifically determine how far and how quickly you advance in your future careers. Second, I cover five core principles that you can put into practice to increase your public speaking effectiveness: managing communication apprehension, staying organized, employing strong verbal and nonverbal delivery skills, working gracefully with your presentation aid, and excelling during the question-and-answer session of your presentation.

Key Assumptions and Guiding Principles

Public Speaking and Perceived Competence

We are all cognitive minimizers. Given the choice, most of us would rather not think too hard. We only have a limited amount of mental bandwidth, so we like to rely on mental shortcuts as often as possible. This is particularly true when we evaluate other people.

Consider a typical job interview. Most first-round interviews last less than 45 minutes—not nearly enough time, of course, for the interviewer to accurately evaluate the depth and breadth of the candidate's intelligence, work ethic, commitment, character, and competence. Yet, interviewers are expected to use what they see in such short periods of time to make accurate assessments about whether candidates would be good hires. We do the same when assessing the competence of public speakers. In our classrooms, houses of worship, and on the job, we pay as much (if not more) attention to a speaker's eye contact, physical appearance, and vocal articulations as we do to technical proficiency. Tim Geithner found this out the hard way. Echoing Susan Cain's research, it is not enough to be smart; you also have to be able to communicate that technical expertise to other people in an effective manner.

Public Speaking and Democracy

Public speaking is fundamentally connected to a healthy, fully functioning democracy. The ancient Greeks—the first to really experiment with democracy—understood this (Brummett, 2000). Citizens gathered regularly in the town square to talk about what the community should do.

Imagine this scenario: Suppose I were to stand up in the town square one day and offer a proposal about why we should raise taxes on olive growers to fund a new university (selfishly, of course, because I need a place to teach).

Now imagine you are an olive grower, and your livelihood depends on keeping taxes at a minimum because you are barely making enough to feed your children as it is. How do you respond? You could pick up a rock and throw it at my head, you could challenge me to a duel, you could tell the authorities I am a treasonous spy, or, more likely, you would need to take your turn in the town square and deliver a speech of your own on why raising taxes is a terrible idea, or why we do not need a new university, or why we should build one but the funding should come from a tax on apples, not olives.

Your livelihood is stake. You would be discouraged from using coercion to get your way (because we have agreed that we all want to live in a society of law and order). Your power would be limited. All you would have is your voice.

This is not an abstract exercise. We all use public address to speak as citizens in a democracy (Palczewski, Ice, & Fritch, 2012). If you were concerned about the prevalence of sexual assault on college campuses, you would use public address; if you were an undocumented student who wanted to advocate for the passage of the Dream Act, you would use public address; or, if you worked at Carl's Jr. and wanted to increase your wages so you could pay tuition, you might participate in a rally focused on raising the minimum wage. And, there, you would be using public address.

Public address matters more to you than to a citizen of North Korea. There, it would likely not make much of a collective difference if a citizen stood up in the town square and delivered a persuasive and passionate speech about freeing markets from centralized control or shifting resources from defense to education. In an autocratic or closed society such as North Korea, public address plays only a limited role because people lack agency—the ability to influence their environments. But, in our open democracy, we all use public address to participate in the construction and affirmation of just and fair political, economic, social, and legal structures so that the interests of our communities are met.

Public Address in a Democracy Induces Cooperation

It is not overly dramatic to say that public address is one of the features that separate humans from other animals (see Chapter 2). Unlike dogs, for example, humans use symbols (words and images) to attach meaning to interactions and experiences. And, we do not do this alone. Rather, we rely on a shared system of symbolic interpretation to make sense of our reality. Therefore, we can study what it means to be human by thinking about what it means to think symbolically (Brummett, 2000; Burke, 1966).

Take an example Kenneth Burke offered in his book *Language as Symbolic Action* (1966): One day Burke was sitting in his college philosophy class when he noticed a trapped bird flying nervously around the ceiling of the classroom. Although several windows were open in other parts of the room, the bird—following its instincts to fly up—kept trying to escape the room by batting against the ceiling rather than simply dipping down and flying out one of the open windows.

How much easier, Burke (1966) wrote, if he could speak the language of the bird and tell it to simply fly down a few feet and escape the room through one of many open windows. Burke's example illustrates how important it is for us to think and speak symbolically (see also: Chapter 6). Once we can do that, we can share ideas that allow us to work together to make decisions about matters of common interest, such as whether we should build a new road or a new school. But, all that first begins with our ability to think symbolically. Consider what it means to engage in **symbolic thinking**—the ability to conceptualize with a malleable and conventional system for referring to the world and thoughts about that world. You could look around right now and find a bunch of different symbols: You may have some symbols in your wallet (money); some people permanently tattoo the name of a motorcycle company on their chest (Harley Davidson); you may be wearing shoes that display an ancient symbol of the Greek goddess of winged victory (the Nike Swoosh). Your choice of jewelry, your hairstyle, or, more simply, the letters you are reading right now are all symbols—signifying a whole set of ideas.

Public Address and Symbols

Words, nonverbal communication, clothing, and money are all symbols that come together to operate as language (see Chapter 2). In order to have language, any language, we need to be able to think symbolically. And, once we have this ability for symbolic thought and language, then all kinds of things become possible. Symbolic action allows for the rhetorical mobilization of symbols to act in the world. Symbols induce cooperation (Palczewski et al., 2012). Through symbols we can share what we have learned and can then organize larger and larger groups of people who can do more and more complex things such as build bridges, schools, and computers. Through symbols, practically everything else in modern life is possible, including acquiring and developing the necessary skills to be an effective employee and an actively engaged citizen in a healthy democracy. Being a citizen in a democracy is not a spectator sport. To participate fully, you need to understand the relationship between symbols, public address, and democracy.

When we are in positions with limited influence—when we are not all-powerful dictators—we must rely on public address to ensure our interests are met. More broadly, in a healthy, fully functioning democracy that does not rely on coercion or brainwashing to keep people in line, we all use public address to make decisions about how our resources will be allocated fairly, in a way we can trust. Iconic historical figures such as Winston Churchill, Fannie Lou Hamer, and Martin Luther King Jr. provide vivid examples. And that was really what Geithner's speech was all about: assuring the U.S. public that we would get through this, that our banks would not fail, and that we would most likely not lose our life savings the next day.

Public Speaking and You

As we shift focus from public address as a social phenomenon, it is important to recognize that most of us understand, on a personal level, how important public speaking is. This is why many of us struggle with apprehension, nervousness, and anxiety when asked to speak publicly. Public opinion polls often put public speaking near snakes, spiders, and death in terms of what people fear most.

But here is the good news: No one is born a competent speaker. Yes, some people seem more comfortable on stage, but it is likely those folks are simply more skilled at masking the same apprehension that all of us feel. When I was in fifth grade, I had a really hard time learning fractions. After a particularly poor performance on a test, I showed my score to my parents after school, but I was quick to remind them that I was "not a math person." Does that sound familiar? My parents would reassure me that my skill set was better suited for social studies or the basketball court. Amy Chua, a Yale law professor and author of *Battle Hymn of the Tiger Mother*, argued that "not being a math person" is a uniquely U.S. phrase. If one of her daughters were to try it, Chua's own Chinese parenting style would respond: "Well, it is true, you may not be a math person *yet*. But from now on, every day after school for six hours you are going to sit at this desk and *become a math person*" (Chua, 2011).

I want to encourage you to adopt the same mindset. Many of us may approach public speaking in our classes and future careers as something we have to get through because "we are not good speakers." Work hard to get rid of that attitude. Develop what social psychologists call a *growth mindset* (demonstrated by Chua's example). You may not be a totally competent public speaker now, but with enough thoughtful effort, most of us can get to the point where we can speak persuasively, gracefully, and competently.

Core Concepts

Communication Apprehension

One of the initial requirements of becoming a competent presenter involves learning to manage the inevitable anxiety that comes with public presentations. Whether you call it apprehension, anxiety, nerves, or butterflies, most of us feel some sort of unease before giving a public presentation (Winslow, Lindemann, Spitzberg, & Rapp, 2015). **Communication apprehension** is an experience of fear or anxiety regarding a real or imagined communication encounter. Those feelings are perfectly normal. In fact, they are a product of thousands of years of human evolution. We do not like to be evaluated, whether we are walking into a party for the first time or standing in front of a classroom. Susan Cain detailed how evolving human beings connected being evaluated with being hunted (2012). We do not like people (or lions) watching us too closely. As products of this evolution, it is perfectly natural for our bodies to respond as if we are being hunted, including sweaty palms, dry throat, blotchy neck, cold hands, or untimely bladder behaviors (think about the evolutionary explanation for that last one: If you were running from a saber-toothed tiger, you would rather have an empty bladder than a full one, right? For that reason, most of us have to use the restroom when we get

nervous).To speak competently, the goal should not be to eliminate feelings of apprehension. They are a natural response to being evaluated. Consider another scenario in which your body might react in a similar manner: If you are running the 400-meter sprint in a track meet or playing the lead role in the school play, your bodily reactions to evaluation and apprehension may actually sharpen your focus and improve your performance. Now, what about meeting your girlfriend's dad for the first time? Or before a job interview? Or before a big presentation? I would like you to consider how beneficial feelings of apprehension might be in those situations. The most effective public speakers still get nervous, but they have learned how to manage their apprehension in a way that actually improves performance.

That should be your goal. It will take years to get there, and plenty of mindful, deliberate practice. But, ideally, you can get to the point at which, rather than be surprised by feelings of apprehension before a presentation or job interview, you can use those feelings to remind yourself that you care about this moment, that you are well prepared, and that you are ready to excel.

Balancing Risk and Reward

Willi Unsoeld was one of the first U.S. citizens to climb Mount Everest, and, in that context, he claimed: "Risk is at the heart of all education." He knew that climbing Mount Everest was not going to be easy, and he knew he would get nervous. But he would not be surprised. In fact, he was looking forward to being nervous. He *wanted* to be nervous because he knew that would make him a better mountain climber. I encourage you to adopt Unsoeld's mindset. It is natural to be nervous. But that does not have to be a bad thing. As Unsoeld wrote, the right amount of nervousness can throw you into a state of total concentration. For our purposes, nervousness can actually make you a more competent public speaker.

But, as Unsoeld also wrote, he does not expect to just let his nervousness magically carry him to the top of the mountain. In your case, you cannot expect to wing it, hope you get nervous, and let that improve your performance. Rather, you first have to master the fundamentals and become competent in technical aspects of what you are doing. Then, when it is time to perform, you can use the inevitable apprehension to excel.

This cognitive shift might be easier said than done, but let me now offer some more specific advice for how you can get to that point. The first step is the simplest: Be prepared.

Be Prepared

The lowest level of apprehension occurs during the preparation stage of the speech. Most of us know this from experience. We tend to get nervous when the assignment is announced, and then again right before it is our turn to speak. We are not as nervous at 2:00 a.m. when we are researching or outlining our speeches alone in our apartments. If you are really worried about apprehension ruining your ability to think clearly and speak eloquently, put as much effort as you can into the preparation stage so that, if you are overcome by debilitating levels of apprehension, you can use the hours you put into preparing for the speech as a default mode to fall back on.

Many students make the mistake of "practicing" by reading over their notecards sitting at their desk. Do not do that. The research says that you want to simulate the environment in which you will be performing as closely as possible (Ishak & Ballard, 2012). Stand up as you would in a speech, film or voice-record yourself, practice in front of people you are slightly intimidated by, and try to practice at least once in the actual room in which you will be speaking. That type of mindful, **deliberate practice** can go a long way in managing any debilitating apprehension you might experience.

Fight Perfection

Set aside the goal of perfection. Gymnasts and figure skaters know this. Such an athlete knows that if perfection is the goal, and even a minor mistake is made (and mistakes are always made), confidence and focus can be lost, triggering a cascade of additional mistakes. Instead, gymnasts and figure skaters aim for **optimal performance**. Where perfect performance implies both ideal form and an absence of mistakes, optimal performance implies the best possible performance in a given situation and audience. You should do the same. Remind yourself that some minor mistakes may make your audience like you even more. It is not necessary to sound like a newscaster in front of your peers. Instead, think about the benefits you are bringing to your audience, not your own hand placement or sock color. *Do not* memorize your speech.

Like the perfectionist gymnast, the speaker who tries to memorize every word of a presentation will inevitably mess up one word, and, like a train going off the tracks, the entire presentation can be derailed. Instead, practice saying the same passages, sentences, and phrases multiple ways so that you do not get stuck on trying to keep each word right.

Release Adrenaline

Recall the evolutionary reactions to being evaluated. When we feel like people are watching us, we feel threatened. In response, our adrenal glands release the hormone **adrenaline** into our bloodstream. This boosts our heart rate and dilates our blood vessels and breathing passages, providing bursts of energy. We evolved adrenal surges to cope with threatening situations, and situations in which survival might be at stake, such as pursuing prey or avoiding becoming prey. But our lives are seldom on the line in public speaking contexts. Still, if our goal is not to eliminate apprehension, but rather to use it to optimize our performance, what should we do?

Taking advice from theatre performers, athletes, and ballerinas, I encourage you to release the adrenaline. Exercise your muscles. If you can, move around before your speech. One of the worst things you can do is to sit still for an hour before you go on stage. You can imagine how all that pent-up adrenaline will come out in your shaky hands, fragile voice, and rapid speech rate. Work out the morning of your speech, walk the hallway right before you go on, or try a technique ballerinas are known to employ—try to push down the wall as a way to exercise the adrenaline out of your arms, back, chest, and legs.

Be a Convincing Actor

The mantra *fake it until you make it* can be helpful, here. If you doubt your public speaking ability, pretend to be a competent speaker. Your audience may not know the difference (of course, do not take this too far; too much pretending and not enough preparation will probably expose you as a fraud). There is not much difference between being confident and pretending to be.

Recall the movie *Forrest Gump*: When Forrest asked his mother if he was stupid, she replied with the iconic line: "Stupid is as stupid does." Ms. Gump indirectly gives us some sage advice here: Courage is as courage does, and confidence is as confidence does. Or, follow Gregg Gillis's advice (better known as the experimental musician Girl Talk), and pretend to have fun up there. Your audience probably will not know the difference.

Visualize Success

Familiarity can limit debilitating levels of apprehension. Baseball players know this well. Many baseball players engage in a series of intense, therapeutic **visualization** sessions before they play—a process of mentally rehearsing idealized images of the performance. Before a game, they might visualize themselves in the batter's box, feel their cleats and batting gloves, see the color of the pitcher's hat, smell the grass and dirt, hear the crowd's murmur, and finish the mental exercise by seeing the bat make solid contact with the ball.

Follow their lead: Before your presentation, imagine what your collared shirt will feel like (especially if you do not normally wear one), see where your boss or teacher will be sitting, listen for the hum of the projector, feel how sweaty your palms will be, and visualize yourself performing optimally. Be ready for minor mistakes. You might say something out of order. You may have a few "um's." Your face may get a little red. And all that is okay. You still have something valuable to contribute to your audience, and they are lucky to hear it.

Be Rational

The source of much of our debilitative apprehension comes from the idea that if something bad can happen, it will, and it will happen to *me*, during *my presentation*. Think about the worst possible scenario that could happen during your speech: Your mind goes blank? You pass out? Your bodily functions act up? (I once had a student who was worried about becoming sexually aroused before his speech; I told him to keep the podium close).

Now think about what is most likely to happen. Most of the people in the room probably have to speak. Your audience is probably rooting for you, including your teacher or boss. You may not give a perfect speech, but you probably will not pass out. Focus on the rational: You will be nervous, but that is okay. You will not be perfect, but, depending on how well you prepared, you will do a solid job, finish, receive applause, sit down, exhale, and learn from the experience.

Organization

As audience members, most of us are selfish. Think about how rare it is for an audience to care more about the subject matter of a speech than the speaker. There may be a few such occasions, but they are not very common, especially when you consider most of the presentations you have given in your classes. If we begin from the premise that our audience is less interested in our subject matter than we are, we can begin to understand why organization is so important. Any chance your audience members have to think about something else—the movies they saw last night, the fights they got into with their partners, how the guy next to them smells—they will take. A competent public speaker will know that the audience members may be apathetic, indifferent, and prone to distraction, and will make adjustments accordingly. These are considerations of what ancient rhetoricians identified as one of the five canons of rhetoric: **disposition**, or the arrangement and organization of a presentation.

The first adjustment should be to keep your presentation short. There are very few situations in which the audience will be disappointed that you ended early. How often have you been upset when an awards ceremony, a worship service, or class presentation ended earlier than you expected? It may happen, but not very often. For this reason, one of the keys to competent public speaking is this: Have an introduction, have a conclusion, and make sure they are not very far apart.

The second adjustment concerns the WIIFM acronym; it stands for "what's in it for me?" Competent speakers know the audience members will constantly be asking that question. Whether the context is a job interview or a client presentation, just because you care about your subject matter does not mean your audience members will. Be audience focused. Make sure your content addresses a genuine interest or need. If it does not, either reorganize it to make sure it does, or cut it out.

Third, be thoughtful about how formatting can help the audience follow your message. Again, if you assume that your audience members care less than you do about your subject matter, you have to also assume they will not be hanging onto your every word, and they can get distracted from your message. It is the speaker's responsibility to account for that and be able to bring the daydreaming and distracted audience members back into the fold of the message of the speech. Following the simple introduction, body, conclusion organizational sequence can help with that.

The Introduction

First, get your audience members' attention. The first 10 seconds of your presentation are vital. Many speakers lose their audience members before they even get warmed up. Audience members can be lost if you, the speaker, thank them for coming, tell them your name, or describe how nervous you are. Avoid that in your introduction. In general, people do not need to be thanked, and they may care what your name is, but just not yet. First, get their attention. Inspire them. Get them to lean forward in their seats and smile. Assure the audience members that the next 5, or 10, or 20 minutes of their lives are not going to be wasted.

Follow Steve Jobs's advice; he said an effective speaker begins every speech with the same sentence: "Let me start by telling you a story" (Issacson, 2011). A sentence like that will hook your audience members; they will lean forward, smile, and pay attention, at least for a little while.

Second, establish your credibility in the introduction. Once your audience members' attention is attracted with a story, answer this question for them: Why should they trust you? You may have a specific title that will gain respect, or years of experience that can bolster your credentials as an expert.

But, what if you do not? You may, at times, be forced to speak about a topic that you do not initially know a lot about, or you may not have specific credentials that attest to your credibility. In that case, try to be introduced by a well-respected authority figure, such as someone the audience already trusts. Mention how much research you have done to prepare for your presentation and that your content is informed by several scholarly articles and tenured professors from well-respected universities. Put another way, give your audience members a reason to trust you. Do not make them wonder.

Third, preview the rest of the speech. Set out a roadmap for your audience. Here is where you can integrate your own introduction, or that of your group members, with your central organizing question, your thesis statement, and your three or four main points. Again, imagine that you may lose a few of your listeners along the way, but if you give them a preview of what is about to come, this will help them get back on track when that does happen.

The Body

Think about this middle section as the guts of your speech. You should provide specific answers to your central organizing question and specific support for your thesis, here. You have several options when considering exactly how to organize that support. Some of the most recognized **organizational templates** are:

- **Chronological**: Tracing a process, story, history, or movement from its early to its later states. For example, a history of the Fukushima nuclear disaster might trace it from the earthquake to the tsunami to the shutdown of the cooling generators, to the evacuation, and so forth.

- **Problem–solution**: Specifying and elaborating the nature and extent of a problem or issue, and then presenting a proposed approach to managing that problem or issue. For example, the Green New Deal identifies the problems associated with anthropogenic climate change, and proposes a set of objectives for reaching a more carbon neutral society.

- **Cause–effect**: To analyze a process, story, history, or event by identifying its cause(s) and the outcome(s) or effect(s). For example, the Fukushima disaster might be discussed in regard to the poor engineering design and planning as the causes, and the effects being a meltdown when nature exceeded engineering specifications.

- **Topical**: To separate basic themes of a given topic. For example, the problem of anthropogenic climate change might be discussed in regard to private sector, public sector, and social or personal approaches to dealing with the crisis.

- **Criterion focused**: This approach identifies the ideals or objectives that specify what the best solution would need to achieve, and then identifies an approach that best meets those objectives. For example, a presenter might identify the criteria of (1) the most easily adopted, (2) fastest, and (3) least economically disruptive approaches to managing climate change, and then argue that a particular approach (e.g., carbon capture and cap-and-trade) is the most ideal approach to meeting those criteria.

Be strategic and thoughtful, here. Consider the perspective of your audience members and try to organize this section in a way that will make listening easier for them.

The Conclusion

Recall how competent speakers start their presentation; use a similar format for your conclusion. Remind the audience of your central question, thesis, and primary pieces of support. This is especially important for a longer presentation during which the audience has more time to get distracted. It is also wise to conclude by giving your audience members something to think about or something specific to do. Assuming you did not just waste their time, remind the audience members what they might have learned, and how this knowledge can impact their lives. Should they change their behavior in some ways? Buy one product or boycott another? Write a letter to their local newspapers? Vote in a specific way? Think differently about an issue or idea?

Be appropriately direct with what you expect of your audience. Answer the "So what?" question forcefully and clearly. Do not be bashful. Point out what the audience members learned and how this knowledge should impact their day-to-day lives (hopefully it has).

Finally, consider how your last sentence or two can function as a bookend. Do this by reminding the audience members of the story you told initially to get their attention. Hopefully, there was some conflict, mystery, urgency, or ambiguity illuminated in that story that the rest of your presentation sorted out, unpacked, and explained. Have the members of your audience recall that story, and in so doing remind them what value they just received from listening to you. The bookend can function as a tight, clean, and professional way to both begin and end your presentation.

Delivery

If we assume that most of the time you will care more about your subject matter than your audience will, we need to put some thought into not only *what* we say, but *how* we say it. Competent public speakers recognize they will be judged not just by their organizational strategies or the credibility of their citations, but also by how they look and sound when standing in front of the audience. Although it is not always fair, audiences do use peripheral and superficial cues (such as tone of voice and physical appearance) to evaluate the more substantive qualities of the speaker (such as intelligence and character). The most competent speakers tailor their delivery so they can balance a sense of confidence, expertise, and professionalism in the minds of their audience members with a sense of likeability, similarity, and charm. The next section offers advice about how to manipulate vocal and nonvocal nonverbal delivery to achieve this balance in the eyes of audience members (see also: Chapter 2).

Vocal Delivery Tools

Tone

Speak conversationally. Avoid the overly formal "speech voice." Do not try to sound like Ron Burgundy on *Anchorman*. You will feel unnatural, and your audience members will think you look phony. But at the same time, elevate your tone beyond what you might normally sound like talking with your friends during a Sunday afternoon Chargers' game. Treat your speech as an interactive conversation in which your tone matches the expectations of the audience, your need to appear credible, and the seriousness of the subject matter.

Rate

Research tells us that competent speakers tend to speak a little faster than average (Daly, 2011a). As listeners, we tend to think those who speak quickly and efficiently must know what they are talking about. Maybe your mother cautioned you against dating a guy who was a "fast talker," or maybe a "fast talking" salesperson got you to overpay for a car you did not really want. This phrase works because we use **rate**—the number of words spoken per minute—as a shortcut to evaluate a speaker's level of expertise.

Recognize this shortcut, but be mindful of how you put it into practice during your public presentations. Most of us are nervous during our presentations, and those nerves will naturally make us speak faster. Be aware of that. Also, speaking too fast the whole time will make it hard for your audience members to track your message.

With those qualifiers acknowledged, it is a good idea to internalize your material well enough so that you can speak efficiently. Know that your audience can comprehend more words per minute than you can speak, so speaking too slowly can hurt your credibility, making you appear unprepared and unintelligent. Work hard to find the right balance between speaking efficiently and making sure you are clearly understood.

Volume

We know we must be heard to impact an audience. Because we are all cognitive minimizers, audience members who have to strain too much to even hear you are likely to divert their attention elsewhere. Let your voice effortlessly hit the back wall without knocking it over. The people in the back should not have to put forth much effort to hear you, but the people in the front should not feel overpowered by your volume.

If you are not sure if your volume is appropriate, pay attention to the audience members' nonverbals to see if they look like they can hear you all right. If you are still unsure, ask if they can hear you; it is better to break up the formality and ask if you are being heard than force your audience to miss out on what you have to say because you are being too quiet.

It is also a good idea to mix up your volume to add a sense of dynamism to your verbal delivery. This is wise with each of these verbal delivery components; we want to work hard to avoid sounding **monotonous** by expressing little or no variety in pitch, pace and volume (see Chapter 2).

The most competent speakers tend to be louder than average; they use volume to show how enthusiastic they are about their topics. But, they also know when to slow down, pause, and lower the volume. This type of strategic vocal variety should be used sparingly, but, at times, it is effective to employ a higher-than-average volume to show passion and urgency, and then switch to a lower-than-average volume to make the audience members think they are getting in on something special.

Pausing

The most competent public speakers use silence to their rhetorical advantage. Integrating deliberate and intentional pauses into a presentation is an effective way to both transition from one point to another and to add emphasis to what was just said.

The best speakers (and the best actors) know that a lot can happen in the moments of silence between words or sentences. Watch a speech by Barack Obama or a movie with Jack Nicholas, and you will be able to see this in action.

Be careful with the pauses, though. Too many unplanned pauses hurt your credibility and make you look unprepared. When employed deliberately and intentionally, a well-timed and well-placed pause can add a lot to a presentation.

Punching

You all know how to italicize parts of a sentence when you are typing, *like this*. **Punching** refers to vocally italicizing important words or phrases. If you pause and punch properly, you can influence audience attention in a strategically advantageous direction. If a speaker were to say, "We have to do this *right* now," with a verbal emphasis placed on *right*, that sentence could take on a totally different meaning than if the speaker punched the word *now*.

The competent public speakers recognize this and deliberately punch important words or phrases during their presentations. Be careful not to overuse this technique. As you can imagine, a speaker who punches every word is really hard to listen to. As I advised with pausing, use this technique strategically and sparingly.

Pitch

If you have ever sung in a choir (or if you have ever seen the delightful movie *The Sound of Music*), you know **pitch** refers to how high or low your voice is on the vocal scale. Research tells us that the lower your voice is on that scale, the more competent you appear in the eyes of your audience (Kawasaki, 2010). Speakers with more bass in their voice—closer to the "Doe, a deer, a female deer" end of the continuum—are thought to be more credible and trustworthy than those whose voices fall higher on the vocal scale.

Consider who plays God in our popular Hollywood movies. We want God sounding like Morgan Freeman and James Earl Jones; we do not want God to sound like Pee Wee Herman or Gilbert Godfrey, known for their high, squeaky voices. Interestingly, in polygamous cultures (where is it socially acceptable to have multiple wives), the men who have more bass in their voice tend to also have more wives.

Our biological evolution can explain why: A voice lower on the vocal scale functions as a shortcut to symbolize physical power. In polygamous cultures, that shortcut is taken seriously so that the men with more bass are thought of as more attractive and virile.

This puts those with high voices at a distinct disadvantage, of course. Tim Geithner, whose story I told at the beginning of the chapter, knows this well. This shortcut is surely a sad reflection of our patriarchal culture and is an example of how careful we should be as audience members with how we use mental shortcuts to evaluate people.

For the speaker, pitch is primarily determined by biology, so there is not a lot that can be done about it. Even so, it is important for those of us with higher voices to be aware of how our chin placements influence where our voices fall on the vocal scale. In general, when your chin is pointing up, your pitch goes up. This is no reason to give our speeches with our chins stuck on our chests; just make sure you are never caught in a situation where you have to *look up* at a microphone or into a telephone. Looking up forces your chin up, and that will cause your pitch to go up and your credibility to go down.

Disfluencies

The most competent speakers avoid distracting the audience with too many verbal fillers. We call these **disfluencies**. For English speakers, the most common are "um" and "uh," but words and phrases such as "like," "actually," "honestly," and "you know" are also common. Spanish speakers are more likely to fill in the pauses between words or sentences with "esta"; Hawaiians use the phrase "da kine" for the same purpose; Mandarin speakers often use an equivalent of this/that as a disfluency.

A few "um"s or "uh"s do not matter that much. In fact, some disfluencies actually make you sound more comfortable and conversational. Speakers without any disfluencies seem robotic and mechanical. But, on the other end of the continuum, I am sure many of you have been in a situation in which you have kept a tally of a speaker's disfluencies. I would bet that it was not merely the number of "um's" or "uh's" (or "mm-kay's," as Mr. Garrison from *South Park* likes to say) that caught your attention. It is likely that you were so bored by everything else the speaker was doing that counting his or her disfluencies was all you could do to stay awake.

This is important to acknowledge because a few disfluencies can be like having a hand in your pocket while you are speaking: It does not matter that much, as long as other aspects of your verbal and nonverbal delivery are strong.

One way to find out if you have too many disfluencies is to record yourself giving a presentation and count them. If you have less than 10 a minute, you are probably okay. If you have many more than that, consider adjusting your preparation techniques so that you become more comfortable with silent pauses between words and sentences. The audience would prefer that over a deluge of filler words.

Nonvocal Delivery Tools

Along with being mindful of vocal delivery, competent public speakers are also aware of how important nonvocal delivery is to effective presentations. Just as we consider rate, pitch, and volume, we use nonvocal components such as gestures, appearance, and movement as peripheral cues that lead to substantive evaluations of a speaker.

Eye Contact

This is one of the most important dimensions of nonverbal delivery. Confident speakers are not afraid to look at their listeners and engage them with their eyes. Research backs this up: More powerful people tend to make more eye contact, hold it longer, and determine when it should be ended (Daly, 2011a). Try this in the hallway sometime as you cross paths with someone you do not know. Assuming the person does not ask you out or punch you in the face, you can probably tell who is more powerful by who breaks off eye contact first. This can be a good (but creepy) way to figure out how powerful you are.

As speakers, we must internalize our content well enough so that we do not need to look at our speaking notes or at the PowerPoint. The most competent speakers know their material well enough and are confident enough in the value of their subject matters that they are willing to come out from behind the podium and make eye contact with everyone, including listeners in the front rows and the far sides of the room.

Eye contact can also be a useful way to figure out if your message is being heard and understood. Look for signs of confusion in the faces of the audience members, or nods of affirmation when they are tracking with your message.

Finally, if you are really nervous, focus on the friendly faces in your audience; find a few people who are looking at you, smiling and nodding, and seem to be rooting for you. Speak specifically to those people as you begin (as opposed to the people who are falling asleep or texting under the table). Doing this—at least for a short period of time—can help you get comfortable being on stage and build up some confidence before you turn your attention to the entire room.

Physical Appearance

The research on the effect of physical appearance and perceived levels of competence is stunning (Hosoda,

Stone-Romero, & Coats, 2003; Jackson, Hunter, & Hodge, 1995; Langlois et al., 2000; Mazzella & Feingold, 1994; Ritts, Atterson, & Tubbs, 1992; Wilson & Sherrell, 1993). Maybe it is not a total surprise that we like physically attractive people. We think they are smarter, kinder, stronger, friendlier, and happier than less attractive people. We also think they are more honest, more sensitive, better organized, and even better romantic partners (Hamermesh, 2010).

In the classroom, physically attractive students receive more teacher attention, score higher grades on standardized tests, have higher positive academic expectancies, and are rated as more favorable by teachers. Attractive politicians receive more votes; attractive criminals are less likely to go to jail; attractive children are even less likely to be physically abused. In professional settings, managerial ratings are significantly higher for attractive candidates than for unattractive candidates. Physically attractive job applicants are rated by interviewers as possessing more sensitivity, organizational awareness, personal impact, leadership ability, and self-objectivity. On almost all dimensions except energy, less attractive people receive lower scores than attractive people.

As we discussed with pitch, much of our attractiveness is determined by our biology, and we cannot do a lot about that. We can mostly thank our parents for our jawlines and hip-to-waist ratios. But, as it applies to the public speaker setting, we can manipulate, to some degree, the aesthetic dimensions of our public presentations to help our audience members perceive us more favorably. For example, audience members use a speaker's grooming, trappings, clothing, and accessories as mental shortcuts to evaluate that speaker's intelligence, and competent speakers use these mental shortcuts to their advantage.

The most useful advice is to consider adopting aesthetic dimensions that put you *one level above* most everyone else in the room. Leaders are often recognizable in a room, and they are usually not wearing sandals, a bro-tank, and cargo shorts. Show your teachers and your employers how serious you take your presentations by dressing one level above your audience: If everyone is in shorts, wear pants; if everyone is in t-shirts, wear a polo-shirt; if a polo-shirt is normal, wear a button-down; if a button-down is normal, put on a tie; if a tie is normal, put on a jacket; if a jacket is normal, go with a suit. The dark suit is usually the ceiling (you probably will not

ever need to show up for work in a tuxedo with a top hat, white gloves, and a cane).

Gestures

Do not let your hands betray your nervousness. Use your gestures to naturally accent and supplement your verbal message. Avoid putting your hands in your pockets, keeping them locked behind your back, or rigidly stuck together in front of you. But as Ricky Bobby demonstrated in *Talladega Nights,* knowing what not to do with your hands is only a start. You should also have a plan for what you should do.

First, notice how you gesture during a normal conversation with a friend in a relaxed setting. Your hands probably accent your message in a natural and effortless way. We want our hands to function the same way when we are on stage. Second, have a **home base** where your hands go when they are not accenting your verbal message. I put one hand loosely inside the other, without my fingers interlocked; I let them sit right below my belt. I have seen other people have their home base near their belly button or rest comfortable near their mid-torso. Find a home that is comfortable for you. Do not keep your hands there the whole speech, of course. Use your home base as the default to which your hands return when not gesturing. Keep in mind, we do not want our gestures to be noticed. If someone were to get compliments on hand placement after a speech, that would be a problem.

Posture and Stance

Develop a home base for your posture and stance as well. In general, have your feet shoulder-width apart, your shoulders back, and your chest out. Do not slouch; that can make you look threatened and cowardly. Host the party, so to speak. Lean forward. Stay open and attentive. As we recommended with your tone, balance the gravity of the event with a sense of poise and confidence. Do not overdo it and stand like a drill sergeant, but, at the same time, signify the importance of the moment by standing confidently. The most common mistake related to posture and stance occurs when speakers cross their legs when they stand. This is a normal bodily reaction to the apprehension that we discussed earlier. It is natural to want to cover your "soft parts" when you are being evaluated and feel threatened. Work hard to avoid this, though, because it is read by the audience—either consciously or unconsciously—as that you have something to hide.

Movement

Competent speakers move naturally and gracefully. Standing in one place the whole time can make you look rigid and uncomfortable. Standing totally still can also make the signals of adrenaline—like a shaky knee or a fidgety hand—more noticeable.

Competent speakers move enough to stay loose. They keep the audience members on both sides of the room engaged and show they, as speakers, are not afraid to be evaluated. At the same time, their movement is not scattered or shifty. As Tim Geithner learned, too much movement can make a speaker look like a shoplifter. Instead, move with purpose. Do not pace or rock back and forth. Be comfortable and active. Occupy space. Use the stage. Do not stay behind the podium. For a more formal presentation, consider planning deliberate and intentional movement within the first minute of your presentation to ensure that you appear poised and confident.

Visual Aids

Many of the formal presentations you will deliver will involve visual aids. Although you have many options—including the white board, document camera, objects, overheads, and handouts—the most common visual aid right now is Microsoft's PowerPoint presentation software. But, here is the problem: Although it is widely used, nothing inhibits effective public speaking as much as PowerPoint, not even stupidity or laziness.

Competent speaking involves explanation, reasoning, questioning, and evidence. PowerPoint too often involves none of those. Research indicates that PowerPoint, compared to other common presentation tools, reduces the analytic quality of presentations, limits the thoughtful exchange of information, and distorts the transmission of complex content (Reynolds, 2012; Tufte, 2006). PowerPoint is not at fault, however. We are. Like a hammer or a car, PowerPoint is a neutral tool that can be good or bad depending on how it is used. In this section, I spend some time contrasting how PowerPoint is commonly used with how it should be used.

Misuses of PowerPoint

PowerPoint as a Crutch

PowerPoint is presenter oriented, not content or audience oriented. This is one of the reasons it is so prevalent. PowerPoint helps with presentation jitters. It also helps lazy speakers who have not put much effort into their preparation. It is not hard to copy and paste notes from a Word document onto some PowerPoint slides, and, presto, an almost-instant presentation is created. You can imagine why reading to the audience off the PowerPoint is so common: It is a natural consequence of using PowerPoint as a crutch rather than doing the hard work of internalizing the content.

PowerPoint as a Sound Bite

Consider why technical research papers are published as analytical reports, not as PowerPoint presentations. PowerPoint is not conducive to complex thought processes, pattern recognition, and narrative arc. PowerPoint presentations, because they are broken up into individual slides, constantly disrupt coherent strands of thought, forcing complex pieces of information into bite-sized chunks.

PowerPoint as Bullet Points

Most formal presentations require the speaker to place evidence within a context and extend the reach of memory beyond tiny clumps of data. PowerPoint has trouble with that. PowerPoint does lists, but lists only communicate logical relationships of sequence, priority, and membership in a set (Tufte, 2006). Bullet points leave critical relationships unspecified, forcing what is often an apathetic and uninformed audience to do the cognitively taxing job of connecting the dots.

PowerPoint as Entertainment

Speakers often use PowerPoint as way to spice up their presentations. Either through sound effects, animations, or cute pictures and images, the lazy speaker relies on PowerPoint to do the hard work of keeping the audience engaged. But, PowerPoint is a cheap way to keep your audience engaged. Stimulate your audience with fascinating content, polished and passionate delivery, and compelling stories, not PowerPoint. The main consideration a presenter should have is to think of PowerPoint as an accent or supplement to a presentation—not a replacement for it.

Competent PowerPoint Tips

Make Your Slides Simple, Natural, and Elegant
Follow the aesthetic models of Apple and Google: Limit the number of different colors you use, and make sure they vividly contrast with each other; recognize how much we appreciate blank space; avoid sound effects; limit transition animations between slides; include only critical information, and keep the number of words per slide below 30. It is better to have 20 slides that are simple, natural, and elegant than 10 slides that are overloaded, wordy, and cumbersome (Reynolds, 2012).

Use PowerPoint as a Persuasive Device
Make the title to each slide an argument, not an overview. Assume your audience members are only going to read the title. Feature your main conclusion there. Include citations on your slides. Let those citations build your credibility.

Supplement PowerPoint With Handouts
Handouts offer a permanent, high-resolution record; they allow audience members to take notes, contrast, contextualize, compare, narrate, and recast evidence within a common view. Supplementing PowerPoint with a written document can make your audience smarter and more attentive. For some general guidelines regarding PowerPoint, see **Table 21.1**.

Excel in the Question-and-Answer Session

By the time you have reached your capstone course and matriculated through your major, I would imagine if you were given enough time and asked to speak on a subject you were familiar with, most of you could pull off a decent presentation. But, what distinguishes a truly competent speaker from an average speaker is not how well that speaker performs during the speech; true competency is displayed in the question-and-answer session. Let me now conclude with a short discussion of how to excel during this part of your presentation—how to handle objections, clarify points, and leave your audience impressed.

Assume We Have Questions
The question-and-answer session is vital. Do not skip it. Watch the end of the PBS *Frontline* clip on Tim Geithner and see how he learned this the hard way (*Frontline*). Competent speakers welcome questions; they look forward to handling objections and clarifying their points

TABLE 21.1: Uses of PowerPoint

Uses of PowerPoint	
Redundancy	PowerPoint allows the speaker to connect to the audience on multiple channels. In addition to hearing the words of the speaker, seeing important words or phrases increases comprehension and retention, especially for non-native English speakers.
Efficiency	It is much easier for the speaker to click a button on the presentation remote or keyboard than to write on the white board or to draw an image on the document camera.
Organization	Research tells us that audiences perceive speakers who use PowerPoint as more organized than speakers who do not. An audience member may be thinking: "Well, I don't know how much effort this guy put into this speech, but at least he prepared a PowerPoint deck."
Image appeal	We have a well-honed appreciation of the visual. PowerPoint can appeal to that. The most competent public speakers recognize that most audiences would rather look at pictures than words. PowerPoint is therefore useful for displaying short words and phrases, graphs, charts, and maps that would otherwise be cumbersome to display in another medium. PowerPoint is also an excellent tool for displaying pictures that can activate the appeal of the image (without diluting that appeal with words on the same slide).

because they trust their expertise. They view the question-and-answer session as a time to assess both whether their message was understood and another opportunity to demonstrate their competency. Cowardly speakers avoid this part of the presentation, and they act surprised when hands go up. Initiate the question-and-answer session by using an open-ended prompt. Do not say, "Do you have any questions?" Assume we do! Demand them; in fact, say, "What are your questions?" or, better yet, "Who has the first question?"

Recognize Face

From an audience's perspective, asking a question can be risky. We have probably all been in a situation in which we have been made to feel stupid for asking a question, or at least we have seen that happen to someone else. The most competent speakers recognize the *face* of the audience member—another's desired public image—and affirm an audience member's participation (see also: Chapters 8 & 15). If you want questions, reward the audience members who ask them. They are helping you out.

Use their names. Let them finish their question completely; fight the urge to cut them off and answer the question, even if you know what it is (you may have heard the question before and know *exactly* what they are going to ask. Bite your tongue anyway. They have probably never asked it before). Let them finish completely, thank them for the question, then answer it as thoroughly but concisely as possible.

Your answer should not be seen as an opportunity to give another speech. If the questioner feels like your answer is too short or incomplete, he or she will probably ask a follow-up.

Handle Objections with Grace and Aplomb

Although it is not common, you may have to deliver a presentation to a hostile audience. The question-and-answer session during this type of presentation can be challenging. Truly competent speakers excel, even in this situation. If the questioner asks more than one question at once, answer the last question they asked first, and then ask them to rephrase the others for you. Try to take multiple questions one at a time. If the question is complex or wordy, paraphrase it, and then offer it back to the questioner to make sure you understood it correctly. This

will not only allow the questioner to possibly ask it in a simpler way, but will buy you some time to think about your answer.

Once you understand the question, you may realize that the questioner has tried to back you into a corner or has raised an objection that you did not consider. Keep your cool. Be ready to acknowledge minor imperfections in your arguments. Keep in mind that your content would not be interesting if it were completely agreeable. No one wants to listen to a speech about why we should wear our seatbelts or avoid cigarettes. Concede that there may be small cracks in your argument, but transcend those objections by bridging, or pivoting, back to your thesis.

Recognize also that in the classroom setting, sometimes students and teachers may ask questions not because they want an answer but because they want to be heard, and they want other people to acknowledge how insightful they are. We have all had classes with these know-it-all types. A competent speaker recognizes those situations and affirms the questioner's need to feel heard. In some situations, it is appropriate to even give the question back to the person who asked it (that is often what the know-it-all wants all along).

In some informal situations, it is even appropriate to see what the rest of the audience members think about a question. Smart phones can be helpful with simple, fact-based questions. Again, this can buy you some time, but also allow for a chance to divert the question in a direction you can more comfortably answer.

When you are totally stumped, make sure not to lie to your audience. If you are asked a question that you should know but do not, admit it, but do not leave it there; tell the questioner you will find out for him or her. Follow up as quickly as possible. Get the questioner's contact information or talk to the questioner in person the next time you can. That follow-up, even if the rest of the audience will not know about it, can go a long way in building rapport with someone who may potentially doubt your qualifications.

End on Your Own Terms

Finally, do not let the last question-and-answer interaction be the final impression left in the audience members' minds (especially if it was a potentially damaging objection). When you have the power to manipulate the format, *end on your terms.* Here is what I mean by that: After the last question has been asked, take 30 seconds and reassert your thesis one final time. Remind the audience of your main argument, key pieces of supporting evidence, and why it matters to them (despite the potential objections raised in the question-and-answer session). Address any new objections brought up in the question-and-answer session and let your audience know that you will be happy to continue the conversation once the formal presentation has ended.

Conclusion

The book *Drunk Tank Pink* (Alter, 2013) identifies public speaking as the number one fear for most U.S. adults. Death is a far second. It is for this reason that Jerry Seinfeld famously remarked that when attending a funeral, most people would rather be in the coffin than giving the eulogy. But, as we have discussed in this chapter, public speaking is vital both for the health of our democracy and for personal development.

Fortunately, competent public communication is a learned skill. Each of us, with enough effective practice, can get better at it. Improvement may not come easy, especially for those of you who consider yourselves introverted. Increasing communication competence requires deliberate practice. We should not expect that simply reading over note cards the night before a speech will improve

our performances. Just like learning to play the violin or hitting a curve ball, if you truly desire to get better at public speaking, expect a little bit of pain. Put yourself into a context in which your existing skill set is stretched; do not just practice in front of friends with whom you are already comfortable. Work on your weaknesses, not just your strengths. Aim to improve these weaknesses one at a time. Videotape your presentations. And, as painful as this will be, watch yourself and observe your strengths and weaknesses. Ask for critical feedback from people who slightly intimidate you. Expect to fail, but learn from that failure and *fail better* the next time. Keep an eye on experienced presenters, either in your classes, in houses of worship, or on TV and shamelessly steal their techniques.

Finally, put yourself out there. Expose yourself to opportunities to speak publicly. Join a toastmaster's public speaking group, volunteer to be the spokesperson during group projects in class, and ask for a leadership position in your social organization when you know giving public presentations is required.

Although these are challenging tasks for most of us, the effort will pay off. Being able to stand and deliver, to speak eloquently and cogently, and to competently express yourself and your ideas to offer uniquely powerful tools to shape our social worlds in ways that align with our interests. I hope this chapter has offered some useful advice about how to do just that.

  CHAPTER 22

Mass Communication

Rachael A. Record

& Brian H. Spitzberg

LEARNING OBJECTIVES

After reading this chapter, you should be able to do the following:

- Outline the major technological and paradigmatic developments in the history of mass communication.
- Identify and differentiate key assumptions and concepts of major theories of mass communication.
- Identify and differentiate strong versus weak forms of media effects models.
- Identify the assumptions of uses and gratifications theory.
- Identify the assumptions of spiral of silence theory.
- Identify the assumptions of agenda-setting theory.
- Identify the assumptions of cultivation theory.
- Identify and sequence the process of social learning as it relates to media consumption.
- Identify and sequence the types of adopters in diffusion of innovations theory.
- Define and differentiate the digital divide and knowledge-gap hypothesis.
- Articulate the implications of mediatization and vertical integration of media.

Humans evolved communication for much the same reason most organisms have—communication has survival value to coordinate actions with others to compete in a challenging environment. The process of communication and language development clearly predates any historical records, but we know from the record that human efforts to symbolize date deeply into our background. Indeed, a recent find in South Africa shows what appears to be a symbolic rock etching resembling "hashtags" in 73,000-year-old cave strata (Henshilwood et al., 2018). The fact that the stone lasted to communicate to us today makes the rock itself a medium of communication. As Kylmälä (2013, p. 133) posits: "the human condition (in its organization and structure) is by default a mediated condition." As illustrated in part by **Figure 2.3** in Chapter 2, and here in **Table 22.1**, the history of communication is marked substantially by the communication media.

The term **medium** (plural: **media**) derives originally from its Latin (i.e., "middle," neuter of *medius*), and in English derives from the 1500s as something intermediate or between in position or nature, or a person or thing that acts as an intermediate agent, instrument, channel, or means (OED Online, 2018). As such, there can be natural

TABLE 22.1: A Select Timeline of Significant Developments in Mass Communication

Date	Medium Development
500,000 BCE?	Verbal speech and protolanguage(s)
30,000 BCE	Cave paintings (Chauvet cave)
30,000 BCE	Lunar calendar markings on ivory, bone, and stone
14,000 BCE	Map markings on bone
12,000 BCE	Protocalendars
9000 BCE	Pictograms (stylized symbolic image with visual resemblance to a physical object independent of language)
8000–10,000 BCE	Petroglyphs (symbolic rock carvings)
6000–7000 BCE	Protowriting systems (nonrepresentational marks that communicate some form of information)
6000–7000 BCE	Ideograms (graphic symbols representing some idea; contemporary: the international "not allowed" red circle with diagonal bar)
3000 BCE	Tattoos
3000 BCE	Writing systems (e.g., cuneiform)
2000 BCE	Alphabetic writing systems
26–37	Signal systems using metal mirrors reflecting sunlight (Roman Emperor Tiberius)
105	Invention of paper
1250	Quill is used for writing
1305	Wood block movable type printing
1520	Ships signal using canon fire (Magellan voyages)
1717	Sun stencils of words (Johann Heinrich Schulze)
1792	First long-distance telegraph line for semaphore code (Claude Chappe)
1801	Punch cards are used to program a fabric loom (Joseph Marie Jacquard)
1816–1827	First photographs in various media experiments (Nicéphore Niépce)
1822	Calculating machine conceived (Charles Babbage)
1839	Daguerreotype process photographs introduced (Louis Daguerre)
1843	First functioning long-distance electric telegraph line for Morse code
1849	The Associated Press develops the Nova Scotia pony express
1876	Telephone (Alexander Graham Bell and Thomas A. Watson)
1877	Photography
1887	Moving photographic image demonstration (Eadweard Muybridge)
1888	First practical easy-use box camera (Kodak)
1891	Kinetoscope motion picture camera (William Kennedy and Laurie Dickson)

(continued)

Date	Medium Development
1895	Cinématographe (Auguste and Louis Lumiére)
1906	Feature-length multireel film (*The Story of the Kelly Gang*)
1920	Radio broadcasting (KDKA, Pittsburgh)
1927	First talkie film (*The Jazz Singer*)
1943–1944	ENIAC (Electronic Numerical Integrator and Calculator; John Mauchly and J. Presper Eckert)
1947	Full-scale commercial broadcast of television
1947	Transistor developed to replace vacuum tubes (William Shockley, John Bardeen, and Walter Brattain of Bell Labs)
1948	Polaroid instant camera (Edwin H. Land)
1949	Information theory (Claude E. Shannon)
1953	COBOL standardized computer language (Grace Hopper)
1954	FORTRAN standardized computer language (John Backus)
1957	Sputnik satellite launched with radio signal, initiating space race and satellite communications era
1958	Integrated circuit (computer chip; Jack Kilby and Robert Noyce)
1963	Communications satellite launched with geosynchronous orbit
1965	Email (first sent at MIT)
1969	Internet ancestor, ARPANET, with four nodes
1971	Floppy disk (Alan Shugart, IBM)
1973	Ethernet for connecting multiple hardware devices (Robert Metcalfe, Xerox)
1976	Personal computer market initiated
1981	Nordic Mobile Telephone introduces automatic mobile phone
1984	Seiko releases first watch to interface with a computer
1991	Optical fiber demonstrated at 32 billion bps (Anders Olsson)
1992	Text messaging demonstrated (Nedil Papworth)
1997	Social networking services introduced (SixDegrees.com)
1999	Peer-to-peer file sharing (Napster)
2000	Apple buys SoundJam MP (launched 1998) and rebrands it as iTunes
2003	Video calling (Skype)
2004	Facebook
2005	YouTube
2006	Twitter
2007	iPhone
2009	WhatsApp; Fitbit tracker
2010	Instagram; Siri (voice recognition) released as a stand-alone app
2011	Snapchat
2014	Amazon Alexa
2018	Facebook Portal
2019	Google Nest (connected home)

Source: Adapted from Wikipedia sources.

media such as rock engravings, beating on logs for sound transmission, and sending smoke or firelight for visual signals, as well as, writing, photography, and, in more contemporary times, broadcasting, telephonic, and Internet communications. In contemporary usage, **communication media** most typically refer to materials or technologies manipulated for the purpose of recording, amplifying or transmitting communications from some source to others. In contemporary usage, mediated communication involves some form of message(s) "passing through technologically-based infrastructures of transmission and distribution ("media")" (Couldry & Hepp, 2013, p. 197).

Contemporary History of Mass Mediated Communication

The history of communication, writ large, has been a trend of communicating more information more efficiently, more quickly, across broader audiences, in less time, and at less cost. In the 20th century, scientific interest grew with economies of scale in mass communication (see **Table 22.1**). Communication becomes **mass communication** when a given source is capable of using media to transmit information to large quantities of potential recipients. There is no bright line determining how many potential recipients constitute mass communication.

As will be elaborated on more specifically later in this chapter, early conceptions of the mass society seemed to fit with the relatively new modes of media such as print, radio, and film, in which large audiences could be reached simultaneously with relatively little societal or political filter between the media content and the individual consumer (McQuail, 2013). The power of propaganda during the rise of the Nazi Party in the lead up to and maintenance of World War II suggested the immense power of rhetoric when communicated *en masse* by institutional sources in the form of propaganda. Such conceptions predicted that media consumer beliefs and behaviors would be influenced in the direction of the media content, and that for the most part: (1) the greater the exposure and consumption, (2) the greater the influence, (3) which would be largely unidirectional from media source to consumer (McQuail, 2013). These assumptions represent a prediction of **strong effects**, sometimes characterized as

a "magic bullet" or "hypodermic needle" paradigm (see also, Chapter 14). Such a media effects paradigm "has played a central role in mass communication research for many decades. It has been the lead actor in the drama of mass communication discourse for close to a century" (Perloff, 2013, pp. 326–327).

The newer paradigm, arising in the 1960s and continuing to contemporary scholarship, is a greater presumption of interactivity, variety and accessibility across messages, meanings, and media. As early as 2004, Bryant and Miron (2004) noted that (1) all media and mass communication processes are undergoing rapid and radical changes in form, content, and substance, in addition to mere technological convergence; (2) media are moving from one-to-many to many-to-many (3) ownership patterns are increasingly shifting toward owner interests rather than public interests; (4) consumption patterns are shifting to be more fragmented across audience segments and media; (5) the traditional unit of observation (i.e., the family) is itself undergoing rapid cultural transformation as a media consumption group; and (6) interactive media are transforming personal relationships, the home, and their media ecologies. Furthermore, with barriers to entering the digital world diminishing, resulting in a shrinking digital divide, people increasingly are engaging in both **consumption** (i.e., viewing, reading, playing, listening, and experiencing media and their contents) and **prosumption** (i.e., the design, creation, production, transmission and distribution of media contents).

Mass Communication Theories

For decades, mass media theories have provided frameworks for examining and understanding communication processes that occur through mediated platforms. Although hundreds of media theories exist, this chapter emphasizes the importance of six predominant theories. Scholarly interest in mass communication began with strong effects assumptions about processes such as propaganda, but scholarship has evolved into a broad range of theories about media effects. These theories were not only the foundation to the field over the last 60 years of technological innovation, but they continue to provide insight into mediated communication processes.

314 | Part III: Knowing Where We Are and What Our Communication Is Doing

Strong vs. Weak Effects Models

Theoretical frameworks surrounding mass mediated communication were originally founded on the perspective that media exposure results in powerful and strong persuasive effects on audiences (Sparks, 2013). Theories and models that embraced this perspective were later classified as **strong effects models**. Arguments for these models grew out of World War I propaganda and viewed audiences as helpless victims that were captive, attentive, and gullible with regard to media exposure (Iyengar & McGrady, 2005; Lubken, 2008). These models were often analogized as representing a hypodermic needle, unlimited effects, direct effects, or magic bullet paradigm.

Two important views of human nature served as foundational principles for these models. The first argues that human nature was partially driven by instinct (DeFleur & DeFleur, 2016). This principle functioned as the basis for the stimulus–response view of human behavior. For instance, the implication for mass media (as a stimulus) is that it possessed the power to influence masses of people (as a response) in a uniform fashion. The second principle posited that unconscious urges served as the driving factor underlying behavior. This implied that when the mass media successfully tapped into these unconscious motivations, individuals who were impressionable could be influenced to conform their behavior to follow these needs and drives (DeFleur & DeFleur, 2016).

As researchers continued to examine effects related to mass mediated exposure, a new perspective began to emerge in the 1940s. This perspective argued that media effects are not strong and direct, but instead passive with selective influence. This framework recognized that audiences are simply composed of individuals interacting with other individuals and groups (Bryant, Thompson, & Finklea, 2012). Therefore, due to these additional influences, effects stemming from mass media exposure were likely to be limited and indirect. Theories and models that embraced this perspective are classified as **weak effects models**. This new emphasis on individual differences and environmental factors helped lay the foundation for theories such as agenda-setting theory (McCombs & Shaw, 1972) and uses and gratifications theory (e.g., Katz, Blumler, & Gurevitch, 1973). In addition, concurrent advances in theories of cognitive psychology (e.g., cultivation theory; Gerbner & Gross, 1976) and social learning theory (Bandura, 1973) facilitated advancing the understanding of cognitive processes underlying mass media effects. These theories and frameworks were predominantly founded in the 1960s, but remain the lens through which much mass mediated communication processes are understood today.

Uses and Gratifications

The **uses and gratifications** perspective (Katz et al., 1974) grew out of a desire to explain why individuals select (and do not select) a particular medium or set of media content. Rubin (2009) articulated the objectives of uses and gratifications to be: "to (a) explain how people use media to gratify their needs, (b) understand motives for media behavior, and (c) identify functions or consequences that follow" (p. 166). These objectives are grounded in five assumptions regarding the relationship between media, selection, humans, and satisfaction.

1. Media selection is an active and purposeful human behavior.

2. People select and use media for satisfaction.

3. Social, environmental, and psychological factors serve as filters for media selection/perceptions.

4. Media compete with other forms of communication in a selection process.

5. People are typically, but not always, more influential than media.

These objectives and assumptions collectively propose that people select media in order to gratify a particular need. Rubin (1981) proposed a typology of gratifications, listing that media selection is motivated by the desire to be satisfied in one of the following ways: passing time, companionship, escape, enjoyment, social interaction, relaxation, information, or excitement. Although modern applications of uses and gratifications have declined since the 1970s and 1980s, more recent research typically incorporates these assumptions with other media effects theories in order to explain media effects beyond simply seeking satisfaction (see LaRose & Eastin, 2004; Rubin, 2009; Song, LaRose, Eastin, & Lin, 2004). Such uses and gratifications are also reflected in contemporary theories of the affordances, or functions, that media technologies provide (Aladwani, 2017; Gill, 2017; Karahanna, Xu, Xu, & Zhang, 2018; Rathnayake & Winter, 2018).

Spiral of Silence

Proposed in an era when one's opinion could not be posted, tweeted, or reshared, Noelle-Neumann's (1974) **spiral of silence** theory posits that the perception that one's own opinion is not shared by the majority of others in a referent group context, the greater the likelihood of remaining silent and not voicing opinion in those contexts. As opposed to expressing the perceived minority opinion, individuals or groups may be compelled to remain silent out of fear of social isolation and a perceived threat of social rejection. A spiral of silence is then initiated as the perceived majority opinion gains traction and the perceived minority opinion receives little or no expression. Such a spiral then disproportionately creates the illusion that the majority opinion is more consensual than it actually is. This perspective rests on four assumptions (Noelle-Neumann, 1991):

1. Society threatens deviant individuals with isolation.

2. Individuals experience fear of isolation continuously.

3. Fear of isolation causes individuals to try to assess the climate of opinion at all times.

4. The results of this estimate affect their behavior in public.

With the advent of the Internet, the ability to find a majority opinion who agree with you is perceived as a matter of opinion. Thus, advanced technology has challenged the premise of spiral of silence. Some research has found the assumptions related to fear of isolation and outspokenness to no longer hold true (e.g., Liu & Fahmy, 2011), but other research finds the premises of the theory to still hold true (e.g., Hampton et al., 2014). Furthermore, the majority of society may now be less the referent group than one's social network.

Research continues to show that a person tends to post opinions when a perceived threshold of agreement or homophilous opinion has been reached by one's social network (Chiang, 2007; Iribarren & Moro, 2011; Mønsted, Sapieżyński, Ferrara, & Lehmann, 2017; Watts & Dodds, 2007). What constitutes a communicator's perceived majority may have shifted from society or culture to social network, producing structure in which the world-view of one group remains relatively silent to other groups ensconced in their own echo chambers of reality.

Agenda Setting

The **agenda-setting** perspective grew out of a famous study, called the Chapel Hill Study, conducted by Maxwell McCombs and Donald Shaw. This study followed media reporting and voter perceptions of presidential elections in the 1960s. Based on the study data, the theory of agenda setting was proposed, which proposes that the media agenda set the public agenda (McCombs & Shaw, 1972). Specifically, data from the study showed consistency between what the media were reporting as important considerations during the presidential election (e.g., economy and job growth) and what voters were saying to be the important considerations. Since the original study, other researchers have found consistent support in the context of elections, as well as civil rights, entertainment, and economics (see McCombs & Reynolds, 2009).

The simple assumption is that there is far more content of issues occurring in the world than can possibly be practically distributed to audiences. Thus, media industries (newspapers, radio stations, television, etc.) engage in a variety of processes to filter what is covered. In the process, the agenda of the media, especially the news, is significantly biased toward the agenda(s) of those who filter the media contents. Thus, for example, a magazine editorial staff engage in selection of what issues to cover, what visual or sequential emphasis these issues receive in the medium, how much information is provided on that issue, and by implication, what topics or issues are excluded or not discussed (see **Figure 22.1**). As a result, the public agenda will begin to reflect the agenda of the media agencies that control the media.

For example, in the 2016 presidential election debates, the issue of climate change was never covered as a question asked of the candidates. If a topic is excluded, the topic may seem less relevant, important, or salient to the public. If climate change is not discussed on the campaign trail or in presidential debates, then even though it is easy to find such discussions somewhere across all the various media, it is not the primary topic of discussion among people at the time. Although some argue that there is no way to know the order of effects (i.e., does the public influence the media, or do the media influence the public?), most media researchers are confident that the persuasive agenda is the media agenda. Thus, although the media do not tell people exactly what to think, they do suggest what people should think and talk about.

FIGURE 22.1: Visual Representation of Agenda-Setting Theory

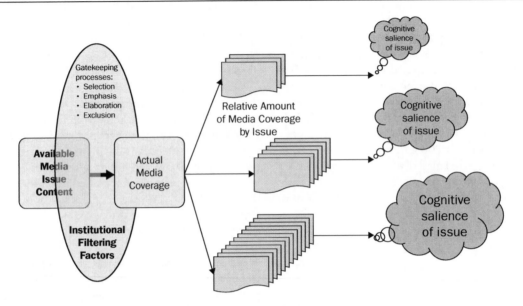

Cultivation

Conceptualized by George Gerbner and colleagues working on a research project entitled the Cultural Indicators Project, **cultivation theory** postulates that heavy viewers of television will cultivate a view of the real world that is reflective of how the world is portrayed on television (Gerbner & Gross, 1976). Specifically, the study concluded that heavy general television viewing cultivated the perception that the world was more violent than it actually was (Gerbner et al., 1980). These findings suggested a phenomenon that Gerbner and colleagues entitled **mean world syndrome**—the idea that people believe the world is a meaner and scarier place than it actually is. Fifty years later, research continues to support the tenets of cultivation theory, building on the violence research to find cultivation effects related to smoking initiation, political participation, and perceptions of stereotypes (see Morgan, Shanahan, & Signorielli, 2009). In addition, modern cultivation research has also moved beyond the examination of general TV exposure toward examining heavy exposure to specific genres, such as medical dramas, reality TV, and crime dramas (see Record, 2018). Thus, cultivation theory does not suggest watching a lot of TV will persuade us how to act, but that watching a lot of television will influence our perceptions of the real world.

Social Learning

Social learning theory is one of a number of behavioral theories proposed by Albert Bandura. This theory suggests that humans learn how to behave by modeling other human behavior (Bandura, 1973, 1978). The behavior modeling process includes four stages:

1. Paying attention to the behavior.

2. Retention of the behavior through repeat exposure.

3. Reproducing the behavior with attention to feedback from the external world.

4. Motivation to continue performing the behavior based on the interpretation of feedback from the modeled behavior.

The key to this process is that individuals who receive negative feedback will not continue to model the behavior. This theory becomes particularly relevant to media to the extent that the behavior we model is from media characters and coverage. For example, if a child continues to watch people on TV smoke, then he or she might try a cigarette. If the world around the child reacts positively or in a neutral manner to the behavior, then the child will likely continue smoking. If the world around the child reacts negatively, however, then the child will likely stop smoking. Thus, the persuasiveness of media on behavior has an indirect effect on behavioral performance—one that is dependent on feedback to behavioral performance. In the era of social media, the models we use to reference our own behavior may be our social networks, mediated through platforms such as Facebook and Instagram. If our public figures become nastier in their language, do we emulate such behavior in our own language?

Diffusion of Innovations

The **diffusion of innovations** theory outlines how innovations (i.e., new objects, ideas, or approaches) spread through mediated channels and become adopted by audiences (Rogers, 1962). Traditionally, the adoption of an innovation referred to the use of technology or tools. Innovation adoption has also been studied, however, as the adoption of new attitudes or ideas. There are two major layers of this theory. First, the theory identifies five subgroups that represent the different types of adopters among the population. **Figure 22.2** depicts the expected percentage of subgroup members regarding any given innovation. Rogers's (1962) descriptions of each subgroup are presented in **Table 22.2**. Second, the theory outlines five stages of innovation adoption. **Figure 22.3** displays these stages. According to the diffusion of innovations

theory, the diffusion process is leveraged through motivating the most influential subgroups (i.e., **early adopters** and **early majority**) in order to move audiences through the stages of innovation adoption. As technology has continued to exponentially grow, interest in examining how topics and tools are diffused within and across media also grows.

Mediatization

Although it may feel like we live a world with more media choices than ever before, all of those choices are owned by a small concentration of corporations (Gómez, 2016, p. 193). The concentration ratio of the top cable system operators increased from less than 42% in 1993 to more than 70% by 2002, while the number of cable operators overall decreased across this time span (Chung, 2017). In fact, Potter (2016) notes that "only seven conglomerates now control well over half of the mass media audience exposure" (p. 200). One study found three trends over a 34-year period. First, although media may not be seriously concentrated yet, the most recent trends are toward a "marked and gradual increase in ownership concentration within the media industry," starting in 2001 (Vizcarrondo, 2013). Second, despite the common assumption that the Internet is far more democratic and heterogenous than

FIGURE 22.2: Typical Population Distribution of Innovation Adopters

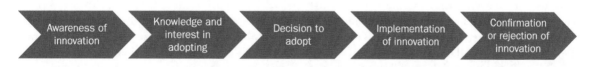

Awareness of innovation → Knowledge and interest in adopting → Decision to adopt → Implementation of innovation → Confirmation or rejection of innovation

TABLE 22.2: Descriptions of Diffusion of Innovation Subgroups

Subgroup	Description
Innovators	Enthusiastic, drive change, not afraid of failure, high tolerance for risk, uncertainty, and ambiguity.
Early adopters	Embrace change, like to be the first to try new things/ideas, inspired by new, trend setters.
Early majority	Accept change, pragmatists, adopt practical change, waits for success in practice.
Late majority	Cautious of change, skeptics, adopts after proven in practice, will follow once strong majority has largely adopted.
Laggards	Change averse, value tradition, suspicious of new innovations, often wait until forced adoption.

See Rogers & Beal (1958, 1962).

FIGURE 22.3: Stages of Innovation Adoption

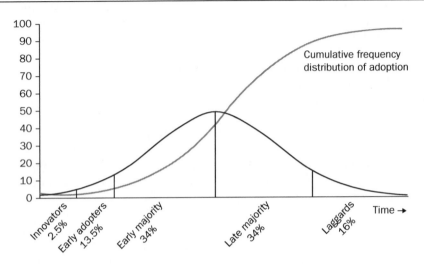

uniform or univocal, it is notable that while there is more and more content from which to select, the dominance of a shrinking number of web portals can distort access to such content (Dewan, Freimer, Seidmann, & Zhang, 2004). Finally, such concentration tends to reflect the values of the owner(s) (Corneo, 2006) and advertisers (Germano & Meier, 2013), and may also reflect more global rather than local content focus (Saffran, 2011). This represents, in part, a **knowledge-gap hypothesis**, which predicts that the diffusion of media will increasingly favor those with economic and institutional power (Hwang & Jong, 2009), which represents an increasingly disparate set of communication competencies or literacies in the **digital divide** (Rowsell, Morrell, & Alvermann, 2017).

This concentration is not exclusive to online news. One of the most dramatic recent illustrations of the potential bias reflected due to concentration of news can be seen in the recent mashup of news announcers working at Sinclair local television news stations. The Sinclair Broadcast Group owns nearly 200 local TV news stations, and is seeking to acquire more. Their footprint represents over 90% of the U.S. population (Chang, 2018). In 2018, newswatchers caught these diverse, local stations mouthing a script about the fairness and objectivity of their reporting; a common script from their corporate leadership, which was imposed upon the local stations to read. A powerful display of homogenized perspective disguised as independent reporting is available at: https://twitter.com/i/status/980175772206993409 (Domonoske, 2018; Fortin & Bromwich, 2018).

Although **vertical integration** increases the efficiency of communication and media interaction, there are also many important cautions. For audiences, the importance of vertical integration is twofold. First, as is demonstrated in the Sinclair example, smaller ownership means more gatekeeping power in fewer hands. The decisions over what content to show (or not to show) will be homogeneous across platforms owned by the same corporations. Potter (2016) conceptualizes this phenomenon as **localism**, or the belief that control and power should be shared by as many people as possible. Second, awareness of vertical integration is essential to critically consuming mediated messages. Unsurprisingly, corporations work very hard to ensure it is not easy to confirm who owns what. Even for those with greater access to information and technology, keeping up with media ownership is a challenge. Going back to the knowledge-gap hypothesis, those with a lower socioeconomic status are at an even greater disadvantage for being aware of, and keep track of, media ownership. These difficulties interfere with the ability to be media literate and a critical consumer of media.

Box 22.1 Ethical Issues

With great power comes great responsibility. There are few things as powerful as the tool of media. Mass media has the power to reach countless people in one click—click of a mouse, click of a remote, or click of a phone. The messages that disseminate from the media are not vetted by any overarching system of morals or values. Thus, it's impossible to consider message dissemination from mass media without considering the ethical implications that stem from such power.

Media Content Regulation

Numerous media effects theories have been developed that outline the expected persuasive impacts related to media exposure. Few of these theories are context based. This means that theoretical outcomes are expected regardless of the content—whether it be positive or hate filled, true or false. Take the spiral of silence for instance. The age of the Internet has made it so that all perspectives can be felt as if they are a majority perspective, even those such as White supremacy and lack of gun regulations. But the truth of the matter is that national data finds these perspectives to be in a small minority of U.S. adults: less than 6% of adults agree with perspectives consistent with White supremacy (Hawley, 2018), and only 8% of adults believe gun laws should stay the same or become less strict (Jackson & Newall, 2018). It's clear that negative, fake, or hateful content disseminated across mass media platforms can have powerful and dangerous effects on society—even more than just swaying opinion. Mass media has been effectively used to recruit terrorists (Lachow & Richardson, 2007) and teach bomb-making (Torok, 2010).

The need to consider ethical dissemination of content often brings about the ethical dilemma of censorship. Censorship is defined as the suppression of speech, public communication, or other information, on the basis that such material is considered objectionable, harmful, sensitive, or "inconvenient." Humans have a long history regarding censorship, including banning (or even burning) books, regulating news, and controlling Internet content. The motives behind censorship vary from religious or moral reasons to political or military reasons. Although many of us would love to ban all content related to topics we disagree with, who are we to say that our perspective is the right perspective or the only perspective? The right to free speech is a right that requires constant battles—but a right that should be fought. As there is no debate over the need to protect freedom of information, we choose to accept the risks of negative and hateful content in hopes that humans are stronger than fear.

The Widening Knowledge Gap

Although it's always fun to buy the newest piece of technology or consumer media from the newest social platforms, the quick-paced technological environment is not easy for everyone to keep up with. The knowledge gap and digital divide get wider the quicker technological innovation is made available. This is not to say that technology should slow down. But whose responsibility is it to ensure that technological advancements are available for everyone, not just those with the most wealth or access? The government? Technology companies? At what point do we, as a society, demand equality in information access for all citizens? Despite being a major concern for many people, this ethical dilemma is rarely at the center of the conversation.

The extent to which media infuse their influences into our everyday lives is broadly reflected in a concern that our society, our culture, our relationships, our consumerism, our government and politics, and our everyday ways of thinking are mediatized—infiltrated, shaded, framed, and constructed through media. In ways even beyond Marshall McLuhan's (1964) early conceptions, mediatization envisions the extent to which the medium is the message, which is our experience of the world in which we live. A critical viewpoint is increasingly required by any given citizen to engage such environments competently, the topic taken up next in Chapter 23.

Conclusion

Media effects research has long explored human communication processes through mediated platforms. Well-established theoretical frameworks provide insight into media effects processes, as well as suggestions for improving communication. Media effects can be unintentional, such as passively watching TV or listening to music, and it can be purposeful, such as through carefully designed campaigns (see Chapters 19 and 20). Regardless, the research is clear that media effects are a central component of communication research.

CHAPTER 23

Mediated Communication

Brian H. Spitzberg & Rachael A. Record

LEARNING OBJECTIVES

After reading this chapter, you should be able to do the following:

- Differentiate interpersonal, mediated, mass, and masspersonal communication.

- Specify some of the implications of media convergence in a polymedia informational ecosystem.

- Identify and relate the major components and processes of the MEDIA model of media competence.

- Discuss how distribution and reach differ between mass and masspersonal communication.

- Designate differences and similarities between transportation and social presence in media use.

- Identify and differentiate media literacy, visual literacy, CMC competence, and media competence.

- Identify and differentiate the major contextual levels of the MEDIA model of media competence.

- Articulate the role of commodification in the media ecology.

From Traditional to Interpersonal to Masspersonal

During most of the 20th century, communication media developments were mostly in the realm of mass communication. Late in the century, however, with the merging of the Internet with smartphones, GPS, and satellite communications, new paradigms of communication research and theory were enabled and required. While there are many possible ways of distinguishing the most recent forms of media from traditional media, new media represent significantly increased (1) role for audience participation and authorship of media contents (Zajc, 2015); (2) greater synchrony, or

321

interactivity, and immediacy of possible responses or feedback; (3) social presence in the form of the richness and sense of being there in a collective communicative space; and (4) reach, in the form of one-to-many distribution (Hall, 2018). In general, the more that media facilitate back-and-forth exchange among interlocutors, the more personal or relational it tends to be (Hall, 2018).

Recognizing these and other changes in the modern media ecology, scholars have begun to identify how media traverse the traditional "mass" versus "personal" spaces of communication. New media increasingly offer a masspersonal mode of communication. **Masspersonal communication** occurs "when (a) individuals use conventional mass communication channels for interpersonal communication, (b) individuals use conventional interpersonal communication channels for mass communication, and (c) individuals engage in mass communication and

interpersonal communication simultaneously" (O'Sullivan & Carr, 2017, p. 1164). **Figure 23.1** illustrates how masspersonal communication media occupy a space that has extensive reach in terms of potential audience, but also provides opportunities for interactivity and representation of and adaptation of messages to individuals in the communicative exchange.

The world is awash in information and mediated messages. The extent to which we rely on media for the negotiation of our everyday identity and relationships is amply evidenced. For example, according to one study of college students involved in a romantic relationship, the amount of time the students estimated they communicate online with their partner averaged over 17 hours per week (Anderson & Emmers-Sommer, 2006). Another estimate that examined types of posts on Twitter found that about 41% of posts by personal users (vs. business or bots) were about "me now,"

FIGURE 23.1: Masspersonal Communication Model (adapted from O'Sullivan & Carr, 2017)

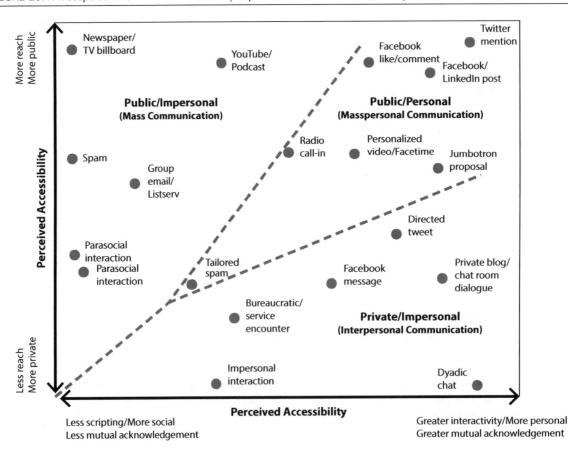

or what the person was experiencing contemporaneously with the post, and approximately 22% reflecting "information sharing," approximately 24% sharing opinions or complaints, and 25% representing "statements and random thoughts" (Naaman, Boase, & Lai, 2010, p. 3). This information exchange function seems to dominate conversational contexts (Dunbar, Duncan, & Marriott, 1997). We use media to tell others who we think we are, who we hope to be, and with whom we want to affiliate.

Media are infused in our everyday lives, but they are far from entirely unobtrusive. Younger people appear more tolerant of cellphone use in social settings compared to older generations. For example, 82% of people report that in group interaction contexts, "when people use their phones in these settings it frequently or occasionally hurts the conversation" (Rainie & Zickuhr, 2015). Despite this general sense of the disruptiveness of interacting with their phone during social interactions, almost 90% of people report engaging in such behavior in their last social gathering, and over 85% report someone else doing so, most commonly involving reading a text or email message. It should be noted, however, that at the same time, over three-quarters of people cited "group-contributing" reasons, such as posting a picture of the gathering itself, sharing something that had occurred in the gathering, seeking information relevant or of interest to the group, or connecting to others in the gathering.

At the same time that people misuse media in various ways that disrupt everyday encounters, they also often rely on them in ways that mislead them. By one estimate, over half of U.S. adults believe at least one conspiracy theory (Oliver & Wood, 2014), and as much as 40% of social media messages about medical issues represent "fake news" (Waszak, Kasprzycka-Waszak, & Kubanek, 2018). In the fall of the 2016 presidential campaign, over a quarter "of Americans read an article from a fake news site on their laptop or desktop computer," with an average of over five articles read (Guess, Lyons, Montgomery, Nyhan, & Reifler, 2018). Between the multitasking across platforms and apps, between business and social mediated life, on-demand access to information, and the sheer infusion of media throughout society, there is reason to believe that the basic attention span of teens (Purcell et al., 2012) and adults (Gausby, 2015) is decreasing, at the cost of our ability to use media competently. A significant priority of education in the future is to ensure media competence across the population.

Media Competence

"No one is born media literate. **Media literacy** must be developed, and this development requires effort from each individual as well as guidance from experts. The development is a long term process that never ends; that is, no one ever reaches a point of total, complete media competence. Skills can always be more highly developed; and if they are not continually improved they will atrophy" (Potter, 2013, p. 422). People who grow up in the digital age (i.e., born after 1980) are referred to as **digital natives**. Digital natives are generally expected to be more acquainted with and skilled at using a variety of media. Even among the digital native generation, however, relational transgressions in social networking sites and messages are common (Tokunaga, 2014).

Media competence can be considered an amalgam of issues both of (1) how people use media in their personal, civic, relational, and professional lives, and (2) how they process the contents of those communications to form behavior patterns and beliefs about the world. The former set of issues concerns computer-mediated communication (CMC) competence, and the latter concerns media competence.

CMC competence refers to the degree to which digital media are used in ways perceived as both appropriate and effective (Spitzberg, 2006; see Chapter 12). In general, the more motivated, knowledgeable, and skilled a person is in using CMC technologies to communicate, the more likely it is that such communication will be viewed as appropriate and effective by those interacting with that person through such media (Bakke, 2010; Hwang, 2011). **Media competence**, in contrast, refers to the ability to critically access, interpret, assess, and use media to both form and express feelings, positions and opinions (Ashley, 2015; Austin, Muldrow, & Austin, 2016; Chen, Wu, & Wang, 2011; Koc & Barut, 2016; Lee, Chen, Li, & Lin, 2015; Lin, Li, Deng, & Lee, 2013; Young, 2015). It involves the understanding and strategic skilled use of images, sounds, symbols, texts, and their manifold contexts and means of creation and transmission. Such competence is increasingly viewed as a central competency for maintaining a civic democracy (Mihalidis & Thevenin, 2013).

The media engagement and dynamic information analysis (MEDIA) model of competence makes a basic assumption—whether media are used for entertainment or more utilitarian tasks, and whether it is composed of image, shape, sound, text, or some combination of these,

FIGURE 23.2: Media Expertise Dynamic Integrated Activity (MEDIA) Model

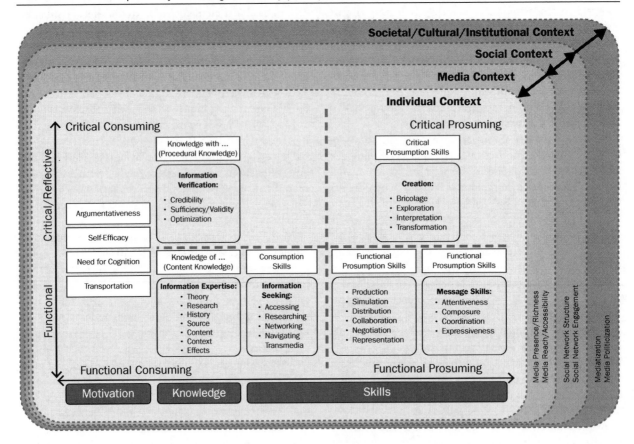

any media creation is in some form and to some degree an argument (see **Figure 23.2**). This is not an uncontroversial position (e.g., Alcolea-Banegas, 2009; Birdsell & Groarke, 2007; Groarke, Palczewski, & Godden, 2016). However, "Because arguments are acts, they cannot be delimited to just being discrete, verbal texts" (Kjeldsen, 2018b, p. 81). Everything from architecture, environmental design (Wood, 2010), film (Alcolea-Banegas, 2009), advertising (Jeong, 2008; Maier, 2012; Slade, 2003), nonverbal icons (Pineda & Sowards, 2007), and sound (Kjeldsen, 2018a; Walker & Bender, 1994) can be productively analyzed as forms of multimodal argument (Tseronis, 2018). The model draws upon numerous existing models of media literacy and competence (Álvarez-Arregui et al., 2017; Ashley, 2015; Austin et al., 2016; Chen et al., 2011; Claro et al., 2018; Groenendijk, Haanstra, & Kárpáti, 2018; Kahn & Idris, 2019; Kędra, 2018; Koc & Barut, 2016; Lee et al., 2015; Lin et al., 2013; Mihalidis & Thevenin, 2013;

Perrin & Ehrensberger-Dow, 2008; Potter, 2013, 2016; Rex, Thomas, & Engel, 2010; Spitzberg, 2006, 2014; Young, 2015).

"The importance of the study of visual arguing is inherent in the times—times in which technological developments (digital communication, the internet, virtual reality, etc.) have made visuals an increasingly pervasive element of communication. People now live in a reality that is not merely visually permeated—it is visually mediated" (Groarke et al., 2016, p. 233). As visual forms of communication are recognized increasingly as significant forms of argument (Warnick, 2002), if all media are not arguments, media competence certainly involves a critical consideration of the potential of such argument in any mediated context. "A complete theorization of argumentation, one that hopes to explain its workings and assess its merits, must recognize and account for features of visual argument emphasized by rhetoricians and logicians" (Groarke, et al., 2016, p, 231). Thus, any use of media can be evaluated in regard to its propositional, its evidentiary, causal, or persuasive force the sender anticipates as an intended effect on its receiver(s) (Boland, 2005; Grancea, 2017; Kjeldsen, 2018b; Roque, 2015). Furthermore, cognitive and neuroimaging studies increasingly demonstrate the integral interplay between ordinary language structures, argument, and the visual processing of arguments (Dove, 2016; Oestermeier & Hesse, 2000).

An important consideration of the MEDIA model is that it is more aspirational than descriptive. That is, in today's media environment in which people often forward YouTube links, tweets, and Instagram posts with relatively little thought, or merely for or due to the convenience of liking, disliking, and forwarding such messages, it seems obvious that much mediated communication occurs with little critical self-reflection. The MEDIA model therefore is less about explaining all of mediated communication that occurs, and more about pointing the path to a more literate and conscious approach to using mediated communication in the interest of a more fully functioning set of personal, social, and civic relationships.

The MEDIA model begins with a continuum between the consumption and the production of communicative content and process. Toffler (1980) predicted that those who traditionally were primarily consumers of media would increasingly take on the role of producers of media content. "Consumption and production are not dualistic opposites, but co-present in and are organized by practices of everyday living" (Hartmann, 2016, p. 4). Chen, et al. (2011) elaborated the key quadrants of this model, composed of the consuming-versus-prosuming competencies, and the functional-versus-critical competencies. The further division of motivation, knowledge, and skills components reflects Spitzberg's (2006) CMC model. Thus, the MEDIA model proposes that a media competence is reflected in a person who is motivated to engage media proficiently, is knowledgeable about how to fully comprehend the implications of such engagement, and who possesses the consumption and production skills that facilitate appropriate and effective media engagement.

Social media represent a clear example in which individuals both consume and create the contents of such communication (Zajc, 2015). For example, **citizen journalism** illustrates a symbiosis between news consumers and producers (Usher, 2017). New media platforms may still be dominated by commercial interests, but they offer the potential for greater interaction between the professional and the amateur, between institutional and personal media, between horizontal rather than vertical relations between producer and consumer, and the development of entrepreneurial and social capital rather than being exploited purely as a commodified consumer product. The MEDIA model envisions theconception of *emirec*, which Aparici and Garcia attribute to Cloutier, in which interlocutors are simultaneously both receivers and transmitters, consumers and creators; "the emirec is an empowered subject that has the potential capacity to introduce critical discourses that question the system's functioning" (Aparici & Garcia, 2018, p. 77).

Motivational Components of Media Competence

Need for cognition is a predisposition to enjoy or have fun engaging in effortful cognitive endeavors or thinking (Ashley, 2015; Austin et al., 2016; Cacioppo, Petty, Feinstein, & Jarvis, 1996). Media consumers higher in need for cognition tend to use media more for information acquisition than entertainment, and within such media, they tend to prefer text over pictures (Strobel, Fleischhauer, Bauer, & Müller, 2014). Media consumers high in cognition need tend to process messages more carefully, are less biased by simple assertions or heuristics, and prefer multiple-sided messages to single-sided messages (Haugtvedt, Petty, & Cacioppo, 1992; Winter & Krämer, 2012). Yet, they are also inclined to consume media even when they do not trust it because they seek the diverse information in forming judgments (Tsfati & Capella, 2005).

Derived originally from Bandura's (1977) social learning theory, **self-efficacy** refers to the belief or degree of conviction that the behaviors needed to successfully achieve a particular goal or objective are available. That is, people high in self-efficacy in a particular area believe they possess the skills needed to achieve a particular outcome in that area. Self-efficacy has demonstrated that it facilitates competence in using the Internet (Kim & Glassman, 2013; Livingstone & Helsper, 2010), social media (Hocevar, Flanagin, & Metzger, 2014), computer-mediated communication in general (Shu, Tu, & Wang, 2011), and specifically in regard to discerning misinformation in such media (Khan & Idris, 2019). As a consequence, such media self-efficacy facilitates the use of social media to develop cultural competence (Hu, Liu, & Gu, 2018).

Argumentation is a cognitive ability underlying conceptual change, mental problem-solving, and various forms of higher-order thinking (Jonassen & Kim, 2010, p. 454). Specifically, **argumentativeness** is a predisposition to defend or advocate positions on controversial issues and articulating criticisms of or challenges to others' positions on such issues (Frankovský, 1995; Hamilton & Hample, 2011; Infante & Rancer, 1982; Rancer, Kosberg & Baukus, 1992; Rancer & Whitecap, 1997). Argumentative persons are more open to new ideas, more tolerant of disagreement, and more inclined to objectively consider multiple possible perspectives in the media (Arpan & Peterson, 2008). Argumentativeness is not only a motivation to engage in argument, but also a tendency to avoid aggression or personal attack (Hamilton & Hample, 2011; Infante & Rancer, 1996). As such, those high in argumentativeness also demonstrate an ability to develop more counterarguments to TV ads, and are more resistant to persuasion by such ads (Kazoleas, 1993). Argumentative individuals tend to be more resistant to persuasion. Furthermore, argumentatives were found to generate greater numbers of counterarguments (Kazoleas, 1993). The intention to argue regarding a given issue is influenced by the argumentativeness of the interlocutor (Levine & Boster, 1996), the personal involvement, and the type of argument topic, whether about personal or public issues (Stewart & Roach, 1998).

Thus, argumentativeness is a motivational tendency to engage in critical skepticism, or a tendency to ask probing questions of media messages, and to reflect upon the argumentative bases of such messages (Thier, 2008). It is what colloquially might be referred to as a healthy skepticism in regard to messages (Robinson & Nilsen, 2002; Venable, 1998), in which content is examined with an eye toward noticing and rectifying any errors or false claims (Venable, 1998). Such critical skepticism is related to the extensive research on media trust, credibility, and hostile media perceptions (McLeod, Wise, & Perryman, 2017). Skeptical media consumers tend to seek out diverse news sources for information surveillance (Tsfati & Peri, 2006). It is a natural component of media literacy as well as an outcome of critical thinking about media messages (Austin et al., 2016). More skeptical media consumers tend to be more motivated to assess the truthfulness of the media source and claims (Zhang, Ko, & Carpenter, 2016).

Transportation in the context of media refers to the extent to which a consumer is transported into a media story, narrative, or context. It represents a tendency toward immersion, engagement, and being drawn into the story of a media message (Nabi & Krcmar, 2004; Thompson et al., 2018). In general, people higher in transportation feel like they "get lost" in a story or narrative (Tal-Or & Cohen, 2010). Narrative transportation theory predicts that increasing transportation tends to result in consumer attitudes, emotions, and behaviors that navigate toward those represented in the narrative (Van Laer, Ruyter, Visconti, & Wetzels, 2014). This theory posits that when people lose themselves in a story—when they are "narratively transported"—their attitudes and intentions change to reflect that story" (Seo et al., 2018, p. 84).

Such transportation into a medium or its narrative may seem to lower a consumer's critical reflection and increase a consumer's persuadability (Hamby, Brinberg, & Jaccard, 2018; Seo, et al., 2018). Transportation appears to promote viral advertising (Seo et al., 2018) and the relative influence by narratives compared to evidentiary or logical means (Hamby et al., 2018). However, there is a difference between feeling immersed in a mediated message and feeling personally influenced or affected by it. There is evidence that such immersion and experience of personal influence also facilitate attentional focus and involvement in evaluating narrative realism, noticing inconsistencies in the narrative, and engaging in counterarguments (Quintero Johnson & Sangalang, 2017).

Knowledge Components of Media Competence

The affect and motivation aspects of media competence activate mental search and analysis processes. Much media content is probably taken in and processed relatively passively. However, once a communicator is motivated to focus attention on a media message, other cognitive processes are activated. Once a media message is of interest, a person's knowledge relevant to that message is accessed and can be further focused on the message, and the more the communicator can evaluate the value of the message. These two forms of knowledge broadly represent the person's media knowledge and critical thinking.

Media knowledge refers to the cognitive or mental faculties that inform our actions, or "the thought processes that precede and accompany communication" in regard to any given media message(s) (Dillard, Anderson,

& Knobloch, 2002, p. 437). How do you know what to say or do in response to a situation or a prior comment by someone? You know from experience, social learning, and you may even have genetic templates of language use regarding such things as the relevance of subject–object or subject–verb agreement, past versus present tense, and so forth. Knowledge can be understood in part by distinguishing content knowledge from procedural knowledge.

Content knowledge broadly refers to the storage and accessibility of cognitive representations of the symbols, syntax, goals, plans, situations, people, objects, and other elements of behavior that are involved in generating and comprehending meaning and messages. Content knowledge is *what* we know about a message or communication event. These elements are dynamically stored and indexed in memory as knowledge structures, and are thought to be guided by efficiency, memory, and means-ends reasoning in retrieval and usage (Beatty, Heisel, Pascual-Ferrá, & Berger, 2015; McCornack, Morrison, Paik, Wisner, & Zhu, 2014). Such knowledge is accessed in order to comprehend the context, its goal formation, and personal interest and capabilities for performance in complex social interactions. Of course, the learning processes involved in developing such knowledge will depend in part on the emotional components and outcomes of such knowledge use in actual communication encounters (Meyer, 2013). Over time as we develop as adults, such knowledge structures become more and more overlearned as they become intuitive or relatively automatic. People lacking in such mental structures are likely to be more inclined toward blurting the first thing that comes to mind, which has been shown to relate to less sophisticated analysis of arguments, more aggressiveness, lying, and less ability to take the perspective of others (Hample, Richards, & Skubisz, 2013).

There could be any number of categorizations of practical bins or structures relevant to media competence. With relatively little neurological research, and only some conceptual effort to examine communication knowledge as it applies to competent media use (e.g., Namkoong, et al., 2017), a more intuitive set of categories is suggested in the MEDIA model of competence. Utilizing the best available research methods, and informed by a knowledge of relevant theories and the history of media, these categories of content knowledge include the acquisition and analysis of the credibility or expertise of the source of any given mediated message, the broader context within which the message occurred, the topical content of the message, and what kinds of effects it had or may yet have. These represent relatively standard *topoi* for acquiring knowledge of any rhetorical event.

Procedural knowledge involves all those aspects of mental access, assembly, and production involved in producing the actual skilled behavior of communication (Greene, 2003). Such knowledge obviously accesses content knowledge, but assembles it based on procedural cognitive units in long-term memory about how such content knowledge can be enacted (Greene, 1997). Such units are activated by experiences in a given encounter, as well as communicative goals and intentions. As just one example, Han (2018) found that frequency of use of social media correlated to the perceived communication competence of tweets. They will be affected by a person's cognitive flexibility, cognitive capacity and load, effort, and prior experience or learning (Hargie, 1993).

In regard to media competence, the general interest is in **critical thinking**, or "the ability to analyze media messages (dig below the surface meaning to recognize senders' motives and alternative meanings) and to evaluate them (for accuracy, credibility, completeness, and usefulness)" (Potter, 2013, p. 422). Some of this comes from experience. In order to think critically, concepts have to be analyzed. *Analysis* represents understanding the extent to which a given issue or referent is comprised of varying elements or processes, and how these elements and processes operate to form the whole (Lee et al., 2015; Lin et al., 2013). **Argument analysis (logos)** involves the use of evidence, claims, reasoning, claims, balance, optimization, acceptability, relevance, sufficiency, and validity of the intended position or stance in the media message.

Abductive analysis represents a type of induction, in which bridging warrants or conclusions are provided for the observation of examples, cases, or instances, often applied to accounting for unusual or surprising experiences or observations. That is, it is a mode of thought that combines induction and deduction in moving from conjectures to tests and back to conjectures, engaging the interactions between explanations and data to formulate the most plausible explanation (Mirza et al., 2014; McKaughan, 2008; Singer, 2008). In the MEDIA model, abduction serves somewhat the same role as Toulmin's rebuttal—the ability to conjure reasonable alternative hypotheses or explanations, and to test these rival explanations against the message under evaluation.

Source analysis (ethos) refers to all the due diligence that needs to be paid to the legitimacy of the source of the media message. Is the source reliable, trustworthy, competent, distracting, or otherwise relevant to the processing of the message. Finally, many media messages seek to evoke emotions as part of their persuasive appeal. *Affect analysis* (*pathos*) refers to the reflective consideration of the ways in which the media message is attempting to (or succeeding or failing in) evoking a particular emotional response in its consumers. "Skillful navigation of persuasive environments … demands a reflective attitude—a kind of self-monitoring that attends to one's engagement with, and responsiveness to, the visuals in their environment" (Groarke et al., 2016, p. 232).

Box 23.1 Ethical Issues

Mediated communication is now the most prominent mode of communication in our society. Many interpersonal and mass communication ethical concerns can be applied here. But many additional ethical concerns also emerge. Most of these new ethical concerns surround the issues of reality and privacy.

Fake Online Accounts

Fake online accounts come in many forms. Some accounts, such as *catfishing*, or the act of creating a fake online profile in order to target an individual, is typically created by a single individual in order to deceive another individual. But other fake accounts, such as bots, are mass created (often managed by *troll farms*) to infiltrate online platforms in order to achieve a larger social goal, such as Russia using attempting to influence the 2016 presidential election (Mueller, 2019). The creation of fake accounts is an ethical concern, but so is the sharing of information from fake accounts. Sometimes we truly believe accounts are real, but other times we don't bother to confirm the legitimacy of the source before we click the share button. In those cases, we become part of the problem of ignorantly sharing un-checked information from fake accounts.

Terms and Conditions

Have you ever read the *terms and conditions* of a social media account from start to finish? Don't worry, you're not alone. A survey of 2,000 adult consumers found 91% of them agree to terms and conditions without reading them first (Deloitte, 2017). The main reason for this is that terms and conditions are purposely written in a manner to deter the desire to read them: small font, long length, convoluted statements, etc. As more and more major media corporations experience data hacks and the loss of "secure" user data, government and voluntary regulations surrounding the ease of understanding—and denying—terms and conditions are slow-growing. But the vast majority of terms and conditions for media companies are designed to be two choices: agree or don't use the service. So most people continue to select agree without bothering to read the conditions.

User Data

In a similar vein, one of the most common conditions that users agree to in media terms and conditions contracts is the collecting of personal data. This data can sometimes directly identify you, such as your bank storing your social security number, and sometimes it's de-identified, such as Facebook marking you a "1" if you select female and a "2" if you select male. Most of this data is used to hypertarget advertisements to your account. This is why that pair of shoes in your Amazon cart continues to show up in advertisements on your Facebook wall. But there are few regulations surrounding the use of this data—or, more important, misuse of this data. The question is, does this data need to be collected? Some argue that collecting personal data is a misuse of corporate power—that is, that it is generally unnecessary and puts users' privacy at risk. Others argue that collecting personal data enhances user experiences and allows for a more integrated information system that makes users' lives easier. Although one could argue the decision to have personal information collected is up to each individual user, the pervious discussion regarding the reading of terms and conditions suggests that's just a fallacy created to make people think they're in control of their data.

Collectively, these forms of critical thinking will inform other forms of thinking important to comprehending media messages, such as synthesizing such knowledge into evaluative interpretations and conclusions about the media message (Lee et al., 2015; Lin et al., 2013). "New communication technologies use rhetorical structures and strategies different from but analogous to more familiar forms of logic and reasoning" (Warnick, 2002, p. 262). When applied to analysis of media arguments, these knowledge processes allow a consumer to engage in *verification*, or the testing of argument validity and evidence adequacy (Osborne, Erduran, & Simon, 2004; Stapleton & Wu, 2015). "What might count as verification of this reflective monitoring?" One criterion is articulability—that is, can someone articulate the persuasive and logical forces that are in play on any given visual occasion?" (Groarke et al., 2016, p. 232). Such verification involves questioning and assessing the extent to which a mediated message involves a claim, whether and how it provides evidence to support that claim, and how visual elements of the message comprise a set of logical relations or argument that complement the message.

As an example of the types of verification that can be applied to media, one can turn to traditional tests of evidence (Deane et al., 2018). For example, if an advertisement has an actor wearing white lab or medical coat speaking from what appears to be a clinical setting, and is narrating information about a new drug, it is reasonable to ask questions of this type of evidence (see **Table 23.1**).

Skills Components of Media Competence

Assuming a competent user has the appropriate motivational stance, and has engaged the media context and content with appropriate knowledge and critical thinking, the remaining concerns of competence are the implementation or translation of such motivation and knowledge into actual messages. Even though mediated messages increasingly involve simultaneous face-to-face feedback in which the roles of sender and receiver are combined (i.e., FaceTime, videoconferencing, multiparty games, virtual reality environments), for the sake of focus, the MEDIA model respects a common distinction between the reception or consumption of such messages, and the production or prosumption of such messages (Chen et al., 2011; Koc & Barut, 2016; Lin et al., 2013). This distinction is important for media competence given the extent to which media still permit communicators to elect more asynchronous modes of message construction and distribution, and the selection of which medium to use is one of the critical skills of competent mediated communication.

The first set of competent media messaging skills involve information-seeking. The process of pursuing requisite information through media, whether to reduce uncertainty about a situation, to purchase an item, or to settle a wager in an argument with a friend, involves a counterintuitively complex set of skills (see, e.g., Robson & Robinson, 2015; Savolainen, 2002, 2017a, 2017b). As immersion in a mediated social environment increases, it is challenging to know which messages to attend to, which to investigate further, and which to absorb or accept as legitimate or important. In the MEDIA model,

TABLE 23.1: Exemplary Evidence Tests of Visual Arguments

Exemplary Verification Queries For an Advertisement
• Is the ad proposing an opinion or fact?
• What details in the ad are relevant to the main idea (i.e., is the drug safe and effective)?
• What is the main purpose of the ad?
• What idea(s), argument(s) support this main purpose?
• How extensive, accurate, and valid are the arguments, evidence, and reasoning?
• In what ways do the visual, auditory, and textual aspects of the ad combine to influence its stance?
• Does the ad take into account reasonable counterarguments or evidence?
• Is the ad ethical (i.e., does it avoid plagiarism, symbolic aggression; is it culturally sensitive, etc.)?

these complex processes are summarized in four basic competencies: Accessing, researching, networking, and navigating.

Accessing refers to the ability to obtain, examine, or retrieve relevant information from media (Chen, et al., 2011). This ability hinges on such processes as locating and establishing the ability to utilize whatever optimal media are available for obtaining relevant information to a given search objective. For example, one of the most common modes of accessing information in today's environment is to simply "Google something" (Georgas, 2015), where the Google search engine has become a verb for accessing needed information. People increasingly access voice-moderated assistants such as Siri. However, only a relatively small percentage of the population has access to the more serious forms of information-seeking, such as the scholarly search engines at research institutions of higher learning (Johnson, Rowley, & Sbaffi, 2016). Given the relative value of scholarly research, and especially the evidentiary advantages of blind peer-reviewed journal scholarship (see Chapter 5), access becomes an important mediator of consuming the most competent media content.

Assuming that a person has access to the best media content, the ability to conduct competent research on that information becomes important. **Researching** here refers to the ability to discern the most credible (reliable, expert, trustworthy) and relevant information from accessible information regarding a specified topic area (Groenendijk et al., 2018). This will involve some of the critical modes of thinking referred to earlier, but adds the actual behaviors involved in research. For example, seeking out multiple sources on any given topic, seeking the most comprehensive sources (e.g., meta-analyses in scholarly peer-reviewed journal articles), using multiple search terms and their derivatives or synonyms, seeking the oldest and historical sources on a topic, and using multiple search platforms, all illustrate best practices for researching any given media content. Finally, although increasingly jejune and arcane to millennial generations, researching includes such activities as using physical libraries, collections, and, of course, direct experience and observation to inform the development of media content (Georgas, 2015).

Search engines and Google will not always resolve a person's interest in a given media message. Consider, for example, the popular app Yelp. It is designed to capitalize on collective social network sources of knowledge.

Frequently we trust the wisdom of the crowd more than we might the website of a given restaurant, or the advice of a single acquaintance. In the explosion of social media, blogs, discussion forums, and mediated social networks organized around common interests, we often seek information from others as sources of insight. This **networking** process involves the ability to interact with strong and weak social network ties to access information not readily available from traditional research methods.

Finally, once media and network sources are accessed, it is important to understand how to move within and across such platforms or modes of information-seeking. This involves the ability of **navigating**, or the ability to utilize multiple transmedia platforms for accessing, researching, and networking for information (Literat, 2014; Young, 2015). For example, approximately 70 to 90% of Google search queries never navigate past the first page of results (Shelton & Forbes Agency Council, 2017).

Some people tend to engage in lurking—observing, reading, listening to, and watching media rather than contributing to such media. However, the norm of reciprocity clearly demonstrates that the vast majority of time that a person receives media messages, the person will seek ways of contributing or responding with media messages (Spitzberg, 2019). Of course, this is particularly true of interactive media such as social media, telephony, personalized email, and business transactions. Thus, a significant part of media competence is not just receiving and evaluating media content, but producing such media content and messages. The MEDIA model proposes two type of skills involved in producing media content: Functional prosumption skills (consisting of construction skills and presentation skills) and critical prosumption skills.

Functional prosumption skills refer to those skills involved in the technical production of media content, as well as the delivery or performance of those skills in the form of an actual message design or content delivery. A competent media user needs to know how to produce certain messages. This *production* skill refers to the ability to utilize transmedia platforms to design and implement mediated messages reflecting intended meanings and influences (Lin et al., 2013). An analogue might be the ability to use a typewriter keyboard, or to use PowerPoint to draw images for a presentation. Many baby boomers, for example, may be able to use Facebook, but more millennials are able to use Instagram. Either group might be able to learn (i.e., gain the knowledge needed), but even then, their skills at using these platforms would tend to vary by generational cohort.

A second functional prosumption skill involves the ability to interpret and develop multiple abstract models of real-world processes, referred to as **simulation** (Literat, 2014; Young, 2015). For example, the conceiving, generating, and use of a PowerPoint or Prezi presentation, using the graphics tools in those platforms, is a form of simulating ideas and intended meanings in visual form to complement or reinforce those meanings. Simulation employs processes of visual, audio, and textual forms of analogy and metaphor to translate one set of ideas into another communicative form to represent those ideas.

When seeking information, communicators often seek out what others in their social networks think about something. They also often need to tap into the knowledge of those social networks when creating media messages. Working on group projects, using Doodle polls to coordinate meetings, employing Dropbox to share and coedit files, and employing media in group network contexts, all engage the skill of **collaboration**, or the ability to navigate across diverse communities to transform social network ties into social and intellectual capital relevant to a media project.

Finally, creating a mediated message does not mean that message gets out to those who are the intended receivers of that message. A significant portion of today's business environment is increasingly oriented to optimizing the distribution and targeting of mediated messages to the most or best audiences. This **distribution** skill represents the ability to transmit and target mediated messages optimally to intended and accessible audiences (Lee et al., 2015; Lin et al., 2013).

Designing and distributing media messages that have low quality, lack finesse or panache, or are awkward or vulgar may sometimes work as intended. Media competence, however, seeks higher qualities in message delivery. Media competence is not just about getting the message out, but in developing better messages. Better messages, whether verbal or nonverbal, mediated or unmediated, will generally be comprised of four general dimensions of quality: attentiveness, composure, coordination, and expressiveness (Spitzberg, 2006, 2013a; see Chapter 13).

Any given media message needs to be adapted to its intended audience. Competent media use is **attentive**: Does the media content, the medium selected for its delivery, its tone, and its perspective respect, show concern for, and relevance to, the intended receiver or audience(s) of that message? Attentiveness means that competent media messages are more likely to be adapted and personalized to, and take into account the perspective of, the audiences that receive the message.

Media competence also involves the ability to demonstrate **composure**, which reflects confidence, assertiveness and coherence in the composition and enactment of mediated messages. Just as confident speakers tend to be viewed as more charismatic and competent, so are those who deliver confidently worded texts and coherently composed visuals, which reflect forethought, self-control, and deliberateness of conception.

As media become more and more synchronous in their technological capacity, we increasingly attend to issues of timing in our use and interaction with media. **Coordination** skill refers to the ability to manage the contextual and chronemic aspects of mediated interaction involving responsiveness, proportionality, and timing of mediated messages. How long should we wait before responding to a media message? How long is too long of a text or email? How is the best way of opening a greeting or salutation, and how do we know that a mediated conversation (e.g., email chain) comes to a mutually negotiated close? These are all aspects of the social etiquette of mediated interaction.

Finally, whether textual, visual, auditory, and/or some combination, mediated messages have the potential to be **expressive**, which involves the ability to infuse animation, sonic creativity, variability, activity, and novelty into mediated messages. A particular example of expressiveness is the ability some media users demonstrate in their ability to incorporate interesting humor, memes, or other interesting devices and tropes into their everyday media messages.

Being able to merely produce and delivery media messages is essential to competent media use. Such use may reflect the majority of everyday or routine media communication with one another. The most competent media use, however, is likely to depend on the degree to which **critical prosumption skills** are used. These highly interrelated and overlapping skills represent the ability to apply interpretive lenses that facilitate or enhance the appropriate, effective, and adapted use of media content and form for optimal audience response.

Creation prosumption skills refer to the ability to innovate of new conceptions or representations of intended mediated messages (Chen et al., 2011; Lee et al., 2015; Lin et al., 2013). It involves imagination, out-of-the-box thinking, and the ability to employ cognitive heuristics to inform the generation of new forms, relationships, concepts, images, sounds, symbolic frames, and texts. It involves novel and adaptive thinking, opportunistic attention, cognitive flexibility, initiative, risk-taking, curiosity, and confidence (Puccio, 2017). Creation involves finding a balance between convergent and divergent creative thinking and practice, fluid intelligence, and reflective thinking (Corgnet, Espin, & Hernán-González, 2016). It has long been understood as an important skill to communicating competently (Branham, 1980; Lefroy & McKinley, 2011), and evidence indicates it can be increased by training in creative thinking and practice (Perry & Karpova, 2017). Creation leans heavily on a process known as **bricolage**, or an ability to make do with what is at hand (Baker & Nelson, 2005; Wu, Liu & Zhang, 2017). Think of a tinkerer in a workshop making something useful with the pieces and parts from different products never originally intended for what the bricoleur is seeking to make. While creation is capable of innovating new ideas from little or nothing, the bricolage process tends to work with what already exists and is available (Duymedjian & Rüling, 2010), including capitalizing on a person's existing social capital (Andersen, 2008).

A skill that is likely to facilitate creation is **exploration**, or the ability to experiment and engage media *qua* media; to pursue media capabilities for the joy or pure playfulness of the experience (Groenendijk et al., 2018). Exploration, or play, reflects people who are able to tinker with and go spelunking into new games, virtual environments, software, hardware, and imaginative uses of new media, whether for personal or problem-solving objectives. This process of exploration will often emerge through, and enable, the experience of flow (Plester & Hutchison, 2016). **Flow** is "a psychological state in which the person feels simultaneously happy, strong, motivated, active, and cognitively efficient" (Moneta & Csikszentmihalyi, 1999, p. 606). Flow involves a skill-based challenge in which action and awareness merge in the context of clear goals and feedback. In this process of focused entrained activity in a media environment, time is experienced differently, a feeling of optimal experience occurs, and paradoxically, one feels both in control of the activity, and yet merged with and immersed in the activity itself (Fang, Zhang, & Chan, 2013). In experiencing flow, highly challenging activity is matched with one's own highly developed skills or competence in performing that activity (Csikszentmihalyi & LeFevre, 1989; Moneta & Csikszentmihalyi, 1996).

Creation and exploration for their own sake is often desirable, but in the context of media competence, they need to be directed toward an interpretative experience. **Interpretation** prosumption skills refer to the ability to create, portray, or perform different intended mediated identities or roles (Groenendijk et al., 2018). Interpretation, or performance, involves taking on and enacting varied identities in cyberspace, including everything from Snapchat photo embellishments to constructing alternate identities. Whether a communicator invests in continual elaboration and refinement of a singular identity, or explores multiple identities and performances across multiple different media platforms and social networks, interpretation reflects critical attention to issues of appropriateness, effectiveness, and satisfaction in media use.

The final critical prosumption skill is transformation. **Transformation** is the ability to comprehend the logic of and create audio and/or visual mediated representations of textual concepts (Kędra, 2018). The difference between transformation and simulation as a functional prosumption skill is the degree to which the logic or ecosystem of the media transformation alters the representation. Imagine the difference between a movie in two dimensions versus 3D movies—successful transformation requires a rethinking of the visual aesthetic, the logic of spatial relations, and what objects in the two-dimensional screen that need to be projected into or emphasized in the third dimension for the greatest effect. When we break up with someone, we can construct such messages in an email (Weisskirch & Delevi, 2012, 2013), but an understanding of the relative coldness and textual poverty of this medium recommends face-to-face, rather than mediated interaction. Transformation involves an astute sensibility about and sensitivity to the medium and its effects on the message being transformed in relation to the audience comprehension and reception of the message.

Contextual Factors of Media Competence

Media competence is contextual. The possession and competent use of motivation, knowledge, and skills in consuming and producing media communication messages will depend in significant ways on a communicator's individual, social, and sociocultural contexts (Spitzberg,

2014). The first of these, the individual context, refers to the degree to which an individual has access to rich media that have the appropriate reach for the intended audiences and communicative goals. The competence with which a communicator uses media will depend on the degree to which the user perceives the media to provide desired or needed technological *affordances* (Aladwani, 2017; Gill, 2017; Karahanna et al., 2018; Rathnayake & Winter, 2018). Affordances are the functions or outcomes to which a medium is put. Two of these affordances are the richness of the medium and its reach.

In general, *media richness* refers to the capacities of a medium for communicating more complex information in ways that can preserve verbal and nonverbal information, synchrony, and a sense of presence or immediacy and immersion (Timmerman & Madhavapeddi, 2008). Richer media provide affordances that allow a medium to better match contextual needs for privacy or confidentiality, immediacy of feedback, social interaction, information representativeness, affect or emotion, relationship management, and accountability (Palvia, Pinjani, Cannoy, & Jacks, 2011; Sheer, 2011).

A second component of the individual context is the reach of the media (O'Sullivan & Carr, 2017). Here, **reach** refers to the degree to which a medium can (1) be directed or targeted, (2) in unilateral or reciprocal ways, (3) to one or many prospective receivers. Twitter and emails, for example, can be narrowcast to individually targeted persons, or broadcast to mass audiences. Other media such as television, radio, skywriting and billboards are inherently more broadcast forms of media. Twitter can be unilaterally sent to followers who do not have to be followed by the sender, but emails typically involve some potential for being responded to by the receiver.

A second level of context is the social context. A communicator can send out very competent messages, but if no one in that communicator's social network engages the messages, they are likely to fall on digitally deaf ears. For example, the vast majority of Twitter users post few or no tweets, such that 2% of users produce 80% of tweets (Ferrara & Yang, 2015; Rogers-Pettie & Hermann, 2015; Stattner, Eugenie, & Collard, 2015; Szell, Grauwin, & Ratti, 2014; Zhi, Hu, Ming, & Tao, 2011). Furthermore, the vast majority of tweets go no more than one hop, never diffusing further outside of the sender's initial receivers. In one large-scale study, "the probability of a given piece of content becoming 'popular'—meaning that it attracts at least 100 adoptions" was one in a thousand (Goel et al., 2016, p. 189; see also: Bakshy, Hofman, Mason, & Watts, 2011; Pei, Muchnik, Tang, Zheng, & Makse, 2015; Weng, Flammini, Vespignani, & Menczer, 2012; Yang & Counts, 2010). Thus, media competence will always be mediated not just by the medium, but by the extent of the social network and its engagement with the messages sent through those medium.

Media are not used just by individuals in their personal social networks. Users and their social networks are themselves embedded in a broader sociopolitical and cultural context. This sociocultural context includes the political and corporate institutions, racial and ethnic groups and their relations, and socioeconomic concerns such as educational access and utilization, wealth distribution, and the control of or democratic access to these various tangible and social resources.

Media are both proliferating and converging. They are proliferating in the sense that technological innovation is developing more media (faster chips, more wearable technology, more charging options, etc.). They are converging in the sense that any given media device is increasingly merging more technological capabilities (cameras, health monitoring, geolocation, cross-platform capability, etc.). In a society with rapidly evolving dependence on proliferating and converging media, media competence will increasingly require competence in working with multiple media and their various affordances. This capability implies competence in using polymedia—or multiple media.

In a **polymediated** environment, in which all media have to be considered in relationship to one another in regard to their communicative implications, media competence will be dependent on the extent of societal mediatization (Madianou & Miller, 2013). **Mediatization** reflects the extent to which communication media infiltrate, integrate into, and frame everyday behavior (Ampuja, Koivisto, & Väliverronen, 2014; Jansson, 2015). The concept echoes earlier conceptions of medium theory by McLuhan (1964; Kylmälä, 2013) and Meyerwitz (1985, 2008), which examined the role of media formats in framing human activity and experience (Jensen, 2013). "Generally speaking, mediatization is a concept used to analyze critically the interrelation between changes in media and communications on the one hand, and changes in culture and society on the other" (Couldry & Hepp, 2013, p. 197). Thus, whereas communication mediation refers to the use of media to communicate, mediatization refers to the processes by which mediated communication collectively influences and changes or molds sociocultural activities and perceptions (Hepp, 2013).

The tendencies through which we increasingly create our identities on and through media (individualization), detach ourselves from the physical or territorial situation and its attachments (deterritorialization), and experience immediacy through social telepresence and instantaneous access (intermediacy) (Hepp, 2009). These trends are both brought about through media, and the drive for innovation of their commercialization, which, in turn, increase the potential for corporate and institutional surveillance (Jansson, 2013). Further, in a mediatized society, media competence will depend increasingly on demographic and socioeconomic cultural factors that facilitate or constrain access to such media, political investment in media infrastructure, industry structure, and social interest in media (Jansson, 2015).

The Once Future, Now Present, of Mediated Communication

New media are often valorized in utopian visions of society, but they are at least as often envisioned in their more dystopian potential. Both Aldous Huxley's *Brave New World* and George Orwell's iconic *1984* painted bleak pictures of the potential for media to either dissolve our individual initiative, or oppress individualism under the yoke of authoritarian control (Varricchio, 1999). There are many visions and many paths that new media may take. Two of the more dystopic paths that have received attention are the shift to big data and the increasing concentration of ownership and control of the media.

Big Data

According to one estimate, 90% of the world's information ever created has been generated within just the past 2 years (BSA, 2015), and the growth of such information and our capacity for generating, storing, and transmitting it are increasing at substantial rates (Hilbert, 2014; Hilbert & López, 2011). Given the increase in merging technologies onto and into the human body, there are today serious discussions of viewing humans as "aggregates of data" (van der Meulen & Bruinsma, 2018). The McKinsey Institute

estimated that in 2012, "80% of the world's online population use social networks on a regular basis" (Chui et al., 2012, p. 6). The IDC organization estimates that "by 2025, an average connected person anywhere in the world will interact with connected devices nearly 4,800 times per day—basically one interaction every 18 seconds" (Reinsel, Gantz, & Rydning, 2018, p. 3). Examining 225 million hours of digital work time on the RescueTime productivity app, across hundreds of thousands of global users, these users jumped from one task to another task an average of around 300 times per day, switching pages or documents about 1,300 times a day. They checked their communication apps 40 times a day (about once every 7.5 minutes of digital work time), comprising 7% of the entire workday spent on social media, checking social media 14 times per day, or about three times an hour of digital worktime (MacKay, 2018). Another study found that the average smartphone user swipes, taps, or pinches their phone 2,617 times a day, but when asked to estimate their touches of their phone, they generally significantly underestimated such usage (dscout, 2016). A 2012 study by Deal (2015) from the Center for Creative Leadership of "executives, managers, and professionals" found that over three-quarters used smartphones but "60% of those who use smartphones for work are connected to work 19.5 or more hours a day five days a week, and spend about five hours on weekends scanning e-mails, for a total of about 72 hours a week connected to work" (p. 2). Communication by email, phone, and in meetings may comprise from 70 to 95% of a typical employee's workweek (Cross & Gray, 2013). Over 90% of U.S. adults have a cellphone, 90% of whom claim the phone is frequently with them, and up to 75% say they never turn it off (Rainie & Zickuhr, 2015). Over 60% of Americans use YouTube and Facebook, with between 20 and 40% using each of the following apps: Instagram, Pinterest, Snapchat, LinkedIn, Twitter, and WhatsApp (Smith & Anderson, 2018). Such adoption of use leads over half of teens to admit to spending too much time on their cellphones (Jiang, 2018). Yet, approximately 40% report feeling anxious and 25% report feeling lonely when they are without their cellphone (Jiang, 2018).

These digital trends increasingly present prospects for the commodification of people through the big data they generate. **Commodification** is the process through which something is treated as a commodity or object for commercial purposes. Consumers participate in their own commodification, or equation of people with commodities, by agreeing to the value of various apps and technologies, in the process providing personal information to companies and institutions that then profit from such information by advancing their ability to transform the information producers into product or service consumers (Ritzer, 2014, 2015). As wearable technologies such as the Apple watch, biometric sensors, wearable or implanted medical monitoring devices, and the manifold social media platforms, digital books and music, and search queries are increasingly generating enormous amounts of information about each online person's everyday behavior and preferences, there is a Faustian exchange of data for the convenience of the technological affordance (Zelenkauskaite, 2017).

Evolving Uses and Gratifications

Affordances are the technological flip-side of media gratifications—instead of what users get out of the medium, affordances are the functions a medium allows (Fox & McEwan, 2017; Karahanna et al., 2018). So, for example, the earliest cellular phones did not have cameras, and there was little consumer demand for such a technology. But once industry installed the cameras into smartphones, the cameras afforded manifold uses and gratifications that were unforeseen when the technology was initially developed. The medium afforded new uses and gratifications.

Such affordances are developing rapidly through an ongoing process of convergence. **Convergence** is the merging or integration of multiple media affordances into increasingly fewer devices or platforms (Walther, 2017). Potter (2013) explains that the trend in convergence has "rendered the distinctions between [different] mass media as relatively unimportant compared to the similarities" (p. 420). For instance, smartphones today

have more computer power than computers that once required a warehouse to occupy; the fact that one device also contains the ability to make a phone call is irrelevant compared to the similarity in their computing capabilities. Each new generation of computer, smartphone, television, watch, and other devices represent an increasing trend toward converging not only technological affordances, but converging humans with a technologically mediated society, economy, and culture.

Conclusion

We are a wired, wireless, wayward, and often wicked society when it comes to communication media. As history demonstrates, humans will continue to push for advancements in communication technology. Although research demonstrates the changes that these advancements can have in communication patterns, media theory consistently demonstrates the presence in media effects for audience. Current trends in media suggest a greater focus on big data and continued vertical integration. Although it has always been difficult to predict technological advancements, there is no doubt that mediated communication continue to be a predominant mode of human communication.

Credit

FIG. 23.1: Adapted from Patrick B. O'Sullivan and Caleb T. Carr, "Masspersonal Communication: A Model Bridging the Mass-Interpersonal Divide," *New Media and Society*, vol. 20, no. 3. Copyright © 2017 by SAGE Publications.

PART IV

Knowing Why Knowing About Communication Matters

CHAPTER 24

College, Communication, and Careers

Brian H. Spitzberg

LEARNING OBJECTIVES

After reading this chapter, you should be able to do the following:

- Identify and differentiate the prototypical characteristics of generational workers.
- Know the implications of earning successive levels of education degree.
- Know the relative importance of applied knowledge/skills based on employer surveys.
- Classify relative population levels along the communication competence continuum.
- Detect the trends of communication in the evolving job market.
- Recognize the relative value of a business degree vis-à-vis a communication degree.
- Know key factors in predicting employability and career success.
- Identify the role of social networks in career success.

W HAT DO YOU WANT TO BE WHEN YOU grow up? What do you want to do after college? Do you still believe in "the American dream" (even though only slightly more than half of U.S. 18- to 24-year-olds still believe "the American dream is alive"? (Institute of Politics, 2017). These are questions commonly experienced during youth. As we do "grow up," our friends and relatives often continue to inquire, in some regard, to what we intend or hope to "go into," or what career we intend to achieve. This question often becomes quite a quandary for communication majors. The conversation may well proceed like this:

Uncle: "How is school? Remind me, what is your major?"
You: "I'm majoring in communication."
Uncle: "Oh. What can you do with that?"

What can you do with that? This *CITE* text presented what the communication major is about, but it has only occasionally discussed what can be done with this knowledge. At a minimum, you should be more prepared now than before the term began to show your abilities to think, appreciate, and state how different perspectives can provide understanding of communication. Prepare yourself to answer the "what can you do with that" question by discussing the value of different perspectives and by articulating your own view of the significances of human communication.

Much has been debated regarding the millennial and Z-generations and their employability in an increasingly STEM-oriented technological marketplace. Whereas different studies characterize recent generations differently, relatively common stereotypes about millennials do contrast with previous generations (see **Table 24.1**). At the same time, the communication discipline continues to establish its identity in that broader marketplace. Communication majors want to know what career trajectories and opportunities might await their degree completion, but the professional associations affiliated with the National Communication Association provide relatively little evidence to address such practical questions. This chapter examines the roles that communication skills and the communication degree play in the postmillennial marketplace.

TABLE 24.1: Prototypical Characteristics of Generational Workers

Time Period (born between)	Characteristics	Prototypical Attitude
Before 1946 *Traditionalists*	• Loyalists who spent a lifetime at one company and expect to be rewarded with a "gold watch." • Disciplined, rule-abiding, respectful of authority, and accustomed to sacrifice. • Want their experience to be valued. • Prefer formal communication and individual work.	• "How can I help you?" • "Flexibility is a code word for less work getting done." • "If I'm not yelling at you, you're doing fine."
1946–1963 *Baby Boomers*	• Worship the Beatles and clawed their way to the top of the organizational ladder. • Work hard for a cause, be the first to question authority, and desire personal fulfillment at work. • Optimistic and hyper involved in all areas of their lives. • Prefer to be team players and communicate in person; they need to be needed.	• "You'll get your feedback; that's what annual performance reviews are for." • "I paid my dues to get more money, a better title, and a swankier office—what are you going to do?" • "We've been in business for 50 years; we must be doing something right."
1964–1979 *Gen-X*	• Loners or "latchkey kids" who learned to be self-reliant when parents left them alone at home. • Cynical, informal, and task-oriented. • Pioneered the concept of portable skill sets. • Prefer direct communication and doing things their way.	• "Company loyalty—what's that?" • "I can manage my own career better than you, thank you very much." • "Give me the skills or give me death."
1980–1995 *Millennials/Gen-Y*	• Techies whose parents taught them they were entitled to the world. • Confident, collaborative, impatient, entrepreneurial, and socially tolerant. • Work by multitasking in real time. • Prefer e-communication and want continuous exposure to challenges and interesting people.	• "Sorry to interrupt, but you haven't told me how I'm doing in the last hour." • "Let's cut out the red tape and cut it out now." • "How can you help me?"

Source: Levit & Licina (2011).

Communication Is Ubiquitous

Communication is ubiquitous—it is everywhere. As water is to fish, communication is the sea in which people swim. We spend more time every day communicating in one form or another than we do any other overt activity (see, e.g., Callejo, 2013; Cohen, White, & Cohen, 2011; Janusik & Wolvin, 2009; Robinson & Lee, 2014; Stepanikova, Nie, & He, 2010). That is, communication is the primary activity binding almost all human experience. Several estimates indicate that the average person spends about 75 to 90% of their waking hours conversing, reading, writing, listening, or engaging with media such as TV or radio (Callejo, 2013; Cohen et al., 2011; Dunbar et al., 1997; Janusik & Wolvin, 2009; Pentland, 2007; Robinson & Lee, 2014; Stepanikova et al., 2010). Other estimates indicate that U.S. adults spend between 11 and 13 hours a day communicating (Chui et al., 2012; Emanuel et al., 2008), and approximately 9 hours of this is spent with media among 13- to 18-year-olds (Rideout, 2016). New media appear to be increasing our immersion in these communication processes (Twenge, Martin, & Spitzberg, 2018; Twenge, Spitzberg, & Campbell, 2019). By one impossible estimate, in a 24-hour day, college students spend over 28 hours in activities that involve one or more of the communicative activities of talking, writing, reading, and/or listening (Hanson, Drumheller, Mallard, McKee, & Schlegel, 2011)!

Communication activities also saturate the workplace (Keyton et al., 2013). By one estimate, communication by email, phone, and in meetings takes up 70 to 95% of a typical employee's workweek (Cross & Gray, 2013). An extensive analysis of available estimates found between 36 and 56 million business meetings a day in the United States (Keith, 2015). One should also consider the implications that these trends suggest for the modern career. A 2012 study by Deal (2015) from the Center for Creative Leadership of "executives, managers, and professionals" found that over three-quarters used smartphones "to enable flexible work," but that "60% of those who use smartphones for work are connected to work 19.5 or more hours a day five days a week, and spend about five hours on weekends scanning e-mails, for a total of about 72 hours a week connected to work" (p. 2).

Therefore, Communication Competence Is Important

Organizations consistently recognize that professionalism and work ethic, teamwork and collaboration, oral and written communication, and leadership are seen as the most important skills needed by entrants into today's workforce (see **Table 24.2**). **Communication competence**, the ability to communicate appropriately and effectively (see Chapter 13), is often seen as the *most important skill* in business (e.g., Clokie & Fourie, 2016; Mikkelson, York, & Arritola, 2015; Steele & Plenty, 2015). A survey by Pew also indicates the importance the public places on students learning communication skills (**Table 24.3**). Even one of the richest persons in the world, Warren Buffett, espouses that communication skills are the most important skills a prospective employee can learn. Buffett believes that

TABLE 24.2: Employer vs. Student Perceptions of Proficiency in Career Readiness Competencies

Rank	Competency	% of Employers Who Rated Recent Grads "Proficient"	% of Students Who Considered Themselves "Proficient"
1	Professionalism/Work Ethic	42.5	89.4
2	Oral/Written Communications	41.6	79.4
3	Critical Thinking/Problem Solving	55.8	79.9
4	Teamwork/Collaboration	77.0	85.1
5	Leadership	33.0	70.5
6	Digital Technology	65.8	59.9
7	Career Management	17.3	40.9
9	Global/Intercultural Fluency	20.7	34.9

Source: National Association of Colleges and Employers (2017).

TABLE 24.3: Skills Considered Important to Getting Ahead

SKILLS: "Regardless of whether you think these skills are good to have, which ones do you think are most important for children to get ahead in the world today?"	% Selecting "Yes"
Communication skills	90
Reading skills	86
Math skills	79
Teamwork skills	77
Logic skills	74
Science skills	58
Athletic skills	25
Music skills	24
Art skills	23

Source: Pew Research Center (2015a).

communication skills and public speaking increase one's earnings potential by 50% over that employee's lifetime (Gallo, 2017).

Hart Research Associates (HRA) conducted an online survey of 318 executives at private-sector and nonprofit organizations, including owners, CEOs, presidents, C-suite level executives, and vice presidents. HRA's survey found that over 90% considered "interpersonal skills" and the ability to "communicate clearly" essential to innovation (Hart Research Associates [HRA], 2013; see **Figure 24.1**). Similarly, a survey of human resources professionals asking the defining characteristics of "professionalism" found

FIGURE 24.1: Skills Employers Consider Essential for Innovation

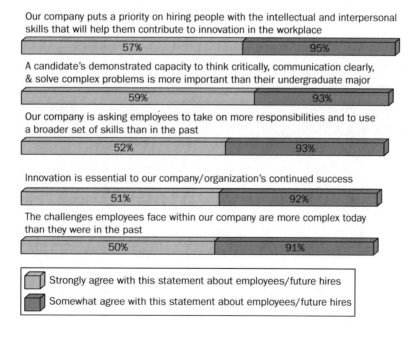

that "the most frequently cited qualities are … interpersonal skills (33.6%), work ethic (27.3%), appearance (25.3%), and communication skills (24.9%)" (Polk-Lepson Research Group, 2012, p. 19). A study of health communication practitioners found that the communication degree is perceived as the most useful field of study for working in health communication (McKeever, 2014). Communication skills are clearly the most commonly sought attributes in candidate resumes (see **Table 24.4**).

Even projections into the future indicate that skills that are foundationally dependent on communication will be important, such as cross-cultural competency, sense making, transdisciplinary literacy, virtual collaboration, and new media literacy (Institute for the Future, 2011). More contemporary surveys of employers continue to demonstrate the importance of communication skills.

Communication Competence Is Becoming More Important

The big picture of the U.S. workforce is that it has changed significantly since the 1970s. Specifically, a strong skill shift in employment is occurring. "The biggest increases by far have been in education and health services, which have more than doubled as a percentage of total jobs; … The overall trend is a giant employment increase in industries based on personal interaction" (Colvin, 2015). This represents a significant **skills shift** in the economy.

These trends are dramatically demonstrated by **Figures 24.2** and **24.3**, from data based on analyses of want ads by Levy and Murnane (2004) (see, Koenig, 2011). Over a period of 30 years, jobs requiring routine tasks have been on the decline, and jobs requiring complex

TABLE 24.4: Attributes Employers Seek on a Candidate's Résumé

Skill	% Employers Seeking
Communication skills (written)	82.0
Problem-solving skills	80.9
Ability to work in a team	78.7
Initiative	74.2
Analytical/quantitative skills	71.9
Strong work ethic	70.8
Communication skills (verbal)	67.4
Leadership	67.4
Detail-oriented	59.6
Technical skills	59.6
Flexibility/adaptability	58.4
Computer skills	55.1
Interpersonal skills (relates well to others)	52.8
Organizational ability	43.8
Strategic planning skills	38.2
Tactfulness	25.8
Creativity	23.6
Friendly/outgoing personality	22.5
Entrepreneurial skills/risk-taker	16.9
Fluency in a foreign language	11.2

Source: National Association of Colleges and Employers (2019).

FIGURE 24.2: Economy Shifting from Blue Collar to Communication-Based Occupations

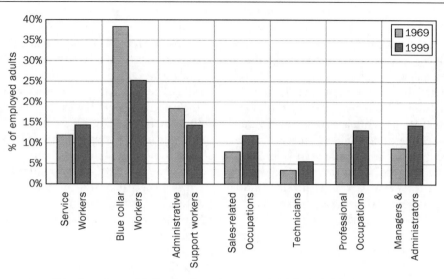

Notes: Occupations are listed in order of increasing average salary. Authors' calculations based on the March 1970 and March 2000 U.S. Census Bureau Current Populations Surveys

communication have increased. In this study, "complex communication" includes skills "eliciting critical information and conveying a convincing interpretation of it" (Koenig, 2011, p. 8). Even currently, among the most sought skills on resumes are problem-solving skills (83%),

ability to work in a team (83%), written communication skills (80%), leadership (73%), verbal communication skills (68%), and interpersonal skills (55%) (NACE, 2017).

A related trend is the extent to which traditional jobs and careers will be displaced by artificial intelligence,

FIGURE 24.3: Proportional Decline of Routine Jobs and Increase in Complex Communication Jobs

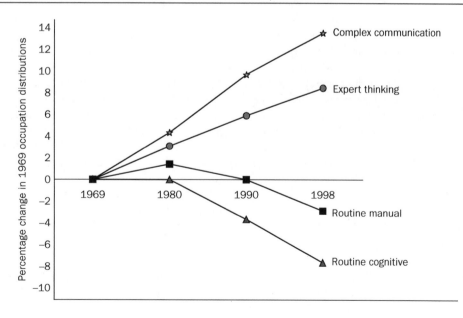

automation, and computerization. By one estimate, up to 47% of today's jobs are at high risk of displacement by technological developments (Frey & Osborne, 2017), although when a variety of mainly communication-related job tasks are accounted for (e.g., exchanging information, training others, presenting, selling, consulting, influencing, etc.), far more jobs are likely to be secure from automation (Arntz, Gregory, & Zierahn, 2017). Moreover, careers at the lowest risk of displacement are in the fine arts, those that require originality and human heuristics, the development of novel ideas and artifacts, and jobs involving negotiation, persuasion, social perceptiveness, and assisting and caring for others. Thus, the lowest-risk careers include "most occupations in education, healthcare, as well as arts and media jobs" (Frey & Osborne, 2017, p. 266).

Given the inexorable trend of the marketplace in general toward more complex, more information-based, more skills-based (Wegman, Hoffman, Carter, Twenge, & Guenole, 2018), and more communication-based occupations, organizations are increasingly likely to expect their new hires to be prepared for such work. According to a LinkedIn (2019) survey of over 5,000 talent professionals in 35 countries, 91% of these professionals indicated that *soft skills* were a trend "very important to the future of recruiting and HR," by far the most important trend noted (p. 3). Soft skills are abilities that facilitate competent and collaborative interaction with others. Such skills also show up in NACE's (2019) research, in which critical thinking and problem solving, teamwork and collaboration, professionalism and work ethic, oral and written communication are rated as the "most essential need" as career competencies. LinkedIn's (2018) own analyses also indicate that "oral communication remains the skill group with the biggest shortage in nearly every city across the country," and that "people with these skills are hired at faster rates than people without these skills." The Institute for the Future (2011) predicted that the future workforce will prioritize skills such as sense-making, social intelligence, novel and adaptive thinking, cross-cultural competence, new media literacy, transdisciplinarity, and virtual collaboration.

People Overestimate Their Own Communication Competence

As millennials pursue fulfillment through their education and careers, a variety of other changes are evolving in the character of future U.S. employees. We are under duress: About half of all incoming college freshmen consider their emotional health to be average or below average, and almost a third feel "overwhelmed" (HERI, 2011). It is not unusual that college students seek fulfillment in their careers. Of freshmen surveyed, substantial majorities rate themselves as above average or in the top 10% of their peers in regard to ability to work cooperatively with diverse people (78%), tolerance of others with different beliefs (72%), seeing the world from someone else's perspective (66%), ability to discuss and negotiate controversial issues (62%), and openness to having their own views challenged (60%) (HERI, 2009). College seniors also have reasonably high opinions of their critical-thinking skills. Based on the HERI survey of college seniors, approximately 85% strongly or somewhat strongly consider their critical-thinking skills and their problem-solving skills as one of their major strengths (HERI, 2014, p. 1).

All of this is consistent with a general *self-referential bias*, referred to as the **better-than-average** or **Wobegon** effect (Kruger, 1999; Kruger & Dunning, 1999; Kruger, Epley, Parker, & Ng, 2005; Varnum, 2015). For example, college students think they are a scale point higher in attractiveness than their friends think those students are (7-point scale; Hitsch, Hortaçsu, & Ariely, 2010a, 2010b; Pozzebon et al., 2012). People think they are "better in bed" than others (Beggan, Vencill, & Garos, 2013). Also, people think that up to 80% of other people overestimate their accuracy of communication (Fay et al., 2010). People are generally not very accurate at assessments regarding their own communication behavior (Gosling, John, Craik, & Robins, 1998; Hicks & McNulty, 2019), much less the impressions that others have of them (Spitzberg, 1993, 1994).

This better-than-average effect applies to graduating seniors in college and to the marketplace to which those seniors aspire. For example, a study by PayScale.com in 2017 found that although "only 50% of managers feel recent grads are prepared for a full-time job, 87% of grads feel they're ready for the big time." Employees systematically tend to rate their own job performance higher than supervisors rate the performance of those employees (Jaramillo, Carrillat, & Locander, 2005; Korsgaard, Maglino, & Lester, 2004). Ironically, as employees inflate their relative self-assessed competence, the worse their actual performance becomes (Atkins & Wood, 2002; Ehrlinger et al., 2008; Eichinger & Lombardo, 2003, 2004). So, it appears that college students overestimate their own skill levels, and thus may remain ignorant of their preparation for the job market.

Communication Incompetence Is Common

A major question arises: Are college freshmen *actually* better than average, or do they only *think* they are? A few objective bases by which a definitive answer can be derived. Some more subjective bases exist. For example, compared to college students in the 1980s, recent U.S. college students are approximately 30% more narcissistic (Twenge et al., 2008), and about 30% less empathic (Konrath et al., 2010).

The research on the population level of communication competence is limited. Existing scarce research indicates that substantial portions of the population cannot communicate in a variety of common encounters and contexts. Summarizing across a variety of studies, Spitzberg (Spitzberg, 2000, 2013a, 2015a, 2015b; Spitzberg & Cupach, 2002) estimates that between 7 and 25% of people in the general population probably experience significant constraints in their communication competence to some consistent degree. Of course, these communication skill deficits vary by situation and over time. A person competent at communicating on a first date might be incompetent in negotiating contracts, and a person competent at negotiating contracts may be incompetent at being humorous at a party (Spitzberg & Brunner, 1991).

One way to think about this is that communication competence is a continuum, ranging from extremely incompetent to extremely competent. The majority of us, the majority of the time, communicate at a moderate level of competence. Only rarely do most of us communicate terribly, and only rarely do we communicate in such a manner that the other interactants leave the encounter with vivid memories of how excellent we did so.

When employers are asked how competent they believe (or experience) their new college graduate hires to be, the results accord with the "moderate" evaluation. For example, **Table 24.5** reveals one survey of employers, indicating that new graduates get a B+ for verbal communication skills and for leadership, but a B for teamwork and a B– for written communication ability.

Cengage (2018) found that a majority of employers found it very or somewhat difficult to find qualified applicants with critical-thinking skills (64%), listening skills (54%), communication skills (55%), and interpersonal skills (55%). In one survey, 99% of employers considered oral and written communication skills as "essential," yet they considered that only 42% of candidates as "proficient" at these skills (NACE, 2017). Surveys of employers and studies of job ads demonstrate that "writing, communication skills, and organizational skills are scarce everywhere. These skills are in demand across nearly every occupation" (Burningglass Technologies, 2015, p. 4).

So millennial college students and graduates may not be quite as well-prepared as they think. If so, then this may call into question the very value of the college degree. Yet, the data continue to indicate that there are few better preparations for the workplace and career development than a college degree.

TABLE 24.5: Employers Rate Recent Graduates on Career Readiness Competencies

Competencies	Average Rating (1 = Not at all proficient; 5 = Extremely proficient)
Teamwork/Collaboration	3.83
Digital Technology	3.76
Critical Thinking/Problem Solving	3.64
Oral/Written Communications	3.49
Professionalism/Work Ethic	3.31
Leadership	3.31
Global/Multi-cultural Fluency	3.13
Career Management	3.05

Source: NACE (2019).

Does College Education Help in General?

Around 1960, about 7% of female and about 15% of male adults 25 to 29 years of age had bachelor's degree or better. By 2013, approximately 35% of female and 30% of male adults 25 to 29 years had a bachelor's degree or higher (Bauman, 2016). As of 2014, 29% of males and 29% females had a bachelor's degree or higher (U.S. Census Bureau, 2014). Today, slightly over 40% of the population aged 18 to 24 is currently enrolled in college/higher education (U.S. Census Bureau, 2014). Importantly, the overall 6-year graduation rate for full-time, first-time undergraduates pursuing a BA is around 60%" (U.S. Department of Education, 2017).

So, a minority of the U.S. population never seeks a college degree, and 40% of those people who start college do not graduate. Thus, less than a majority of the U.S. population seeks higher education, a relatively small percentage of the U.S. population is currently enrolled in higher education, and a substantial proportion of those who begin college do not finish. As a result, only approximately one-third of the U.S. population has a bachelor's degree or higher, with substantially fewer still attaining a graduate degree. Only 21% of recent communications and journalism majors have completed a graduate degree (Carnevale, Cheah, & Hanson, 2015).

What do college students expect from their degree? Nationwide in 1967, "86% of respondents checked 'developing a meaningful philosophy of life,' more than double the number who said 'being very well off financially'" (Bauerlein, 2015). In a 2015 survey, by dramatic contrast, 46% checked "developing a meaningful philosophy of life," and 82% checked "being very well off financially" (Eagan et al., 2016, p. 53).

These results are qualified by research from a big data approach to assess the zeitgeist of the U.S. population. If the dollar dominates the consciousness of the current generation, so does an interest in personal fulfillment through work. Using Google's nGram search engine (Google Books, n.d.), **Figure 24.4** (Panels A and B) indicate that the phrase "a secure career" is plummeting in common usage, whereas "a fulfilling career" is trending (Newport, 2012).

College graduates tend to subjectively believe that their time and effort were justified. "Among survey respondents who graduated from a four-year college, 74% say their college education was very useful in helping them grow intellectually; 69% say it was very useful in helping them grow and mature as a person; and 55% say it was very useful in helping them prepare for a job or career" (Taylor et al., 2011, p. 2). Furthermore, in a large-scale survey of 2014 college graduating seniors, "among students planning to work full time, 35.7% of students rate their preparedness for employment as 'a major strength,' 37.2% rate it 'somewhat strong,' and 19.8% rate it 'average.' Over a fifth of these seniors intended to pursue further graduate studies prior to entering the job market to attain even further preparation" (HERI, 2014, p. 1). In short, several bases exist upon which a college degree, in general, and for most people, result in ***net value*** relative to the costs and investments involved, both personally and societally.

FIGURE 24.4: Google nGram for "A Secure Career" (Panel A) and for "A Fulfilling Career" (Panel B)

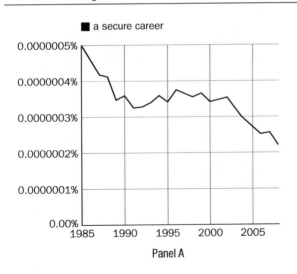

Panel A

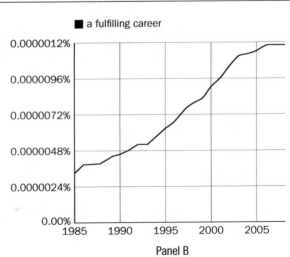

Panel B

Earnings Benefits

As the United States, and much of the developed world, has shifted increasingly away from an agrarian to a manufacturing, to a service, and, more recently, to an information economy, higher education has become increasingly essential. Good jobs in manufacturing have been declining, especially for those with only a high school education or less (Carnevale, Ridley, Cheah, Strohl, & Campbell, 2019). The influences of globalization, automation, upskilling and the replacement of manufacturing with skilled service-related professions such as health care and new media "have coalesced to make postsecondary education and training the dominant pathway to good jobs that pay a median of $65,000" (Carnevale, Strohl, Ridley, & Gulish, 2018, p. 5). This appears to continue a trend. A 2012 survey of alumni of five MA programs in health communication concurred that "there remains a strong market for health communication graduates" (Edgar et al., 2015, p. 365; see also: Edgar et al., 2016). The nature of the job market is moving toward a more educated workforce.

The **earnings benefits** of a college degree do not go unnoticed by their recipients. Consider the following lifetime earnings as relative benefits of higher education:

- In the U.S. in 2017, those having less than a high school diploma earn approximately $500 a week.
- Those with a high school diploma but no or only some college earn approximately $750 a week.
- Those with an Associate degree earn over $800 a week.
- Those with a Bachelor's degree earn almost $1,200 a week.
- Those with a Master's degree earn $1,400 a week.
- Those with a Doctoral or Professional degree earn between $1,740 and $1,835 a week (Torpey, 2018).

When accumulated over the working lifespan of a worker, compared to those with just a high school degree, a BA degree represents approximately $900,000 added salary for men and $630,000 for women, whereas a graduate degree represents an added $1.5 million for men and $1.1 million for women (Tamborini, ChangHwan, & Sakamoto, 2015).

It is also noteworthy that 97% of CEOs of the Standard and Poor stock market index top 500 have college degrees (SpencerStuart, 2004).

As Berger observed "Advanced degrees have greater salary impact on any given role" than most other single factors (2017).

So college has benefits, but is it cost-beneficial? An analysis by this author of data from *Money Magazine* (*Money*, 2017) shows that the cost of a college degree (not including financial aid) is correlated almost .30 ($r = .29$) with the early career earnings of graduates from those colleges. The same data show that the average cost of the education ($M = \$44.917$) achieves a greater return on that investment in the initial earnings of the graduate ($M = \$46,813$); that is, the cost of the entire education pays for itself in initial earnings, on average. An economic scenario analyzed by Johnson, Mejia, Ezekiel, and Zeiger (2013) indicates that college is still an exceptional value, even taking into account the escalating costs and loan burdens involved in contemporary higher education (Abel & Deitz, 2014b). As Athreya and Price (2013) conclude: "Even taking into account the rising costs of higher education, investing in a bachelor's degree remains highly lucrative for most college-ready students" (p. 1).

As a result of such trends, a bachelor's degree or greater is increasingly considered the necessary key to the door to the middle class:

> [T]he middle class is dispersing into two opposing streams of upwardly mobile college-haves and downwardly mobile college-have-nots … since 1983, among prime-age workers between the ages of 25 and 54: Earnings of people with some college or an Associate's degree have increased by 15%; earnings of people with Bachelor's degrees have increased by 34%; [and] earnings of people with graduate degrees have increased by 55%. (Carnevale et al., 2010, pp. 3–4).

In brief, people without college degrees increasingly will be left behind, and those with college degrees will have likely success in achieving a position in the middle class or better.

(Un)Employment Benefits

The economic benefits of college education extend well beyond earnings while employed—they also apply to the likelihood of being employed in general, and avoid being unemployed—an **employment benefit**. College-educated people are substantially less likely to ever experience unemployment. College graduates are far less likely to be the employees laid off in times of economic recession (Carnevale, Jayasundera, & Gulish, 2016). The value of a college degree is also expected to protect employability from automation and robotic types of displacement in the marketplace. One analysis found that up to 30% of the country's workforce is at risk of robotic replacement by the 2030s, and workers without a college degree are almost four times more likely to be displaced by automation than workers with a college degree (PricewaterhouseCoopers, 2017).

Health Benefits

Health is distributed inequitably based on socioeconomic status, ethnicity, and a variety of other factors. Adjusting for such factors, however, by very conservative estimates, every year of education adds approximately 4 to 6% to quality life years of health (Furnée, Groot, & van den Brink, 2008; Silles, 2009), and reduces likelihood of dying (e.g., Ljungdahl & Bremberg, 2015; Smith, Anderson, Salinas, Horvatek, & Baker, 2015). Naturally, some of these results may occur because educated people tend to make better life choices and engage in fewer health risk behaviors.

Does the Communication Degree Help in Particular?

There is substantial emphasis in the press, and perhaps in the form of parental pressures on college-bound children, to pursue **STEM** (science, technology, engineering, and mathematics) degrees and majors. Notably, "74 percent of those who have a bachelor's degree in science, technology, engineering and math—commonly referred to as STEM—are not employed in STEM occupations" (U.S. Census Bureau, 2014). This coincides with research that shows, on average, only about 27.3% of college majors have careers that match their degrees (Abel & Deitz, 2014a). More importantly, a detailed study by Deming (2015) concluded that

> social skill-intensive occupations have grown by nearly 10 percentage points as a share of the U.S. labor force, and that wage growth has also been particularly strong for social skill-intensive occupations. Jobs that require high levels of cognitive skill and social skill have fared

particularly well, while high math, low social skill jobs (including many STEM, or Science, Technology, Engineering and Math, occupations) have fared especially poorly. (p. 30)

This has led many to emphasize the inclusion of the arts to complement such technical occupations (i.e., **STEAM**).

The ubiquitous business major is the most common major (U.S. Census Bureau, 2014), whereas communication and journalism represent only about 5% of U.S. college majors (Carnevale et al., 2015). Business majors will therefore be competing with the largest cohort of individuals with the same degree. Those with STEM degrees do tend to fare better than business majors and communication majors in the job market by most criteria, but the value of most majors depends significantly on what the individual with the major does with the degree (Abel, Deitz, & Su, 2014). The top occupations of communication degree holders are marketing and sales managers, administrative, assistants to human resources or training and development officers, and labor relations specialists, (Altonji, Blom, & Meghir, 2012).

The Marketability of the Communication Degree

Being able to communicate competently is an essential aspect of everyday life in general, and in the workplace in particular. Yet, "fewer than half (43%) of Americans agree that college graduates in the country are well-prepared for success in the workplace, and just 14% strongly agree with this statement" (Gallup/Lumina, 2014, p. 10). According to a Pew Research Center survey, "A majority of Americans (57%) say the higher education system in the United States fails to provide students with good value for the money they and their families spend. An even larger majority—75%—says college is too expensive for most Americans to afford" (Taylor et al., 2011). Employers also find that college graduates, although more skilled than their less-educated counterparts, are still often deficient in core competencies.

Recent degree holders in communications and journalism are still experiencing hangovers from the great recession and are having a harder time getting jobs than a lot of other majors (Carnevale & Cheah, 2015). Nevertheless, communication remains one of the most highly valued competencies among organizational leaders, even if they do not recognize that the communication degree is a route to such competencies. Organizations seek communication competence from their hires, but does this translate to any substantial degree into the career relevance of the communication degree?

Research by Carnevale, Cheah, and Strohl (2012; see also NACE, 2015) finds that communication-degree holders compete reasonably well compared to many other disciplines. Communication-degree holders are relatively comparable to agriculture and natural resources, humanities and liberal arts, and recreation, and are somewhat better than psychology and social work, and arts. The Center for Education and the Workforce provides ample data on the degrees they label "Advertising and public relations," "Communication and mass media," and "Journalism" (Carnevale et al., 2015). Across all degree fields, each successive degree step represents a significant improvement in earnings and a significant decrease in the likelihood of unemployment. It is also worth noting that according to the NACE 2014 salary survey, "driving the sizable overall salary increase are the gains made by the communications and computer science disciplines, which are the biggest for Class of 2014 graduates" (NACE, 2015, p. 3).

Berger and Gan (2016) surveyed almost 300 U.S. hiring managers, asking how hard it was to find candidates with soft skills for each of the jobs they were hiring for. Fifty-nine percent of hiring managers' responses were that soft skills are "difficult" to find. They speculate that "one potential reason why more fundamental soft skills—like communication, teamwork, and critical thinking—are more in-demand among employers, is that they're applicable to every job function, industry, and level of seniority."

The Intersection of Marketplace and Matriculation

A few conclusions from the evidence reviewed deserve summary. First, the current generation in the United States is brimming with self-confidence, but the more narcissistic aspects of this confidence may not be well-founded (Twenge et al., 2008). Second, a 4-year college degree is increasingly a necessary but insufficient stepping stone to middle-class aspirations—college grads earn substantially more and are far less likely to be unemployed, compared to nondegreed individuals. Third, each successive degree step is substantially *more* likely to result in substantial earnings and employment benefits. Fourth, a four-year degree in communication is similar in its competitiveness to many other degrees. Fifth, employers believe strongly in the importance of communication skills to their organizations, even though they may or may not associate such skills with the communication major.

In regard to the general employment prospects for students of communication, the Bureau of Labor Statistics (BLS, 2018) reports 2018 median pay for PR specialists at $60,000/year with a typical entry-level education of a BA and no experience, with a slightly higher than average growth prospect (9%) through 2026. For the job category of "reporters, correspondents, and broadcast news analysts," BLS reports the median salary is $43,490 with a typical BA with no experience, but a below average (–9%) growth prospect through to 2026. For "advertising, promotions, and marketing managers" with a typical BA and no experience, the median pay is $132,620, and a higher than average growth prospect (10%) to 2026. Training and development specialists with a BA and less than 5 years' experience are estimated to earn around $60K/year, with a higher than average growth rate to 2026.

Some Select Recommendations for Communication Majors

So what is a communication major, and by indirect implication, their professors, to do in order to survive after their degree? Certainly one should avoid many communication behaviors. For example, surveys of employers illustrate their attention to mistakes candidates make in their resumes (see **Figure 24.5**). Even a single minor typo on a resume or cover letter diminishes a candidate's hirability (Scott et al., 2014). Also, one should not keep challenging content on social media and online profiles. As many as 70% of employers investigate the social media of their candidates (Salm, 2017), and over half of employers decided not to hire candidates because of what they found on social media (CareerBuilder, 2018). This does not mean, however, to erase your social media or online profile, because almost half of employers report they would be reluctant to hire a candidate that they cannot find online (CareerBuilder, 2018). Still, you should investigate what your online profile appears to say about you, and whether it is consistent with the professional qualifications you intend to project.

First, students are well-advised to seek forms of experience. A primary form of experience is an internship. There is no experience like experience. Evidence

FIGURE 24.5: Common Mistakes Made in Interviews

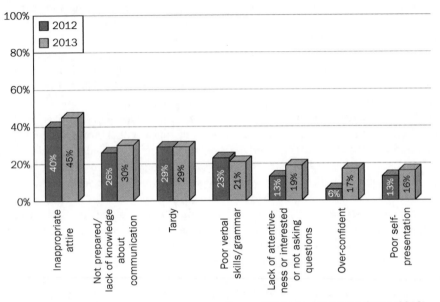

Source: Polk-Lepson Research Group (2013).

demonstrates that internships tend to pay off across the long run. "The starting annual salary for college graduates who completed a paid internship was $52,000, compared to $36,000 for those who completed an unpaid internship and $37,000 for those who did not complete an internship" (Carnevale & Hanson, 2015, p. 83). Another study "found that the gap in job offer rates between students with internship experience and those without grew from 12.6% in 2011 to 20% in 2015 (56.5% versus 36.5%)" (Collins, 2016, p. 25). Furthermore, the share of college graduates who received a job offer was 63% for those who completed a paid internship, compared to 37% for those who completed an unpaid internship and 35% for those who did not complete an internship" (Carnevale et al., 2015, p. 16). Similarly, the HERI (2014) survey of over 13,000 college seniors found that "[f]or students who plan to work full time and who participated in an internship program, 48.1% already had a job offer compared to 30.1% who want to work full time but who did not have an internship." An alternative form of experience is to study abroad. Resrach indicates that employers value the kinds of skills and experiences that students gain from studying abroad, including communication skills, flexibility and adaptability, intercultural skills, intepersonal skills, language skills, leadership, and teamwork (Farrugia & Sanger, 2017).

Second, students should engage and expand their professional newtworks and social ties. Increasingly sophisticated research indicates that the ability to work across teams, departments, and networks in an organization is one of the most important competencies in organizations. Research by Burt (2014) finds that employees who bridge, or link, the social capital of different social networks within an organization tend to peform better. Not being too isolated, nor too embedded within a particular group, is important in an organization. Employees who demonstrate higher performance metrics are those who interact across diverse groups in order to fill **structural holes** in organizations where one network has little interaction with other networks or groups. This particular **network bridging** role, also known as **social capital brokerage**, was found to account for over half of an employee's evaluation, early promotion, and team efficiency. This imortant role for networking may in part explain the advantages that cities have over rural areas for matching college degrees to occupations (Abel & Dietz, 2013).

Third, students need to look to success. One study looked at the best predictors of earning over $100K/year

(Burke & Attridge, 2011). Among other demographics, which are inflexible to change, the following factors were predictive:

- Transformational leadership style
- Resilience/flexibility
- Political use of interpersonal skills
- Experiencing a mentoring relationship

Harrell and Alpert (1989; and Harrell, Harrell, McIntyre, & Weinberg, 1977) conducted a study of Stanford MBA grads with 5-, 10-, and 20-year follow-up, looking for the best predictors of high earnings. At the 10-year mark, the factors "most important for high earnings were social extroversion, ascendance or social boldness, and general activity or energy" (p. 640). At the 20-year mark, the most consistent predictor was "a desire to talk … to be able to get others to listen, and … to be persuaded by what one has to say," which also correlated .71 with an extraversion measure (Harrell & Alpert, 1989, p. 318). "The only valid personality factor for predicting compensation [is] social extroversion" (p. 321). Graduates' best asset is their ability to interact and communicate in ways that leave a positive impression on others.

Conclusion

Cream rises to the top in most settings. Getting by in college tends to predict just getting by in life. Students have probably all heard a professor say something to the effect of "Do you expect people in the 'real world'

to accept such excuses?" There is a reason they ask that. "The top 25% of communications and journalism majors earn more than $80,000 annually, while the bottom 25% earn less than $40,000" (Carnevale et al., 2015, p. 63). How students apply themselves in college is a predictor of how well they will apply themselves in their prospective careers.

Communication constitutes almost everything that matters between people. The coordination of human activity is impossible without communication, and nothing great gets accomplished without communication functioning competently. Perhaps it is time for you to see what greatness you can accomplish.

Credits

FIG. 24.1: Hart Research Associates, It Takes More Than a Major: Employer Priorities for College Learning and Student Success. Copyright © 2013 by Association of American Colleges & Universities.

FIG. 24.2: Adapted from F. Levy and R. J. Murnane, "Education and the Changing Job Market," *Educational Leadership*, vol. 62, no. 2. Copyright © 2004 by Association for Supervision and Curriculum Development.

FIG. 24.3: Adapted from F. Levy and R. J. Murnane, "Education and the Changing Job Market," *Educational Leadership*, vol. 62, no. 2. Copyright © 2004 by Association for Supervision and Curriculum Development.

FIG. 24.4: Source: https://books.google.com/ngrams/info.

FIG. 24.5: Source: Polk-Lepson Research Group, "2013 Professionalism in the Workplace." Copyright © 2013 by York College of Pennsylvania.

Glossary

abduction: A form of reasoning in which various reasonable explanations for a surprising or unexpected observation are compared. A process by which the best available evidence is formulated as hypotheses, which are then tested against additional evidence in continuous comparison to the best alternative explanations or hypotheses.

abductive analysis: A type of induction, in which bridging warrants or conclusions are provided for the observation of examples, cases, or instances, often applied to accounting for unusual or surprising experiences or observations.

ability: The capacity for goal-driven, repeatable behavior.

ableism: Privileging people who are nondisabled or able-bodied and discrimination against those with physical, developmental, or cognitive disabilities or differences.

accessibility: The degree to which evidence can be verified, observed, authenticated, and inspected by others.

accessing: The ability to obtain, examine, or retrieve relevant information from media.

accommodating: A party who cares little for his or her own self-interests in a particular situation, but realizes that it is very important to the other party.

account: Any tactic intended to explain, manage, or repair a perceived or accused transgression.

action: An entryway into the practical applications of intercultural communication, comprising an active, sustained, and complex process of contemplation and self-reflection incorporated into one's own actions.

action orientation: Team members who are willing to do something; making a deliberate effort to make something happen.

action projection: A speaker's current turn at talk projects the relevance of a next turn, because talk amounts to action and action projects relevance.

ad hoc groups: Groups that come together for a restricted time to solve a problem and then cease working together when their goals are met (e.g., to treat a rare illness).

adrenaline: A hormone that boosts the heart rate and dilates blood vessels and breathing passages, providing a burst of energy.

aesthetics: Aesthetic judgments tend to revolve around criteria such as beauty, skill, originality, genre appropriateness, expressiveness, emotion, and balance. Also, the narrative fidelity, aesthetic satisfaction, and/or perceiver interest in a theory.

affect analysis (pathos): Reflective consideration of the ways in which a media message is attempting to (or succeeding or failing in) evoking a particular emotional response in its consumers.

affection exchange theory: A neo-Darwinian theory that situates human's fundamental need for relationships in which the body rewards affection in the short term through improvements to physical health.

affordance: The functions a medium allows a user to perform or achieve through a given medium or technology.

agency: The ability to control material circumstances and exert influence in avenues of power.

agenda setting: A process of making certain issues more salient than others (i.e., more on a person's agenda of relevant topics or concerns). Describes how media exert influence on audiences; focuses on the saliences of the news media and the incorporation of a shared set of interests into political attitudes, effectively making the media's priorities become the voters' priorities. Agenda-setting theory predicts that media messages do not determine what people think but instead determine what they think *about*.

aggravation–mitigation continuum: A dimension that represents the degree to which an account functions to deescalate or escalate the intensity or negativity of the encounter.

aggression: A conflict motivated to hurt another person psychologically, relationally, or physically, using any combination of verbal or physical means.

alternative dispute resolution (ADR): A process in which a neutral third-party attempts to facilitate a cooperative communication process through which the conflicting parties can achieve their own enforceable resolution to the conflict.

analogic communication: A nonarbitrary code based on the connection between the referent and the reference (e.g., tears from crying index an interior emotional state).

analogic messages: Continuously observable and understood as broadly iconic, or something that directly or naturally reflects something else.

analysis: Understanding the extent to which a given issue or referent is composed of varying elements or processes, and how these elements and processes operate to form the whole.

antecedent variable: A variable that comes before both independent and dependent variables.

anticipatory socialization: The first stage of organizational socialization when new members first begin to think about joining and becoming a part of the organization.

apologies: Statements or actions that attempt to imply some degree of responsibility, along with regret or sympathy, for the victim of the transgression.

apprenticeship model: Model of education involving students working with an experienced person, whether scholar, engineer, artist, or other profession, with the goal of eventually moving onto a career in that area.

appropriated structures: Structures adopted by groups from larger structures.

appropriateness: The contextual legitimacy of behavior.

analysis (media): Understanding the extent to which a given issue or referent is comprised of varying elements or processes, and how these elements and processes operate to form the whole.

arbitration: A form of negotiation in which a third party (e.g., a judge, an arbitrator) has some degree of authority to make an enforceable decision in resolving the conflict.

argument: Any form of consensus-seeking discourse that uses logical structure and/or reasons to gain some degree of audience ascension to the claim(s) of the argument.

argument analysis (logos): The use of evidence, claims, reasoning, claims, balance, optimization, acceptability, relevance, sufficiency, and validity of the intended position or stance in the media message.

argumentativeness: A predisposition to defend or advocate positions on controversial issues and articulating criticisms of or challenges to others' positions on such issues.

asides: Short, written reflections during data analysis meant to spur thinking about analytic categories, themes, or patterns in the ethnographic data.

assessments: When a speaker claims knowledge of that which he or she is assessing, relying on experiences to provide an assessment.

Association for Education in Journalism and Mass Communication (AEJMC): An international professional association (https://www.aejmc.org/) of academics, scholars, professionals and practitioners of journalism, media arts and sciences, public relations, adversitising, and mass communication, founded in 1912.

attachment style (avoidant, dismissive, preoccupied, or secure): General predispositions to behave based upon the degree to which self and others are viewed positively or negatively. Those with positive views of self and others tend to experience interpersonal relationships and interaction with a secure style. Those with positive views of self but negative views of others tend to experience interpersonal relationships and interaction with a dismissive style. Those with negative views of self but positive views of others tend to experience interpersonal relationships and interaction with a preoccupied style. Finally, those with negative views of self and others tend to experience interpersonal relationships and interaction with an avoidant style.

attentiveness: Adapting and personalizing the message to, and taking into account the perspective of, the audience receiving the message. The ability to demonstrate attention to, interest in, and concern for others in a conversation.

attitude: A person's evaluation of an object.

attributes: The options participants can choose from when answering questions.

autoethnography: Ethnographic research that incorporates the reflection on and interrogation of researcher's own experience with relationship to the topic of study or the research process itself.

avoidant: A party who examines a situation and concludes that there is very little worth fighting for in that situation, but who also sees little interest in the other party's goals or objectives, is likely to take an avoidant strategic approach to the conflict.

axiology: The branch of philosophy concerned with the nature and function of values.

baby boomers: The U.S. generation born between 1946 and 1963.

backing: In (Toulmin) argument theory, the evidentiary, observational, statistical, visual, exemplary, or illustrative bases providing support for claims or warrants. See also *grounds*.

backstage: All areas in which we, as everyday actors, might prepare to perform our roles. This might include bathrooms, bedrooms, cars, offices, and locker rooms.

behavioral intention: The intention (mental decision) to enact a behavior.

better-than-average effect: The tendency to view self as better than average, or better than self is viewed by others. See also *Wobegon effect*.

Big Five: A model of personality comprising the following traits: openness, extraversion, neuroticism, conscientiousness, and agreeableness.

big rhetoric: A rhetorical perspective that approaches truth and knowledge as fundamentally rhetorical, meaning that truth and knowledge are always deeply shaped by prevailing historical and cultural contexts and power dynamics, and are always partly produced and contested through language or discourse. Big rhetoric therefore implies a constitutive perspective.

biological theory: Theory that biological characteristics of sexes are foundational to the difference between men and women.

biomedical model: Patient care based on the assumption that the human body is like a machine that can be diagnosed and corrected. Biomedical care tends to emphasize the provider's authority and expertise and is based heavily on medical interviewing.

354 | The Communication Capstone

biopsychosocial model: An alternative to the biomedical model of patient care; integrative care that treats patients' physical, social, emotional, and spiritual well-being in the context of care.

blind peer review: A process of anonymous review or evaluation in which there are no explicit cues to the identity of the author(s), and the reviewer is unaware of the authorship of the manuscript under review.

Boolean: Using conditional combinations of search terms to narrow or expand a search, typically involving "and" or "or" combinations of search terms.

boundary specification: A theory must indicate the domain of its legitimate scope and relevance.

bourgeoisie: A concept used by Karl Marx to describe a class of people who have ownership and control over the land, instruments, and technologies needed to produce commodities.

brain hemisphere (right brain/left brain): The hemispheric hypothesis is that different forms of information processing are emphasized in the bilateral sides of the human brain. In general, the right hemisphere is associated with greater emphasis of analogic, nonlinguistic, visual, and spatial information processing, and the left hemisphere is associated with greater emphasis of symbolic, digital, and verbal information processing.

breadth: The scope or range of a theory.

bricolage: A process of creation that uses the miscellaneous resources available, which may not have had any prior connection; tinkering; assemblage.

burnout: The exhaustion, fatigue, and frustration that result when stress exceeds a person's capacity for withstanding a given level of stress.

causation: An association between two variables in which one causes the other, established by time, order, correlation, and nonspuriousness.

cause–effect: An organizational template for organizing a presentation by analyzing a process, story, history, or event by identifying its cause(s) and the outcome(s) or effect(s).

census: Data collection from an entire population when analyzing the data collected from a sample.

central route: A predominantly thoughtful, conscious, mindful, analytical, and critical process of information evaluation.

cheating: The act of obtaining or attempting to obtain credit for academic work by the use of dishonest, deceptive, or fraudulent means.

chronological: An organizational template for organizing a presentation by tracing a process, story, history, or movement from its early to its later states.

cisgender: The prefix *cis* means "same as." Thus, the gender performance is consistent with what society deems appropriate for sex assigned at birth.

citationality: The properties of texts (or performances) that necessarily invoke other texts when readers (or audience) are attempting to make sense of them.

citizen journalism: A symbiosis between news consumers and producers in which laypersons and nonprofessional media consumers produce leads and content for professional journalists to investigate and publish.

claim: The conclusion, or the particular proposition (e.g., hypothesis, value judgment, belief statement, etc.), that contextualizes the reasonableness of data.

claiming insufficient knowledge: A stated inability to know about, or remember, events or activities that constrain speakers from making a knowledgeable assessment (e.g., "I don't know" or "I can't remember").

climate: The collective employee experience of the organizational culture.

close-ended questions: Questions that require respondents to choose from a fixed set of answer options.

CMC competence: Computer-mediated communication competence refers to the degree to which digital media are used in ways perceived as both appropriate and effective.

coaching style: A leadership style suited to followers need high task direction and high relational supportiveness.

cocultures: Patterns of behavior, beliefs, values, customs, and rituals of subgroups of individuals.

code: A set of conventions or modalities for understanding and action.

codebook: The part of a coding scheme that outlines the coding rules. A codebook will (at minimum) explain how to identify the unit of analysis, provide the conceptualizations of all variables, and attribute explanations for each variable.

coding form: The sheet of items, paper or electronic, that each coder completes for each unit of analysis.

coding scheme: Used for content analysis, a coding scheme includes two parts: a codebook and a coding form.

coercive power: Influence based on a person's ability to punish other group members for their behaviors and actions.

cognitive dissonance: The degree to which a message is inconsistent with preexisting behavior or perspective.

collaborating: A party who recognizes the importance of the interests of both parties in the conflict.

collaboration: the ability to navigate across diverse communities to transform social network ties into social and intellectual capital relevant to a media project.

collective rationalization: A common symptom of groupthink in which early warnings and signs of danger that run against the prevailing position are discredited or discounted.

command: The capacity for behavior to imply some definition of the nature of the connection, history, meaning state, or disposition between them.

commentaries: Extended asides, often using complete sentences, designed to move the ethnographic researcher closer to discrete categories or themes for the final analysis.

commodification: The process through which something is treated as a commodity or object for commercial purposes.

communal coping: Mutually supportive conversations that revolve around a shared stressor. When the stress one individual faces is shared by the other.

communibiological paradigm: A paradigm of communication that assumes (a) communication behaviors are based on traits, (b) that are heritable, and (c) that account for a majority of communication behavior.

Communication: Creating and exchanging meaning through the use of symbols. The processes by which one person may affect another through behavior.

communication apprehension: An experience of fear or anxiety regarding a real or imagined communication encounter.

communication competence: The degree to which a person interacts in a way that is perceived by self and/or others as both appropriate and effective.

communication functions: Shaper of opinion, language use, information transmission, relationship development, and cultural construction.

communication history: The modern convergence of the speech and journalism traditions of scholarship and professional activity.

communication media: Materials or technologies manipulated for the purpose of recording, amplifying, or transmitting communications from some source to others, typically involving some form of message(s) exchanged through technological means and distribution infrastructure.

communication network: The informal network through which cultural information is shared within the organization.

communication skill deficits: Relative inabilities to demonstrate literacy or minimum capability in communication tasks or functions.

communicative constitution of organizations (CCO): Perspective toward organizations based on the premise that communication is inherently organizing of organizational practice and behavior.

communitas: A spontaneous feeling of community that arises among groups of people during cultural rituals and often in liminal spaces such as sports stadiums or music concerts.

community analysis: The first step in launching a community-level intervention where a profile of important qualities, such as resources, norms, beliefs, and values, that characterize the community is developed.

community change theory: A framework for understanding the use of theory to transform a community by achieving change at individual, organizational, societal, and environmental levels.

comparative theoretical quality: An evaluative standard for evaluating the status of a theory determined by the degree to which the evidence for or against a theory is the best available for assessing its status as a theory.

competence styles (maximizing, minimizing, sufficing, optimizing): The tendency of a person to communicate in a way that is generally perceived as appropriate and/or effective. Those who interact in a manner perceived as both inappropriate and ineffective represent a minimizing style. Those who interact in a manner perceived as inappropriate but effective represent a maximizing style. Those who interact in a manner perceived as appropriate but ineffective represent a sufficing style. Finally, those who interact in a manner perceived as both appropriate and effective represent an optimizing style of communication.

competition principle: The extent to which a theory competes favorably vis-à-vis its rivals.

competitive: A party who cares greatly for his or her own interests, in a manner that greatly outweighs the perceived interests of the other party.

complementary interactions: Responses that fit or harmonize with the previous interactant's action.

compliance-gaining tactics: Relatively singular message constructions that attempt to influence the behavior of another by using persuasive strategies.

composure: Communication that reflects confidence, assertiveness and coherence in the composition and enactment of mediated messages. With regard to public speaking, the ability to demonstrate confidence, calmness, comfort, spontaneity, appropriate assertiveness, self-control, and directedness of behavior.

compromising: Strong interest one's self-interests, but also recognizing the importance of the other party's interests.

conceptual battleground: Contestations and struggles over different meanings of, approaches to, and perspectives on culture and intercultural communication.

conceptual definition: A statement formally specifying the requisite features that characterize a component of a theory or model.

conceptualization: The explanation or definition of a variable.

conditional relevance: Design of a talk for specific recipients that projects the relevance of some (not just any) range of appropriate and next actions.

confederate: An individual trained by the researcher who is also a part of the study but is not known to have been trained by the researcher.

confidentiality: Situations where although sensitive participant information could potentially be linked back to participants, it is kept private.

conflict: Any expressed struggle between two or more parties. In general, at least one of these parties will perceive some degree of interdependence on, and obstruction from, the other party or parties in regard to a perceived scarcity of preferred outcomes.

conformity: The process by which a person alters his or her behavior in an effort to correspond or match responses of other individuals.

confounder: A third variable that explains or qualifies the relationship between the independent variable and the dependent variable.

connotative: The contextualized inference of meaning of a word or symbol, typically based on informal or conventional associations between the word and the things that co-occur with the word.

constitutive perspective: Whereas a foundationalist view sees language as able to *represent* preexisting truths, a constitutive view says truth and reality are always partly produced by and contested through language and communication. See also *big rhetoric* and *constructivist conception of language*.

construct and conditionship specification: A theory must indicate the nature of the constructs and the relationships among these constructs (e.g., necessity, sufficiency, parameters, function form, generality, etc.).

constructed descriptions: The more nebulous and affective features of a candidate's personality; constructed through language, adjectives, or buzz; constructed descriptions often influence a candidate's likability and relatability.

constructivist conception of language: A perspective toward rhetoric that became increasingly prominent in the modern world and which sees symbols as central to the negotiation of reality. From a constructivist perspective, the historical, cultural, and social value of symbols are embodied in and produced by everyday habits and practices. See also *big rhetoric* and *constitutive perspective*.

consumption: The passive and active perception and interpretation of media content.

contemporary period of intercultural communication study: Formalization and institutionalization of the academic study of intercultural communication within the communication discipline since the 1960s.

contempt: A specific emotion state indicating a direct disgust, frustration, or resentment for having the original demand so disregarded and contested.

content: Awareness and comprehension of the topic represented by media. The more denotative or literal meaning of the content of a message or behavior.

content analysis: A methodology that follows structured guidelines (i.e., systematic) that foster unbiased data analysis (i.e., objective) resulting in numerical estimations (i.e., quantitative) of the specified content.

content knowledge: The storage and accessibility of cognitive representations of the symbols, syntax, goals, plans, situations, people, objects, and other elements of behavior that are involved in generating and comprehending meaning and messages.

context: Awareness and comprehension of the components, factions, institutions, and cultural processes in the media ecology of a given mediated event or topic. In conversation analytic studies, context is not treated as external to or removed from communication, but achieved through interaction.

context shaping and renewing: Social actions are both context shaping as speakers tailor them to prior and immediate circumstances, and context renewing, as speakers contribute to evolving and subsequent actions.

contract cheating: The act of contracting with, or soliciting, another person or agent to produce a textual document that is then presented as one's own.

contradictory structuration: When one social structure undermines or contradicts another social structure already in place.

Control: The potential for strategic manipulation of phenomena being theorized.

control group: A group in an experiment not exposed to manipulations of the independent variable.

control variable: A variable that accounts for changes in the dependent variable that are not accounted for by the independent variable and can help researchers eliminate third variables as potential explanations for observed relationships.

controllability: The belief that making better choices is within one's own control, as opposed to dependent on the choices of other people.

convergence: The degree to which a given medium incorporates functions of other media technologies.

conversation analysis (CA): The systematic study of naturally occurring audio and video recordings, in unison with carefully produced transcriptions, to discover the sequential organization of social actions in conversations and institutional interactions.

conversation analytic (CA) methods: Methods driven by the assumption that because communicators accomplish everyday life based only on the behaviors they display through their communication (as opposed to reading each other's minds), researchers can understand such behaviors best by observing and precisely analyzing such naturally occurring activities.

coordination: The ability to manage the contextual and chronemic aspects of mediated interaction involving responsiveness, proportionality, and timing of mediated messages. The ability to manage timing, ebb and flow, and the initiation and ending of speaking turns, conversations, and episodes and sequences of interaction.

correlation: A measure for the degree to which two variables are associated with each other.

correspondence with observables: The extent to which the components or concepts of a theory are observable.

countersuggestiveness: The ability of a theory to suggest contrary, paradoxical, or critical perspectives toward the status quo.

creation: The ability to innovate of new conceptions or representations of intended mediated messages.

crisis: The messages that occur during and immediately after a disaster that attempt to mitigate social harm and disruption.

criteria for theory evaluation: Standards for assessing the relative value of a theory.

criterion focused: An organizational template for organizing a presentation by identifying the ideals or objectives that specify what the best solution would need to achieve, and then identifying an approach that best meets those objectives.

critical race rhetoric: The study and critique of how Whiteness has become a privileged norm and cultural ideal.

critical and rhetorical methods: Methods driven by the assumption that reality is always influenced by underlying systems of often hidden influence and power, and such structures must be evaluated through an evaluative perspective that reveals these hidden forces, thereby presenting opportunities for pursuing more noble or practical ends.

critical approach to rhetoric: A perspective that critiques the ways that language and other symbols naturalize what are in fact historically rooted and therefore contestable power disparities such as those based on race, class, sexuality, ability, or between humans and nonhumans.

critical approach to intercultural communication: Studying intercultural communication with particular attentions to power relations, macro structures, and dominant ideologies for the goals of promoting liberation and social justice.

critical prosumption skills: The ability to apply interpretive lenses that facilitate or enhance the appropriate, effective, and adapted use of media content and form for optimal audience response.

critical skepticism: The tendency to examine media content with an eye toward noticing and rectifying any errors or false claims, to engage in extensive research on media trust, credibility, and hostile media perceptions, and to seek out diverse news sources through information surveillance.

critical theoretical qualities: Standards for evaluating the status of a theory determined by those characteristics of a theory that provide better directions or guidelines for pursuing future action.

critical thinking (media): Ability to analyze and evaluate media messages for their validity and utility.

critical/cultural theory: Claims one can never truly understand sex/gender unless they study it within the broader cultural context.

cross-cultural communication: Comparisons and contrasts of communication patterns within at least two different cultures.

cross-sectional survey: A research design that allows researchers to take a cross-section or snapshot of a group of individuals at a specific time point.

cultivation theory: The conjecture that extensive exposure to media messages, especially television, biases the perception of reality toward the content of the media consumed.

cultural appropriation: Adoption and adaptation of minority others' cultural practices into one's own, especially for material and monetary gain.

cultural perspective: The perspective toward organizations viewing them as collective forms of symbolic behavior, constituted through stories, metaphors, and rituals through which members create their realities.

culture: All the intergenerational patterns of behaviors, beliefs, values, customs, and rituals of an identifiable group. Identification with, membership in, acceptance into, or access to resources shared by members of a group based on nationality, race, ethnicity, sex and gender, ability, citizenship, socioeconomic status, profession, sexual orientation, sexuality, immigrant status, political affiliation, or others that impact communication.

curvilinear relationship: A relationship that starts out as positive or negative but reverses direction after crossing a certain threshold.

damn strange coincidences principle: The extent to which a theory predicts facts that could not be understood or sought without the theory.

data: Artifacts, observations, cases, examples, or counts of something, which become meaningful in the crucible of argument.

data analysis: The process of reading and rereading field notes, interview transcriptions, and other documents for the purpose of understanding communicative meanings constructed by participants, often accompanied by written reflections on the data.

debriefing: Represents a process by which researchers correct any deception introduced through the experiment, restate the purpose and value of the study, and thank the respondents for their participation.

deduction: A particular process of inference in which a general principle or law is used to conclude aspects or characteristics of that principle as they apply to a particular

358 | The Communication Capstone

instance. In reference to theory construction in the social sciences, it typically takes the form of a deductive tripartite syllogism, such that the first and second premise entail the conclusion (e.g., If A occurs, B occurs. If B occurs, C occurs. Therefore, if A occurs, C occurs). Drawing a conclusion that is entailed by prior premises. Logical reasoning that begins with a general or universal law from which particular instances are then inferred. The opposite of *induction*.

deductive reasoning: A form of reasoning from generalization to particulars (i.e., specific cases).

defensive climates: The communicative context resulting from defensive communication.

defensive communication: Communication that tends to threaten another person's sense of self, thereby evoking and eliciting reactionary, ego-involved behavior that focuses on protecting face and self-esteem. A communicative attempt to deny responsibility or fault, in a way that generally either criticizes the accuser as being unjust or denies the accuser's position.

definition: An equation of one concept or term with another concept or set of terms.

delegating style: A leadership style suited to followers need low relationship supportiveness and low task direction.

deliberate practice: A specific type of intentional and mindful presentation preparation where the speaker seeks out opportunities to expand his or her public communication skills by simulating the speaking environment while practicing; receiving immediate, critical, and expert feedback; and applying that feedback toward the goal of incremental improvement.

delivery: The actual presentation of the content, in a lively fashion and, with adjustments for actual conditions, in a manner similar to how one planned the presentation.

demand: A general term for a one-up action that implies the other party did something wrong.

demarcation criterion: A conceptual or empirical form of evidence that distinguishes science from non-scientific or pseudo-scientific forms of knowledge claims.

denotative: The literal or dictionary meaning of a term.

dependent variable: A variable measured for changes as a result of variations in independent variables.

descriptive decision-making models: Procedures or templates for managing task interaction that represents what groups normatively or typically engage in, without proposing a particular approach.

descriptive norms: Norms that reference what is typically done or what typically occurs.

descriptive statistics: Statistics usually used in early stages of data analysis to summarize or describe data.

design and initiation of campaign activities: The second step in launching a community-level intervention, where partnerships with community are organized, community participation with the campaign efforts is increased, and the framework for a full launch of the campaign to the wider community is laid down.

desirable theoretical quality: Evaluative standards that identify features of a theory that connote generally higher general quality; the more of these characteristics (e.g., parsimony) the theory possesses, the more desirable it is.

determining effectiveness: The fifth step in launching a community-level intervention that includes analysis of campaign activities in achieving objectives for community change, identification of lessons learned for improving future campaign activities, revision of the community analysis for future campaign efforts, and identification of campaign's aspects that worked well, in addition to which parts functioned less optimally.

development communication: Applications of communication research, theories, and technologies to promote positive social change and evaluation.

devil terms: Symbols (such as "terrorism") that represent what a society considers to be most evil or at odds with its values. Devil terms are the opposite of *god terms*.

dialectical method: A method first proposed by Plato that seeks to discover universal, transcendent, and eternal philosophical truths about human nature, morality, ethics, and justice. This method is enacted in conversation by defining key terms, seeking to avoid logical contradictions, and deriving rational conclusions that all participants in the conversation can agree on.

dialogue: An entryway into the practical applications of intercultural communication, comprised by facilitating an adaptation and reaching out across intercultural differences in order to experience, imagine, conceptualize and engage creatively with others.

difference: Signifies the extent to which an individual or group of individuals differs or diverges from another.

diffusion of innovations: The process by which innovations (i.e., new objects, ideas, or approaches) spread through mediated channels and become adopted by audiences.

digital: Signals or symbols dichotomized categorically into one and zero.

digital communication: A conventional system of code, or discrete symbols or symbol system (e.g., language, mathematics, computer code).

digital divide: The degree of disparity in the degree to which access to, and abilities to engage and use, the various technologies associated with digital communication media (e.g., Internet, smartphones, software and programming, etc.) based on factors such as race, culture, socioeconomic status, age, language, or other factors.

digital native(s): People who grow up in the digital age (i.e., born after 1980).

direct–indirect dimension: The degree to which behaviors clearly address the key issues at stake in the conflict.

directing style: A leadership style suited to followers who need high task direction and low relationship supportiveness.

disfluency: Vocalized breaks, irregularities, or non-lexical vocalities that occur within the flow of the speech; the most common include "um's" and "uh's."

displacement: The capacity of language to refer to things not present in time or space.

displays: Characteristics and behaviors enacted by everyday actors that convey meanings to audiences about the person and his or her role. When conscious and intentional, these might be used to achieve a desired effect in an audience (e.g., persuade them about one's credibility). When unconscious or unintentional, displays may break a frame of understanding between performer and audience and may make the performer seem incompetent.

disposition: Organizing the content into a coherent presentation. The canon of rhetoric concerned with the arrangement and organization of a presentation.

disproof: In regard to a non-mathematical sense, the logical ability to reasonably falsify a general principle through observation.

distal factors: Factors in the deep past of a person or group or institution or of a society or culture that influences the process. Factors distant in time to an event.

distribution: The ability to transmit and target mediated messages optimally to intended audiences.

door-in-the-face effect: In regard to sequential influence strategies, a message strategy by which a request is made that expects recipient rejection, such that subsequent compliance with a smaller request is more likely.

doxa: Common opinion. For Plato and Aristotle, doxa is aligned with the physical, deceptive, context-specific world of sensory perception and opinion, in contrast to real, nonphysical truth and knowledge (episteme). Rhetoric, for Plato and Aristotle, deals only with doxa, or endoxa, respectively, not episteme. For the Sophists, in contrast, all truth and knowledge are fully doxastic.

dramatism: A perspective developed by Kenneth Burke that views humans as creating and performing meaning in everyday life through the use of symbols. In this view, humans construct meaning through symbols and stories much like actors do in a play.

dual concern model: A four-quadrant typology of conflict goals or motives defined by the dimensions of concern for self and concern for other.

early adopters: With regard to diffusion of innovations theory, the second stage of the population adopting a decision, idea, product, service, etc.

early majority: With regard to diffusion of innovations theory, the third stage of the population adopting a decision, idea, product, service, etc.

early period of intercultural communication study: Intercultural communication trainings and programs at the Foreign Service Institute during the 1940s and 1950s

earnings benefit: The relative value of higher education on earnings.

economic rhetoric: The study and critique of how economic power influences human communication at both the micro and macro levels of society.

effectiveness: The degree to which relatively rewarding outcomes are achieved in or across interactions.

effects: Awareness and comprehension of outcomes and causal implications of a media-related topic or process.

ego-defensive attitudes: Attitudes that defend one's self-image.

elaboration likelihood model: Conceptualizes persuasion as a result of dual information processing routes, with a central route involving careful, conscious and analytic thinking, and a peripheral route involving more intuitive, affective, and unconscious decision-making.

embodied activities: Gesture, eye gaze, facial expressions, body positioning, touch, and other behaviors that accompany and provide meaningful understandings for talk in interaction. The use of instruments, objects, and spatial orientations influencing, and influenced by, talk in interaction.

emic: The emergent quality of themes or patterns derived during the coding process.

emotional state: A temporary reaction to environmental stimuli. Such states vary by their tendencies, physiological reactions, subjective experiences, and environmental context.

emotional support: A form of social support, where support provider(s) seek(s) to improve affective state of support receiver(s).

empathy: The degree to which a person can feel, perceive, or experience the perspective or feelings of another person.

empirical: Observable. In social science, a paradigm of study is considered empirical to the extent it focuses on observable phenomena, and generally, phenomena on which multiple observers could agree.

empirical description: Something that can be measured, such as a candidate's educational background or voting record.

empirical novelty: The ability of a theory to predict phenomena or observations that were previously unanticipated by existing theories.

empirical/analytic dimension: The degree to which a scholar believes evidence is primarily located in the observed and measured world, or in the mental categories and judgments our mind uses to make sense of the world.

employment benefit: The relative value of higher education in facilitating employment and protecting from unemployment.

enacted support: The supportive actions offered by support provider(s) to support receiver(s) during a stressful event.

end on your own terms: The final summary the speaker ends with after the question-and-answer session.

endoxa: Informed opinion that rises above the particularity of individual observation. According to Aristotle, rhetoric, at its best, deals with endoxa because it provides contextually specific truths about human persuasion. For Aristotle, endoxa is inferior to episteme, which provides access to deductive truths that exist independently of particular situated contexts.

enthymeme: A syllogism with one or more suppressed propositions that is filled in by the audience.

entropy: A process or description of system decay, typically into disorder, randomness, or lack of (predictable or patterned) information. A state of systems, especially closed systems, in which the system default tendency is toward deterioration or decline.

environment: The external context and systems with which a given system interacts and by which it influences and by which it is influenced.

episteme: Genuine knowledge. For Plato and Aristotle, episteme refers to real, non-physical, eternal truths that philosophy, not rhetoric, can enable us to access. For modern rhetoricians, however, rhetoric can enable us to access epistemic knowledge because knowledge, they argue, can only ever be known in historically and culturally specific ways.

epistemic: The premise that communication and rhetoric function more to create what is known (i.e., reality) more so than reflecting what is known.

epistemic authority: What speakers experience and know, who claims to know more or less about relevant concerns, and how territorial preserves of knowledge and action are defended and violated.

epistemology: The study of how we know what we think we know.

equifinality: A property of systems in which any given way or path may result in multiple possible outcomes.

esteem support: Behavior that seeks to promote another person's preferred identity.

ethnography: A methodological approach to observation and interpretation of human behavior consisting of fieldwork, reflexivity, interviews, and document analysis.

ethnography of communication: The investigation, discovery, and explication of rules that govern appropriate behavior in a speech community, and a speech community is a cultural group that shares common and functional speech codes based on a specific situation.

ethos: The credibility or expertise of the source of the evidence.

etic: The process of using existing theoretical or scholarly constructs and categories to better understand ethnographic data; the quality of themes or patterns derived from overlaying existing categories over raw data.

eudaimonia: A human ethic involving both reason and virtue, from the words *eu* ("good") and *daimōn* ("spirit"); typically referring to the highest good in human action. See also *flourishing*.

eugenics: A racially motivated set of beliefs and practices, often overseen by state and/or nonstate institutions, that promote the segregation and even murder of human populations believed to be physically, biologically, and/or cognitively inferior, undesirable, or disabled.

evaluation: The critical judgment regarding the validity, legitimacy, or acceptability of media content and selection.

evidence tests: Criteria applicable to arguments, using evidence and the relative quality of that evidence (i.e., observations, experiences, research, quotations, etc.).

excuses: Statements or actions that attempt to diminish the transgressor's responsibility, typically by either externalizing the cause of a transgression or attributing the cause to an uncontrollable source, such as an accident.

expectancy: A cognitive schema involving a projection of anticipated process or outcomes.

experiment: A quantitative method that uses a manipulation of an independent variable in order to see its effects on a dependent variable.

experimental group: A group in an experiment exposed to manipulations of the independent variable.

experimental methods: Methods involving procedures to manipulate (true experiment) or observe existing differences in (quasi-experiment) stimuli (i.e., independent variables) representing distinct conditions in which a variety of other potentially relevant factors can be controlled or accounted for in observing the effects of such conditions on some outcome (dependent) variable(s). The primary form of control in true experiments is random assignment.

expert power: Influence based on a person's specific knowledge or experience that other group members may not have.

explanatory power: The theory must provide a sensible account of the phenomena of concern.

exploration: The ability to experiment and engage media *qua* media; to pursue media capabilities for the joy or pure playfulness of the experience.

expressiveness: The ability some media users demonstrate in their ability to incorporate interesting humor, memes, or other interesting tropes into their everyday media messages. The ability to demonstrate animation and variability of behavior, especially in regard to affect, emotion expression, vocabulary, imagery, narrative, humor, and vivacity of enactment.

external consistency: The degree to which evidence is representative of the domain/population of the external phenomena to which it is applied. The theory must avoid contradiction of "known" data.

external validity: The extent to which a researcher is able to generalize the findings of a study to a population and to situations not directly examined as part of the research.

face: The impression an actor wants to impress on others. Your public image; who you want to be seen as.

factorial experiment: An experiment where the researcher manipulates more than one independent variable.

falsifiable: The quality of a hypothesis that it can be tested empirically and shown to be false or incorrect.

fantasy: Any message that does not refer to the immediate "here and now" of a group.

fantasy chaining: When group members begin to tell a story as a collaborative whole.

fatal attraction: When the characteristic(s) that makes someone else seem like an attractive partner ends up being the thing that drives the relationship apart.

feedback: The signals that actions and actors provide regarding a group's or system's process. Systematic monitoring of feedback allows the system to adapt to changes in its environment.

feminine: Behaviors such as: being polite, kind, caring, nurturing, and attentive to their physical appearance.

feminism: A social movement seeking equality for women, often divided into three major overlapping waves. The first wave fought primarily for formal civic equality. The second wave fought primarily for equality within the private and cultural sphere. The third wave emphasizes an intersectional perspective that appreciates how gender identity always involves multiple dimensions—such as race, class, sexuality, and ability—at once. Politics and movement to end sexism and social oppression of all sexes.

field: The collection of places and spaces in which a particular topic or phenomenon might occur.

field notes: Transcribed head notes and scratch notes made in the field, consisting of complete sentences and paragraphs, and usually incorporating imagery, metaphor, and other figures of speech.

fieldwork: The process of researchers immersing themselves in the field, scene, and setting where a phenomenon is believed to be occurring, including interacting with participants *in situ*.

fight: A particularly intense conflict.

first-wave feminism: The social and political movements in early 20th century associated with early political achievements such as the right to vote in 1920 and to join the work force during World War II.

flourishing: Overall life well-being or happiness. See also *eudaimonia*.

flow: The psychological state of feeling happy, efficacious, motivated and efficient.

focus theory of normative conduct: Conjecture that in order to influence behavior, a norm must be in focus (i.e., relevant in the mind of the individual) prior to acting.

focused research: Seeking particular research studies in a search engine or process based on a narrowed set of topic terms based on a topic statement or title.

foot-in-the-door effect: In regard to sequential influence strategies, a message strategy by which a communicator attempts to convince a recipient to comply with a small initial request in order to increase the likelihood that the recipient will comply with a subsequent larger request.

formative campaign evaluation: Campaign design stage in which campaign planners make critical decisions regarding the theoretical framework, goals, audience, channel(s), and materials related to the campaign.

formulae: Formats for storytelling that are culturally bound. When aspects of a particular formulae are followed, they may serve to key an audience to expect certain things from a storytelling event. For example, when a speaker says "Once upon a time ..." audiences expect a fairytale and the requisite plot points and ending.

foundational/reflexive dimension: The degree to which a scholar believes reality preexists the observer and abides by causal principles, or is cocreated by social actors and the observer-participant.

foundationalist view: A theory and orientation toward reality that understands truth and knowledge as eternal, stable, and unchanging.

four horsemen of the apocalypse pattern: Any sequential pattern of conflict typified by at least four interaction markers of demand, defensiveness, contempt, and withdrawal.

frame: An imaginary bracket placed around certain communication interactions by one or more people, often activated by *keying* behavior. Misunderstandings and disagreements among participants can lead to *frame slippage* (in which shared understandings move from one meaning to another—e.g., what starts out as teasing turns serious) and *frame breakage* (e.g., when playing one child yells "Time out!" and other children stop playing and step out of the play frame).

framing: An entryway into the practical applications of intercultural communication, comprised by awareness of multiple perspectives, alternative interpretations, and frames of reference while fostering mindfulness regarding the unique facets of each of these perspectives and reference points.

front stage: The places in which we enact roles and scripts appropriate to certain concepts (e.g., a classroom is the *front stage* for a teacher).

functional approach: An approach to group decision-making emphasizing the role group members play in communicating with one another, assumes groups are goal oriented, and that certain communication functions need to be performed in order for a group to solve problems effectively.

functional decision-making models: Approaches to managing task interaction that identify key task functions that contribute to decision-making.

functional model of social support: See *stress-buffering model of social support.*

functional prosumption skills: The abilities involved in the technical production of media content, as well as the delivery or performance of those skills in the form of an actual message design or content delivery.

gender: Also considered gender role. Social symbolic construction and performance. Varies across cultures.

gender binary: Organization of sexes based on a two-sex system (male/female or masculine/feminine).

gender performance: Outward expression of gender role.

genderlect: The degree to which biological sex and/or psychological sex-based identity (i.e., gender) are reflected in language behavior.

generalizability: Beginning with single case studies, analysts employ a procedure of constant comparison to examine how larger collections of instances reflect generalized actions and patterns across diverse settings, speakers, topics, and cultures. The potential for an idea or conclusion to apply to relevant instances in other contexts, observers, and times. When the findings of the study (using a sample of a population in the real world) approach or resemble what a researcher would expect to find among members of the study population in the real world.

generative capacity: The ability of a theory to stimulate or formulate new theoretical perspectives, questions, and views.

Gen-X: The U.S. generation born between 1964 and 1979.

god terms: Symbols (such as democracy) that represent a society's ultimate, overarching ideals and values. God terms are the opposite of *devil terms.*

grade inflation: Giving higher grades than are deserved by the quality of the student work.

ground rules: Specified or negotiated understandings explicitly stating group expectations.

grounds: In (Toulmin) argument theory, the evidentiary, observational, statistical, visual, exemplary, or illustrative bases providing support for claims or warrants. See also *backing.*

group: Three or more individuals interacting for the achievement of some common goal, who influence and are influenced by each other.

group input: All the factors, resources, information, personal characteristics, and abilities and skills that are brought to the group.

groupthink: A premature consensus-seeking tendency in a group.

haptics (touch behavior): The study of how the use of touch or physical contact communicate.

head notes: Mental notes researchers make if they are unable to write them down while doing fieldwork.

health: In contrast to a mere absence of disease or illness, health is a state of physical, psychological and social well-being.

health campaigns: Planned and organized collective communication efforts to facilitate public health-promoting attitudes, values, beliefs, and/or behaviors regarding a particular health-related domain of activity or risk.

healthcare professionals: Any individual who works in the business of caring for patients.

healthcare teams: A group of direct or indirect health providers (e.g., ad hoc, nominal care, unidisciplinary, multidisciplinary, interdisciplinary, transdisciplinary).

hegemonic masculinity: The privileging of masculinity from a White, upper-class, wage-earning, heterosexual, athletic perspective.

hegemony: Process where dominant group controls and oppresses other groups without question from the oppressed (in a sense of taken for granted knowledge/practices).

heroes: The people in the organization (past and present) who have represented or enacted the values of the organization.

heteronormativity: The view that heterosexuality is the only natural, normal, or preferred sexual orientation among humans. Critical and queer scholarship and activists argue, in contrast, that heteronormativity is historically produced and argue for recognizing LGBTQI identities as equally normal and valid.

heurism: The extent to which a theory suggests new scholarly questions and endeavors.

heuristic shortcuts: Used heavily by U.S. voters to navigate what might be an unmanageably complex political climate, these shortcuts rely on affect to activate the intuitive and automatic thought processes that influence how voters feel, not what they cognitively, analytically, and deliberately know.

history: Awareness and comprehension of the history of a media-related topic and processes.

holism (nonsummative): The characteristic of systems that specify that the interrelationships among system elements and processes are so interdependent and complex that the system can only be understood as a "whole" or at a very inclusive level of analysis.

holism (synergy): A property of systems in which the total outcomes of any system are different than the sum of its parts.

home base: The default hand position used when the speaker is not gesturing.

homeostasis: A property of systems in which the tendency of the system is to maintain balance, maintaining a steady state without excess or dearth.

hospice care: A health service that aims to provide comfort care, including pain and symptom management, for the terminally ill.

human relations: A theoretical perspective toward organizations viewing individual needs as vital to the organizational success.

humanistic: Approaches or perspectives toward knowledge that emphasize the interpretation and exploration of myriad meanings of personal and human existence and its possibilities, typically using analytic, critical, or interpretive methods in the exploration of texts.

humanities: academic disciplines or fields of scholarship involving approaches or perspectives toward knowledge that emphasize the interpretation and exploration of myriad meanings of personal and human existence and its possibilities, typically using analytic, critical, or interpretive methods in the exploration of texts.

hypothesis: A proposal or statement regarding the relationship between variables. A verbal or symbolic statement of relationship between two or more variables, or how changes in one concept correspond to changes in another concept.

hypothesis testing: The use of inferential statistics to help a researcher arrive at a decision about whether to accept or reject the null hypothesis.

identification (rhetorical): In a Burkean sense, the process by which persuasion occurs in which rhetors use symbols in ways that reflect commonalities or allow recognition of one's own self in the symbolic meanings expressed.

identity: How self is perceived or evaluated.

ideology: A system of beliefs that shape attitudes and perceptions, and inform organizational culture. A system of ordered values, ideas and ideals, often implying a particular evaluative perspective toward social behavior (e.g., Marxism and feminism generally entail evaluative criteria or ideals for society).

idiosyncratic: Particular or unique; a "one-off" or characteristic specific to an individual or encounter or episode.

illness model: A model that assumes that all illnesses are due to a specifiable disease. The illness model is the basis for the biomedical model.

illusion of invulnerability: A typical symptom of groupthink in which there is a climate of extreme optimism; group members ignore signs of danger and engage in risk-taking actions.

illusion of morality: A typical symptom of groupthink in which group members are convinced their decisions are morally right while ignoring their ethical implications.

illusion of unanimity: A typical symptom of groupthink in which group members assume others agree with prevailing position whether expressed or not.

image appeal: The principle that audiences often respond better when there are visual cues, analogies, or representations of verbally expressed ideas.

implementation: The third step in launching a community-level intervention, involving careful monitoring and refinement of the campaign strategy and coordination between the campaign and its community partners.

inclusion: The critical rhetoric strategy used, for example, by early feminist rhetoric scholars to identify and introduce noteworthy but neglected women rhetors into the discipline's official canons and history books. Despite its importance, other feminist scholars have critiqued this strategy for reinforcing problematic, male-centric standards for what constitutes "good" rhetoric. See also *pluralistic inclusion* and *transformative approaches.*

independent variable: A variable that when altered or manipulated produces a change in a dependent variable.

individual roles: A group member's tendency for a group member to pursue self-goals or interests independent of, or at the expense of, group goals or interests.

individualism/collectivism: The extent to which individuals are supposed to look after themselves or remain integrated into groups that they belong to such as the family.

induction: Inferring a general law from particular instances. The opposite of *deduction.* The process of observing many specific instances of something and drawing a general conclusion about what these instances have in common.

inductive reasoning: A form of reasoning from particulars (i.e., specific cases) to generalizations.

ineffability: An experience that cannot be adequately expressed, voiced, or articulated.

inferential statistics: Statistics typically calculated at more advanced stages of data analysis in order to infer or draw conclusions about a population based on the sample used in the study.

informational support: A form of social support, where support provider(s) give(s) advice, instructions, or other forms of guidance to support receiver(s). Behavior that seeks to provide utilitarian guidance, advice, or instruction to another person.

injunctive norms: Norms that refer to what is socially approved or disapproved.

innovation adoption: A decision to accept an idea, practice, or object that an individual, group, or institution perceives as new.

innovators: With regard to diffusion of innovations theory, the initial stage of the population creating or initiating a decision, idea, product, service, etc.

input: In systems, the process variables that contribute to the system.

inquiry: An entryway into the practical applications of intercultural communication, comprised of motivations to know, question, and learn.

instrumental communication: Communication that functions to achieve specified goals or functions.

instrumental conflict: A struggle over what goals to achieve.

instrumentality (positive, negative, zero): The belief that a certain level of performance will lead to an outcome. Positive instrumentality indicates a belief that performance will lead to achieving an outcome; a negative instrumentality indicates a belief that performance will prevent an outcome from occurring; and a zero instrumentality represents no expectation of a relationship between performance and outcome.

intentionality: The assumption that there are states of conscious awareness and goal-orientation to behavior activation.

interact: A two-part sequence of two turns at talk or behavior by two or more interactants.

intercoder reliability: Consistency of responses between coders.

intercultural communication: An interactive, dynamic, and negotiated process of communicating one's self with members of different cultural groups and/or representing cultural others to members of one's own cultural group.

intercultural praxis: A critical, reflective, and practical process of being, thinking, feeling, analyzing, and acting in the world as an ethical intercultural communicator for social justice.

interdependence: A property of systems in which the system's components depend on each other for effective functioning. A change in one component changes all components because they are mutual dependent on each other. One party's objectives, goals, preferences, and/or behaviors are contingent on the other party's actions or at least are perceived to be contingent on those actions. The degree to which one person's goals or outcomes depend on the actions of another person or persons.

interdisciplinary teams: Healthcare teams composed of healthcare professionals from various subfields of medicine who work together at the same time and in the same setting to accomplish patient health goals (e.g., a surgical team that includes a primary surgeon, nurses, and an anesthesiologist).

intergenerational transmission hypothesis: The prediction that characteristics are heritable, and therefore the traits of the parents will be reflected significantly in the traits of the children.

internal consistency: The coherence of evidence. The theory must maintain logical consistency of all statements of conditionship, assumptions, and units.

internal validity: The extent a researcher can be confident in the cause-effect relationship observed in a study.

international communication: Similarities and differences between mass communication and/or mediated communication between two or more countries.

International Communication Association (ICA): A global academic professional association (https://www.icahdq.org/) of scholars and interested parties (e.g., government, media, business law, technology, health, etc.), founded in 1950.

interpersonal communication: The process of interaction and relationships (or relational communication) will be defined as the product of interpersonal interaction.

interpersonal relationships: Relationships that are more intimate than role relationships. Interpersonal relationships involve repeated interactions, a feeling of uniqueness about the relationship, and some degree of personal (as opposed to just role) interdependence.

interpretation: The ability to create, portray or perform different intended mediated identities or roles.

interpretative approach: Studying intercultural communication for the goals of understanding and appreciating how individuals as cultural members come to be, know, experience, enact, or negotiate their everyday communication interactions.

interpretive and ethnographic methods: Methods driven by the assumption that reality is socially constructed—that there are as many realities as there are people perceiving and influencing such perceptions through their communication.

interprofessional health communication: Communication occurring between individuals who identify as healthcare professionals.

interprofessional teams: Healthcare teams in which communication is occurring between individuals who identify as healthcare professionals.

intersectionality: Interpretive, often critical, perspectives toward knowledge claims that emphasize how race interacts with other social dimensions, such as class and gender, to collectively and variably produce particular subjective experiences.

intervening variable: Variables that can explain the effect of an independent variable on a dependent variable.

interviewing: The process of posing to participants a series of questions or prompts to better understand the ethnographic scene and setting.

intimate partner violence (IPV): Behavior intended to harm a person physically in the context of an established personal relationship.

intraboundary generality: The theory must provide statements of relationship that hold across all phenomena of concern.

intuitive ways of knowing: Everyday, layperson impressions; ways of thinking that apply personal rather than systematic normative procedures or methods.

invention: Constructing the content to be presented.

irreversibility: Communication cannot reverse the arrow of time—every new communication act is re-contextualized by what has been previously communicated and what has previously occurred.

journalism history: A distinctive early focus on the content of newspapers and magazines and how news was perceived by the public.

justifications: Statements or actions that accept responsibility but attempt to provide a rationale for the legitimacy of the transgression.

keying: Communication that signals the establishment of a frame among interactants. For example, a tone of voice or facial expression may signal that your friend is teasing you; while the insult may be something he or she would *really* say if trying to hurt you, the keying establishes a frame that *metacommunicates* to you not to take him or her seriously.

kinesics (body language): The study of how bodily movements communicate.

knowledge function: Attitudes that organize and process information and events.

knowledge-gap hypothesis: The prediction that that the diffusion of media will increasingly favor those with economic and institutional power.

kurtosis: The degree to which a distribution is peaked or flat.

laggards: With regard to diffusion of innovations theory, the last stages of population adopting a decision, idea, product, service, etc.

land-grant institutions: Originally oriented more toward agriculture and industry, significant donations of land to institutions of higher education to facilitate their development and access.

language/verbal communication: The use of digital (i.e., conventional discrete) symbols systems organized by syntax, semantics, phonemics, morphology, recursivity, displacement, and productivity.

language: The use of a conventional symbol system for communicating among organisms. To be considered linguistic, a symbol system generally has to meet several additional criteria, such as morphology, phonemics, syntax, semantics, productivity, recursivity, and displacement.

late majority: With regard to diffusion of innovations theory, the next-to-the-last stage of population adopting a decision, idea, product, service, etc.

latitude of acceptance: A cognitive range of attitudes regarding some topic within which a person will consider plausible, agreeable, or legitimate.

latitude of noncommitment: A cognitive range of attitudes regarding some topic within which a person has little or no involvement or care, or is ambivalent.

latitude of rejection: A cognitive range of attitudes regarding some topic within which a person will consider implausible, disagreeable, or illegitimate.

lay ideas: General understanding among non-expert audiences regarding causes and effects of health-related issues.

leader member relations: In the situational theory of leadership, the relationship leaders build with their members through interaction.

leadership: The process of motivating organizational members, involving change.

least preferred co-worker (LPC): In the situational theory of leadership, the leader's evaluation of the worker(s) in regard to their ability to achieve a task. Leaders who rate LPCs positively tend to be relationship oriented, whereas leaders who rate LPCs negatively tend to be task oriented in leadership style.

legitimate power: Influence based on a person's position or title granted by a higher power.

levels perspective: A paradigm for conceptualizing and studying communication based on context, primarily indexed by the number of people involved, but also taking into account factors such as formality and media.

liminality: From the Latin *limen*, meaning "threshold," it is a state of "betwixt and between," coined by Victor Turner to refer to the in-between role often experienced in rites of passage (e.g., a boy going off on a hunt and returning to the village a "man"; when on the hunt, he is neither boy nor man in the eyes of the villagers).

little rhetoric: The view, advanced by Plato and Aristotle, in distinct versions, that rhetoric is inferior to philosophy but can play a beneficial role when used in the service of philosophy. For Aristotle, in addition, rhetoric is the best practice in the civic, political domain specifically, which requires persuading a reason-deficient public based on situated, partly improvisational knowledge on ever-changing topics. Contrasted with *big rhetoric*.

logic: The underlying rationale or system of reasoning underlying some process or set of claims.

longitudinal survey: A research design that permits researchers to examine how individuals change over time.

localism: The belief that control and power should be shared by as many people as possible.

long-term/short-term orientation: The extent to which a cultural group conditions its members to accept or avoid delayed gratification of their materials, social, and emotional needs.

magisteria: A domain or set of types of inquiry and asking questions. Most associated with Stephen Jay Gould's argument that the sciences and religion ask different and relatively non-overlapping types of questions.

main effects model of social support (also known as structural support): The direct of effects of inclusion in strong and enduring social networks on individuals' psychophysiological health.

maintaining and consolidating campaign efforts: The fourth step in launching a community-level intervention, where campaign elements are incorporated into the community for the long-term by preserving volunteer effort and further merging campaign activities with existing community structures.

maintenance roles: A group member's tendency to reinforce and culminate the groups' social atmosphere.

management: A process of administering the status quo of an organization.

manipulation: Altering aspects or levels of an independent variable and measuring a dependent variable for any changes that result from that manipulation.

manipulation check: A procedure that allows a researcher to see if participants are in fact receiving the correct stimulus and/or the intended level of exposure to stimulus.

masculine: Behaviors such as independent play, roughness, aggression, being emotionally controlled, and being physically active.

masculinity/femininity: The degree to which the distribution of emotional roles between the sexes and genders are distinct and specific to gender roles or are allowed to overlap

mass communication: When a given source is capable of using media to transmit information to large quantities of potential recipients.

masspersonal communication: Occurs whenindividuals use conventional mass communication channels for interpersonal communication, individuals use conventional interpersonal communication channels for mass communication, and individuals engage in mass communication and interpersonal communication simultaneously.

mean: The average value of a variable.

mean world syndrome: With regard to cultivation theory, the state in which people believe the world is more criminal, violent, exploitative, and scary than it actually is.

meaning: The conscious formulation of an interpretation of the intent, purpose, significance, or implication of some symbolic or nonsymbolic set of thoughts or stimuli.

measurement: The process of systematic observation and assignment of numbers to phenomena, according to rules.

measures of dispersion: Designed to capture the variability, or how close or far away each value is from the mean score, these measures include range, variance, and standard deviation.

media competence: The ability to critically access, interpret, assess, and use media to both form and express feelings, positions and opinions.

media knowledge: The cognitive or mental faculties that inform our actions in regard to any given media message(s).

media literacy: The ability to critically access, interpret, assess, and use media to both form and express feelings, positions, and opinions.

media richness: The capacities of a medium for communicating more complex information in ways that can preserve verbal and nonverbal information, synchrony, and a sense of presence or immediacy and immersion.

media/medium: Something intermediate or between in position or nature, or a person or thing that acts as an intermediate agent, instrument, channel or means. Electronic communication technologies, such as radio, television, print, and the Internet, whose purpose is to attract audiences by disseminating information; a fragmented, multi-dimensional set of electronic communities that have become a fundamentally important part of our political ecology; effectively function as the facilitator of shortcuts between political candidates and the public.

median: The representation of the 50th percentile of the data—the point at which half of the values fall below or above.

mediating variables: Factors or constructs that account for the relationship between two variables.

mediation: A form of alternative dispute resolution (ADR), which is a process in which a third party attempts to facilitate a cooperative communication process through which the conflicting parties can achieve their own enforceable resolution to the conflict.

mediation structuration: One structure mediates another when its production and reproduction involve the reproduction of the other.

mediatization: The extent to which communication media infiltrate, integrate into, and frame everyday behavior.

member checking: Asking participants to comment on the veracity of observations, initial analysis, and/or conclusions, sometimes done in interviews but often done while negotiating interactions in the field.

memory: The ability to keep all the pieces of presentation in one's head.

memos: Lengthy elaborations of commentaries roughly two pages in length, written in complete sentences and paragraphs, in which the researcher attempts to utilize relevant research to frame initial themes or patterns in ethnographic data.

mental models: Cognitive schema that organize information associated with some experience of the world (e.g., attachment figures) into relatively stable structures or ways of thinking and perceiving.

metamorphosis: The final stage of organizational socialization in which members begin to change their expectations and behaviors to adapt to and become a vital part of the organizational culture.

methodological pluralism: The integration of multiple methodologies, just as many developed societies have begun to recognize the value of cultural pluralism.

micro/macro: In reference to relationship development theories, macro approaches conceptualize stages or developmental phases through which relationships evolve, and micro approaches focus on the dynamic processes of everyday interaction within relationships.

Millennials/Gen-Y: The U.S. generation born between 1980 and 1995.

mimetic conception of language: A *representational* view of symbols. From a mimetic standpoint, symbols seek to capture an objective reality that exists prior to and independently of the symbols that represent them.

mind-guarding: In an effort to preserve cohesion and group functioning, some group members may insulate the group from information if it potentially threatens group dynamics.

mirror neurons: A synapse that activates (i.e., fires) either when an animal engages in an action, or when observing that same action. The assumption is that mirror neurons activate at the observance of emotional expressions by others and thereby activate the same emotion state in the observing animal.

Mode: A measure of central tendency of a distribution of scores or values, representing the most commonly or frequently occurring score or value.

model: A visual (and sometimes mathematical) simplification of concepts that exist in both a hypothesized conceptual form and an actual or potential observed form.

moderating variables: Factors or constructs that influence the direction and/or strength of a relationship between two or more concepts.

Modern Language Association (MLA): A professional association (https://www.mla.org/) of scholars and teachers of language, literature, and linguistic form, founded in 1883.

money in the bank principle: The extent to which a theory has survived past attempts to falsify it.

monotone: The continuous sound of someone's voice that is unchanging in pitch, without intonation or expressiveness.

morphology: Rules for word formation.

Morrill Act: An act in 1862 that facilitated land grants in states to institutions of higher education.

motivation: The degree to which a member is driven or incentivized to pursue a given path of behavior.

multichanneled: The degree to which communication occurs simultaneously across multiple media or codes of expression (e.g., happiness can be communicated through laugher and vocalics, squinting eyes and oculesics, and the kinesics of bending over in laughter).

multidisciplinary teams: Healthcare teams composed of healthcare professionals from various subfields of medicine who work together but function independently (e.g., a health department consisting of health educators, nurses, and board members), all of whom perform required tasks independently.

multifinality: A property of systems in which any given way or path may result in multiple possible outcomes.

multiracial feminism: Intersectional approach to feminism, drawing into question perspectives other than the White, Western woman.

narrative coherence: Walter Fisher's first criteria for evaluating effective arguments. It concerns how consistent the speaker's values are with the story he or she tells, or how well the two things (speaker and story) "hang together."

narrative fidelity: Walter Fisher's second criteria for evaluating effective arguments. It centers on the audience in a rhetorical interaction and asks whether the story being told rings true to their particular experiences or not.

National Communication Association (NCA): A professional association of academics, scholars and teachers (https://www.natcom.org/) with a mission to advance and promote the communication discipline in all its forms, modes, media, and humanistic, social scientific, and aesthetic paradigms of inquiry, founded in 1914.

National Council of Teachers of English (NCTE): A U.S.-based professional and academic association of scholars and teachers (http://www2.ncte.org/) with a mission to advance and promote the teaching and learning of language arts and the English language, founded in 1911.

naturalistic generalizations: From Stake and Trumbull (1982), the use of writing to get the reader to feel what the participants and/or researcher experienced; the transferability of emotions and feelings from the researcher and participations to the reader.

naturally occurring: Interactions that would be occurring whether or not a recording device is present. Content of talk is not prescripted, idealized, or hypothetical.

nature versus nurture paradigm: The debate regarding the extent to which human behavior, including communication, is derived from heritable genetic traits (nature) or from environmental learning processes (nature).

navigating: The ability to utilize multiple transmedia platforms for accessing, researching, and networking for information.

need for cognition: a predisposition to enjoy or have fun engaging in effortful cognitive endeavors or thinking.

negative affect reciprocity: Responding to one person's negative comments or criticisms with one's own criticisms or insults.

negative relationship: A change in one variable creates a change in the opposite direction for the other variable.

negotiation: Any conflict in which all parties involved begin the interaction with a presumption of potential mutual benefit.

net value of higher education: The relative value of earnings adjusted by the cost of higher education.

network bridging: How densely interconnected a person is with people who are homogenous and tightly interconnected.

networking: the ability to interact with strong and weak social network ties to access information not readily available from traditional research methods.

neutral relationship: A change in one variable creates no change for the other variable.

New Orleans Conference: A 1968 conference of selected developed by the Speech Association of America (later, NCA) scholars to make communication a central part of speech scholarship.

nominal care teams: Healthcare groups that provide patient care through the oversight of the primary care physician (e.g., primary care physician recommends appointments with a physical therapist as part of a broader plan of care).

nonprobability sample: A sample in which each member of the population does not have an equal chance of being selected for the sample.

nonregulated couples: Relational couples with an exchange ratio of positively to negatively valenced communication approximating one to one.

nonresponse bias: Arises when the participants who do not answer a specific question or set of questions differ in important ways from the participants who did answer.

nonverbal communication: Meaningful behavior that is not linguistic in its code.

norm of reciprocity: A universal tendency to respond in kind to the actions of others.

normative beliefs: The degree to which others pressure someone to behave in certain ways.

null hypothesis: The proposition that no relationship exists between two variables.

observation: Conducted during fieldwork, the process of witnessing the goings-on in a particular scene or setting; the researcher may be completely involved in interactions (complete participant) or completely detached from interactions (complete observer), or somewhere in-between.

observational analysis: A quantitative method that investigates the actual interaction of people communicating. Both verbal and nonverbal communication behavior are examined.

oculesics (eye behavior): The study of how ocular or eye behaviors (e.g., gaze, contact, pupil dilation, etc.) communicate.

openness: Communication that fosters an environment open to the promotion and exchange of ideas.

operationalization: The techniques used to observe or measure a variable given its conceptualization.

optimal performance: Where perfect performance implies both ideal form and an absence of mistakes, optimal performance implies the best possible performance in a given situation and audience.

optimal tolerance: The same thing as the curvilinearity hypothesis, that individuals have preferable ranges for most social behaviors and that too little or too much of a behavior will activate displeasure or dis-preference.

order at all points: Patterned actions produced in the first instance as meaningful, and thus in meaningful ways, by participants.

organizational encounter: The second stage of organizational socialization in which the member joins the organization—the formal entry stage of socialization.

organizational grace: Acceptance, forgiveness, awareness, and caring, extends from healthy spirituality in a manner that recognizes, rewards, and respects another person.

organizational identification: The active process through which members experience their connection to the various aspects of the social context of the organization.

organizational templates: Standard heuristic guides for arranging the sequence of topics in a presentation (e.g., chronological, topical, etc.).

outcomes: The dependent variable(s), or the effects that result from the distal, proximal, moderating and mediating factors.

outliers: Extreme scores that can potentially influence results of an analysis.

output: In systems, the products and byproducts that come out of the system.

oxytocin: A hormone produced in the hypothalamus and released by the pituitary gland that facilitates sexual reproductive motivation, social bonding, and attachment.

panel design: A study design that follows the same group of individuals over time.

paradigm: A collective set of practices and beliefs shared by a group of scholars.

parameters: Mathematical estimates derived from the analysis of census data related to a population.

parsimony: The elegance or simplicity of a theory.

patriarchy: Systems of ideology, social structure, and practices created by men, which reflect the values and priorities of this group.

patterns of Interaction: Sequences of behavior that specify how one person's communicative behavior is followed by another person's communicative behavior.

peer review: A process by which people with comparable or topical expertise evaluate a project, manuscript, or body of scholarly work.

perceived behavioral control: Perceived capability of performing the behavior.

performance: The aesthetically shaped display of verbal, nonverbal, and mediated communication within a frame of meaning established by a communicator and intended to be shared with an audience.

performative methods: Methods seeking visceral engagement of audiences with the knowledge produced by interpretive and ethnographic means—by actual enactment of voice in performance settings.

performativity: Originated in Austin's notion of *performative utterances*, it is the property of written, spoken, and nonverbally displayed communication to *bring into being new understandings or meanings*. For Butler, the performativity of gender means enacted behaviors create commonplace understandings and make gender seem "natural" when gender is an ongoing construction.

peripheral route: A predominantly mindless, intuitive, subconscious, and uncritical process of information evaluation.

personal relationships: The most intimate and significant relationships people typically develop throughout their lifetimes that are highly interdependent; the parties involved in those relationships see one another as irreplaceable.

personal space bubble: The area surrounding an individual perceived to belong to and move with that individual, usually indicating a set of comfort zones that are variously permeable depending on contextual features such as the type of situation and relationship to others.

personal style: The factor affecting groups that refers to team members' display of a negative or positive attitude.

persuasion: An intentional effort that succeeds in influencing another person's mental state through some act or acts of communication in which the persuadee has relative freedom to choose.

phases: Distinct or identifiable period of time in which interaction reveals different functions or forms (e.g., openings, reason provision/solicitation, verbal history, diagnosis, detailing treatment, termination of consultation).

phases of group decision-making: An interval in the progression of group interaction in which certain behaviors, functions or patterns of behavior occur more prominently than in other intervals; for example, (1) orientation, (2) conflict, (3) emergence, and (4) reinforcement.

phonemics: Rules for sounding and pronunciation.

phylogeny (phylogenetic): The evolutionary history of a type or species of organism.

physical appearance: The features of a person's tangible features (e.g., dress, complexion, etc.) available to the perception of others when communicating.

pitch: Ordering of sound on a frequency-related scale.

place: One of the four Ps of marketing; denotes how and where target audience can gain access to the product.

plagiarism: The act of representing creative, textual, visual, musical, mathematical or other symbolic works as one's own when such work was actually directly or indirectly derived from another original source.

pluralistic inclusion: A critical rhetoric strategy that seeks to include neglected figures and voices from marginalized groups but in a way that recognizes and values their own ways of speaking, rather than measuring them against the standards of dominant groups. Continues to accept deeply held assumptions about rhetoric, however, such as its use by individual citizens to promote the goals of their states. See also *inclusion* and *transformative approaches*.

political communication: The study of how we use language and symbols to make sense of how goods and resources are dispensed and withheld.

political communication campaigns: Planned and organized collective communication efforts to pursue political objectives (e.g., election to office, policy change, social movement activation, etc.).

politics: The process by which a democratic polity makes decisions about how to dispense and withhold goods and resources.

polymedia: an environment, in which all media have to be considered in relationship to one another in regard to their communicative implications.

population: The entire set of people, objects, observations, or scores that have a characteristic in common.

position power: The leader's ability to either reward or punish members.

positionality: A researcher's stance in relation to the relevant social, cultural, and political dimensions of the context of research.

positioning: An entryway into the practical applications of intercultural communication, comprised by inviting appreciation and understanding of our own geographic, societal, economic, political, and historic positions. Strategy used to position the product in the context of competitors, often used in conjunction with the four p's of marketing.

positive relationship: A change in one variable creates a change in the same direction for the other variable.

power: A person's ability to influence or control some other person or decision. Dimension of relationship-level meaning that expresses the degree to which a person is equal to, dominant over, or deferential to others.

power distance: The extent to which the less powerful members of an organization, institution, or country accept and expect unequal distribution of power.

precision: The degree to which a theory allows for prediction of phenomena.

prescriptive decision-making models: procedures or templates for managing task interaction that represents what groups ought to, or are advised to pursue.

presenteeism: A state in which employees are present at work but limited in job performance by a health problem.

pressure to conform: A typical symptom of groupthink in which Group members apply strong social pressure against disagreement with the prevailing position.

price: One of the four Ps of marketing; involves addressing target audience's barriers to adopting the new behavior or idea.

probability level: The level of confidence (or confidence interval) used to reject the null hypothesis (e.g., no relationship or difference). Can be calculated by taking the percentile of the desired confidence level (e.g., 95%) and subtracting it from 1 (e.g., 1 − .95 = .05).

probability sample: A sample in which each member of the population has an equal chance of being selected for the sample.

probability theory: According to this theory, the score appearing most frequently in the sample will coincide with the score most frequently observed in the population. Also implicit in probability theory is the assumption that larger samples will more probably represent the population than will smaller samples.

probability value: Also called p-value. See *probability level.*

problem–solution: An organizational template for organizing a presentation by specifying and elaborating the nature and extent of a problem or issue, and then presenting a proposed approach to managing that problem or issue.

procedural knowledge: Involves all those aspects of mental access, assembly, and production involved in producing the actual skilled behavior of communication.

process campaign evaluation: Stage of campaign implementation that monitor the campaign plan, including the implementation of campaign materials, to confirm everything is going accordingly.

product: One of the four Ps of marketing; representing the new behavior or idea being "sold" and what benefits it offers the target audience when adopted.

production: The design, implementation and enactment of communication through a medium or media.

productivity: The capacity of language to generate new words and language.

progressive: The degree to which theories and knowledge in a paradigm become better at solving puzzles that previous or existing theories seem incapable of solving.

proletariat: A concept used by Karl Marx to describe the class of people who work for the bourgeoisie. This class owns nothing except their own labor, which they are forced to sell to the *bourgeoisie* class for an exploitative wage.

promotion: One of the four Ps of marketing involves development and implementation of the communication strategy used to convey and publicize the message or content about the product.

propaganda: An institutional or group-based systematic and deliberate set of efforts intended to shape the perceptions, thoughts and behaviors to achieve some outcomes preferred by the propagandist.

prosumption: The process of producing communication through media.

proxemics (spatial behavior): The study of the use of spatial, distance, and locational forms of communication.

proximal factors or influences: Factors close in time to an event. Factors that occur in the immediate context that influence the phenomenon of interest.

psychological theories: Emphasize internal psychological processes in early childhood development and through interpersonal interactions with primary caregivers.

public narrative: Sequences of characters and actions connected by a meaningful thread or through-line.

punching: Vocally italicizing important words or phrases during a public presentation.

qualifier: A component of the Toulmin model that brings attention to the probabilistic character of arguments.

qualitative: methods driven by the assumption that there are meanings and interpretations that can be extracted through focused attention, expertise, and insight into (typically textual) human behavior.

quality of work life (QWL): The multidimensional (i.e., physical, psychological, social, and spiritual) forms of health in a work context.

Quantitative methods: Research approaches that answer questions by using numbers to quantify a phenomenon.

quasi-experimental design: An experimental design that does not use random assignment to assign participants to study conditions.

queer theory: Theory that social categories artificially restrict people's perceptions and thus should be critically examined.

questionnaire: A form comprised of different sets of questions.

random assignment: A primary form of experimental control in which each member of the population has an equal chance of being assigned to an experimental or control group in an experiment.

range: The distance between the highest and lowest value, which can be computed by subtracting the lowest value from the highest value.

rate: The number of words spoken per minute.

reach: The number of targets capable of receiving a message through a given medium.

reasoned action: Models of persuasion that assume behavior is a function of reasoning that involves behavioral intentions, evaluation of norms, and beliefs relevant to such behavior.

rebuttal/qualifier: In (Toulmin) argument theory, a statement or disclaimer that places a form of exception or probability to the claim(s) being posited. A component of the Toulmin model that specifies the conditions under which an argument could fail.

recency: The timeliness of evidence. Also, in persuasion theory, the degree to which a message was included early or late (i.e., recently) in a broader presentation or campaign.

recipient design: Talk is sensitive to recipient design as next actions reveal how speakers hear and orient to specific and local social actions comprising prior speakers' utterances.

reciprocity: The matching of one party's actions with a similar response; the general tendency for such a response is referred to as the norm of reciprocity.

recursivity: Capable of self-reference, or using itself to refer to itself, such as in dictionaries, or asking someone "What did you mean by that [gesture, statement, etc.]?"

redundancy: The extent to which multiple channels or codes of communication contain and complement or reinforce one another's information or meaning. The principle that communicating an idea across multiple verbal and visual channels increases the likelihood of audience impact.

reference/thought: A meaningful cognition or idea.

referent: A thing or set of things in the objective sensory world to which messages and referents refer; a thing signified.

referent power: Influence based on a person's ethos, character, trust, and charisma.

reflection: An entryway into the practical applications of intercultural communication, comprising the ability to learn and grow from self-reflection upon oneself in interaction and relationship to others.

reflective thinking: A multistep process groups use to solve problems. The following steps are involved in reflective thinking: identify the problem, analyze the problem, determine the criteria by which decisions will be made, suggest possible solutions, engage in brainstorming, evaluate the possible solutions using set criteria, test and implement the best solution.

reflexivity: The process of critically reflecting on the research process, the researcher's attempts to understand the data, and the researcher's own relevant personal experience as it relates to the research topic.

regulated couples: Relational couples with a predominant exchange of positively valenced communication relative to their negatively valenced communication exchanges.

relational maintenance behaviors: Actions, behaviors, and communication processes used in order to sustain preferred relational definitions or tendencies.

relationship: Connection or link between variables.

relevance: The logical, practical, and reasonable connection of evidence to the claim being made.

reliability: How consistently a variable measure will produce the same results. In conversation analysis, recordings and transcriptions allow for repeated rehearings, reviewings, and reinspections of actual and determinate social events and activities, moments which can be made available for public inspection to provide readers/observers with the opportunity to agree and/or disagree with claims being advanced.

representation: The ways of writing and structuring of the report that researchers choose to present themselves and their participants in the study.

research: Awareness and comprehension of credible research on a media-related topic and processes.

researching: The ability to discern the most credible (reliable, expert, trustworthy) and relevant information from accessible information regarding a specified topic area.

response rate: The percentage of participants who return a survey in relation to the percentage invited to participate.

reward power: Influence based on a person's ability to give rewards to other members.

rhetorical vision: The composite vision for a group created by its character formations, plots, scene, and sanctioning agents.

rhizomatic learning: Pedagogical or learning practices that evolve and renew themselves based on student and educational circumstances. The analogy is based on rhizome root systems of plants in which the older stem of the root dies off as the emergent parts of the root are constantly creating new forms of themselves.

rites: Formal events that serve to reinforce the cultural values of the organization.

rituals: everyday "ways of doing things" in the organization.

role relationships: relatively standardized or normative definitions of functions and organized sets of behavioral expectations for social or institutional behavior. A distinctive feature of role relationships is that the occupants are somewhat interchangeable.

sample: The group of selected people, objects, observations, or scores to be included in an actual research study.

sampling bias: Any distortion in which a sample of observations from a population result in the sample not representing the population from which it is drawn.

sampling frame: A list of all potential participants within the feasible population.

scene: A particular geographic location within the field of study.

scholarly journal: A periodical publication in which original scholarly works are published based on peer review, and often blind review, and based on the decision of an editor or editorial staff appointed to oversee a process intended to be fair, impartial, and rigorous.

scholarly ways of knowing: A process of apprenticed inquiry that presupposes the potential for continued and progressive accumulation, refinement, and expansion of expertise on subject matters.

science(s): The systematic application of method and observation in the pursuit of discovery and testing of reasoned conjectures regarding the description and explanation of worldly phenomena. Or, the systematic search for explicable and replicable pattern(s). The systematic application of method and observation in the pursuit of discovery and testing of reasoned conjectures regarding the description and explanation of worldly phenomena (or, the systematic search for explicable pattern).

scientific: Scholarly approach to understanding or knowledge systematically employing methods and observation in the pursuit of discovery and testing of reasoned conjectures regarding the description and explanation of worldly phenomena, typically involving procedures such as experimental control, inferential analysis, and coding processes that seek intersubjective agreement and/or replicability across observers and investigations.

scientific management: An historically early approach to leadership concerned with the technical elements needed to organize and manage people, seeking the single optimal technique to maximize efficiency to increase optimal output.

scratch notes: Jottings made in the field to later be transcribed into field notes.

second-wave feminism: The social and political movement associated with identifying and challenging broader and more diverse sex-based disparities beyond first wave feminism.

secondary citation: An instance in which ideas or content originally published, written, spoken, or created by one entity (entity A) is cited by another entity (entity B), and a new author cites A based only on direct knowledge of B (e.g., "According to Jones, 2004, as cited by Smith, 2011) .

self-censorship: A typical symptom of groupthink in which group members with dissenting opinions refrain from opinion expression.

self-disclosure: The multidimensional process of revealing personal information about oneself to another.

self-efficacy: The belief in one's own ability to engage in a behavior (e.g., make healthier choices). The belief that one is competent or able to accomplish a task.

self-plagiarism: Using one's own text from previously completed (e.g., submitted and graded paper) or published content without attribution or citation to that prior work and authorship.

self-reflexivity: A focused conscious awareness, and often overt articulation, of the role of self in the process of observation and inquiry.

semantics: Rules for meaning attribution to words and sentences.

sense-making: The ongoing organizational process through which people continually try and make sense of the process they are experiencing—a process constituted in and by communication.

sequential influence strategies: Techniques that involve a series of persuasion tactics to convince a recipient to alter a behavior.

sequential organization: The turn-by-turn and action-by-action character of unfolding interactional participation.

sex: Biologically determined category that is conceived by chromosomes.

sign/symbol: Anything that is conventionally used to stand for something else; signs are often considered to have a more restrictive link between the sign and the signified, whereas symbols are considered more flexible in usage.

significance testing: A way of comparing the statistical test or result of a given study to the probability that that particular result will occur by chance alone.

simulation: The processes of using visual, audio, and textual forms of analogy and metaphor to translate one set of ideas into another communicative form to represent those ideas.

situational perspective: A theory of leadership based on the fit between the leader's task or relationship orientation and leader–member relations, task structure, and leader power or status.

skewness: When values of a variable tend to cluster to one side of the distribution.

skill: An ability (i.e., the capacity for goal-driven, repeatable behavior) that has been internalized to some degree of efficiency, stability, or other criterion of quality.

skills shift: An employment and economic trend toward less physical labor and toward more complex communication, service, and interaction-based occupations.

social capital: Resources that are available to individuals as a function of membership in their existing and ongoing social networks. The sum of all a person's social support.

social capital brokerage: The ability to connect multiple social networks of people in an organization.

social cognitive theory: Presumes that behavior is mediated by mental appraisals and environmentally learned behaviors.

social drama: Turner's process, based on established understandings of stage dramas, by which a community deals with a break in its cultural norms and values, consiting of a *breach* (an important norm or value is violated), *crisis* (the community isn't sure how to reconcile the violation and proceed), *redress* (community members advocate a way to address and/or solve the crisis resulting from this violation), and *reintegration* and *schism* (depending on the redress, a community reintegrates the violator(s) or accepts a permanent schism between members).

social exchange model: Employing a marketplace investment analogy, the process by which the interaction between people is understood as the interdependent transfer of perceived costs, rewards, alternatives, and foregone alternatives.

social influence: Persuasion occurring in routine, ordinary, and typically interpersonal settings.

social judgment theory: The conjecture that persuasive messages are evaluated (i.e., judged) based on pre-existing attitudes.

social justice: Both a process and a goal of promoting fair treatments of all and more equitable distributions of resources.

social learning theory: The conjecture that humans learn how to behave by modeling other human behavior theory that focuses on interpersonal interactions between child and caregiver and the rewards and punishments of gender role performance.

social marketing: The practice of applying effective marketing techniques developed in the commercial sector to developing campaigns that are prosocial in nature and designed to promote social good through products, price, promotions, and positioning.

social network support: Behavior that seeks to facilitate linkages between a person in need and others who may be able to help.

social penetration stages (orientation, exploratory affective exchange, affective exchange, stable exchange): The degree to which two or more persons in an interaction or relationship achieve both breadth (i.e., number of topics) and depth (i.e., intimacy of topics) in their communication. In order from the broadest and most superficial to the most intimate stages of penetration are *orientation* (the period of initial interaction), *exploratory affective exchange* (the period of experimentation with more personal topics), *affective exchange* (a personal relationship with the discussion of numerous personal topics), and *stable exchange* (arriving at the psychosocial core of the other).

social presence: The extent to which a medium conveys social, contextual, visual and nonverbal cues of the message and/or its source.

social science: Seeks to predict, explain, and understand social processes. Studying intercultural communication for the goals of explaining and predicting communication choices and behaviors based on cultural backgrounds.

social support: The perceived or actual degree to which a person does or can receive tangible, informational, emotional, or behavioral care or assistance from others in his or her social network(s). Verbal and nonverbal behavior produced with the intention of providing assistance to others perceived as needing that aid.

socialization: The process by which new members become assimilated into the organization and how they learn and adapt to the organizational culture.

socially constructed and constructive: A conjectured process in which language and social interaction substantially alters, mediates, or creates perceived reality, often to such a degree that reality itself is altered directly or indirectly (e.g., exposure to negative messages can result in an eating disorder or depression).

sociofugal space: Physical environments that inhibit social interaction.

sociopetal space: Physical environments that facilitate social interaction.

soft skills: Abilities that facilitate competent and collaborative interaction with others.

Sophists: The world's first professional speaking instructors who taught ancient Greek citizens how to communicate effectively and win arguments. The sophists believed language played an active role in shaping reality and truth and were proponents of a *big rhetoric* perspective, which Plato and Aristotle both rejected.

source: Awareness and comprehension of qualifications, credibility and relative expertise of a media source.

source analysis (ethos): Analysis and evaluation of the legitimacy, reliability, trustworthiness, and competence of the source of a media message.

speech code: A system of symbols, premises, meanings, rules, and agreements that are socially constructed and shared by members of a speech community to guide their communication conducts.

speech history: A distinctive focus on public speaking, persuasive messages, and the communication processes affecting group discussion.

spiral model: A pattern of decision-making in which a group swings back and forth through phases of interaction in a cyclical pattern.

spiral of silence: The conjecture that when an individual or group perceives to hold an opinion that is not held by the majority of other individuals or groups, that individual or group member elects to remain silent rather than articulate a minority opinion.

stakeholders: Any entity or party (e.g., community members, target audience, etc.) whose outcomes are affected by the health risk or campaign and whose support is important for reaching campaign objectives.

standard deviation: Indicates, on average, how much each value differs from the mean value.

standpoint theory: Theory that focuses on the influence of gender, race, class, and other social categories on people's lives. The key point of view with this perspective is reflection.

statistics: Mathematics that use data—information gathered, recorded, or observed—from a sample to make an estimation about what we can expect to occur in a population.

status: A person's ability to influence based on position or importance in a group.

STEM/STEAM: Science, technology, engineering, (arts), and mathematics focused education.

stereotyping: A typical symptom of groupthink in which group members generate or reinforce negative stereotypes of rivals or outgroups.

strategic choice model: A four-quadrant typology of conflict defined by the dimensions of directness–indirectness and positive valence–negative valence.

strategies: The use of similar tactics across an entire conflict episode.

stress: A person's psychological and physiological reaction to a potential real or perceived threat.

stress-buffering model of social support: Model focusing on "buffering" or protective functions of social support (e.g., emotional, informational, appraisal, tangible, and relational) against stress.

strong effects models: A media frameworks perspective that assumes media exposure results in powerful and strong persuasive effects on audiences.

structural holes: Gaps in interaction links between groups or social networks in an organization.

structuration: The process of producing and reproducing various social systems through the appropriation of rules, and resources.

structured interviews: Informal interviews, often conversational in nature, designed to elicit short narratives or lengthier stories, depending on the goal of the researcher.

style: Using language appropriate to the audience and to make the message clear.

style guide: An official set of rules for composition of a written work, typically authorized by a professional or publishing organization.

styles (conflict): The tendency of a person to do the same thing across conflicts with a given person or across conflict situations.

subjective norm: The perception of others' views of performing or not performing a behavior.

sufficiency: The degree to which there is adequate quantity and quality of evidence to generalize.

summative campaign evaluation: Evaluation stage were the extent to which the publication health communication campaign was effective at achieving its goals is determined.

superior–subordinate interaction: The everyday interpersonal or dyadic interactions between members of lower and higher status in an organization.

supporting style: The style of leadership in which members need high relational supportiveness and low task direction.

supportive climate: The communicative context resulting from supportive communication.

supportive communication: Communication that engenders trust, which opens communication channels.

survey: A method used in social science research that seeks to learn more about individuals or groups by directly asking participants questions about their perceptions, opinions, knowledge, and behaviors.

syllogism: A deductive form of reasoning that arrives at an unstated conclusion based on shared premises. For example: "All men are mortal (premise 1), Socrates is a man (premise 2); therefore, Socrates is mortal (conclusion)." A tripartite system of statements in which the conclusion is logically entailed by the two preceding premises.

symbolic action: Kenneth Burke's term for what he saw as the uniquely human domain of creative meaning-making. See also *dramatism* and *constructivist conception of language.*

symbolic convergence: The sense-making function of communication, focusing on how groups create a common language of shared emotions, motives, and meanings that bring a group into a cohesive unit.

symbolic thinking: The ability to conceptualize with a malleable and conventional system for referring to the world and thoughts about that world

symmetry: The interact-based sequence in which a party responds with the same behavior as the previous party just enacted.

synchrony: the extent to which a medium permits or facilitates immediacy of response to messages.

syntax: Rules for word arrangement in phrases and sentences.

synthesis: The facilitation of organizing and including existing ideas and information.

system: Any set of interdependent parts that function as a whole.

systems perspective of community: Perspective that considers community to be part of a larger dynamic system connected to other sectors and organizations and where a change in one sector signifies a change in others.

systems theory: A theory that considers organizations and the broader environment within which they must operate and adapt.

tactics: Specific types of behavior.

tangible support: A form of social support where support provider(s) give necessary (usually physical) resources and perform(s) behaviors such as lending money and domestic and/or professional duties for the support receiver(s).

task roles: A group member's tendency to work toward, focus on, and facilitate a group's goal achievement.

task structure: Whether a task is highly structure or accomplished in a number of different ways.

teams: A group that also has characteristics of high interdependence, cohesion, identity, commitment, and complementary skillsets.

teamwork factors: Openness, supportiveness, personal style, and action orientations that differentiate effective from ineffective team members.

technologists: In reference to communication history, the scholarly focus on the technologies or media of communication and information flow, exemplified by the Bell Laboratories research, and Shannon and Weaver's information theory.

telos: A predetermined endpoint or goal that a particular living thing or rhetorical activity seeks to realize.

terministic screens: A concept developed by Kenneth Burke which conveys that language never functions simply as a neutral, objective mirror that reflects or *represents* reality as it really is, but functions instead as a kind of "symbolic filter" that always selects or includes some aspects of reality while deflecting or excluding others.

theoretical population: An ideal population of all participants that can possibly be studied to answer a research question or test a hypothesis.

theory of normative behavior: The conjecture that a norm's influence on behavior can be explained by the desired level of social approval (e.g., strength of injunctive directives), the perceived benefits of performing the behavior (e.g., outcome expectancies), and the degree to which an individual aspires to be similar to the group endorsing the norm (e.g., group identity).

theory of planned behavior: The variables of attitude, subjective norm, and behavioral control are used to predict intention to change behavior, which in turn predicts actual behavior.

theory of reasoned action: A family of conjectures that posit behavior is a function of attitude, subjective norms, and behavioral intentions.

Theory X: Classical management style where managers believed that workers had an inherent dislike for work and that workers needed to be controlled and told what to do.

Theory Y: A management style in which work could be viewed as natural as play and that workers learned under the proper conditions and workers could show self-direction and control.

theory: A framework within which information is organized and therefore comprehended in a single explanatory perspective. A set of statements that explain or predict a phenomenon. A verifiable conceptual system of interrelated propositions explaining conditionship among a set of phenomena.

thick description: Writing (typically ethnographically) in a vivid way that provides extensive details of observation that contextualize and ground cultural patterns and social relations in and through those details

third-wave feminism: The social and political movement associated with more post-modern expansion of the meanings of gender- and sex-based norms and identities.

thriving: In contrast to surviving (coping with but not exceeding the basic well-being requirements of a workplace), thriving implies the achievement of positive work-life balance.

throughput: In systems theory is the process and interactions group members go through in reaching their goal. the process by which decisions and processes are formulated within the system.

topical: An organizational template for organizing a presentation by separating basic themes of a given topic.

Toulmin model: A model developed by Stephen Toulmin that makes explicit the implicit assumptions of syllogistic arguments. The model allows us to see how all arguments are historical, normative, and context-specific and thus always rhetorical. See *warranting model*.

traditionalists: The U.S. generation born before 1946.

trait: Relatively enduring individual differences or characteristics.

trait (perspective): A theory of leadership emphasizing the stable characteristics and individual differences that distinguished between leaders and non-leaders.

transactional leadership: A theory proposing that leadership consists primarily of management, or preserving the status quo of an organization and its members.

transdisciplinary teams: Healthcare teams comprised of members who are sufficiently knowledgeable about, and able to provide skills from, the other health fields of the team members (e.g., when a social worker on a hospice team is able to explain a patient's dietary requirements).

transformation: the ability to comprehend the logic of and create audio and/or visual mediated representations of textual concepts.

transformational leadership: A theory proposing that leadership changes and transforms of others, much like the definition of leadership itself.

transformative approaches: A critical rhetoric strategy that seeks to fundamentally transform traditional conceptions of rhetoric and argumentation by critically examining even its most basic assumptions such as rhetoric's use by individual citizens to promote the goals of their nation-states. Transformative approaches thus radically affirm alternative ways of speaking and arguing, including even those of noncitizens, non-Westerners, and indigenous communities. See also *inclusion* and *pluralistic inclusion.*

transportation: The extent to which a consumer is transported into a media story, narrative, or context.

trend design: A study design that follows different groups of individuals over time.

triangulation: using multiple data sources to see if they concur or agree with observer interpretations

tropes: Prototypical figurative forms of speech, expression, or representation. Commonly used oxymorons (e.g., "deafening silence") and metaphors (e.g., "thirst for knowledge") are examples of tropes.

troubles talk: The conversations that close relational partners share in the face of troubling or uncertain situations.

true experimental design: An experimental design that uses random assignment to assign participants to study conditions.

twice-behaved behavior: Schechner's notion that performance—staged and everyday—is a recreation of previously observed behavior. But, just as one can never step into the same river twice, these recreations are actually new creations as they slightly change the repeated behavior each time.

two-step flow: Early model of communication in which media (step 1) create a minor influence on conversation (step 2), which subsequently has a more substantial effect on attitudes, beliefs and behavior.

Type I error: Happens when a researcher rejects a null hypothesis when it should have been accepted.

Type II error: Happens when a researcher incorrectly accepts the null hypothesis in concluding that there is no relationship.

ubiquity of communication: The primacy of interaction and symbolic behavior in everyday life, relative to other activities.

uncertainty avoidance: The degree to which a cultural group conditions and controls its members to feel either comfortable or uncomfortable in unstructured situations that are novel or different from usual.

uncertainty reduction theory: A theory that posits that a lack of predictability (i.e., uncertainty) significantly drives a variety of interpersonal communication processes, especially in initial interaction encounters.

unidisciplinary teams: healthcare teams comprised of collections of healthcare professionals from the same subfields of medicine (e.g., cardiovascular physicians coming together to propose a new surgical approach).

units of analysis: Data points selected for coding. The particular data points selected for coding.

universal audience: An audience that adheres to a general conception of "reasonableness," this is composed of a diverse population. The universal audience changes historically.

universal/cross-cultural: The extent to which a given communicative form of expression and/or meaning is common across the human species, regardless of cultural or geographic context.

uses and gratifications: A theoretical framework that seeks to (a) explain how people use media to gratify their needs, (b) understand motives for media behavior, and (c) identify functions that follow from needs, motives, and behaviors.

utilitarian attitudes: Attitudes that help people maximize benefit and minimize cost.

valence: An individual's attitude, or preference, toward a particular outcome.

valence dimension: The emotional tone of the behavior, referring to the degree to which the values expressed are positive or negative in nature.

validity: Empirical findings (a) are grounded within and exemplified through close inspections of naturally occurring interactional materials, rather than preselected (ungrounded) categories or abstract assumptions about communication practices, and (b) preserve the integrity and distinctiveness of conversational activities. How accurately a measure assesses the intended variable.

value-expressive attitudes: Attitudes that reflect central values and self-images.

variable: Any construct or concept that can be observed to take on different values. It takes the form of X = fY. Anything that can assume more than one value.

variance: The average distance between the values in a variable from the mean value.

verbal: Pertaining to the use or form of words or language.

verifiability/falsifiability: The degree to which a theory's components can be observed and tested.

vertical integration: The degree to which all aspects of media are owned by one (monopoly), or a few (oligopoly) persons or institutions, thereby significantly distorting a marketplace toward the values and influences of that ownership. The degree to which an organization or industry owns and/or controls all aspects of media production, from content acquisition to distribution, and/or across media platforms.

violence: A conflict involving physical contact, restraint (e.g., kidnapping, imprisonment), and the potential for physical injury.

visualization: A mental process of mentally rehearsing idealized images of the performance.

vocalics (paralinguistic communication): The study of how nonlinguistic features of vocal expression (e.g., pitch, range, volume, inhaling, sighing, laughter, etc.) communicate.

warrant: In (Toulmin) argument theory, the bridging statement or reason that logically connects data to a claim as a rationale or justification. The reason(s), rationale(s), or answer(s) to the question, "why should I believe the claim being made by this research?"

warranting model: An abstract template of argument elements, consisting most basically of data, claim, and warrant (or reasons).

weak effects models: A media frameworks perspective that assumes effects from media exposure are passive with selective influence.

whiteness: A cultural norm and ideal in dominant Western culture that has historically been privileged. Strategic rhetoric used, consciously or unconsciously, to maintain the racial status quo.

withdrawal: Any behavior attempting to avoid further conflict (also known as stonewalling).

Wobegon effect: The tendency to view self as better than average, or better than self is viewed by others. See also *better-than-average effect.*

working knowledge factors: Experience and problem-solving and factors that differentiate effective from ineffective team members.

work–life balance: The degree of homeostasis that permits a person to cope with a stress level without experiencing dysfunction or trauma. A work–life balance generally means that a worker experiences a physically, emotionally, and psychologically healthy work life.

References

Abel, J. R., & Deitz, R. (2013). Do big cities help college graduates find better jobs? Liberty Street Economics. Retrieved from: http://libertystreeteconomics.newyorkfed.org/2013/05/do-big-cities-help-college-graduates-find-better-jobs.html

Abel, J. R., & Deitz, R. (2014a, December). Agglomeration and job matching among college graduates. *Federal Reserve Bank of New York* (Staff Report No. 587). Retrieved from: https://www.newyorkfed.org/medialibrary/media/research/staff_reports/sr587.pdf

Abel, J. R., & Deitz, R. (2014b). Do the benefits of college still outweigh the costs? *Current Issues in Economics and Finance, 20*(3), 1–12.

Abel, J. R., Deitz, R., & Su, Y. (2014). Are recent college graduates finding good jobs? *Current Issues in Economics and Finance, 20*(1). Retrieved from: https://www.newyorkfed.org/medialibrary/media/research/current_issues/ci20-1.pdf

Acuna, A. (2013, May 21). How much time to managers spend on conflict? *Learning4Management.* Retrieved from: https://learning-4managers.com/dir/conflict_management/

Adams, K. M., Hester, P. T., Bradley, J. M., Meyers, T. J., & Keating, C. B. (2014). Systems theory as the foundation for understanding systems. *Systems Engineering, 17*(1), 112–123.

Afifi, W. A., & Weiner, J. L. (2004). Toward a theory of motivated information management. *Communication Theory, 14*(2), 167–190.

Aikens, J. E., Nease, D. E., & Klinkman, M. S. (2008). Explaining patients' beliefs about the necessity and harmfulness of antidepressants. *The Annals of Family Medicine, 6*(1), 23–29.

Ajzen, I. (1985). From intentions to actions: A theory of planned behavior. In J. Kuhl & J. Beckmann (Eds.), *Action-control: From cognition to behavior* (pp. 1–39). Heidelberg, Germany: Springer.

Akins, S. (2009). Racial segregation, concentrated disadvantage, and violent crime. *Journal of Ethnicity in Criminal Justice, 7*(1), 30–52.

Aladwani, A. M. (2017). Compatible quality of social media content: Conceptualization, measurement, and affordances. *International Journal of Information Management, 37*(6), 576–582.

Alcolea-Banegas, J. (2009). Visual arguments in film. *Argumentation, 23*(2), 259–275.

Alicke, M. D., & Govorun, O. (2005). The better-than-average effect. In M. D. Alicke, D. A. Dunning, & J. I. Krueger (Eds.), *The self in social judgment* (pp. 85–106). New York, NY: Psychology Press.

Allen, B. J. (1996). Feminist standpoint theory: A black woman's (re)view of organizational socialization. *Communication Studies, 47*(4), 257–271.

Allen, J. A., Beck, T., Scott, C. W., & Rogelberg, S. G. (2014). Understanding workplace meetings: A qualitative taxonomy of meeting purposes. *Management Research Review, 37*(9), 791–814.

Allen, J. A., Sands, S. J., Mueller, S. L., Frear, K. A., Mudd, M., & Rogelberg, S. G. (2012). Employees' feelings about more meetings: An overt analysis and recommendations for improving meetings. *Management Research Review, 35*(5), 405–418.

Alter, A. (2013). *Drunk tank pink: And other unexpected forces that shape how we think, feel, and behave.* New York, NY: The Penguin Press.

Altman, I., & Taylor, D. A. (1973). *Social penetration: The development of interpersonal relationships.* Oxford, UK: Holt, Rinehart & Winston.

Altonji, J. G., Blom, E., & Meghir, C. (2012, April). Heterogeneity in human capital investments: High school curriculum, college major, and careers (NBER Working Paper No. 17985). JEL No. I21, J24. Retrieved from: https://www.frbatlanta.org/-/media/Documents/news/conferences/2011/employment-education/altonji.pdf

Álvarez-Arregui, E., Rodríguez-Martín, A., Madrigal-Maldonado, R., Grossi-Sampedro, B-Á., & Arreguit, X. (2017). Ecosystems of media training and competence: International assessment of its implementation in higher education. *Comunicar, 25*(51), 105–114.

Alvesson, M., & Deetz, S. A. (2006). Critical theory and postmodernism approaches to organizational studies. In S. Clegg, C. Hardy, T. Lawrence, and W. Nord (Eds.), *The SAGE Handbook of Organization Studies* (2nd ed., pp. 255–283). Thousand Oaks, CA: SAGE Publications.

Amato, P. R. (1996). Explaining the intergenerational transmission of divorce. *Journal of Marriage and Family, 58*(3), 628–640.

American Psychological Association. (2010). *Publication manual of the American Psychological* Association (6th ed.). Washington, DC: Author.

Ampuja, M., Koivisto, J., & Väliverronen, E. (2014). Strong and weak forms of mediatization theory. *NORDICOM Review, 35*, 111–123.

Andersen, O. J. (2008). A bottom-up perspective on innovations: Mobilizing knowledge and social capital through innovative processes of bricolage. *Administration & Society, 40*(1), 54–78.

Andersen, P. A. (1986). Consciousness, cognition, and communication. *Western Journal of Speech Communication, 50*(1), 87–101.

Andersen, P. A. (2008). *Nonverbal communication: Forms and functions.* Long Grove, Il: Waveland Press.

Andersen, P. A., Garrison, J. P., & Andersen, J. F. (1979). Implications of a neurophysiological approach for the study of nonverbal communication. *Human Communication Research, 6*(1), 74–89.

Andersen, P. A., & Guerrero, L. K. (1998). Principles of communication and emotion in social interaction. In P. A. Andersen & L. K. Guerrero (Eds.), *Handbook of communication and emotion: Research, theories, applications, and contexts* (pp. 49–96). San Diego, CA: Academic Press.

Anderson, J. A. (1996). *Communication theory.* New York, NY: Guilford.

Anderson, J. A., & Baym, G. (2004). Philosophies and philosophic issues in communication, 1995–2004. *Journal of Communication, 54*(4), 589–615.

Anderson, P., & Spitzberg, B. (2009). Myths and maxims of risk and crisis communication. In R. Heath & D. O'Hair (Eds.), *Handbook of risk and crisis communication* (pp. 205–226). New York, NY: Routledge.

Anderson, T., & Emmers-Sommer, T. (2006). Predictors of relationship satisfaction in online romantic relationships. *Communication Studies, 57*(2), 153–172.

Aparici, R., & García-Marín, D. (2018). Prosumers and emirecs: Analysis of two confronted theories. *Comunicar, 26*(55), 71–79.

Apker, J. (2012). *Communication in health organizations.* Cambridge, MA: Polity Press.

Arazy, O., Yeo, L., & Nov, O. (2013). Stay on the Wikipedia task: When task-related disagreements slip into personal and procedural conflicts. *Journal of the American Society for Information Science and Technology, 64*(8), 1634–1648.

Aristotle. (1994–2009). Physics. In D. C. Stevenson (Ed.), R. P. Hardie & R. K. Gay (Trans.), *The Internet classics archive.* http://classics.mit.edu/Aristotle/physics.4.iv.html

Aristotle. (2006). *On rhetoric: A theory of civic discourse* (G. Kennedy, Trans.). Oxford, UK: Oxford University Press.

Arizona State University. (n.d.). https://humancommunication.clas.asu.edu/research-and-initiatives/transformation-project

Arntz, M., Gregory, T., & Zierahn, U. (2017). Revisiting the risk of automation. *Economics Letters, 159*, 157–160.

Arpan, L. M., & Peterson, E. M. (2008). Influence of source liking and personality traits on perceptions of bias and future news source selection. *Media Psychology, 11*(2), 310–329.

Asante, M. K. (1980). Intercultural communication: An inquiry into research directions. *Communication Yearbook, 4*(1), 401–410.

Ashcraft, K. L. (2005). Feminist organizational communication studies: Engaging gender in public and private. In S. May & D. K. Mumby (Eds.), *Engaging organizational communication theory and research: Multiple perspectives* (pp. 141–169). Thousand Oaks, CA: SAGE Publications,

Ashcraft, K. L. (2007). Appreciating the "work" of discourse: Occupational identity and difference as organizing mechanisms in the case of commercial airline pilots. *Discourse and Communication, 1*, 9–36.

Ashcraft, K. L. (2011). Knowing work through the communication of difference: A revised agenda for difference studies. In D.K. Mumby (Ed.), *Reframing difference in organizational communication studies: Research, pedagogy, practice* (pp. 3–29). Thousand Oaks, CA: SAGE Publications.

Ashley, S. (2015). Media literacy in action? What are we teaching in introductory college media studies courses? *Journalism & Mass Communication Educator, 70*(2), 161–173.

Athreya, K., & Price, D. A. (2013, June). *Implications of risks and rewards in college decisions* (Paper EB13-06). Richmond, VA: Federal Reserve Bank of Richmond. Retrieved from http://www.mybudget360.com/does-a-college-degree-protect-your-career-unemployment-rate-for-college-graduates-highest-on-record/

Atkin, C. K., & Freimuth, V. (2013). Guidelines for formative evaluation research in campaign design. In R. E. Rice & C. K. Atkin (Eds.), *Public communication campaigns* (4th ed., pp. 53–68). Thousand Oaks, CA: SAGE Publications.

Atkin, C. K., & Rice, R. E. (2013). Theory and principles of public communication campaigns. In R. E. Rice & C. K. Atkin (Eds.), *Public communication campaigns* (4th ed., pp. 3–20). Thousand Oaks, CA: SAGE Publications.

Atkins, P. W. B., & Wood, R. E. (2002). Self-versus others' ratings as predictors of assessment center ratings: Validation evidence for 360-degree feedback programs. *Personnel Psychology, 55*(4), 871–903.

Atkinson, J. M., & Drew, P. (1979). *Order in court: The organisation of verbal interaction in judicial settings.* London, UK: Macmillan.

Atkinson, J. M., & Heritage, J. (Eds.). (1984). *Structures of social action: Studies in conversation analysis.* London, UK: Cambridge University Press.

Aune, J. A. (1994). *Rhetoric and Marxism.* New York, NY: Westview Press.

Austin, E. W., Muldrow, A., & Austin, B. W. (2016). Examining how media literacy and personality factors predict skepticism toward alcohol advertising. *Journal of Health Communication, 21*(5), 600–609.

Austin, J. L. (1975). *How to do things with words: The William James Lectures delivered at Harvard University* (2nd ed.). Cambridge, MA: Harvard University.

Avinun, R., & Knafo, A. (2014). Parenting as a reaction evoked by children's genotype: A meta-analysis of children-as-twins studies. *Personality & Social Psychology Review, 18*(1), 87–102.

Babbie, E. R. (1973). *Survey research methods.* Belmont, CA: Wadsworth.

Baker, L. A., & Emery, R. E. (1993). When every relationship is above average: Perceptions and expectations of divorce at the time of marriage. *Law and Human Behavior, 17*(4), 439–450.

Baker, T., & Nelson, R. E. (2005). Creating something from nothing: Resource construction through entrepreneurial bricolage. *Administrative Science Quarterly, 50*(3), 329–366.

Bakke, E. (2010). A model and measure of mobile communication competence. *Human Communication Research, 36*(3), 348–371.

Bakshy, E., Hofman, J., Mason, W. A., & Watts, D. J. (2011, February). Everyone's an influencer: Quantifying influence on Twitter. *Proceedings of the fourth ACM international conference on Web search and data mining* (pp. 65–74). Hong Kong, China.

Bales, R. F. (1950). *Interaction process analysis; a method for the study of small groups.* Oxford, England: Addison-Wesley.

Balint, M. (1957). *The doctor, his patient and the illness.* Oxford, UK: International Universities Press.

Ballif, M. (2001). *Seduction, sophistry, and the woman with the rhetorical figure.* Carbondale, IL: Southern Illinois Univeristy Press.

Bandura, A. (1973). *Aggression: A social learning theory analysis.* Upper Saddle River, NJ: Prentice Hall.

Bandura, A. (1977). Self-efficacy: Toward a unifying theory of behavioral change. *Psychological Review, 84*(2), 191.

Bandura, A. (1978). Social learning theory of aggression. *Journal of Communication, 28*(3), 12–29.

Bandura, A. (1998). Health promotion from the perspective of social cognitive theory. *Psychology and Health. Special Issue: Self-Regulation and Health, 13*(4), 623–649.

Bandura, A. (2002). Social cognitive theory of mass communication. In B. Jennings & D. Zillman (Eds.), *Media effects: Advances in theory and research* (2nd ed, pp. 121–153). Mahwah, NJ: Erlbaum.

Bandura, A., & Walters, R. H. (1963). *Social learning and personality development.* New York, NY: Holt, Rinehart, & Winston.

Banks, G. C., Batchelor, J. H., Seers, A., O'Boyle, E. J., Pollack, J. M., & Gower, K. (2014). What does team–member exchange bring to the party? A meta-analytic review of team and leader social exchange. *Journal of Organizational Behavior, 35*(2), 273–295.

Barbour, A. (1995). *Caring for patients: A critique of the medical model.* Stanford, CA: Stanford University Press.

Barge, J. K., & Fairhurst, G. T. (2008). Living leadership: A systemic constructionist approach. *Leadership, 4*(3), 227–251.

Barker, J. R. (1993). Tightening the iron cage: Concertive control in self-managing teams. *Administrative Science Quarterly, 38*(3), 408–437.

Barlett, C. P. (2013). Excuses, excuses: A meta-analytic review of how mitigating information can change aggression and an exploration of moderating variables. *Aggressive Behavior, 39*(6), 472–481.

Barna, L. M. (1994). Stumbling blocks in intercultural communication. In L. A. Samovar & R. E. Porter (Eds.), *Intercultural communication: A reader* (pp. 337–346). Belmont, CA: Wadsworth.

Bartholomew, K., & Horowitz, L. M. (1991). Attachment styles among young adults: A test of a four-category model. *Journal of Personality and Social Psychology, 61*(2), 226–264.

Bass, B. M. (1985). *Leadership and performance beyond expectations.* New York: The Free Press.

Bass, B. M. (1990). From transactional to transformational leadership: Learning to share the vision. *Organizational Dynamics, 18,* 19–31.

Bass, B. M., Avolio, B. J., Jung, D. I., & Berson, Y. (2003). Predicting unit performance by assessing transformational and transactional leadership. *Journal of Applied Psychology, 88*(2), 207–218.

Bastien, D. T., McPhee, R. D., & Bolton, K. A. (1995). A study and extended theory of the structuration of climate. *Communication Monographs, 62*(2), 87–109.

Bateson, G. (1972). *Steps to an ecology of mind.* New York, NY: Ballantine Books.

Bauer, K., Orvis, K., Ely, K., & Surface, E. (2016). Re-examination of motivation in learning contexts: Meta-analytically investigating the role type of motivation plays in the prediction of key training outcomes. *Journal of Business and Psychology, 31*(1), 33–50.

Bauerlein, M. (2015, May 9). What's the point of a professor? *New York Times* (online). Retrieved from https://www.nytimes.com/2015/05/10/opinion/sunday/whats-the-point-of-a-professor.html

Bauman, K. (2016, March 31). *College completion by cohort, age and gender, 1967 to 2015.* Paper presented at the Annual Meetings of the Population Association of America, Washington, DC. Retrieved from https://www.census.gov/content/dam/Census/library/working-papers/2016/demo/SEHSD-WP2016-04.pdf

Bauman, R. (1977). *Verbal art as performance.* Prospect Heights, IL: Waveland Press.

Baumeister, R. F., & Leary, M. R. (1995). The need to belong: Desire for interpersonal attachments as a fundamental human motivation. *Psychological Bulletin, 117*(3), 497–529.

Baxter, L. A. (2004). A tale of two voices: Relational dialectics theory. *Journal of Family Communication, 4*(3), 181–192.

Beach, W. A. (1990a). On (not) observing behavior interactionally. *Western Journal of Speech Communication, 54*(4), 603–612.

Beach, W. A. (1990b). Language as and in technology: Facilitating topic organization in a videotex focus group meeting. In M. J. Medhurst (ed.), *Communication and the culture of technology* (pp. 197–220). Pullman, WA: Washington State University Press.

Beach, W. A. (1991a). Avoiding ownership for alleged wrongdoings. *Research on Language and Social Interaction, 24,* 1–36.

Beach, W. A. (1991b). Searching for universal features of conversation. *Research on Language and Social Interaction, 24,* 349–366.

Beach, W. A. (1993). Transitional regularities for 'casual' "okay" usages. *Journal of Pragmatics, 19*(4), 325–352.

Beach, W. A. (1995). Preserving and constraining options: "Okays" and 'official' priorities in medical interviews. In G. H. Morris & R. J. Cheneil (Eds.), *The talk of the clinic: Explorations in the analysis of medical and therapeutic discourse* (pp. 259–289). Hillsdale, NJ: Erlbaum.

Beach, W. A. (1996). *Conversations about illness: Family preoccupations with bulimia.* Mahwah, NJ: Erlbaum.

Beach, W. A. (2000). Inviting collaborations in stories about a woman. *Language in Society, 29*(3), 379–407.

Beach, W. A. (2008). Conversation analysis. In W. Donsbach (Ed.), *The international encyclopedia of communication* (Vol. 3; pp. 989–995). London, UK: Blackwell Publishing, Ltd.

Beach, W. A. (2009). *A natural history of family cancer: Interactional resources for managing illness.* Cresskill, NJ: Hampton Press.

Beach, W. A. (2013a). Conversation analysis and communication. In J. Sidnell & T. Stivers (Eds.), *The handbook of conversation analysis* (pp. 674–687). Hoboken, NJ: Wiley-Blackwell.

Beach, W. A. (Ed.). (2013b). *Handbook of patient–provider interactions: Raising and responding to concerns about life, illness, and disease.* Cresskill, NJ: Hampton Press, Inc.

Beach, W. A. (2013c). Patients' efforts to justify wellness in a comprehensive cancer clinic. *Health Communication, 28,* 577–591.

Beach, W. A. (2015). Doctor–patient interactions. In K. Tracy (Ed.), *Encyclopedia of language and social interaction* (pp. 476–493). New York, NY: John Wiley & Sons.

Beach, W. A., Buller, M. K., Dozier, D. M., Buller, D. B., & Gutzmer, K. (2014). The Conversations About Cancer (CAC) project: Assessing feasibility and audience impacts from viewing *The Cancer Play.* *Health Communication, 29*(5), 462–472.

Beach, W. A., & Dixson, C. N. (2001). Revealing moments: Formulating understandings of adverse experiences in a health appraisal interview. *Social Science and Medicine (1982), 52*(1), 25–44.

Beach, W. A., & Dozier, D. M. (2015). Fears, uncertainties, and hopes: Patient-initiated actions and doctors' responses during oncology interviews. *Journal of Health Communication, 20*(11), 1243–1254.

Beach, W. A., Dozier, D. M., Buller, M. K., Gutzmer, K., Fluharty, L., Myers, V. H., & Buller, D. B. (2016). The Conversations About Cancer (CAC) Project—Phase II: National findings from viewing *When Cancer Calls* … and implications for entertainment–education (E–E). *Patient Education and Counseling, 99*(3), 393–399.

Beach, W. A., Easter, D. W., Good, J. S., & Pigeron, E. (2005). Disclosing and responding to cancer "fears" during oncology interviews. *Social Science and Medicine, 60*(4), 893–910.

Beach, W. A., & Metzger, T. R. (1997). Claiming insufficient knowledge. *Human Communication Research, 23,* 562–588.

Beach, W. A., & Powell, T. (2019). *A journey through breast cancer* [documentary film].

Beatty, M. J., Heisel, A. D., Hall, A. E., Levine, T. R., & La France, B. H. (2002). What can we learn from the study of twins about genetic and environmental influences on interpersonal affiliation, aggressiveness, and social anxiety?: A meta-analytic study. *Communication Monographs, 69*(1), 1–18.

Beatty, M. J., Heisel, A. D., Pascual-Ferrá, P., & Berger, C. R. (2015). Electroencephalographic analysis in communication science: Testing two competing models of message production. *Communication Methods and Measures, 9*(1/2), 101–116.

Beatty, M. J., & McCroskey, J. C. (2000). Theory, scientific evidence, and the communibiological paradigm: Reflections on misguided criticism. *Communication Education, 49*(1), 36–44.

Beatty, M. J., McCroskey, J. C., & Valencic, K. (2001). *The biology of communication: A communobiological perspective*. Cresskill, NJ: Hampton Press.

Beckman, H. B., & Frankel, R. M. (1984). The effect of doctor behavior on the collection of data. *Annals of Internal Medicine, 101*(5), 692–696.

Bedeian, A. G. (2016). A note on the aphorism "there is nothing as practical as a good theory." *Journal of Management Theory, 22*(2), 236–242.

Beebe, S. A., & Masterson, J. T. (2000). *Communicating in small groups: Principles and practices*. New York, NY: Longman.

Beebe, S. A., & Masterson, J. T. (2006). *Communicating in small groups: Principles and practices*. Boston, MA: Pearson.

Beggan, J. K., Vencill, J. A., & Garos, S. (2013). The good-in-bed effect: College students' tendency to see themselves as better than others as a sex partner. *Journal of Psychology: Interdisciplinary and Applied, 147*(5), 415–434.

Bem, S. (1974). The measurement of psychological androgyny. *Journal of Counseling and Clinical Psychology, 42*, 155–162.

Benne, K. D., & Sheats, P. (1948). Functional roles of group members. *Journal of Social Issues, 4*, 41–49.

Bennis, W., & Nanus, B. (1985). *Leaders: The strategies for taking charge*. New York: AMACOM.

Benoit, W. L. (1995). *Accounts, excuses, and apologies: A theory of image restoration strategies*. Albany, NY: SUNY Press.

Berger, C. R., & Calabrese, R. J. (1975). Some explorations in initial interaction and beyond: Toward a developmental theory of interpersonal communication. *Human Communication Research, 1*(2), 99–112.

Berger, G. (2017). *Linkedin's state of salary report 2017*. Retrieved from: https://www.linkedin.com/jobs/blog/linkedin-2017-us-state-of-salary-report

Berger, G., & Gan, L. (2016, August 30). Soft skills are increasingly crucial to getting your dream job. Retrieved from: https://www.linkedin.com/pulse/soft-skills-increasingly-crucial-getting-your-dream-guy-berger-ph-d-?articleId=8846425096220875376

Berger, P. L., & Luckmann, T. (1966). *The social construction of reality: A treatise in the sociology of knowledge*. Garden City, NY: Doubleday.

Berlo, D. K. (1960). *The process of communication*. New York, NY: Holt, Rinehart & Winston.

Berry, K. (2013). Spinning autoethnographic reflexivity, cultural critique, and negotiating selves. In S. Holman Jones, T. E. Adams, & C. Ellis (Eds.), *Handbook of autoethnography*. Walnut Creek, CA: Left Coast Press.

Berscheid, E., & Peplau, L. A. (1983). The emerging science of relationships. In H. H. Kelley, E. Berscheid, A. Christensen, J. H. Harvey, T. L. Huston, E. Levinger, E. McClintock, L. A. Peplau, & D. R. Peterson (Eds.), *Close relationships* (pp. 1–19). New York, NY: W. H. Freeman.

Bettencourt, M. F. (2015). *Triumph of the heart: Forgiveness in an unforgiving world*. New York, NY: Hudson Street Press.

Biesecker, B. (1992). Coming to terms with recent attempts to write women into the history of rhetoric. *Philosophy and Rhetoric, 25*(2), 140–161.

Biesecker, B. A. (2002). Remembering World War II: The rhetoric and politics of national commemoration at the turn of the 21st century. *Quarterly Journal of Speech, 88*(4), 393–409.

Biesecker, B. A. (2011). Whither ideology?: Toward a different take on enjoyment as a political factor. *Western Journal of Communication, 75*(4), 445–450.

Biesecker, B. A. (2017). From general history to philosophy: Black Lives Matter, late neoliberal molecular biopolitics, and rhetoric. *Philosophy & Rhetoric, 50*(4), 409–430.

Bigdon, C., & Sachitanandam, S. A. (2003). *Community mobilization principles and practice guidebook*. Trincomalee, Sri Lanka: Integrated Food Security Program.

Bilić-Zulle, L., Frković, V., Turk, T., Ažman, J., & Petrovečki, M. (2005). Prevalence of plagiarism among medical students. *Croatian Medical Journal, 46*(1), 126–131.

Birdsell, D. S., & Groarke, L. (2007). Outlines of a theory of visual argument. *Argumentation and Advocacy, 43*(3/4), 103–113.

Blackless, M., Charuvastra, A., Derryck, A., Fausto-Sterling, A., Lauzanne, K., & Lee, E. (2000). How sexually dimorphic are we? Review and synthesis. *American Journal of Human Biology, 12*, 151–166.

Bohns, V. K., Lucas, G. M., Molden, D. C., Finkel, E. J., Coolsen, M. K., Kumashiro, M., … Higgins, E. T. (2013). Opposites fit: Regulatory focus complementarity and relationship well-being. *Social Cognition, 31*(1), 1–14.

Bok, S. (1979). *Lying: Moral choice in public and private life*. New York, NY: Vintage.

Boland, J. E. (2005). Visual arguments. *Cognition, 95*(3), 237–274.

Bolden-Barrett, V. (2017, March 14). Study: CFOs spend 15% of their time resolving staff conflicts. *HR Dive*. Retrieved from: https://www.hrdive.com/news/study-cfos-spend-15-of-their-time-resolving-staff-conflicts/438013/

Bolen, R. M. (2000). Validity of attachment theory. *Trauma, Violence, and Abuse, 1*(2), 128–153.

Bolhuis, J. J., Tattersal, I., Chomsky, N., & Berwick, R. C. (2014). How could language have evolved? *PLOS Biology, 12*(8).

Bolotova, A. K. (2012). Time parameters of nonverbal communication and personal communicative competence. *Psychology in Russia: State of the Art, 5*(1), 289–300.

Bormann, E. G. (1972). Fantasy and rhetorical vision: The rhetorical criticism of social reality. *Quarterly Journal of Speech, 58*, 396–407.

Bormann, E. G. (1981). Ethical standards for interpersonal/small group communication. *Communication, 6*, 267–286.

Bormann, E. G. (1982). I. Fantasy and rhetorical vision: Ten years later. *Quarterly Journal of Speech, 68*(3), 288.

Bormann, E. G. (1985). Symbolic convergence theory: A communication formulation. *Journal of Communication, 35*(4), 128–138.

Borman, E. G., Cragan, J. F., & Shields, D. C. (1994). In defense of symbolic convergence theory: A look at the theory and its criticisms after two decades. *Communication Theory 4*(4), 259–294.

Borrell-Carrió, F., Suchman, A. L., & Epstein, R. M. (2004). The biopsychosocial model 25 years later: Principles, practice, and scientific inquiry. *Annals of Family Medicine, 2*(6), 576–582.

Bost, M., & Greene, R. W. (2011). Affirming rhetorical materialism: Enfolding the virtual and the actual. *Western Journal of Communication, 75*(4), 440–444.

Bowlby, J. (1969/1981). *Attachment and loss: Volume I. Attachment: Attachment and loss*. New York, NY: Basic Books.

Bracht, N., Kingsbury, L., & Rissel, C. (1999). Community organization principles in health promotion: A five-stage model. In N. Bracht (Ed.), *Health promotion at the community level 2: New advances* (pp. 83–104). Thousand Oaks, CA: SAGE Publications.

Brahic, C. (2014). Oldest hand stencil found in Indonesia. *New Scientist, 224*(2990), 10.

Branham, R. J. (1980). Ineffability, creativity, and communication competence. *Communication Quarterly, 28*(3), 11–21.

Broeckelman-Post, M. A., & Pyle, A. S. (2017). Public speaking versus hybrid introductory communication courses: Exploring four outcomes. *Communication Education, 66*(2), 210–228.

Brouwer, D. C. (2001). ACT-ing UP in congressional hearings. In R. Asen & D. Brouwer. (Eds.), *Counterpublics and the state* (pp. 87–109). Albany, NY: SUNY Press.

Brown, E., & Males, M. (2011). Does age or poverty level best predict criminal arrest and homicide rates? A preliminary investigation. *Justice Policy Journal, 8*(1), 1–30.

Brown, L. L., Acevedo, B., & Fisher, H. E. (2013). Neural correlates of four broad temperament dimensions: Testing predictions for a novel construct of personality. *PLOS One, 8*(11), e78734.

Brummans, B. H. J. M., Cooren, F., Robichaud, D., & Taylor, J. R. (2014). Approaches to the communicative constitution of organizations. In L. L. Putnam & D. K. Mumby (Eds.), *The SAGE handbook of organizational communication: Advances in theory, research, and methods*. Thousand Oaks, CA: SAGE Publications.

Brummett, B. (1976). Some implications of "process" or "intersubjectivity": Postmodern rhetoric. *Philosophy and Rhetoric, 9*(1), 21–51.

Brummett, B. (2000). *Reading rhetorical theory*. Fort Worth, TX: Harcourt.

Bruni, F. (2013, May 12). America the clueless. *New York Times*, p. 3—Sunday Review. Retrieved from: https://www.nytimes.com/2013/05/12/opinion/sunday/bruni-america-the-clueless.html

Bryant, C. A., Brown, K. R. M., McDermott, R. J., Forthofer, M. S., Bumpus, E. C., Calkins, S. A., & Zapata, L. B. (2007). Community-based prevention marketing: Organizing a community for health behavior intervention. *Health Promotion Practice, 8*(2), 154–163.

Bryant, C. A., Courtney, A. H., McDermott, R. J., Alfonso, M. L., Baldwin, J. A., Nickelson, J., … & Zhu, Y. (2010). Promoting physical activity among youth through community-based prevention marketing. *Journal of School Health, 80*(5), 214–224.

Bryant, J., & Miron, D. (2004). Theory and research in mass communication. *Journal of Communication, 54*(4), 662–704.

Bryant, J., Thompson, S., & Finklea, B. W. (2012). *Fundamentals of media effects*. Prospect Heights, IL: Waveland Press.

Bryman, A. (2007). Barriers to integrating quantitative and qualitative research. *Journal of Mixed Methods Research, 1*(1), 8–22.

BSA. (2015). *What's the big deal with data?* Washington DC: BSA Software Alliance. https://data.bsa.org/wp-content/uploads/2015/12/bsadatastudy_en.pdf

Buckley, W. (1967). *Sociology and modern systems theory*. Oxford: Prentice Hall.

Bugental, D. B. (2000). Acquisition of the algorithms of social life: A domain-based approach. *Psychological Bulletin, 126*(2), 187–219.

Bureau of Labor Statistics (2014, June 18). American time use survey-2013 results. Washington, DC: U.S. Department of Labor. Retrieved from: https://www.bls.gov/news.release/archives/atus_06182014.pdf

Bureau of Labor Statistics. (2018). *Occupational Outlook Handbook*. Retrieved from: https://www.bls.gov/ooh/media-and-communication/public-relations-specialists.htm

Burgoon, J. K., Dunbar, N. E., & Elkins, A. (2017). Analyzing video and audio nonverbal dynamics: Kinesics, proxemics, haptics, and vocalics. In A. VanLear & D. J. Canary (Eds.), *Researching interactive communication behavior* (pp. 35–44). Thousand Oaks, CA: SAGE Publications.

Burke, J. M., & Attridge, M. (2011). Pathways to career and leadership success: Part 1—A psychosocial profile of $100K professionals. *Journal of Workplace Behavioral Health, 26*(3), 175–206.

Burke, K. (1939). Rhetoric of Hitler's battle. *Southern Review, 5*, 1–21.

Burke, K. (1945). *A grammar of motives*. New York, NY: Prentice Hall.

Burke, K. (1950). *A rhetoric of motives*. Berkeley, CA: University of California Press.

Burke, K. (1966). *Language as symbolic action: Essays on life, literature, and method*. Berkeley, CA: University of California Press.

Burke, K. (1969a). *A rhetoric of motives*. Berkeley, CA: University of California Press.

Burke, K. (1969b). *A grammar of motives*. Berkeley, CA: University of California Press.

Burke, K. (1970). *The rhetoric of religion: Studies in logology*. Berkeley, CA: University of California Press.

Burleson, B. (2003). The experience and effects of emotional support: What the study of cultural and gender differences can tell us about close relationships, emotion and interpersonal communication. *Personal Relationships, 10*(1), 1–23.

Burleson, B. R. (2009). Understanding the outcomes of supportive communication: A dual-process approach. *Journal of Social and Personal Relationships, 26*(1), 21–38.

Burleson, B. R., & MacGeorge, E. L. (2002). Supportive communication. In M. L. Knapp & J. A. Daly (Eds.), *Handbook of interpersonal communication* (3rd ed., pp. 374–424). Thousand Oaks, CA: SAGE Publications.

Burleson, B. R., Wilson, S. R., Waltman, M. S., Goering, E. M., Ely, T. K., & Whaley, B. B. (1988). Item desirability effects in compliance-gaining research seven studies documenting artifacts in the strategy selection procedure. *Human Communication Research, 14*(4), 429–486.

Burningglass Technologies. (2015). *The human factor: The hard time employers have finding soft skills*. Retrieved from: https://www.burning-glass.com/wp-content/uploads/Human_Factor_Baseline_Skills_FINAL.pdf

Burns, J. M. (1978). *Leadership*. New York, NY: Harper & Row Publishers

Burrell, N. A., & Gross, C. (2017). Quantitative research, purpose of. In M. Allen (Ed.), *The SAGE encyclopedia of communication research methods*. Los Angeles, CA: SAGE Publications.

Burstein, D. D. (2013). *Fast future: How the millennial generation is shaping our world*. Boston, MA: Beacon Press.

Burt, R. S. (2014, August). Network structure and strategic leadership [39802 syllabus, Slide 7]. Retrieved from: http://faculty.chicago-booth.edu/ronald.burt/teaching/syllabi/AoM2014slides.pdf

Butler, J. (1990). *Gender trouble: Feminism and the subversion of identity*. New York, NY: Routledge.

Butler, J. (1993). *Bodies that matter: On the discursive limits of sex*. New York, NY: Routledge.

Butler, J. (1998). Performative acts and gender constitution. *Theatre Journal, 40*(4), 519–531.

Buzzanell, P. M., & Stohl, C. (1999). The Redding tradition of organizational communication scholarship: W. Charles Redding and his legacy. *Communication Studies, 50*(4), 324–337.

Byrne, P. S., & Long, B. E. L. (1976). *Doctors talking to patients: A study of the verbal behaviors of doctors in the consultation.* London, UK: HMSO.

Byron, K., & Khazanchi, S. (2010). When and how rewards increase creative performance: A theoretically-derived meta-analysis. *Academy of Management Annual Meeting Proceedings,* 1–6.

Cacioppo, J. T., Cacioppo, S., Gonzaga, G. C., Ogburn, E. L., & VanderWeele, T. J. (2013). Marital satisfaction and break-ups differ across on-line and off-line meeting venues. *PNAS Proceedings of the National Academy of Sciences of the United States of America, 110*(25), 10135–10140.

Cacioppo, J. T., Petty, R. E., Feinstein, J. A., & Jarvis, W. B. G. (1996). Dispositional differences in cognitive motivation: The life and times of individuals varying in need for cognition. *Psychological Bulletin, 119*(2), 197–253.

Cain, S. (2012). *Quiet: The power of introverts in a world that can't stop talking.* New York, NY: Crown.

Calafell, B. M., & Moreman, S. T. (2009). Envisioning an academic readership: Latina/o performativities per the form of publication. *Text and Performance Quarterly, 29*(2), 123–130.

Callejo, J. (2013). Media time use among adolescents and young adults: analysis of differences. *Comunicación Y Sociedad, 26*(2), 1–26.

Calmes, J., & Lublin, J. S. (2004, May 13). Crisis veterans offer advice to Bush. *Wall Street Journal.* Retrieved from: http://www.wsj.com/articles/SB108440228857710045

Campbell, K. K. (1989). *Man cannot speak for her: A critical study of early feminist rhetoric (Vols. 1 & 2).* New York, NY: Greenwood Press.

Camras, L. A. (1982). Ethological approaches to nonverbal communication. In R. S. Feldman (Ed.), *Development of nonverbal vehavior in children* (pp. 3–28). New York, NY: Springer-Verlag.

Canary, D. J. (2017). Observing relational conflict. In A. VanLear & D. J. Canary (Eds.), *Researching interactive communication behavior* (pp. 3–16). Thousand Oaks, CA: SAGE Publications.

Canary, D. J., Brossmann, J. E., & Weger, H. (1995). Toward a theory of minimally rational argument: Analyses of episode-specific effects of argument structures. *Communication Monographs, 62*(3), 183–212.

Canary, D. J., Cody, M. J., & Manusov, V. L. (2008). *Interpersonal communication: A goals-based approach* (4th ed.). Boston, MA: Bedford/St. Martin's.

Canary, D. J., & Lakey, S. (2013). *Strategic conflict.* New York, NY: Routledge.

Canary, D. J., & Seibold, D. R. (2010). Origins and development of the conversational argument coding scheme. *Communication Methods and Measures, 4*(1–2), 7–26.

Canary, D. J., & Spitzberg, B. H. (1987). Appropriateness and effectiveness perceptions of conflict strategies. *Human Communication Research, 14,* 93–118.

Canary, D. J., & Spitzberg, B. H. (1989). A model of competence perceptions of conflict strategies. *Human Communication Research, 15,* 630–649.

Canary, D. J., & Spitzberg, B. H. (1990). Attribution biases and associations between conflict strategies and competence outcomes. *Communication Monographs, 57,* 139–151.

Canary, D. J., Spitzberg, B. H., & Semic, B. A. (1998). The experience and expression of anger in interpersonal settings. In P. A. Andersen

& L. K. Guerrero (Eds.), *Handbook of communication and emotion: Theory, research, and applications* (pp. 189–213). San Diego, CA: Academic Press.

Canary, D. J., & Stafford, L. (1992). Relational maintenance strategies and equity in marriage. *Communication Monographs, 59*(3), 243–267.

Canary, D. J., & Stafford, L. (1994). Maintaining relationships through strategic and routine interaction. In D. J. Canary & L. Stafford (Eds.), *Communication and relational maintenance* (pp. 3–22). San Diego, CA: Academic Press.

Canary, D. J., & Stafford, L., & Semic, B. A. (2002). A panel study of the associations between maintenance strategies and relational characteristics. *Journal of Marriage and Family, 64,* 395–406.

Canary, H. E., & Jennings, M. M. (2008). Principles and influence in codes of ethics: A centering resonance analysis comparing pre- and post-Sarbanes-Oxley codes of ethics. *Journal of Business Ethics, 80,* 263–278.

Canary, H. E., & Tarin, C. A. (2017). Structuration theory. *The international encyclopedia of organizational communication.* New York, NY: Wiley.

Cancelliere, C., Cassidy, D. J., Ammendolia, C., & Côté, P. (2011). Are workplace health promotion programs effective at improving presenteeism in workers? A systematic review and best evidence synthesis of the literature. *Biomedical Central (BMC) Public Health, 11,* 395–405.

Caplan, B. (2007). *The myth of the rational voter. Why democracies choose bad policies.* Princeton, NJ: Princeton University Press.

CareerBuilder. (2018, August 9). More than half of employers have found content on social media that caused them not to hire a candidate, Retrieved April 23, 2019. https://www.prnewswire.com/news-releases/more-than-half-of-employers-have-found-content-on-social-media-that-caused-them-not-to-hire-a-candidate-according-to-recent-careerbuilder-survey-300694437.html

Carlson, M. (2004). *Performance: A critical introduction* (2nd ed.). London, UK: Routledge.

Carnevale, A. P., & Cheah, B. (2015). *From hard times to better times.* Washington, DC: Georgetown University Center on Education and the Workforce. Retrieved from: https://cew-7632.kxcdn.com/wp-content/uploads/HardTimes2015-Report.pdf

Carnevale, A. P., Cheah, B., & Hanson, A. R. (2015). *The economic value of college majors.* Washington, DC: Georgetown University Center on Education and the Workforce. Retrieved from: https://cew-7632.kxcdn.com/wp-content/uploads/The-Economic-Value-of-College-Majors-Full-Report-web-FINAL.pdf

Carnevale, A. P., Cheah, B., & Strohl, J. (2012). *Hard times: College majors, unemployment and earnings.* Washington, DC: Georgetown University Center on Education and the Workforce.

Carnevale, A. P., & Hanson, A. (2015). Learn and earn: Career pathways for youth in the 21st century. *E-Journal of International and Comparative Labour Studies, 4*(1), 76–89.

Carnevale, A. P., Jayasundera, T., & Gulish, A. (2016). *America's divided recovery: College haves and have-nots.* Washington, DC: Georgetown University Center on Education and the Workforce. Retrieved from: https://cew-7632.kxcdn.com/wp-content/uploads/Americas-Divided-Recovery-web.pdf

Carnevale, A. P., Ridley, N., Cheah, B., Strohl, J., & Campbell, K. P. (2019). *Upskilling and downsizing in American manufacturing.* Washington, DC: Georgetown University Center on Education and the Workforce. Retrieved from: https://1gyhoq479ufd3yna29x7ubjn-wpengine.netdna-ssl.com/wp-content/uploads/Manufacturing_FR.pdf

Carnevale, A. P., Strohol, J., Ridley, N., & Gulish, A. (2018). *Three educational pathways to good jobs: High school, middle skills, and bachelor's degree.* Washington, DC: Georgetown University Center on Education and the Workforce. Retrieved from: https://1gyhoq479ufd3yna29x7ubjn-wpengine.netdna-ssl.com/wp-content/uploads/3ways-FR.pdf

Carpenter, C. J. (2015). A meta-analysis of the ELM's argument quality × processing type predictions. *Human Communication Research, 41*(4), 501–534.

Carr, N. (2011). *The shallows: What the Internet is doing to our brains.* New York, NY: W. W Norton & Company.

Carrère, S., & Gottman, J. M. (1999). Predicting divorce among newlyweds from the first three minutes of a marital conflict discussion. *Family Process, 38*(3), 293–301.

Cassell, E. J. (1985). *Talking with patients: Volumes I and II.* Cambridge, MA: MIT Press.

Cassirer, E. (1953). *The philosophy of symbolic forms* (Vol. 1, R. Manheim, Transl.). New Haven, CT: Yale University.

Cavanagh, K., Dobash, R. E., Dobash, R. P., & Lewis, R. (2001). 'Remedial work': Men's strategic responses to their violence against intimate female partners. *Sociology, 35,* 695–714.

Cengage. (2018). *The people factor: Uniquely human skills tech can't replace at work.* Morning Consult/Cengage. Retrieved from: https://www.cengage.com/todays-learner/career-readiness#skillssurvey

Census Scope (2010). Percent multiracial ranking: States ranked by percent of population identifying as multiracial. Retrieved June 11, 2019: http://www.censusscope.org/us/rank_multi.html

Centers for Disease Control and Prevention. (n.d.). Gateway to health communication and social marketing practice. https://www.cdc.gov/healthcommunication/healthbasics/WhatIsHC.html

Chan, C., Ying Ho, P. S., & Chow, E. (2002). A body-mind-spirit model in health: An Eastern approach. *Journal of Social Work in Healthcare, 34*(3–4), 261–282.

Chang, A. (2018, April 6). Sinclair's takeover of local news, in one striking map. Vox.com. Retrieved from: https://www.vox.com/2018/4/6/17202824/sinclair-tribune-ma

Chaput, C. (2010). Rhetorical circulation in late capitalism: Neoliberalism and the overdetermination of affective energy. *Philosophy and Rhetoric, 43*(1), 1–25.

Charon, R. (2006). *Narrative medicine: Honoring the stories of illness.* New York, NY: Oxford University Press.

Charon, R. (2009). Narrative medicine as a witness for the self-telling body. *Journal of Applied Communication Research, 37*(2), 118–131.

Chávez, K. R. (2015). Beyond inclusion: Rethinking rhetoric's historical narrative. *Quarterly Journal of Speech, 101*(1), 162–172.

Chávez, K. R., & Griffin, C. L. (2014). Women's studies in communication still matters. *Women's Studies in Communication, 37,* 262–265.

Chen, D -T., Wu, J., & Wang, Y. -M. (2011). Unpacking new media literacy. *Journal of Systemics, Cybernetics and Informatics, 9*(2), 84–88.

Chen, G -M., & Starosta, W. J. (1998). *Foundations of intercultural communication.* Boston, MA: Allyn & Bacon.

Chen, Y. W., & Nakazawa, M. (2009). Influences of culture on self-disclosure as relationally situated in intercultural and interracial friendships from a social penetration perspective. *Journal of Intercultural Communication Research, 38*(2), 77–98.

Cheney, G. (1983). On the various and changing meanings of organizational membership: A field study of organizational identification. *Communication Monographs, 50*(4), 342–362.

Cheney, G., & Tompkins, P. K. (1988). On the facts of the text as the basis of human communication research. In J. Anderson (Ed.), *Communication yearbook, 11,* 455–481. Newbury Park, CA: SAGE Publications.

Cherney J. L., Lindemann, K., & Hardin, M. (2015). Research in communication, disability, and sport. *Communication and Sport, 3,* 8–26.

Chiang, Y. (2007). Birds of moderately different feathers: Bandwagon dynamics and the threshold heterogeneity of network neighbors. *Journal of Mathematical Sociology, 31*(1), 47–69.

Chomsky, N. (2011). Language and other cognitive systems. What is special about language? *Language Learning and Development, 7*(4), 263–278.

Chua, A. (2011). *Battle hymn of the tiger mother.* New York, NY: Penguin Press.

Chui, M., Manyika, J., Bughin, J., Dobbs, R., Roxburgh, C., … , Westergren, M. (2012, July). *The social economy: Unlocking value and productivity through social technologies.* New York, NY: McKinsey Global Institute.

Chung, J. W. (2017). Concentration and diversity in the cable television industry under regulatory uncertainty. *Journal of Broadcasting and Electronic Media, 61*(2), 430–448.

Cialdini, R. B., & Goldstein, N. J. (2004). Social influence: Compliance and conformity. *Annual Review of Psychology, 55,* 591–621.

Cialdini, R. B., Kallgren, C. A., & Reno, R. R. (1991). A focus theory of normative conduct: A theoretical refinement and reevaluation of the role of norms in human behavior. *Advances in Experimental Social Psychology, 24,* 201–234.

Cialdini, R. B., Reno, R. R., & Kallgren, C. A. (1990). A focus theory of normative conduct: Recycling the concept of norms to reduce littering in public places. *Journal of Personality and Social Psychology, 58*(6), 1015–1026.

Cialdini, R. B., & Trost, M. R. (1999). Social influence: Social norms, conformity, and compliance. In D. Gilbert, S. Fiske, & G. Lindzy (Eds.), *The handbook of social psychology* (Vol. 2, pp. 151–192). Boston, MA: McGraw-Hill.

Cialdini, R. B., Vincent, J. E., Lewis, S. K., Catalan, J., Wheeler, D., & Darby, B. L. (1975). Reciprocal concessions procedure for inducing compliance: The door-in-the-face technique. *Journal of Personality and Social Psychology, 31*(2), 206.

Cicero, M. T. (1948). *On the orator* (E. W. Sutton & H. Rackham, Trans.). Cambridge, MA: Harvard University Press.

CIPD. (2008, October). *Leadership and the management of conflict at work.* London, UK: Chartered Institute of Personnel and Development. Retrieved from: http://www2.cipd.co.uk/NR/rdonlyres/E426E492-7AED-46A6-B8F5-92B9CF9725C5/0/4545Leadershipconflict.pdf

Clampitt, P. G., & Downs, C. W. (1993). Employee perceptions of the relationship between communication and productivity: A field study. *Journal of Business Communication, 30*(1), 5–28.

Clark, R. P. (2010). *The glamour of grammar: A guide to the magic and mystery of practical English*. New York, NY: Little, Brown and Company.

Clark, R. W. (1984). Einstein. Retrieved from: http://todayinsci.com/E/Einstein_Albert/EinsteinAlbert-Quotations.htm

Claro, M., Salinas, A., Cabello-Hutt, T., San Martín, E., Preiss, D. D., … & Jara, I. (2018). Teaching in a Digital Environment (TIDE): Defining and measuring teachers' capacity to develop students' digital information and communication skills. *Computers & Education, 121*, 162–174.

Clokie, T. L., & Fourie, E. (2016). Graduate employability and communication competence. *Business & Professional Communication Quarterly, 79*(4), 442–463.

Cloud, D. L. (1994). The materiality of discourse as oxymoron: A challenge to critical rhetoric. *Western Journal of Communication, 58*(3), 141–163.

Cloud, D. L. (1998). *Control and consolation in American culture and politics: Rhetoric of therapy*. Thousand Oaks, CA: SAGE Publications.

Cody, M. J., & McLaughlin, M. L. (1980). Perceptions of compliance-gaining situations: A dimensional analysis. *Communications Monographs, 47*(2), 132–148.

Cohen, D. J., White, S., & Cohen, S. B. (2011). A time use diary study of adult everyday writing behavior. *Written Communication, 28*(1), 3–33.

Cohen, S., Doyle, W. J., Alper, C. M., & Skoner, D. P. (2003). Sociability and susceptibility to the common cold. *Psychological Science, 14*(5), 389–395.

Cohen, S., Gottlieb, B. H., & Underwood, L. G. (2000). Social relationships and health. In S. Cohen, L. G. Underwood, & B. H. Gottlieb (Eds.), *Social support measurement and interventions: A guide for health and social scientists* (pp. 3–25). Oxford, UK: Oxford University Press.

Cohen, S., & Wills, T. (1985). Stress, social support, and the buffering hypothesis. *Psychological Bulletin, 98*(2), 310–357.

Collier, M. J., Hegde, R. S., Lee, W., Nakayama, T., & Yep, G. A. (2002). Dialogue on the edges: Ferment in communication and culture. In M. J. Collier (Ed.), *Transforming communication about culture: Critical new directions* (Vol. 24, pp. 219–280). Thousand Oaks, CA: SAGE Publications.

Collier, M. J., & Thomas, M. (1988). Cultural identity: An interpretive perspective. In Y. Y. Kim & W. B. Gudykunst (Eds.), *Theories in intercultural communication* (pp. 94–120). Newbury Park, CA: SAGE Publications.

Collins, M. (2016, May). The employment outlook for the class of 2016 communication graduates. *Spectra, 52*(2), 24–27.

Colonnesi, C., Draijer, E. M., Jan, J. M., Stams, G., Van der Bruggen, C. O., Bögels, S. M., & Noom, M. J. (2011). The relation between insecure attachment and child anxiety: A meta-analytic review. *Journal of Clinical Child and Adolescent Psychology, 40*(4), 630–645.

Colvin, G. (2015). Humans are underrated. *Fortune, 172*(2), 100–113. Retrieved from: http://fortune.com/2015/07/23/humans-are-underrated/

Condit, C. M. (2000a). Toward new 'sciences' of human behavior. *Communication Education, 49*(1), 29–35.

Condit, C. M. (2000b). Culture and biology in human communication: Toward a multi-causal model. *Communication Education, 49*(1), 7–24.

Condit, C. M. (2013). How ought critical communication scholars judge, here, now? *Western Journal of Communication, 77*(5), 550–558.

Condon, J. C., & Yousef, F. S. (1975). An introduction to intercultural communication (Vol. 19: The Bobbs-Merrill series in speech communication). Indianapolis, IN: Bobbs-Merrill.

Connell, R. W. (1982). Class, patriarchy, and Sartre's theory of practice. *Theory and Society, 11,* 305–320.

Conquergood, D. (1985). Performing as a moral act: Ethical dimensions of the ethnography of performance. *Literature in Performance, 5*(2), 1–13.

Conquergood, D. (1991). Rethinking ethnography: Towards a critical cultural politics. *Communication Monographs, 58*(2), 179–194.

Consigny, S. P. (2001). *Gorgias, sophist and artist*. Columbia, SC: University of South Carolina Press.

Cook, J. (2014). Quantifying the consensus on anthropogenic global warming in the scientific literature: A re-analysis: Reply. *Energy Policy, 73*, 706–708.

Cook, J., Nuccitelli, D., Green, S. A., Richardson, M., Winkler, B., … Skuce, A. (2013). Quantifying the consensus on anthropogenic global warming in the scientific literature. *Environmental Research Letters, 8*(2), 1–7.

Cook, T. D., & Campbell, D. T. (1979). *Quasi-experimentation: Design and analysis issues for field settings*. New York, NY: Rand McNally & Co.

Corgnet, B., Espín, A. M., & Hernán-González, R. (2016). Creativity and cognitive skills among millennials: Thinking too much and creating too little. *Frontiers in Psychology, 7*. Retrieved from: a.espin@mdx.ac.uk

Corneo, G. (2006). Media capture in a democracy: The role of wealth concentration. *Journal of Public Economics, 90*(1/2), 37–58.

Corrigan, R., & Denton, P. (1996). Causal understanding as a developmental primitive. *Developmental Review, 16*(2), 162–202.

Cortese, A. (1990). *Ethnic ethics: The restructuring of moral theory*. Albany, NY: SUNY Press.

Cott, C. (1997). We decide, you carry it out: A social network analysis of multidisciplinary long-term care teams. *Social Science and Medicine, 45*(9), 1411–1421.

Couldry, N., & Hepp, A. (2013). Conceptualizing mediatization: Contexts, traditions, arguments. *Communication Theory, 23*(3), 191–202.

Craig, R. T. (1993). Why are there so many communication theories? *Journal of Communication, 43*(3), 26–33.

Craig, R. T. (1999). Communication theory as a field. *Communication Theory, 9*(2), 119–161.

Craig, R. T. (2007). Pragmatism in the field of communication theory. *Communication Theory, 17*(2), 125–145.

Credé, M., Roch, S. G., & Kieszczynka, U. M. (2010). Class attendance in college: A meta-analytic review of the relationship of class attendance with grades and student characteristics. *Review of Educational Research, 80*(2), 272–295.

Crites, L., & Crites, B. (2003). *The call to Hawaii: A wellness vacation guidebook*. Honolulu, HI: Aloha Wellness Publications.

Cross, R., & Gray, P. (2013). Where has all the time gone? Addressing collaboration overload in a networked economy. *California Management Review, 56*(1), 50–66.

Csikszentmihalyi, M., & LeFevre, J. (1989). Optimal experience in work and leisure. *Journal of Personality and Social Psychology, 56,* 815–822.

Cupach, W. R., & Canary, D. J. (2007). *Competence in interpersonal conflict*. Long Grove, IL: Waveland Press.

Cupach, W. R., Canary, D. J., & Sptizberg, B. H. (2010). *Competence in interpersonal conflict* (2nd ed.). Prospect Heights, IL: Waveland Press.

Cupach, W. R., Spitzberg, B. H., Bolingbroke, C. M., & Tellitocci, B. S. (2011). Persistence of attempts to reconcile a terminated romantic relationship: A partial test of relational goal pursuit theory. *Communication Reports, 24*(2), 99–115.

Currah, P. & Mulqueen, T. (2011). Securitizing gender: Identity, biometrics, and transgender bodies at the airport. *Social Research: An International Quarterly, 78,* 557–582.

Curry-Johnson, S. (1993). Weaving an identity tapestry. In. B. Findlen (Ed.), *Listen up: Voices from the next feminist generation* (pp. 51–58). New York, NY: Seal Press.

Cutrona, C. E., & Suhr, J. A. (1992). Controllability of stressful events and satisfaction with spouse support behaviors. *Communication Research, 19*(2), 154–174.

Czech, K., & Forward, G. L. (2010). Leader communication: Faculty perceptions of the department chair. *Communication Quarterly, 58*(4), 431–457.

Czech, K., & Forward, G. L. (2013). Communication, leadership, and job satisfaction: Perspectives on supervisor-subordinate relationships. *Studies in Media and Communication, 1*(2), 11–24.

D'enbeau, S. (2011). Transnational feminist advocacy online: Identity recreation through diversity, transparency, and co-construction. *Women's Studies in Communication, 34,* 64–83.

Dailey, R., Lee, C. M., & Spitzberg, B. H. (2007). Psychological abuse and communicative aggression. In B. H. Spitzberg & W. R. Cupach (Eds.), *The dark side of interpersonal communication* (2nd ed., pp. 297–326). Mahwah, NJ: Erlbaum.

Dailey, R. M., Lee, C. M., & Spitzberg, B. H. (2012). Charting dangerous territory: The family as a context of violence and aggression. In A. L. Vangelisti (Ed.), *Handbook of family communication* (pp. 479–495). New York, NY: Routledge.

Dainton, M., & Stafford, L. (2000). Predicting maintenance enactment from relational schemata, spousal behavior, and relational characteristics. *Communication Research Reports, 17*(2), 171–180.

Daly, J. A. (2011a). *Advocacy: Championing ideas and influencing others.* New Haven, CT: Yale.

Daly, J. A. (2011b). Personality and interpersonal communication. In M. L. Knapp & J. A. Daly (Eds.), *The SAGE handbook of interpersonal communication* (pp. 131–167). Thousand Oaks, CA: SAGE Publications.

Daniels, T., Spiker, B., & Papa, M. (1997). *Organizational communication: Perspectives and trends.* Thousand Oaks, CA: SAGE Publications.

Das, K., & Pegu, U. K. (2016). Ethical complexities in communicating conflict. *Global Media Journal: Indian Edition, 7/8*(2/1), 1–15.

Davis, D. (2011). Creaturely rhetorics. *Philosophy & Rhetoric, 44*(1), 88–94.

Davis, O. I. (2007). Locating Tulsa in the souls of Black women folk: Performing memory as survival. *Performance Research, 12,* 124–136.

de Beauvoir, S. (1952). *The second sex.* New York, NY: Vintage Books.

De Coster, S., Heimer, K., & Wittrock, S. M. (2006). Neighborhood disadvantage, social capital, street context, and youth violence. *Sociological Quarterly, 47*(4), 723–753.

de Guinea, A. O., Webster, J., & Staples, D. S. (2012). A meta-analysis of the consequences of virtualness on team functioning. *Information and Management, 49*(6), 301–308.

De Neve, J-E., Mikhaylov, S., Dawes, C. T., Chistakis, N. A., & Fowler, J. H. (2013). Born to lead? A twin design and genetic association study of leadership role occupancy. *Leadership Quarterly, 24,* 45–60.

de Saussure, F. (1959). *Course in general linguistics.* New York, NY: Philosophical Library.

Deal, J. J. (2015). *Always on, never done? Don't blame the smartphone.* San Diego, CA: Center for Creative Leadership (white paper). Retrieved from: http://www.ccl.org/wp-content/uploads/2015/04/AlwaysOn.pdf

Deal, T. E., & Kennedy, A. A. (1982). *Corporate cultures: The rites and rituals of corporate life.* Reading, MA: Addison-Wesley.

Deane, P., Song, Y., Rijn, P., O'Reilly, T., Fowles, M., Bennett, R., … Zhang, M. (2018). The case for scenario-based assessment of written argumentation. *Reading and Writing: An Interdisciplinary Journal, 32*(6), 1575–1606.

Dearing, J. W., Gaglio, B., & Rabin, B. A. (2011). Community organizing research approaches. In T. L. Thompson, R. Parrott, & J. F. Nussbaum (Eds.), *The Routledge handbook of health communication* (pp. 546–559). New York, NY: Taylor & Francis.

DeChurch, L. A., & Mesmer-Magnus, J. R. (2010). The cognitive underpinnings of effective teamwork: a meta-analysis. *Journal of Applied Psychology, 95*(1), 32–53.

Dediu, D., & Levinson, S. C. (2013). On the antiquity of language: The reinterpretation of Neandertal linguistic capacities and its consequences. *Frontiers in Psychology, 4.*

Dediu, D., & Levinson, S. C. (2014). The time frame of the emergence of modern language and its implications. In D. Dor, C. Knight, & J. Lewis (Eds.), *The social origins of language* (pp. 184–195). New York, NY: Oxford University Press.

DeFleur, M. L., & DeFleur, M. H. (2016). *Mass communication theories: Explaining origins, processes, and effects.* New York, NY: Routledge.

Deloitte. (2017). *2017 global mobile consumer survey: US edition.* New York, NY: Deloitte. https://www2.deloitte.com/content/dam/Deloitte/us/Documents/technology-media-telecommunications/us-tmt-2017-global-mobile-consumer-survey-executive-summary.pdf

DeLuca, K. M. (2012). *Image politics: The new rhetoric of environmental activism.* New York, NY: Routledge.

Deming, D. J. (2015, August). The growing importance of social skills in the labor market (NBER Working Paper 21473). Cambridge, MA: National Bureau of Economic Research. Retrieved from: http://www.nber.org/papers/w21473.pdf

Denes, A., Affifi, T. D., & Hesse, C. (2017). Physiological outcomes of communication behavior. In A. VanLear & D. J. Canary (Eds.), *Researching interactive communication behavior* (pp. 45–60). Thousand Oaks, CA: SAGE Publications.

Dennison, R. P., Koerner, S. S., & Segrin, C. (2014). A dyadic examination of family-of-origin influence on newlyweds' marital satisfaction. *Journal of Family Psychology, 28*(3), 429–435.

Derrida, J. (1978). *Of grammatology* (G. C. Spivak, Trans.). Baltimore, MD: Johns Hopkins University Press.

Derue, D. S., Nahrgang, J. D., Wellman, N., & Humphrey, S. E. (2011). Trait and behavioral theories of leadership: An integration and meta-analytic test of their relative validity. *Personnel Psychology, 64*(1), 7–52.

Derzon, J. H. & Lipsey, M. W. (2002). A meta-analysis of the effectiveness of mass-communication for changing substance-use knowledge, attitudes, and behavior. In W. D. Crano & M. Burgoon (Eds.), *Mass media and drug prevention: Classic and contemporary theories and research* (pp. 231–258). Mahwah, NJ: Erlbaum.

Deutsch, M., & Gerard, H. B. (1955). A study of normative and informational social influences upon individual judgment. *The Journal of Abnormal and Social Psychology, 51*(3), 629–636.

Deutschman, A. (2007). *Change or die.* New York, NY: Harper Collins.

Dewan, R. M., Freimer, M. L., Seidmann, A., & Jie Zhang. (2004). Web portals: Evidence and analysis of media concentration. *Journal of Management Information Systems, 21*(2), 181–199.

Dewey, J. (1910). *How we think.* Lexington, MA: DC Heath.

Diamond, I., & Quinby, L. (1988). Introduction. In *Feminism & Foucault: Reflections on resistance* (pp. iv–xv). Boston: Northeastern University Press.

Dillard, J. P., Anderson, J. W., & Knobloch, L. K. (2002). Interpersonal influence. In M. L. Knapp & J. A. Daly (Eds.), *Handbook of interpersonal communication* (3rd ed., pp. 423–474). Thousand Oaks, CA: SAGE Publications.

Dillard, J. P., Hunter, J. E., & Burgoon, M. (1984). Sequential-request persuasive strategies. *Human Communication Research, 10*(4), 461–488.

Dindia, K. (2006). Men are from North Dakota, women are from South Dakota. In K. Dindia & D. J. Canary (Eds.), *Sex differences and similarities in communication* (2nd ed., pp. 3–20). Mahwah, NJ: Erlbaum.

Dishman, E. (2002). Performative interventions: Designing future technologies through synergetic performance. In N. Stucky & C. Wimmer (Eds.), *Teaching performance studies* (pp. 235–246). Carbondale, IL: Southern Illinois University.

Dolmage, J. T. (2014). *Disability rhetoric.* Syracuse, NY: Syracuse University Press.

Domonoske, C. (2018, April 2). Video reveals power of Sinclair, as local news anchors recite script in unison. NPR.org. Retrieved from: https://www.npr.org/sections/thetwo-way/2018/04/02/598794433/video-reveals-power-of-sinclair-as-local-news-anchors-recite-script-in-unison

Donner, Y., & Hardy, J. (2015). Piecewise power laws in individual learning curves. *Psychonomic Bulletin and Review, 22*(5), 1308–1319.

Dorfman, L., & Wallack, L. (2012). Putting policy into health communication. In R. E. Rice & C. K. Atkin (Eds.), *Public communication campaigns* (pp. 335–348). Los Angeles, CA: SAGE Publications.

Dove, I. J. (2016). Visual scheming: Assessing visual arguments. *Argumentation and Advocacy, 52*(4), 254–264.

Drew, P. (1992). Contested evidence in courtroom cross-examination: The case of a trial for rape. In R. Pirard (Ed.), *Anthropologiques, IV* (pp. 470–520). Louvain: Peeters.

Drew, P. (2013). The voice of the patient: Non-alignment between patients and doctors in the consultation. In W. A. Beach (Ed.), *Handbook of patient–provider interactions: Raising and responding to concerns about life, illness, and disease* (pp. 299–306). New York, NY: Hampton.

Drew, P., & Heritage, J. (Eds.). (1992). *Talk at work: Interaction in institutional settings.* Cambridge, UK: Cambridge University Press.

Drucker, P. (1954). *The practice of management.* New York: Harper & Row.

dscout, Inc. (2016, June 15). *Mobile touches: dscout's inaugural study on humans and their tech.* Retrieved from: https://blog.dscout.com/hubfs/downloads/dscout_mobile_touches_study_2016.pdf

du Pré, A. (2014). *Communicating about health: Current issues and perspectives* (4th ed.). New York, NY: Oxford University Press.

Duck, S. (1988). *Relating to others.* Stony Stratford, UK: Open University Press.

Dunbar, N. E. (2017). Nonverbal communication. In M. Allen (Ed.), *The SAGE encyclopedia of communication research methods.* Los Angeles, CA: SAGE Publications.

Dunbar, R. I. M., Duncan, N. D. C., & Marriott, A. (1997). Human conversational behavior. *Human Nature, 8*(3), 231–246.

Dunn, D. S., & Dougherty, S. B. (2008). Flourishing: Mental health as living life well. *Journal of Social and Clinical Psychology, 27,* 314–316.

Dunning, D., Heath, C., & Suls, J. M. (2004). Flawed self-assessment: Implications for health, education, and the workplace. *Psychological Science in the Public Interest, 5*(3), 69–106.

Duranti, A., & Goodwin, C (Eds.). (1992). *Rethinking context: Language as an interactive phenomenon.* Cambridge, UK: Cambridge University Press.

Duymedjian, R., & Rüling, C.-C. (2010). Towards a foundation of bricolage in organization and management theory. *Organization Studies, 31*(2), 133–151.

Eadie, W. F. (2011). Stories we tell: Fragmentation and convergence in communication disciplinary history. *Review of Communication, 11*(3), 161–176.

Eagan, K., Stolzenberg, E. B., Bates, A. K., Aragon, M. C., Suchard, M. R., & Rios-Aguilar, C. (2016). *The American freshman: National norms Fall 2015.* Los Angeles, CA: Higher Education Research Institute, UCLA. Retrieved from: http://heri.ucla.edu/monographs/TheAmericanFreshman2015.pdf

Eastin, M. S., & LaRose, R. (2000). Internet self-efficacy and the psychology of the digital divide. *Journal of Computer-Mediated Communication, 6*(1).

Edgar, T., Gallagher, S. S., Silk, K. J., Cruz, T. B., Abroms, L. C., Evans, W. D., … Miller, G. A. (2015). Results From a National Survey of Health Communication Master's Degree Recipients: An Exploration of Training, Placement, Satisfaction, and Success. *Journal of Health Communication, 20*(3), 354–366.

Edgar, T., Silk, K. J., Abroms, L. C., Cruz, T. B., Evans, D. W., Gallagher, S. S. … Sheff, S. E. (2016). Career paths of recipients of a master's degree in health communication: Understanding employment opportunities, responsibilities, and choices. *Journal of Health Communication, 21*(3), 356–365.

Edwards, P. (1999). Unstoried: Teaching literature in the age of performance studies. *Theatre Annual, 52,* 1–147.

Ehrlinger, J., Johnson, K., Banner, M., Dunning, D., & Kruger, J. (2008). Why the unskilled are unaware: Further explorations of (absent) self-insight among the incompetent. *Organizational Behavior and Human Decision Processes, 105*(1), 98–121.

Eibl-Eibesfeldt, I. (1979). Universals in human expressive behavior. In A. Wolfgang (Ed.), *Nonverbal behavior, applications and cultural implications* (pp. 17–30). New York, NY: Academic Press.

Eichinger, R. W., & Lombardo, M. M. (2003). Knowledge summary series: 360-degree assessment. *Human Resource Management, 26,* 34–44.

Eichinger, R. W., & Lombardo, M. M. (2004). Patterns of rater accuracy in 360-degree feedback. *Human Resource Management, 27*(4), 23–25.

Einstein, A. (1919). Induction and deduction in physics. In *The collected papers of Albert Einstein, Vol. 7: The Berlin Years: Writings, 1918–1921* (English translation supplement, transl. A. Engel, Doc. #28). Princeton, NJ: Princeton University Press. Retrieved from: http://einsteinpapers.press.princeton.edu/vol7-trans/

Eisenberg, A. M., & Smith, R. R., Jr. (1971). *Nonverbal communication.* Indianapolis: Bobbs-Merrill.

Eisenberg, E. M. (1990). Jamming: Transcendence through organizing. *Communication Research, 17*(2),139–164.

Eisenberg, E. M., Monge, P. R., & Farace, R. V. (1984). Coorientation on communication rules in managerial dyads. *Human Communication Research, 11*(2), 261–271.

Ekman, P., & Friesen, W. V. (1975). *Unmasking the face: A field guide to recognizing emotions from facial clues.* Englewood Cliffs, NJ: Prentice Hall.

Elfenbein, H. A., & Ambady, N. (2002). On the universality and cultural specificity of emotion recognition: A meta-analysis. *Psychological Bulletin, 128*(2), 203–235.

Ellen, R. (2009). A modular approach to understanding the transmission of technical knowledge. *Journal of Material Culture, 14*(2), 243–277.

Ellingson, L. L. (2017). *Doing embodiment in qualitative research.* New York, NY: Routledge.

Emanuel, R., Adams, J., Baker, K., Daufin, E. K., Ellington, C., Fitts, E., … Okeowo, D. (2008). How college students spend their time communicating. *International Journal of Listening, 22*(1), 13–28.

Emerson, R. M., Fretz, R. I., & Shaw, L. L. (2011). *Writing ethnography fieldnotes.* Chicago, IL: University of Chicago Press.

Endres, D., & Gould, M. (2009). 'I am also in the position to use my whiteness to help them out': The communication of whiteness in service learning. *Western Journal of Communication, 73*(4), 418–436.

Engel, G. L. (1977). The need for a new medical model: A challenge for biomedicine. *Science, 196*(4286), 129–136.

Ensari, N., Riggio, R. E., Christian, J., & Carslaw, G. (2011). Who emerges as a leader? Meta-analyses of individual differences as predictors of leadership emergence. *Personality and Individual Differences, 51*(4), 532–536.

Entman, R. (2004). *Projections of power: Framing news, public opinion, and U.S. foreign policy.* Chicago, IL: University of Chicago Press.

Epstein, R. M., & Street R. L., Jr. (2007). *Patient-centered communication in cancer care: Promoting healing and reducing suffering.* Bethesda, MD: National Cancer Institute.

Esser, J. K. (1998). Alive and well after 25 years: A review of groupthink research. *Organizational Behavior and Human Decision Processes, 73*(2-3), 116–141.

Exline, J. J., Deshea, L., & Holeman, V. T. (2007). Is apology worth the risk? Predictors, outcomes, and ways to avoid regret. *Journal of Social and Clinical Psychology, 26*(4), 479–504.

Fahs, B. (2008). The radical possibilities of Valerie Solanas. *Feminist Studies, 34*(3), 591–617.

Falk, E., & Scholz, C. (2018). Persuasion, influence, and value: Perspectives from communication and social neuroscience. *Annual Review of Psychology, 69*, 329–356.

Fang, X., Zhang, J., & Chan, S. S. (2013). Development of an instrument for studying flow in computer game play. *International Journal of Human-Computer Interaction, 29*(7), 456–470.

Farrell, A., & Geist-Martin, P. (2005). Communicating social health: Perceptions of wellness at work. *Management Communication Quarterly, 18*, 543–592.

Farrugia, C., & Sanger, J. (2017, October). *Gaining an employment edge: The impact of study abroad on 21st century skills and career prospects in the United States, 2013–2016.* New York, NY: Institute of International Education Center for Academic Mobility.

Fârte, G.-I. (2016). How to change people's beliefs? Doxastic Coercion vs. Evidential Persuasion. *Argumentum: Journal the Seminar of Discursive Logic, Argumentation Theory & Rhetoric, 14*(2), 49–78.

Faulkner, W. (2000). The power and the pleasure? A research agenda for "making gender stick" to engineers. *Science, Technology, and Human Values, 25*, 87–119.

Fausto-Sterling, A. (2000). *Sexing the body: Gender politics and the construction of sexuality.* New York, NY: Basic Books.

Fawkes, J. (2007). Public relations models and persuasion ethics: a new approach. *Journal of Communication Management, 11*(4), 313–331.

Fay, N., Page, A. C., & Serfaty, C. (2010). Listeners influence speakers' perceived communication effectiveness. *Journal of Experimental Social Psychology, 46*(4), 689–692.

Fayol, H. (1949). *General and industrial management.* London: Sir Isaac Pitman and Sons.

Fearn-Banks, K. (2011). *Crisis communications: A casebook approach.* New York, NY: Routledge.

Fehr, R., Gelfand, M. J., & Nag, M. (2010). The road to forgiveness: A meta-analytic synthesis of its situational and dispositional correlates. *Psychological Bulletin, 136*(5), 894–914.

Felmlee, D. (1995). Fatal attractions: Affection and disaffection in intimate relationships. *Journal of Social and Personal Relationships, 12*(2), 295–311.

Fenske, M., & Goltz, D. B. (2013). Disciplinary dedications and extradisciplinary experiences: Themes on a relation. *Text and Performance Quarterly, 34*(1), 1–8.

Fernando, C., Valijärvi, R., & Goldstein, R. A. (2010). A model of the mechanisms of language extinction and revitalization strategies to save endangered languages. *Human Biology, 82*(1), 47–75.

Ferrara, E., & Yang, Z. (2015). Measuring emotional contagion in social media. *PLOS One, 10*(11).

Festinger, L. (1957). *A theory of cognitive dissonance.* Stanford, CA: Stanford University Press.

Feyerabend, P. K. (1970). Against method: Outline of an anarchistic theory of knowledge. In M. Radner & S. Winokur (Eds.), *Minnesota studies in the philosophy of science* (Vol. 4, Analyses of theories and methods of physics and psychology, pp. 17–130). Minneapolis, MN: University of Minnesota.

Feyerabend, P. K. (1975). *Against method: Outline of an anarchistic theory of knowledge.* London, UK: NLB.

Fiedler, F. E. (1967). *A theory of leadership effectiveness.* New York: McGraw-Hill.

Field, T. (2002). Infant's need for touch. *Human Development, 45*, 100–103.

Fine, M. (1994). Working the hyphens: Reinventing self and other in qualitative research. In N. K. Denzin & Y. S. Lincoln (Eds.), *Handbook of qualitative research* (pp. 70–82). Thousand Oaks, CA: SAGE Publications.

Finkel, E. J., Simpson, J. A., & Eastwick, P. W. (2017). The psychology of close relationships: Fourteen core principles. *Annual Review of Psychology, 68,* 383–411.

Finn, A. N., Schrodt, P., Witt, P. L., Elledge, N., Jernberg, K. A., & Larson, L. M. (2009). A meta-analytical review of teacher credibility and its associations with teacher behaviors and student outcomes. *Communication Education, 58*(4), 516–537.

Fishbein, M. (2000). The role of theory in HIV prevention. *AIDS Care, 12*(3), 273–278.

Fishbein, M., & Ajzen, I. (1975). *Belief, attitude, intention, and behavior: An introduction to theory and research.* Reading, MA: Addison-Wesley.

Fishbein, M., & Ajzen, I. (2010). *Predicting and changing behavior: The reasoned action approach.* New York, NY: Psychology Press.

Fisher, B.A. (1980). *Small group decision making.* New York, NY: McGraw-Hill.

Fisher, B.A., & Ellis, D.G. (1992). *Small group decision making: Communication and the group process.* New York, NY: McGraw-Hill.

Fisher, W. R. (1978). Toward a logic of good reasons. *Quarterly Journal of Speech, 64*(4), 376–384.

Fisher, W. R. (1989). *Human communication as narration: Toward a philosophy of reason, value, and action.* Columbia, SC: University of South Carolina Press

Fitzpatrick, M. A., Witteman, H., & Vance, L. (1984). Interpersonal communication in the casual interaction of marital partners. *Journal of Language and Social Psychology, 3*(2), 81–95.

Flanagin, A. J. (2017). Online social influence and the convergence of mass and interpersonal communication. *Human Communication Research, 43*(4), 450–463.

Fleeson, W., & Gallagher, P. (2009). The implications of Big Five standing for the distribution of trait manifestation in behavior: Fifteen experience-sampling studies and a meta-analysis. *Journal of Personality and Social Psychology, 97*(6), 1097–1114.

Fleischmann, A. A., Spitzberg, B. H., Andersen, P. A., & Roesch, S. C. (2005). Tickling the monster: Jealousy induction in relationships. *Journal of Social and Personal Relationships, 22*(1), 49–73.

Fleming, P. & Spicer, A. (2008). Beyond power and resistance: New approaches to organizational politics. *Management Communication Quarterly, 21*(3), 301–309.

Flew, T. (2014). Changing influences on the concept of "media influence." *International Journal of Digital Television, 5*(1), 7–18.

Flores, L. A. (2003). Constructing rhetorical borders: Peons, illegal aliens, and competing narratives of immigration. *Critical Studies in Media Communication, 20*(4), 362–387.

Floyd, K. (2002). Human affection exchange: V. Attributes of the highly affectionate. *Communication Quarterly, 50*(2), 135–152.

Floyd, K. (2006). *Communicating affection: Interpersonal behavior and social context.* Cambridge, UK: Cambridge University Press.

Floyd, K. (2011). *Interpersonal communication* (2nd ed.). Boston, MA: McGraw-Hill.

Floyd, K. (2014). Humans are people, too: Nurturing an appreciation for nature in communication research. *Review of Communication Research, 2*(1).

Floyd, K., & Denes, A. (2015). Attachment security and oxytocin receptor gene polymorphism interact to influence affectionate communication. *Communication Quarterly, 63*(3), 272–285.

Floyd, K., Hess, J., Miczo, L., Halone, K., Mikkelson, A. C., & Tusing, K. (2005). Human affection exchange: VIII. Further evidence of the benefits of expressed affection. *Communication Quarterly, 53*(3), 285–303.

Floyd, K., & Hesse, C. (2017). Affection deprivation is conceptually and empirically distinct from loneliness. *Western Journal of Communication, 81*(4), 446–465.

Floyd, K., & Pauley, P. M. (2011). Affectionate communication is good, except when it isn't: On the dark side of expressing affection. In W. R. Cupach & B. H. Spitzberg (Eds.), *The dark side of close relationships II* (pp. 145–173). New York, NY: Routledge/Taylor & Francis.

Floyd, K., Pauley, P. M., & Hesse, C. (2010). State and trait affectionate communication buffer adults' stress reactions. *Communication Monographs, 77*(4), 618–636.

Floyd, K., Pauley, P. M., Hesse, C., Veksler, A. E., Eden, J., & Mikkelson, A. C. (2014). Affectionate communication is associated with markers of immune and cardiovascular system competence. In J. M. Honeycutt, C. R. Sawyer, & S. A. Keaton (Eds.), *The influence of communication on physiology and health* (pp. 115–130). New York, NY: Peter Lang.

Fortin, J., & Bromwich, E. (2018, April 2). Sinclair made dozens of local news anchors recite the same script. *New York Times.* Retrieved from: https://www.nytimes.com/2018/04/02/business/media/sinclair-news-anchors-script.html

Forward, G. L., Czech, K., & Lee, C. M. (2011). Assessing Gibb's supportive and defensive communication climate: An examination of measurement and construct validity. *Communication Research Reports, 28*(1), 1–15.

Foss, K. A., & Foss, S. K. (1983). The status of research on women and communication. *Communication Quarterly, 31*(3), 195–204.

Foster, E. (2010). My eyes cry without me: Illusions of choice in the transition to motherhood. In S. Hayden & L. O'Brien Hallstein (Eds.), *Contemplating maternity in an era of choice: Explorations into discourses of reproduction* (pp. 139–158). Lanham, MD: Lexington Books.

Foucault, M. (1990a). *The history of sexuality, vol 1: An introduction* (R. Hurley, Trans.). New York, NY: Vintage.

Foucault, M. (1990b). *The history of sexuality, vol. 2: The use of pleasure* (R. Hurley, Trans.). New York, NY: Vintage.

Foucault, M. (1994). *Power: The essential works of Foucault, 1954–1984, vol. 3.* (R. Hurley, Trans., J. D. Faubion, Ed.). New York, NY: New Press.

Fowler, C., Gasiorek, J., & Afifi, W. (2018). Complex considerations in couples' financial information management: Extending the theory of motivated information management. *Communication Research, 45*(3), 365–393.

Fowler, F. J. (1993). *Survey research methods* (2nd ed.). Newbury Park, CA: SAGE Publications.

Fox, J., & McEwan, B. (2017). Distinguishing technologies for social interaction: The perceived social affordances of communication channels scale. *Communication Monographs, 84*(3), 298–318.

Fox, R. (2013). "You are not allowed to talk about production": Narratization on (and off) the set of CBS's *Big Brother. Critical Studies in Media Communication, 30*(3), 189–208.

Fraley, R. C. (2002). Attachment stability from infancy to adulthood: Meta-analysis and dynamic modeling of developmental mechanisms. *Personality and Social Psychology Review, 6*(2), 123–151.

Frankovský, M. (1995). Multidimensional scale of argumentativeness. *Studia Psychologica, 37*(3), 157–158.

Franz, R. S. (1998). Task independence and personal power in teams. *Small Group Research, 29*, 226–253.

Fredal, J. (2008). Why shouldn't the sophists charge fees? *Rhetoric Society Quarterly, 38*(2), 148–170.

Fredrickson, B. L., & Losada, M. F. (2005). Positive affect and complex dynamics of human flourishing. *American Psychologist, 60*(7), 678–686.

Freire, P. (1996). *Pedagogy of the oppressed* (M. B. Ramos, Trans., 20th anniversary ed.). New York, NY: Cantinuum.

Freitas, K. B., & Dixon, P. W. (1997). A cosmology of Hawaiian and Western values. *Social Behavior and Personality, 25*(1), 59–76.

French, J. R. P., & Raven, B. H. (1959). The bases of social power. In D. Cartwright (Ed.), *Studies in social power.* 150–167.

Frey, B. B., Ellis, J. D., Bulgreen, J. A., Hare, J. C., & Ault, M. (2015). Development of a test of scientific argumentation. *Electronic Journal of Science Education, 19*(4).

Frey, C. B., & Osborne, M. A. (2017). The future of employment: How susceptible are jobs to computerisation? *Technological Forecasting & Social Change, 114*, 254–280.

Frey, L. R. (Ed.). (1999). *The handbook of group communication and research.* Thousand Oaks, CA: SAGE Publications.

Frick, R. W. (1985). Communicating emotion: The role of prosodic features. *Psychological Bulletin, 97*(3), 412–429.

Fried, C. (1978). *Right and wrong.* Cambridge, MA: Harvard University Press.

Friedan, B. (2001). *The feminine mystique* (reprint.). New York, NY: W. W. Norton.

Friedman, R. (2014). *The best place to work: The art and science of creating an extraordinary workplace.* New York, NY: Perigee.

Fritsche, I. (2002). Account strategies for the violation of social norms: Integration and extension of sociological and social psychological typologies. *Journal for the Theory of Social Behaviour, 32*(4), 371–394.

Frontline. (2012). Money, power, and Wall Street. Retrieved from: http://www.pbs.org/wgbh/pages/frontline/business-economy-financial-crisis/money-power-wall-street/the-buzz-around-that-tim-geithner-scene/

Frosch, D. L., & Kaplan, R. M. (1999). Shared decision making in clinical medicine: Past research and future directions. *American Journal of Preventive Medicine, 17*(4), 285–294.

Frye, M. (2000). Feminism; First-wave/Second-wave feminism; Third-wave feminism. In L. Code (Ed.), *Encyclopedia of feminist theories* (pp. 195–197; 208–210; 474). New York, NY: Routledge.

Fuchs, S. (2001). What makes sciences "scientific"? In J. H. Turner (Ed.), *Handbook of sociological theory* (pp. 21–35). New York, NY: Kluwer Academic/Plenum.

Fugard, A. (1990). *My children! My Africa!* Boston, MA: Faber and Faber.

Furnée, C. A., Groot, W., van den Brink, H. M. (2008). The health effects of education: A meta-analysis. *European Journal of Public Health, 18*(4), 417–421.

Furnham, A., & Baguma, P. (1999). Cross-cultural differences in explanations for health and illness: A British and Ugandan comparison. *Mental Health, Religion and Culture, 2*(2), 121–134.

Galland, L. (2005). *Textbook of functional medicine.* Gig Harbor, WA: Institute for Functional Medicine.

Gallo, C. (2017, January 5). The 1 skill Warren Buffett says will raise your value by 50%. Retrieved from: https://www.inc.com/carmine-gallo/the-one-skill-warren-buffett-says-will-raise-your-value-by-50.html?cid=email

Gallup. (2019). *Evolution, creationism, intelligent design.* Gallup.com. Retrieved from: https://news.gallup.com/poll/21814/evolution-creationism-intelligent-design.aspx

Gallup/Lumina Foundation. (2014, February 25). *What America needs to know about higher education redesign.* Washington, DC: Author. Retrieved from: https://www.luminafoundation.org/files/resources/2013-gallup-lumina-foundation-report.pdf

Gamble, C. N., & Hanan, J. S. (2016). Figures of entanglement: Special issue introduction. *Review of Communication, 16*(4), 265–280

Garner, J. T., Ragland, J. P., Leitre, M., Young, J., Bergquist, G., … Ivy, T. (2016). A long look back: An analysis of 50 years of organizational communication research (1964–2013). *Review of Communication Research, 4.*

Garro, L. C. (2000). Remembering what one knows and the construction of the past: A comparison of cultural consensus theory and cultural schema theory. *Ethos, 28*(3), 275–319.

Gass, R. H., & Seiter, J. S. (2014). *Persuasion, social influence, and compliance-gaining* (5th ed.). New York, NY: Pearson.

Gausby, A. (2015, Spring). *Attention spans: Mississauga, ON, Canada: Microsoft Canada.* Retrieved from: https://www.scribd.com/document/265348695/Microsoft-Attention-Spans-Research-Report

Geertz, C. (1980). Blurred genres: The refiguration of social thought. *American Scholar, 49*(2), 165–182.

Geertz, C. (1983). *Local knowledge.* New York, NY: Basic Books.

Geimer, J. L., Leach, D. J., DeSimone, J. A., Rogelberg, S. G., & Warr, P. B. (2015). Meetings at work: Perceived effectiveness and recommended improvements. *Journal of Business Research, 68*(9), 2015–2026.

Geist-Martin, P., Becker, C. Carnett, S., & Slauta, K. (2008). The call to Hawaii: Holistic practitioners' perspectives of their communication practices of healing. *Communication and Medicine, 5*, 133–144.

Geist-Martin, P., & Bell, K. K. (2009). "Open your heart first of all": Perspectives of holistic providers in Costa Rica about communication in the provision of health care. *Health Communication, 24*(7), 631–646.

Geist-Martin, P., Bollinger, B. J., Wiechert, K. N., Plump, B., & Sharf, B. F. (2016). Challenging integration: Clinicians' perspectives of communicating collaboration in a center for integrative medicine. *Health Communication, 31*(5), 544–556.

Geist-Martin, P., Carnett, S., & Slauta, K. (2008). Dialectics of doubt and accomplishment: Re-counting what counts in cultural immersion and adaptation. In L. A. Samovar, R. E. Porter, & E. R. McDaniel (Eds.), *Intercultural communication: A reader* (pp. 401–412). Belmont, CA: Wadsworth.

Geist-Martin, P., & Dreyer, J. (2001). Accounting for care: Different versions of different stories in the health care context. In S. L. Herndon & G. L. Kreps (Eds.), *Qualitative research: Applications in organizational communication* (2nd ed., pp. 121–149). Cresskill, NJ: Hampton Press.

Geist-Martin, P., & Freiberg, K. L. (1992, October). *The saving grace of organizational communication.* Paper presented at the annual convention of the Speech Communication Association, Chicago, IL.

Geist-Martin, P., Horsley, K., & Farrell, A. (2003). Working well: Communicating individual and collective wellness initiatives. In T. L. Thompson, A. M. Dorsey, K. I. Miller, & R. Parrott (Eds.), *Handbook of health communication* (pp. 423–443). Mahwah, NJ: Erlbaum.

Geist-Martin, P., Ray, E. B., & Sharf, B. F. (2011). *Communicating health: Personal, cultural, and political complexities*. Long Gove, IL: Waveland Press.

Geist-Martin, P., & Scarduzio, J. A. (2011). Working well: Reconsidering health communication at work. In T. L. Thompson, R. Parrott, & J. F. Nussbaum (Ed.), *Handbook of health communication* (2nd ed., pp. 117–131). Mahwah, NJ: Erlbaum.

Geist-Martin, P., & Scarduzio, J. A. (2017). Workplace wellness as flourishing: Communicating life quality at work. In J. Yamasaki, P. Geist-Martin, & B. F. Sharf (Eds.), *Storied health and illness: Communicating personal, cultural, and political complexities* (pp. 157–190). Long Grove, IL: Waveland Press.

Geist-Martin, P., Sharf, B. F, & Jeha, N. (2008). Communicating healing holistically. In H. Zoller & M. J. Dutta (Eds.), *Emerging perspectives in health communication: Meaning, culture, and power* (pp. 85–112). New York, NY: Routledge.

Geithner, T. F. (2014). *Stress test: Reflections on financial crises*. New York, NY: Crown.

Georgas, H. (2015). Google vs. the Library (Part III): Assessing the quality of sources found by undergraduates. *Portal: Libraries and the Academy, 15*(1), 133–161.

Gerbner, G., & Gross, L. (1976). Living with television: The violence profile. *Journal of Communication, 26*(2), 172–201.

Gerbner, G., Gross, L., Morgan, M., Signorielli, N., & Hirsch, P. M. (1980). Comments and letters: Some additional comments on cultivation analysis. *Public Opinion Quarterly, 44*(3), 408–413.

Gergen, K. J. (1994). *Toward transformation in social knowledge* (2nd ed.). London, UK: SAGE Publications.

Gersick, C. J. (1988). Time and transition in work teams: Toward a new model of group development. *Academy of Management Journal, 31*(1), 9–41.

Gersick, C. J. (1991). Revolutionary change theories: A multilevel exploration of the punctuated equilibrium paradigm. *The Academy of Management Review, 16*(1), 10–36.

Gibb, J. R. (1961). Defensive communication. *Journal of Communication, 11,* 141–148.

Giddens, A. (1983). Comments on the theory of structuration. *Journal for the Theory of Social Behaviour, 13*(1), 75–80.

Gilbert, K. L., Quinn, S. C., Goodman, R. M., Butler, J., & Wallace, J. (2013). A meta-analysis of social capital and health: A case for needed research. *Journal of Health Psychology, 18*(11), 1385–1399.

Gill, M. (2017). Adaptability and affordances in new media: Literate technologies, communicative techniques. *Journal of Pragmatics, 116,* 104–108.

Gill, V. T. (1998). Doing attributions in medical interaction: Patients' explanations for illness and doctors' responses. *Social Psychology Quarterly, 61*(4), 342–360.

Gilligan, C. (1982). *In a different voice: Psychological theory and women's development*. Cambridge, MA: Harvard University Press.

Gilovich, T., & Savitsky, K. (1999). The spotlight effect and the illision of transparency: Egocentric assessments of how we are seen by others. *Current Directions in Psychological Science, 8*(6), 165-168.

Giovannini, E., Hall, J., Morrone, A., & Ranuzzi, G. (2011). A framework to measure the progress of societies. *Revue d'économie politique, 121,* 93–118.

Glenn, P. (2003). *Laughter in interaction*. Cambridge, UK: Cambridge University Press.

Glenn, P., LeBaron, C., & Mandelbaum, J. (Eds.). (2002). *Studies in language and social interaction: In honor of Robert Hopper*. Mahwah, NJ: Erlbaum.

Godfrey, E., & Parker, L. (2010). Mapping the cultural landscape in engineering education. *Journal of Engineering Education, 99,* 5–22.

Goehring, C., Renegar, V., & Puhl, L. (2017). "Abusive furniture": Visual metonymy and the Hungarian stop violence against women campaign. *Women's Studies in Communication, 40*(4), 440–457.

Goel, S., Anderson, A., Hofman, J., & Watts, D. J. (2016). The structural virality of online diffusion. *Management Science, 62*(1), 180–196.

Goffman, E. (1959). *The presentation of self in everyday life*. New York, NY: Doubleday.

Goffman, E. (1963). *Stigma: Notes on the management of spoiled identity*. New York, NY: Simon & Schuster.

Goffman, E. (1981). *Forms of talk*. Philadelphia, PA: University of Pennsylvania Press.

Goffman, E. (1986). *Frame analysis: An essay on the organization of experience*. Boston, MA: Northeastern University Press.

Goh, J., Pfeffer, J., & Zenios, S. A. (2016). The relationship between workplace stressors and mortality and health costs in the United States. *Management Science, 62*(2), 608–628.

Goldberg, L. R. (1993). The structure of phenotypic personality traits. *American Psychologist, 48*(1), 26–34.

Goldsmith, D. J. (2004). *Communicating social support*. Cambridge, UK: Cambridge University Press.

Goldsmith, D. J., & Albrecht, T. L. (2011). Social support, social networks, and health. In T. L. Thompson, R. Parrott, & J. F. Nussbaum (Eds.), *The Routledge handbook of health communication* (pp. 335–348). New York, NY: Taylor & Francis.

Goldstein, N. J., Cialdini, R. B., & Griskevicius, V. (2008). A room with a viewpoint: Using social norms to motivate environmental conservation in hotels. *Journal of Consumer Research, 35*(3), 472–482.

Gómez, R. (2016). Communication industries in North America after 20 years of North American Free Trade Agreement: Media policy, regulatory bodies and concentration. *International Communication Gazette, 78*(3), 177–199.

Goodall, H. L., Jr. (1991). *Living in the rock n roll mystery: Reading context, self, and others as clues*. Carbondale, IL: Southern Illinois University Press.

Goodall, H. L., Jr. (1996). *Divine signs: Connecting spirit to community*. Carbondale, IL: Southern Illinois University.

Goodhart, C. (2013). Group-think and the current financial crisis. In J. Pixley & G. Harcourt (Eds.) *Financial crises and the nature of capitalist money* (pp. 70–78). London, UK: Palgrave Macmillan.

Google Books. (n.d.). Ngram viewer. Retrieved from: https://books.google.com/ngrams/info

Gosling, S. D., John, O. P., Craik, K. H., & Robins, R. W. (1998). Do people know how they behave? Self-reported act frequencies compared with on-line codings by observers. *Journal of Personality and Social Psychology, 74*(5), 1337–1349.

Gottman, J. M. (1994). *What predicts divorce? The relationship between marital processes and marital outcomes*. Hillsdale, NJ: Erlbaum.

Gottman, J. M. (1996). *What predicts divorce? The measures*. Mahwah, NJ: Erlbaum.

Gottman, J. M. (1999). *The marriage clinic: A scientifically based marital therapy*. New York, NY: W. W. Norton.

Gottman, J. M., Coan, J., Carrere, S., & Swanson, C. (1998). Predicting marital happiness and stability from newlywed interactions. *Journal of Marriage and Family, 60*(1), 5–22.

Gottman, J. M., & Levenson, R. W. (2000). The timing of divorce: predicting when a couple will divorce over a 14-year period. *Journal of Marriage and Family, 62*(3), 737–745.

Gottman, J., Markman, J., & Notarius, C., (1977). The topography of marital conflict: A sequential analysis of verbal and nonverbal behavior. *Journal of Marriage and Family, 39*, 461–477.

Gould, S. J. (1999). *Rocks of ages: Science and religion in the fullness of life*. New York, NY: Ballantine.

Gould, S. J. (2003). *The hedgehog, the fox, and the magister's pox: Mending the gap between science and the humanities*. New York, NY: Harmony Books.

Gouran, D. (1990). *Making decisions in groups*. Longview, IL: Waveland Press.

Gouran, D. S., & Hirokawa, R. Y. (1996). Functional theory and communication in decision-making and problem-solving groups: An expanded view. In R. Y. Hirokawa & M. S. Poole (Eds.), *Communication and group decision making* (2nd ed., pp. 55–80). Thousand Oaks, CA: SAGE Publications.

Graham, E. E., Papa, M. J., & McPherson, M. B. (1997). An applied test of the functional communication perspective of small group decision-making. *Southern Communication Journal, 62*(4), 269.

Gramsci, A. (1971). *Selections form the prison notebooks of Antonio Gramsci*. New York, NY: International Publishers.

Grancea, I. (2017). Types of visual arguments. *Argumentum: Journal the Seminar of Discursive Logic, Argumentation Theory and Rhetoric, 15*(2), 16–34.

Gray, G. W. (1946). Precepts of Kagemni and Ptah-Hotep. *Quarterly Journal of Speech, 32*, 446–454.

Gray, J. (1992). *Men are from Mars, women are from Venus*. New York, NY: HarperCollins.

Greene, J. O. (1997). A second generation action assembly theory. In J. O. Greene (Ed.), *Message production: Advances in communication theory* (pp. 151–170). Mahwah, NJ: Erlbaum.

Greene, J. O. (2003). Models of adult communication skill acquisition: Practice and the course of performance improvement. In J. O. Greene & B. R. Burleson (Eds.), *Handbook of communication and social interaction skills* (pp. 51–92). Mahwah, NJ: Erlbaum.

Greene, R. W. (2004). Rhetoric and capitalism: Rhetorical agency as communicative labor. *Philosophy and Rhetoric, 37*(3), 188–206.

Gries, L. (2015). *Still life with rhetoric: A new materialist approach for visual rhetorics*. Boulder, CO: University of Colorado Press.

Griffiths, M. (2013). The money maze: Another look at the psychology of casino environments. *Psychology Today*. Retrieved from: https://www.psychologytoday.com/blog/in-excess/201307/the-money-maze

Grimshaw, A. D. (1990). Talk and social control. In M. Rosenberg, R. H. Turner, M. Rosenberg, R. H. Turner (Eds.), *Social psychology: Sociological perspectives* (pp. 200–232). Piscataway, NJ: Transaction Publishers.

Groarke, L., Palczewski, C. H., & Godden, D. (2016). Navigating the visual turn in argument. *Argumentation and Advocacy, 52*(4), 217–235.

Groenendijk, T., Haanstra, F., & Kárpáti, A. (2018). A new tool for developmental assessment based on the Common European Framework of Reference for Visual Literacy—An international usability study. *International Journal of Education through Art, 14*(3), 353–378.

Guerrero, L. K., & Andersen, P. A. (1998). The dark side of jealousy and envy: Desire, delusion, desperation, and destructive communication. In B. H. Spitzberg & W. R. Cupach (Eds.), *The dark side of close relationships* (pp. 33–70). Mahwah, NJ: Erlbaum.

Guerrero, L. K., Andersen, P. A., & Afifi, W. A. (2011). *Close encounters: Communication in relationships* (4th ed.). Thousand Oaks, CA: SAGE Publications.

Guerrero, L., & Farinelli, L. (2009). The interplay of verbal and nonverbal codes. In W. Eadie (Ed.), *21st century communication: A reference handbook* (pp. 239–249). Thousand Oaks, CA: SAGE Publications.

Guerrero L. K., & Floyd, K. (2006). *Nonverbal communication in close relationships*. Mahwah, NJ: Erlbaum.

Guerrero, L. K., & Ramos-Salazar, L. (2015). Nonverbal skills in emotional communication. In A. Hannawa & B. H. Spitzberg (Eds.), *Communication competence* (Vol. 22, pp. 131–152). Boston, MA: De Gruyter Mouton.

Guess, A., Lyons, B., Montgomery, J. M., Nyhan, B., & Reifler, J. (2018). Fake news, Facebook ads, and misperceptions: Assessing information quality in the 2018 U.S. midterm election campaign. Washington DC: Democracy Fund report. http://www.dartmouth.edu/~nyhan/fake-news-2018.pdf

Gulley, H. E. (1968). *Discussion, conference, and group process* (2nd ed.). New York, NY: Holt, Rinehart and Winston.

Gully, S. M., Joshi, A., Incalcaterra, K. A., & Beaubien, J. M. (2002). A meta-analysis of team-efficacy, potency, and performance: Interdependence and level of analysis as moderators of observed relationships. *Journal of Applied Psychology, 87*(5), 819–832.

Gutzmer, K., & Beach, W. A. (2015). "Having an ovary this big is not normal": Physicians' use of normal to assess wellness and sickness during oncology interviews. *Health Communication, 30*(1), 8–18.

Guzzo, R. A., & Dickson, M. W. (1996). Teams in organizations: Recent research on performance and effectiveness. *Annual Review of Psychology, 47*(1), 307–338.

Haakana, M. (2001). Laughter as a patient's resource: Dealing with delicate aspects of medical interaction. *Text, 21*, 187–220.

Hacking, I. (2013). What logic did to rhetoric. *Journal of Cognition and Culture, 13*(5), 419–436.

Hackman, M., & Johnson, C. (2013). *Leadership: A communication perspective* (6th ed.) Long Grove, IL: Waveland Press.

Hadden, B. W., Smith, C. V., & Webster, G. D. (2014). Relationship duration moderates associations between attachment and relationship quality: Meta-analytic support for the temporal adult romantic attachment model. *Personality and Social Psychology Review, 18*(1), 42–58.

Hahn, D. F. (2003). *Political communication: Rhetoric, government, and citizens*. State College, PA: Strata.

Haig, K. M., Sutton, S., & Whittington, J. (2006). SBAR: A shared mental model for improving communication between clinicians. *Joint Commission Journal on Quality and Patient Safety, 32*(3), 167–175.

Half, R. (2011, March 15). Keeping the peace: Accountemps survey: Managers spend nearly a full day each week dealing with staff conflicts. Retrieved from: http://rh-us.mediaroom.com/2011-03-15-Keeping-The-Peace

Halkowski, T. (2013). 'Occasional' drinking: Some uses of a non-standard temporal metric in primary care assessment of alcohol use. In W. A. Beach (Ed.), *Handbook of patient–provider interactions: Raising and responding to concerns about life, illness, and disease* (pp. 321–332). New York, NY: Hampton.

Hall, E. T. (1959). *The silent language.* Garden City, NY: Doubleday.

Hall, E. T. (1968). Proxemics. *Current Anthropology, 9*(2–3), 83–109.

Hall, J., Giovannini, E., Morrone, A., & Ranuzzi, G. (2010). A framework to measure the progress of societies. *OECD Statistics Working Papers, 5.*

Hall, J. A., Kearney, M. W., & Xing, C. (2019). Two tests of social displacement through social media use. *Information, Communication & Society, 22*(10), 1396–1413.

Halualani, R. T., & Nakayama, T. K. (2010). Critical intercultural communication studies at a crossroads. In T. K. Nakayama & R. T. Halualani (Eds.), *The handbook of critical intercultural communication* (pp. 1–16). West Sussex, UK: Wiley-Blackwell.

Halualani, R. T., Mendoza, S. L., & Drzewiecka, J. A. (2009). "Critical" junctures in intercultural communication studies: A review. *The Review of Communication, 9*(1), 17–35.

Hamby, A., Brinberg, D., & Jaccard, J. (2018). A conceptual framework of narrative persuasion. *Journal of Media Psychology: Theories, Methods, and Applications, 30*(3), 113–124.

Harms, L. S. (1973). *Intercultural communication.* New York, NY: Harper & Row.

Hamermesh, D. S. (2011). *Beauty pays: Why attractive people are more successful.* Princeton, NJ: Princeton University Press.

Hamilton, M. A., Buck, R. W., Chory, R. M., Beatty, M. J., & Patrylak, L. A. (2009). Individualistic and cooperative affect systems as determinants of aggressive or collaborative message choice. In M. J. Beatty, J. C. McCroskey, & K. Floyd (Eds.), *Biological dimensions of communication: Perspectives, research, and methods* (pp. 227–250). Cresskill, NJ: Hampton Press.

Hamilton, M. A., & Hample, D. (2011). Testing hierarchical models of argumentativeness and verbal aggressiveness. *Communication Methods and Measures, 5*(3), 250–273.

Hample, D., Richards, A. S., & Skubisz, C. (2013). Blurting. *Communication Monographs, 80*(4), 503–532.

Hampton, K. N., Rainie, H., Lu, W., Dwyer, M., Shin, I., & Purcell, K. (2014, August). *Social media and the 'spiral of silence'.* Washington, DC: Pew Research Center. Retrieved from: http://www.pewinternet.org/2014/08/26/social-media-and-the-spiral-of-silence/

Han, K. (2018). How do you perceive this author? Understanding and modeling authors' communication quality in social media. *PLOS One, 13*(2), e0192061.

Hanan, J. S. (2010). Home is where the capital is: The culture of real estate in an era of control societies. *Communication and Critical/Cultural Studies, 7*(2), 176–201.

Hanan, J. S. (2013). The ecology of empire: Wal-Mart's rhetoric of environmental stewardship and the constitutive power of the multitude. *Environmental Communication: A Journal of Nature and Culture, 7*(4), 529–547.

Hanan, J. S. (2019). Subjects of technology: An auto-archeology of attention deficit disorder in neoliberal time(s). *Cultural Studies↔Critical Methodologies, 19*(2), 105–115.

Handy, E. S. C., & Pukui, M. K. (1977). *The Polynesian family system in Ka-U, Hawaii.* Rutland, VT: Charles Tuttle.

Hanna, J. L. (2003). Aesthetics: Whose notions of appropriateness and competency, what are they, and how do we know? *The World of Music, 45*(3), 29–55.

Hanson, T. L., Drumheller, K., Mallard, J., McKee, C., & Schlegel, P. (2011). Cell phones, text messaging, and Facebook: Competing time demands of today's college students. *College Teaching, 59*(1), 23–30.

Hargie, O. D. W. (1993). Communication as skilled performance. In O. D. W. Hargie (Ed.), *The handbook of communication skills* (2nd ed., pp. 7–28). New York, NY: Routledge.

Hargie, O., Tourish, D., & Wilson, N. (2002). Communication audits and the effects of increased automation: A follow-up study. *Journal of Business Communication, 39*(4), 414–436.

Harrell, M. S., Harrell, T. W., McIntyre, S. H., & Weinberg, C. B. (1977). Predicting compensation among MBA graduates five and ten years after graduation. *Journal of Applied Psychology, 62*(5), 636–640.

Harrell, T. W., & Alpert, B. (1989). Attributes of successful MBAs: A 20-year longitudinal study. *Human Performance, 2*(4), 301–322.

Harris, R. (2012). A different way of knowing: With respect to John C. (Jack) Condon. *International Journal of Intercultural Relations, 36*(6), 798–809.

Hart Research Associates. (2013, April 10). *It takes more than a major: Employer priorities for college learning and student success.* Retrieved from: https://www.aacu.org/sites/default/files/files/LEAP/2013_EmployerSurvey.pdf

Hart, R. (1997). *Modern rhetorical criticism.* Boston, MA: Allyn & Bacon.

Hart, R. (1999). *Seducing America: How television charms the modern voter.* Thousand Oaks, CA: SAGE Publications.

Hartmann, B. J. (2016). Peeking behind the mask of the prosumer: Theorizing the organization of consumptive and productive practice moments. *Marketing Theory, 16*(1), 3–20.

Hartnett, S. J. (2013) "Tibet is burning": Competing rhetorics of liberation, occupation, resistance, and paralysis on the roof of the world. *Quarterly Journal of Speech, 99*(3), 283–316.

Haugtvedt, C. P., Petty, R. E., & Cacioppo, J. T. (1992). Need for cognition and advertising: understanding the role of personality variables in consumer behavior. *Journal of Consumer Psychology, 1*(3), 239–260.

Haut, M. (2007). A salty tongue: At the margins of satire, comedy and polemic in the writing of Valerie Solanas. *Feminist Theory, 8*(1), 27–41.

Hawhee, D. (2011). Toward a bestial rhetoric. *Philosophy and Rhetoric, 44*(1), 81–87.

Hawley, G. (August 2018). *The demography of the alt right.* Retrieved from https://ifstudies.org/blog/the-demography-of-the-alt-right.

Hay, M. C. (2008). Reading sensations: Understanding the process of distinguishing "fine" from "sick." *Transcultural Psychology, 45*(2), 198–229.

Haynes, A. B., Weiser, T. G., Berry, W. R., Lipsitz, S. R., Breizat, A. S., Dellinger, E. P., & Gawande, A. A. (2009). A surgical safety checklist to reduce morbidity and mortality in a global population. *New England Journal of Medicine, 360*, 491–499.

Hazan, C., & Shaver, P. (1987). Romantic love conceptualized as an attachment process. *Journal of Personality and Social Psychology, 52*(3), 511–524.

Hazel, M., Karst, J., Saezkleriga, G., Wongprasert, T. K., & Ayres, J. (2017). Testing the communibiological paradigm: The similarity of fraternal and identical twins across three communication variables. *Northwest Journal of Communication, 45*(1), 37–51.

Heath, C. (1986). *Body movement and speech in medical interaction.* Cambridge, UK: Cambridge University Press.

Heath, C. (2002). Demonstrative suffering: The gestural (re)embodiment of symptoms. *Journal of Communication, 52*(3), 597–617.

Hefner, V. (2017). Variables, moderating types. In M. Allen (Ed.), *The SAGE encyclopedia of communication research methods.* Los Angeles, CA: SAGE Publications.

Heisenberg, W. (1971). Physics and beyond: Encounters and conversations. Retrieved from: http://todayinsci.com/E/Einstein_Albert/EinsteinAlbert-Quotations.htm

Helgeson, V. (2003). Social support and quality of life. *Quality of Life Research: An International Journal of Quality of Life Aspects of Treatment, Care & Rehabilitation, 12*(Supplement 1), 25–31.

Hellweg, S. A., & Andersen, P. A. (1989). An analysis of source valence instrumentation in the organizational communication literature. *Management Communication Quarterly, 3*(1), 132–159.

Helme, D. W., Savage, M. W., & Record, R. A. (2015). Campaigns and interventions. In N. G. Harrington (Ed.), *Health communication: Theory, method, and application* (pp. 397–427). Thousand Oaks, CA: SAGE Publications.

Hendrix, K. G., & Jackson, R. L., II. (2016). The contours of progress: Parsing diversity and difference studies. *Communication Education, 65*(2), 245–249.

Henningsen, D., Henningsen, M., Eden, J., & Cruz, M. G. (2006). Examining the symptoms of groupthink and retrospective sensemaking. *Small Group Research, 37*(1), 36–64.

Henshilwood, C. S., d'Errico, F., van Niekerk, K. L., Dayet, L. O., Queffelec, A., & Pollarolo, L. (2018). An abstract drawing from the 73,000-year-old levels at Blombos Cave, South Africa. *Nature, 562*, 115–118.

Hepp, A. (2009). Differentiation: Mediatization and cultural change. In Lundby, K. (Ed.) *Mediatization: Concept, changes, consequences* (pp. 139–157). New York: Peter Lang.

Hepp, A. (2013). The communicative figurations of mediatized worlds: Mediatization research in times of the 'mediation of everything.' *European Journal of Communication, 28*(6), 615–629.

Heritage, J. (1984). *Garfinkel and ethnomethodology.* Cambridge, UK: Polity Press.

Heritage, J. (2005). Revisiting authority in physician-patient interaction. In J. F. Duchan & D. Kovarsky (Eds.), *Diagnosis as cultural practice* (pp. 83–102). New York, NY: Mouton De Gruyter.

Heritage, J. (2012). Universal dilemmas and collateralized practices. *Current Anthropology, 53*(3), 322–323.

Heritage, J., & Maynard, D. W. (Eds.). (2006). *Communication in medical care: Interactions between primary care physicians and patients.* Cambridge, MA: Cambridge University Press.

Heritage, J., & Raymond, G. (2005). The terms of agreement: Indexing epistemic authority and subordination in talk-in-interaction. *Social Psychology Quarterly, 68*(1), 15–38.

Herkert, J. R., Wetmore, J., Canary, H. E., & Ellison, K. (2009). Integrating microethics and macroethics in graduate science and engineering education: Developing instructional models. *Proceedings of the 2009 American Society for Engineering Education Annual Conference.* Retrieved from: https://peer.asee.org/5190

Hersey, P., & Blanchard, K. (1969). *Management of organizational behavior: Utilizing human resources.* Englewood Cliffs, NJ: Prentice Hall.

Herve, P., Zago, L., Petit, L., Mazoyer, B., & Tzourip-Mazoyer, N. (2013). Revisiting human hemispheric specialization with neuroimaging. *Trends in Cognitive Sciences, 17*(2), 60–80.

Hesse, C., Pauley, P. M., & Frye-Cox, N. E. (2015). Alexithymia and marital quality: The mediating role of relationship maintenance behaviors. *Western Journal of Communication, 79*(1), 45–72.

Hicks, L. L., & McNulty, J. K. (2019). The Unbearable Automaticity of Being... in a Close Relationship. *Current Directions in Psychological Science, 28*(3), 254–259.

Higher Education Research Institute at UCLA (HERI). (2009, January). *The American freshman: National norms for Fall 2008* (Research brief). Los Angeles, CA: Author.

Higher Education Research Institute at UCLA (HERI). (2010, January). *Findings from the 2009 administration of the Your First College Year (YFCY): National aggregates.* Los Angeles, CA: Author.

Higher Education Research Institute at UCLA (HERI). (2011, January). *The American freshman: National norms for Fall 2010* (Research brief). Los Angeles, CA: Author.

Higher Education Research Institute at UCLA (HERI). (2014, December). *Findings from the 2014 college senior survey.* Los Angeles, CA: Cooperative Institutional Research Program, University of California at Los Angeles. Retrieved from: http://www.heri.ucla.edu/briefs/CSS-2014-Brief.pdf

Hilbert, M. (2014c). What is the content of the world's technologically mediated information and communication capacity: How much text, image, audio, and video? *Information Society, 30*(2), 127–143.

Hilbert, M., & López, P. (2011). The world's technological capacity to store, communicate, and compute information. *Science, 332*(6025), 60–65.

Hirneise, G. (2016, September 25). Students are using ADHD medication as academic steroids. Retrieved from: https://www.statepress.com/article/2016/09/spopinion-performance-enhancing-drugs-in-the-academic-world.

Hirokawa, R. Y., & Pace, R. (1983). A descriptive investigation of the possible communication-based reasons for effective and ineffective group decision making. *Communication Monographs, 50*(4), 363–379.

Hitsch, G. J., Hortacsu, A., & Ariely, D. (2010a). Matching and sorting in online dating. *American Economic Review, 100*(1), 130–163.

Hitsch, G. J., Hortacsu, A., & Ariely, D. (2010b). What makes you click?—Mate preferences in online dating. *Quantitative Marketing and Economics, 8*(4), 393–427.

Ho, D. Y-F. (1976). On the concept of face. *American Journal of Sociology, 81*(4), 867–884.

Hocevar, K. P., Flanagin, A. J., & Metzger, M. J. (2014). Social media self-efficacy and information evaluation online. *Computers in Human Behavior, 39*, 254–262.

Hochschild, A. (2003). *The second shift: Working parents and the revolution at home* (Rev. Ed.). New York, NY: Viking/Penguin.

Hoffman, B. J., Woehr, D. J., Maldagen-Youngjohn, R., & Lyons, B. D. (2011). Great man or great myth? A quantitative review of the relationship between individual differences and leader effectiveness. *Journal of Occupational and Organizational Psychology, 84*(2), 347–381.

Hoffmann, B. (1972). Albert Einstein: Creator and rebel. Retrieved from: http://todayinsci.com/E/Einstein_Albert/EinsteinAlbert-Quotations.htm

Hofstede, G. (2001). *Culture's consequences: Comparing values, behaviors, institutions, and organizations across nations* (2nd ed.). Thousand Oaks, CA: SAGE Publications.

Hogan, J. M. (2013). Persuasion in the rhetorical tradition. In J. P. Dillard & L. Shen (Eds), *The SAGE handbook of persuasion* (2nd ed., pp. 2–19). Thousand Oaks, CA: SAGE Publications.

Hogan, T. P., & Palmer, C. L. (2005). Information preferences and practices among people living with HIV/AIDS: Results from a nationwide survey. *Journal of the Medical Library Association, 93*(4), 431.

Holman, T. B., & Jarvis, M. O. (2003). Hostile, volatile, avoiding, and validating couple-conflict types: An investigation of Gottman's couple-conflict types. *Personal Relationships, 10*(2), 267–282.

Holman Jones, S., Adams, T. E., & Ellis, C. (Eds.). (2013). *Handbook of autoethnography.* Walnut Creek, CA: Left Coast Press.

Holt-Lunstad, J., Smith, T. B., & Layton, J. B. (2010). Social relationships and mortality risk: A meta-analytic review. *PLoS Medicine, 7*(7), 1–20.

Holt-Lunstad, J., Smith, T. B., Baker, M., Harris, T., & Stephenson, D. (2015). Loneliness and social isolation as risk factors for mortality: A meta-analytic review. *Perspectives on Psychological Science, 10*(2), 227–237.

Hook, C., & Geist-Martin, P. (2018). Cultivating communities of care: A qualitative investigation of the communication of support between incarcerated women. *Communication and Critical/Cultural Studies, 15*(2), 127–143.

Hook, C., Plump, B., & Geist-Martin, P. (2018). Advocating for integrative medicine: Providers' narratives of communicating to educate and promote. *Qualitative Research and Healthcare, 2*(1), 30–44.

hooks, b. (2000). *Feminism is for everybody: Passionate politics.* New York, NY: Villard.

hooks, b. (2004). *We real cool: Black men and masculinity.* New York, NY: Routledge.

Hopper, R. (1989). Conversation analysis and social psychology as descriptions of interpersonal communication. In D. Roger & P. Bull (Eds.), *Conversation* (pp. 48–66). Clevedon, England: Multilingual Matters, Ltd.

Hopper, R., & LeBaron, C. (1998). How gender creeps into talk. *Research on Language and Social Interaction, 31*(3–4), 59–74.

Hornik, J., Ofir, C., & Rachamim, M. (2016). Quantitative evaluation of persuasive appeals using comparative meta-analysis. *Communication Review, 19*(3), 192–222.

Hosoda, M., Stone-Romero, E. F., & Coats, G. (2003). The effects of physical attractiveness on job-related outcomes: A meta-analysis of experimental studies. *Personnel Psychology, 56*(2), 431–462.

House, R. J. (1976). A 1976 theory of charismatic leadership. In J. G. Hunt & L. L. Larson (Eds.), *Leadership: The cutting edge* (pp. 189–207). Carbondale, IL: Southern Illinois University Press.

Houston, M. (2004). When Black women talk with White women: Why the dialogues are difficult. In A. González, M. Houston, & V. Chen (Eds.), *Our voices: Essays in culture, ethnicity, and communication* (4th ed., pp. 119–125). New York, NY: Oxford University Press.

Houston, R. (2009). "Being homeless and gay or lesbian is a difficult combination": An invisible population. In E. Kirby & M. C. McBride (Eds.), *Gender actualized: Cases in communicatively constructing realities* (pp. 16–18). Dubuque, IA: Kendall/Hunt.

Hoyningen-Huene, P. (2008). Systematicity: The nature of science. *Philosophia, 36*(2), 167–180.

Hu, S., Liu, H., & Gu, J. (2018). What role does self-efficacy play in developing cultural intelligence from social media usage? *Electronic Commerce Research & Applications, 28*, 172–180.

Hullett, C. R. (2005). The impact of mood on persuasion: A meta-analysis. *Communication Research, 32*(4), 423–442.

Humbad, M. N., Donnellan, M. B., Klump, K. L., & Burt, S. A. (2011). Development of the Brief Romantic Relationship Interaction Coding Scheme (BRRICS). *Journal of Family Psychology, 25*(5), 759–769.

Hursthouse, R. (1999). *On virtue ethics.* Oxford, UK: Oxford University Press.

Hutto, D. (2002). Ancient Egyptian rhetoric in the old and middle kingdoms. *Rhetorica: A Journal of the History of Rhetoric, 20*(3), 213–233.

Hwang, Y. (2011). Is communication competence still good for interpersonal media?: Mobile phone and instant messenger. *Computers in Human Behavior, 27*(2), 924–934.

Hwang, Y., & Jeong, S-H. (2009). Revisiting the knowledge gap hypothesis: A meta-analysis of thirty-five years of research. *Journalism and Mass Communication Quarterly, 86*(3), 513–532.

Iarocci, G., Yager, J., & Elfers, T. (2007). What gene–environment interactions can tell us about social competence in typical and atypical populations. *Brain and Cognition, 65*(1), 112–127.

Imahori, T. T., & Cupach, W. R. (2005). Identity management theory. In W. B. Gudykunst (Ed.), *Theorizing about intercultural communication* (pp. 195–210). Thousand Oaks, CA: SAGE Publications.

Impey, C. (2013). What students know about science. *International Journal of Science in Society, 4*(3), 167–180.

Infante, D. A., & Rancer, A. S. (1982). A conceptualization and measure of argumentativeness. *Journal of Personality Assessment, 46*(1), 72–80.

Infante, D. A., & Rancer, A. S. (1996). Argumentativeness and verbal aggressiveness: A review of recent theory and research. *Communication Yearbook, 19*, 319–351.

Institute for the Future. (2011). *Future work skills 2020.* Palo Alto, CA: The University of Phoenix Research Institute. Retrieved from: cdn.theatlantic.com/static/front/docs/sponsored/phoenix/future_work_skills_2020.pdf Institute of Politics. (2017). *Survey of young Americans' attitudes toward politics and public service* (28th ed.). Boston, MA: John F. Kennedy School of Government, Harvard University. https://iop.harvard.edu/sites/default/files/content/docs/171128_Harvard%20IOP_Fall%202017%20Topline.pdfInternational

Internet Marketing Ninjas. (2017). *Google organic click through study: Comparison of Google's CTR by position, industry, and query type.* Retrieved from: https://www.internetmarketingninjas.com/additional-resources/IMN-CTR-whitepaper.pdf

Iribarren, J. L., & Moro, E. (2011). Affinity paths and information diffusion in social networks. *Social Networks, 33*(2), 134–142.

Ishak, A. W., & Ballard, D. I. (2012). Time to re-group: A typology and nested phased model for action teams. *Small Group Research, 43*(1), 3–29.

Ison, D. C. (2012). Plagiarism among dissertations: Prevalence at online institutions. *Journal of Academic Ethics, 10*, 227–236.

Issacson, W. (2011) *Steve Jobs*. New York, NY: Simon & Schuster.

Iverson, J. M., & Goldin-Meadow, S. (1997). What's communication got to do with it? Gesture in children blind from birth. *Developmental Psychology, 33*(3), 453–467.

Iyengar, S., & McGrady, J. (2005). Mass media and political persuasion. In T. C. Brock & M. C. Green (Eds.), *Persuasion: Psychological insights and perspectives* (2nd ed., pp. 225–248). Thousand Oaks, CA: SAGE Publications.

Jablin, F. M. (1979). Superior–subordinate communication: The state of the art. *Psychological Bulletin, 86*(6), 1201–1222.

Jablin, F. M. (2001). Organizational entry, assimilation, and disengagement/exit. In F.M. Jablin & L.L. Putnam (Eds.), *The new handbook of organizational communication* (pp. 732–818). Thousand Oaks, CA: SAGE Publications.

Jackson, C. & Newall, M. (February 2018). *Ipsos/NPR poll: Majority of Americans support policies aimed to keep guns out of hands of dangerous individuals*. Retrieved from https://www.ipsos.com/en-us/news-polls/npr-ipsos-poll-majority-americans-support-policies-aimed-keep-guns-out-hands-dangerous-individuals.

Jackson, L. A., Hunter, J. E., & Hodge, C. N. (1995). Physical attractiveness and intellectual competence: A meta-analytic review. *Social Psychology Quarterly, 58*(2), 108–122.

Jackson, R. L. (1999). *The negotiation of cultural identity: Perceptions of European Americans and African Americans*. Westport, CT: Praeger.

Jackson, S. (2004). *Professing performance: Theatre in the academy from philology to performativity*. Cambridge, UK: Cambridge University Press.

Jameson, D. A. (2007). Reconceptualizing cultural identity and its role in intercultural business communication. *Journal of Business Communication, 44*(3), 199–235.

Jameson, F. (1981). *The political unconscious: Narrative as socially symbolic act*. Ithaca, NY: Cornell University Press.

Janis, I. L. (1972). *Victims of groupthink: A psychological study of foreign-policy decisions and fiascoes*. Boston, MA: Houghton Mifflin.

Janis, I. L. (1982). *Groupthink* (2nd ed.). Boston: MA: Houghton Mifflin.

Janis, I. L., & Mann, L. (1977). *Decision making: A psychological analysis of conflict, choice, and commitment*. New York, NY: Free Press.

Jansson, A. (2013). Mediatization and social space: Reconstructing mediatization for the transmedia age. *Communication Theory, 23*(3), 279–296.

Jansson, A. (2015). The molding of mediatization: The stratified indispensability of media in close relationships. *Communications: The European Journal of Communication Research, 40*(4), 379–401.

Janusik, L. A., & Wolvin, A. D. (2009). 24 hours in a day: A listening update to the time studies. *International Journal of Listening, 23*(2), 104–120.

Jaramillo, F., Carrillat, F. A., & Locander, W. B. (2005). A meta-analytic comparison of managerial ratings and self-evaluations. *Journal of Personal Selling and Sales Management, 25*(4), 315–328.

Jarvis, S. E., Barberena, L. A., & Davis, A. J. (2007, May). "Civics, not government: Redirecting social studies in the nation's schools." The Annette Strauss Institute. Report prepared for the Bill and Melinda Gates Foundation.

Jefferson, G. (1980). On 'trouble premonitory' response to inquiry. *Sociological Inquiry, 50*, 153–185.

Jefferson, G. (1984a). On the organization of laughter in talk about troubles. In J. M. Atkinson & J. Heritage (Eds.), *Structures of social action: Studies in conversation analysis* (pp. 347–369). London: Cambridge University Press.

Jefferson, G. (1984b). On stepwise transition from talk about a trouble to inappropriately next-positioned matters. In J. M. Atkinson & J. Heritage (Eds.), *Structures of social action: Studies in conversation analysis* (pp. 191–222). London: Cambridge University Press.

Jefferson, G. (1996). A case of transcriptional stereotyping. *Journal of Pragmatics, 26*(2), 159–170.

Jefferson, G. (2004). Glossary of transcript symbols with an introduction. In G. H. Lerner (Ed.), *Conversation analysis: Studies from the first generation* (pp. 13–31). Amsterdam, Netherlands: Benjamins.

Jensen, K. B. (2013). Definitive and sensitizing conceptualizations of mediatization. *Communication Theory, 23*(3), 203–222.

Jensen, P. R., & Meisenbach, R. J. (2015). Alternative organizing and invisibility: Managing tensions of transparency and autonomy in a nonprofit organization. *Management Communication Quarterly, 29*(4), 564–589.

Jeong, S-H. (2008). Visual metaphor in advertising: Is the persuasive effect attributable to visual argumentation or metaphorical rhetoric? *Journal of Marketing Communications, 14*(1), 59–73.

Jeong, S-H, Cho, H., & Hwang, Y. (2012). Media literacy interventions: A meta-analytic review. *Journal of Communication, 62*(3), 454–472.

Jiang, J. (2018, August). *How teens and parents navigate screen time and device distractions*. Washington, DC: Pew Research Center. Retrieved from: http://www.pewinternet.org/2018/08/22/how-teens-and-parents-navigate-screen-time-and-device-distractions/

Johannesen, R. L., Valde, K. S., & Whedbee, K. E. (2008). *Ethics in human communication* (6th ed.). Long Grove, IL: Waveland Press.

Johnson, A. (2013). Antoine Dodson and the (mis)appropriation of the Homo Coon: An intersectional approach to the performative possibilities of social media. *Critical Studies in Media Communication, 30*(2), 152–170.

Johnson, A. J. (2002). Beliefs about arguing: A comparison of public issue and personal issue arguments. *Communication Reports, 15*, 99–111.

Johnson, C. E., & Hackman, M. Z. (2018). *Leadership: A communication perspective* (7th ed.). Long Grove, IL: Waveland Press.

Johnson, F., Rowley, J., & Sbaffi, L. (2016). Exploring information interactions in the context of Google. *Journal of the Association for Information Science and Technology, 67*(4), 824–840.

Johnson, H., Mejia, M. C., Ezekiel, D., & Zeiger, B. (2013, June). *Student debt and the value of a college degree*. Public Policy Institute of California. Retrieved from: http://www.ppic.org/content/pubs/report/R_613HJR.pdf

Joint Commission. (2012). Sentinel event. Retrieved from http://www.jointcommission.org/sentinel_event.aspx

Jonassen, D. H., & Kim, B. (2010). Arguing to learn and learning to argue: Design justifications and guidelines. *Educational Technology Research and Development, 58*(4), 439–457.

Joordens, J. C. A., d'Errico, F., Wesselingh, F. P., Munro, S., de Vos, J., Wallinga, J., … Reijmer, J. J. G. (2015). Homo erectus at Trinil on Java used shells for tool production and engraving. *Nature, 518*(7538), 228–231.

Jordan, P., & Shennan, S. (2003). Cultural transmission, language, and basketry traditions amongst the California Indians. *Journal of Anthropological Archaeology, 22*(1), 42.

Jowett, G. S., & O'Donnell, V. (2014). *Propaganda and persuasion.* Thousand Oaks, CA: SAGE Publications.

Judd, T., & Kennedy, G. (2011). Expediency-based practice? Medical students' reliance on Google and Wikipedia for biomedical inquiries. *British Journal of Educational Technology, 42*(2), 351–360.

Juslin, P. N., & Laukka, P. (2003). Communication of emotions in vocal expression and musical performance: Different channels, same code? *Psychological Bulletin, 129*(5), 770–814.

Juslin, P. N., Sakka, L. S., Barradas, G. T., & Liljeström, S. (2016). No accounting for taste? Idiographic models of aesthetic judgment in music. *Psychology of Aesthetics, Creativity and the Arts, 10*(2), 157–170.

Khan, M. L., & Idris, I. K. (2019). Recognise misinformation and verify before sharing: A reasoned action and information literacy perspective. *Behaviour & Information Technology,* Online first: https://doi.org/10.1080/0144929X.2019.1578828

Kahneman, D. (2011) *Thinking, fast and slow.* New York, NY: Farrar, Straus and Giroux.

Kallgren, C. A., Reno, R. R., & Cialdini, R. B. (2000). A focus theory of normative conduct: When norms do and do not affect behavior. *Personality and Social Psychology Bulletin, 26*(8), 1002–1012.

Kanahele, G. H. S. (1986). *Ku Kanaka—stand tall: A search for Hawaiian values.* Honolulu, HI: University of Hawaii Press.

Kane, E. (2006). "No way my boys are going to be like that!" Parents' responses to children's gender nonconformity. *Gender and Society, 20,* 149–176.

Kane, H. S., Jaremka, L. M., Guichard, A. C., Ford, M. B., Collins, N. L., & Feeney, B. C. (2007). Feeling supported and feeling satisfied: How one partner's attachment style predicts the other partner's relationship experiences. *Journal of Social and Personal Relationships, 24*(4), 535–555.

Karahanna, E., Xu, S. X., Xu, Y., & Zhang, N. (2018). The needs–affordances–features perspective for the use of social media. *MIS Quarterly, 42*(3), 737–756.

Karazsia, B. T., Berlin, K. S., Armstrong, B., Janicke, D. M., & Darling, K. E. (2014). Integrating mediation and moderation to advance theory development and testing. *Journal of Pediatric Psychology, 39*(2), 163–173.

Karl, K. A., & Kopf, J. M. (1994). Will individuals who need to improve their performance the most, volunteer to receive videotaped feedback? *Journal of Business Communication, 31*(3), 213–223.

Kassing, J. W. (2008). Consider this: A comparison of factors contributing to employees' expressions of dissent. *Communication Quarterly, 56*(3), 342–355.

Katz, D. (1960). The functional approach to the study of attitudes. *Public Opinion Quarterly, 24*(2), 163–204.

Katz, D., & Kahn, R. L. (1966). *The social psychology of organizations.* New York, NY: Wiley.

Katz, E., Blumler, J. G., & Gurevitch, M. (1973). Uses and gratifications research. *The Public Opinion Quarterly, 37*(4), 509–523.

Katz, E., & Lazarsfeld, P. F. (1955). *Personal influence: The part played by people in the flow of mass communications.* New York, NY: The Free Press.

Katz, J. (2012). Violence against women—it's a men's issue [Video file]. Retrieved from: https://www.ted.com/talks/jackson_katz_violence_against_women_it_s_a_men_s_issue?language=en

Katz, J. (2013). *Tough guise, 2.* Northampton, MA: Media Education Foundation.

Katzenbach, J. R., & Smith, D. K. (1993). *The wisdom of teams: Creating the high performance organization.* Boston, MA: Harvard Business School Press.

Kaufman, J. M. (2005). Explaining the race/ethnicity–violence relationship: Neighborhood context and social psychological processes. *Justice Quarterly, 22*(2), 224–251.

Kawasaki, G. (2010). *Enchantment: The art of changing hearts, minds, and actions.* New York, NY: Portfolio/Penguin.

Kazoleas, D. (1993). The impact of argumentativeness on resistance to persuasion. *Human Communication Research, 20*(1), 118–137.

Keck, K. L., & Samp, J. A. (2007). The dynamic nature of goals and message production as revealed in a sequential analysis of conflict interactions. *Human Communication Research, 33*(1), 27–47.

Kędra, J. (2018). What does it mean to be visually literate? Examination of visual literacy definitions in a context of higher education. *Journal of Visual Literacy, 37*(2), 67–84.

Kedrowicz, A. A. & Taylor, J. L. (2019). Ideologies of gender: Culture clash between the disciplines. In M. A. Mathison (Ed.), *Sojourning in disciplinary cultures: A case study of teaching writing in engineering* (pp. 166–188). Boulder, CO: University Press of Colorado.

Keeling, D. M. (2017). Feral rhetoric: Common sense animals and metaphorical beasts. *Rhetoric Society Quarterly, 47*(3), 229–237.

Keith, E. (2015, December 4). 55 million: A fresh look at the number, effectiveness, and cost of meetings in the U.S. Retrieved from: https://blog.lucidmeetings.com/blog/fresh-look-number-effectiveness-cost-meetings-in-us

Kellermann, K., & Cole, T. (1994). Classifying compliance-gaining messages: Taxonomic disorder and strategic confusion. *Communication Theory, 4*(1), 3–60.

Kelly, C. R. (2011). Blood-speak: Ward Churchill and the racialization of American Indian identity. *Communication and Critical/Cultural Studies, 8*(3), 240–265.

Kelly, S., & Westerman, C. K. (2014). Immediacy as an influence on supervisor-subordinate communication. *Communication Research Reports, 31*(3), 252–261.

Kendall, B. E. (2008). Personae and natural capitalism: Negotiating politics and constituencies in a rhetoric of sustainability. *Environmental Communication, 2*(1), 59–77.

Kennedy, G. A. (1992). A hoot in the dark: The evolution of general rhetoric. *Philosophy and Rhetoric, 25*(1), 1–21.

Kenney, K. (2002). Building visual communication theory by borrowing from rhetoric. *Journal of Visual Literacy, 22*(1), 53–80.

Keysar, B., Converse, B. A., Wang, J., & Epley, N. (2008). Reciprocity is not give and take: Asymmetric reciprocity to positive and negative acts. *Psychological Science, 19*(12), 1280–1286.

Keyton, J., Caputo, J. M., Ford, E. A., Fu, R., Leibowitz, S. A., Liu, T., … Wu, C. (2013). Investigating verbal workplace communication behaviors. *Journal of Business Communication, 50*(2), 152–169.

Khan, M. L., & Idris, I. K. (2019). Recognise misinformation and verify before sharing: A reasoned action and information literacy perspective. *Behaviour and Information Technology* (online first).

Khemlani, S. S., Barbey, A. K., & Johnson-Laird, P. N. (2014). Causal reasoning with mental models. *Frontiers in Human Neuroscience, 8*, 1–15.

Kibler, R. J., & Barker, L. L. (1969). *Conceptual frontiers in speech-communication: Report of the New Orleans Conference on Research and Instructional Development.* New York, NY: Speech Association of America.

Kim, S.-Y., Allen, M., Preiss, R., & Peterson, B. (2014). Meta-analysis of counterattitudinal advocacy data: Evidence for an additive cues model. *Communication Quarterly, 62*(5), 607–620.

Kim, Y., & Glassman, M. (2013). Beyond search and communication: Development and validation of thee internet self-efficacy scale (ISS). *Computers in Human Behavior, 29*, 1421–1429.

Kimmel, M. (2008). *Guyland: The perilous world where boys become men.* New York, NY: HarperCollins.

King, C. L. (2016). Beyond persuasion: The rhetoric of negotiation in business communication. *Journal of Business Communication, 47*(1), 69–78.

Kinsbourne, M. (2006). Gestures as embodied cognition. A neurodevelopmental interpretation. *Gesture, 6*(2), 205–214.

Kirzinger, A. E., Weber, C., & Johnson, M. (2012). Genetic and environmental influences on media use and communication behaviors. *Human Communication Research, 38*(2), 144–171.

Kjeldsen, J. E. (2018a). The rhetoric of sound, the sound of arguments three propositions, three questions, and an afterthought for the study of sonic and multimodal argumentation. *Argumentation and Advocacy, 54*(4), 347–354.

Kjeldsen, J. E. (2018b). Visual rhetorical argumentation. *Semiotica, 2018*(220), 69–94.

Knapp, M. L. (1978). *Social intercourse: From greeting to goodbye.* Needham Heights, MA: Allyn & Bacon.

Knapp, M. L., & Daly, J. A. (2011). Background and current trends in the study of interpersonal communication. In M. L. Knapp & J. A. Daly (Eds.), *The SAGE handbook of interpersonal communication* (pp. 3–22). Thousand Oaks, CA: SAGE Publications.

Knapp, M. L., & Vangelisti, A. L. (2005). *Relationship stages: A communication perspective. Interpersonal communication and human relationships* (5th ed). Boston: Allyn & Bacon.

Knapp, M. L., Vangelisti, A. L., & Caughlin, J. P. (2014). *Interpersonal communication and human relationships* (7th ed.). Boston, MA: Allyn & Bacon

Kneupper, C. W. (1978). Teaching argument: an introduction to the Toulmin model. *College Composition & Communication, 29,* 237–241.

Knibb, R. C., & Horton, S. L. (2008). Can illness perceptions and coping predict psychological distress amongst allergy sufferers? *British Journal of Health Psychology, 13*(1), 103–119.

Koc, M., & Barut, E. (2016). Development and validation of New Media Literacy Scale (NMLS) for university students. *Computers in Human Behavior, 63,* 834–843.

Koenig, J. A. (2011). *Assessing 21st century skills: Summary of a workshop.* Washington, DC: National Academies Press.

Kohn, L. T., Corrigan, J. M., & Donaldson, M. S. (Eds.). (2000). *To err is human: Building a safer health system.* Washington, DC: National Academies Press.

Konrath, S. H., O'Brien, E. H., & Hsing, C. (2011). Changes in dispositional empathy in American college students over time: A meta-analysis. *Personality and Social Psychology Review, 15*(2), 180–198.

Korsgaard, M. A., Meglino, B. M., & Lester, S. W. (2004). The effect of other orientation on self-supervisor rating agreement. *Journal of Organizational Behavior, 25*(7), 873–891.

Korzybsky, A. (1933). *Science and sanity: An introduction to non-Aristotelian systems and general semantics.* New York, NY: International Non-Aristotelian Library.

Kościński, K. (2014). Assessment of waist-to-hip ratio attractiveness in women: An anthropometric analysis of digital silhouettes. *Archives of Sexual Behavior, 43*(5), 989–997.

Kotter, J. P. (1990). *A force for change: How leadership differs from management.* New York: Free Press.

Kozinets, R. V. (2015). *Netnography: Redefined.* Thousand Oaks, CA: SAGE Publications.

Kroeber, A. L., & Kluckhohn, C. (1952). *Culture: A critical review of concepts and definitions* (Vol. 47). Cambridge, MA: Harvard University Peabody Museum of American Archeology and Ethnology.

Kruger, J. (1999). Lake Wobegon be gone! The "below-average effect" and the egocentric nature of comparative ability judgments. *Journal of Personality and Social Psychology, 77*(2), 221–232.

Kruger, J., & Dunning, D. (1999). Unskilled and unaware of it: How difficulties in recognizing one's own incompetence lead to inflated self-assessments. *Journal of Personality and Social Psychology, 77*(6), 1121–1134.

Kruger, J., Epley, N., Parker, J., & Ng, Z. (2005). Egocentrism over e-mail: Can we communicate as well as we think? *Journal of Personality and Social Psychology, 89*(6), 925–936.

Kuhn, T. S. (1970). *The structure of scientific revolutions* (2nd ed.). Chicago, IL: University of Chicago.

Kuncel, N. R., Credé, M., & Thomas, L. L. (2005). The validity of self-reported grade point averages, class ranks, and test scores: A meta-analysis and review of the literature. *Review of Educational Research, 75*(1), 63–82.

Kylmälä, T. P. (2013). Medium, the human condition and beyond. *Empedocles: European Journal for the Philosophy of Communication, 4*(2), 133–151.

Lachow, I., & Richardson, C. (2007). Terrorist use of the Internet: The real story. *Joint Force Quarterly, 45*(2), 100–103.

LaFasto, F., & Larson, C. (2001). *When teams work best: 6,000 team members and leaders tell what it takes to succeed.* Thousand Oaks, CA: SAGE Publications.

LaFrance, M., & Mayo, C. (1978). *Moving bodies: Nonverbal communication in social relationships.* Monterey, CA: Brooks/Cole.

Lakatos, I. (1970). Falsification and the methodology of scientific research programmes. In I. Lakatos & A. Musgrave (Eds.), *Criticism and the growth of knowledge* (Proceedings of the International Colloquium in the Philosophy of Science, Vol. 4, pp. 91–195). Cambridge, UK: Cambridge University Press.

Lake, R. A. (1991). Between myth and history: Enacting time in Native American protest rhetoric. *Quarterly Journal of Speech, 77*(2), 123–151.

Lancaster, A. L., Dillow, M. R., Ball, H., Borchert, K., & Tyler, W. J. C. (2016). Managing information about a romantic partner's relationship history: An application of the Theory of Motivated Information Management. *Southern Communication Journal, 81*(2), 63–78.

Langlois, J. H., Kalakanis, L., Rubenstein, A. J., Larson, A., Hallam, M., & Smoot, M. (2000). Maxims or myths of beauty? A meta-analytic and theoretical review. *Psychological Bulletin, 126*(3), 390–423.

LaRose, R., & Eastin, M. S. (2004). A social cognitive theory of internet uses and gratifications: Toward a new model of media attendance. *Journal of Broadcasting & Electronic Media, 48*(3), 358–377.

Lavelli, M. & Fogel, A. (2005). Developmental changes in the relationship between infants' attention and emotion during early face-to-face communication: The two-month transition. *Developmental Psychology, 41*(1), 265–280.

Lawrence, P. R., & Lorsch, J. W. (1967). *Organization and environment.* Boston: Harvard University.

Lazarsfeld, P., Berelson, B., & Gaudet, H. (1944). *The people's choice: How the voter makes up his mind in a presidential campaign.* New York, NY: Columbia University Press.

Lazarus, R. S. (1991). *Emotion and adaptation.* New York, NY: Oxford University Press.

Lee, J., & Jablin, F. M. (1995). Maintenance communication in superior-subordinate work relationships. *Human Communication Research, 22*(2), 220–257.

Lee, L., Chen, D.-T., Li, J.-Y., & Lin, T.-B. (2015). Understanding new media literacy: The development of a measuring instrument. *Computers and Education, 85*, 84–93.

Lee, N. R., & Kotler, P. (2011). *Social marketing: Influencing behaviors for good.* Los Angeles, CA: SAGE Publications.

Leeds-Hurwitz, W. (1990). Notes in the history of intercultural communication: The Foreign Service Institute and the mandate for intercultural training. *Quarterly Journal of Speech, 76*(3), 262–281.

LeFebvre, L. (2017a). Variables, conceptualization. In M. Allen (Ed.), *The SAGE encyclopedia of communication research methods.* Los Angeles, CA: SAGE Publications.

LeFebvre, L. (2017b). Variables, defining. In M. Allen (Ed.), *The SAGE encyclopedia of communication research methods.* Los Angeles, CA: SAGE Publications.

Lefroy, J., & McKinley, R. K. (2011). Skilled communication: Comments further to 'Creativity in clinical communication: From communication skills to skilled communication.' *Medical Education, 45*(9), 958.

LeGreco, M., & Tracy, S. J. (2009). Discourse tracing as qualitative practice. *Qualitative Inquiry, 15*, 1516–1543.

Lehmann-Willenbrock, N., Rogelberg, S. G., Allen, J. A., & Kello, J. E. (2018). The critical importance of meetings to leader and organizational success: Evidence-based insights and implications for key stakeholders. *Organizational Dynamics, 47*(1), 32–36.

Lerner, G. (Ed.). (2004). *Conversation analysis: Studies from the first generation* (pp. 109–129). Amsterdam, Netherlands: John Benjamins Publishing.

Lerner, G. H. (1989). Notes on overlap management in conversation: The case of delayed completion. *Western Journal of Speech Communication, 53*(2), 167–177.

Leung, T., & Kim, M. (2007). Eight conflict handling styles: Validation of model and instrument. *Journal of Asian Pacific Communication, 17*(2), 173–198.

Leventhal, H., Leventhal, E. A., & Cameron, L. (2001). Representations, procedures and affect in self-regulation: A perceptual–cognitive model. In A. Baum, T. A. Revenson, & J. E. Singer (Eds.), *Handbook of health psychology* (pp. 19–48). Mahwah, NJ: Erlbaum.

Levine, T. R. (2014). Truth-default theory (TDT): A theory of human deception and deception detection. *Journal of Language and Social Psychology, 33*(4), 378–392.

Levine, T. R., & Boster, F. J. (1996). The impact of self and others' argumentativeness on talk about controversial issues. *Communication Quarterly, 44*(3), 345–358.

Levine, T. R., Weber, R., Hullett, C., Park, H. S., & Lindsey, L. M. (2008). A critical assessment of null hypothesis significance testing in quantitative communication research. *Human Communication Research, 34*(2), 171–187.

Levine, T. R., Weber, R., Park, H. S., & Hullett, C. R. (2008). A communication researchers' guide to null hypothesis significance testing and alternatives. *Human Communication Research, 34*(2), 188–209.

Levit, A., & Licina, S. (2011). *How the recession shaped millennial and hiring manager attitudes about millennials' future careers.* Washington, DC: Career Advisory Board, DeVry University.

Levy, F., & Cannon, C. (2016, February 9). The Bloomberg job skills report 2016: What recruiters want. Retrieved from: https://www.bloomberg.com/graphics/2016-job-skills-report

Levy, F., & Murnane, R. J. (2004). Education and the changing job market. *Educational Leadership, 62*(2), 80–83.

Levy, K. N., Ellison, W. D., Scott, L. N., & Bernecker, S. L. (2011). Attachment style. *Journal of Clinical Psychology, 67*(2), 193–201.

Lewin, K. (1943). Psychology and the process of group living. *Journal of Social Psychology, 17*(1), 113–131.

Lewis, N. (2013). Priming effects of perceived norms on behavioral intention through observability. *Journal of Applied Social Psychology, 43*(S1), E97–E108.

Lewis, N., Martinez, L. S., Freres, D. R., Schwartz, J. S., Armstrong, K., Gray, S. W., … Hornik, R. C. (2012). Seeking cancer-related information from media and family/friends increases fruit and vegetable consumption among cancer patients. *Health Communication, 27*(4), 380–388.

Likert, R. (1976). *New ways of managing conflict.* New York, NY: McGraw-Hill.

Lim, T.-S., & Bowers, J. W. (1991). Facework: Solidarity, approbation, and tact. *Human Communication Research, 17*(3), 415–450.

Lin, C., Standing, C., & Liu, Y.-C. (2008). A model to develop effective virtual teams. *Decision Support Systems, 45*(4), 1031–1045.

Lin, T-B., Li, J-Y., Deng, F., & Lee, L. (2013). Understanding new media literacy: An explorative theoretical framework. *Journal of Educational Technology and Society, 16*(4), 160–170.

Lindemann, K. (2005). Live(s) online: Narrative performance, presence, and community in LiveJournal.com. *Text and Performance Quarterly, 25*(4), 354–372.

Lindemann, K. (2008). "I can't be standing up out there": Communicative performances of (dis)ability in wheelchair rugby. *Text and Performance Quarterly, 28*(1–2), 98–115.

Lindemann, K. (2010a). Cleaning up my (father's) mess: Narrative containments of "leaky" masculinities. *Qualitative Inquiry, 16*(1), 29–38.

Lindemann, K. (2010b). Self-reflection and our sporting lives: Communication research in the community of sport. *Electronic Journal of Communication, 14*(3–4). Retrieved from: http://www.cios.org/getfile/019344_EJC

Lindemann, K. (2011). Performing (dis)ability in the classroom: Pedagogy and (con)tensions. *Text and Performance Quarterly, 31*(3), 285–302.

Lindemann, K. (2012). Access-ability and disability: Performing stigma, writing trauma. *Journal of the Northwest Communication Association, 40*, 129–149.

Lindemann, K., & Cherney, J. L. (2008). Communicating in and through "Murderball": Masculinity and disability in wheelchair rugby. *Western Journal of Communication, 72*, 107–125.

LinkedIn. (2018, December 13). LinkedIn's 2018 U.S. emerging jobs report. Retrieved July 11, 2019: https://economicgraph.linkedin.com/research/linkedin-2018-emerging-jobs-report

LinkedIn. (2019). *Global talent trends: The 4 trends transforming your workplace.* https://business.linkedin.com/content/dam/me/business/en-us/talent-solutions/resources/pdfs/global-talent-trends-2019.pdf

Liszkowski, U., Brown, P., Callaghan, T., Takada, A., & de Vos, C. (2012). A prelinguistic gestural universal of human communication. *Cognitive Science, 36*(4), 698–713.

Literat, I. (2014). Measuring New Media Literacies: Towards the Development of a Comprehensive Assessment Tool. *Journal of Media Literacy Education, 6*(1), 15–27.

Littlejohn, S. W., Foss, K. A., & Oetzel, J. G. (2017). *Theories of human communication* (11th ed.). Long Grove, IL: Waveland Press.

Liu, D., & Campbell, W. K. (2017). The Big Five personality traits, Big Two metatraits and social media: A meta-analysis. *Journal of Research in Personality, 70*, 229–240.

Liu, X., & Fahmy, S. (2011). Exploring the spiral of silence in the virtual world: Individuals' willingness to express personal opinions in online versus offline settings. *Journal of Media and Communication Studies, 3*(2), 45–57.

Livingstone, S., & Helsper, E. (2010). Balancing opportunities and risks in teenagers' use of the internet: The role of online skills and internet self-efficacy. *New Media and Society, 12*(2), 309–329.

Lizza, R. (2016, July 20). Three problems with the Melania Trump plagiarism admission. *New Yorker.* Retrieved from: http://www.newyorker.com/news/news-desk/three-problems-with-the-melania-trump-plagiarism-admission

Ljungdahl, S., & Bremberg, S. G. (2015). Might extended education decrease inequalities in health?—A meta-analysis. *European Journal of Public Health, 25*(4), 587–592.

Locke, E. A. (1976). The nature and causes of job satisfaction. In M. D. Dunnette (Ed.), *Handbook of industrial and organizational psychology* (pp. 1297–1349). Chicago, IL: Rand McNally.

Lofland, J., & Lofland, L. H. (1995). *Analyzing social settings: A guide to qualitative observation and analysis* (3rd ed.). Belmont, CA: Wadsworth.

Lubken, D. (2008). Remembering the straw man: The travels and adventures of hypodermic. In D. Park & J. Pooley (Ed.), *The history of media and communication research: Contested memories* (pp. 19–42). New York, NY: Peter Lang.

Lucaites, J. L., & Hariman, R. (2001). Visual rhetoric, photojournalism, and democratic public culture. *Rhetoric Review, 20*(1/2), 37–42.

Luhmann, N. (2000). *Organisation and entscheidung.* Opladen, Germany: Westdeutscher Verlag.

Lusty, N. (2009). Valerie Solanas and the limits of speech. *Australian Literary Studies, 24*(3/4), 144–154.

Ma, L., Yang, B., Wang, X., & Li, Y. (2017). On the dimensionality of intragroup conflict. *International Journal of Conflict Management (Emerald), 28*(5), 538–562.

Mabry, E. A. (1999). The systems metaphor in group communication. In L. Frey, D. S. Gouran, & M. S. Poole (Eds.), *The handbook of group communication theory and research* (pp. 71–91). Thousand Oaks, CA: SAGE Publications.

MacKay, J. (2018, January 4). *What we learned about productivity from analyzing 225 million hours of working time in 2017.* Retrieved from: https://blog.rescuetime.com/225-million-hours-productivity/

MacNeilage, P. F., Rogers, L. J., & Vallortigara, G. (2009, July). Origins of the left and right brain. *Scientific American, 301*, 60–67.

Madianou, M., & Miller, D. (2013). Polymedia: Towards a new theory of digital media in interpersonal communication. *International Journal of Cultural Studies, 16*(2), 169–187.

Madlock, P. (2006). Do differences in displays of nonverbal immediacy and communication competence between male and female supervisors affect subordinates, job satisfaction? *Ohio Communication Journal, 44*, 61–78.

Madlock, P. E. (2008). The link between leadership style, communicator competence, and employee satisfaction. *Journal of Business Communication, 45*(1), 61–78.

Madlock, P. E., Martin, M. M., Bogdan, L., & Ervin, M. (2007). The impact of communication traits on leader–member exchange. *Human Communication, 10*(4), 451–464.

Maier, C. D. (2012). Mediating argumentative deconstruction of advertising discourses: A new means of multimodal learning. *Learning, Media and Technology, 37*(2), 163–176.

Maier, M. A., & Burrell, N. A. (2017). Conflict, mediation, and negotiation. In M. Allen (Ed.), *The SAGE encyclopedia of communication research methods.* Thousand Oaks, CA: SAGE Publications.

Makau, J. M. (1991). The principles of fidelity and veracity: Guidelines for ethical communication. In K. J. Greenberg (Ed.), *Conversations on communication ethics* (pp. 111–120). Norwood, NJ: Ablex.

Makau, J. M. (2009). Ethical and unethical communication. In W. F. Eadie (Ed.), *21st-century communication: A reference handbook* (pp. 435–443). Thousand Oaks, CA: SAGE Publications.

Mandel, J. V., & Shapiro, D. A. (Producers), & Rubin, H. A., & Shapiro, D. A. (Directors). (2005). *Murderball* [Motion picture]. Paramount Pictures.

Mandelbaum, J. (1991). Ethnography and conversation analysis after *Talking Culture. Research on Language and Social Interaction, 24*, 333–350.

Margolin, G., Oliver, P. H., Gordis, E. B., Garcia O'Hearn, H., Medina, A. M., Ghosh, C. M., & Morland, L. (1998). The nuts and bolts of behavioral observation of marital and family interaction. *Clinical Child and Family Psychology Review, 1*, 195–213.

Marlow, S. L., Lacerenza, C. N., Paoletti, J., Burke, C. S., & Salas, E. (2018). Does team communication represent a one-size-fits-all approach?: A meta-analysis of team communication and performance. *Organizational Behavior and Human Decision Processes, 144*, 145–170.

Martin, J. N., & Nakayama, T. K. (1999). Thinking dialectically about culture and communication. *Communication Theory, 9*(1), 1–25.

Martin, J. N., & Nakayama, T. K. (2013). *Intercultural communication in contexts* (6th ed.). New York, NY: McGraw-Hill.

Martin, J. N., Nakayama, T. K., & Carbaugh, D. (2012). The history and development of the study of intercultural communication and applied linguistics. In J. Jackson (Ed.), *The Routledge handbook of language and intercultural communication* (pp. 17–36). New York, NY: Routledge.

Martin, R., Guillaume, Y., Thomas, G., Lee, A., & Epitropaki, O. (2016). Leader–member exchange (LMX) and performance: A meta-analytic review. *Personnel Psychology, 69*(1), 67–121.

Martindale, D. (1979). Ideologies, paradigms, and theories. In W. E. Snizek, E. R. Fuhrman, & M. K. Miller (Eds.), *Contemporary issues in theory and research: A metasociological perspective* (pp. 7–24). Westport, CT: Greenwood.

Martinez, L. S. (2014). Explaining the effects of anticipated regret messages on young women's intention to consume folic acid: A moderated-mediation model. *Journal of Health Communication, 19*, 115–132.

Marvel, M. K., Epstein, R. M., Flowers, K., & Beckman, H. B. (1999). Soliciting the patient's agenda: Have we improved? *Journal of the American Medical Association, 281*(3), 283–287.

Marwell, G., & Schmitt, D. R. (1967). Dimensions of compliance-gaining behavior: An empirical analysis. *Sociometry, 30*(4), 350–364.

Marx, K. (1867/1992) *Capital: Volume one.* New York, NY: Penguin.

Matsumoto, D. (2006). Culture and nonverbal behavior. In V. Manusov & M. L. Patterson (Eds.), *The SAGE handbook of nonverbal communication* (pp. 219–235). Thousand Oaks, CA: SAGE Publications.

Mattern, K. D., Burrus, J., & Shaw, E. (2010). When both the skilled and unskilled are unaware: Consequences for academic performance. *Self and Identity, 9*(2), 129–141.

Matthews, N. L., & Weaver, A. J. (2013). Skill gap: Quantifying violent content in video game play between variably skilled users. *Mass Communication and Society, 16*(6), 829–846.

May, M. S. (2009). Spinoza and class struggle. *Communication and Critical/Cultural Studies, 6*(2), 204–208.

May, V. (2015). *Pursuing intersectionality, unsettling dominant.* New York, NY: Routledge.

Maynard, D. W. (1996). On 'realization' in everyday life: The forecasting of bad news as a social relation. *American Sociological Review, 61*(1), 109–131.

Maynard, D. W. (1997). The news delivery sequence: Bad news and good news in conversational interaction. *Research on Language and Social Interaction, 30*, 93–130.

Maynard, D. W. (2003). *Good news, bad news: A benign order in conversations, clinics, and everyday life.* Chicago, IL: University of Chicago Press.

Mazzella, R., & Feingold, A. (1994). The effects of physical attractiveness, race, socioeconomic status, and gender of defendants and victims on judgments of mock jurors: A meta-analysis. *Journal of Applied Social Psychology, 24*(15), 1315–1344.

McAndrew, F. T. (2009). The interacting roles of testosterone and challenges to status in human male aggression. *Aggression and Violent Behavior, 14*, 330–335.

McCombs, M. E., & Reynolds, A. (2009). How the news shapes our civic agenda. In J. Bryant & M. B. Oliver (Eds.), *Media effects: Advances in theory and research* (3rd ed., pp. 1–16). New York, NY: Taylor & Francis.

McCombs, M. E., & Shaw, D. L. (1972). The agenda-setting function of mass media. *Public Opinion Quarterly, 36*(2), 176–187.

McCornack, S. A., Morrison, K., Paik, J. E., Wisner, A. M., & Zhu, X. (2014). Information manipulation theory 2: A propositional theory of deceptive discourse production. *Journal of Language and Social Psychology, 33*(4), 348–377.

McCroskey, J. C., & Beatty, M. J. (2000). The communibiological perspective: Implications for communication in instruction. *Communication Education, 49*(1), 1–6.

McDonald, J. (2015). Organizational communication meets queer theory: Theorizing relations of "difference" differently. *Communication Theory, 25*, 310–329.

McEwan, D., Ruissen, G. R., Eys, M. A., Zumbo, B. D., & Beauchamp, M. R. (2017). The effectiveness of teamwork training on teamwork behaviors and team performance: A systematic review and meta-analysis of controlled interventions. *PLOS One, 12*(1).

McGhee, H. (2012, February 10) "Heather McGhee on the millennial generation." Moyers & Company. Retrieved from: http://billmoyers.com/segment/heather-mcghee-on-the-millennial-generation/

McGregor, D. (1960). *The human side of enterprise.* Boston, MA: McGraw-Hill.

McKaughan, D. J. (2008). From ugly duckling to swan: C. S. Peirce, abduction, and the pursuit of scientific theories. *Transactions of the Charles S. Peirce Society, 44*, 446–468.

McKeever, B. W. (2014). The status of health communication: Education and employment outlook for a growing field. *Journal of Health Communication, 19*(12), 1408–1423.

McKerrow, R. E. (1989). Critical rhetoric: Theory and praxis. *Communications Monographs, 56*(2), 91–111.

McKewon, T. (1988). *The origins of human disease.* Oxford, UK: Basil Blackwell.

McLeod, D. M., Wise, D., & Perryman, M. (2017). Thinking about the media: A review of theory and research on media perceptions, media effects perceptions, and their consequences. *Review of Communication Research, 5*, 35–83.

McLuhan, M. (1964). *Understanding media: The extensions of man.* New York, NY: McGraw-Hill.

McPhail, M. L. (1998). From complicity to coherence: Rereading the rhetoric of Afrocentricity. *Western Journal of Communication, 62*(2), 114–140.

McPhee, R. D., Poole, M. S., & Iverson, J. (2013). Structuration theory. In L. L. Putnam & D. K. Mumby (Eds.), *The SAGE handbook of organizational communication: Advances in theory* (pp. 75–100). Thousand Oaks, CA: SAGE Publications.

McPhee, R. D., & Zaug, P. (2000). The communicative constitution of organizations: A framework for explanation. *Electronic Journal of communication, 10*. http://www.cios.org/EJCPUBLIC/010/1/01017.html

McQuail, D. (2013). Reflections on paradigm change in communication theory and research. *International Journal of Communication, 7*, 216–229.

Mead, G. H. (1934). *Mind, self, and society.* C. W. Morris (Ed.). Chicago, IL: University of Chicago Press.

Meehl, P. E. (1990). Appraising and amending theories: The strategy of Lakatosian defense and two principles that warrant it. *Psychological Inquiry, 1*(2), 108–141.

Men, L. R. (2014). Why leadership matters to internal communication: Linking transformational leadership, symmetrical communication, and employee outcomes. *Journal of Public Relations Research, 26*(3), 256–279.

Men, L. R., & Stacks, D. W. (2013). The impact of leadership style and employee empowerment on perceived organizational reputation. *Journal of Communication Management, 17*(2), 171–192.

Mendez-Luck, C. A., Bethel, J. W., Goins, R. T., Schure, M. B., & McDermott, E. (2015). Community as a source of health in three racial/ethnic communities in Oregon: A qualitative study. *BMC Public Health, 15*, 127.

Merkin, R., Taras, V., & Steel, P. (2014). State of the art themes in cross-cultural communication research: A systematic and meta-analytical review. *International Journal of Intercultural Relations, 38*, 1–23.

Merkle, J. A. (1980). *Management and ideology: The legacy of the international scientific management movement.* Berkeley, CA: University of California Press.

Merolla, A. J. (2010). Relational maintenance during military deployment: Perspectives of wives of deployed US soldiers. *Journal of Applied Communication Research, 38*(1), 4–26.

Mesmer-Magnus, J. R., DeChurch, L. A., Jimenez-Rodriguez, M., Wildman, J., & Shuffler, M. (2011). A meta-analytic investigation of virtuality and information sharing in teams. *Organizational Behavior & Human Decision Processes, 115*(2), 214–225.

Metts, S. (1997). Introduction. *Personal Relationships, 4*(3), 201–202.

Metzger, T. R., & Beach, W. A. (1996). Preserving alternative versions: Interactional techniques for organizing courtroom cross-examination. *Communication Research, 23*(6), 749–765.

Meyer, J. R. (2013). Contemplating regretted messages: Learning-oriented, repair-oriented, and emotion-focused reflection. *Western Journal of Communication, 77*(2), 210–230.

Meyrowitz, J. (1985). *No sense of place: The impact of electronic media on social behavior.* New York, NY: Oxford University Press.

Michell, G. (1984). Women and lying: A pragmatic and semantic analysis of "telling it slant." *Women's Studies International Forum, 7*(5), 375–383.

Mieth, D. (1997). The basic norm of truthfulness: Its ethical justification and universality. In C. Christians & M. Traber (Eds.), *Communication ethics and universal values* (pp. 87–104). Thousand Oaks, CA: SAGE.

Mihailidis, P., & Thevenin, B. (2013). Media literacy as a core competency for engaged citizenship in participatory democracy. *American Behavioral Scientist, 57*(11), 1611–1622.

Mikkelson, A. C., York, J. A., & Arritola, J. (2015). Communication competence, leadership behaviors, and employee outcomes in supervisor–employee relationships. *Business and Professional Communication Quarterly, 78*(3), 336–354.

Miller, G. R. (1975). Humanistic and scientific approaches to speech communication inquiry: Rivalry, redundancy, or rapprochement. *Western Speech Communication, 39*(4), 230–239.

Miller, G., Boster, F., Roloff, M., & Seibold, D. (1977). Compliance-gaining message strategies: A typology and some findings concerning effects of situational differences. *Communication Monographs, 44*(1), 37–51.

Mirivel, J. (2014). *The art of positive communication: Theory and practice.* New York, NY: Peter Lang.

Mirza, N. A., Akhtar-Danesh, N., Noesgaard, C., Martin, L. & Staples, E. (2014). A concept analysis of abductive reasoning. *Journal of Advanced Nursing, 70*(9), 1980–1994.

Mischel, W. (1966). A social learning view of sex differences in behavior. In E. E. Maccoby (Ed.), *The development of sex differences* (pp. 93–106). Stanford, CA: Stanford University.

Mishler, E. G. (1984). *The discourse of medicine: Dialectics of medical interviews.* Norwood, NJ: Ablex.

Miyagawa, S., Berwick, R. C., & Okanoya, K. (2013). The emergence of hierarchical structure in human language. *Frontiers in Psychology, 4.*

Mokuau, N., & Browne, C. (1994). Life themes of native Hawaiian female elders: Resources for cultural preservation. *Social Work, 39*, 43–49.

Moneta, G. B., & Csikszentmihalyi, M. (1996). The effect of perceived challenges and skills on the quality of subjective experience. *Journal of Personality, 64*(2), 275–310.

MONEY/PayScale. (2017). 2,400 colleges + 27 data points = 711 best colleges for your money. Retrieved from: http://new.money.com/money/best-colleges/rankings/best-colleges/

Monge, P. R. (1977). Systems perspective as a theoretical basis for the study of human communication. *Communication Quarterly, 25*, 19–29.

Monge, P. R. (1982). Systems theory and research in the study of organizational communication: The correspondence problem. *Human Communication Research, 8*, 245–261.

Mongeau, P. A., & Henningsen, M. L. M. (2008). Stage theories of relationship development. In L. A. Baxter and D. O. Braithwaite (Eds.), *Engaging theories in interpersonal communication: Multiple perspectives* (pp. 363–375). New York, NY: SAGE Publications.

Moneta, G. B., & Csikszentmihalyi, M. (1999). Models of concentration in natural environments: A comparative approach based on streams of experiential data. *Social Behavior & Personality: An International Journal, 27*(6), 603–637.

Mønsted, B., Sapieżyński, P., Ferrara, E., & Lehmann, S. (2017). Evidence of complex contagion of information in social media: An experiment using Twitter bots. *PLOS One, 12*(9), 1–12.

Moon, D. G. (1996). Concepts of "culture": Implications for intercultural communication research. *Communication Quarterly, 44*(1), 70–84.

Morgan, G. (1986). *Images of organization* (updated edition) Thousand Oaks, CA: SAGE Publications.

Morgan, M., Shanahan, J., & Signorielli, N. (2009). Growing up with television: Cultivation processes. In J. Bryant & M. B. Oliver (Eds.), *Media effects: Advances in theory and research* (3rd ed., pp. 34–49). New York, NY: Taylor & Francis.

Morris, C. E. III (Ed.). (2007). *Queering public address: Sexualities in American historical discourse.* Columbia, SC: University of South Carolina Press.

Morris, C. E. III (2009). Hard evidence: The vexations of Lincoln's queer corpus. In Biesecker and Lucaites (Eds.), *Rhetoric, materiality politics* (pp. 185–213). New York, NY: Peter Lang.

Morris, C. E. III, & Sloop, J. M. (2006). "What lips these lips have kissed": Refiguring the politics of queer public kissing. *Communication and Critical/Cultural Studies, 3*(1), 1–26.

Mosley, E., & Irvine, D. (2015). *The power of thanks: How social recognition empowers employees and creates a best place to work.* Southborough, MA: Globoforce.

Mueller, R. S. (2019, March). *Report on the investigation into Russian interference in the 2016 presidential election* (Vols. I–II). Washington DC: U. S. Department of Justice. https://www.justice.gov/storage/report.pdf

Mullen, B., & Copper, C. (1994). The relation between group cohesiveness and performance: An integration. *Psychological Bulletin, 115*(2), 210–227.

Müller, M., Höfel, L., Brattico, E., & Jacobsen, T. (2010). Aesthetic judgments of music in experts and laypersons—An ERP study. *International Journal of Psychophysiology, 76*(1), 40–51.

Mumby, D. K. (1988). *Communication and power in organizations: Discourse, ideology, and domination.* Norwood: NJ, Ablex.

Mumby, D. K. (2001). Power and politics. In F. M. Jablin & L. L. Putnam (Eds.), *The new handbook of organizational communication: Advances in theory, research, and methods* (pp. 585–623). Newbury Park, CA: SAGE Publications.

Mumby, D. K. (2013). *Organizational communication: A critical approach.* Thousand Oaks, CA: SAGE Publications.

Mumby, D. K., & Putnam, L. L. (1992). The politics of emotion: A feminist reading of bounded rationality. *The Academy of Management Review, 17*(3), 465–486.

Mumby, D. K., & Stohl, C. (1996). Disciplining organizational communication studies. *Management Communication Quarterly, 10*(1), 50–72.

Musk, J. (2014, June 5). Love. fear. sex. (+ the power of radical listening) [Blog post]. Retrieved from: http://justinemusk.com/2014/06/05/how-to-end-the-battle-of-the-sexes/

Naaman, M., Boase, J., & Lai, C-H. (2010). Is it really about me? Message content in social awareness streams. *Proceedings of the 2010 ACM Conference on Computer Supported Cooperative Work* (pp. 189–192). New York, NY: ACM.

Nabi, R. L., & Krcmar, M. (2004). Conceptualizing media enjoyment as attitude: implications for mass media effects research. *Communication Theory (1050-3293), 14*(4), 288–310.

Nabokov, V. (1996). *Vladimir Nabokov: Novels 1969–1974.* New York, NY: Literary Classics of the United States.

Nagy, E., Liotti, M., Brown, S., Waiter, G., Bromiley, A., Trevarthen, C., & Bardos, G. (2010). The neural mechanisms of reciprocal communication. *Brain Research, 1353,* 159–167.

Nakayama, T. K., & Krizek, R. L. (1995). Whiteness: A strategic rhetoric. *Quarterly Journal of Speech, 81*(3), 291–309.

Namkoong, K., Shah, D. V., McLaughlin, B., Chih, M.-Y., Moon, T. J., Hull, S., & Gustafson, D. H. (2017). Expression and reception: An analytic method for assessing message production and consumption in CMC. *Communication Methods and Measures, 11*(3), 153–172.

National Association of Colleges and Employers (NACE). (2014a). *Job outlook 2015.* Bethlehem, PA: Author. Retrieved from: https://www.umuc.edu/upload/NACE-Job-Outlook-2015.pdf

National Association of Colleges and Employers (NACE). (2014b, January). *Salary survey: Starting salaries for new college graduates—data reported by employers (Executive summary).* Bethlehem, PA: Author. Retrieved from: http://career.sa.ucsb.edu/files/docs/handouts/2014-september-salary-survey-executive-summary.pdf

National Association of Colleges and Employers (NACE). (2015, January). *Salary survey: Starting salaries for new college graduates—data reported by employers (Executive summary).* Bethlehem, PA: Author. Retrieved from: https://www.naceweb.org/uploadedfiles/content/static-assets/downloads/executive-summary/2015-january-salary-survey-executive-summary.pdf

National Association of Colleges and Employers (NACE). (2016, June). *First destinations for the college class of 2015.* Bethlehem, PA: Author. Retrieved from: http://www.naceweb.org/uploadedfiles/pages/surveys/first-destination/nace-first-destination-survey-executive-summary.pdf

National Association of Colleges and Employers (NACE). (2017, November). *Job outlook 2018.* Bethlehem, PA: NACE. Retrieved from: http://careerservices.wayne.edu/pdfs/2018-nace-job-outlook-survey.pdf

National Association of Colleges and Employers (NACE). (2019, November). *Job outlook 2019.* Bethlehem, PA: NACE. https://www.odu.edu/content/dam/odu/offices/cmc/docs/nace/2019-nace-job-outlook-survey.pdf

National Communication Association. (2018, February). *Employment outlook for communication graduates.* Retrieved from: https://www.natcom.org/reports-discipline/employment-outlook-communication-graduates

National Institutes of Health. (2002). *Human participant protections education for research teams.* Washington, DC: U.S. Department of Health and Human Services National Institutes of Health. Retrieved May 10, 2019: http://people.oregonstate.edu/~acock/hdfs361/NIH%20training%20on%20human%20subjects.pdf

Neighbors, C., Lee, C. M., Lewis, M. A., Fossos, N., & Larimer, M. E. (2007). Are social norms the best predictor of outcomes among heavy-drinking college students? *Journal of Studies on Alcohol and Drugs, 68*(4), 556–565.

Ness, A. M., & Connelly, S. (2017). Situational influences on ethical sensemaking: Performance pressure, interpersonal conflict, and the recipient of consequences. *Human Performance, 30*(2–3), 57–78

NetMarketShare. (n.d.). Search engine market share. Retrieved from: https://www.netmarketshare.com/search-engine-market-share.aspx

Neuendorf, K. A. (2016). *The content analysis guidebook.* Los Angeles, CA: SAGE Publications.

Neuliep, J. W. (2018). *Intercultural communication: A contextual approach* (7th ed.). Los Angeles, CA: SAGE Publications.

Neuman, W. R., and Guggenheim, L. (2011). The evolution of media effects theory: A six-stage model of cumulative research. *Communication Theory, 21*(2), 169–196.

Neumann, M., Scheffer, C., Tauschel, D., Lutz, G., Wirtz, M., & Edelhäuser, F. (2012). Physician empathy: Definition, outcome-relevance and its measurement in patient care and medical education. *GMS Zeitschrift Für Medizinische Ausbildung, 29*(1), Doc11.

Newport, C. (2012, September 18). Solving Gen Y's passion problem. *Harvard Business Review.* Retrieved from: https://hbr.org/2012/09/solving-gen-ys-passion-problem

Newport, F., & Dugan, A. (2015, March 26). *College-educated Republicans most skeptical of global warming.* Gallup.com. Retrieved from: https://news.gallup.com/poll/182159/college-educated-republicans-skeptical-global-warming.aspx

Newton, P. M. (2018). How common is commercial contract cheating in higher education and is it increasing? A systematic review. *Frontiers in Education, 3*(67), 1–18.

Nicholson, L. (2013). Feminism in "waves": Useful metaphor or not? In C. Mccann & S-K. Kim (Eds.) *Feminist theory reader: Local and global perspectives* (pp. 49–55). New York, NY: Routledge.

Nicotera, A. M., Steele, J., Catalani, A., & Simpson, N. (2012). Conceptualization and test of an aggression competence model. *Communication Research Reports, 29*(1), 12–25.

Nilsen, T. R. (1974). *Ethics of speech communication* (2nd ed.). Indianapolis, IN: Bobbs-Merrill.

Noack, R., & Gamio, L. (2015, April 23). The world's languages in 7 maps and charts. *Washington Post* (online). Retrieved from: https://www.washingtonpost.com/news/worldviews/wp/2015/04/23/the-worlds-languages-in-7-maps-and-charts/?noredirect=on&utm_term=.d615917d5895

Noar, S. M. (2006). A 10-year retrospective of research in health mass media campaigns: Where do we go from here? *Journal of Health Communication, 11*(1), 21–42.

Noelle-Neumann, E. (1974). The spiral of silence a theory of public opinion. *Journal of Communication, 24*(2), 43–51.

Noelle-Neumann, E. (1991). The theory of public opinion: The concept of the spiral of silence. In J. Anderson (Eds.), *Communication Yearbook, 14* (pp. 256–287). Newbury Park, CA: SAGE Publications.

Noelle-Neumann, E. (1993). *The spiral of silence: Public opinion, our social skin* (2nd ed., pp. 11–15). Chicago, IL: University of Chicago Press.

Noller, P., & Fitzpatrick, M. A. (1993). *Communication in family relationships.* Englewood Cliffs, NJ: Prentice Hall.

Norris, F. (2014, September 12). Young households: Even educated ones, lose ground in income. *New York Times.* Retrieved from: http://www.nytimes.com/2014/09/13/business/economy/young-households-are-losing-ground-in-income-despite-education.html?_r=0

Northhouse, P. G. (2013). *Leadership: Theory and practice* (6th ed.). Thousand Oaks, CA: SAGE Publications.

Notarius, C., Markman, H., & Gottman, J. (1983). The couples' interaction scoring system: Clinical applications. In E. E. Filsinger (Eds.), *A sourcebook of marriage and family assessment* (pp. 117–136). Beverly Hills, CA: SAGE Publications.

Núñez, R., & Cooperrider, K. (2013). The tangle of space and time in human cognition. *Trends in Cognitive Sciences, 17*(5), 220–229.

Nussbaum, E. M. (2011). Argumentation, dialogue theory, and probability modeling: Alternative frameworks for argumentation research in education. *Educational Psychologist, 46*(2), 84–106.

Nyqvist, F., Pape, B., Pellfolk, T., Forsman, A. K., & Wahlbeck, K. (2016). Structural and cognitive aspects of social capital and all-cause mortality: A meta-analysis of cohort studies. *Social Indicators Research, 116*(2), 545–566.

O'Brien, C. (2019, May 9). Conan O'Brien: Why I decided to settle a lawsuit over alleged joke stealing. *Variety.* Retrieved from: https://variety.com/2019/biz/news/conan-obrien-jokes-lawsuit-alex-kaseberg-settlement-1203210214/

O'Keefe, D. J. (2013). The elaboration likelihood model. In J. P. Dillard & L. Shen (Eds), *The SAGE handbook of persuasion* (2nd ed., pp. 137–149). Thousand Oaks, CA: SAGE Publications.

O'Keefe, D. J. (2002). *Persuasion: Theory and research* (2nd ed.). Thousand Oaks, CA: SAGE Publications.

O'Keefe, D. J. (2016). *Persuasion: Theory and research* (3rd ed.). Thousand Oaks, CA: SAGE Publications.

O'Neill, T., Allen, N., & Hastings, S. (2013). Examining the "pros" and "cons" of team conflict: A team-level meta-analysis of task, relationship, and process conflict. *Human Performance, 26*(3), 236–260.

O'Sullivan, P. B., & Carr, C. T. (2018). Masspersonal communication: A model bridging the mass–interpersonal divide. *New Media and Society, 20*(3), 1161–1180.

Ocaña, A. M., Chamberlain, K. A., & Carlson, G. B. (2005). Sex differences and satisfaction in conflict resolution methods: A meta-analysis. *North Dakota Journal of Speech and Theatre, 18*, 1–12.

Odermatt, I., König, C. J., Kleinmann, M., Nussbaumer, R., Rosenbaum, A., Olien, J. L., & Rogelberg, S. G. (2017). On leading meetings: Linking meeting outcomes to leadership styles. *Journal of Leadership and Organizational Studies, 24*(2), 189–200.

OED Online. (2018, December). Media. Oxford University Press. Accessed February 13, 2019.

Oestermeier, U., & Hesse, F. W. (2000). Verbal and visual causal arguments. *Cognition, 75*(1), 65–104.

Oetzel, J. G. (2009). *Intercultural communication: A layered approach.* New York, NY: Vango Books.

Oetzel, J. G., Ting-Toomey, S., Masumoto, T., Yokochi, Y., Pan, X., Takai, J., & Wilcox, R. (2001). Face and facework in conflict: A cross-cultural comparison of China, Germany, Japan, and the United States. *Communication Monographs, 68*(3), 235–258.

Ogden, C. K., & Richards, I. A. (1923). *The meaning of meaning: A study of the influence of language upon thought and of the science of symbolism.* Cambridge, UK: Cambridge University Press.

Oleinik, A. (2015). The language of power: A content analysis of presidential addresses in North America and the former Soviet Union, 1993–2012. *International Journal of the Sociology of Language, 2015*(236), 181–204.

Oliver, J. E., & Wood, T. J. (2014). Conspiracy theories and the paranoid style(s) of mass opinion. *American Journal of Political Science, 58*(4), 952–966.

Oliver, R. (1962). *Culture and communication: The problem of penetrating national and cultural boundaries.* Springfield, IL: Thomas.

Ono, K. A., & Pham, V. (2009). *Asian Americans and the media.* Cambridge, UK: Polity.

Ono, K. A., & Sloop, J. M. (1995). The critique of vernacular discourse. *Communications Monographs, 62*(1), 19–46.

Ono, K. A., & Sloop, J. M. (2002). *Shifting borders: Rhetoric, immigration, and California's Proposition 187.* Philadelphia, PA: Temple University Press.

Opotow, S. (1990). Moral exclusion and injustice: An introduction. *Journal of Social Issues, 46*, 1–20.

Ordoñana, J. R., Bartels, M., Boomsma, D. I., Cella, D., Mosing, M., Oliveira, J. R., … Sprangers, M. G. (2013). Biological pathways and genetic mechanisms involved in social functioning. *Quality of Life Research: An International Journal of Quality of Life Aspects of Treatment, Care and Rehabilitation, 22*(6), 1189–1200.

Organisation for Economic Co-operation and Development. (2011). *Development co-operation report 2011.* Retrieved from: http://www.oecd.org/dac/developmentco-operationreport2011.htm

Organisation for Economic Co-operation and Development. (2014), *Education at a glance 2014: OECD indicators.* Washington, DC: OECD Publishing.

Organization for Migration. (2018). *World migration report 2018.* Geneva, Switzerland: Author. https://publications.iom.int/system/files/pdf/wmr_2018_en.pdf

Orlitzky, M., & Hirokawa, R. Y. (2001). To err is human, to correct for it divine: A meta-analysis of research testing the functional theory of group decision-making effectiveness. *Small Group Research, 32*(3), 313–341.

Osborne, J., Erduran, S., & Simon, S. (2004). Enhancing the quality of argumentation in school science. *Journal of Research in Science Teaching, 41*(10), 994–1020.

Ott Anderson, J., & Geist-Martin, P. (2003). Narratives and healing: Exploring one family's stories of cancer survivorship. *Health Communication, 15,* 133–143.

Overall, N. C., Fletcher, G. O., Simpson, J. A., & Sibley, C. G. (2009). Regulating partners in intimate relationships: The costs and benefits of different communication strategies. *Journal of Personality and Social Psychology, 96*(3), 620–639.

Pacanowsky, M. E., & O'Donnell-Trujillo, N. (1983). Organizational communication as cultural performance. *Communication Monographs, 50*(2), 126–147.

Pagel, M. (2009). Human language as a culturally transmitted replicator. *Nature Reviews Genetics, 10*(6), 405–415.

Palczewski, C. H., DeFrancisco, V. P., & McGeough D. D. (2019). *Gender in communication: A critical introduction* (3rd ed.). Thousand Oaks, CA: SAGE Publications.

Palczewski, C. H., Ice, R. & Fritch, J. (2012). *Rhetoric in civic life.* State College, PA: Strata.

Pallini, S., Baiocco, R., Schneider, B. H., Madigan, S., & Atkinson, L. (2014). Early child–parent attachment and peer relations: A meta-analysis of recent research. *Journal of Family Psychology, 28*(1), 118–123.

Palmer, J. L. (1988). *From the greenroom to the boardroom: Performance studies as management training.* San Dimas, CA: Communication Excellence Institute.

Palvia, P., Pinjani, P., Cannoy, S., & Jacks, T. (2011). Contextual constraints in media choice: Beyond information richness. *Decision Support Systems, 51*(3), 657–670.

Papa, M. J., Singhal, A., Law, S., Pant, S., Sood, S., Rogers, E. M., & Shefner-Rogers, C. L. (2000). Entertainment-education and social change: An analysis of parasocial interaction, social learning, collective efficacy, and paradoxical communication. *Journal of Communication, 50*(4), 31–55.

Pappano, L. (2014, April 8). Courses with a twist. *New York Times, Education Life.* Retrieved from: http://www.nytimes.com/2014/04/13/education/edlife/10-courses-with-a-twist.html?_r=0

Park, W. (2000). A comprehensive empirical investigation of the relationships among variables of the groupthink model. *Journal of Organizational Behavior, 21*(8), 873–887.

Parker, K., & Livingston, G. (2016). *6 facts about American fathers.* Pew Research Center. Retrieved from http://www.pewresearch.org/fact-tank/2016/06/16/fathers-day-facts/

Parkinson, B. (2005). Do facial movements express emotions or communicate motives? *Personality and Social Psychology Review, 9*(4), 278–311.

Parrott, S., & Parrott, C. T. (2015). Law & disorder: The portrayal of mental illness in U.S. crime dramas. *Journal of Broadcasting and Electronic Media, 59*(4), 640–657.

Paul, A. (2014). Is online better than offline for meeting partners? Depends: Are you looking to marry or to date? *Cyberpsychology, Behavior and Social Networking, 17*(10), 664–667.

Pauley, P. M., Morman, M. T., & Floyd, K. (2011). Expressive writing improves subjective health among testicular cancer survivors: A pilot study. *International Journal of Men's Health, 10*(3), 199–219.

Pavitt, C. (2000). Answering questions requesting scientific explanations for communication. *Communication Theory, 10*(4), 379–404.

Pavitt, C., & Johnson, K. K. (2002). Scheidel and Crowell revisited: A descriptive study of group proposal sequencing. *Communication Monographs, 69*(1), 19–32.

PayScale.com. (2016, August 31). Which American workers have the biggest egos? Retrieved from: http://www.payscale.com/data-packages/big-ego-jobs

PayScale.com. (2017). Leveling up: How to win in the skills economy. Retrieved from: http://www.payscale.com/data-packages/job-skills

Pearson, J. C., & Spitzberg, B. H. (1990). *Interpersonal communication: Concepts, components, and contexts* (2nd ed.). Dubuque, IA: William C. Brown.

Peck, D. L. (1993). The fifty percent divorce rate: Deconstructing a myth. *Journal of Sociology and Social Welfare, 20*(3), 135–144.

Pei, S., Muchnik, L., Tang, S., Zheng, Z., & Makse, H. A. (2015). Exploring the complex pattern of information spreading in online blog communities. *PLOS One, 10*(5), 1–18. e0126894.

Pelias, R. J., & VanOosting, J. (1987). A paradigm for performance studies. *Quarterly Journal of Speech, 73*(2), 219–231.

Pennebaker, J. W. (1997). Writing about emotional experiences as a therapeutic process. *Psychological Science, 8*(3), 162–166.

Pennebaker, J. W. (2000). Telling stories: The health benefits of narrative. *Literature and Medicine, 19*(1), 3–18.

Pentland, A. (2007). Automatic mapping and modeling of human networks. *Physica A, 378,* 59–67.

PeopleMetrics. (2011). *Employee engagement trends report.* Philadelphia, PA: Author. Retrieved from: http://info.peoplemetrics.com/hs-fs/hub/221727/file-2078153457-pdf/PDFs/2011_Employee_Engagement_Trends_Report_PeopleMetrics.pdf

Peräkylä, A. (1998). Authority and accountability: The delivery of diagnosis in primary health care. *Social Psychology Quarterly, 61*(4), 301–320.

Peräkylä, A. (2002). Agency and authority: Extended responses to diagnostic statements in primary care encounters. *Research on Language and Social Interaction, 35*(2), 219–247.

Peräkylä, A., & Sorjonen, M. L. (Eds.). (2012). *Emotion in interaction.* Oxford, UK: Oxford University Press.

Perelman, C., & Olbrechts-Tyteca, L. (1958). *The new rhetoric: A treatise on argumentation* (J. Wilkinson and P. Weaver, Trans). Notre Dame, IN: Notre Dame University Press.

Perez, T. L., & Dionisopoulos, G. N. (1995). Presidential silence, C. Everett Koop, and the Surgeon General's report on AIDS. *Communication Studies, 46*(1–2), 18–33.

Perloff, R. M. (2013). Progress, paradigms, and a discipline engaged: A response to Lang and reflections on media effects research. *Communication Theory, 23*(4), 317–333.

Perrin, D., & Ehrensberger-Dow, M. (2008). Media competence. In G. Rickheit & H. Strohner (Eds.), *Handbook of communication competence* (pp. 277–312). New York, NY: Mouton de Gruyter.

Perrow, C. (1973). The short and glorious history of organizational theory. *Organizational Dynamics, 2*(1), 2–15.

Perry, A., & Karpova, E. (2017). Efficacy of teaching creative thinking skills: A comparison of multiple creativity assessments. *Thinking Skills and Creativity, 24,* 118–126.

Pervin, L. A. (1978). Definitions, measurements, and classifications of stimuli, situations, and environments. *Human Ecology, 6*(1), 71–105.

Peters, J. D. (2001). *Speaking into the air: A history of the idea of communication.* Chicago, IL: University of Chicago Press.

Peterson, L. W., & Albrecht, T. L. (1999). Where gender/power/politics collide: Deconstructing organizational maternity leave policy. *Journal of Management Inquiry, 8,* 168–181.

Petronio, S. (2002). *Boundaries of privacy: Dialectics of disclosure.* Albany, NY: SUNY Press.

Pettit Jr., J. D., Goris, J. R., & Vaught, B. C. (1997). An examination of organizational communication as a moderator of the relationship between job performance and job satisfaction. *Journal of Business Communication, 34*(1), 81–98.

Petty, R. E., & Cacioppo, J. T. (1986). *Communication and persuasion: Central and peripheral routes to attitude change.* New York, NY: Springer-Verlag.

Pew Research Center. (2011, May 15). Is college worth it? Retrieved from: http://www.pewsocialtrends.org/2011/05/15/is-college-worth-it/

Pew Research Center. (2013, December). Public's views on human evolution. Retrieved from: http://www.pewforum.org/files/2013/12/Evolution-12-30.pdf

Pew Research Center. (2014, September). *2014 Pew Research Center's American trends panel.* Retrieved from: http://www.pewresearch.org/methodology/u-s-survey-research/american-trends-panel/

Pew Research Center. (2015a, February). *The skills Americans say kids need to succeed in life.* Retrieved from: http://static1.squarespace.com/static/5633a3ade4b02b1547969346/t/5633dccbe4b03d18620c942c/1446239435953/The+skills+Americans+say+kids+need+to+succeed+in+life+_+Pew+Research+Center.pdf

Pew Research Center. (2015b, July 1). *Americans, politics and science issues.* Washington, DC: Author. Retrieved from:bhttp://assets.pewresearch.org/wp-content/uploads/sites/14/2015/07/2015-07-01_science-and-politics_FINAL-1.pdf

Pew Research Center (2017, January). *After seismic political shift, modest changes in public's policy agenda.* Washington DC: Author. Retrieved from: http://assets.pewresearch.org/wp-content/uploads/sites/5/2017/01/24114242/1-24-17-Priorities-release.pdf

Pew Research Center's Internet & American Life Project. (2012). *How teens do research in the digital world.* Washington DC: Author.

Pezzullo, P. C., & Cox, R. (2017). *Environmental communication and the public sphere.* Thousand Oaks, CA: SAGE Publications.

Pfister, D. S. (2015). A short burst of inconsequential information: Networked rhetorics, avian consciousness, and bioegalitarianism. *Environmental Communication, 9*(1), 118–136.

Philipsen, G. (1975). Speaking "like a man" in Teamsterville: Culture patterns of role enactment in an urban neighborhood. *Quarterly Journal of Speech, 61*(1), 13–22.

Philipsen, G., Coutu, L. M., & Covarrubias, P. (2005). Speech codes theory: Restatement, revisions, and response to criticisms. In W. B. Gudykunst (Ed.), *Theorizing about intercultural communication* (pp. 55–68). Thousand Oaks, CA: SAGE Publications.

Pierce, J. R. (1961). *Symbols, signals and noise: The nature and process of communication.* New York, NY: Harper & Brothers.

Pincus, J. D. (1986). Communication satisfaction, job satisfaction, and job performance. *Human Communication Research, 12*(3), 395–419.

Pineda, R. D., & Sowards, S. K. (2007). Flag waving as visual argument: 2006 immigration demonstrations and cultural citizenship. *Argumentation and Advocacy, 43*(3/4), 164–174.

Pirsig, R. A. (1991). *Lila: An inquiry into morals.* New York, NY: Bantam.

Pitard, J. (2017). A journey to the centre of the self: Positioning the researcher in autoethnography. *Forum: Qualitative Social Research, 18*(3), Art. 10.

Plato (1998a). *Gorgias* (J. H. Nichols Jr., Trans). Ithaca, NY: Cornell University Press.

Plato (1998b). *Phaedrus* (J. H. Nichols Jr., Trans). Ithaca, NY: Cornell University Press.

Plester, B., & Hutchison, A. (2016). Fun times: The relationship between fun and workplace engagement. *Employee Relations, 38*(3), 332–350.

Plump, B., & Geist-Martin, P. (2013). Collaborative intersectionality: Negotiating identity, liminal spaces, and ethnographic research. *Liminalities, 9*(2). http://liminalities.net/9-2/collaborative.pdf

Polk-Lepson Research Group (2012, January). *2012 Professionalism in the workplace study.* York, PA: Center for Professional Excellence, York College of Pennsylvania. Retrieved from: http://www.ycp.edu/media/york-website/cpe/2012-Professionalism-in-the-Workplace-Study.pdf

Polk-Lepson Research Group (2013, January). *2013 Professionalism in the workplace study.* York, PA: Center for Professional Excellence, York College of Pennsylvania. Retrieved from: http://www.ycp.edu/media/york-website/cpe/York-College-Professionalism-in-the-Workplace-Study-2013.pdf

Pollio, H. R., Jensen, P. R., & O'Neil, M. A. (2014). The semantics of time and space: A thematic analysis. *Journal of Psycholinguistic Research, 43*(1), 81–104.

Pollock, D. (1998). Performing writing. In P. Phelan & J. Lane (Eds.), *The ends of performance* (pp. 73–103). New York, NY: NYU Press.

Pomerantz, A. (1984). Agreeing and disagreeing with assessments: Some features of preferred/dispreferred turn shapes. In J. M. Atkinson & J. Heritage (Eds.), *Structures of social action: Studies in conversation analysis* (pp. 57–101). Cambridge, England: Cambridge University Press.

Pomerantz, A. (1990). Conversation analytic claims. *Communication Monographs, 57,* 231–235.

Pomerantz, A., Gill, V. T., & Denvir, P. (2007). When patients present serious health conditions as unlikely: Managing potentially conflicting issues and constraints. In A. Hepburn & S. Wiggins (Eds.), *Discourse research in practice: New approaches to psychology and interaction* (pp. 127–146). Cambridge, MA: Cambridge University Press.

Poole, M. S. (1983). Decision development in small groups, III: A multiple sequence model of group decision development. Communication Monographs, 50(4), 321.

Poole, M. S. (1983). Decision development in small groups: II A study of multiple sequences in decision making. *Communication Monographs, 50*(3), 206–232.

Poole, M. S. (1983). Decision development in small groups: III A multiple sequence model of group decision development. *Communication Monographs, 50*(4), 321–341.

Poole, M. S. (1999). Group communication theory. In L. R. Frey (Ed.), *The handbook of group communication theory and research* (pp. 37–70). Thousand Oaks, CA: SAGE Publications.

Poole, M. S. (2000). *Organizational change and innovation processes: Theory and methods for research.* New York, NY: Oxford.

Poole, M. S., & Real, K. (2003) Groups and teams in health care: Communication and effectiveness. In T. L. Thompson, A. M. Dorsey, K.

I. Miller, & R. Parrott (Eds.), *Handbook of health communication* (pp. 369–402). Mahwah, NJ: Erlbaum.

Poole, M. S., Seibold, D. R., & McPhee, R. D. (1985). Group decision-making as a structurational process. *Quarterly Journal of Speech, 71*(1), 74–102.

Popkin, S. (1996). *The reasoning voter: Communication and persuasion in presidential campaigns.* Chicago, IL: University of Chicago Press.

Popper, K. (1959). *The logic of scientific discovery.* New York, NY: Basic Books.

Popper, K. (1980). Science: Conjectures and refutations. In E. D. Klemke, R. Hollinger, & A. D. Kline (Eds.), *Introductory readings in the philosophy of science* (pp. 19–34). Buffalo, NY: Prometheus.

Porter, H., Wrench, J. S., & Hoskinson, C. (2007). The influence of supervisor temperament on subordinate job satisfaction and perceptions of supervisor sociocommunicative orientation and approachability. *Communication Quarterly, 55*(1), 129–153.

Postmes, T., Spears, R., & Cihangir, S. (2001). Quality decision making and group norms. *Journal of Personality and Social Psychology, 80,* 918–930.

Potter, J. W. (2004). Argument for the need for a cognitive theory of media literacy. *American Behavioral Scientist, 48*(2), 266–272

Potter, J. W. (2013). *Media literacy* (6th ed.). Thousand Oaks, CA: SAGE Publications.

Potter, J. W. (2016). *Introduction to media literacy.* Thousand Oaks, CA: SAGE Publications.

Poulakos, J. (1983). Toward a sophistic definition of rhetoric. *Philosophy and Rhetoric, 16*(1), 35–48.

Pourcain, B. S., Skuse, D. H., Mandy, W. P., Kai, W., Hakonarson, H., Timpson, N. J., … Smith, G. D. (2014). Variability in the common genetic architecture of social-communication spectrum phenotypes during childhood and adolescence. *Molecular Autism, 5*(1), 1–26.

Powell, L., & Cowart, J. (2013). *Political communication: Inside and out.* Boston, MA: Pearson.

Powell, L., Richmond, V. P., & G. Cantrell-Williams (2012). The "drinking-buddy" scale as a measure of para-social behavior. *Psychological Reports, 110*(3), 1029–1037.

Powers, J. H. (1995). On the intellectual structure of the human communication discipline. *Communication Education, 44,* 191–222.

Pozzebon, J. A., Visser, B. A., & Bogaert, A. F. (2012). Do you think you're sexy, tall and thin? The prediction of self-rated attractiveness, height, and weight. *Journal of Applied Social Psychology, 42,* 2671–2700.

Pratt, T. C., Turanovic, J. J., & Cullen, F. T. (2016). Revisiting the criminological consequences of exposure to fetal testosterone: A meta-analysis of the 2d:4d digit ratio. *Criminology: An Interdisciplinary Journal, 54*(4), 587–620.

PricewaterhouseCoopers LLP (2017, March). *UK economic outlook.* London: Author. Retrieved from: http://www.pwc.co.uk/economic-services/ukeo/pwc-uk-economic-outlook-full-report-march-2017-v2.pdf

Prior, M. E. (1962). *Science and the humanities.* Evanston, IL: Northwestern University Press.

Proulx, C. M., Helms, H. M., & Buehler, C. (2007). Marital quality and personal well-being: A meta-analysis. *Journal of Marriage and Family, 69*(3), 576–593.

Puccio, G. J. (2017). From the dawn of humanity to the 21st century: Creativity as an enduring survival skill. *The Journal of Creative Behavior, 51*(4), 330–334.

Purcell, K., Rainie, L., Heaps, A., Buchanan, J., Friedrich, L., … Zickuhr, K. (2012). *How teens do research in the digital world.* Washington, DC: Pew Research Center's Internet & American Life Project. Retrieved from http://pewinternet.org/Reports/2012/Student-Research

Putnam, L. L., & Pacanowsky, M. E. (Eds.). (1983). *Communication and organizations: An interpretive approach.* Beverly Hill, CA: SAGE Publications.

Qin, Z., Andreychik, M., Sapp, D. A., & Arendt, C. (2014). The dynamic interplay of interaction goals, emotion, and conflict styles: Testing a model of intrapersonal and interpersonal effects on conflict styles. *International Journal of Communication (19328036), 8,* 534–557.

Quintero Johnson, J. M., & Sangalang, A. (2017). Testing the explanatory power of two measures of narrative involvement: An investigation of the influence of transportation and narrative engagement on the process of narrative persuasion. *Media Psychology, 20*(1), 144–173.

Rahim, M. A. (2014). A model of managerial power bases: Alternative explanations of reported findings. *Current Topics in Management, 17,* 23–40.

Rainie, L., & Zickuhr, K. (2015, August). *Americans' views on mobile etiquette.* Washington, DC: Pew Research Center. Retrieved from: http://www.pewinternet.org/2015/08/26/americans-views-on-mobile-etiquette/

Ramsay, R. (2010, February 17). Meet the Flintstones. *The Texas Tribune* (online). Retrieved from: https://www.texastribune.org/2010/02/17/texans-dinosaurs-humans-walked-the-earth-at-same/

Rancer, A. S., Kosberg, R. L., & Baukus, R. A. (1992). Beliefs about arguing as predictors of trait argumentativeness: Implications for training in argument and conflict management. *Communication Education, 41*(4), 375–387.

Rancer, A. S., & Whitecap, V. G. (1997). Training in argumentativeness: Testing the efficacy of a communication training program. *Communication Education, 46*(4), 273.

Rand, E. J. (2012). Gay pride and its queer discontents: ACT UP and the political deployment of affect. *Quarterly Journal of Speech, 98*(1), 75–80.

Rasnic, S. R. (2016, July 21). Yes, it was plagiarism. *Inside Higher Education.* Retrieved from: https://www.insidehighered.com/views/2016/07/21/why-plagiarism-melania-trumps-speech-matters-essay

Rathnayake, C., & Winter, J. S. (2018). Carrying forward the uses and grats 2.0 agenda: An affordance-driven measure of social media uses and gratifications. *Journal of Broadcasting and Electronic Media, 62*(3), 371–389.

Raymond, G., & Heritage, J. (2006). The epistemics of social relations: Owning grandchildren. *Language in Society, 35*(5), 677–705.

Real, K., & Buckner, M. M. (2015). Interprofessional communication. In N. G. Harrington (Ed.), *Health communication: Theory, method, and application* (pp. 147–178). New York, NY: Routledge.

Real, K., & Poole, M. S. (2011). Health care teams: Communication and effectiveness. In T. L. Thompson, R. Parrott, & J. Nussbaum (Eds.), *The Routledge handbook of health communication* (2nd ed., pp. 100–116). New York, NY: Routledge.

Record, R. A. (2014). *Increasing compliance with a tobacco-free policy via a campus campaign* (Doctoral dissertation). University of Kentucky Theses and Dissertations-Communication.

Record, R. A. (2018). Genre-specific television viewing: State of the literature. *Annals of the International Communication Association, 42*(3), 155–180.

Record, R. A., Staricek, N., & Pavelek, M. (2014, November). The markings in your stall: A content analysis of bathroom graffiti in college-area bars. Paper presented at the National Communication Association Conference, Visual Communication Division, Chicago, IL.

Redding, C. (1972). *Communication within the organization: An interpretive review of theory and research.* New York, NY: Industrial Communication Council.

Reed, C., & Rowe, G. (2005). Translating Toulmin diagrams: Theory neutrality in argument representation. *Argumentation, 19*(3), 267–286.

Reinsel, D., Gantz, J., & Rydning, J. (2018, November). *The digitization of the world: From edge to core* (Data age 2025—IDC White Paper, Doc#US44413318). Cupterino, CA: Seagate. https://www.seagate.com/files/www-content/our-story/trends/files/idc-seagate-data-age-whitepaper.pdf

Retzinger, S. M. (1991). *Violent emotions: Shame and rage in marital quarrels.* Newbury Park, CA: SAGE Publications.

Rex, L. A., Thomas, E. E., & Engel, S. (2010). Applying Toulmin: Teaching logical reasoning and argumentative writing. *English Journal, 99*(6), 56–63.

Reynolds, G. (2012). *Presentation Zen: Simple ideas on presentation design and delivery.* Berkeley, CA: New Riders.

Rhodes, N., & Ewoldsen, D. R. (2013). Outcomes of persuasion: Behavioral, cognitive, and social. In J. P. Dillard & L. Shen (Eds.), *The SAGE handbook of persuasion* (2nd ed., pp. 53–69). Thousand Oaks, CA: SAGE Publications.

Rice, J. E. (2008). The new "new": Making a case for critical affect studies. *Quarterly Journal of Speech, 94*(2), 200–212.

Rice, R. E., & Foote, D. (2013). A systems-based evaluation planning model for health communication campaigns in developing countries. In R. E. Rice & C. K. Atkin (Eds.), *Public communication campaigns* (pp. 69–82). Los Angeles, CA: SAGE Publications.

Richardson, L. (2000). Writing: A method of inquiry. In N. K. Denzin & Y. S. Lincoln (Ed.), *Handbook of qualitative research* (2nd ed., pp. 923–948). Thousand Oaks, CA: SAGE Publications.

Rickert, T. (2013). *Ambient rhetoric: The attunements of rhetorical being.* Pittsburgh, PA: University of Pittsburgh Press.

Rideout, V. (2016). Measuring time spent with media: The Common Sense census of media use by US 8- to 18-year-olds. *Journal of Children and Media, 10*(1), 138–144.

Rimal, R. N., & Real, K. (2005). How behaviors are influenced by perceived norms a test of the theory of normative social behavior. *Communication Research, 32*(3), 389–414.

Risen, J. L., & Gilovich, T. (2007). Target and observer differences in the acceptance of questionable apologies. *Journal of Personality and Social Psychology, 92*(3), 418–433.

Ritts, V., Patterson, M. L., & Tubbs, M. E. (1992). Expectations, impressions, and judgments of physically attractive

Ritzer, G. (2014). Prosumption: Evolution, revolution, or eternal return of the same? *Journal of Consumer Culture, 14*(1), 3–24.

Ritzer, G. (2015). The "new" world of prosumption: Evolution, "return of the same," or revolution? *Sociological Forum, 30*(1), 1–17.

Roberto, A. J., Murray-Johnson, L., & Witte, K. (2011). International health communication campaigns in developing countries. The

Routledge handbook of health communication (pp. 220–234). New York, NY: Taylor & Francis.

Robinson, D. N. (1989). *Aristotle's psychology.* New York, NY: Columbia University Press.

Robinson, J. D. (2003). An interactional structure of medical activities during acute visits and its implications for patients' participation. *Health Communication, 15*(1), 27–57.

Robinson, J. D. (2004). The sequential organization of "explicit" apologies in naturally occurring English. *Research on Language and Social Interaction, 37*(3), 291–330.

Robinson, J. P., & Lee, C. W. (2014). Society's (virtually) time-free transition into the digital age. *Social Indicators Research, 117*(3), 939–965.

Robinson, J., & Nilsen, A. P. (2002). Skepticism: A literacy for our times. *Teaching English in the Two-Year College, 29*(3), 285–296.

Robles, T. F., Slatcher, R. B., Trombello, J. M., & McGinn, M. M. (2013). Marital quality and health: A meta-analytic review. *Psychological Bulletin, 140*(1), 140–187.

Robson, A., & Robinson, L. (2015). The information seeking and communication model. *Journal of Documentation, 71*(5), 1043–1069.

Rockstuhl, T., Dulebohn, J. H., Ang, S., & Shore, L. M. (2012). Leader–member exchange (LMX) and culture: A meta-analysis of correlates of LMX across 23 countries. *Journal of Applied Psychology, 97*(6), 1097–1130.

Roethlisberger, F. L., & Dickson, W. (1939). *Management and the worker.* New York, NY: John Wiley & Sons.

Rogelberg, S. G., Shanock, L. R., & Scott, C. W. (2012). Wasted time and money in meetings: Increasing return on investment. *Small Group Research, 43*(2), 236–245.

Rogers, E. M. (1962). *Diffusion of innovations.* New York, NY: The Free Press.

Rogers, E. M. (1997). *A history of communication study.* New York, NY: The Free Press.

Rogers, E. M., & Beal, G. M. (1958). The importance of personal influence in the adoption of technological changes. *Social Forces, 36,* 329–335.

Rogers, E. M., & Hart, W. B. (2002). The histories of intercultural, international, and development communication. In W. B. Gudykunst & B. Mody (Eds.), *Handbook of international and intercultural communication* (2nd ed., pp. 1–18). Thousand Oaks, CA: SAGE Publications.

Rogers, E. M., Hart, W. B., & Miike, Y. (2002). Edward T. Hall and the history of intercultural communication: The United States and Japan. *Keio Communication Review, 24,* 3–26.

Rogers-Pettie, C., & Herrmann, J. (2015). Information diffusion: A study of Twitter during large scale events. In S. Cetinkaya & J. K. Ryan (Eds.), *Proceedings of the 2015 Industrial and Systems Engineering Research Conference.* Retrieved from: http://www.isr.umd.edu/~jwh2/papers/Pettie-Herrmann-ISERC-2015.pdf

Roloff, M. E. (1981). *Interpersonal communication: The social exchange approach* (Vol. 6). Thousand Oaks, CA: SAGE Publications.

Roloff, M. E., & Wright, C. N. (2009). Message construction and editing. In Eadie, W. F. (Ed.), *21st Century communication: A reference handbook* (pp. 101–109). Thousand Oaks, CA: SAGE Publications.

Roque, G. (2015). Should visual arguments be propositional in order to be arguments? *Argumentation, 29*(2), 177–195.

Rose, S. (2013, November/December). The value of a college degree. *Change, 45*(6), 24–32.

Rose, S. M. (1984). How friendships end: Patterns among young adults. *Journal of Social and Personal Relationships, 1*, 267–277.

Rosenberg, R. (2014). Man arrested for stalking 'GMA's' Robin Roberts. *New York Post*. Retrieved from: http://pagesix.com/2014/07/30/creep-arrested-for-stalking-and-threatening-robin-roberts/

Rost, J. C. (1991). *Leadership for the twenty-first century*. New York, NY: Praeger.

Roter, D. L., & Hall, J. A. (2004). Physician gender and patient-centered communication: A critical review of empirical research. *Annual Review of Public Health, 25*, 497–519.

Roter, D. L., & Hall, J. A. (2006): *Doctors talking with patients/Patients talking with doctors* (2nd ed.). Westport, CT: Auburn House.

Roter, D. L., Stewart, M., Putnam, S. M., Lipkin, M., Stiles, W., & Inui, T. S. (1997). Communication patterns of primary care physicians. *JAMA: Journal of the American Medical Association, 277*(4), 350–356.

Rowe, D. D. (2013). Performative (re)writing: Valerie Solanas and the politics of scribble. *Women and Language, 36*(2), 107–113.

Rowe, W. E. (2014). Positionality. In D. Coghlan & M. Brydon-Miller (Eds.), *The SAGE encyclopedia of action research* (p. 628). Los Angeles, CA: SAGE Publications.

Rowold, J., Borgmann, L., & Diebig, M. (2015). A 'Tower of Babel'?—Interrelations and structure of leadership constructs. *Leadership and Organization Development Journal, 36*(2), 137–160.

Rowsell, J., Morrell, E., & Alvermann, D. E. (2017). Confronting the digital divide: Debunking brave new world discourses. *Reading Teacher, 71*(2), 157–165.

Rubin, A. M. (1981). An examination of television viewing motives. *Communication Research, 8*, 141–165.

Rubin, A. M. (2009). Uses-and-gratifications perspective on media effects. In J. Bryant & M. B. Oliver (Eds.), *Media effects: Advances in theory and research* (3rd ed., pp. 165–184). New York, NY: Routledge.

Rufo, K. (2009). Shades of Derrida: Materiality as the mediation of *différance*. In B. Biesecker and R. Lucaites (Eds.), *Rhetoric, materiality, and politics* (pp. 229–251). New York, NY: Peter Lang.

Rule, B. G., Bisanz, G. L., & Kohn, M. (1985). Anatomy of a persuasion schema: Targets, goals, and strategies. *Journal of Personality and Social Psychology, 48*(5), 1127–1140.

Rumpf, R. E. (2012). The predictors of parasocial interaction and their effects on perceived persuasiveness (Unpublished master's thesis). San Diego State University, San Diego, CA.

Russill, C. (2008). Tipping point forewarnings in climate change communication: Some implications of an emerging trend. *Environmental Communication, 2*(2), 133–153.

Sacks, H. (1984a). Notes on methodology. In J. M. Atkinson & J. Heritage (Eds.), *Structures of social action: Studies in conversation analysis* (pp. 21–27). Cambridge, England: Cambridge University Press.

Sacks, H. (1984b). On doing 'being ordinary'. In J. M. Atkinson & J. Heritage (Eds.), *Structures of social action: Studies in conversation analysis* (pp. 413–429). Cambridge, England: Cambridge University Press.

Sacks, H. (1992). *Lectures on conversation: Volumes I & II*. (G. Jefferson, Ed.). Hoboken, NJ: Wiley Blackwell.

Sacks, H., Schegloff, E., & Jefferson, G. (1974). A simplest systematics for the organization of turn-taking for conversation. *Language, 50*(4), 696–735.

Saffran, M. J. (2011). Effects of local-market radio ownership concentration on radio localism, the public interest, and listener opinions and use of local radio. *Journal of Radio and Audio Media, 18*(2), 281–294.

Salm, L. (2017, June 15). 70% of employers are snooping candidates' social media profiles. Retrieved from: https://www.careerbuilder.com/advice/social-media-survey-2017

Samovar, L. A., & Porter, R. E. (1972). *Intercultural communication: A reader*. Belmont, CA: Wadsworth.

Samp, J. A., & Humphreys, L. R. (2007). "I said what?" Partner familiarity, resistance, and the accuracy of conversational recall. *Communication Monographs, 74*(4), 561–581.

Sattel, J. (1976). The inexpressive male: Tragedy or sexual politics? *Social Problems, 23*(4), 469–477.

Savolainen, R. (2002). Network competence and information seeking on the Internet: From definitions towards a social cognitive model. *Journal of Documentation, 58*(2), 211–226.

Savolainen, R. (2017a). Contributions to conceptual growth: The elaboration of Seo, Y., Li, X., Choi, Y. K., & Yoon, S. (2018). Narrative transportation and paratextual features of social media in viral advertising. *Journal of Advertising, 47*(1), 83–95.

Savolainen, R. (2017b). Contributions to conceptual growth: The elaboration of Ellis's model for information-seeking behavior. *Journal of the Association for Information Science & Technology, 68*(3), 594–608.

Sawyer, C. R., & Behnke, R. R. (2009). Psychophysiological patterns of arousal in communication. In M. J. Beatty, J. C. McCroskey, & K. Floyd (Eds.), *Biological dimensions of communication: Perspectives, research, and methods* (pp. 197–210). Cresskill, NJ: Hampton Press.

Scanlon, P. M., & Neumann, D. R. (2002). Internet plagiarism among college students. *Journal of College Student Development, 43*(3), 374–385.

Scarduzio, J. A., & Geist-Martin, P. (2016). Workplace wellness campaigns: The four dimensions of a whole person approach. In T. Harrison & E. Williams (Eds.), *Organizations, health, and communication* (pp. 172–186). New York, NY: Routledge.

Schechner, R. (2002). *Performance studies: An introduction*. London, UK: Routledge.

Schechner, R. (2003). *Performance theory*. London, UK: Routledge.

Schechner, R., & Appel, W. (1990). *By means of performance: Intercultural studies of theatre and ritual*. Cambridge, UK: Cambridge University.

Schegloff, E. A. (1968). Sequencing in conversational openings. *American Anthropologist, 70*, 1075–1095.

Schegloff, E. A. (1986). The routine as achievement. *Human Studies, 9*, 111–151.

Schegloff, E. A. (1987). Some sources of misunderstanding in talk-in-interaction. *Linguistics: An Interdisciplinary Journal of the Language Sciences, 25*(1 [287]), 201–218.

Schegloff, E. A. (1991). Reflections on talk and social structure. In D. Boden & D. H. Zimmerman (Eds.), *Talk and social structure* (pp. 44–70). Cambridge, England: Polity Press.

Schegloff, E. A. (1996a). Issues of relevance for discourse analysis: contingency in action, interaction and co-participant context. In E. H. Hove & D. R. Scott (Eds.), *Computational and conversational discourse: Burning issues-an interdisciplinary account* (pp. 3–35). Berlin: Springer.

Schegloff, E. A. (1996b). Turn organization: One intersection of grammar and interaction. *Interaction and Grammar, 52–133*.

Schegloff, E. A. (1997). Whose text? Whose context? *Discourse & Society: An International Journal for the Study of Discourse and Communication in their Social, Political and Cultural Contexts, 8*(2), 165–187.

Schegloff, E. A. (2006). Interaction—the infrastructure for social institutions, the natural ecological niche for language, and the arena in which culture is enacted. *Roots of Human Sociality: Culture, Cognition and Interaction*, 70–96.

Schegloff, E. A. (2007). *Sequence organization in interaction: A primer in conversation analysis.* Cambridge, UK: Cambridge University Press.

Scheidel, T. M., & Crowell, L. (1964). Idea development in small discussion groups. *Quarterly Journal of Speech, 50*, 140–145.

Schein, E. H. (1993). *Organizational culture and leadership.* San Francisco, CA: Jossey-Bass.

Schiappa, E. (1990). Did Plato coin rhetorike? *American Journal of Philology, 111*(4), 457–470.

Schnake, M. E., Dumler, M. P., Cochran Jr., D. S., & Barnett, T. R. (1990). Effects of differences in superior and subordinate perceptions of superiors' communication practices. *Journal of Business Communication, 27*(1), 37–50.

Schönbach, P. (1980). A category system for account phases. *European Journal of Social Psychology, 10*(2), 195–200.

Schriesheim, C. A., Tepper, B. J., & Tetrault, L. A. (1994). Least preferred co-worker score, situational control, and leadership effectiveness: A meta-analysis of contingency model performance predictions. *Journal of Applied Psychology, 79*(4), 561–573.

Schultz, A., Moore, J., & Spitzberg, B. H. (2014). Once upon a midnight stalker: A content analysis of stalking in films. *Western Communication Journal, 78*(5), 612–636.

Schütz, A. (1999). It was your fault! Self-serving biases in autobiographical accounts of conflict in married couples. *Journal of Social and Personal Relationships, 19*, 193–208.

Schwarz, A. (December 14, 2013). The selling of attention deficit disorder. *New York Times.* Retrieved from: https://www.nytimes.com/2013/12/15/health/the-selling-of-attention-deficit-disorder.html

Schweitzer, N. J. (2008). Wikipedia and psychology: Coverage of concepts and its use by undergraduate students. *Teaching of Psychology, 35*(2), 81–85.

Scott, C. W., Shanock, L. R., & Rogelberg, S. G. (2012). Meetings at work: Advancing the theory and practice of meetings. *Small Group Research, 43*(2), 127–129.

Scott, G. G., Sinclair, J., Short, E., & Bruce, G. (2014). It's not what you say, it's how you say it: Language use on Facebook impacts employability but not attractiveness. *Cyberpsychology, Behavior, and Social Networking, 17*(8), 562–566.

Scott, R. L. (1967). On viewing rhetoric as epistemic. *Central States Speech Journal, 18*(1), 9–16.

Scott, R. L. (1976). On viewing rhetoric as epistemic: Ten years later. *Central States Speech Journal, 27*, 258–266.

Scott, S. D. (1993). Beyond reason: A feminist theory of ethics for journalism. *Feminist Issues, 13*, 23–40.

Searle, J. R. (1995). *The construction of social reality.* New York, NY: Free Press.

Sedikides, C., Gaertner, L., & Toguchi, Y. (2003). Pancultural self-enhancement. *Journal of Personality and Social Psychology, 84*(1), 60–79.

Seelig, C. (1956). Albert Einstein: A documentary biography. Retrieved from: http://todayinsci.com/E/Einstein_Albert/EinsteinAlbert-Quotations.htm

Seibold, D. R., Cantrill, J. G., & Meyers, R. A. (1985). Communication and interpersonal influence. In M. L. Knapp & G. R. Miller (Eds.), *Handbook of interpersonal communication* (pp. 551–611). Beverly Hills, CA: SAGE Publications.

Seligman, C., Bush, M., & Kirsch, K. (1976). Relationship between compliance in the foot-in-the-door paradigm and size of first request. *Journal of Personality and Social Psychology, 33*(5), 517–520.

Sellers, M. N. S. (2003). *Republican legal theory.* New York, NY: Macmillan.

Seo, Y., Li, X., Choi, Y. K., & Yoon, S. (2018). Narrative transportation and paratextual features of social media in viral advertising. *Journal of Advertising, 47*(1), 83–95.

Seyfarth, B. (2000). Structuration theory in small group communication: A review and agenda for future research. In M. E. Roloff (Ed.), *Communication Yearbook.* (Vol. 23, pp. 341–379). Thousand Oaks, CA: SAGE Publications.

Shafir, E. (Ed.). (2012). *The behavioral foundations of public policy.* Princeton, NJ: Princeton University Press.

Shafritz, J. M., & Ott, J. S. (2001). *Classics of organization theory* (5th ed.). Fort Worth, TX: Harcourt College Publishers.

Shannon, C. E., & Weaver, W. (1949). *The mathematical theory of communication.* Urbana, IL: University of Illinois Press.

Sharf, B. F., & Geist-Martin, P. (2014). Integrative medicine. In T. Thompson (Eds.) *Encyclopedia of health communication* (Vol. 2, pp. 727–729). Thousand Oaks, CA: SAGE Publications.

Sharf, B. F., Geist-Martin, P., Cosgriff-Hernandez, K. K., & Moore, J. (2012). Trailblazing healthcare: Institutionalizing and integrating complementary medicine. *Patient Education and Counseling, 89*(3), 434–438.

Sharf, B. F., Geist-Martin, P., & Moore, J. (2012). Communicating healing in a third space: Real and imagined forms of integrative medicine. In L. Harter (Ed.), *Imagining new normals: A narrative framework for health communication* (pp. 125–147). Dubuque, IA: Kendall Hunt.

Sharf, B. F., Harter, L. M., Yamasaki, J., & Haidet, P. (2011). Narrative turns epic: Continuing developments in health narrative scholarship. In T. L. Thompson, R. Parrott, & J. F. Nussbaum (Eds.). *The Routledge handbook of health communication* (2nd ed., pp. 36–51). New York, NY: Routledge.

Shaver, P. R., & Mikulincer, M. (2006). Attachment theory, individual psychodynamics, and relationship functioning. In A. L. Vangelisti & D. Perlman (Eds.), *The Cambridge handbook of personal relationships* (pp. 251–271). Cambridge, UK: Cambridge University Press.

Shaw, L. A. (2010). Divorce mediation outcome research: A meta-analysis. *Conflict Resolution Quarterly, 27*(4), 447–467.

Shaw, M. E. (1976). *Group dynamics: The psychology of small group behavior.* New York, NY: McGraw-Hill.

Sheer, V. (2011). Teenagers' use of MSN features, discussion topics, and online friendship development: The impact of media richness and communication control. *Communication Quarterly, 59*(1), 82–103.

Shelton, K., & Forbes Agency Council. (2017, October 30). The value of search results rankings. *Forbes.* Retrieved from: https://www.forbes.com/sites/forbesagencycouncil/2017/10/30/the-value-of-search-results-rankings/#fc7612c44d3a

Shen, X., Cheung, C. K., & Lee, M. O. (2013). What leads students to adopt information from Wikipedia? An empirical investigation into the role of trust and information usefulness. *British Journal of Educational Technology, 44*(3), 502–517.

Sherif, C., Sherif, M., & Nebergall, R. E. (1995). *Attitude and social change*. Philadelphia, PA: Saunders.

Sherif, M., & Hovland, C. I. (1965). *Social judgement*. New Haven, CT: Yale University Press.

Shields, D. C. (2000). Symbolic convergence and special communication theories: Sensing and examining dis/enchantment with the theoretical robustness of critical autoethnography. *Communication Monographs, 67*(4), 392–421.

Shin, C. I., & Jackson, R. L., II. (2003). A review of identity research in communication theory: Reconceptualizing cultural identity. In W. J. Starosta & G.-M. Chen (Eds.), *Ferment in the intercultural field: Axiology/value/praxis* (pp. 211–240). Thousand Oaks, CA: SAGE Publications.

Shin, Y. J., & Lu, Y. (2017). Hypothesis formulation. In M. Allen (Ed.), *The SAGE encyclopedia of communication research methods*. Los Angeles, CA: SAGE Publications.

Shu, Q., Tu, Q., & Wang, K. (2011). The Impact of computer self-efficacy and technology dependence on computer-related technostress: A social cognitive theory perspective. *International Journal of Human-Computer Interaction, 27*(10), 923–939.

Shuter, R. (1990). The centrality of culture. *Southern Communication Journal, 55*(3), 237–249.

Shuter, R. (2011). Robert T. Oliver: Trailblazer in intercultural communication. *China Media Research, 7*(2), 121–126.

Sidnell, J., & Stivers, T. (2013). *Handbook of conversation analysis*. Cambridge, England: Cambridge University Press.

Sillars, A. L., Canary, D. J., & Tafoya, M. (2004). Communication, conflict, and the quality of family relationships. In A. L. Vangelisti, A. L. Vangelisti (Eds.), *Handbook of family communication* (pp. 413–446). Mahwah, NJ: Erlbaum.

Sillars, A. L., Coletti, S. F., Parry, D., & Rogers, M. A. (1982). Coding verbal conflict tactics: Nonverbal and perceptual correlates of the 'avoidance–distributive–integrative' distinction. *Human Communication Research, 9*(1), 83–95.

Sillars, A. L. & Overall, N. C. (2017). Coding observed interaction. In In A. VanLear & D. J. Canary (Eds.), *Researching interactive communication behavior* (pp. 199–216). Thousand Oaks, CA: SAGE Publications.

Sillars, A. L., Roberts, L. J., Leonard, K. E., & Dun, T. (2000). Cognition during marital conflict: The relationship of thought and talk. *Journal of Social and Personal Relationships, 17*, 479–502.

Silles, M. A. (2009). The causal effect of education on health: Evidence from the United Kingdom. *Economics of Education Review, 28*(1), 122–128.

Simmons, N. (2014). "We're a culture, not a costume": Ethical analysis of a college student-led organization's anti-racism campaign. *Public Voices, 14*(1), 97–114.

Simons, D. J. (2013). Unskilled and optimistic: Overconfident predictions despite calibrated knowledge of relative skill. *Psychonomic Bulletin and Review, 20*(3), 601–607.

Sims, S. (2004). *Big Island Edition: Healing Vacations in Hawaii*. Honolulu, HI: Watermark Publishing.

Singer, B. (2008). Comment: Implication analysis as abductive inference. *Sociological Methodology, 38*(1), 75–83.

SINTEF. (2013, May 22). Big data, for better or worse: 90% of world's data generated over last two years. *ScienceDaily*. Retrieved July 10, 2019 from www.sciencedaily.com/releases/2013/05/130522085217.htm

Slade, C. (2003). Seeing reasons: Visual argumentation in advertisements. *Argumentation, 17*(2), 145.

Slocum, D., Allan, A., & Allan, M. M. (2011). An emerging theory of apology. *Australian Journal of Psychology, 63*(2), 83–92.

Slovic, P., Zionts, D., Woods, A. K., Goodman, R., & Jinks, D. (2013). Physic numbing and mass atrocity. In E. Shafir (Ed.), *Behavioral foundations of public policy* (pp. 126–142), Princeton, NJ: Princeton University Press.

Small, M. L., Morgan, N., Abar, C., & Maggs, J. L. (2011). Protective effects of parent-college student communication during the first semester of college. *Journal of American College Health, 59*(6), 547–554.

Smith, A., & Anderson, M. (2018, March). *Social media use in 2018*. Washington, DC: Pew Research Center. Retrieved from: www.pew-internet.org/2018/03/01/social-media-use-in-2018/

Smith, K. K. (2017). Organizational communication. In M. Allen (Ed.), *The SAGE encyclopedia of communication research methods*. Los Angeles, CA: SAGE Publications.

Smith, T. J., III (1988). Diversity and order in communication theory: The uses of philosophical analysis. *Communication Quarterly, 36*(3), 28–40.

Smith, W. (2002). From prevention vaccines to community care: New ways to look at program success. In R. C. Hornik (Ed.), *Public health communication: Evidence for behavior change* (pp. 327–356). Mahwah, NJ: Erlbaum.

Smith, W. C., Anderson, E., Salinas, D., Horvatek, R., & Baker, D. P. (2015). A meta-analysis of education effects on chronic disease: The causal dynamics of the population education transition curve. *Social Science and Medicine, 127*, 29–40.

Snow, C. P. (1959). *The two cultures*. London, UK: Cambridge University Press.

Snyder, L. B., & LaCroix, J. M. (2013). How effective are mediated health campaigns? A synthesis of meta-analyses. In R. E. Rice & C. K. Atkin (Eds.), *Public communication campaigns* (4th ed., pp. 113–132). Thousand Oaks, CA: SAGE Publications.

Solanas, V. (1967). *SCUM Manifesto*. London: Verso.

Sommer, R. (1967). Sociofugal space. *American Journal of Sociology, 72*(6), 654–660.

Song, I., LaRose, R., Eastin, M. S., & Lin, C. A. (2004). Internet gratifications and internet addiction: On the uses and abuses of new media. *CyberPsychology & Behavior, 7*(4), 384–394.

Sontag, S. (1977). *Illness as metaphor*. New York, NY: Farrar, Straus, and Giroux.

Sorrells, K. (2013). *Intercultural communication: Globalization and social justice*. Los Angeles, CA: SAGE Publications.

Sorrells, K., & Nakagawa, G. (2008). Intercultural communication praxis and the struggle for social responsibility and social justice. In O. Swartz (Ed.), *Transformative communication studies: Culture, hierarchy, and the human condition* (pp. 17–43). Leicester, UK: Troubador.

Soulliere, D., Britt, D. W., & Maines, D. R. (2001). Conceptual modeling as a toolbox for grounded theorists. *Sociological Quarterly, 42*(2), 253–269.

Sparks, G. G. (2013). *Media effects research: A basic overview*. Boston, MA: Wadsworth

Speer, S. A. (2014). Reflecting on the ethics and politics of collecting interactional data: Implications for training and practice. *Human Studies, 37*, 279–286

Speer, S. A., & Stokoe, L. (2011). *Gender and conversation*. Cambridge, UK: Cambridge University Press.

SpencerStuart, Inc. (2004). 2004 CEO study: A statistical snapshot of leading CEOs. Retrieved from: http://www.antolin-davies.com/research/ceos.pdf

Spender, D. (1980). *Man-made language*. Boston, MA: Routledge.

Spitzack, C., & Carter, K. (1987). Women in communication studies: A typology for revision. *The Quarterly Journal of Speech, 73*(4), 401–423.

Spitzberg, B. H. (1989). Issues in the development of a theory of interpersonal competence in the intercultural context. *International Journal of Intercultural Relations, 13*, 241–268.

Spitzberg, B. H. (1993). The dialectics of (in)competence. *Journal of Social and Personal Relationships, 10*(1), 137–158.

Spitzberg, B. H. (1994). The dark side of (in)competence. In W. R. Cupach & B. H. Spitzberg (Eds.), *The dark side of interpersonal communication* (pp. 25–49). Hillsdale, NJ: Erlbaum.

Spitzberg, B. H. (1997). Intimate violence. In W. R. Cupach & D. J. Canary, *Competence in interpersonal conflict* (pp. 174–201). New York, NY: McGraw-Hill.

Spitzberg, B. H. (2000). What is good communication? *Journal of the Association for Communication Administration, 29*(1), 103–119.

Spitzberg, B. H. (2006). Preliminary development of a model and measure of computer-mediated communication (CMC) competence. *Journal of Computer-Mediated Communication, 11*(2), 629–666.

Spitzberg, B. H. (2007). *CSRS: The conversational skills rating scale—An instructional assessment of interpersonal competence* (NCA Diagnostic Series, 2nd ed.). Annandale, VA: National Communication Association.

Spitzberg, B. H. (2009a). Aggression, violence, and hurt in close relationships. In A. L. Vangelisti (Ed.), *Feeling hurt in close relationships* (pp. 209–232). Cambridge, UK: Cambridge University Press.

Spitzberg, B. H. (2009b). Axioms for a theory of intercultural communication competence *Annual Review of English Learning and Teaching,* [Japanese Association of Communication and English Teachers] *No.14*, 69–81.

Spitzberg, B. H. (2010a). Intimate partner violence and aggression: Seeing the light in a dark place. In W. R. Cupach & B. H. Spitzberg (Eds.), *The dark side of close relationships* (2nd ed., pp. 327–380). New York, NY: Routledge.

Spitzberg, B. H. (2010b). Intimate violence. In W. R. Cupach, D. J. Canary, & B. H. Spitzberg (Eds.), *Competence in interpersonal conflict* (2nd ed., pp. 211–252). Long Grove, IL: Waveland Press.

Spitzberg, B. H. (2011). The interactive media package for assessment of communication and critical thinking (IMPACCT©): Testing a programmatic online communication competence assessment system. *Communication Education, 60*(2), 145–173.

Spitzberg, B. H. (2013a). (Re)Introducing communication competence to the health professions. *Journal of Public Health Research, 2*(3), 126–135.

Spitzberg, B. H. (2013b). Intimate partner violence. In J. G. Oetzel & S. Ting-Toomey (Eds.), *The SAGE handbook of conflict communication* (2nd ed., pp. 187–210). Thousand Oaks, CA: SAGE Publications.

Spitzberg, B. H. (2014). Toward a model of meme diffusion (M³D). *Communication Theory, 24*, 311–339.

Spitzberg, B. H. (2015a). Assessing the state of assessment: Communication competence. In A. F. Hannawa & B. H. Spitzberg (Eds.), *Communication competence* (Vol. 22, pp. 559–584). Boston, MA: De Gruyter Mouton.

Spitzberg, B. H. (2015b). Epilogue: Problems, paradoxes, and prospects in the study of communication competence. In A. F. Hannawa & B. H. Spitzberg (Eds.), *Communication competence* (Vol. 22, pp. 745–755). Boston, MA: De Gruyter Mouton.

Spitzberg, B. H. (2015c). Is past prologue, or just passed and lacking presence? *International Journal of Intercultural Relations, 48*, 24–26.

Spitzberg, B. H. (2015d). The composition of competence: Communication skills. In A. F. Hannawa & B. H. Spitzberg (Eds.), *Communication competence* (Vol 22, pp. 237–269). Boston, MA: De Gruyter Mouton.

Spitzberg, B. H. (2019). Traces of pace, place and space in personal relationships: The chronogeometrics of studying relationships at scale [Distinguished Scholar lead essay]. *Personal Relationships, 26*(2), 184–208.

Spitzberg, B. H., & Brunner, C. C. (1991). Toward a theoretical integration of context and competence inference research. *Western Journal of Speech Communication, 56*, 28–46.

Spitzberg, B. H., Canary, D. J., & Cupach, W. R. (1994). A competence-based approach to the study of interpersonal conflict. In D.D. Cahn (Ed.), *Conflict in personal relationships* (pp. 183–202). Hillsdale, NJ: Erlbaum.

Spitzberg, B. H., & Cupach, W. R. (2002). Interpersonal skills. In M. L. Knapp & J. A. Daly (Eds.), *Handbook of interpersonal communication* (3rd ed., pp. 564–611). Newbury Park, CA: SAGE Publications.

Spitzberg, B. H., & Cupach, W. R. (2009). Unwanted communication, aggression, and abuse. In W. F. Eadie (Ed.), *21st century communication* (pp. 454–462). Thousand Oaks, CA: SAGE Publications.

Spitzberg, B. H., & Cupach, W. R. (2011). Interpersonal skills. In M. L. Knapp & J. A. Daly (Eds.), *Handbook of interpersonal communication* (4th ed., pp. 481–524). Newbury Park, CA: SAGE Publications

Spitzberg, B. H., & Cupach, W. R. (2014). *The dark side of relationship pursuit: From attraction to obsession and stalking* (2nd ed.). New York, NY: Routledge.

Spitzberg, B. H., Cupach, W. R., Hannawa, A. F., & Crowley, J. (2014). A preliminary test of a relational goal pursuit theory of obsessive relational intrusion and stalking. *Studies in Communication Sciences, 14*(1), 29–36.

Stafford, L. (2011). Measuring relationship maintenance behaviors: Critique and development of the revised relationship maintenance behavior scale. *Journal of Social and Personal Relationships, 28*(2), 278–303.

Stafford, L., & Canary, D. J. (1991). Maintenance strategies and romantic relationship type, gender and relational characteristics. *Journal of Social and Personal Relationships, 8*(2), 217–242.

Stafford, L., & Canary, D. J. (2006). Equity and interdependence as predictors of relational maintenance strategies. *Journal of Family Communication, 6*(4), 227–254.

Stafford, L., & Daly, J. A. (1984). Conversational memory: The effects of recall mode and memory expectancies on remembrances of natural conversations. *Human Communication Research, 10*(3), 379–402.

Stake, R. E., & Trumbull, D. J. (1982). Naturalistic generalizations. *Review Journal of Philosophy and Social Science, 7*(1), 1–12.

Stapleton, P., & Wu, Y. (2015). Assessing the quality of arguments in students' persuasive writing: A case study analyzing the relationship between surface structure and substance. *Journal of English for Academic Purposes, 17,* 12–23.

Stattner, E., Eugenie, R., & Collard, M. (2015). How do we spread on Twitter? *Proceedings of the IEEE 9th International Conference on Research Challenges in Information Science (RCIS).* (pp. 334–341). Retrieved from: https://ieeexplore.ieee.org/stamp/stamp.jsp?arnumber=7128894

Steele, G. A., & Plenty, D. (2015). Supervisor–subordinate communication competence and job and communication satisfaction. *International Journal of Business Communication, 52*(3), 294–318.

Stepanikova, I., Nie, N. H., & He, X. (2010). Time on the Internet at home, loneliness, and life satisfaction: Evidence from panel time-diary data. *Computers in Human Behavior, 26*(3), 329–338.

Stephen, T. D. (2008). Measuring the reputation and productivity of communication programs. *Communication Education, 57*(3), 297–311.

Stephen, T., & Geel, R. (2007). Normative publication productivity of communication scholars at selected career milestones. *Human Communication Research, 33*(1), 103–118.

Stern, C. S., & Henderson, B. B. (1993). *Performance studies: Texts and contexts.* London, UK: Longman Publishing Group.

Stern, D. (1980). *The first relationship: Mother and infant.* Cambridge, MA: Harvard University Press.

Stewart, R. A., & Roach, K. D. (1998). Argumentativeness and the theory of reasoned action. *Communication Quarterly, 46*(2), 177–193.

Stivers, T. (2007). *Prescribing under pressure: Physician-parent conversations and antibiotics.* New York, NY: Oxford University Press.

Stodgill, R. M. (1974). *Handbook of leadership.* New York: The Free Press.

Stogdill, R. M. (1948). Personal factors associated with leadership; a survey of the literature. *Journal of Psychology: Interdisciplinary and Applied, 25,* 35–71.

Stolzenberg, L., Eitle, D., & D'Alessio, S. J. (2006). Race, economic inequality, and crime. *Journal of Criminal Justice, 34*(3), 303–316.

Stormer, N., & McGreavy, B. (2017). Thinking ecologically about rhetoric's ontology: Capacity, vulnerability, and resilience. *Philosophy and Rhetoric, 50*(1), 1–25.

Storms, M. (1973). Videotape and the attribution process: Reversing actors' and observers' points of view. *Journal of Personality and Social Psychology, 27,* 165–175.

Streeck, J., Goodwin, C., & LeBaron, C. (2011). *Embodied interaction. Language and body in the material world.* Cambridge, UK: Cambridge University Press.

Street, R. L., Krupat, E., Bell, R. A., Kravitz, R. L., & Haidet, P. (2003). Beliefs about control in the physician-patient relationship: Effect on communication in medical encounters. *Journal of General Internal Medicine, 18*(8), 609–616.

Strine, M. S., Long, B. W., & Hopkins, M. F. (1991). Research in interpretation and performance studies: Trends, issues and priorities. In G. M. Phillips & J. T. Wood (Ed.), *Speech communication: Essays to commemorate the 75th anniversary of the Speech Communication Association.* (pp. 191–201). Carbondale, IL: Southern Illinois University Press.

Strobel, A., Fleischhauer, M., Bauer, D., & Müller, S. (2014). The relation of need for cognition to information acquisition and media usage. *Personality and Individual Differences, 60,* S9.

Sunnafrank, M. (1986). Predicted outcome value during initial interactions: A reformulation of uncertainty reduction theory. *Human Communication Research, 13*(1), 3–33.

Swift, A. (2017, May 22). *In U.S., belief in creationist view of humans at new low.* Gallup.com. Retrieved from: https://news.gallup.com/poll/210956/belief-creationist-view-humans-new-low.aspx

Syfers, J. (2000). I want a wife. In E. Ashton-Jones, G. A. Olson, & M. G. Perry (Eds.), *The gender reader* (2nd ed., pp. 390–393). Boston, MA: Allyn & Bacon.

Szell, M., Grauwin, S., & Ratti, C. (2014). Contraction of online response to major events. *PLOS One, 9*(2), 1–9. e89052.

Tal-Or, N., & Cohen, J. (2010). Understanding audience involvement: Conceptualizing and manipulating identification and transportation. *Poetics, 38,* 402–418.

Tamborini, C. R., ChangHwan K., & Sakamoto, A. (2015). Education and lifetime earnings in the United States. *Demography, 52,* 1383–1407. doi: 10.1007/s13524-015-0407-0

Tannen, D. (1990). *You just don't understand.* New York, NY: Ballantine Books.

Tannenbaum, M. B., Hepler, J., Zimmerman, R. S., Saul, L., Jacobs, S., Wilson, K., & Albarracín, D. (2015). Appealing to fear: A meta-analysis of fear appeal effectiveness and theories. *Psychological Bulletin, 141*(6), 1178–1204.

Taylor, D. A., & Altman, I. (1987). Communication in interpersonal relationships: Social penetration processes. In M. E. Roloff, G. R. Miller, M. E. Roloff, & G. R. Miller (Eds.), *Interpersonal processes: New directions in communication research* (pp. 257–277). Thousand Oaks, CA: SAGE Publications.

Taylor, F. W. (1947). *Principles of scientific management.* New York: Harper & Brothers.

Taylor, J. L. (2013). *"What can you teach me?": (Re)thinking responses to difference for multidisciplinary teamwork.* Conference Proceedings from the American Society for Engineering Education, Atlanta, GA. Retrieved from: http://www.asee.org/public/conferences/20/papers/7065/view

Taylor, J. L. & Canary, H. E. (2017). Organizing prostitution through silence^discourse: Unveiling masks of a masquerade. *Western Journal of Communication, 81,* 21–42.

Taylor, J. R., & Van Every, E. J. (2000). *The emergent organization.* Mahwah, NJ: Erlbaum

Taylor, P., Parker, K., Fry, R., Cohn, D., Wang, W., Velasco, G., & Dockterman, D. (2011, May 16). Is college worth it? College presidents, public assess value, quality and mission of higher education. Washington, DC: Pew Research Center. Retrieved from: http://www.pewsocialtrends.org/2011/05/15/is-college-worth-it/

Tennyson, A. (1850). *In memoriam A. H. H.* Retrieved from: https://en.wikipedia.org/wiki/In_Memoriam_A.H.H.

Teven, J. J. (2007). Effects of supervisor social influence, nonverbal immediacy, and biological sex on subordinates' perceptions of job satisfaction, liking, and supervisor credibility. *Communication Quarterly, 55*(2), 155–177.

Thier, M. (2008). Media and science: Developing skepticism and critical thinking. *Science Scope, 32*(3), 20–23.

Third, A. (2006). "Shooting from the hip": Valerie Solanas, SCUM and the apocalyptic politics of radical feminism. *Hecate, 32*(2), 104–132.

Thomas, G. F., Zolin, R., & Hartman, J. L. (2009). The central role of communication in developing trust and its effect on employee involvement. *Journal of Business Communication, 46*(3), 287–310.

Thompson, B., & Kinne, S. (1999). Social change theory: Applications to community health. In N. Bracht (Ed.), *Health promotion at the community level: New advances* (2nd ed., pp. 29–46). Thousand Oaks, CA: SAGE Publications.

Thompson, J. M., Teasdale, B., Duncan, S., van Emde Boas, E., Budelmann, F., Maguire, L., & Dunbar, R. I. M. (2018). Individual differences in transportation into narrative drama. *Review of General Psychology, 22*(2), 210–219.

Thompson, T. L., Robinson, J. D., & Brashers, D. E. (2011). Interpersonal communication and health care. In M. L. Knapp & J. A. Daly (Eds.), *The SAGE handbook of interpersonal communication* (4th ed., pp. 633–677). Thousand Oaks, CA: SAGE Publications.

Thompson, T. L., Whaley, B. B., & Stone, A. M. (2011). Issues concerning the co-construction of explications. *The Routledge handbook of health communication* (pp. 293–305). New York, NY: Taylor & Francis.

Thulman, D. (2014). The role of nondeclarative memory systems in the inference of long-term population continuity. *Journal of Archaeological Method and Theory, 21*(4), 724–749.

Tian, X., Schrodt, P., & Carr, K. (2016). The theory of motivated information management and posttraumatic growth: emerging adults' uncertainty management in response to an adverse life experience. *Communication Studies, 67*(3), 280–301.

Timmerman, C. E., & Madhavapeddi, S. N. (2008). Perceptions of organizational media richness: Channel expansion effects for electronic and traditional media across richness dimensions. *IEEE Transactions on Professional Communication, 51*(1), 18–32.

Ting-Toomey, S. (1999). *Communicating across cultures.* New York, NY: Guilford.

Toffler, A. (1980). *The third wave.* New York, NY: William Morrow.

Tokunaga, R. S. (2014). Relational transgressions on social networking sites: Individual, interpersonal, and contextual explanations for dyadic strain and communication rules change. *Computers in Human Behavior, 39*, 287–295.

Tolstoy, L. (1899). *Anna Karénina* (Vol. 1). New York, NY: Thomas Y. Crowell.

Tompkins, P. K. (1993). *Organizational communication imperatives: Lessons of the space program.* Los Angeles, CA: Roxbury.

Torok, R. (2010). "Make a bomb in your mums kitchen": Cyber recruiting and socialisation of 'white moors' and home grown Jihadists. *Proceedings of the 1st Australian Counter Terrorism Conference.* Sidney, Australia.

Torpey, E. (2018, April). Measuring the value of education. *Career Outlook.* Washington, DC: U.S. Bureau of Labor Statistics. Retrieved September, 10, 2019: https://www.bls.gov/careeroutlook/2018/data-on-display/education-pays.htm

Toulmin, S. (1958). *The uses of argument.* Cambridge, UK: Cambridge University Press.

Towns, A. R. (2015). The (racial) biases of communication: Rethinking media and blackness. *Social Identities, 21*(5), 474–488.

Tracy, S. J. (2010). Qualitative quality: Eight "big-tent" criteria for excellent qualitative research. *Qualitative Inquiry, 16*(10), 837–851.

Tracy, S. J. (2013). *Qualitative research methods: Collecting evidence, crafting analysis, communicating impact.* Malden, MA: Wiley-Blackwell.

Trager, G. L. (1958) Paralanguage: A first approximation. *Studies in Linguistics, 13*, 1–12.

Trethewey, A. (1999). Disciplined bodies: Women's embodied identities at work. *Organizational Studies, 20*, 423–450.

Trippe, B., & Baumoel, D. (2015). Beyond the Thomas–Kilmann model: Into extreme conflict. *Negotiation Journal, 31*(2), 89–103.

Trujillo, N. (1985). Organizational communication as cultural performance: Some managerial considerations. *Southern Speech Communication Journal, 50*(3), 201–224.

Tseronis, A. (2018). Multimodal argumentation: Beyond the verbal/visual divide. *Semiotica, 2018*(220), 41–67.

Tsfati, Y., & Cappella, J. N. (2005). Why do people watch news they do not trust? The need for cognition as a moderator in the association between news media skepticism and exposure. *Media Psychology, 7*(3), 251–271.

Tsfati, Y., & Peri, Y. (2006). Mainstream media skepticism and exposure to sectorial and extranational news media: The case of Israel. *Mass Communication and Society, 9*(2), 165–187.

Tufte, E. R. (2006). *The cognitive style of PowerPoint: Pitching out corrupts within.* Cheshire, CT: Graphics Press.

Turanovic, J. J., Pratt, T. C., & Piquero, A. R. (2017). Exposure to fetal testosterone, aggression, and violent behavior: A meta-analysis of the 2d:4d digit ratio. *Aggression and Violent Behavior, 33*, 51–61.

Turner, J. H. (1985). In defense of positivism. *Sociological Theory, 3*(2), 24–30.

Turner, J. H. (1986). The theory of structuration. *American Journal of Sociology, 91*, 969–977.

Turner, J. H. (1990). The misuse and use of metatheory. *Sociological Forum, 5*(1), 37–53.

Turner, J. H. (1991). Developing cumulative and practical knowledge through metatheorizing. *Sociological Perspectives, 34*(3), 249–268.

Turner, V. (1982). *From ritual to theatre: The human seriousness of play.* New York, NY: Performing Arts Journal Publications.

Turner, V. (1990). Are there universals of performance in myth, ritual and drama? In R. Schechner & W. Appel (Eds.), *By means of performance: Intercultural studies of theatre and ritual* (pp. 8–18.). Cambridge, UK: Cambridge University Press.

Turner, V. (2002). Liminality and communitas. In H. Bial (Ed.), *The performance studies reader* (pp. 79–87). London, UK: Routledge.

Turnitin. (2012). *What's wrong with Wikipedia? Evaluating the sources used by* students. Oakland, CA: iParadigms, LLC. Retrieved from: http://pages.turnitin.com/rs/iparadigms/images/Turnitin_White-Paper_EvaluatingSources.pdf

Twenge, J. M., Konrath, S., Foster, J. D., Campbell, W. K., & Bushman, B. J. (2008). Egos inflating over time: A cross-temporal meta-analysis of the narcissistic personality inventory. *Journal of Personality, 76*(4), 875–902.

Twenge, J. M., Martin, G. N., & Campbell, W. K. (2018). Decreases in psychological well-being among American adolescents after 2012 and links to screen time during the rise of smartphone technology. *Emotion.* Online first: doi: 10.1037/emo0000403

Twenge, J. M., Martin, G. N., & Spitzberg, B. H. (2018). Trends in U.S. adolescents' media use, 1976–2015: The rise of the Internet, the decline of TV, and the (near) demise of print. *Psychology of Popular Media Culture*. Advance online publication: http://dx.doi.org/10.1037/ppm0000203/

Twenge, J. M., & Park, H. (2018). The decline in adult activities among U.S. adolescents, 1976–2016. *Child Development*. Online first.

Twenge, J., Spitzberg, B. H., & Campbell, W. K. (2019). Less in-person social interaction with peers among U.S. adolescents in the 21st century and links to loneliness. *Journal of Social and Personal Relationships, 36*(6), 1892–1913.

U.S. Centers for Disease Control. (2019). Defining health literacy. *Health Literacy for Public Health Professionals*. Retrieved from: https://www.cdc.gov/healthliteracy/training/page572.html

U.S. Census Bureau. (2012). 2010 Census shows interracial and interethnic married couples grew by 28 percent over decade. Retrieved from: https://www.census.gov/newsroom/releases/archives/2010_census/cb12-68.html

U.S. Census Bureau. (2014, July 10). Census Bureau reports majority of STEM college graduates do not work in STEM occupations. Retrieved from: http://www.census.gov/newsroom/press-releases/2014/cb14-130.html

U.S. Department of Education. (2016, November). Fact Sheet: Department of Education announces release of new program-level gainful employment earnings data. Washington, DC: Author. Retrieved from: http://www2.ed.gov/documents/press-releases/ge-fact-sheet-online.pdf

Unsoeld, W. (n.d.). *Willi Unsoeld: Brief biography & quotes*. Retrieved from: http://www.wilderdom.com/Unsoeld.htm

Uranowitz, S. W. (1975). Helping and self-attributions: A field experiment. *Journal of Personality and Social Psychology, 31*(5), 852–854.

Usher, N. (2017). The appropriation/amplification model of citizen journalism. *Journalism Practice, 11*(2/3), 247–265.

Valente, T. W., & Kwan, P. P. (2013). Evaluating communication campaigns. In R. E. Rice & C. K. Atkin (Eds.), *Public communication campaigns* (4th ed., pp. 83–98). Thousand Oaks, CA: SAGE Publications.

Valenzuela, S., Halpern, D., & Katz, J. E. (2014). Social network sites, marriage well-being and divorce: Survey and state-level evidence from the United States. *Computers in Human Behavior, 36*, 94–101.

van de Vliert, E., & Euwema, M. C. (1994). Agreeableness and activeness as components of conflict behaviors. *Journal of Personality and Social Psychology, 66*(4), 674–687.

van der Goot, M. H., Tomasello, M., & Liszkowski, U. (2014). Differences in the nonverbal requests of great apes and human infants. *Child Development, 85*(2), 444–455.

van der Meulen, S., & Bruinsma, M. (2018). Man as 'aggregate of data'. *AI and Society*. Online first: https://doi.org/10.1007/s00146-018-0852-6

Van Eerde, W., & Thierry, H. (1996). Vroom's expectancy models and work-related criteria: A meta-analysis. *Journal of Applied Psychology, 81*(5), 575–586.

Van Laer, T., Ruyter, K. D., Visconti, L. M., & Wetzels, M. (2014). The extended transportation-imagery model: A meta-analysis of the antecedents and consequences of consumers' narrative transportation. *Journal of Consumer Research, 40*(5), 797–817.

VanLear, C. A. (2017). Modeling and analyzing behaviors and the dynamics of behavioral interaction. In A. VanLear & D. J. Canary, *Researching interactive communication behavior: A sourcebook of methods and measures*, pp. 235–260. Thousand Oaks, CA: Sage.

Van Maanen, J. (1988). *Tales of the field: On writing ethnography*. Chicago, IL: University of Chicago Press.

VanLear, A., & Canary, D. J. (Eds.). (2017). *Researching interactive communication behavior: A sourcebook of methods and measures*. Thousand Oaks, CA: SAGE Publications.

Varnum, M. W. (2015). Higher in status, (even) better-than-average. *Frontiers in Psychology, 6*.

Varricchio, M. (1999). Power of images/images of power in *Brave New World* and *Nineteen Eighty-Four*. *Utopian Studies, 10*(1), 98–114.

Velázquez-Quesada, F. R. (2015). Reasoning processes as epistemic dynamics. *Axiomathes: An International Journal in Ontology and Cognitive Systems, 25*(1), 41–60.

Venable, T. L. (1998). Errors as teaching tools—the mass media mistake. *Journal of College Science Teaching, 28*(1), 33–37.

Verhage, M. L., Schuengel, C., Madigan, S., Fearon, R. P., Oosterman, M., Cassibba, R., … van Ijzendoorn, M. H. (2016). Narrowing the transmission gap: A synthesis of three decades of research on intergenerational transmission of attachment. *Psychological Bulletin, 142*(4), 337–366.

Villagran, M., & Weathers, M. R. (2015). Providers' perspectives on health communication: Influences, processes, and outcomes. In N. G. Harrington (Ed.), *Health communication: Theory, method, and application* (pp. 87–115). New York, NY: Routledge.

Viswesvaran, C., Schmidt, F. L., & Ones, D. S. (2002). The moderating influence of job performance dimensions on convergence of supervisory and peer ratings of job performance. *Journal of Applied Psychology, 87*(2), 345–354.

Vitanza, V. J. (1997). *Negation, subjectivity, and the history of rhetoric*. Albany, NY: SUNY Press.

Vizcarrondo, T. (2013). Measuring concentration of media ownership: 1976–2009. *JMM: The International Journal on Media Management, 15*(3), 177–195.

Voelker, T., Love, L., & Pentina, I. (2012). Plagiarism: What don't they know? *Journal of Education for Business, 87*(1), 36–41.

von Bertalanffy, L. (1951a). General system theory: A new approach to unity of science. 1. Problems of general system theory. *Human Biology, 23*(4), 302–312.

von Bertalanffy, L. (1951b). General system theory: A new approach to unity of science. 5. Conclusion. *Human Biology, 23*(4), 337–345.

von Bertalanffy, L. (1968). *General systems theory: Foundations, development, applications* (Rev. ed.). New York, NY: George Braziller.

von Bertalanffy, L. (1975). *Perspectives on general systems theory*. New York, NY: George Braziller.

Vosoughi, S., Roy, D., & Aral, S. (2018). The spread of true and false news online. *Science, 359*(6380), 1146–1151.

Vroom, V. H. (1964). *Work and motivation*. New York, NY: Wiley.

Wade, D. T., & Halligan, P. W. (2004). Do biomedical models of illness make for good healthcare systems? *BMJ: British Medical Journal, 329*, 1398–1401.

Walker, G. B., & Bender, M. A. (1994). Is it more than rock and roll?: Considering music video as argument. *Argumentation and Advocacy, 31*(2), 64.

Wallace, K. R. (1955). An ethical basis of communication. *The Speech Teacher, 4,* 1–9.

Walster, E., Berscheid, E., & Walster, G. W. (1973). New directions in equity research. *Journal of Personality and Social Psychology, 25*(2), 151–176.

Walter, N., Cody, M. J., Xu, L. Z., & Murphy, S. T. (2018). A priest, a rabbi, and a minister walk into a bar: A meta-analysis of humor effects on persuasion. *Human Communication Research, 44*(4), 343–373.

Walter, N., Tukachinsky, R., Pelled, A., & Nabi, R. (2019). Meta-analysis of anger and persuasion: An empirical integration of four models. *Journal of Communication, 69*(1), 73–93.

Walter, T. (1991). Modern death: Taboo or not taboo? *Sociology, 25*(2), 293–310.

Walther, J. B. (2017). The merger of mass and interpersonal communication via new media: Integrating metaconstructs. *Human Communication Research, 43*(4), 559–572.

Wang, G., Oh, I., Courtright, S. H., & Colbert, A. E. (2011). Transformational leadership and performance across criteria and levels: A meta-analytic review of 25 years of research. *Group and Organization Management, 36*(2), 223–270.

Wang, Q., Fink, E. L., & Cai, D. A. (2012). The effect of conflict goals on avoidance strategies: What does not communicating communicate? *Human Communication Research, 38*(2), 222–252.

Wanzer, D. A. (2012). Delinking rhetoric, or revisiting McGee's fragmentation thesis through decoloniality. *Rhetoric and Public Affairs, 15*(4), 647–657.

Warner, B. R. (2017). Hypothesis testing, logic of. In M. Allen (Ed.), *The SAGE encyclopedia of communication research methods.* Los Angeles, CA: SAGE Publications.

Warnick, B. (2002). Analogues to argument: New media and literacy in a posthuman era. *Argumentation and Advocacy, 38*(4), 262.

Warren, J. E. (2010). Taming the warrant in Toulmin's model of argument. *English Journal, 99*(6), 41–46.

Waszak, P. M., Kasprzycka-Waszak, W., & Kubanek, A. (2018). The spread of medical fake news in social media—the pilot quantitative study. *Health Policy and Technology.* Online first: https://doi.org/10.1016/j.hlpt.2018.03.002

Watts, D. J., & Dodds, P. S. (2007). Influentials, networks, and public opinion formation. *Journal of Consumer Research, 34*(4), 441–458.

Watzlawick, P., Beavin, J. H., & Jackson, D. D. (1967). *Pragmatics of human communication: A study of interactional patterns, pathologies, and paradoxes.* New York, NY: W. W. Norton.

Wayne, L. (2005). Neutral pronouns: A modest proposal whose time has come. *Canadian Woman Studies, 24,* 85–91.

Weaver, D. (1994). Media agenda setting and elections: Voter involvement or alienation? *Political Communication, 11*(4), 347–356.

Weaver, R. M. (1953/1995). *The ethics of rhetoric.* New York, NY: Routledge.

Weaver, W. (1949). Recent contributions to the mathematic theory of communication. In C. E. Shannon & W. Weaver (Eds.), *The mathematical theory of communication* (pp. 94–117). Urbana, IL: University of Illinois Press.

Weber, M. (1946). *Essays in sociology.* New York, NY: Oxford University Press.

Weedon, C. (1997). *Feminist practice and poststructuralist theory* (2nd ed.). Cambridge, UK: Blackwell.

Wegman, L. A., Hoffman, B. J., Carter, N. T., Twenge, J. M., & Guenole, N. (2018). Placing job characteristics in context: Cross-temporal meta-analysis of changes in job characteristics since 1975. *Journal of Management, 44*(1), 352–386.

Weick, K. E. (1979). *The social psychology of organizing.* Reading: MA, Addison-Wesley.

Weick, K. E. (1989). Theory construction as disciplined imagination. *Academy of Management Review, 14*(4), 516–531.

Weick, K. E. (1995). *Sensemaking in organizations.* Beverly Hills, CA: SAGE Publications.

Weick, K. E. (2001). *Making sense of the organization.* MA: Blackwell.

Weigel, D. J., & Ballard-Reisch, D. S. (1999). All marriages are not maintained equally: Marital type, marital quality, and the use of maintenance behaviors. *Personal Relationships, 6*(3), 291–303.

Weisskirch, R. S., & Delevi, R. (2012). Its ovr b/n u n me: Technology use, attachment styles, and gender roles in relationship dissolution. *Cyberpsychology, Behavior, and Social Networking, 15*(9), 486–490.

Weisskirch, R. S., & Delevi, R. (2013). Attachment style and conflict resolution skills predicting technology use in relationship dissolution. *Computers in Human Behavior, 29*(6), 2530–2534.

Weng, L., Flammini, A., Vespignani, A., & Menczer, F. (2012). Competition among memes in a world with limited attention. *Scientific Reports, 2*(335), 1–8.

West, C., & Zimmerman, D. (1987). Doing gender. *Gender and Society, 1,* 124–151.

West, R., & Turner, L.H. (2006). *Introducing communication theory: Analysis and application* (3rd ed.). Boston, MA: McGraw-Hill.

Weymouth, B. B., Buehler, C., Zhou, N., & Henson, R. A. (2016). A meta-analysis of parent–adolescent conflict: Disagreement, hostility, and youth maladjustment. *Journal of Family Theory and Review, 8*(1), 95–112.

Wheeless, L. R., Wheeless, V. E., & Howard, R. D. (1984). The relationships of communication with supervisor and decision-participation to employee job satisfaction. *Communication Quarterly, 32*(3), 222–232.

Whithaus, C. (2012). Claim-evidence structures in environmental science writing: Modifying Toulmin's model to account for multimodal arguments. *Technical Communication Quarterly, 21*(2), 105–128.

Whitman, B. J., & Guthrie, J. (n.d.). *PRSA & ethics: A history of our commitment to integrity and education.* https://www.prsa.org/wp-content/uploads/2019/01/BEPS_Handbook_2018.pdf

Wiener, N. (1948). *Cybernetics, or control and communication in the animal and the machine.* New York, NY: John Wiley & Sons.

Wikipedia. (n.d.). Timeline of the evolutionary history of life. Retrieved from: https://en.wikipedia.org/wiki/Timeline_of_the_evolutionary_history_of_life

Wild, R. (1975). *Work organization: A study of manual work and mass production.* New York, NY: Wiley

Wilden, A. (1972). Analog and digital communication: On the relationship between negation, signification, and the emergence of the distinct element. *Semiotica, 6*(1), 50–82.

Wilden, A. (1980). *System and structure.* New York, NY: Tavistock Publications.

Willis-Rivera, J. (2010). *The essential guide to intercultural communication.* Boston, MA: Bedford/St. Martin.

Wilson, E. J., & Sherrell, D. L. (1993). Source effects in communication and persuasion research: A meta-analysis of effect size. *Journal of the Academy of Marketing Science, 21*(2), 101–112.

Wilson, J. C., & Lewiecki-Wilson, C. (2001). Disability, rhetoric, and the body. In James C. Wilson and Cynthia Lewiecki-Wilson (Eds.), *Embodied rhetorics: Disability in language and culture* (pp. 1–24). Carbondale, IL: Southern Illinois University Press.

Wilson, K. H. (1999). Towards a discursive theory of racial identity: The souls of black folk as a response to nineteenth-century biological determinism. *Western Journal of Communication, 63*(2), 193–215.

Wimmer, C. (2002). "I dwell in possibility__": Teaching consulting applications for performance studies. In S. Nathan & C. Wimmer (Eds.), *Teaching performance studies* (pp. 219–234). Carbondale, IL: Southern Illinois University.

Winslow, L. (2017). Pastors of profit: Marketplace ministries and the rhetorical acquisition of affective allegiance. *Communication and Critical/Cultural Studies, 14*(3), 203–220.

Winslow, L., Lindemann, K., Spitzberg, B.H., & Rapp, M. (2015). Communication presentations: A white paper for San Diego State University instructors and students, with practical advice on giving and assessing public speeches and presentations. *Pedagogical White Paper,* San Diego State University.

Winter, S., & Krämer, N. C. (2012). Selecting science information in Web 20: How source cues, message sidedness, and need for cognition influence users' exposure to blog posts. *Journal of Computer-Mediated Communication, 18*(1), 80–96.

Wiseman, R. L., & Schenck-Hamlin, W. (1981). A multidimensional scaling validation of an inductively-derived set of compliance-gaining strategies. *Communication Monographs, 48*(4), 251–270.

Witte, E., & Davis, J. H. (1996). *Understanding group behavior: Consensual action by small groups* (Vol. 1). Mahwah, NJ: Erlbaum.

Witte, K. (1992). Putting the fear back into fear appeals: The extended parallel process model. *Communications Monographs, 59*(4), 329–349.

Wood, D. A. (2010). Structures as argument: The visual persuasiveness of museums and places of worship. *Rhetoric and Public Affairs, 13*(3), 530–533.

Wood, J. T. (1997). Clarifying the issues. *Personal Relationships, 4*(3), 221–228.

Wood, J. T. (2002). A critical response to John Gray's Mars and Venus portrayals of men and women. *Southern Communication Journal, 67*(2), 201–210.

Wood, J. T., & Fixmer-Oraiz, N. (2017). *Gendered lives: Communication, gender and culture* (12th ed.). Boston, MA: Cengage.

Woodin, E. M. (2011). A two-dimensional approach to relationship conflict: Meta-analytic findings. *Journal of Family Psychology, 25*(3), 325–335.

World Health Organization (WHO). (1948). *Preamble to the constitution of the World Health Organization as adopted by the International Health Conference.* Retrieved from: http://www.who.int/governance/eb/who_constitution_en.pdf

Wrench, J. W., Thomas-Maddox, C., Richmond, V. P., & McCroskey, J. C. (2015). *Quantitative research methods for communication* (3rd ed.). New York, NY: Oxford University Press.

Wu, L., Liu, H., & Zhang, J. (2017). Bricolage effects on new-product development speed and creativity: The moderating role of technological turbulence. *Journal of Business Research, 70*, 127–135.

Yamasaki, J., Geist-Martin, P., & Sharf, B. F. (Eds.). (2016). *Storied health and illness: Communicating personal, cultural, and political complexities.* Long Grove, IL: Waveland Press.

Yang, J., & Counts, S. (2010, May). Predicting the speed, scale, and range of information diffusion in Twitter. *Proceedings of the Fourth International Conference on Weblogs and Social Media, ICWSM 2010.* Washington, DC. Retrieved from: https://www.microsoft.com/en-us/research/wp-content/uploads/2016/12/TwitterSpeedScaleRangeICWSM10.pdf

Yanovitzky, I., & Rimal, R. N. (2006). Communication and normative influence: An introduction to the special issue. *Communication Theory, 16*(1), 1–6.

Ye, Y., & Ward, K. E. (2010). The depiction of illness and related matters in two top-ranked primetime network medical dramas in the United States: A content analysis. *Journal of Health Communication, 15*(5), 555–570.

Yep, G. A. (2004). Approaches to cultural identity: Personal notes from an auto-ethnographical journey. In M. Fong & R. Chuang (Eds.), *Communicating ethnic and cultural identity* (pp. 69–81). Lanham, MD: Rowman & Littlefield.

YouGov. (2015, June). *Over 40% of Americans believe humans and dinosaurs shared the planet.* Retrieved from: https://d25d2506s-fb94s.cloudfront.net/cumulus_uploads/document/ukwe10eses/tabs_OPI_jurassic_world_20150617.pdf

YouGov. (2015, July). *Astrology.* Retrieved from: https://d25d2506s-fb94s.cloudfront.net/cumulus_uploads/document/rd948socdc/Results%20for%20YouGovNY%20(Astrology)%20149%2007.25.2017%20(version%201).pdf

Young, J. A. (2015). Assessing new media literacies in social work education: The development and validation of a comprehensive assessment instrument. *Journal of Technology in Human Services, 33*(1), 72–86.

Yu, T.-K., Lin, M.-L., & Liao, Y.-K. (2017). Understanding factors influencing information communication technology adoption behavior: The moderators of information literacy and digital skills. *Computers in Human Behavior, 71*, 196–208.

Zajc, M. (2015). Social media, prosumption, and dispositives: New mechanisms of the construction of subjectivity. *Journal of Consumer Culture, 15*(1), 28–47.

Zaleznik, A. (2004). Managers and leaders. Are they different? 1977. *Harvard Business Review, 82*(1), 74–81.

Zaragoza, A. (2017). A Chicano community in San Diego is outraged over a White woman's attempt to open a 'modern fruteria'. Retrieved from: https://wearemitu.com/things-that-matter/san-diegos-barrio-logan-community-is-fighting-against-a-modern-fruteria-and-the-gentrification-it-embodies/

Zeidler, E. (1995). Applied functional analysis: Main principles and their applications. Retrieved from: http://todayinsci.com/E/Einstein_Albert/EinsteinAlbert-Quotations.htm

Zietlow, P. H., & Sillars, A. L. (1988). Life-stage differences in communication during marital conflicts. *Journal of Social and Personal Relationships, 5*(2), 223–245.

Zelenkauskaite, A. (2017). Remediation, convergence, and big data: Conceptual limits of cross-platform social media. *Convergence: The International Journal of Research into New Media Technologies, 23*(5), 512–527.

Zelizer, B. (2016). Communication in the fan of disciplines. *Communication Theory, 26*(3), 213–235.

Zhang, X., Ko, M., & Carpenter, D. (2016). Development of a scale to measure skepticism toward electronic word-of-mouth. *Computers in Human Behavior, 56*, 198–208.

Zhi, Z., Hu, X., Ming, S., and, S., & Tao, Z. (2011). Empirical analysis on the human dynamics of a large-scale short message communication system. *Chinese Physics Letters, 28*(6), 068901.

Zimmerman, D. H. (1988). On conversation: The conversation analytic perspective. In J. A. Anderson (Ed.), *Communication Yearbook, 11* (pp. 406–432). Newbury Park, CA: SAGE Publications.

Zorich, Z. (2016). New dates for the oldest cave paintings. *Archaeology, 69*(4), 12.

Zuckerman, M., Kuhlman, D., Joireman, J., Teta, P., & Kraft, M. (1993). A comparison of three structural models for personality: The big three, the big five, and the alternative five. *Journal of Personality and Social Psychology, 65*(4), 757–768.

Zuckerman, M., Silberman, J., & Hall, J. A. (2013). The relation between intelligence and religiosity: A meta-analysis and some proposed explanations. *Personality and Social Psychology Review, 17*(4), 325–354.

Index

422 | The Communication Capstone

About the Editors/Authors

Volume Editors/Authors

BRIAN H. SPITZBERG (PhD, University of Southern California) is Senate Distinguished Professor Emeritus in the School of Communication at San Diego State University, and a certified threat manager (CTM™). He is author or coauthor of over 140 scholarly articles and book chapters, and coauthor and coeditor of several scholarly books. He received the 2009 Western States Communication Association Scholar Award, the 2011 National Communication Association Larry Kibler Memorial Award, and the 2017 Mark Knapp NCA Award for career contribution to the study of interpersonal communication. His coauthored book *The Dark Side of Relationship Pursuit* won both the biennial International Association for Relationship Research Book Award (1st ed.: 2008) and the NCA Gerald Miller Book Award (2nd ed., 2015). He was Co-PI on two National Science Foundation grants. His primary areas of research involve meme diffusion, assessment, communication skills, threats, coercion, stalking, and the dark side of communication.

HEATHER E. CANARY (PhD, Arizona State University) is Professor and Director of the School of Communication at San Diego State University (SDSU). Before coming to SDSU, Dr. Canary was on faculties of Arizona State University and the University of Utah. Her research interests include organizational, family, and health communication. Dr. Canary's recent projects include interventions to improve surgical team communication and to improve policy communication and compliance at a research university. Dr. Canary's research has been supported by the National Science Foundation and the National Institutes of Health. Her teaching interests include leadership and organizational communication, family communication, communication theory, and health communication.

DANIEL J. CANARY (PhD, University of Southern California) is Lecturer in the School of Communication at San Diego State University. A current or previous member of 15 editorial boards, Dan has coauthored more than 40 research articles, 10 scholarly books, 4 textbooks, and 45 chapters, plus other academic contributions. A recipient of the Herberger Professorship at Arizona State University, he is a former president of the Western States Communication Association and the International Network on Personal Relationships. He received the prestigious 2017 Western States Communication Association Distinguished Service Award. His research interests include communicative processes regarding interpersonal conflict management, relational maintenance strategies, and conversational argument.

Authors

PETER A. ANDERSEN (PhD, Florida State University) is Professor Emeritus at San Diego State University. He is author of more than 150 book chapters and journal articles. His books include *The Handbook of Communication and Emotion* (1998, coedited with Laura Guerrero), *Nonverbal Communication: Forms and Functions* (1999, 2008), *The Complete Idiots' Guide to Body Language* (2004), and *Close Encounters: Communication in Relationships* (2000, 2007, 2011, 2014; coauthored with Laura Guerrero and Walid Afifi). He was president of the Western Communication Association and editor of *The Western Journal of Communication*. He was coinvestigator on a number of major grants from the National Cancer Institute and the Center for Disease Control. His primary areas of research and teaching include nonverbal communication, relational communication, interpersonal communication, and health communication.

WAYNE A. BEACH (PhD, University of Utah) is Professor in the School of Communication at San Diego State University (SDSU), and Director of the *Center for Communication, Health, and the Public Good*. He is also faculty on the UCSD/SDSU joint doctoral program in public health, Adjunct Professor, Department of Surgery, and Member of the Moores Cancer Center, University of California, San Diego (UCSD). Recent honors include two Distinguished Scholar Awards from the National Communication Association (2018) and the Western States Communication Association (2017). He has pioneered diverse studies focusing on the social organization of verbal and embodied features of everyday talk and action, including ordinary conversations, interactions about cancer in homes and during clinical encounters, and emerging work on genetic counseling and family decision-making when managing uncertain futures and health risks. External funding has been provided by the National Cancer Institute (NCI), American Cancer Society (ACS), and several philanthropic foundations in San Diego.

YEA-WEN CHEN (PhD, University of New Mexico) is Associate Professor in the School of Communication at San Diego State University. Her research examines how communication—including silence—about cultural identities impacts diversity, inclusion, and social justice across contexts such as identity-based nonprofit organizations. She is the winner of numerous top paper awards at regional, national, and international communication conferences. Dr. Chen has published over 40 works, including peer-reviewed articles in *Communication Monographs, Journal of International and Intercultural Communication, and Departures in Critical Qualitative Research*. She coedited *Our Voices: Essays in Culture, Ethnicity, and Communication* (6th ed., Oxford University Press, 2015). In 2019, she was appointed a Provost's Professor of Equity in Education at San Diego State University.

KATHLEEN CZECH (EdD, University of San Diego) is Lecturer and Director of internships and study abroad programs in the School of Communication at San Diego State University. Her major area of research is organizational communication. She has published several peer-reviewed articles on defensive versus supportive communication in organizations. She also teaches interpersonal, leadership, and intercultural communication, among many other courses. Before joining the faculty at SDSU she was a Professor of Communication at Point Loma Nazarene University.

TIFFANY DYKSTRA-DeVETTE (PhD, University of Utah) is Assistant Professor in the School of Communication at San Diego State University. Her research focuses on non-profit organizing, empowerment, and forced migration. She has been published in journals such as *Organization Studies*. In the past, she has served as a debate coach and enjoys teaching courses on organizational communication, social movements, and communication theory.

WILLIAM F. EADIE (PhD, Purdue University) is former Director of the School of Communication at San Diego State University, where he was responsible for leadership of a large program that encompassed all aspects of communication, media, and journalism. Prior to joining the SDSU faculty in 2001, he was associate director of the National Communication Association (NCA) in Washington, DC. He served as the first editor of *The Journal of Applied Communication Research* after it became an NCA publication. He has also served as president of the Western States Communication Association and as editor of *The Western Journal of Communication*. His scholarship has focused on the development of the communication discipline. He has received the NCA Golden Anniversary Award for outstanding articles published in the field's journals. He has also been elected a member of Phi Kappa Phi, Golden Key, and Phi Beta Delta, all national honorary societies.

CHRISTOPHER GAMBLE (MS, Pennsylvania State University) is a doctoral student at the University of Washington. His interests are in rhetoric, communication technology, and new materialisms. More specifically, his research focuses on the changes in human–nonhuman relations from Homeric to Classical Greece. He has taught courses on environmental communication and persuasion.

PATRICIA GEIST-MARTIN (PhD, Purdue University) is Senate Distinguished Professor Emeritus in the School of Communication at San Diego State University. She is the author of five books, including *Falling in Love with the Process: A Stroke Survivor's Story of Recovery and Advocacy* (coauthored with Sarah Parsloe), *Storied Health and Illness* (coedited with Jill Yamasaki and Barbara Sharf), *Communicating Health* (coauthored with Eileen Berlin Ray and Barbara Sharf), *Courage of Conviction: Women's Words, Women's Wisdom* (coedited with Linda A. M. Perry), and *Negotiating the Crisis* (coauthored with Monica Hardesty). She has published over 70 articles and book chapters focusing on individuals' stories of negotiating identity and control in their personal and professional lives. She has conducted research on holistic and integrative medicine in Hawaii, Cuba, Guatemala, Mexico, Costa Rica, and San Diego. In 2011, she was awarded NCA's Francine Merritt Award for outstanding contributions to the lives of women in communication.

JOSHUA HANAN (PhD, University of Texas at Austin) is Associate Professor and Director of undergraduate studies for the Department of Communication Studies at the University of Denver. His scholarship explores rhetorical theory and practice from the critical standpoints of historical materialism, cultural materialism, and new materialism. His work is published in a number of journals both inside and outside of the discipline of communication studies, including *Communication and Critical/Cultural Studies, Quarterly Journal of Speech, Rhetoric and Public Affairs, Advances in the History of Rhetoric*, and *Argumentation and Advocacy*. Dr. Hanan is the chair of a new NCA Division that he helped found called Economics, Communication, and Society, and in 2014 he published an edited book (with Mark Hayward) titled *Communication and the Economy: History, Value, and Agency*. His interdisciplinary teaching interests include rhetorical theory, cultural studies, rhetorical materialism, publics and counterpublics, the rhetoric of economics, and disability rhetoric.

KURT LINDEMANN (PhD, Arizona State University) is Professor and Director of graduate studies in the School of Communication at San Diego State University. Dr. Lindemann also serves as director of the Center for the Study of Media and Performance, an interdisciplinary center housed at SDSU that is focused on the critical inquiry of live art and screen culture. His teaching interests include performance studies, ethnography, critical theory, and organizational communication. His work primarily examines communicative performances of identity in organizational and mediated contexts. Most recently, his research has been focused on men's narratives of grief. In addition to publishing articles on this topic, he has adapted for the stage and performed his research in numerous performance venues. His work has appeared in a variety of scholarly journals, books, and popular press magazines, including *Qualitative Inquiry, Text and Performance Quarterly, The Western Journal of Communication, Southern Journal of Communication*, and *Rebel* magazine.

work focuses primarily on tobacco control and cancer communication.

LOURDES S. MARTINEZ (PhD, University of Pennsylvania) is Associate Professor in the School for Communication at San Diego State University and Associate Director in the Center for Human Dynamics in the Mobile Age (HDMA). She received her BA (2004) in public health from Johns Hopkins University. Her research focuses on identifying ways in which individuals actively seek and share health-related information within their social environment, and how these processes influence health-related decisions and behavior. Her current research investigates how individuals engage with information on social media, and ways this information engagement can be used to understand prevention and risk behaviors. Her research has been published in several journals, including *Cyberpsychology, Behavior & Social Networking, Patient Education and Counseling, Journal of Health Communication, Health Communication*, and *Communication Methods and Measures.*

PERRY M. PAULEY (PhD, Arizona State University, 2009) is the Director of the Health Communication Continuing Medical Education Program at San Diego State University and a Faculty Associate in the Hugh Downs School of Communication at Arizona State University. His research and teaching focuses broadly on the intersection of relational communication and health with a particular emphasis on the ways in which positive forms of communication—things like affection, empathy, compassion, and support—improve psychological and physical health outcomes for recipients and providers alike.

MEGHAN BRIDGID MORAN (PhD, University of Southern California) is Assistant Professor in the Department of Health, Behavior, and Society at Johns Hopkins University. She is a health communication scholar studying how health information can best be communicated to individuals in different contexts and through different channels. She studies both micro-level processes of persuasion and social influence, as well as the more macro-level health communication that occurs in society, with particular interest in how media and pop culture influence health. Her research areas leverage expertise in persuasion, message design, media effects, and health behavior. Her

COLTER D. RAY (PhD, Arizona State University, 2018) is Assistant Professor of Interpersonal and Health Communication at San Diego State University. His research focuses on social support following a cancer diagnosis and aims to improve communication between people with cancer and their supporters. Specifically, his research focuses on the "dark side" of supportive interactions, including instances of unwanted support or times when people purposefully avoid communicating support to people they know with cancer. His recent research explores instances of "mixed messages" of support that simultaneously convey positive statements of love and negative statements of criticism. He also directs the Human Communication Laboratory at SDSU and is a core researcher in SDSU's Center for Communication, Health, and the Public Good.

RACHAEL A. RECORD (PhD, University of Kentucky) is Associate Professor in the School of Communication at San Diego State University and the Associate Director of the Thirdhand Smoke Resource Center. Her research, typically grounded in behavior change theories, employs mixed methods to examine campaign and intervention strategies to improve health behavior outcomes, particularly within the context of tobacco use and among medically underserved populations In addition, she explores how social media is used among the general public for health management. Most recently, she is focusing on campaign efforts for increasing education and awareness of thirdhand tobacco pollution.

MATTHEW SAVAGE (PhD, Arizona State University) is Associate Professor of Health and Interpersonal Communication at San Diego State University. His research interests are at the intersection of health, interpersonal, and mass communication. His scholarship is conducted within the context of creating and supporting health communication campaigns aimed to deter negative and risky behaviors among adolescents and young adults. Much of his research is embedded in strong partnerships with educational institutions, government organizations, and nonprofits. Currently, he is working on various projects addressing adolescent bullying/cyberbullying, oral health promotion, and reciprocal violence. He is recognized with prestigious university teaching awards at the University of Kentucky, the University of Hawaii, and Arizona State University.

WILLIAM B. SNAVELY (PhD, University of Nebraska-Lincoln) is Professor Emeritus and the former Director of the School of Communication at San Diego State University. He earned his MS in communication from West Virginia University in 1974 and his BA degree in speech communication at Illinois State University in 1973. His areas of research focus have included social style theory, communication competence, Russian business culture, and job stress. His work has appeared in a number of journals, including *Communication Monographs, Communication Quarterly, Journal of Applied Communication Research, Business Horizons*, and *Journal of Leadership and Organizational Studies*. His teaching interests include leadership, organizational communication, intercultural communication, organizational behavior, and communication skills in business.

JULIE L. TAYLOR (PhD, University of Utah) is an Assistant Professor in the Department of Communication Studies at California State University San Bernardino. Her research interests include organizational, policy, and gender communication. Dr. Taylor's recent projects include investigating organizing elements of sex for sale around policy construction and enactment. Dr. Taylor has published articles in *Communication Education, The Western Journal of Communication*, and *The Journal of*

Human Trafficking, among other scholarly journals and outlets. Her teaching interests include organizational communication, gender communication, and interdisciplinary teaching initiatives.

LUKE WINSLOW (PhD, The University of Texas at Austin) is Professor of Rhetorical Studies in the School of Communication at San Diego State University. His teaching and research interests include contemporary rhetorical theory and criticism, political communication, and rhetoric and social justice. His essays have appeared in *Communication and Critical/Cultural Studies, Critical Studies in Media Communication, Rhetoric and Public Affairs, Western Journal of Communication, Southern Journal of Communication, Communication Studies,* and *the Journal of Communication and Religion.* His first book, *Economic Injustice and the Rhetoric of the American Dream,* was published in 2017, and his second, *American Catastrophe: Fundamentalism, Climate Change, Gun Rights, and the Rhetoric of Donald J. Trump* (The Ohio State University Press) is in progress. He lives in San Diego with his wife and two sons.